First published in 2007 by
Amnesty International USA
5 Penn Plaza
New York, NY 10001
USA

© Copyright
Amnesty International 2007
ISBN: 978-1-887204-46-0
ISSN: 0309-068X
AI Index: POL 10/001/2007
Original language: English

Printed by:
The Alden Press
De Havilland Way, Witney
United Kingdom

Cover design by John Finn

Regional maps by András Bereznay
www.historyonmaps.com

Photographs: All photographs appear
with full credits and captions elsewhere
in the report.

Thanks to: Mary Gray, Simon Long and
John Palmer.

www.amnestyusa.org

AMNESTY INTERNATIONAL
REPORT 2007
THE STATE OF THE
WORLD'S HUMAN RIGHTS

This report covers the period January to December 2006.

ABOUT THIS REPORT

The *Amnesty International Report* 2007 documents human rights issues of concern to Amnesty International (AI) during 2006.

AI's approach to tackling human rights abuses is informed by both the challenges and opportunities for change in a given country or region. The strategic goals that AI identifies in a country or region determine AI's work. As a result, AI addresses particular issues in

specific countries. Its coverage of individual issues, as reflected in the content of this report, is focused rather than comprehensive. If an issue is not covered in a country entry, this should not be taken as a statement by AI that abuses within this category did not occur. Nor can the absence of an entry on a particular country or territory be taken to imply that no human rights abuses of concern to AI took place there during 2006. In particular, the length of individual entries cannot be used as the basis for a comparison of the extent and depth of AI's concerns.

Regional maps have been included in this report to indicate the location of countries and territories, and each individual country entry begins with some basic information about the country. Neither the maps nor the country information may be interpreted as AI's view on questions such as the status of disputed territory.

AMNESTY INTERNATIONAL

Amnesty International (AI) is a worldwide movement of people who campaign for internationally recognized human rights to be respected and protected.

AI's vision is for every person to enjoy all of the human rights enshrined in the Universal Declaration of Human Rights and other international human rights standards. AI's mission is to conduct research and take action to prevent and end grave abuses of all human rights — civil, political, social, cultural and economic. From freedom of expression and association to physical and mental integrity, from protection from discrimination to the right to shelter — these rights are indivisible.

AI has 2.2 million members and supporters in more than 150 countries and territories. Funded largely by its membership and public donations, AI is independent of any government, political ideology, economic interest or religion. No funds are sought or accepted from governments for investigating and campaigning against human rights abuses.

AI is a democratic movement. Major policy decisions are taken by a two-yearly International Council made up of representatives from all national sections. The Council elects an International Executive Committee which carries out its decisions. The Committee's members elected for 2005-7 were Soledad García Muñoz (Argentina), Ian Gibson (Australia), Lilian Gonçalves-Ho Kang You (Netherlands, Chair from September 2006), Petri Merenlahti (Finland), Claire Paponneau (France), Vanushi Rajanayagam (New Zealand), Hanna Roberts (Sweden), and David Weissbrodt (USA). AI's Secretary General is Irene Khan (Bangladesh).

CONTENTS

ABBREVIATIONS

The following abbreviations are used in this report:

■ UN Children's Convention refers to the Convention on the Rights of the Child.

■ UN Convention against Racism refers to the International Convention on the Elimination of All Forms of Racial Discrimination.

■ UN Convention against Torture refers to the Convention against Torture and Other Cruel, Inhuman or Degrading Treatment or Punishment.

■ UNHCR, the UN refugee agency, refers to the UN High Commissioner for Refugees.

■ UNICEF refers to the UN Children's Fund.

■ UN Migrant Workers Convention refers to the International Convention on the Protection of the

Rights of All Migrant Workers and Members of Their Families.

■ UN Refugee Convention refers to the Convention relating to the Status of Refugees.

■ UN Women's Convention refers to the Convention on the Elimination of All Forms of Discrimination against Women.

■ European Committee for the Prevention of Torture refers to the European Committee for the Prevention of Torture and Inhuman or Degrading Treatment or Punishment.

■ European Convention on Human Rights refers to the (European) Convention for the Protection of Human Rights and Fundamental Freedoms.

Children survive by selling refuse from the municipal dump, La Chureca, Nicaragua. © Dermot Tatlow/Panos Pictures

AMNESTY INTERNATIONAL
REPORT 2007
PART 1

Women tortured at the former Khiam Detention Centre run by the Israeli-backed South Lebanon Army speak to AI Secretary General Irene Khan in December. © Sarah Hunter

IRENE KHAN
FREEDOM FROM FEAR

On 10 December 2006, while the world celebrated International Human Rights Day, I was in Jayyus on the West Bank. The small village is now divided by the Wall — or more accurately a high iron fence. Built in defiance of international law, and ostensibly to make Israel more secure, the Wall's main effect has been to cut off the local Palestinian population from their citrus groves and olive orchards. A once prosperous farming community is now impoverished.

"Every day I have to suffer the humiliation of checkpoints, petty obstructions and new restrictions that stop me from getting to my orchard on the other side. If I cannot cultivate my olives, how will I survive?" cried one angry Palestinian farmer.

As I listened to him, I could see in the distance the neat red roofs and white walls of a large and prosperous Israeli settlement. I wondered if those who lived there believed that a Wall threatening the future of their neighbours could truly enhance their security.

Earlier that week, I had visited Sderot, a small town in the south of Israel, which had been subjected to rocket attacks from Palestinian groups in Gaza.

"We are frightened," one young woman resident told me. "But we know that there are women like us on the other side who are also suffering, who are also afraid, and who are in a worse situation than us. We feel empathy for them, we want to live in peace with them, but instead our leaders promote our differences and create more distrust. So we live in fear and insecurity."

FEAR DESTROYS OUR SHARED UNDERSTANDING AND OUR SHARED HUMANITY

This brave Israeli woman understood what many world leaders fail to comprehend: that fear destroys our shared understanding and our shared humanity. When we see others as a threat, and are ready to negotiate their human rights for our security, we are playing a zero-sum game.

Her message is sobering at a time when our world is as polarized as it was at the height of the Cold War, and in many ways far more dangerous. Human rights — those global values, universal principles and common standards that are meant to unite us — are being bartered away in the name of security today as they were then. Like the Cold War times, the agenda is being driven by fear — instigated, encouraged and sustained by unprincipled leaders.

Fear can be a positive imperative for change, as in the case of the environment, where alarm about global warming is forcing politicians belatedly into action. But fear can also be dangerous and divisive when it breeds intolerance, threatens diversity and justifies the erosion of human rights.

In 1941, US President Franklin Roosevelt laid out his vision of a new world order founded on "four freedoms": freedom of speech and of religion; freedom from fear and from want. He provided inspirational leadership that overcame doubt and unified people. Today far too many leaders are trampling freedom and trumpeting an ever-widening range of fears: fear of being swamped by migrants; fear of "the other" and of losing one's identity; fear of being blown up by terrorists; fear of "rogue states" with weapons of mass destruction.

Fear thrives on myopic and cowardly leadership. There are indeed many real causes of fear but the approach being taken by many world leaders is short-sighted, promulgating policies and strategies that erode the rule of law and human rights, increase inequalities, feed racism and xenophobia, divide and damage communities, and sow the seeds for violence and more conflict.

The politics of fear has been made more complex by the emergence of armed groups and big business that commit or condone human rights abuses. Both – in different ways – challenge the power of governments in an increasingly borderless world. Weak governments and ineffective international institutions are unable to hold them accountable, leaving people vulnerable and afraid.

History shows that it is not through fear but through hope and optimism that progress is achieved. So, why do some leaders promote fear? Because it allows them to consolidate their own power, create false certainties and escape accountability.

The Howard government portrayed desperate asylum-seekers in leaky boats as a threat to Australia's national security and raised a false alarm of a refugee invasion. This contributed to its election victory in 2001. After the attacks of 11 September 2001, US President George W Bush invoked the fear of terrorism to enhance his executive power, without Congressional oversight or judicial scrutiny. President Omar al-Bashir of Sudan whipped up fear among his supporters and in the Arab world that the deployment of UN peacekeepers in Darfur would be a pretext for an Iraq-style, US-led invasion. Meanwhile, his armed forces and militia allies continued to kill, rape and plunder with impunity. President Robert Mugabe of Zimbabwe played on racial fears to push his own political agenda of grabbing land for his supporters.

Only a common commitment based on shared values can lead to a sustainable solution. In an inter-dependent world, global challenges, whether of poverty or security, of migration or marginalization, demand responses based on global values of human rights that bring people together and promote our collective well-being. Human rights provide the basis for a sustainable future. But protecting the security of states rather than the sustainability of people's lives and livelihoods appears to be the order of the day.

FEAR THRIVES ON MYOPIC AND COWARDLY LEADERSHIP

FEAR OF MIGRATION AND MARGINALIZATION

In developed countries, as well as emerging economies, the fear of being invaded by hordes of the poor is being used to justify ever tougher measures against migrants, refugees and asylum-seekers, violating international standards of human rights and humane treatment.

Driven by the political and security imperatives of border control, asylum procedures have become a means for exclusion rather than protection.

Across Europe, refugee recognition rates have fallen dramatically over the years, although the reasons for seeking asylum – violence and persecution – remain as high as ever.

The hypocrisy of the politics of fear is such that governments denounce certain regimes but refuse to protect those escaping from them. The harsh policies of the North Korean government have been condemned by western governments but these same governments are far less vocal about the fate of some 100,000 North Koreans reportedly hiding in China, hundreds of whom are deported forcibly to North Korea every week by the Chinese authorities.

Migrant workers fuel the engine of the global economy – yet they are turned away with brutal force, exploited, discriminated against, and left unprotected by governments across the world, from the Gulf states and South Korea to the Dominican Republic.

Six thousand Africans drowned or were missing at sea in 2006 in their desperate bid to reach Europe. Another 31,000 – six times higher than the number in 2005 – reached the Canary islands. Just as the Berlin Wall could not stop those who wanted to escape Communist oppression, tough policing of the borders of Europe is failing to block those seeking to escape abject poverty.

In the long term, the answer lies not in building walls to keep people out but in promoting systems that protect the rights of the vulnerable while respecting the prerogative of states to control migration. International instruments provide that balance. Attempts to weaken the UN Refugee Convention or shun the UN Migrant Workers Convention – which no western country has ratified – are counter-productive.

If unregulated migration is the fear of the rich, then unbridled capitalism, driven by globalization, is the fear of the poor. Booming markets are creating enormous opportunities for some, but also widening the gap between the "haves" and the "have-nots". The rewards of globalization are heavily skewed, both across the world and within countries. Latin America is burdened with some of the highest levels of inequality in the world. In India, there have been average growth rates of 8 per cent over the past three years, but more than a quarter of its population still lives below the poverty line.

These statistics reveal the dark underbelly of globalization. The marginalization of large swathes of humanity should not be treated as the inevitable cost of global prosperity. There is nothing inevitable about policies and decisions that deny individuals their economic and social rights.

Amnesty International's growing programme of work on economic and social rights is laying bare the reality of people's fear: that in many parts of the world people are being tipped into poverty and trapped there by corrupt governments and greedy businesses.

As the demands for mining, urban development and tourism put pressure on land, across Africa, Asia and Latin America, entire communities – millions of people - are being forcibly evicted from their homes with no due process, compensation or alternative shelter. Often, excessive force is used to uproot them. Development-induced displacement is not a new problem, yet little appears to have been learnt from past experience. In Africa alone more than 3 million people have been affected since 2000, making forced evictions one

MILLIONS OF PEOPLE ARE BEING FORCIBLY EVICTED FROM THEIR HOMES WITH NO DUE PROCESS, COMPENSATION OR ALTERNATIVE SHELTER of the most widespread and unrecognized human rights violations on the continent. Carried out in the name of economic progress, in reality they leave the poorest of the poor homeless and often without access to clean water, health, sanitation, jobs or education.

Africa has long been the victim of the greed of western governments and companies. Now, it faces a new challenge from China. The Chinese government and Chinese companies have shown little regard for their "human rights footprint" on the continent. The deference to national sovereignty, antipathy to human rights in foreign policy, and readiness to engage with abusive regimes, are all endearing China to African governments. But for those same reasons, African civil society has been less welcoming. The health and safety standards and treatment of workers by Chinese companies have fallen short of international standards. As the biggest consumer of Sudan's oil and a major supplier of its weapons, China has shielded the Sudanese government against pressure from the international community – although there are some signs that it may be modifying its position.

Weak, deeply impoverished, and often profoundly corrupt states have created a power vacuum into which corporations and other economic actors are moving. In some of the most resource-rich countries with the poorest populations, big business has used its unbridled power to gain concessions from governments that deprive local people of the benefits of the resources, destroy their livelihoods, displace them from their homes and expose them to environmental degradation. Anger at the injustice and denial of human rights has led to protests that are then brutally repressed. The oil-rich Niger Delta in southern Nigeria, torn by violence for the past two decades, is a case in point.

Corporations have long resisted binding international standards. The United Nations must confront the challenge, and develop standards and promote mechanisms that hold big business accountable for its impact on human rights. The need for global standards and effective accountability becomes even more urgent as multinational corporations from diverse legal and cultural systems emerge in a global market.

CORPORATIONS HAVE LONG RESISTED BINDING INTERNATIONAL STANDARDS

The push for land, timber and mineral resources by big conglomerates is threatening the cultural identity and daily survival of many Indigenous communities in Latin America. Subjected to racial discrimination and driven into extreme poverty and ill-health, some of the groups are on the brink of collapse.

Against this background, the failure of the 2006 UN General Assembly to adopt the Declaration on the Rights of Indigenous Peoples was yet another unfortunate testimony to powerful interests trumping the very survival of the vulnerable.

Although the rich are getting richer every day, they do not necessarily feel any safer. Rising crime and gun violence are a source of constant fear, leading many governments to adopt policies that are purportedly tough on crime but in reality criminalize the poor, exposing them to the double jeopardy of gang violence and brutal policing. Ever higher levels of criminal and police violence in São Paulo and the presence of the army on the streets of Rio de Janeiro in 2006 demonstrated the failure of Brazil's public security policies. Providing security to one group of people at the expense of the rights of another does not work. Experience shows that public security is best strengthened through a comprehensive approach that combines better policing alongside provision of basic services such as health, education and shelter to the poor communities; so that they feel they too have a stake in a secure and stable society.

At the end of the day, promoting economic and social rights for all is the best approach to addressing the fears of the rich as well as the poor.

FEAR BREEDS DISCRIMINATION

Fear feeds discontent and leads to discrimination, racism, persecution of ethnic and religious minorities and xenophobic attacks against foreigners and foreign-born citizens.

When governments turn a blind eye to racist violence, it can become endemic. In Russia hate crimes against foreigners and minorities are common but until recently were rarely prosecuted because they fed into the nationalist propaganda of the authorities.

As the European Union expands eastwards, the acid test of its commitment to equality and non-discrimination will be the treatment of its own Roma population.

From Dublin to Bratislava, anti-Roma attitudes remain entrenched, with segregation and discrimination in education, health and housing and exclusion from public life persistent in some countries.

In many western countries, discrimination has been generated by fears of uncontrolled migration and, post-9/11, aggravated by counter-terrorism strategies targeting Arabs, Asians and Muslims. Fear and hostility on one side have led to alienation and anger on the other.

Increasing polarization has strengthened the hands of extremists at both ends of the spectrum, reducing the space for tolerance and dissent. Incidents of Islamophobia and anti-Semitism are increasingly evident. In many parts of the world, anti-western and anti-American sentiments are at an all-time high, as demonstrated by the ease with which some groups fomented violence following the publication in Denmark of cartoons that many Muslims found offensive.

The Danish government rightly upheld free speech but failed to affirm strongly and immediately its commitment to protect Muslims living in Denmark from discrimination and social exclusion. The Iranian President called for a debate to promote the denial of the historical fact of the Holocaust. The French parliament passed a bill making it a crime to deny that the Armenians suffered genocide at the hands of the Ottomans.

Where should the line be drawn between protecting free speech and stopping incitement of racial hatred?

The state has an obligation to promote non-discrimination and prevent racial crimes but it can do that without limiting freedom of speech. Freedom of expression should not be lightly restricted. Yes, it can be used to propagate lies as well as truth, but without it there is no way to argue against lies, no way to seek truth and justice. That is why speech should be curtailed only where there is clear intent to incite racial or religious hatred, not where the purpose is to express opinion, however distasteful.

In *Albert-Engelman-Gesellschaft MBH v Austria* (January 2006) the European

> SPEECH SHOULD BE
> CURTAILED ONLY
> WHERE THERE IS
> CLEAR INTENT TO
> INCITE RACIAL OR
> RELIGIOUS HATRED

Court of Human Rights described freedom of expression as "one of the essential foundations of a democratic society and one of the basic conditions for its progress and each individual's self-fulfilment... freedom is applicable not only to 'information' or 'ideas' [that are deemed acceptable] but also to those that offend, shock or disturb; such are the demands of pluralism, tolerance and broadmindedness without which there is no 'democratic society'."

FEAR OF DISSENT

Freedom of expression is fundamental to the right to dissent. Where there is no dissent, the right to free speech is endangered. Where there is no dissent, democracy is stifled. Where there is no dissent, tyranny raises its head.

Yet, freedom of expression and dissent continue to be suppressed in a variety of ways, from the prosecution of writers, journalists and human rights defenders in Turkey, to political killings of left-wing activists in the Philippines.

In the US prison camp at Guantánamo Bay, the only form of protest arguably left to detainees is hunger strike. In 2006 some 200 detainees who resorted to it were force fed by tubes inserted through the nose — a particularly painful and humiliating method. When three men were reported to have committed suicide, the US taskforce commander at Guantánamo described it as "asymmetrical warfare".

National security has often been used as an excuse by governments to suppress dissent. In recent years heightened fears about terrorism and insecurity have reinforced repression — or the risk of it — in a variety of ways.

"Old fashioned" abuses of freedom of expression, assembly and association have gained a new lease of life in North Africa and the Middle East. In liberal democracies the ever-widening net of counter-terrorism laws and policies poses a potential threat to free speech. In 2006, for example, the UK adopted legislation to create a vaguely defined crime of "encouraging terrorism", incorporating the even more baffling notion of "glorifying terrorism".

HEIGHTENED FEARS ABOUT TERRORISM AND INSECURITY HAVE REINFORCED REPRESSION

In the USA the authorities showed more interest in hunting down the source of the leak behind the story in *The Washington Post* on CIA "black sites", than in investigating the policies that led to the establishment of these secret prisons in the first place in contravention of international and US laws.

The authoritarian drift in Russia has been devastating for journalists and human rights defenders. Having intimidated or taken over much of the Russian press, President Vladimir Putin turned his attention to Russian and foreign non-governmental organizations (NGOs) in 2006 with a controversial law to regulate their funding and activities. In a public relations exercise just prior to the meeting of the G8, he met with a group of international NGOs, including Amnesty International. Informed of the damaging impact of his NGO law on civil society in Russia and urged to suspend it pending further consultations on amendments, he responded: "We did not pass this law to have it repealed." Three months later the Russian Chechen Friendship Society, a human rights NGO working to expose violations in Chechnya, was closed down under the new law.

Unfortunately, Russia is not the only country seeking to silence independent voices on human rights. From Colombia to Cambodia, Cuba to Uzbekistan, governments have introduced laws to restrict human rights organizations and the work of activists, branding them disloyal or subversive, prosecuting those who dare to expose human rights violations, and launching smear campaigns with the help of unscrupulous media in an effort to instil fear and de-legitimize the work of activists.

In an age of technology, the Internet has become the new frontier in the struggle for the right to dissent. With the help of some of the world's biggest IT companies, governments such as those in Belarus, China, Egypt, Iran, Saudi Arabia and Tunisia are monitoring chat rooms, deleting blogs, restricting search engines and blocking websites. People have been imprisoned in China, Egypt, Syria, Uzbekistan and Viet Nam for posting and sharing information online.

Everyone has the right to seek and receive information and to express their peaceful beliefs without fear or interference. Amnesty International, with the support of the UK newspaper *The Observer* (which published Amnesty International's first appeal in 1961), launched a campaign in 2006 to show that human rights activists will not be silenced, online or offline, by governments or big business.

> IN AN AGE OF TECHNOLOGY, THE INTERNET HAS BECOME THE NEW FRONTIER IN THE STRUGGLE FOR THE RIGHT TO DISSENT

FREEDOM FOR WOMEN

The pernicious relationship between discrimination and dissent is playing out most vividly in the arena of gender. Women activists have been arrested for demanding gender equality in Iran, murdered for promoting education of girls in Afghanistan, and subjected to sexual violence and vilification around the world. Women working on issues of sexual orientation and reproductive rights have been especially targeted, marginalized and attacked.

Women human rights defenders are doubly endangered: as activists and as women – for their work as well as for their identity. They are attacked by both state and society, not only because they expose human rights abuses, but also because they challenge patriarchal power structures and social and cultural conventions that subjugate women, condone discrimination and facilitate gender violence.

Women's human rights have suffered in recent years from the twin trends of backlash and backtrack. The backlash on human rights in the context of counter-terrorism has affected women as well as men. And in an environment of fear and religious fundamentalism, governments have backtracked on their promise to promote gender equality.

Violence against women – in all societies around the world – remains one of the gravest and most common human rights abuses today.

It thrives because of impunity, apathy and inequality. One of the most blatant examples of impunity is the conflict in Darfur, where incidents of rape rose in 2006 as armed conflict increased and spread to neighbouring areas of Chad. One of the most insidious examples of apathy is Guatemala, where more than 2,200 women and girls have been murdered since 2001, but very few cases have been investigated and even fewer prosecuted. There are many examples of the impact of inequality, but possibly one of the saddest is the high levels of maternal and infant mortality – for example in Peru – due to discrimination in health services.

Billions of dollars are being spent to fight the "war on terror" – but where is the political will or the resources to fight sexual terror against women? There was universal outrage against racial apartheid in South Africa – where is the outrage against gender apartheid in some countries today?

Whether the perpetrator is a soldier or a community leader, whether the violence is officially sanctioned by the authorities or condoned by culture and custom, the state cannot shirk its responsibility to protect women.

The state has the obligation to safeguard a woman's freedom of choice, not restrict it. To take an example, the veil and headscarf of Muslim women have become a bone of contention between different cultures, the visible symbol of oppression according to one side, and an essential attribute of religious freedom according to the other. It is wrong for women in Saudi Arabia or Iran to be compelled to put on the veil. It is equally wrong for women or girls in Turkey or France to be forbidden by law to wear the headscarf. And it is foolish of western leaders to claim that a piece of clothing is a major barrier to social harmony.

In the exercise of her right to freedom of expression and religion, a woman should be free to choose what she wants to wear. Governments and religious leaders have a duty to create a safe environment in which every woman can make that choice without the threat of violence or coercion.

The universality of human rights means that they apply equally to women as well as to men. This universality of rights — universality both in understanding and in application — is the most powerful tool against gender violence, intolerance, racism, xenophobia and terrorism.

FEAR OF TERRORISM

It is in the sphere of terrorism and counter-terrorism that fear's most harmful manifestations flourish. Whether in Mumbai or Manhattan, people have the right to be secure and governments have the duty to provide that security. However, ill-conceived counter-terrorism strategies have done little to reduce the threat of violence or to ensure justice for victims of attacks, and much to damage human rights and the rule of law.

Thwarted in 2004 by the courts from pursuing its policy of detaining people indefinitely without charge or trial, the UK government has resorted increasingly to deportation, or to "control orders" that allow the Home Secretary effectively to place people under house arrest without criminal prosecution. Suspects are thus condemned without ever being convicted. The essence of the rule of law is subverted while its form is preserved.

Japan introduced a law in 2006 to fast-track deportation of anyone deemed by the Minister of Justice to be a "possible terrorist". People's fate will no longer be determined on the basis of what they have done but on the omniscient ability of governments to predict what they might do!

Unfettered discretionary executive power is being pursued relentlessly by the US administration, which treats the world as one big battlefield for its "war on terror": kidnapping, arresting, detaining or torturing suspects either directly or with the help of countries as far apart as Pakistan and Gambia, Afghanistan and Jordan. In September 2006, President Bush finally admitted what Amnesty International has long known — that the CIA had been running secret detention centres in circumstances that amount to international crimes.

Nothing so aptly portrays the globalization of human rights violations as the US government's programme of "extraordinary renditions". Investigations by the Council of Europe, the European Parliament and a Public Enquiry in Canada, have provided compelling evidence confirming Amnesty

IT IS IN THE SPHERE OF TERRORISM AND COUNTER-TERRORISM THAT FEAR'S MOST HARMFUL MANIFESTATIONS FLOURISH

**A CLEAR MOMENTUM
HAS BEEN CREATED IN
FAVOUR OF
TRANSPARENCY,
ACCOUNTABILITY AND
AN END TO IMPUNITY**

International's earlier findings of the complicity, collusion or acquiescence of a number of European and other governments — whether democratic like Canada or autocratic like Pakistan. Over the past few years, hundreds of people have been unlawfully transferred by the USA and its allies to countries such as Syria, Jordan and Egypt. In this shadowy system they risk enforced disappearance, torture and other ill-treatment. Some have ended up in Guantánamo, US-run prisons in Afghanistan or CIA "black sites".

Lawyers cannot petition the authorities, seek judicial review or demand fair trial for those held in secret detention for the simple reason that no one knows where and by whom they are being held. International monitoring is impossible for the same reasons.

The US administration's double speak has been breathtakingly shameless. It has condemned Syria as part of the "axis of evil", yet it has transferred a Canadian national, Maher Arar, to the Syrian security forces to be interrogated, knowing full well that he risked being tortured. Pakistan is another country that the US administration has courted and counted as an ally in its "war on terror" — notwithstanding concerns about its human rights record.

Thankfully, there appears to be a growing realization in many countries that security at all costs is a dangerous and damaging strategy. European institutions are becoming more rigorous in their demand for accountability and courts less willing to give in to governments' claims. The Public Enquiry in Canada called for an apology and compensation by the US authorities for Maher Arar and for investigation into other similar cases. Reports by the Council of Europe and the European Parliament are leading to calls for greater scrutiny of security services. Arrest warrants have been issued in Italy and Germany against CIA agents.

A clear momentum has been created in favour of transparency, accountability and an end to impunity.

But the USA has yet to surrender. President Bush persuaded a Congress in pre-election fever to adopt the Military Commissions Act, negating the impact of the 2006 Supreme Court judgement in *Hamdan v Rumsfeld*, and making lawful that which world opinion found immoral. *The New York Times* described it as "a tyrannical law that will be ranked with the low points in American democracy".

The US administration remains deaf to the worldwide calls for closing down Guantánamo. It is unrepentant about the global web of abuse it has spun in the name of counter-terrorism. It is oblivious to the distress of thousands of detainees and their families, the damage to the rule of international law and human rights, and the destruction of its own moral authority, which has plummeted to an all-time low around the world — while the levels of insecurity remain as high as ever.

US Supreme Court Justice Brennan wrote in 1987: "After each perceived security crisis ended, the United States has remorsefully realized that the abrogation of civil liberties was unnecessary. But it has proven unable to prevent itself from repeating the error when the next crisis came along."

A new US Congress raises hopes that things may yet take a different turn, and that Democrats and Republicans will come to see a bipartisan interest in restoring respect for human rights at home and abroad, demanding accountability, setting up a commission of inquiry and either repealing or changing the Military Commissions Act substantially in line with international law.

FREEDOM FROM VIOLENCE

When global values of human rights are swept aside with impunity, parochial interests raise their head, often driven by sectarian, ethnic and religious groups, sometimes using violence. Although their practices are often contrary to human rights, in a number of countries they are gaining support with ordinary people because they are seen to be addressing the injustices that governments and the international community are ignoring.

Meanwhile governments are failing to provide the leadership to bring these groups to account for their abuses, and instead appear to be feeding the very factors that foster them.

In Afghanistan, the government and the international community have squandered the opportunity to build an effective, functioning state based on human rights and the rule of law. Rampant insecurity, impunity and corrupt and ineffective government institutions, combined with high unemployment and poverty, have sapped public confidence, while thousands of civilian deaths resulting from US-led military operations have fuelled resentment. The Taleban has capitalized on the political, economic and security vacuum to gain control over large parts of the south and east of the country.

A misguided military adventure in Iraq has taken a heavy toll on human rights and humanitarian law, leaving the population embittered, armed groups empowered and the world a much less secure place. The insurgency has morphed into a brutal and bloody sectarian conflict. The government has shown little commitment to protect the human rights of all Iraqis. The Iraqi police forces, heavily infiltrated by sectarian militia, are feeding violations rather than restraining them. The Iraqi justice system is woefully inadequate, as former President Saddam Hussain's flawed trial and grotesque execution confirmed.

If there is to be any hope of a shift in the apocalyptic prognosis for Iraq, the Iraqi government and those who support it militarily must set some clear human rights benchmarks — to disarm the militia, reform the police, review the justice system, stop sectarian discrimination and ensure the equal rights of women.

In the Palestinian Occupied Territories the cumulative impact of measures by the Israeli authorities, including increasingly severe restrictions on freedom of movement, expansion of settlements and the building of the Wall inside the West Bank, has strangled the local economy. Ordinary Palestinians are caught between interfactional fighting of Hamas and Fatah, and the reckless shelling of the Israeli army. With no justice and no end to occupation in sight, a predominantly young Palestinian population is being radicalized. No truce will survive and no political process will succeed in the Middle East if impunity is not addressed, and human rights and security of people are not prioritized.

In Lebanon, sectarian divisions have further deepened in the aftermath of the war between Israel and Hizbullah. The lack of accountability for current

> GOVERNMENTS ARE FAILING TO ... BRING THESE GROUPS TO ACCOUNT FOR THEIR ABUSES, AND INSTEAD APPEAR TO BE FEEDING THE FACTORS THAT FOSTER THEM

and past abuses — including during this recent war, and political assassinations and enforced disappearances during the civil war (1975-1990) — is a source of grievance that is being exploited by all sides. The government is under pressure to concede more space to Hizbullah. There is a real risk that the country could plunge into sectarian violence once again.

One commentator predicts a nightmare scenario of failing states from the Hindu Kush to the Horn of Africa, with Pakistan, Afghanistan and Somalia as bookends, and Iraq, the Occupied Territories and Lebanon at the core of this band of instability. Others speak of the revival of a Cold War mindset of "them and us" in which powerful states seek to fight their enemies through proxy wars in someone else's backyard. The prognosis for human rights is dire.

A FUTURE FREE OF FEAR

One can get sucked into the fear syndrome or one can take a radically different approach: an approach based on sustainability rather than security.

The term sustainability may be more familiar to development economists and environmentalists, but it is crucial too for human rights activists. A sustainable strategy promotes hope, human rights and democracy, while a security strategy addresses fears and dangers. Just as energy security is best provided through sustainable development, human security is best pursued through institutions that promote respect for human rights.

Sustainability requires rejecting the Cold War tradition of each super power sponsoring its own pool of dictatorships and abusive regimes. It means promoting principled leadership and enlightened policies.

Sustainability requires strengthening the rule of law and human rights — nationally and internationally. Elections have drawn a lot of international attention, from Bolivia to Bangladesh, Chile to Liberia. But as the Democratic Republic of the Congo and Iraq have shown, creating the conditions in which people can cast their ballots is not enough. A bigger challenge is to promote good governance, including an effective legal and judicial structure, the rule of law based on human rights, a free press and a vibrant civil society.

A properly functioning system of rule of law at the national level is the ultimate safeguard for human rights. But such a system of law, if it is to be truly just, must embrace women and the poor. The majority of poor people today live outside the protection of the law. Including them in a meaningful way requires giving effect to economic and social rights in public policy and programmes. In too many countries women continue to be denied equality before the law. Equal access of women to all human rights is not only a precondition for sustaining human rights, but also for economic prosperity and social stability.

Sustainability requires revitalizing UN human rights reform. Humiliated and sidelined by its most powerful members and ignored by governments such as Sudan and Iran, the credibility of the UN Security Council has suffered badly. Yet when the UN fails, the authority of its powerful member states is also eroded. It is in the USA's own interest to discard the "pick and choose" approach to the UN and recognize the value of multilateralism as a crucial means of promoting greater stability and security through human rights.

The UN Human Rights Council appears to be displaying some worrying signs of factionalism reminiscent of its predecessor institution. But it is not

SUSTAINABILITY REQUIRES STRENGTHENING THE RULE OF LAW AND HUMAN RIGHTS – NATIONALLY AND INTERNATIONALLY too late to change. Member countries can play a constructive role – and some, including India and Mexico, are indeed doing so – to make the Council more willing to tackle human rights crises and less open to political selectivity and manipulation.

The new UN Secretary General too must assert himself to show leadership as a champion of human rights. The UN's responsibility for human rights is a unique one that no other entity can usurp. All organs and officials of the UN must live up to it.

Sustainability in human rights terms means nurturing hope. From the many examples in 2006, we can draw lessons for the future.

The ending of the decade-long conflict in Nepal, with its attendant human rights abuses, was a clear example of what can be achieved through collective effort. The UN and interested governments, working with national political leaders and human rights activists in the country and abroad, responded to the powerful call from the people of Nepal.

International justice is critical for sustaining respect for human rights, and in 2006 Nigeria finally handed over former Liberian President Charles Taylor to the Special Court for Sierra Leone to be tried for war crimes and crimes against humanity. The International Criminal Court (ICC) began its first prosecution against a warlord from the Democratic Republic of the Congo for recruiting child solders. The Lord's Resistance Army, a Ugandan rebel group, is next on the ICC's list, as are perpetrators of the atrocities in Darfur. In pressing for accountability of armed groups as well as government actors, the ICC is setting an important precedent at a time when armed groups are flexing their muscles with brutal consequences for human rights.

A massive campaign by civil society organizations moved the UN General Assembly in 2006 to adopt a resolution to start work on an Arms Trade Treaty. Proliferation of arms is a major threat to human rights and the willingness of governments to bring it under control is an important step towards achieving "freedom from fear".

These positive developments – and many more – have happened because of the courage and commitment of civil society. Indeed, the single most significant sign of hope for transforming the human rights landscape is the human rights movement itself – millions of defenders, activists and ordinary people, including members of Amnesty International, who are demanding change.

Marches, petitions, virals, blogs, t-shirts and armbands may not seem much by themselves, but by bringing people together they unleash an energy for change that should not be underestimated. Darfur has become a household word for international solidarity thanks to the efforts of civil society. The killings unfortunately have not stopped, but civil society will not allow world leaders to forget Darfur as long as its people are unsafe. Gender justice has a long journey still to make, but the campaign by Iranian human rights activist and Nobel Peace Prize winner Shirin Ebadi for equality of women in Iran is lighting a flame that will not die down until the battle has been won. The campaign for the abolition of the death penalty goes from strength to strength thanks to civil society.

People power will change the face of human rights in the 21st century. Hope is very much alive.

CIVIL SOCIETY WILL NOT ALLOW WORLD LEADERS TO FORGET DARFUR AS LONG AS ITS PEOPLE ARE UNSAFE

At the end of 2006, nearly 400 detainees were still held without charge or trial at the US detention centre in Guantánamo Bay, Cuba.

© Brennan Linsley/AP/Empics

More than 2 million people have been displaced by the conflict in Sudan, 130,000 of whom are in the Gereida camp in Darfur. © Reuters/Zohra Bensemra®

REGIONAL OVERVIEWS

AFRICA

The human rights situation in many parts of Africa remained precarious in 2006. Armed conflict, under-development, extreme poverty, widespread corruption, inequitable distribution of resources, political repression, marginalization, ethnic and civil violence, and the HIV/AIDS pandemic continued to undermine the enjoyment of human rights across the region.

Although armed conflicts generally were on the decrease, they still affected many countries. As a result, several million refugees and internally displaced people, including children and the elderly, remained without basic shelter, protection and care.

Most states suppressed dissent and the free expression of opinion. Some governments authorized or condoned extrajudicial executions, arbitrary arrests, torture and other ill-treatment, or harassment of opposition political activists, human rights defenders and journalists. Across the region, suspects in criminal investigations continued to be at high risk of torture in part because of poor police training and supervision, as well as public pressure on police to tackle high rates of crime.

The enjoyment of economic, social and cultural rights such as the rights to food, shelter, health and education remained a mere illusion for the vast majority of people in Africa. Corruption and under-investment in social services contributed to entrenched poverty.

ARMED CONFLICTS

At least a dozen countries in Africa were affected by armed conflict. Marginalization of certain communities, small arms proliferation and struggles for geo-political power and control of natural resources were some of the underlying causes of the conflicts.

Although there were numerous peace and international mediation processes, Burundi, Central African Republic (CAR), Chad, Côte d'Ivoire, Democratic Republic of the Congo (DRC), Eritrea, Ethiopia, the Republic of Congo, Senegal, Sudan and Somalia were among the countries still engaged in or affected by conflict. In all these countries, civilians continued to suffer human rights abuses, and the most affected were women, children and the elderly. The conflicts in CAR, Chad, Sudan and Somalia (with the involvement of Ethiopia), represented an escalation of conflict in central and east Africa.

Even in countries where peace processes were under way, such as in Côte d'Ivoire, the DRC and Sudan, civilians continued to face attacks and were inadequately protected by their governments.

Conflict continued in the Darfur region of Sudan, despite the Darfur Peace Agreement. The Sudanese government failed to disarm the armed militia known as the Janjawid, which attacked civilians in Sudan and eastern Chad. Tens of thousands of Darfuris who escaped the killing, rape and pillage were living in refugee camps in CAR and Chad, unable to return to their villages. At least 200,000 people had died and 2.5 million internally displaced by the end of 2006.

Armed opposition groups in Chad, Côte d'Ivoire and Sudan carried out human rights abuses, and in CAR, Chad and Sudan they continued to launch attacks against their respective government forces using other countries as bases.

Despite presidential and legislative elections in the DRC in July and October, the peace process and future stability of the country remained under serious threat, particularly because of the failure to reform the new national army into a professional and apolitical force that respects human rights. The new army committed numerous serious human rights violations and the government failed to exclude suspected perpetrators from its ranks. Congolese armed groups, as well as foreign armed groups from Burundi, Rwanda and Uganda present in the DRC, also threatened the peace and committed human rights abuses. Lack of security limited humanitarian access to many areas in the east.

Proliferation of small arms remained a serious problem, particularly in Burundi, the DRC, Somalia and Sudan, contributing to a vicious cycle of violence, instability, poor human rights situations and humanitarian crises.

In Angola, the Memorandum of Understanding for Peace and Reconciliation in Cabinda was signed by the government and the Cabindan Forum for Dialogue, formally ending the armed conflict in Cabinda. However, sporadic attacks by both sides against civilians persisted.

Despite intense diplomatic efforts, notably by the UN and the African Union (AU), human rights abuses continued to be reported in Côte d'Ivoire. Government security forces and the Forces Nouvelles (New Forces), a coalition of armed groups in control of the north since September 2002, were implicated. Both protagonists repeatedly postponed disarmament and demobilization, and the reintegration programme remained deadlocked because of disagreement over the timetable.

In Somalia, the militias of the Union of Islamic Courts, which had conquered Mogadishu in June, were defeated in December by an Ethiopian force supporting the internationally recognized Transitional Federal Government. Uncertainties remained about the deployment of an AU peace support force to protect this government, as authorized by the UN Security Council.

The border dispute between Ethiopia and Eritrea continued to be a source of tension.

ECONOMIC, SOCIAL AND CULTURAL RIGHTS

The realization of economic, social and cultural rights remained illusory in virtually all countries in Africa. Struggling economies, under-development, under-investment in basic social services, corruption, and marginalization of certain communities were some of the factors behind the failure to realise these basic human rights. In countries such as Angola, Chad, the DRC, Equatorial Guinea, Nigeria, the Republic of Congo and Sudan, the presence of oil and other minerals continued to blight rather than enhance people's lives because of conflicts, corruption and power struggles.

Hundreds of thousands of people in many African countries were deliberately rendered homeless. By forcibly evicting people without due process of law, adequate compensation or provision of alternative shelter, governments violated people's internationally recognized human right to shelter and adequate housing.

Such evictions, which were often accompanied by disproportionate use of force and other abuses, were known to have taken place in Angola, Equatorial Guinea, Kenya, Nigeria and Sudan. In one incident in August, bulldozers arrived unannounced in Dar al-Salam, a settlement for displaced people 43 kilometres south of Khartoum, Sudan, and began demolishing the homes of some 12,000 people, many of whom had fled drought, famine, the north-south civil war and, most recently, the conflict in Darfur. Some 50,000 other people in Sudan continued to face eviction as a result of the building of the Meroe dam; in 2006 a total of 2,723 households in the Amri area were given six days to evacuate their homes and reportedly given no shelter, food or medicine.

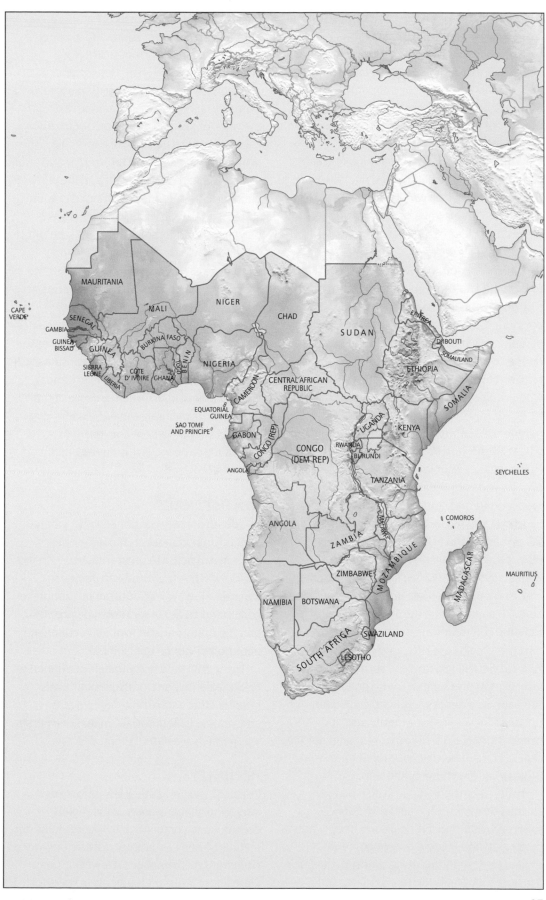

The HIV/AIDS pandemic continued to pose a threat to millions of Africans. According to UNAIDS (the Joint UN Programme on HIV/AIDS), the virus caused 2.1 million deaths in 2006 and 2.8 million people were newly infected, bringing to 24.7 million the total number of people living with HIV/AIDS on the continent.

Women and girls in Africa remained 40 per cent more likely to be infected with the virus than men, and often carried the main burden as carers. Violence against women and girls in some countries also increased their risk of HIV infection.

National responses to HIV/AIDS continued to be scaled up throughout the continent. The roll-out of anti-retroviral treatment continued, albeit unevenly. In June UNAIDS estimated that more than one million people on the continent were receiving life-saving anti-retroviral therapy – 23 per cent of those who required it.

In South Africa, the country with the largest number of people living with HIV/AIDS, the government showed signs of greater openness to the participation of civil society organizations in achieving a more effective response to the pandemic.

At the AU Special Summit on HIV/AIDS, Tuberculosis and Malaria in Abuja, Nigeria, in May, African governments committed themselves to "universal access to treatment, care and prevention services for all people by 2010." This call was reiterated, albeit with few tangible commitments, at the UN General Assembly High Level Review Meeting on HIV/AIDS (UNGASS Review) shortly afterwards. UN member states committed themselves to working towards achieving universal access to treatment, care and prevention by 2010. Countries throughout the region were developing national targets and indicators for achieving this aim.

Tuberculosis and malaria also posed a serious threat in many areas. In 2006 tuberculosis killed over 500,000 people across the region and around 900,000 people in Africa, most of them young children, died from acute cases of malaria.

REPRESSION OF DISSENT

Repression of dissent continued in many countries. The authorities in Eritrea, Ethiopia, Rwanda, Sudan, Uganda and Zimbabwe were among those that used a licensing/accreditation system to restrict the work of journalists and consequently impinged on the freedom of expression. The promulgation and use of anti-terror and public order laws to restrict dissent and the work of human rights defenders continued in some states, and human rights defenders were particularly vulnerable in Burundi, the DRC, Ethiopia, Rwanda, Somalia, Sudan and Zimbabwe.

In Ethiopia, for example, opposition party leaders, journalists and human rights defenders who were prisoners of conscience were tried on capital charges such as treason, attempted genocide and armed conspiracy. In Eritrea, members of minority evangelical churches were imprisoned because of their faith, and former government leaders, members of parliament and journalists continued to be held without trial, many of them feared dead.

DEATH PENALTY

The death penalty continued to be widely applied and prisoners remained under sentence of death in several countries in the region, including around 600 people in Rwanda. However, the Tanzanian authorities commuted all death sentences during 2006, and the ruling party in Rwanda recommended abolition of capital punishment.

In the DRC military tribunals continued to pass the death penalty after unfair trials, although there were no reports of state executions. In Equatorial Guinea, one person was publicly executed for murder.

IMPUNITY

Police officers and other law enforcement personnel in many parts of the region continued to commit human rights violations, including unlawful killings, torture or other ill-treatment, with impunity. However, there were important developments in the efforts to end impunity for war crimes and other serious crimes under international law.

Following the referral of the situation in Darfur by the UN Security Council in March 2005, the Office of the Prosecutor of the International Criminal Court (ICC) visited Khartoum in 2006.

Warrants of arrest issued in 2005 against senior members of the Ugandan armed political group, the Lord's Resistance Army (LRA) – including Joseph Kony, Vincent Otti, Okot Odhiambo and Dominic Ongwen – remained in force, but the accused were not apprehended. The LRA leaders argued that the warrants should be withdrawn before they would commit to a peace agreement, but the warrants remained in force at the end of the year.

In the DRC, Thomas Lubanga Dyilo, leader of an Ituri armed group, the Union of Congolese Patriots, was arrested and charged with war crimes – specifically, recruiting and using in hostilities children aged under 15. He was subsequently transferred to the ICC in The Hague, the Netherlands.

In March, former Liberian President Charles Taylor was handed over to Liberia by Nigeria, where he had been living. He was then transferred to the Special Court for Sierra Leone to face trial on charges of war crimes and crimes against humanity committed during the armed conflict in Sierra Leone. In addition, three trials before the Special Court continued of those bearing the greatest responsibility for crimes against humanity, war crimes and other serious violations of international law committed in the civil war in Sierra Leone after 30 November 1996.

In Ethiopia, the 12-year trial of former President Mengistu Hailemariam ended in December with his conviction for genocide, mass killings and other crimes. Along with 24 other members of the Dergue military government (1974-1991), he was tried in his absence while in exile in Zimbabwe. Zimbabwe President Robert Mugabe had refused to extradite him for trial.

In July 2006, the AU Assembly of Heads of State and Government asked Senegal to try Hissène Habré, Chad's former President, for crimes against humanity he committed while in power (1982-1990). He had been living in Senegal since he was ousted from office. In 2005 a Belgian judge issued an international arrest warrant for torture and other crimes committed during his rule. In November 2006 Senegal's Council of Ministers adopted a draft law allowing Hissène Habré to be tried.

Trials of prominent genocide suspects continued before the International Criminal Tribunal for Rwanda (ICTR), which held 57 detainees at the end of 2006. Ten trials were ongoing. The UN Security Council asked the ICTR to complete all trials by the end of 2008. However, the ICTR failed to indict or prosecute leaders of the former Rwandese Patriotic Front widely believed to have authorized, condoned or carried out war crimes and crimes against humanity in 1994.

In Rwanda, concerns remained about the impartiality and fairness of gacaca tribunals (a community-based system of tribunals established in Rwanda in 2002 to try people suspected of crimes during the 1994 genocide).

VIOLENCE AGAINST WOMEN AND GIRLS

Violence against women and girls remained pervasive and only a few countries were considering laws to address the problem. Parliaments in Kenya, Nigeria, South Africa and Zimbabwe continued to discuss draft legislation on domestic violence and sexual offences.

In South Africa and Swaziland in particular, the pervasiveness of gender-based violence continued to place women and girls at risk of HIV/AIDS directly or through obstructing their access to information, prevention and treatment. Gender-based violence, as well as stigma and discrimination, also affected access to treatment for those already living with HIV/AIDS.

The practice of female genital mutilation remained widespread in some countries, particularly Sierra Leone, Somalia and Sudan.

In the DRC, women and girls were raped by government security forces and armed groups and had little or no access to adequate medical treatment. In Darfur, rape of women by Janjawid militias continued to be systematic. The number of women attacked and raped while searching for firewood around Kalma Camp near Nyala, South Darfur, increased from about three or four a month to some 200 a month between June and August.

In Nigeria there were frequent reports of sexual violence, including rape, by state officials. Such abuses were committed with impunity. In Côte d'Ivoire there were continuing reports of sexual violence against women in the government-controlled areas and the region held by the Forces Nouvelles.

REGIONAL INSTITUTIONS AND HUMAN RIGHTS

Although the Constitutive Act of the AU underscores the centrality of the promotion and protection of human rights throughout the continent, the AU fell short of its commitment to human rights generally. The AU continued to demonstrate a deep reluctance to publicly criticize African leaders who failed to protect human rights, especially in Sudan and Zimbabwe.

A combination of lack of political will and capacity of the AU to halt continuing conflicts in places such as Darfur, and the apathy of an international community that had the capacity but lacked the will to act, left millions of civilians at the mercy of belligerent governments and ruthless warlords.

Many of the institutions referred to under the Constitutive Act of the AU became fully operational in 2006 but they made little or no impact on people's lives. However, the election of 11 judges to the newly established African Court on Human and Peoples' Rights enhanced the prospects of developing a culture that would respect the rule of law and human rights regionally. The Court held its first meeting in July and the judges began drafting the Court's rules of procedure. A draft legal instrument relating to the establishment of a merged court comprising the African Court on Human and Peoples' Rights and the African Court of Justice was being negotiated at the end of the year.

The African Peer Review Mechanism completed the review of Ghana, Rwanda and South Africa but failed to make its findings public. The African Commission on Human and Peoples' Rights, which remained the only functional regional human rights body, continued to be denied the much needed human, material and financial resources to fully respond to the many human rights problems in the region.

Overall, widespread and massive corruption in Africa continued to contribute to a vicious cycle of extreme poverty, manifesting itself in violations of internationally recognized human rights, especially economic and social rights, weak institutions and leadership, and marginalization of the most vulnerable sectors of the population, including women and children.

AMERICAS

The Americas remained an extraordinarily diverse region, encompassing some of the world's most economically advantaged populations in North America as well as some of the world's poorest countries in the Caribbean and Latin America. Common to the whole region, however, were a range of complex and pressing political, social and economic challenges that impinge on the fulfilment of fundamental human rights.

The USA, unrivalled in military and economic terms in the region and the world, continued to maintain a dual discourse on human rights as it pursued its "war on terror". It claimed to be the leading force for the promotion of human rights and the rule of law, while simultaneously pursuing policies and practices that flouted some of the most basic principles of international law. In so doing, it undermined not only long-term security of which the rule of law is a central pillar, but also its own credibility on the international stage.

Nowhere was the erosion of US credibility and influence more marked than in Latin America. Growing numbers of South American countries in particular have sought to dissociate themselves from political, economic and security policies promoted by the USA, and relations between the US and several Latin American governments have become increasingly fractious. Political tensions and mutual criticisms were sharpest between the USA and Venezuela.

A key feature of 2006 was the continuing strengthening of democratic processes and the consolidation of democratic institutions. Eleven countries held presidential elections, some combined with legislative and state elections. The transition of power was peaceful, despite legal challenges by some losing candidates, such as in Mexico. In general, the elections were judged by observers to have been fair.

Cuba, the only one-party state in the region, also underwent a transfer of power as Fidel Castro's brother Raúl was temporarily appointed President.

The peaceful transfer of government power in so many countries was a significant achievement in a region that has been plagued by political instability and violent electoral campaigns. Many of the new governments were elected on anti-poverty agendas imposed by electorates increasingly frustrated by the failure of prevailing economic policies to reduce poverty. The consolidation of democratic processes provided an unprecedented opportunity for the region's governments to tackle persistent human rights violations and pervasive poverty.

Indeed, after decades of neglect of deep-rooted social and economic problems, there were encouraging signs that some governments in Latin America in particular were moving beyond a rhetorical commitment to human rights towards the adoption and implementation of social and economic policies that could begin to address the region's long-standing inequities.

Among the promises made by some new governments were reforms to address structural flaws, such as inequitable land tenure, entrenched discrimination in the justice system and lack of access to basic services, which underpin violations of human rights.

However, progress was slow and Latin America remained one of the most economically inequitable parts of the world. Poverty remained endemic and access to basic services such as health and education continued to be denied or limited for most people. The poor rural populations in particular were denied access to justice and basic services — vast rural areas were neglected by the state leaving large numbers of people isolated and insecure.

High expectations risk being dashed as democracy and good governance were threatened by chronically weak institutions and undermined by lack of independence of the judiciary, impunity and endemic corruption.

Civil society in the Americas continued to play an increasingly prominent role in challenging governments' lack of accountability and the lack of access to public services and to the justice system for the region's poor. Human rights defenders were key in the struggle for political, economic and social rights. Their work contributed to highlighting the social and economic inequalities in the region and they played a crucial role in legitimizing the struggle of the most vulnerable sectors of society, including Indigenous peoples, women, and lesbian, gay, bisexual and transgender (LGBT) people.

Public opposition to governments frequently led to massive and protracted social protests, which often met a repressive response from security forces. For example, the political crisis in Oaxaca, Mexico, sparked by a mass strike by teachers, resulted in huge protests against the state governor over many months. Despite the fact that only some protesters were violent, the state authorities and their sympathizers reportedly responded by targeting all individuals and organizations perceived as sympathetic to the opposition movement.

INSECURITY AND CONFLICT

High levels of violent crime and lack of public security continued to be major public concerns. Poverty, violence and the proliferation of small arms — daily realities for millions of people in the Americas — created and sustained environments where human rights abuses flourished.

Governments have traditionally resorted to repressive law enforcement strategies to deal with the consequences of state neglect, discrimination and social exclusion. Such policies have resulted in poor communities sinking deeper into violence and insecurity, particularly in urban centres. In cities in Brazil, El Salvador, Guatemala, Haiti, Honduras and Jamaica, youth and armed criminal gangs posed a serious threat. Several states increasingly resorted to military "containment" of neighbourhoods, leaving many inhabitants exposed to the violence of both the gangs that dominate the communities and repressive state forces.

One of the more visible consequences of states' repressive security measures was rampant violence in the region's overcrowded and out-of-control prisons. The phenomenon of prisons as "no go" areas to the security forces spread in Central and South America. In Brazil, for example, a criminal gang in São Paulo's prison system orchestrated simultaneous riots in around 70 prisons in the state. At the same time, the gangs' leaders from within the detention system ordered criminal attacks across the state, which resulted in the killing of over 40 law enforcement officers and widespread damage. Police killed over 100 suspects during the confrontation, and many others died in suspected "death-squad"-style retaliations.

In Colombia, which has endured one of the world's most intractable conflicts, the humanitarian crisis continued. The security forces, army-backed paramilitaries and guerrilla groups were responsible for many human rights abuses, including war crimes and crimes against humanity. Human rights defenders, trades unionists, and indigenous and community leaders were particularly vulnerable.

In addition, the Colombia conflict continued to affect the rights of people living near the borders in neighbouring countries. In Ecuador, Panama and Venezuela, rural populations were particularly exposed to threats from armed forces, both state and non-state, and the risk of forced recruitment into armed groups.

'WAR ON TERROR'

Further evidence emerged of a systematic pattern of abuse by the USA and its allies in the context of the "war on terror", including secret detention, enforced disappearance, prolonged incommunicado and arbitrary detention, and torture or other cruel, inhuman or degrading treatment. At the end of 2006, thousands of detainees continued to be held in US custody without charge or trial in Iraq, Afghanistan and Guantánamo Bay, Cuba.

Despite several adverse judicial rulings, the US administration persisted in pursuing policies and practices inconsistent with human rights standards. The US Congress, despite some positive initiatives, gave its stamp of approval to human rights violations committed by the USA in the "war on terror" and turned bad executive policy into bad domestic law.

In sharp contrast to positive developments in Latin America, there was a continued failure to hold senior US government officials accountable for torture and ill-treatment of "war on terror" detainees, despite evidence that abuses had been systematic.

A shift in the balance of power in the US Congress as a result of the November mid-term elections raised the possibility of greater congressional oversight and investigation of executive actions, and of improved legislation.

DISCRIMINATION: STEPS FORWARD, STEPS BACK

Violence against women continued to be widespread throughout the Americas. Governments failed to uphold laws that criminalize violence against women in the home and the community, nor did they provide support and protection for victims of violence. Lack of judges and prosecutors specialized in gender-based violence as well as a lack of gender-sensitive police units and adequate and sufficient shelters demonstrated a fundamental lack of political will to end the endemic violence against women.

Despite national and international indignation, the pattern of killings of women continued in Colombia, El Salvador, Guatemala, Honduras and Mexico, among other countries.

However, women's rights, including their sexual and reproductive rights, were high on the agendas of political and civil society. In Chile, for example, the authorities successfully petitioned in the courts to allow the distribution without parental consent of the "morning-after pill" to girls over the age of 14. In Peru, the Constitutional Tribunal ruled that the "morning-after pill" should be available to every woman. In Colombia, abortion was decriminalized in cases of rape in certain situations.

In contrast, the Constitutional Court in Ecuador ruled that emergency contraception should not be available, and the authorities in Nicaragua repealed the law that had allowed abortion in certain cases of rape.

Violations of the rights of Indigenous peoples, including violence against women and girls, were reported throughout the region. Indigenous peoples continued to face entrenched racism and discriminatory treatment. Denied adequate protection of their right to live on and use the lands and territories vital to their cultural identity and their daily survival, Indigenous communities were often driven into extreme poverty and ill-health.

During 2006 the trend of reassertion of Indigenous identity continued to grow. In the Andean countries in particular, this trend was reflected in the emergence of Indigenous peoples as a political force at the national level, as in Bolivia, and at a local level. Parallel to this, growing ethnic divisions became apparent in Andean countries with the largest proportion of Indigenous people. In Bolivia, ethnic divisions were aggravated by demands for greater regional autonomy by the mainly non-Indigenous departments of Santa Cruz, Tarija, Beni and Pando.

The LGBT community continued to suffer stigma, discrimination and abuse in many countries in the Americas, although they also gained visibility and some acceptability, particularly in major cities.

In Nicaragua, lesbian and gay relationships remained criminalized and in Caribbean countries a number of "sodomy laws" were still in force. However, there were positive moves in some countries to ensure equality before the law. Mexico City passed a landmark ruling recognizing same-sex unions. The Congress in Colombia discussed a bill that if approved would give same-sex couples the same social security rights as those enjoyed by couples of the opposite sex.

IMPUNITY ROLLED BACK

Several countries in Latin America faced the painful legacy of past human rights violations. The issues of truth, justice and reparation were high on the agenda of civil society, the judiciary and some governments, and action was taken against several former senior officials.

In Argentina, Miguel Etchecolatz, former Director of Investigations of the Buenos Aires Province Police, was convicted of murder, torture and kidnappings during the period of the military government (1976-1983) and sentenced to life imprisonment in September. The three judges in the case ruled that he was responsible for crimes against humanity.

Former Peruvian President Alberto Fujimori was granted bail in May in Chile pending a decision by the Chilean Supreme Court of Justice on whether to extradite him to Peru to face charges of corruption and human rights violations. The Supreme Court established that Alberto Fujimori was not allowed to leave the country until a decision was reached.

The prosecution in Mexico of former senior officials accused of crimes against humanity committed in the 1960s, 1970s and 1980s continued to collapse. However, in November a federal court ordered the rearrest of former President Luis Echeverría to stand trial on the charge of genocide in connection with the murder of students in Tlatelolco Square in 1968.

In November, a Uruguayan judge ordered the detention and trial of former President Juan María Bordaberry (1971-1976) and former Minister of Foreign Affairs Juan Carlos Blanco. They were charged in connection with the killings of legislators Zelmar Michelini and Héctor Gutiérrez Ruiz, as well as Rosario Barredo and William Whitelaw, members of the Tupamaro guerrilla group Movement of National Liberation, in Argentina in 1976. The judicial decision was appealed.

The need for speedier justice was thrown into stark relief by the death on 10 December of former Chilean ruler Augusto Pinochet before he had faced trial for atrocities during his 17-year rule. Just weeks before his death he faced new charges in connection with 35 kidnappings, one homicide and 24 cases of torture. Former Paraguayan President Alfredo Stroessner died in exile in Brazil without ever having been brought to trial for the widespread human rights violations committed during his rule between 1954 and 1989.

Universal jurisdiction continued to play a key role in tackling the legacy of past human rights violations in Latin America. A judge in Spain issued arrest warrants for Guatemala's former President General Efraín Ríos Montt and several former senior army officials, who faced charges of genocide, torture, terrorism and illegal detention. However, former General Efraín Ríos Montt remained free after the Guatemalan authorities considered only part of the case presented by the Spanish National Court. Two other former officials were in custody and a third was a fugitive from justice.

REGIONAL DEVELOPMENTS

The Inter-American Commission on Human Rights and the Inter-American Court of Human Rights, the human rights mechanisms of the Organization of American States (OAS), issued a number of significant decisions. If implemented by states parties, these should not only address particular cases of denials or violations of human rights of individuals but also set important precedents for systematic change across the region.

No progress was made on negotiations for a free trade agreement for the Americas; such an agreement was viewed in many countries with scepticism or rejection. However, progress was made on strengthening trading partnerships within Latin America.

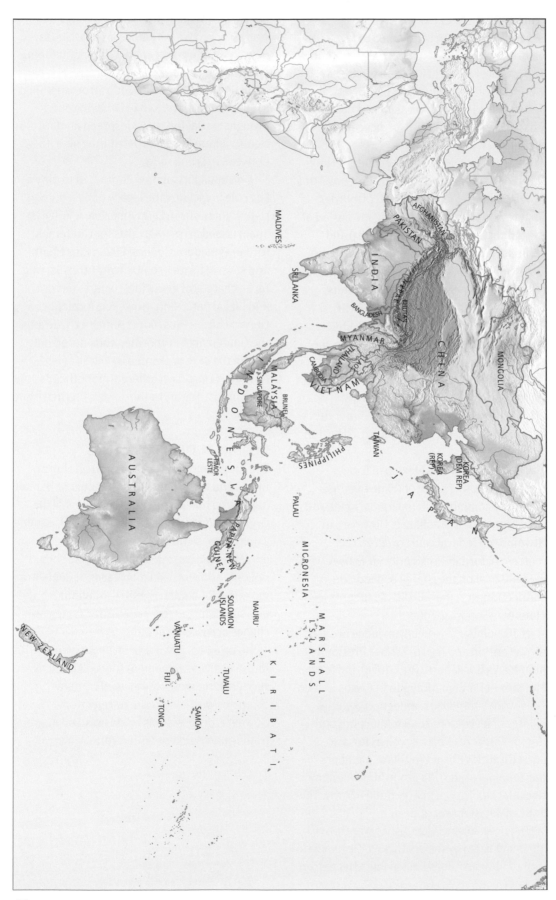

ASIA-PACIFIC

2006 was a year of dramatic events and much change in Asia and the Pacific. Political upheavals provided the context for accounts of fear, deprivation and discrimination. These included political unrest in Timor-Leste, Tonga and the Solomon Islands, and the declaration of a state of emergency in the Philippines that sparked fears of increased political killings. In Bangladesh, politically motivated violence marred the run-up to delayed elections, and in Myanmar the authorities continued their policy of incarceration and repression of political opposition. Sri Lankan peace talks collapsed and a ceasefire barely held; thousands of killings and mass displacement occurred through the year and in November the ceasefire was declared "defunct" by the opposition armed group Liberation Tigers of Tamil Eelam (LTTE). Coups took place in Thailand and Fiji. Alongside the anxiety, suffering and despair was hope and opportunity in Nepal where, after years of conflict and political stalemate, people came together to demand peace, human rights and democratic transition. Their voices were heard and the opportunity for peaceful transition appeared to have been seized when the King and political parties agreed a way forward that saw a comprehensive peace agreement signed in November.

The Asia-Pacific region is home to six of the 10 most populous states in the world, and alone they account for half the world's people. Several events in 2006 reflected the region's growing role on the world stage. China's global commercial and political influence grew, and its preparations for the 2008 summer Olympic games generated a climate of pride and some debate. Viet Nam was set to become the World Trade Organization's (WTO's) 150th member in January 2007 after its membership was approved by the WTO's General Council in late 2006. A South Korean, Ban Ki-Moon, was chosen to be the next UN Secretary-General.

In terms of human rights developments, governments' words and deeds were not always well matched. Ten countries in the region joined the new UN Human Rights Council and made admirable statements on human rights. The Association of Southeast Asian Nations (ASEAN) took steps towards a greater role for human rights in its work. However, Asia and the Pacific remained alone in having no regional human rights mechanism, and on the ground improvements in human rights protections were patchy.

GLOBALIZATION: PROSPERITY, POVERTY AND MIGRATION

Globalization continued to have a profound impact in the region. China and India in particular notched up envied rates of economic growth while strengthening their economic ties with each other. However, such developments did not bring benefits to everyone. Some industrialization and development projects brought displacement and human rights abuses, and millions of the most disadvantaged people remained in poverty as the benefits of development were enjoyed disproportionately by those better educated, housed and skilled. According to the UN, more than 28 per cent of people in India remained below the national poverty line. The figures were 50 per cent in Bangladesh, 40 per cent in Mongolia and 33 per cent in Pakistan.

In particular, the rural-urban divide meant that economic development had yet to have a positive effect on the lives of many rural populations. In India, for example, overall unemployment increased, despite the booming service sector, and desperation in rural areas was reflected in a disturbingly high number of suicides by farmers – the government reported that 16,000 took place annually between 2003 and 2006, and 100,000 in the preceding 10 years.

China continued to witness vast numbers of people moving out of poverty as well as shocking disparity between living standards in rural and urban communities. Reports published in 2006 estimated that earnings in towns were almost four times higher than in rural areas. Life expectancy in urban China was reportedly between 10 and 15 years longer than that for a farmer, despite appalling health and safety conditions for many industrial workers in various sectors.

Economic development held great promise but failed to improve the lives of the many who are marginal or suffer discrimination, such as women and ethnic minorities, as underlying structures of inequality remained deeply embedded. The processes of wealth creation benefited limited numbers, as large swathes of the region's population remained in poverty with little or no access to adequate health care, education or housing.

Although globalization and the freer flow of goods, services and finance across borders was largely welcomed in the region, migration was often the only way for people to benefit from the new employment and earning opportunities but such movement remained limited and dangerous. Migrants were treated badly in many Asian and Pacific states, with governments failing to protect their rights.

Other dynamics affecting the movement of people were conflicts and pervasive forms of discrimination. In 2006, armed conflicts displaced at least 213,000 people in Sri Lanka and 16,000 in Myanmar's Karen state. Some 150,000 refugees remained on the Thai/Myanmar border; 100,000 North Koreans were reportedly in China, having fled hunger; and around 7,000 Lao Hmong refugees remained in a camp in Thailand.

SECURITY CONCERNS

The "war on terror" continued to claim lives and to be associated with enforced disappearances, particularly in Afghanistan and Pakistan.

In Afghanistan, the security situation in the south and south-east deteriorated rapidly. The spread of the insurgency in the country, coupled with lawlessness, led to increased social unrest. The escalating conflict resulted in the deaths and injuries of thousands of civilians. Serious breaches of international humanitarian law were committed by all parties to the conflict, including international and Afghan security forces, and the Taleban. The continuing inability of the international community and the Afghan government to ensure good governance and the rule of law added to the culture of impunity, further fuelling local resentments. Government administrators, teachers and human rights defenders, many of them women, faced threats and violent attacks, sometimes leading to death, by the Taleban and local power-holders. Pervasive poverty, food shortages and a lack of safe drinking water exacerbated by drought added to the suffering of people and internal displacement.

In Thailand, violence continued in the mainly Muslim southern provinces. Armed groups bombed, beheaded or shot Muslim and Buddhist civilians, including monks and teachers, and members of the security forces. Those who tried to take action on these and other abuses faced death threats and violent attacks, sometimes leading to death. Under the Emergency Decree, scores of people were detained arbitrarily without charge or trial, denied access to lawyers, and some were tortured or otherwise ill-treated during interrogation.

In Australia anti-terror legislation raised many concerns about the protection of human rights, and in India the debate continued about the introduction of a "war on terror" law.

A nuclear test by North Korea in October heightened tension in north-east Asia and beyond, prompting fears of an arms race in the region, while hunger continued to blight the lives of untold numbers in the country. There were also calls for changes to Japan's anti-war constitutional provisions, while across Asia and beyond, the survivors of Japan's system of military sexual slavery — before and during World War II — continued their dignified call for justice, despite their dwindling numbers and lack of full reparations.

HUMAN RIGHTS: WORDS AND DEEDS

Ten states from the Asia-Pacific region became members of the new UN Human Rights Council – Bangladesh, China, India, Indonesia, Japan, Malaysia, Pakistan, the Philippines, South Korea and Sri Lanka. Each promised to respect human rights, co-operate with UN human rights mechanisms and special procedures, create or maintain strong national human rights frameworks, and ratify and uphold international human rights standards. However, many of these pledges had yet to bear fruit in practice by the end of 2006. Relatively few states in the region, and only one of the new Human Rights Council members, had ratified the Rome Statute of the International Criminal Court. Applications by UN Special Rapporteurs to visit several states in the region remained pending; in some cases requests had been pending for over a decade, such as that made in 1993 by the Special Rapporteur on torture to visit India.

The dire human rights situation in Myanmar was placed on the agenda for the first time by the UN Security Council in 2006, and the UN Under-Secretary-General for Political Affairs, Ibrahim Gambari, visited the country in May. Meanwhile, Nobel Peace Prize winner and opposition leader Aung San Suu Kyi remained under house arrest in Myanmar, and there was continuing conflict, harassment of political activists, use of forced labour and defiance by the authorities of international criticism, including by ASEAN.

The Asia-Pacific region also lagged behind the steady global march towards abolition of the death penalty and hosted shocking numbers of executions, although some progress was made. China, India, Japan, Malaysia, North Korea, Pakistan, Singapore, Thailand and Viet Nam featured among an alarmingly long list of countries in the region that retained the death penalty despite continued campaigning for abolition from within and beyond their borders. However, the Philippines abolished capital punishment in 2006 and South Korea spent another year considering legislation to abolish the death

penalty while maintaining an unofficial moratorium on its use.

In various parts of the region the space for dissent was limited during 2006, and there was a continuing need to strengthen protections for human rights activists. For example, political killings in the Philippines created widespread fear among political activists as well as human rights defenders wanting to speak out against unlawful killings and the lack of investigations into them.

Entrenched traditional practices that curtail the rights of women and often result in them suffering violence and even death remained widespread across the region but were often marginalized in public debate and policy. Rape, forced marriage, "honour" crimes and the abuse of women and girls in conflicts all continued. In Papua New Guinea, for example, sexual violence remained an everyday experience for many women, and accusations of sorcery resulted in the killing or abduction of women. Despite this, the authorities did little to stop such crimes. In Afghanistan, early and forced marriage and traditional practices such as exchange of girls as a means of dispute settlement remained a continuing threat to the well-being of girls and women.

However, the work of women activists in the region did bear some fruit. In Pakistan, the crimes of rape and sexual violence were amended to ensure that a complaint of rape can no longer be converted into a charge of adultery or fornication. In India, a law on violence against women was finally introduced.

The human rights of lesbian, gay, bisexual and transgender (LGBT) people continued to be regarded as a sensitive subject in many parts of the region. However, LGBT rights activism increased in several countries, including China, India and the Philippines. In India, a hundred public figures, including writers, academics and celebrities, signed an open letter calling for the repeal of Article 377 of the Penal Code which criminalizes homosexuality; in Hong Kong, a young gay activist successfully challenged a law which provides for a higher age of consent for same-sex couples than for heterosexual couples; and in the Philippines, activists lobbied hard for the adoption of a proposed Anti-Discrimination Bill aimed at preventing discrimination against LGBT people.

Leadership on human rights issues emerged in different countries at different levels across the region. At the state level, the Philippines heeded calls to abolish the death penalty. At a popular level, the people of Nepal provided an inspiring demonstration of their strength in moving towards peace and an end to the abuses linked to conflict. Human rights defenders, including women, environmental, indigenous and many other activists, continued to challenge powerful interests to defend basic rights. Collectively, the forces for human rights reform showed courage and determination in confronting resistance to progress from within their own societies as well as multiple forms of state repression. Ultimately, the Asia-Pacific region showed strong demand and great potential for progress across the full spectrum of human rights, with the primary challenge one of political will by governments. The dynamic that made states declare their human rights credentials when contending for membership of the UN Human Rights Council in 2006 should build the momentum towards delivering the full range of economic, social and cultural as well as civil and political rights.

EUROPE - CENTRAL ASIA

Issues of statehood, security and migration continued to be major preoccupations across the region.

Europe's newest state, Montenegro, emerged in June from the continuing break-up of the former Yugoslavia, but a decision on the final status of Kosovo, which formally remained part of Serbia, was postponed until early 2007. No significant progress was made in resolving the status of the region's internationally unrecognized entities, situated within the borders of Azerbaijan, Georgia and Moldova, but remaining outside these states' de facto control. Cyprus continued to be a divided island. In Spain the armed Basque group Euskadi Ta Askatasuna (ETA) declared a "permanent ceasefire" in March but dialogue with the government ended in December after an airport bomb killed two people. In Turkey, there was an overall increase in 2006 in fighting between security forces and the armed Kurdistan Workers Party (PKK), and a rise in bomb attacks on civilians by other armed groups. Impunity as a result of conflicts across the region persisted.

Many countries remained a magnet for those attempting to escape poverty, violence or persecution. Changing migration patterns from Africa saw over 30,000 people arrive on the Canary Islands, with an unknown number of others feared lost on the journey in unsafe boats. However, European states continued to disregard the rights of refugees and migrants, adopting repressive approaches to irregular migration that included forcible detention and expulsion without access to fair and individualized asylum procedures. In the context of the "war on terror", governments also violated their international obligations by returning people to countries despite the risk that they faced serious human rights violations including torture.

Two further countries — Bulgaria and Romania — were set to join the European Union (EU) at the beginning of 2007. While enlargement continued to profile human rights as a prime symbol of candidates' readiness to join, the EU as a beacon "union of values" looked increasingly ambivalent. Further evidence emerged of the EU Council's reluctance to confront the USA in its conduct of the "war on terror" and its failure to "practice what you preach" in relation to migration. An institutional minimalist approach to human rights within the EU's borders, which saw the establishment of a Fundamental Human Rights Agency largely barred from addressing human rights abuses by member states, added to the erosion of credibility domestically and globally on human rights issues.

Racism and discrimination continued across the region. There was a failure of leadership in many countries to convincingly challenge racist and xenophobic ideas and ideologies, to implement comprehensive programmes to combat them, and to act with due diligence to prevent, investigate and prosecute racially motivated attacks. In some countries it was the authorities themselves that discriminated against minorities by failing to uphold their rights. Discrimination was frequently on grounds of identity and legal status — or lack of it — and led to barriers in access to a range of human rights, including economic, social and cultural rights.

SECURITY AND HUMAN RIGHTS

Further evidence emerged of complicity by Europe's governments in the US programme of renditions — an unlawful practice in which numerous men have been illegally detained and secretly flown to countries where they have suffered additional crimes, including torture and enforced disappearance. It became increasingly clear, including through inquiries actively pursued by the Council of Europe and the European Parliament, that

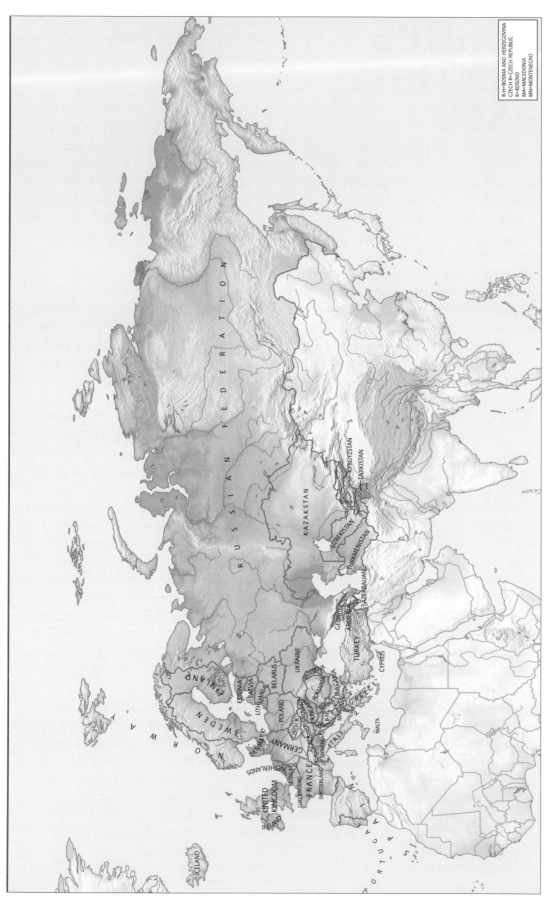

B-H=BOSNIA AND HERZEGOVINA
CZECH R=CZECH REPUBLIC
K=KOSOVO
MA=MACEDONIA
MN=MONTENEGRO

many European governments had adopted a "see no evil, hear no evil" approach when it came to rendition flights using their territory.

Some were willing partners with the US Central Intelligence Agency (CIA) in facilitating abuses. Complicity by states such as Bosnia and Herzegovina, Germany, Italy, Macedonia, Sweden and the UK ranged from acceptance and concealment of renditions, secret detentions and torture or other ill-treatment (and use of information gained from such treatment) to direct involvement in abductions and illegal transfers. There was evidence, furthermore, that security forces of Germany, Turkey and the UK had taken advantage of the situation by interrogating individuals who had been subjected to rendition.

In other areas too, security drove the agenda over fundamental human rights — to the detriment of both. There were grave concerns that the governments of Kazakstan, Kyrgyzstan, Russia and Ukraine, in co-operating with Uzbekistan in the name of regional security and the "war on terror", were violating their obligations under human rights and refugee law by returning people to Uzbekistan despite the risk that they faced serious violations including torture.

The UK government continued to undermine the universal ban on torture by trying to deport people they deemed to be terror suspects to countries with a history of torture or other ill-treatment. The UK authorities sought to rely on inherently unreliable and ineffective "diplomatic assurances" featured in memorandums of understanding agreed with states that had a well-documented record of torture.

In Turkey, the new Law to Fight Terrorism contained sweeping and draconian provisions that could in practice contravene international human rights law and facilitate violations. People charged under existing anti-terrorism legislation in Turkey continued to face unending trials, with some people still detained for more than a decade pending a final verdict in their case.

However, there were other indications — aside from the inquiries into renditions — of a refusal to tolerate such abuses. In a landmark case in Spain, the Supreme Court in July quashed a six-year prison sentence and ordered the immediate release of a man previously held in US detention at Guantánamo Bay, Cuba, on the grounds that evidence obtained while he was there was inadmissible. The court ruled that Guantánamo Bay constituted a legal limbo without guarantees or control and therefore all evidence or procedures originating from it should be declared null and void.

In November, a UN human rights body confirmed that the Swedish authorities had been responsible for multiple human rights violations in connection with a summary expulsion to Egypt. The Swedish government reacted by reiterating that any such finding was not legally binding, and continued to refuse to provide reparation, including compensation, to the victims. In December, Italian prosecutors asked a judge to indict 26 CIA agents accused of kidnapping an Egyptian cleric in the Italian city of Milan and participating in his rendition to Egypt where he was allegedly tortured.

REFUGEES, ASYLUM-SEEKERS AND MIGRANTS

There remained a consistent pattern of human rights violations linked to the interception, detention and expulsion by states of foreign nationals, including those seeking international protection. One year on, there was still no outcome to investigations into the deaths in 2005 of 13 migrants killed while trying to enter the Spanish enclaves of Ceuta and Melilla from Morocco. Three other people died in similar incidents in July 2006.

Men, women and children continued to face obstacles in accessing asylum procedures. Some in Greece, Italy, Malta and the UK were unlawfully detained and others were denied necessary guidance and legal support. Many were unlawfully expelled before their claims could be properly heard, including from Greece, Italy, Malta and Spain. Some were sent to countries where they were at risk of human rights violations.

In response to shifting migration patterns, joint sea patrol missions by various EU countries and co-ordinated by the EU external border control agency Frontex were set up, intended to intercept migrants' boats at sea and return the migrants to their country of origin. This raised serious concerns with respect to fundamental rights, such as the right to seek and enjoy asylum, the right to leave one's own country, and the principle of *non-refoulement*.

New legislation in some countries further restricted the rights of asylum-seekers and migrants. In Switzerland this included refusal of access to the asylum procedure for people without national identity documents. In France a new law tied residence permits for migrants to pre-existing work contracts, putting migrants at risk of exploitation in the workplace.

RACISM AND DISCRIMINATION

Across the region identity-based discrimination was rife against Roma, who remained largely excluded from public life and unable to enjoy full access to rights such as housing, employment and health services. In some countries the authorities failed to fully integrate Romani children into the education system, tolerating or promoting the creation of special classes or schools, including those where a reduced curriculum was taught. Roma were also among those subjected to hate crimes by individuals, as were Jews and Muslims. In Russia, violent racism remained widespread.

Many people faced discrimination on account of their legal status. In Azerbaijan people internally displaced by the Nagorny Karabakh conflict had restricted opportunities to exercise their economic and social rights, including by a cumbersome internal registration process linking eligibility for employment and social services to a fixed place of residence. In Montenegro over 16,000

Roma and Serbs displaced from Kosovo continued to be denied civil, political, economic and social rights because they were refused civil registration. Similar problems faced thousands of people in Slovenia — all from other former Yugoslav republics — who had been unlawfully "erased" from the register of permanent residents. In Estonia, members of the Russian-speaking minority faced limited access to the labour market owing to restrictive linguistic and minority rights.

Authorities in Latvia, Poland and Russia continued to foster a climate of intolerance against the lesbian, gay, bisexual and transgender (LGBT) communities, obstructing public events organized by LGBT groups amid openly homophobic language used by some highly placed politicians.

IMPUNITY AND ACCOUNTABILITY

Although some progress was made in tackling impunity for crimes committed on the territory of the former Yugoslavia during the wars of the 1990s, a lack of full co-operation with the International Criminal Tribunal for the former Yugoslavia together with insufficient efforts by domestic courts meant that many perpetrators of war crimes and crimes against humanity continued to evade justice.

Torture and other ill-treatment, often race-related and frequently used to extract confessions, continued to be reported across the region — routinely so in some countries. Victims described a catalogue of abuses, including mock executions; beatings with fists, plastic bottles full of water, books, truncheons and poles; suffocation; deprivation of food, water and sleep; threats of rape; and electro-shocks to different parts of the body. Obstacles to tackling impunity for such abuses included police circumvention of safeguards, lack of prompt access to a lawyer, victims' fear of reprisals, and lack of a properly resourced and independent system for monitoring and investigating complaints. In Russia, Turkey and Uzbekistan in particular, failures to conduct prompt, thorough and impartial investigations perpetuated an entrenched culture of impunity. Such failures at domestic level in some countries meant that people continued to seek redress at the European Court of Human Rights, adding to its overburdened case load.

DEATH PENALTY

Significant progress continued to be made towards abolition of the death penalty throughout the region. In June, Moldova abolished the death penalty in law, and in November Kyrgyzstan adopted a new Constitution which removed previous provisions on the use of the death penalty.

When the Soviet Union collapsed, all 15 newly independent states retained the death penalty. At the close of 2006, only two of them continued to apply the death penalty in law and practice. These were Belarus and Uzbekistan, both of which continued to cloak in secrecy the exact number of people sentenced to death and executed annually. Uzbekistan even insisted that no death sentence had been passed for two years, even though credible non-governmental organizations in the country reported that at least eight such sentences had been handed down.

While Europe in general followed the global trend towards abolition, the President of Poland sought to buck it by calling in July for the reintroduction of capital punishment in Poland and throughout Europe. Another less positive note were conditions on death row in the region, with some prisoners believed to have been kept in very harsh conditions for many years. In addition, death row inmates in countries (and unrecognized entities) with a moratorium on executions continued to suffer uncertainty about their ultimate fate.

VIOLENCE AGAINST WOMEN

Violence in the home against women and girls remained pervasive across the region for all ages and social groups. It was manifested through a range of verbal and psychological abuse, physical and sexual violence, economic control and killings. Commonly, only a small proportion of women reported this abuse, deterred among other things by fear of

reprisals from abusive partners; fear of prosecution for other offences; self-blame; fear of bringing "shame" on their family; financial insecurity; lack of shelters or other effective measures such as restraining orders to ensure protection for them and their children; and the widespread impunity enjoyed by perpetrators. Women also frequently lacked confidence that the relevant authorities would regard the abuse as a crime, rather than a private matter, and deal with it effectively as such. Failure to bridge that confidence gap in reporting not only hampered justice in individual cases but also impeded efforts to tackle such abuses across society by hiding the full extent and nature of the problem.

While there were some positive moves on legislative protection in this area, other crucial gaps remained. These included the absence in some countries of laws specifically criminalizing domestic violence and a failure to collect comprehensive statistical data. While the new domestic violence law in Georgia was welcome, the failure to approve a national action plan on domestic violence – as stipulated by the law – raised doubts about the authorities' commitment to eradicate domestic violence. In Switzerland, a new law permitted expulsion of an aggressor from the shared home if requested by the victim of domestic violence. However, migrant women living in Switzerland for less than five years remained vulnerable to expulsion if they stopped cohabiting with the partner named on their residence permit.

Trafficking of human beings, including of women and girls for forced prostitution, continued to thrive on poverty, corruption, lack of education and social breakdown. Trafficking of human beings in and to Europe was widespread. Many states failed to ensure that the focus of policy and action in this area was on respect for and protection of the rights of trafficked persons. However, a positive development towards that end included the ratification in 2006 by three countries of the

Council of Europe Convention on Action against Trafficking in Human Beings, which will enter into force when 10 countries become parties.

REPRESSION OF DISSENT

In many areas across the region, there was shrinking space for independent voices and civil society as freedom of expression and association remained under attack. Turkey's restrictive law on "denigrating Turkishness" muzzled peaceful dissenting opinion, with a steady flow of prosecutions against individuals from across the political spectrum.

In Uzbekistan, in the wake of the 2005 Andizhan clashes in which hundreds of people died, fewer and fewer independent or dissenting voices were able to find an outlet to express their opinion without fear of reprisal. Reprisals came in the form of harassment, intimidation and imprisonment. In Azerbaijan, the authorities encouraged a climate of impunity for physical attacks on independent journalists, imprisoned others on questionable charges, and harassed independent media outlets through a range of administrative measures. The clampdown on civil society continued in Belarus, with an increase in the number of activists convicted as legal changes limiting freedom of association came into effect. The outright assault on any form of peaceful dissent intensified in Turkmenistan, where people were dismissed from their jobs and barred from travelling abroad simply because they were related to a dissident, and where the authorities targeted human rights defenders, portraying their activities as "treason" and "espionage".

Controversial new legislation in Russia undermined rather than enabled civil society by giving the authorities increased power of scrutiny of funding and activities of Russian and foreign non-governmental organizations. The legislation introduced a regulatory framework that could be arbitrarily applied, had key provisions which lacked a precise legal definition, and imposed sanctions that were disproportionate. In Chechnya and the wider North Caucasus region of Russia, people seeking justice faced intimidation and death threats, with the murder of leading activist and human rights journalist Anna Politkovskaya in October sending a chilling message about the dangers facing all those who dared to speak out as she had done.

In spite of threats, intimidation and detention, however, human rights defenders across the region remained resolute in continuing their work, inspiring others to join them in aiming for lasting change and respect for the human rights of all.

MIDDLE EAST-NORTH AFRICA

Armed conflict and the legacy of former conflicts overshadowed other developments in the Middle East and North Africa region in 2006. Throughout the year, against the backdrop of foreign military presence, Iraq continued its inexorable descent into civil war as long-standing political, ethnic and religious fault lines were increasingly exposed amid unrelenting sectarian violence. By the end of the year, the country was enmeshed in killings and other violence, primarily by Sunni and Shi'a groups, that threatened the stability of the whole region.

The long struggle between Israelis and Palestinians in the Occupied Territories continued to take a heavy toll in civilian lives despite wide international recognition that the conflict was a major cause of political instability in the region and beyond. The 40-year unresolved struggle entered a new phase after Hamas won January's Palestinian elections, defeating the Fatah party led by Palestinian President Mahmoud Abbas. Frequent Israeli air and artillery attacks resulted in the deaths of more than 650 Palestinians, mostly in the Gaza Strip and mostly in the second half of the year. Further deaths of Palestinians, again mostly in the Gaza Strip, resulted from internecine fighting between members of armed groups linked to the rival Hamas and Fatah parties. Meanwhile, social and economic conditions for Palestinians living under Israeli occupation continued to go from bad to worse as Israel pushed forward its construction of settlements and the building of a 700-kilometre fence/wall in the West Bank, increased or tightened the blockades and restrictions on Palestinian movements, and withheld customs duties due to the Palestinian Authority.

The uneasy relationship between Israel and Arab countries exploded into open conflict in July, when an attack on Israeli soldiers by members of the armed wing of Hizbullah sparked off a 34-day war involving Israel and Lebanon. Around 1,300 people were killed before an internationally negotiated ceasefire took effect on 14 August. Civilians on both sides bore the brunt of the conflict, particularly in Lebanon, where some 1,200 people, including more than 300 children, were killed in Israeli air attacks and artillery bombardment. Much of Lebanon's infrastructure was destroyed or damaged. After the fighting ended, civilians in south Lebanon continued to be killed and maimed by cluster bomblets, some four million of which were fired into the area by Israeli forces in the last days of the war. Both Israeli forces and Hizbullah combatants showed a wanton disregard for civilians and committed gross violations of human rights and international humanitarian law, including war crimes.

Tensions between Iran and the international community continued to grow over the Iranian government's determination to pursue its nuclear enrichment programme. In December the UN Security Council agreed a programme of sanctions against Iran.

IMPUNITY AND ACCOUNTABILITY

The war between Hizbullah and Israel was a war fought without accountability. When the peace came, neither side took any steps to hold to account those who had committed war crimes and other grave abuses during the conflict, and there was virtually no pressure from the international community for them to do so. But this was not surprising. Rather, it reflected a wider pattern of impunity that remained deeply entrenched throughout the Middle East and North Africa region.

In many countries, security forces were allowed virtual carte blanche to detain, intimidate and torture political opponents and criminal suspects. By failing to hold them to

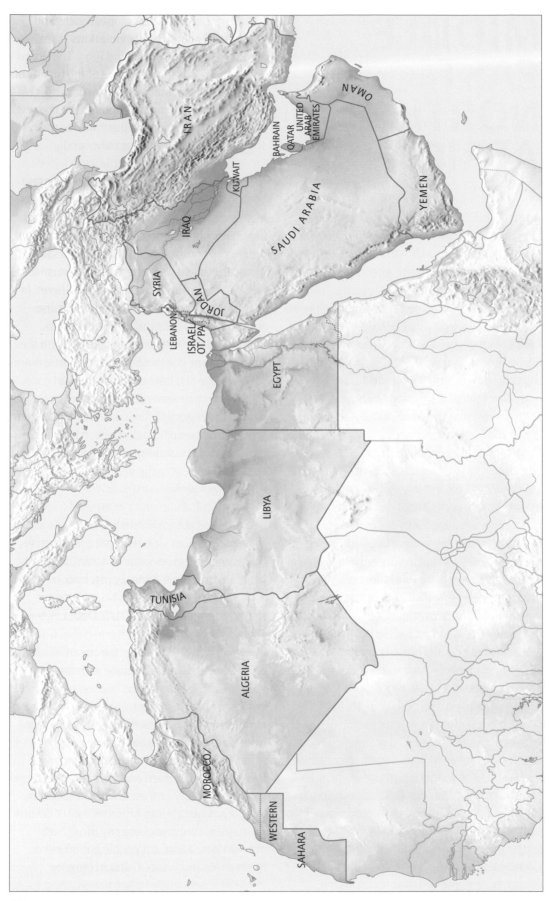

account, the governments to whom these forces reported betrayed their own willingness to condone or acquiesce in such abuses. In Egypt, Jordan, Syria, Tunisia and Yemen, political and terrorism suspects were tried before special and military courts. In many cases they were convicted on the basis of contested confessions by judges who rarely showed any inclination to investigate allegations that defendants had been tortured in pre-trial detention. Such courts were intended to provide a veneer of legitimacy, but the abusive systems of which they formed a part — based on prolonged incommunicado detention, torture or other ill-treatment and the extraction of confessions — were fundamentally rotten. They delivered convictions, long sentences and even, in some cases, the death penalty, but they did not deliver justice.

Impunity was also the watchword in Algeria, which through the 1990s experienced an internal conflict estimated to have claimed as many as 200,000 lives. Many were killed by armed groups or by government security forces, while thousands of others were tortured in custody or became victims of enforced disappearances after arrest. In most cases, the individual perpetrators remained unknown and in 2006 there was further evidence that the Algerian authorities intended to keep it that way. President Bouteflika's government enacted amnesty measures to confer legal immunity on members of armed groups and the security forces responsible for serious abuses, and on their political masters. At the same time, it was made a crime to accuse the security forces of violating human rights, raising the prospect that victims and survivors of such violations could be imprisoned for demanding justice.

In neighbouring Morocco, the government continued to address directly some of the wrongs of the past. The Human Rights Advisory Board was charged by King Mohamed VI with following up on the groundbreaking work undertaken previously by the Equity and Reconciliation Commission, which had

investigated enforced disappearances and other grave human rights violations committed between 1956 and 1999. The Board began to inform some families of the results of the investigation but progress was disappointingly slow even though the process aimed only to obtain and disseminate the truth, not to bring accountability and justice.

In Iraq, former President Saddam Hussain and seven others were tried for human rights violations in connection with the killings of 148 people from the town of al-Dujail following an assassination attempt on Saddam Hussain in 1982. The trial was billed as an exercise in accountability, and so it should have been. In practice, however, the trial was unfair and undermined by political interference. Its outcome was a foregone conclusion, with the tribunal's appeal chamber acting as little more than a rubber stamp body, and Saddam Hussain was sentenced to death and in December executed. The trial had represented an opportunity to turn the page in Iraq and establish accountability through justice and without recourse to the death penalty. It was an opportunity missed.

TERROR AND TORTURE

Torture and other ill-treatment continued to be widespread in several countries in the region, including Algeria, Egypt, Iraq, Iran and Jordan. Such abuses were also reported in Kuwait, Libya, Morocco, Saudi Arabia, Syria, Tunisia and Yemen.

The USA and some of its European allies remained keen to collaborate with the Algerian authorities in the "war on terror", despite Algeria's shameful amnesty measures and human rights record. The UK government strove unsuccessfully to obtain a "memorandum of understanding" such as it had previously agreed with Lebanon, Libya and Jordan, whereby untried terrorism suspects could be returned forcibly from the UK despite the risk that they would be tortured. Such agreements, based not on law but on mere "diplomatic assurances" that a returnee would not be tortured or executed, were symptomatic of the willingness of the USA and some European countries to engage actively in eroding key human rights safeguards that they had previously helped to develop and to which they had long proclaimed allegiance.

The main symbols of this corrosive pattern were the US detention camp at Guantánamo Bay, Cuba, the majority of whose inmates came from countries in the Middle East and North Africa region, and the secret renditions of suspected terrorists by the US government, in which a range of Middle Eastern and North African governments were complicit. Little by little, information continued to emerge about this murky multilateral conspiracy of secret detention and interrogation of terrorist suspects and their unlawful transfer from one country to another, pointing to the close involvement of Egyptian, Jordanian and Syrian security and intelligence agencies among others with the US Central Intelligence Agency (CIA). Three Yemeni nationals, who were released more than a year after they were returned to Yemen from US custody, reported that they had been held for long periods at unknown locations as suspects in the US "war on terror". Other such suspects were repatriated to Kuwait, Libya, Morocco, Saudi Arabia, Yemen and other states after years spent at Guantánamo Bay. Some were subsequently released but others were charged with terrorism-related offences in their home countries.

In Iraq, the US-led Multinational Force continued to hold thousands of detainees without charge or trial, although batches of detainees were released periodically during the year. After the scandal of torture and other abuses at Abu Ghraib in 2004, greatest concern focused on the plight of those detained by Iraqi police and other security forces, some units of which were largely drawn from supporters of Shi'a armed groups. There were continuing reports of torture and other ill-treatment of detainees held by some of these forces, and the Iraqi authorities showed little appetite to investigate or take action against those who abused prisoners.

WOMEN'S RIGHTS

Women remained in a subordinate position — legally, politically and in practice — across the region as a deep-seated culture of gender discrimination continued to hold sway. However, some advances were achieved that offered encouragement to a growing women's rights movement.

In Kuwait, women participated for the first time in national elections and in Bahrain 18 women candidates stood in elections for the House of Representatives, although only one was successful. The Moroccan government announced that it would withdraw its reservations to the UN Convention on the Elimination of All Forms of Discrimination against Women (CEDAW) and took steps to strengthen legislation on domestic violence, and Oman acceded to CEDAW. In Saudi Arabia, there was some movement towards establishing a specialized court to deal with cases of domestic violence, but women continued to face pervasive forms of discrimination, including severe restrictions on their freedom of movement.

These and other developments represented a step forward but only a small and halting one, underlining just how much more needs to be done to give real substance to the notion of women's rights. "Honour killings" persisted in Jordan, the Palestinian Authority, Iraq, Syria and other states in which the perpetrators benefited from laws that belittled their crimes. Throughout the region women were inadequately protected against other violence within the family. There were also worrying reports of trafficking of women in Oman, Qatar and other states.

In Iran, the all-male Council of Guardians ruled ineligible at least 12 women who wished to stand as candidates in elections for the important Assembly of Experts. Demonstrators who called for an end to legal discrimination against women were violently dispersed by the security forces. Despite this, the country's resilient women's rights activists were anything but deterred; they launched a campaign to collect a million signatures nationally in support of their demand for an end to legal discrimination.

DISCRIMINATION

Discrimination on the basis of religion, ethnicity, sexual orientation and other grounds was prevalent in a number of countries in the region, while the religious sectarianism of the Iraq conflict raised tensions between Sunnis and Shi'as. In Iran, members of the Arab, Azerbaijani, Kurdish and Baluchi minorities were increasingly restive in the face of continuing discrimination and repression, while members of religious minorities – Baha'is, Nematollahi Sufis and Christians – were detained or harassed on account of their faith. Baha'is were also subject to discrimination in Egypt, where they were required to present themselves as members of other faiths in order to obtain official documents such as identity cards and birth certificates. In Syria, discrimination continued against the Kurdish minority, with thousands of Syrian Kurds effectively made stateless and so denied equal access to basic social and economic rights, while in Qatar the cases of some 2,000 people deprived of their nationality in previous years remained unresolved.

The Israeli authorities imposed further discriminatory measures against Palestinians living under Israeli military occupation, including by reinforcing the system of segregated roads and checkpoints established on behalf of Israeli settlers residing in the Occupied Territories.

REFUGEES, ASYLUM-SEEKERS AND MIGRANTS

Unsurprisingly, the conflict in Iraq and the war between Hizbullah and Israeli forces caused widespread internal displacement and large outflows of refugees into neighbouring countries. In both Israel and Lebanon, most of those displaced returned to their villages and neighbourhoods once the fighting stopped, although many Lebanese people did so only to find that their homes had been destroyed and their fields and orchards contaminated by

unexploded cluster bomblets. Some 200,000 other Lebanese people were still displaced at the end of the year. Syria, together with Jordan, absorbed most of the refugees who fled the violence in Iraq; estimates suggested that more than half a million Iraqis had taken refuge in Syria by the end of 2006. In Lebanon, around 300,000 Palestinian refugees, in most cases refugees from events surrounding the creation of the state of Israel and the Arab-Israeli war of 1948, maintained a precarious existence, tolerated but far from fully accepted by Lebanese authorities who continued to deny or limit their access to certain basic rights.

In North Africa, refugees and migrants from countries to the south, many of them seeking entry to European Union states, were liable to detention and summary expulsion by security forces in Morocco, Algeria and Libya. There were three further deaths of migrants at the hands of security forces at the border fence between Morocco and the Spanish enclave of Melilla. Even recognized refugees were swept up and expelled by police in Morocco and allegedly abused and robbed in the process. In Libya, the authorities announced that they had increased expulsions of migrants tenfold compared to 2004.

In the Gulf and elsewhere, migrant workers had their rights abused amid a mix of inadequate legal protection, exploitative employers and government complacency. However, in Kuwait, where there were complaints about the treatment of South Asian and Filipino nationals, new legislation was introduced to afford some protection to migrant domestic workers, and in the UAE the government announced new measures to improve living and working conditions for migrant workers. In Oman, the right of workers to form trade unions was set out in law for the first time, although domestic workers were excluded.

DEATH PENALTY

This ultimate form of cruel, inhuman and degrading punishment was used extensively throughout much of the region, although

Algeria, Morocco and Tunisia continued to refrain from carrying out executions. In Iran, at least 177 people were executed, including one minor and three others whose crimes were committed when they were minors, and there were at least 39 executions in Saudi Arabia, mostly of foreign nationals. Bahrain carried out three executions, the first since 1996. Here too, those executed were foreigners. The execution of Saddam Hussain at the very end of the year was particularly significant and controversial, due to its timing, its especially grotesque and degrading manner, and the widespread sense within the region and beyond that it represented no more than "victor's justice" and an act of vengeance, rather than true justice or accountability.

DISSENT

The limits of dissent remained tightly drawn in most of the region by governments intolerant of opposition and by other forces anxious to control debate. In most countries, the media operated within strict constraints and under threat of criminal prosecution should they cause insult or offence to government leaders or officials. Journalists were prosecuted under defamation laws in Algeria, Egypt and Morocco, while in Iran, newspapers continued to be closed down and journalists detained and abused. State controls also extended to use of the Internet. In Bahrain, the government banned several sites; the Syrian authorities blocked access to sites providing news and comment on Syria; and bloggers who criticized the authorities were detained in Egypt and Iran.

The publication in Denmark of cartoons offensive to many Muslims sparked violent reactions, and in Jordan, Lebanon and Yemen editors and journalists were prosecuted for republishing them. Subsequently, Iran's President caused similar offence by publicly questioning the Holocaust. However, the Iranian authorities promptly closed *Iran* newspaper after it published a cartoon found to be offensive to the country's Azerbaijani minority.

Human rights defenders continued to speak up for tolerance in the face of intolerance, and for freedom of expression and the right to dissent, despite harassment and intimidation, the threat of arrest and prosecutions. They did so at particular risk to themselves in Iran, Syria, Tunisia and Western Sahara, but also faced threats and intimidation in other countries, including Algeria and Lebanon.

Political activists in Bangladesh demand electoral reform.

AMNESTY INTERNATIONAL
REPORT 2007
PART 2

Federal police in Oaxaca, Mexico, face protesters during unrest which began in May with a teachers' strike. By December several civilians had been killed and scores injured.

AFGHANISTAN

AFGHANISTAN
Head of state and government: Hamid Karzai
Death penalty: retentionist
International Criminal Court: ratified

The government and its international partners were unable to ensure security and a climate of political uncertainty grew in the course of the year. Armed conflict, marked by aerial bombardments and suicide bombings, escalated in southern parts of the country. At least 1,000 civilians were killed. Poor governance, the power of regional commanders and the impact of narcotics undermined the rule of law and human rights. Government security bodies committed human rights violations with impunity. There was little reform of judicial, law enforcement and security agencies. Women continued to face violence. Human rights defenders, including women, were targeted and killed. It became increasingly dangerous to speak out against human rights abuses and for justice.

Background

In February, the Afghanistan Compact was adopted outlining reforms and priorities for the next five years. Through the Compact, the Afghan government and its international partners agreed new financial and institutional support and oversight mechanisms. Key areas of the Afghanistan Compact are security, governance, rule of law and human rights, as well as economic and social development.

Lack of good governance and the rule of law contributed to the climate of impunity. Government officials and local power-holders were not held accountable for their actions and there was little or no access to justice.

Escalating conflict caused widespread social unrest. Violations of international humanitarian and human rights law were committed with impunity by all parties to the conflict, including international and Afghan security forces and the Taleban.

Human rights defenders, many of them women, faced harassment, intimidation and in at least one case murder, as they sought to protect human rights. It became more dangerous to speak out. Schools were burned down and teachers were attacked and killed by those opposed to the government and the education of girls.

Conflict, drought and floods in different parts of the country caused forced displacement throughout the year, while neighbouring Iran and Pakistan sought to reduce the number of Afghan asylum-seekers. The number of Afghans returning from these countries decreased.

Conflict

The conflict in the south and east grew in intensity and had a detrimental effect on governance in other parts of the country. Thousands of Afghans were forced to flee their homes because of conflict and drought.

The NATO-led International Security Assistance Force (ISAF) widened its area of operation to the south of Afghanistan, focusing on stabilization and security. The US-led Operation Enduring Freedom (OEF) continued to carry out operations purportedly to counter terrorism.

Human rights bodies and the UN expressed grave concern at the conduct of Afghan and international forces. The UN in Afghanistan routinely condemned the killing of civilians by the Taleban and repeatedly called on the Afghan and US authorities to ensure the safety of civilians while battling the insurgents.

US forces continued to deny detainees at Bagram some of their basic rights. Although there appeared to be fewer allegations of gross abuses, lack of information about detainees and denial of access to families were continuing concerns. ISAF handed detainees into the custody of Afghan authorities; there was insufficient monitoring of how these detainees were subsequently treated. Aerial bombardments during OEF and ISAF operations were, on occasion, disproportionate.

In July the UN Secretary-General's Special Representative to Afghanistan expressed concern about the deteriorating security situation in the south and called for more development work as well as further military and diplomatic intervention to curb the growing violence.

◻ During a joint military operation on 21 and 22 May by the government and OEF forces in Panjwayi, Kandahar, 16 civilians, including children and the elderly, were reportedly killed in Azizi village.

◻ Tensions over the presence of international troops were shown by violent protests after a fatal traffic accident in Kabul involving a US military vehicle on 29 May. In ensuing riots, at least eight people were killed and 100 injured. Shops were looted and police vehicles, government buildings in the city and offices belonging to international non-governmental organizations (NGOs) were damaged.

◻ In July, areas near to Tarin Kowt, Uruzgan, were bombed by US-led coalition forces, reportedly resulting in the death of at least 60 civilians. According to the Afghanistan Independent Human Rights Commission in Kandahar, at least 22 civilians were killed in two separate houses in Ghachi Zari. President Karzai ordered an inquiry into the bombing in Uruzgan.

◻ On 24 October, Zangawat village in the Panjwayi district was bombed in an ISAF operation in which at least 70 civilians were reportedly killed, including children.

◻ In late May, more than 3,000 villagers from Panjwayi and 200 from Zhari Dasht, Kandahar, were displaced following fighting between US and Afghan forces and the Taleban. They reportedly fled to Kandahar.

◻ Between July and October, it was estimated that approximately 15,000 people had been forcibly displaced by conflict, including hundreds displaced by aerial bombardments in Kandahar, Uruzgan and Helmand provinces.

Resurgence of the Taleban

Benefiting from a climate of lawlessness, notably in the south, the Taleban enjoyed a significant resurgence. Their forces were responsible for breaches of international humanitarian law by undertaking indiscriminate and disproportionate acts of violence; by killing those not involved in combat; and by ill-treating and torturing those over whom they had effective control. For example, in the context of quasi-judicial processes, at least 11 people were killed. The true number may have been far higher.

▢ On 28 August, a suicide blast attributed to the Taleban in a market in Lashkar Gah, Helmand, killed 17 people, many of them civilians.

▢ At least 19 individuals, including 13 civilians, were killed and another 20 injured on 26 September when a suicide bomber attacked a security post near a mosque in Lashkar Gah. Civilians had gathered outside the mosque to sign up for the Haj, or pilgrimage to Mecca.

Weak government

The reach of the central government was restricted. Parallel systems of governance and dispute resolution prevailed.

Insecurity undermined the rule of law and created a climate of impunity. Governors in some provinces acted independently of central government and violated human rights with impunity. Despite the appointment of Supreme Court judges and other high-ranking officials, reform and rebuilding of the judicial sector remained sluggish. The Afghan security forces, particularly the police and representatives of the National Security Directorate (NSD), were accused of illegal detentions and torture and other ill-treatment.

The legal status of international forces appeared to put them beyond the reach of Afghan law, and their failure to provide effective redress for violations undermined the rule of law.

Corruption and involvement in the drugs trade further undermined the delivery of justice by the government. Private jails continued to be administered by regional commanders. In November, the Attorney-General declared a "jihad" (holy war) against corruption.

In early March, government officials, backed by international forces, brought to a close a prison uprising in which at least five people died. Detainees associated with the Taleban in Pol-e Charkhi prison had protested against a new uniform regime and had taken control of part of the prison.

▢ In July, the government reportedly announced plans to re-establish the Department for the Promotion of Virtue and Prevention of Vice, a government body that committed numerous human rights violations, notably against women, during the rule of the Taleban. Assurances were given that the department would not be given the same duties as before.

Detention by international forces

US forces continued to hold around 500 detainees in Bagram airbase who were accused of links with the Taleban and al-Qa'ida.

▢ In January, a military court in Bagram found a US military official guilty of mistreating detainees and sentenced him to four months' detention. He was found to have punched detainees in the chest, arms and shoulders at a base in Uruzgan province in July 2005.

Around 35 Afghans were released from US custody at Guantánamo Bay and returned to Afghanistan. Refurbishment of Pol-e Charkhi high security prison continued in advance of the expected transfer in 2007 of the remaining Afghan detainees at Guantánamo Bay.

Rights of women and human rights defenders

The situation for human rights defenders deteriorated. Members of the Afghanistan Independent Human Rights Commission and representatives of national human rights organizations faced threats.

Legal reforms designed to protect women were not implemented and women continued to be detained for breaching social mores. There was a rise in cases of "honour" killings of women and self-immolation by women.

▢ On 25 September, Safiye Amajan, head of the Kandahar regional Department of Women's Affairs (DoWA) was shot dead by gunmen on a motorcycle. Individuals associated with Hezb-e Eslami were arrested in connection with her death. Other DoWA heads in other provinces also faced threats and intimidation.

Transitional justice

The government took a few steps to support the Transitional Justice Action Plan, adopted in late 2005. A mechanism for vetting political appointments was established, and in December the President officially launched the action plan. However, efforts failed to bring to justice those accused of human rights violations.

▢ Asadullah Sarwari, a former government minister and former head of the intelligence service, was sentenced to death on 23 February for war crimes committed between 1978 and 1992, under communist rule. His trial was grossly unfair. For most of his 13 years in custody Asadullah Sarwari did not have access to a lawyer.

Freedom of expression

Freedom of expression was reasonably well respected, although there were attempts to limit it.

The NSD sought to ban open discussion of the security situation and the Speaker of Parliament proposed limiting parliamentarians' freedom to speak to the press.

▢ Abdul Rahman was arrested in February and threatened with the death penalty for converting from Islam to Christianity more than 15 years previously, while working in Peshawar, Pakistan. In March, under heavy pressure from foreign governments, the court returned his case to prosecutors, citing "investigative gaps" and he was released from prison. He fled to Italy and was granted asylum.

AI country reports/ visits

Reports

- Afghanistan: UN Security Council mission must ensure international commitment to human rights is long term (AI Index: ASA 11/018/2006)
- Afghanistan: Open letter to His Excellency Sibghatullah Mojaddedi on the occasion of the 15 November 2006 visit to the Meshrano Jirga by military and civil leaders of the International Security Assistance Force (ISAF) (AI Index: ASA 11/019/2006)
- Afghanistan: NATO must ensure justice for victims of civilian deaths and torture (AI Index: ASA 11/021/2006)

ALBANIA

REPUBLIC OF ALBANIA
Head of state: Alfred Moisiu
Head of government: Sali Berisha
Death penalty: abolitionist
International Criminal Court: ratified

Violence against women was common and few perpetrators were brought to justice. Women and children were trafficked for forced prostitution and other forms of exploitation. Detainees frequently alleged ill-treatment by police officers during, or in the hours following, arrest. Investigations and prosecutions related to such allegations were rare, although in some cases police officers were disciplined. Conditions of detention, especially pre-trial detention, were harsh.

Background

In September the European Parliament ratified a Stabilisation and Association Agreement between the European Union (EU) and Albania, a significant step in the process of Albania's accession to the EU. In November the Albanian parliament approved ratification of Protocol 13 to the European Convention on Human Rights, thereby abolishing the death penalty in all circumstances. Public debates about corruption and incompetence within the ranks of judges and prosecutors were frequent but highly politicized; public confidence in the judiciary remained low. Certain legislative reforms were delayed because of political disputes related to forthcoming local elections, which led to the boycott of some parliamentary sessions by opposition deputies.

Violence against women

Domestic violence was not specifically prohibited in the Criminal Code, although it was generally recognized that such violence, particularly against women and children, was widespread. In its report, issued in November, the Organization for Security and Co-operation in Europe (OSCE) noted that "domestic violence is under-reported, under-investigated, under-prosecuted and under-sentenced", and that "the overwhelming majority of perpetrators are granted impunity". There were signs, however, that official and general public awareness of this issue had increased. In July the Director General of the State Police directed the police to implement recommendations made by AI in its report on domestic violence issued in March. He ordered police to respond promptly to all reports of domestic violence, to document complaints made by victims and order their examination by forensic doctors, and to liaise with local non-governmental organizations (NGOs) offering legal assistance and shelter to victims of domestic violence.

In December parliament adopted a law "On measures against violence in family relations" drafted by a group of domestic NGOs. This law aimed both to prevent such violence and to introduce procedures to give victims of domestic violence effective protection. The law was not due to come into force until mid-2007.

☐ Between mid-July and the beginning of August, the wife and daughter of NT reported him three times to Berat police because of his alleged violence towards them and to three younger children. However, apart from briefly detaining NT, the police apparently took no effective action. On 12 October, he was again detained by police after his alleged further violence, but escaped from the police station the same day.

Trafficking

Despite increased, and to some extent successful, measures to counter trafficking, Albania continued to be a source country for the trafficking of women, often minors, for sexual exploitation. Children, many of them Roma, continued to be trafficked to be exploited as beggars, for cheap labour, crime or for adoption. According to official statistics, in the first six months of the year, 119 criminal proceedings were registered with the Serious Crimes Prosecutor's Office relating to charges of trafficking women for prostitution, and five to charges of trafficking children.

In February Albania and Greece signed an agreement, subsequently ratified by parliament, dealing with the protection, repatriation and rehabilitation of trafficked children. In July regional anti-trafficking committees were established in Albania to identify and overcome problems in implementing the national anti-trafficking strategy.

☐ In January, a man was arrested in Saranda on a charge of trafficking two 12-year-old boys to Greece as drug couriers. The children had reportedly been arrested by Greek police two months earlier while crossing the border with a bag of cannabis.

☐ In April, three men were jointly convicted by the Serious Crimes Court of trafficking six babies to Greece between 1997 and 2003. They received sentences of up to 21 years' imprisonment.

There were also reports of trials and convictions of defendants on charges of having trafficked women abroad for sexual exploitation. Those convicted received sentences of up to 15 years' imprisonment. However, witness protection was weak and prosecutors complained that prosecutions often failed because at trial the victims of trafficking tended to withdraw their testimony under pressure from traffickers or their own families.

Police ill-treatment

Detainees frequently alleged that they had been ill-treated by police during arrest or during questioning following arrest. In some cases minors who had been questioned by police without a parent, lawyer or psychologist present complained of physical and psychological ill-treatment. At initial remand hearings prosecutors and judges rarely initiated investigations when a defendant complained of ill-treatment or bore clear marks of injury.

In July the European Committee for the Prevention of Torture (CPT) published its reports on visits to Albania in 2003 and 2005. The CPT reported that during both visits most of the detainees interviewed alleged that they had been beaten by police, often during questioning. In some cases the alleged beatings amounted to torture. In a number of cases a medical examination of the complainant found injuries consistent with these allegations. A report by the OSCE published in November, Analysis of the Criminal Justice System in Albania, reached similar conclusions.

⌔ In March, Dorian Leci was allegedly hit on the head with a pistol butt, kicked and beaten by police officers during his arrest in Tirana. He filed a criminal complaint against a police officer, alleging the use of force, abuse of office and torture. The prosecutor decided not to open an investigation into this complaint and reportedly did not inform Dorian Leci of this decision, as required by law.

⌔ In June, Amarildo Përfundi, aged 17, committed suicide at home a few days after Korça police officers questioned him for six hours. The Ombudsperson later concluded that police officers had psychologically and physically ill-treated Amarildo Përfundi and had questioned him without a parent, psychologist or a lawyer being present – in violation of the law. Korça police denied that police officers had ill-treated the boy. A criminal investigation was started against a police officer but had not been completed by the end of the year.

The Ministry of the Interior was reported as stating that during 2006 more than 40 police officers accused of ill-treating people, taking bribes or other misconduct in relation to the treatment of suspects at police stations had been punished administratively and referred to prosecutors' offices for investigation. However, few were brought to trial, and it appeared that none had been prosecuted under Article 86 of the Criminal Code dealing with "torture and any other degrading or inhuman treatment". Trial proceedings before Tirana District Court against two police officers on lesser charges of "arbitrary acts" – generally punished by non-custodial sentences – had not been concluded by the end of 2006.

Conditions of detention

Despite an EU-supported programme of prison reform and some improvements to detention conditions, these were still generally very poor and characterized by overcrowding, poor hygiene and sanitation, and inadequate diet and health care. Contrary to Albanian law and international standards, minors were still sometimes held together with adult detainees, and remand and convicted prisoners shared cells. Mentally ill prisoners were often held in prisons instead of being sent for medical treatment in specialized institutions in accordance with court decisions.

Detainees held in remand cells in police stations suffered particularly harsh conditions, and there were frequent complaints. Conditions were particularly poor, largely due to overcrowding, in Durrës, Elbasan and Korça police stations.

AI country reports/ visits
Report
- Albania: Violence against women in the family – "It's not her shame" (AI Index: EUR 11/002/2006)

Visit

AI delegates visited Albania in March.

ALGERIA

PEOPLE'S DEMOCRATIC REPUBLIC OF ALGERIA
Head of state: Abdelaziz Bouteflika
Head of government: Abdelaziz Belkhadem (replaced Ahmed Ouyahia in May)
Death penalty: abolitionist in practice
International Criminal Court: signed

The government introduced new amnesty laws entrenching impunity for gross human rights abuses in a stated effort to bring closure to the internal conflict of the 1990s, and criminalizing criticism of past violations by government forces. It made no progress in investigating cases of enforced disappearance and other serious human rights abuses committed during the 1990s or in clarifying the fate of the victims of enforced disappearance. Some 2,200 people who had been imprisoned or detained on terrorism-related charges were released under the amnesty laws and members of armed groups who surrendered were offered exemption from prosecution. However, fighting between armed groups and security forces continued, claiming over 300 lives, including more than 70 civilians. There were persistent reports of torture and ill-treatment of suspects detained by the authorities and accused of terrorism-related activities and there were concerns over the fairness of trials in terrorism-related and politically motivated cases. Journalists, trade unionists and human rights defenders were subject to harassment and prison sentences.

Background

Algeria continued to be affected by the legacy of the long and bloody internal conflict of the 1990s in which as many as 200,000 people are believed to have been killed as a result of attacks and abuses by both armed groups and government security forces. The government branded its policy of "national reconciliation" as the definitive solution to overcoming this brutal legacy. It introduced blanket amnesty measures and exemptions from prosecution for those responsible for past abuses, compensation payments for some categories of victims, social benefits for former armed group members and their families, and measures aimed at reintegrating people who had been ostracized due to their suspected support for the Islamic Salvation Front (Front islamique du salut, FIS). The FIS, whose election success in 1992 had sparked the army's intervention and the ensuing internal conflict, remained banned and excluded from the political process although some of its former leaders actively supported the government's "reconciliation" plan.

Algeria was an important ally in the US-led "war on terror". Violence by residual armed groups persisted, often in connection with criminal activities such as smuggling, protection rackets and money-laundering. The government continued its armed campaign against these groups, which it claimed were aligned with al-Qa'ida. Despite the persistent risk of torture in terrorism-related cases, Algerians were deported from several countries where governments alleged they were a risk to national security. Some countries apparently received assurances from the Algerian authorities that returnees would not be tortured or ill-treated, but Algeria refused independent monitoring of detainees who had been returned from other countries.

Raised oil and gas prices led to high revenues which allowed the government to repay some two thirds of its foreign debt. International financial institutions warned that urgent reforms were needed to diversify growth and create employment. Violent protests over social and economic conditions remained rife amid widespread allegations of corruption.

Impunity

There was no progress towards investigating the numerous gross abuses, including torture, killings, abductions and enforced disappearances, committed by armed groups and state security forces during the conflict of the 1990s. The government continued to fail to co-operate effectively with relevant UN human rights bodies and mechanisms in addressing the human rights legacy of the conflict.

Impunity was entrenched further by amnesty laws issued under presidential decrees in February, which were said by the government to implement the Charter for Peace and National Reconciliation, a framework document adopted by national referendum in 2005. Human rights groups and associations of victims staged public demonstrations to protest against the new legislation, describing it as unconstitutional.

The amnesty laws declared that any complaint against the security forces and those who acted in conjunction with them would be inadmissible, effectively granting them blanket immunity for human rights violations committed during the years of internal conflict. Moreover, the laws threatened with imprisonment those who speak out about abuses by the security forces. During the 1990s, security forces and state-armed militias carried out widespread torture and thousands of extrajudicial executions and enforced disappearances, all crimes under international law. The amnesty laws contravene Algeria's international obligation to investigate these crimes and hold the perpetrators to account, thereby denying victims and their families an effective remedy for the wrongs to which they were subjected.

The amnesty laws also enlarged the scope of earlier measures granting exemption from prosecution to members of armed groups who surrendered to the authorities within a six-month period, in a stated effort to end fighting by armed groups. The law provided insufficient safeguards to ensure that those who had committed serious crimes, for example killings of civilians, would be prosecuted. According to official statements, up to 300 armed group members surrendered before the deadline expired, but it was not known how many of them were exempted from prosecution and by what process. The authorities announced that those giving themselves up in future would benefit from similar measures beyond expiry of the deadline.

The laws also provided for the release under an amnesty of those detained or imprisoned for alleged involvement in terrorist activities except for collective killings, rape and bomb attacks. According to official statements, some 2,200 people who had been charged with or convicted of involvement in terrorist activities were freed from detention in March and in the following months, but the names of those released and the process for determining eligibility were not published. Several people charged with involvement in international terrorism were initially released, although they were not entitled under the terms of the law. Some of them were later rearrested and detained. Other detainees who would have been eligible for release were still in detention at the end of the year.

🗀 In August the UN Human Rights Committee ruled that Malik Medjnoun, who had been detained without trial for nearly seven years, should be tried immediately or released, and that human rights violations he had allegedly suffered in detention should be investigated. However, the government was not known to have taken any action in response to this decision and Malik Medjnoun remained detained without trial at the end of the year. In 2000, he was charged with participation in the 1998 killing of Lounes Matoub, a prominent singer, a crime which has not yet been fully, impartially and independently investigated.

In 1999 and 2000 Malik Medjnoun was held in unacknowledged and secret detention for seven months during which he was reportedly tortured.

Political killings

More than 300 people were reported to have been killed by either armed groups or government security forces during the year, including over 70 civilians.

Armed groups continued to carry out attacks on military and, to a lesser extent, civilian targets. Military forces carried out search operations and attacks in areas where armed group violence persisted, killing alleged armed group members. There were concerns that some of these killings might have been extrajudicial executions and that some of those killed were women and children related to armed group members, but details were difficult to obtain.

Violations in counter-terrorism

Torture continued to be used with impunity. There were persistent reports of torture and other ill-treatment in the custody of the Department for Information and Security (Département du renseignement et de la sécurité, DRS), a military intelligence agency which carries out terrorism-related arrests and investigations. Detainees held in DRS custody said they were beaten, tortured with electric shocks, suspended from the ceiling, and forced to swallow large amounts of dirty water, urine or chemicals. They were held by the DRS in secret locations for up to several months, during which they were denied contact with the outside world, in violation of the law. Reports of torture and ill-treatment were not known to have been investigated, despite new provisions criminalizing torture introduced in 2004. At least three people convicted of belonging to a terrorist group were sentenced to death in their absence.

◻ Hadj Djilali Bouazza, an Algerian national resident in Belgium, was arrested in March, some 10 days after arriving on a visit to Algeria. He was detained in DRS custody for three months during which he was not permitted contact with the outside world and reportedly abused by being stamped on, blindfolded and beaten on the side of his head, causing temporary deafness in one ear. An independent medical examination requested by his lawyer did not take place. He remained in prison awaiting trial for alleged terrorist activities in Algeria and abroad.

◻ Ahmed Chergui was arrested in Boumerdes province, east of Algiers, at the end of June. He was held by gendarmerie officers for three days, during which time he was reportedly stripped and threatened with a dog. He was then transferred to DRS custody and allegedly subjected to further torture, including severe beatings on his legs. Despite extensive bruising to his thighs, a medical certificate reportedly stated that he had no traces of injuries. He was charged with terrorism-related activities and remained in detention awaiting trial.

Enforced disappearances

No steps were taken to clarify the fate of thousands of victims of enforced disappearance between 1993 and 2002. Dozens of court cases brought by their families had not led to full judicial investigations or prosecution of the alleged perpetrators. The laws on "national reconciliation" barred courts from investigating complaints against those responsible.

◻ In March the UN Human Rights Committee issued its first rulings on cases of enforced disappearance in Algeria. The Committee found that the state had violated several provisions of the International Covenant on Civil and Political Rights in failing to protect the rights and life of Salah Saker and Riad Boucherf who had disappeared in 1994 and 1995 respectively. The Committee also recognized that the treatment by the authorities of their relatives, who remained without news of their fate or whereabouts, amounted to ill-treatment.

The laws on "national reconciliation" included provisions to compensate families of victims of enforced disappearance, but no payments had been made by the end of the year. In the absence of any investigations or judicial proceedings, many families rejected the compensation offer, fearing that the payments were intended to silence their calls for truth and justice.

Several dozen families of victims of enforced disappearance who had appealed to the authorities for help in previous years were summoned by security forces and given written notification of the death of their loved ones, a prerequisite for any compensation claims. The documents, however, refuted the families' claims that their loved ones had been arrested by security forces, stating instead that they had been killed by unidentified men or while participating in an armed group.

Families of victims of enforced disappearance were intimidated and some were prosecuted in connection with documentation they had produced and their campaigning activities on behalf of victims of enforced disappearance in Algeria or because of their peaceful protests against the government's national reconciliation policies.

Intimidation of human rights defenders and journalists

There were continuing restrictions on freedom of expression and assembly, and several independent organizations, including organizations of families of victims of enforced disappearance, continued to be denied legal status. Some of the restrictions were linked to the state of emergency, imposed in 1992, which remained in force.

The amnesty laws introduced in February criminalized free speech about the conduct of the security forces. Under these new laws, anyone exposing human rights violations or wishing to generate debate about them could face prosecution and up to five years' imprisonment, or 10 years in the case of a second offence. By the end of the year, the laws were not known to have been applied, but victims of human rights abuses and their families, human rights defenders, journalists and trade unionists faced a range of other forms of harassment and intimidation, including the threat of court action for exercising rights guaranteed under international law.

Algerian media reported that some 20 journalists were prosecuted for defamation after complaints by public officials. Some 15 prison terms of up to one year were imposed, but most journalists remained at liberty pending appeals.

In July, President Bouteflika decreed a pardon for all journalists convicted in connection with laws restricting free speech. Dozens of journalists sentenced to prison sentences and fines benefited from the measure. This followed a similar announcement in May which had, in practice, benefited very few of the 200 or so journalists it was officially aimed at. This was because it covered only journalists whose sentences had been confirmed, and most of those prosecuted were at liberty awaiting the outcome of appeals.

Trumped-up charges were brought against lawyers Hassiba Boumerdesi and Amine Sidhoum in September in an apparent attempt to intimidate them and deter them from carrying out human rights work. They remained at liberty pending trial for violating laws governing the organization and security of prisons.

Refugees and migrants

Irregular migrants were at risk of detention and collective expulsion. There were also reports of ill-treatment of irregular migrants by Algerian border police. Thousands of irregular migrants, including possible asylum-seekers, were deported to countries in sub-Saharan Africa without being able to make asylum applications or to appeal against deportation orders.

AI country reports/visits
Reports
- Algeria: Unrestrained powers – Torture by Algeria's Military Security (AI Index: MDE 28/004/2006)
- Algeria: New amnesty law will ensure atrocities go unpunished (AI Index: MDE 28/005/2006)
- Algeria: Torture in the "war on terror" – a memorandum to the Algerian President (AI Index: MDE 28/008/2006)

Visit
AI informed the government in May that it wished to visit Algeria, but was denied access to the country.

ANGOLA

REPUBLIC OF ANGOLA
Head of state: José Eduardo dos Santos
Head of government: Fernando da Piedade Dias dos Santos
Death penalty: abolitionist for all crimes
International Criminal Court: signed

Forced evictions continued and hundreds of families were left without shelter. There were reports of human rights violations by police, including unlawful killings and torture. Little progress was made towards eradicating impunity. One police officer was prosecuted and 10 others dismissed for various offences. In Cabinda, human rights violations continued despite the signing of a peace agreement with a separatist movement. Human rights defenders and political activists were harassed and some were briefly detained, while a human rights organization was banned.

Background

In February, a cholera epidemic broke out and spread to all provinces. By the end of the year more than 2,000 people had died from the disease.

Elections planned for late 2006 were postponed to late 2007. However, voters' registration only started in November and only in a few areas. Opposition leaders and others expressed concern at the number of small arms, including AK-47 rifles, held by civilians (estimated at between 1.5 and four million) and called for disarmament ahead of the election.

In February the National Assembly approved a new Press Law, which prohibits media censorship and guarantees access to information. The new law abolished the article which prevented journalists from defending themselves in court in cases of defamation of the President of the Republic.

In August Angola ratified the United Nations Convention against Corruption.

Forced evictions

The Council of Ministers approved two of the four regulations for the implementation of the land laws approved in 2004.

Although on a smaller scale than the previous year, forced evictions occurred in several neighbourhoods in Luanda. Between January and June, there were several forced evictions in Cidadania and Cambamba I and II neighbourhoods. In some cases, the police, municipal fiscal agents and private security personnel used excessive force, including firing live ammunition, against residents who resisted the evictions. There were no investigations into the forced evictions or the excessive use of force by police.

In March, the UN Special Rapporteur on the right to adequate housing expressed concern about the persistent practice of forced evictions in Angola. He called on the government to comply with its human rights obligations and to address promptly violations of human rights.

In March at least 330 families from the neighbourhoods of Cambamba I, Cambamba II and Banga Wé, were forcibly evicted by police and private security guards who used excessive force.

National police officers, private security guards and people in civilian clothes demolished 200 houses in Cambamba II on 13 March. They were reinforced by about 100 heavily armed riot police officers who shot into the air and on the ground. They also beat and kicked residents, mainly women, children and the elderly who stood in front of their houses and refused to move. A pregnant woman was beaten and started to bleed. A boy of about four was hit by a bullet in the knee. Nine people, including a 14-year-old boy and four women – Eunice Domingos, Amélia José Faustino, Aida Cardoso and Isabel Miguel Francisco – were arrested, apparently for resisting the evictions. They were all released without charge by the end of the following day.

Also on 13 March, police and private security guards used excessive force when forcibly evicting families in the Cambamba I neighbourhood, where they demolished 130 houses. Police and security guards pushed to the ground and beat those who resisted the evictions. A security guard reportedly shot around the feet of a youth as he was fleeing. Then he and several police officers surrounded the youth, beat him with a hose and kicked him. Several people were arrested and briefly detained, including two members of the non-governmental organization (NGO) SOS-Habitat and four women, one of whom was pregnant and three who had young children with them. Several days later the police returned to Cambamba I and demolished the shelters that families had rebuilt.

There were several forced evictions in May in the Cidadania neighbourhood of Luanda.

On 5 May, police officers and municipal fiscal agents demolished a number of houses in Cidadania. Two men, Rafael Morais, a member of SOS-Habitat, and João Manuel Gomes, a resident, were arrested. They were handcuffed together and kept in the sun for over four hours, before being released uncharged. A police officer beat João Manuel Gomes with a hose and Rafael Morais was kept without his shoes or shirt.

Policing and human rights

Human rights violations committed by police continued, including the unlawful killing, torture and ill-treatment of detainees. Disciplinary measures were taken against some police officers accused of committing human rights violations during the year. The measures, which included dismissal from the police force, were publicized. However, only one police officer was prosecuted during 2006, despite a statement by a police spokesperson that the dismissals would not preclude criminal or civil proceedings.

In May police shot two young street vendors in Luanda, killing one. The police alleged that they suspected the two of possessing stolen mobile phones,

and that one youth fled when they tried to search his bag. He was captured and was then deliberately shot and killed by a police officer. The second youth was shot when the police tried to disperse a group of people who had gathered and were protesting against the shooting. The police officer responsible for the death was reportedly dismissed from the police force in June. However, he had not faced criminal charges by the end of the year.

In May police officers were reported to have tortured four detainees for several days in the Sixth Police Station in Luanda. The four were Mateus Inácio Martins, Faustino Penhafu, Zeferino Muipile and Santos João Francisco. The officers were among a group of 10 officers reportedly dismissed from the police force in June for various offences, including bribery, torture and unlawful killing.

In August the Benguela Provincial Court in Lobito city convicted a police officer of the murder of Antoninho Tchiswugo in January 2005, and sentenced him to 17 years' imprisonment.

Human rights defenders

Human rights defenders remained at risk of persecution. In September, members of the Provincial Criminal Investigative Police (DPIC) arbitrarily arrested human rights defender Raul Danda at the airport in Cabinda city. He was unlawfully detained at the DPIC headquarters for more than the 48 hours allowed by law. He was charged with instigating, inciting and condoning crimes against the security of the state, and transferred to the Cabinda Civil Prison. He was released four weeks later pending trial, but his trial had not started by the end of the year. Raul Danda is a member of the human rights organization Mpalabanda – Cabinda Civic Association, which was banned by the Cabinda Provincial Court in July for alleged involvement in political activities. An appeal against the ban had not been heard by the end of the year.

Cabinda

In August the government and the Cabindan Forum for Dialogue (Forum Cabindés para o Diálogo, FCD) signed a peace agreement to end the armed conflict in the province. The agreement provided for the demilitarization of combatants of the armed Front for the Liberation of the Cabinda Enclave (Frente de Libertação do Enclave de Cabinda, FLEC) and their integration in the Angolan Armed Forces (Forças Armadas Angolanas, FAA) and government. It also provided for an amnesty for crimes against the security of the state committed in the context of the armed conflict, which was subsequently approved by the National Assembly. However, FLEC and other organizations rejected the agreement, saying that it had been signed by a former President of the FCD who had been expelled from the organization in April and that he did not represent their views. Following the signing of the peace agreement there were unconfirmed reports of fighting between FAA and FLEC combatants.

There were no known investigations into numerous reports of human rights violations by the police and the

FAA in Cabinda, including extrajudicial executions, torture, rape and arbitrary detentions.

◻ In January Francisco Banheva was beaten by soldiers who found him and his wife working their fields in the Mbata-Missinga area of Ncutu commune, disobeying a FAA order specifying the days that people in the area could tend their fields. He reportedly died as a result of the beating the next day.

In June, the new Catholic bishop, whose appointment in February 2005 from outside the province had provoked violent protests, took office. Following the swearing-in ceremony, police reportedly arrested 28 members of Mpalabanda who were meeting to discuss the establishment of good relations with the new bishop. They were released without charge later that day.

AI country reports/ visits
Reports
- Angola: Call on Government to end forced evictions and excessive use of force immediately (AI Index: AFR 12/004/2006)
- Angola: Human rights organization banned (AI Index: AFR 12/006/2006)
- Angola: A step towards ending police impunity (AI Index: AFR 12/007/2006)

ARGENTINA

ARGENTINE REPUBLIC
Head of state and government: Néstor Kirchner
Death penalty: abolitionist for ordinary crimes
International Criminal Court: ratified

There were reports of attacks and threats to individuals involved in trials of former members of the security forces. Some trials for human rights violations were concluded. Prison conditions did not improve. Indigenous communities' economic social and cultural rights continued to be violated.

Justice
Several former members of the security forces accused of committing human rights abuses during the military governments (1976-83) went on trial. Judges, prosecution witnesses, non-governmental organizations and relatives of former victims involved in the trials were attacked and threatened in the last four months of the year. The trials followed a ruling by the Supreme Court in 2005 that the Laws of Final Stop and Due Obedience were unconstitutional.

In September the Senate passed a bill implementing the Rome Statute of the International Criminal Court.

The bill was approved by the Chamber of Deputies in December.

Miguel Etchecolatz, former Director of Investigations of the Buenos Aires Province Police, was convicted of murder, torture and kidnappings during the military government and sentenced to life imprisonment in September. The three judges in the case ruled that he was responsible for crimes against humanity committed within the framework of genocide. Jorge Julio López, a main witness and complainant in the trial, went missing in September. There were fears that he may have been a victim of enforced disappearance.

Land issues and Indigenous people
Indigenous communities in Chaco and Salta Provinces, including the Toba, Wichi and Mocovi groups, staged hunger strikes, established roadside camps and submitted petitions to the authorities. Their petitions included requests for a reasonable budget for the Indigenous Institute of Chaco, provisions for housing and health and a halt to the irregular sale and distribution of state-owned land to lumber companies and soybean producers.

◻ In August members of the Wichi community in the General Mosconi area, Salta Province, established a roadside camp beside National highway No. 34 to call for the return of communal land. The land had been exploited by private companies and the local water company had cut off the water supply to the communities.

Prison conditions
Conditions of detention continued to be harsh in most prisons and detention centres and detainees were ill-treated. Detainees were reportedly seriously injured in fires in prisons and police stations, allegedly because of lack of help.

◻ In March, Walter Daniel Lescano died as a result of burns acquired during a fire in the punishment cell where he was held in the men's prison in Santiago del Estero, Santiago del Estero Province. He had complained of ill-treatment by prison guards. An investigation was reportedly initiated into the circumstances surrounding the fire.

◻ In January, three detainees — Sergio Daniel Romero, 16-year-old Matías Martínez and 17-year-old Ricardo Edgar Pared — died and one, Hugo Ariel Escobar, suffered serious burns in a fire at the 7th Police Station in Corrientes, Corrientes Province. The four detainees had been handcuffed to the cell bars after being beaten by members of the police. An investigation was reportedly initiated.

AI country reports/ visits
Statements
- Argentina: Possible "disappearance"/Fear for safety — Jorge Julio López (AI Index: AMR 13/004/2006)
- Argentina: Human rights cases endangered by new wave of threats (AI Index: AMR 13/005/2006)

ARMENIA

REPUBLIC OF ARMENIA
Head of state: Robert Kocharian
Head of government: Andranik Markarian
Death penalty: abolitionist for all crimes
International Criminal Court: signed

Conscientious objectors continued to be imprisoned. There were reports of intimidation of independent journalists. The Ombudsperson was removed from her post in January by a presidential decree that she alleged was unconstitutional.

Conscientious objectors

Armenia did not release conscientious objectors to military service, in defiance of its obligations and commitments undertaken when acceding to the Council of Europe to respect the right to freedom of thought, conscience and religion, and despite the introduction of an alternative civilian service to military service in national legislation in July 2004. Conscientious objectors continued to complain that in both its legislative framework and implementation, Armenia's alternative service was under the supervision and control of the military and so did not constitute a real civilian alternative to military service. As of November there were reportedly 48 Jehovah's Witnesses and one Molokan (a member of a Russian religious minority) in detention for draft evasion. Forty-four of the Jehovah's Witnesses had been tried and sentenced to terms ranging from 18 to 48 months' imprisonment. The remaining four were charged and awaiting trial.

In January an amendment to the criminal code was adopted making conscripts who refuse to perform alternative service liable to imprisonment. In May, 19 men, all Jehovah's Witnesses, filed an appeal with the European Court of Human Rights to prevent retrospective prosecution for their abandonment of the alternative service in 2004. Fifteen of the 19 applicants had been arrested in August 2005 and sentenced to between two and three and a half years' imprisonment under existing articles of the criminal code dealing with desertion from military service rather than refusal to perform alternative service. Although their convictions were later overturned and all were subsequently released, the courts refused to formally acquit the men. The case was dropped in November when all 19 were acquitted and all charges against them dropped.

◻ In October a decision of the Court of Appeal granted a prosecutor's request for a stricter sentence to be handed down to Jehovah's Witness Hayk Avetisian. His sentence was increased from 24 to 30 months.

Freedom of expression

Human rights activists and the Ombudsperson's Office expressed concern over incidents of intimidation and harassment against independent journalists, including two assaults, death threats and the stoning of personal property.

◻ On 6 September, Hovannes Galajian of the *Iravunk* newspaper was beaten by two unidentified men outside his home. The attack followed the publication of a number of articles criticizing prominent officials.

◻ In July the network of independent journalists *Hetq Online* received threats of reprisals, including death threats, if its journalists continued to publish articles concerning the illegal acquisition of land for redevelopment.

Ombudsperson removed from office

Ombudsperson Larisa Alaverdian was removed from her post in January by presidential decree and her duties entrusted to an interim three-member commission. She alleged that her removal and replacement were unconstitutional because a presidential prerogative either to dismiss the Ombudsperson or to replace that post by another body was not provided for in Armenian law. She and other human rights activists alleged that her removal had been prompted by her criticism of government policies and practices. A new Ombudsperson was elected by the National Assembly in February.

Human rights lawyer released on bail

Lawyer Vahe Grigorian, known for his advocacy work for families resisting forced eviction for government-led redevelopment programmes in central Yerevan, was released on bail in February. He had been held since October 2005 on charges of fraud which he alleged were unfounded and politically motivated. The charges against him were not dropped and the case was still pending at the end of the year.

AI country reports/ visits
Reports
- Europe and Central Asia: Summary of Amnesty International's concerns in the region, January-June 2006 (AI Index: EUR 01/017/2006)
- Commonwealth of Independent States: Positive trend on the abolition of the death penalty but more needs to be done (AI Index: EUR 04/003/2006)

Visit
AI delegates visited Armenia in April.

AUSTRALIA

AUSTRALIA
Head of state: Queen Elizabeth II, represented by Michael Jeffery
Head of government: John Howard
Death penalty: abolitionist for all crimes
International Criminal Court: ratified

Violence against women and low rates of prosecution, and in remote communities a lack of support services for Indigenous women were serious concerns. New counter-terrorism measures posed a threat to human rights. Harsh new legislation against asylum-seekers was rejected. Hundreds of refugees remained in limbo under the Temporary Protection Visas system.

Indigenous people

In May, a report by the Crown Prosecutor for Central Australia exposed numerous cases of sexual abuse and violence against women and children in remote Indigenous communities. The report revealed a lack of support services available for Indigenous women in remote communities and a lack of appropriate action by the authorities.

During a visit to Australia in August, the UN Special Rapporteur on adequate housing expressed concern at poor housing conditions in Indigenous communities.

In September an inquest found that a police officer was responsible for the death in custody of Mulrunji Domadgee, an Indigenous man from Palm Island, in 2004.

Violence against women

The UN Committee on the Elimination of Discrimination against Women expressed concern about the high level of violence against women, and the low rates of prosecution and convictions in sexual assault cases. The Committee was also concerned about the continued violence and discrimination faced by women in Indigenous, refugee and migrant communities. There were concerns about the lack of appropriate action against the trafficking of women into Australia.

Human rights and security

Joseph "Jack" Thomas, who was charged with a terrorism-related offence, was subjected to the country's first Control Order, resulting in restrictions on his movement and his freedom to associate and communicate with others.

The Attorney General rejected recommendations by the Security Legislation Review Committee, including those to remove from the Attorney General the power to proscribe organizations as "terrorist" and to make this a judicial process.

Australian citizen David Hicks entered his fifth year in detention at Guantánamo Bay. The Australian government continued to support trial by the US Military Commission, which fell below international standards.

Refugees and asylum-seekers

Forty-three asylum-seekers from the Indonesian province of Papua were recognized as refugees after arriving in Australia by boat in January. Under new legislation proposed by the government, all asylum-seekers without documentation arriving by sea would be processed in other locations in the Pacific Ocean, and those granted refugee status would be settled outside Australia. The bill was withdrawn by the Prime Minister due to lack of support.

In October, an inquiry by the Human Rights and Equal Opportunity Commission found that the Department of Immigration had not provided adequate care to an Iraqi woman after she had been held in an all-male compound in an immigration detention centre.

Approximately 1,100 refugees remained on three-year Temporary Protection Visas. In November the High Court ruled that refugees granted these visas were not entitled to further protection if, after three years, they were unable to prove the continued need for protection and if the government considered their country of origin to be safe.

AI country reports/ visits
Statements

- Australia: One step forward, two steps back — Amnesty International calls for an immediate halt to proposed legislation to punish asylum seekers arriving by boat (AI Index: ASA 12/002/2006)
- Australia: "First things first" — Amnesty International Seeks Australia-Indonesia Declaration on Respect for Human Rights (AI Index: ASA 12/003/2006)
- Australia: Open letter to Prime Minister John Howard calling for David Hicks to be brought home (AI Index: ASA 12/006/2006)

AUSTRIA

REPUBLIC OF AUSTRIA
Head of state: Heinz Fischer
Head of government: Wolfgang Schüssel
Death penalty: abolitionist for all crimes.
International Criminal Court: ratified

Police officers were found guilty of crimes that effectively amount to torture. Austria does not specify the crime of torture. New legal provisions allowing forced feeding of certain groups of people came into force.

Torture and ill-treatment
◻ In August, four police officers were found guilty of beating and threatening Bakary J, a Gambian national, with a mock execution. In April, police officers drove Bakary J, whose deportation had been stopped, to an empty warehouse in Vienna where he was handcuffed, kicked, beaten and threatened with a mock execution. The officers later took him to a hospital and told staff that he had been injured while attempting to escape, and he was eventually returned to a detention centre. Neither the police officers nor medical staff at the hospital reported the events, and criminal investigations were not initiated until Bakary J's wife made a complaint. According to medical documentation, Bakary J's skull was fractured in several places and he had several bruises.

At the end of August the Higher Criminal Court in Vienna ruled that the police officers had inflicted or abetted Bakary J's injuries. They were given suspended sentences of eight and six months' imprisonment for tormenting Bakary J and for neglect, respectively. The judge defined the incident as a "lapse", and as a mitigating factor referred to the stressful conditions under which deportation occurs. In December the disciplinary commission of the Vienna Police sentenced the officers to fines of between one and five months' salary.

Aliens Police Act
◻ At the end of August, Geoffrey A, a Nigerian national, went on hunger strike while in detention awaiting deportation. Under provisions in the Aliens Police Act, which came into force in January, he was transferred to prison, where he was not given any medical attention. He was released after 41 days on hunger strike in a very weakened state. No one was notified of his release, and on his way home he collapsed and was taken to an intensive care unit of a Vienna hospital.

Geoffrey A was detained under provisions of the Aliens Police Act. Inherent inconsistencies in the law mean that, rather then being released on grounds of ill-health – as was formerly the practice – people awaiting deportation who are on hunger strike can continue to be kept in detention in order to be force-fed, while, in recognition of medical ethics, doctors are not legally obliged to force-feed the detainee. The result in practice is that hunger strikers can be detained until they die or, as in the case of Geoffrey A, after suffering serious damage to their health, they are released without effective medical supervision.

AZERBAIJAN

REPUBLIC OF AZERBAIJAN
Head of state: Ilham Aliyev
Head of government: Artur Rasizade
Death penalty: abolitionist for all crimes
International Criminal Court: not ratified

Rights to freedoms of expression and assembly were restricted. Police routinely used force to disperse demonstrations. Opposition journalists were attacked, imprisoned or fined on criminal defamation or dubious drugs-related charges. Opposition politicians were denied rights to due process and reportedly in some cases medical care and access to legal counsel of their own choosing. A journalist was extradited to Turkey despite being at risk of torture or other ill-treatment. People internally displaced by the conflict in Nagorny Karabakh in 1991-94 had restricted opportunities to exercise their economic and social rights.

Freedom of expression under attack
Rights to freedoms of expression and assembly were routinely restricted. Police dispersed authorized and unauthorized meetings, reportedly with excessive force on occasion.
◻ Two serious assaults on opposition journalists Fikret Hüseynli and Baxaddin Xaziyev, attacked in March and May respectively by unidentified assailants, were unsolved at the end of 2006.
◻ Two further assaults by unidentified men took place in late December. Ali Orucov, press secretary of the opposition Azerbaijan National Independence Party, suffered bruising and a fractured finger. Nicat Hüseynov, a journalist with the *Azadlıq* newspaper, was hospitalized with head and internal injuries and a stab wound after being attacked in the street in broad daylight.
◻ No progress was made in investigating the murder in 2005 of newspaper editor Elmar Hüseynov, widely believed to have been killed because of his criticism of political corruption.
◻ Criminal defamation proceedings were brought against several individuals and newspapers. They resulted in the imprisonment of two journalists, who

were pardoned and released in October, and a number of suspended sentences and heavy fines, in one case leading to the closure of independent newspaper *Realny Azerbaydzhan*.

Well-known satirist and government critic Sakit Zahidov of the *Azadlıq* newspaper was arrested on charges of drug-dealing in June. He claimed drugs had been forcibly planted on him after he was abducted and then arrested by plain clothes policemen. After no evidence of drug-dealing was presented at his trial, the charge was reduced to use of illegal drugs. However, a urine test at the time of arrest reportedly showed no evidence of drug usage, and doctors called as witnesses admitted that their diagnosis of Sakit Zahidov as a drug addict was based on 30 minutes' visual observation only. He was sentenced to three years' imprisonment. His appeal was rejected in December; reportedly no new evidence or witnesses were presented at the hearing.

On 24 November the *Azadlıq* and *Bizim Yol* newspapers, the Institute for Reporter Freedom and Safety (a media freedom non-governmental organization with close links to *Azadlıq*), the independent journalists' association Yeni Nesil and the *Turan* news agency were forcibly removed by police from their premises in Baku following a legal ruling they claimed was unfounded and politically motivated. Also on 24 November the National Radio and Television Council decided not to extend the broadcasting licence of the ANS television company, widely regarded as the most independent in the country. The cessation of ANS broadcasting further ended the retransmissions on ANS frequencies of international radio stations such as the BBC, Radio Liberty and the Voice of America. Following international and national appeals, on 12 December ANS was reinstated temporarily pending completion of a tender for its frequencies scheduled for January 2007.

Unfair trial concerns

Three leaders of the Yeni Fikir youth movement arrested in 2005 on charges of plotting a coup d'état were imprisoned in July after an unfair trial. At the trial, only witnesses for the prosecution gave evidence and no jury was appointed, in contravention of Azerbaijani law. Allegations of torture in the case of one of the accused, Ruslan Başirli, were not investigated, and medical care was reportedly denied to another, Said Nuri.

Opposition party activist Qadir Müsayev was imprisoned in May for seven years following conviction on charges of drug dealing. Reports suggested the charges were fabricated because of his refusal to sign fraudulent election result protocols when serving as a polling station official.

Former Minister for Economic Development Farhad Aliyev and his brother Rafiq (no relation to President Aliyev), arrested in October 2005 on charges of plotting to violently overthrow the government, were allegedly denied due process in pre-trial detention. According to reports, their right to legal counsel of their choosing was consistently denied from the time of their arrest, and Farhad Aliyev was not allowed access to appropriate medical care. No hearings have been heard in the brothers' case, and no trial date set. Their property has been expropriated and family members allegedly intimidated.

Risk of torture

On 13 October, Kurdish journalist Elif Pelit was extradited to Turkey, where she was detained on charges of membership of the Kurdish Workers' Party (PKK). In 1999 she had been granted asylum, and subsequently citizenship, in Germany. She was first arrested in Azerbaijan on 4 November 2004, for crossing the border illegally from Iraq while on assignment for *Mesopotamia*, a Kurdish news agency linked to the PKK. Fined and released in March 2005, she was immediately rearrested under Turkey's extradition order, and her extradition was confirmed by the Supreme Court in October 2005.

Restricted rights for the displaced

People internally displaced by the conflict in Nagorny Karabakh continued to have their freedom of movement restricted by a cumbersome internal registration process linking eligibility for employment and social services to a fixed place of residence. Although there was progress in moving the displaced out of temporary shelters and providing housing, many new purpose-built settlements were located in remote and economically depressed areas. People re-housed in these settlements faced a lack of jobs and access to basic services such as education and health care.

AI country reports/ visits
Reports
- Europe and Central Asia: Summary of Amnesty International's concerns in the region, January-June 2006 (AI Index: EUR 01/017/2006)
- Commonwealth of Independent States: Positive trend on the abolition of the death penalty but more needs to be done (AI Index: EUR 04/003/2006)
Visits
AI delegates visited Azerbaijan in April and July.

BAHAMAS

COMMONWEALTH OF THE BAHAMAS
Head of state: Queen Elizabeth II, represented by Arthur Hanna (replaced Paul Adderley in February)
Head of government: Perry Gladstone Christie
Death penalty: retentionist
International Criminal Court: signed

Death sentences continued to be handed down by the courts. Asylum-seekers and migrants, the majority of whom were black Haitians, were deported. Some were reportedly ill-treated. Reports of abuses by members of the security forces, including excessive use of force, continued.

Death penalty
In March, the UK-based Judicial Committee of the Privy Council, the highest court of appeal for the Bahamas, abolished the mandatory death sentence for murder. Following this ruling, the Attorney General announced that re-sentencing hearings would be held for all inmates currently on death row.

Several new death sentences were issued after the decision. At least two people were sentenced to death in 2006 and 26 remained on death row. No executions took place.

Abuses by the security forces
There were reports of abuses, including excessive use of force, by members of the security forces.
◻ Neil Brown was reportedly shot dead while handcuffed as he was being transported back to Fox Hill Prison in January. He had been recaptured following a prison escape in which a prison guard was killed. A prison officer was subsequently found guilty of his murder by a coroner's jury, but the verdict was deferred pending a constitutional review; the officer remained on duty at the end of the year.
◻ On 27 March, Deron Bethel, aged 20, was fatally shot three times outside his home by a police officer who claimed he mistook him for a criminal suspect. Investigations were ongoing at the end of the year.

Asylum-seekers and migrants
Immigrants, the vast majority from Haiti, continued to be deported in large numbers. Some were reportedly ill-treated. On 8 April, 187 Haitians, including children, on the island of Eleuthera were rounded up and detained. It was later found that 166 of them had legal documents and 27 also had permanent residence.

Corporal punishment
In October Alutus Newbold was sentenced to 16 years' imprisonment and eight strokes of the rod for an attack on an 83-year-old woman in her home in 2004. The ruling sparked a debate about the continued use of corporal punishment.

AI country reports/ visits
Reports
- Bahamas: Privy Council abolishes mandatory death sentence (AI Index: AMR 14/001/2006)
- Bahamas: Flogging — Alutus Newbold (AI Index: AMR 14/005/2006)

BAHRAIN

KINGDOM OF BAHRAIN
Head of state: King Hamad bin 'Issa Al Khalifa
Head of government: Shaikh Khalifa bin Salman Al Khalifa
Death penalty: retentionist
International Criminal Court: signed

The authorities imposed restrictions on freedom of expression. A group of detainees complained of physical abuse during their detention. The King ratified a law imposing the death penalty. Three people were executed for murder.

Background
In September Bahrain acceded to the International Covenant on Civil and Political Rights. Elections to a new 40-seat House of Representatives took place in November. Although political parties were officially banned in Bahrain, the al-Wefaq National Islamic Society, the main Shi'a Muslim opposition which had boycotted the previous parliamentary elections in 2002, won 17 seats, and two Sunni Muslim groups, the al-Menbar National Islamic Society and the al-Asala Islamic Society, won a total of 12 seats. Pro-government candidates won 10 seats. Latifa al-Ga'ood was the only one of 18 women candidates to be elected.

Guantánamo Bay detainees
A Bahraini national, Salah al-Balooshi, who had been detained by the US authorities at Guantánamo Bay, Cuba, was returned to Bahrain in October and released. Two other Bahraini nationals, 'Issa 'Abdullah al-Murbati and Juma'a Mohammed al-Dossari, continued to be held at Guantánamo Bay throughout 2006.

New counter-terrorism law
In August the King, Shaikh Hamad bin 'Issa Al Khalifa, ratified a new counter-terrorism law which had been approved by both the elected House of Representatives and the appointed Shura (Consultative) Council in July. The new law extended the use of the death penalty and prior to its introduction was criticized by both the UN

Committee against Torture and the Special Rapporteur on the promotion and protection of human rights while countering terrorism, who expressed concern that it could be used to penalize the peaceful exercise of human rights.

Freedom of expression and association
In July the House of Representatives approved amendments to Decree no. 18 of 1973 on Public Meetings, Processions and Gatherings, and referred it to the Shura Council. Certain provisions of the decree, as well as some of the proposed amendments, imposed serious restrictions on the rights to freedom of expression and of assembly. For example, the definition of "public gathering" was very broad, and even meetings held in private and involving a small number of people were subject to prior official notification. Article 10(a) prohibited political rallies and meetings for non-citizens, while Article 10(b) banned demonstrations for election purposes. The King ratified the new law in July after its approval by the Shura Council.

In October the High Criminal Court ordered a ban on the publishing of any information relating to a report issued in September by Salah al-Bandar, a UK national and adviser to the Bahraini government. The report alleged that officials had planned to manipulate the outcome of the November parliamentary elections at the expense of the majority Shi'a Muslim population. He was deported to the UK the same month and later charged with "illegally seizing government documents and stealing two cheques". He denied the charges.

In October the Minister of Information issued an order banning seven internet websites on the basis of Articles 19 and 20 of the Press and Publications Law of 2002. The reasons for the ban were not clear but were believed to be connected with the report published by Salah al-Bandar. A number of other websites were also banned during the year.

Human rights activists
During the year several human rights activists were reportedly subjected to harassment in the form of anonymous threatening telephone calls telling them to cease their human rights activities. For example, human rights activists received calls warning them to stop referring to Salah al-Bandar's report in their work.

Abuses of detainees
In August, 19 detainees, most of whom were being held at the Dry-Dock prison on the Island of Muharraq, were beaten by riot police after a court session, apparently after they announced their intention to go on a hunger strike. They were protesting against their detention without bail and repeated postponements of the court sessions. The 19 detainees were arrested allegedly for holding an illegal gathering and sabotaging property in the town of Sanabis. After they appeared before the High Criminal Court, they were reportedly taken outside the prison grounds, their hands tied behind their backs, and forced to lie face-down in the heat of the sun for more than two hours,

during which time they were allegedly beaten with sticks and kicked. The men were released in September after a pardon from the King. However, no investigation into their alleged ill-treatment was known to have been carried out.

Death penalty
In November the King ratified the death sentences against three people. Mohammad Hanif Atta Mohammad, a Pakistani national, had been found guilty of the murder in August 2003 of Ibrahim al-Asmawi, a Bahraini national. He was sentenced to death by the High Criminal Court and the sentence was upheld on appeal. In a separate case two Bangladeshi nationals, Jasmine Anwar Hussain, a female domestic worker, and Mohammad Hilaluddin, were sentenced to death in November 2004. Their death sentences were upheld on appeal in December 2005. All three were executed by firing squad in December 2006. These were the first executions to be carried out in Bahrain since 1996.

BANGLADESH

PEOPLE'S REPUBLIC OF BANGLADESH
Head of state: Iajuddin Ahmed
Head of government: Iajuddin Ahmed (replaced Begum Khaleda Zia in October)
Death penalty: retentionist
International Criminal Court: signed

Human rights abuses by gangs linked to political parties continued in the context of widespread political violence. Police used excessive force against protesters seeking improved economic conditions, and against opposition rallies. Mass arbitrary arrests of political activists took place. Scores of people were killed in bomb attacks or in violent clashes between the opposition and ruling party supporters. Women continued to face violence, including acid attacks. Death sentences were handed down and one execution was carried out.

Background
Escalating tension between the ruling coalition parties and the opposition alliance led to several violent clashes leaving scores of people dead and hundreds more injured.

In waves of mass protests, opposition parties led by the Awami League called for the resignation of the Chief Election Commissioner, claiming that he was a supporter of the ruling Bangladesh Nationalist Party.

They objected to the composition of the Election Commission and declared the compilation of the voters list to be biased and flawed.

The government relinquished office in late October as scheduled. Following mass violent clashes between the outgoing ruling party members and their opposition, the designated Chief Adviser for the caretaker government turned down the post. President Iajuddin Ahmed appointed himself as the Chief Adviser amid unresolved controversy that his decision was in breach of the Constitution.

There were waves of strikes and mass demonstrations by garment factory workers, farmers and primary school teachers seeking improved economic conditions.

Cycle of violence and abuses

Bomb blasts occurred but apparently on a much lower scale than in previous years. Targets were mainly opposition party members and court premises.

◻ On 31 October, a bomb attack took place in Rajshahi aimed at several opposition parties, including Gono Forum. They claimed it was carried out by the Bangladesh Islamichatra Shibir cadres, the youth wing of the Jamaat-e-Islami party. On 15 November, eight people were reportedly wounded when a series of small bombs exploded near the offices of the Awami League. No one was known to have been brought to justice.

By the end of the year no one had been brought to justice for the August 2004 grenade attacks against the Awami League leader Sheikh Hasina.

Electoral violence

Scores of people died in clashes between the ruling and opposition parties in the run-up to the general elections. No one was known to have been brought to justice.

◻ According to the human rights group Odhikar, at least 50 people were killed and more than 250 injured between 27 October and 5 November in violence that erupted between the two main parties over opposition demands which included the resignation of the Chief Election Commissioner.

Police brutality

Police repeatedly attacked opposition rallies, targeted leading activists and subjected them to severe beatings.

◻ Senior Awami League leader Saber Hossain Chowdhury suffered head injuries when he was severely beaten on 6 September by more than 12 police officers.

◻ Asaduzzaman Noor, an opposition member of parliament, was beaten by police on 12 September and taken to hospital with severe back injuries. None of the police officers involved was brought to justice.

Police continued to use excessive force including live ammunition against demonstrators, causing dozens of deaths and injuries to hundreds more.

◻ At least 17 people were killed in protests relating to electricity shortages in the northern town of Kansat in April after police fired live ammunition, rubber bullets and tear gas to dispel the crowds. No independent investigation was initiated into the killings.

◻ At least five people were killed and more than 100 injured in Phulbari on 26 August when police and the paramilitary force Bangladesh Rifles (BDR) fired live ammunition into a crowd protesting against the establishment of an open-pit coalmine by the British firm Asia Energy Corporation. The government eventually agreed to some of their demands, giving assurances that no one would be forcibly evicted or lose their livelihoods because of the mine.

Mass arbitrary arrests

Thousands of people were arrested ahead of planned rallies by opposition parties, and thousands more were detained on suspicion of involvement in criminal activity. The families of detainees were not informed of their arrest and were forced to search for them in police stations. Many were held without charge or trial for weeks while others were released on bail after a few days.

Violence against women

Reports of women beaten to death or strangled for not meeting their husbands' dowry demands continued. Women were subjected to acid attacks. Domestic workers were ill-treated or killed if they failed to work excessive hours.

◻ According to reports compiled by the Bangladesh Institute of Labour Studies, at least 169 female domestic workers were killed between 2000 and 2005 in Dhaka alone. Another 122 were critically injured and 52 were raped. A significant proportion of the victims were reportedly children.

Death penalty

At least 130 people were sentenced to death and one man was executed.

AI country reports/ visits

Reports

- Bangladesh: Briefing to political parties for a human rights agenda (AI Index: ASA 13/012/2006)
- Bangladesh: Handover to caretaker government marked by violence (AI Index: ASA 13/014/2006)

BELARUS

REPUBLIC OF BELARUS
Head of state: Alyaksandr Lukashenka
Head of government: Sergei Sidorsky
Death penalty: retentionist
International Criminal Court: not ratified

The clampdown on civil society continued. The number of convictions of civil society activists increased as legal changes limiting freedom of association introduced at the end of 2005 came into effect. Opposition activists were subjected to harassment and arbitrarily detained. Mass detentions of peaceful demonstrators took place after presidential elections in March. The government did not adequately protect women against violence in the home. Use of the death penalty continued. No progress was made in investigations into four cases of enforced disappearance.

Background
Violations of the rights to freedom of expression and assembly were repeatedly condemned by the international community. The Election Observation Mission of the Organization for Security and Co-operation in Europe criticized the conduct of the presidential elections on 19 March. It found that "arbitrary use of state power and widespread detentions showed a disregard for the basic rights of freedom of assembly, association and expression". In conclusions passed on 10 April, the Council of the European Union (EU) criticized the elections and condemned the violence used by the Belarusian authorities against demonstrators and the arrests of demonstrators and members of the opposition. The EU instituted restrictive measures against 31 officials responsible for violations of international electoral standards and for the crackdown on civil society and democratic opposition. The list of officials against whom such restrictive measures would be applied was added to subsequently. On 18 May the EU froze the assets of President Lukashenka and 35 other officials.

Clampdown on freedom of association
Non-governmental organizations continued to face stringent controls and checks on their activities. A number of civil society activists were detained or charged under Article 193 of the Criminal Code which was amended in November 2005 to include a prison sentence of up to three years for "organizing and running an unregistered organization that infringes the rights of citizens".

⌗ Four members of the non-governmental organization Initiative Partnership, which was planning to monitor the presidential elections, were arrested at their offices on 21 February by officers from the Committee for State Security (KGB). The KGB initially claimed that Mikalay Astreyka, Enira Branizkaya, Alyaksandr Shalayka, and Tsimafey Dranchuk were organizing fraudulent exit polls and planning a violent uprising. In August the four were convicted of "organizing and running an unregistered organization that infringes the rights of citizens". Mikalay Astreyka was sentenced to two years' imprisonment, Tsimafey Dranchuk to one year, and Enira Branizkaya and Alyaksandr Shalayka to six months each. All four were released before the end of 2006.

⌗ At the end of December 2005 the Supreme Economic Court renewed its investigation into alleged tax evasion by the Belarusian Helsinki Committee, the only remaining national human rights organization still operating in the country. On 1 March, Tatiana Protko, the chair, was accused of not paying tax on a grant provided by an EU programme. A 1994 memorandum, agreed by the Belarusian authorities and the EU, granted tax exemption for this programme. Two court decisions in 2004 had confirmed that the organization's activities were lawful. As a result of the renewed investigation, the organization faced a potential fine of US$70,000 for tax evasion, and possible closure. On 23 June, the Ministry of Justice lodged a separate claim with the Supreme Court for the closure of the organization on the grounds that it had violated tax laws. This case was continuing at the end of the year. On 1 November the Belarusian Economic Court decided to confiscate property worth US$118,300 towards payment of the tax that it ruled was owing. The property was removed on 5 December. On 19 December the property department of the presidential administration informed the organization that they must vacate their office premises by 20 January 2007. Without a legally registered address the organization would cease to be legal.

Detentions of peaceful demonstrators
Large numbers of peaceful demonstrators were detained and beaten by riot police and anti-terrorist forces during demonstrations following the March elections. According to the human rights group Vyasna, a total of 686 people were detained during the period 19-25 March. Most of those detained were charged with administrative offences, such as participation in unsanctioned meetings or hooliganism, which carry sentences of 10 to 15 days' detention.

⌗ On 27 April, five leading members of the Belarusian opposition were tried and convicted under Article 167 of the Administrative Code, of "organizing an unsanctioned meeting". The charges related to a peaceful march to commemorate the 20th anniversary of the Chernobyl nuclear disaster on 26 April. The marchers had received permission to march to Bangalore Square in Minsk where speeches were to take place. However, Alyaksandr Milinkevich reportedly addressed the crowd before the march began. He and two others — Vintsuk Vyachorka and Alyaksandr Bukhvostov — were sentenced to 15 days' imprisonment. Zmitser Dashkevich and Sergei Kalyakin were sentenced to 14 days.

Harassment of opposition activists

Opposition activists were harassed and intimidated and increasingly sentenced for criminal offences in an attempt to discredit them.

On 10 May, Artur Finkevich, a member of the Malady Front youth political movement, was sentenced to two years' corrective labour by the court of Pershamajski district for writing political graffiti. Artur Finkevich was charged under Article 339, Part 2 of the Criminal Code with "malicious hooliganism". In the past, youth opposition activists were sentenced under the Administrative Code to short-term sentences for graffiti writing. There was concern that the authorities may have used the Criminal Code for political reasons to deter other activists.

Prisoners of conscience

Eleven prisoners of conscience were held during the year.

On 13 July, Alyaksandr Kazulin, presidential candidate in the March elections, was sentenced to five and a half years' imprisonment for "hooliganism" and "organizing group activities that breach public order or actively participating in similar activities". There was concern that these charges were part of an ongoing, systematic campaign of harassment, intimidation and obstruction by the Belarusian authorities against Alyaksandr Kazulin.

In April Mikhail Marinich, a prominent opposition activist and presidential candidate in 2001, was released early for health reasons. He had been convicted in December 2004 of fabricated charges of "embezzlement by means of abuse of his official position executed on a large scale" and sentenced to five years' imprisonment later reduced to three and a half.

Valerii Levonevskii was released on 15 May, having served the full two years of his sentence. Valerii Levonevskii and Alexander Vasiliev, the president and vice-president respectively of the national strike committee of market traders, had been sentenced to two years in prison in September 2004 for publicly insulting President Lukashenka in a satirical leaflet. Alexander Vasiliev had been released from prison on 7 July 2005 under an amnesty announced by the President to commemorate the end of the Second World War.

Violence against women

Despite some progress, measures to protect women from violence in the family remained inadequate. There was a lack of mandatory government training programmes for police, judges and medical staff. Key agencies such as law enforcement officers and the courts failed to record cases of domestic violence in a systematic manner.

There were no accurate statistics on the numbers of victims of domestic violence, but in 2005, 166 people were murdered in the home, and 2,736 women were victims of crimes in the home. The lack of public awareness and support meant many women were unable to escape violent situations.

Death penalty

According to press reports nine death sentences were passed during 2006. There was no official information on the number of executions carried out and death sentences imposed.

Update

No progress was made in establishing the fate of four people who may have been the victims of enforced disappearance in 1999 and 2000 and who were widely believed to have been killed by state agents.

AI country reports/visits

Reports

- Europe and Central Asia: Summary of Amnesty International's concerns in the region, January-June 2006 (AI Index: EUR 01/017/2006)
- Commonwealth of Independent States: Positive trend on the abolition of the death penalty but more needs to be done (AI Index: EUR 04/003/2006)
- Belarus: Domestic Violence – more than a private scandal (AI Index: EUR 49/014/2006)

Visit

AI delegates visited Belarus in February.

BELGIUM

KINGDOM OF BELGIUM
Head of state: King Albert II
Head of government: Guy Verhofstadt
Death penalty: abolitionist for all crimes
International Criminal Court: ratified

Poor conditions in immigration centres and police ill-treatment of migrants and asylum-seekers continued. Migrant minors were held in closed detention centres for illegal immigrants and failed asylum-seekers. Irregular migrants occupied public buildings and went on hunger strike to support demands for legislative reforms. The murder of a woman and child in Antwerp and other incidents reflected the persistence of racist violence. Overcrowding and sub-standard prison conditions prompted strikes by staff. New evidence indicated that secret US flights may have landed on Belgian territory. Belgium became the first country to ban cluster bombs.

Asylum and immigration

New asylum laws in July required new asylum petitions, including appeals, to be processed within 12 months. The asylum procedure was reformed to grant subsidiary protection for those not covered by the 1951 UN Refugee Convention but who risk serious rights violations if they return to their country of origin. However, the new legislation did not address the situation of irregular migrants. The number of asylum applications continued to decline.

Throughout 2006 a number of churches and public buildings were occupied by irregular migrants and failed asylum-seekers demanding regularization of their situation, an end to expulsions and the shutting down of closed detention centres. The government regularized the status of many of the migrants who occupied the church of Saint Boniface in Brussels in February and March. In May, there were hunger strikes in four asylum reception centres.

Migrant children continued to be detained in closed detention centres in violation of international law.

Police ill-treatment

Police officers allegedly ill-treated individuals being forcibly deported.

☐ On 1 August a third attempt was made to expel Hawa Diallo, a failed asylum-seeker from the Republic of Guinea, but was aborted after passengers disembarked in protest at her treatment. The evening before, she had been separated from her 19-month-old baby until the time of the flight. The five police officers accompanying her were reported to have assaulted and racially insulted her. Following the failed deportation, she was freed under orders to leave Belgium within five days. From hiding, she lodged a complaint of ill-treatment with the Permanent Commission for Control of Police Services.

☐ In a landmark ruling on 12 October the European Court of Human Rights found that Belgium was in violation of the prohibition of inhuman treatment and right to respect of private and family life guaranteed under the European Convention on Human Rights. In 2002 an unaccompanied five-year-old asylum-seeker had been detained and subsequently deported unaccompanied back to the Democratic Republic of the Congo, her country of origin, where there was no family member to meet her.

Racism and discrimination

Under a March directive, the police started to record crimes motivated by racism. The Centre for Equal Opportunities said it received 1,000 complaints of racism a year, noting that many attacks were never reported.

☐ In April, Daniel Féret, president of the National Front party, was convicted of inciting racial hatred and sentenced to 10 years' exclusion from political office and 250 hours of community service. He had distributed election materials likening immigrants to criminals, savages and terrorists. The National Front's website manager was also convicted and fined. The court did not order dissolution of the party for lack of evidence linking it to the offending texts. The Court of Appeal confirmed the conviction in October.

☐ On 11 May an 18-year-old resident of Antwerp shot and killed a pregnant black woman and the white child in her care, and seriously wounded a Turkish woman.

He openly stated that he had targeted foreigners. Preliminary investigations were concluding at the end of 2006, but the trial date had not yet been fixed.

'War on terror'

In March press reports alleged there had been at least two secret flights by the US Central Intelligence Agency (CIA) that landed briefly at Deurne airport in Antwerp in July 2002. It was not known whether the planes were transporting detainees. An investigation by the European Parliament found that, of 1,080 stopovers by suspected CIA flights in Europe, four concerned Belgium. A Belgian Senate committee in July found there was insufficient supervision of operations by foreign intelligence services on Belgian territory, making it impossible to ascertain the destination and purpose of such flights.

Prison conditions

Prisoner numbers reached a new high. One third of prisoners were on remand. Specialized centres for minors were overcrowded, and juvenile offenders were sometimes held in mainstream prisons. A law on youth assistance passed in May included plans to construct a special prison for 200 juvenile offenders.

In April the European Committee for the Prevention of Torture reported allegations of ill-treatment in police custody. The Committee condemned overcrowding at the psychiatric unit in Namur prison, cage-like cells at the law courts in Liège, and poor conditions for people refused admission to the country at the detention centre at Brussels airport.

In April there was a strike at Forest prison in Brussels. The GCPS (public services trade union) attacked prison overcrowding, poor conditions, buildings it considered breached health, hygiene and safety requirements, and the "wholly insufficient" six-week basic training for staff. In August staff at the prison in Termonde went on strike in protest at overcrowding and understaffing following the escape of 28 prisoners. In September they renewed strike action, claiming that promised improvements had not materialized.

Arms control

Belgium became the first country to ban cluster bombs when Parliament adopted a law banning their production, stockpiling, transportation and trade on 8 June. In 1995, Belgium was the first country to prohibit anti-personnel landmines.

AI country reports/visits
Report
- Europe and Central Asia: Summary of Amnesty International concerns in the region, January-June 2006 (AI Index: EUR 01/017/2006)

BOLIVIA

REPUBLIC OF BOLIVIA
Head of state and government: Evo Morales Ayma
(replaced Eduardo Rodríguez Veltzé in January)
Death penalty: abolitionist for ordinary crimes
International Criminal Court: ratified

Peasants were killed during a joint security force operation to eradicate coca crops. There were demonstrations calling for the right to land. Deaths were reported during violent clashes between miners. Prison conditions were poor.

Background
President-elect Evo Morales Ayma, the leader of the Movement to Socialism party (Movimiento al Socialismo, MAS), took office in January. A National Development Plan to improve access to fundamental rights such as health, education and justice and to end discrimination was announced. However, no information was forthcoming on its implementation.

A programme of reforms was initiated, including the formation of the Constituent Assembly which was inaugurated in August to rewrite the Constitution. A decree was passed in May to nationalize oil and gas and renegotiate contracts with foreign investors and companies, to raise taxes and to set terms for the acquisition of shares by the State. A programme of land reform was launched in June which included the distribution of state-owned land to peasants and Indigenous people.

In November, following demonstrations by Indigenous groups calling for further reforms, a law for agrarian reform was passed by Congress and signed by the President. Under the new law, unproductive private land could be expropriated by the government for redistribution to peasants. This reform was opposed by landowners in the Departments of Santa Cruz, Beni and Pando which, along with the Department of Tarija, sought autonomy during the year.

In December, civilian groups, members of Indigenous non-governmental organizations, political groups, journalists and community leaders, clashed in Santa Cruz Department in the context of the local consultation for regional autonomy. Premises of the MAS and offices of Indigenous community centres were set on fire, and members of Indigenous groups had their houses ransacked. Investigative journalists were attacked in the streets of Santa Cruz city and radio stations were forced to stop transmission due to harassment.

Bolivia ratified the Optional Protocol to the UN Convention against Torture in May, the Additional Protocol to the American Convention on Human Rights in the Area of Economic, Social, and Cultural Rights, known as the "Protocol of San Salvador" in July, and the Inter-American Convention to Prevent and Punish Torture in November.

Children
In July a study by the UN Development Programme and UNICEF reported that over 230 babies in Bolivia died per day through lack of proper care, six out of 10 children and minors lacked basic needs and five out of 10 lived below the poverty line. The report called on Bolivia to recognize the role played by children in the country's development and to implement health, education and other programmes to tackle the lack of protection for children and to defend their rights.

Eradication of coca leaf crops
In September two peasants were killed and one wounded during the eradication of coca leaf crops around the Carrasco National Park in the region of Yungas de Vandiola, Department of Cochabamba, by a patrol of the Joint Task Forces made up of members of the police and army.

Miners conflict
In October, at least nine miners were killed and dozens injured in clashes between state-employed miners and members of an independent co-operative in the mining town of Huanuni, La Paz Department. The confrontation, in which dynamite and firearms were allegedly used, was sparked by a dispute over the access rights to working areas in the tin mine. An investigation was launched.

Prison conditions
There were reports of poor prison conditions. In Palmasola prison in the city of Santa Cruz, five inmates were killed in April, allegedly as a result of a fight between rival gangs of prisoners who were attempting to impose their rule inside the prison.

In November, inmates in 19 prisons around the country started a hunger strike demanding prompt trials and better prison conditions.

Impunity
In December, the Attorney General's Office charged former President Gonzalo Sánchez de Lozada and two former ministers with the killing of at least 60 people during demonstrations in October 2003. The authorities were seeking Gonzalo Sánchez de Lozada's extradition from the USA to try him for the killings.

Intergovernmental organizations
In November, after a visit to Bolivia, the Inter-American Commission on Human Rights highlighted the lack of access to justice, particularly in rural areas, and the lack of co-operation by the security and armed forces in providing relevant information to the judicial authorities. It expressed concern about poor conditions and the high level of overcrowding in prisons and the fact that over 70 per cent of prisoners had not been sentenced. It also noted that minors were held with adult prisoners.

AI country reports/ visits
Statement
- Bolivia: Open letter to the President of the Republic of Bolivia, Evo Morales Ayma (AI Index: AMR 18/001/2006)

BOSNIA AND HERZEGOVINA

BOSNIA AND HERZEGOVINA
Head of state: rotating presidency – Željko Komšić, Nebojša Radmanović, Haris Silajdžić
Head of government: Adnan Terzić
President of the Federation of Bosnia and Herzegovina: Niko Lozančić
President of the Republika Srpska: Milan Jelić (replaced Dragan Čavić in November)
Death penalty: abolitionist for all crimes
International Criminal Court: ratified

Many perpetrators of war crimes and crimes against humanity during the 1992-95 war continued to evade justice, and thousands of enforced disappearances remained unresolved. Lack of full co-operation with the International Criminal Tribunal for the former Yugoslavia (Tribunal) by the Republika Srpska (RS) was an obstacle to justice. Progress was made in the domestic prosecution of war crimes, including in proceedings at the War Crimes Chamber in Sarajevo, although efforts to bring perpetrators to justice were insufficient. Minorities faced discrimination, including in employment and in access to education. Approximately 3,600 refugees and internally displaced people had returned to their homes by October.

Background

Bosnia and Herzegovina (BiH) remained divided in two semi-autonomous entities, the RS and the Federation of Bosnia and Herzegovina (FBiH), with a special status granted to the Brčko District.

The international community continued to exert significant influence over the country's political process, in particular through a High Representative with executive powers nominated by the Peace Implementation Council (PIC), an intergovernmental body monitoring the implementation of the Dayton Peace Agreement. In June the PIC began preparing the closure in June 2007 of the Office of the High Representative (OHR). The engagement of the international community was expected to continue through a strengthened European Union (EU) Special Representative. Approximately 6,000 troops of the EU-led peacekeeping force EUFOR remained. EUFOR's mandate was extended by the UN Security Council in November for a further year.

General elections in October, the first to be fully administered by local authorities, showed that the electorate remained divided along ethnic lines. Widespread nationalist rhetoric included calls for a referendum on independence for the RS. A new government had not been formed by the end of 2006.

International prosecutions for war crimes

The Tribunal continued to try alleged perpetrators of serious violations of international humanitarian law. Former Serbian President Slobodan Milošević died at the Tribunal Detention Unit following a heart attack on 11 March. He had been on trial before the Tribunal for war crimes and crimes against humanity in BiH, Croatia and Kosovo, and for genocide in BiH.

In March, Enver Hadžihasanović and Amir Kubura, former Army of Bosnia and Herzegovina (ABiH) commanders, were sentenced to five and two and a half years' imprisonment, respectively. They were convicted of failing to prevent or punish crimes against non-Bosniaks by volunteer foreign fighters, Enver Hadžihasanović for crimes including murder and cruel treatment, and Amir Kubura for the plunder of villages.

In May, Ivica Rajić, a former commander of the Croatian Defence Council (HVO), the Bosnian Croat armed forces, was sentenced to 12 years' imprisonment for his involvement in the attack on the village of Stupni Do. The Tribunal found that forces under his command wilfully killed at least 37 people. He had admitted charges of wilful killing, inhuman treatment, appropriation of property, and extensive, unlawful and wanton destruction not justified by military necessity.

In June, Dragan Zelenović, former sub-commander of the RS military police and paramilitary leader in Foča, was transferred to the Tribunal's custody. He had been arrested in the Russian Federation in 2005. He faced charges of torture and rape as war crimes and crimes against humanity against the non-Serb population in Foča, for allegedly raping, sexually assaulting and participating in the gang rape of detained women.

Also in June Naser Orić, former commander of the Srebrenica Armed Forces Staff, was convicted of failing to prevent murders and the cruel treatment of Bosnian Serb prisoners in 1992 and 1993. He was sentenced to two years' imprisonment.

In September, Momčilo Krajišnik, who held high-ranking positions in the Bosnian Serb leadership between 1991 and 1995, was sentenced to 27 years' imprisonment for the persecution, extermination, murder, deportation and forced transfer of non-Serbs. He was acquitted of genocide and complicity in genocide charges.

Co-operation between the RS and the Tribunal remained inadequate and no progress was made by the RS in locating former Bosnian Serb leader Radovan Karadžić, indicted by the Tribunal on charges including genocide and still at large. In December, in her address to the UN Security Council, the Tribunal Prosecutor noted that central institutions were not working efficiently and that the RS authorities, despite some recent improvements, had not shown a robust willingness to arrest Radovan Karadžić and Stojan Župljanin, the fugitives most likely to be in BiH.

Under a "completion strategy" laid down by the UN Security Council, the Tribunal was expected to conclude all cases in 2010. As a result of the tight deadlines imposed by the strategy, the Tribunal continued to refer cases involving lower level perpetrators to national jurisdictions in the former Yugoslavia. In 2006 cases involving seven suspects were transferred to BiH.

Domestic prosecutions for war crimes
The War Crimes Chamber within the BiH State Court, set up to try particularly sensitive cases or cases referred by the Tribunal, issued its first convictions.
▭ In April, former member of Bosnian Serb forces Neđo Samardžić was convicted of unlawful imprisonment, rape, and aiding and abetting sexual slavery of non-Serb victims in the Foča area. He was sentenced to 13 years and four months' imprisonment. In September the verdict was quashed and a re-trial before an appellate panel in December raised the prison sentence to 24 years.
▭ In May, Dragoje Paunović, a former local commander of Bosnian Serb forces, was sentenced to 20 years' imprisonment for crimes against humanity in 1992. He was convicted of persecuting Bosniak civilians, for his command and individual responsibility for killings and other inhuman acts. The verdict was confirmed on appeal in November.
▭ In July former RS police officer Boban Šimšić was convicted of assisting members of the Bosnian Serb Army (VRS) in enforced disappearances and rapes of non-Serbs in 1992. He was sentenced to five years' imprisonment.
▭ Marko Samardžija, a former VRS commander, was convicted of crimes against humanity, including for his role in the killing of at least 144 Bosniak detained men, and sentenced to 26 years' imprisonment in November.
▭ Also in November, the War Crimes Chamber rendered its first judgement in a case transferred by the Tribunal. Radovan Stanković was convicted of crimes against humanity against the non-Serb population in the Foča area. A former VRS member, he was found to have participated in the rape of women detained by Bosnian Serb forces and sentenced to 16 years' imprisonment.
▭ In December, Nikola Andrun, a former HVO member, was sentenced to 13 years' imprisonment for war crimes committed in his capacity as Deputy Commander of the Gabela detention camp, including the torture and intimidation of non-Croat detainees.
Some war crimes trials of low-level perpetrators were also held in local courts, including in the RS, which continued to have difficulties in dealing with these cases because of a lack of staff and effective witness protection programmes.

Enforced disappearances unresolved
According to estimates of the International Commission on Missing Persons (ICMP), approximately 13,000 people who went missing during the war were still unaccounted for. Many of them were victims of enforced disappearances, whose perpetrators enjoyed impunity.
Progress was slow in transferring competencies from the missing persons commissions of the FBiH and RS to the national Missing Persons Institute. The Institute's

directors were appointed in March, and Steering and Supervisory Board members in December.
Approximately 2,500 sets of human remains were exhumed from various locations in BiH.
▭ In August the exhumation of a mass grave in Kamenica, near Zvornik, uncovered 1,009 incomplete and 144 complete skeletons. The site is believed to contain the remains of victims killed by Bosnian Serb forces in Srebrenica in 1995, and was reportedly the biggest mass grave excavated since the end of the war.
▭ In January the OHR ordered the RS authorities to implement a 2001 decision by the BiH Human Rights Chamber to form a commission to investigate the enforced disappearance of Avdo Palić. The ABiH war-time commander in the UN "safe haven" of Žepa, Avdo Palić was last seen negotiating the surrender of Žepa to the VRS in 1995 and was later reportedly detained by Bosnian Serb forces. His fate and whereabouts have remained unknown. A Commission was appointed, and in April presented a report to the OHR, claiming to contain information on the location of his remains. However, this information proved insufficient for an exhumation and no progress was made in the case. The Commission was reportedly reactivated in December.

Right to return
Of an estimated 2.2 million people displaced during the conflict, more than a million refugees and internally displaced persons (IDPs) were estimated to have returned to their homes. Progress on returns was limited. UNHCR, the UN refugee agency, registered approximately 3,600 returns between January and October. Of these, some 3,000 returned to areas where they were part of a minority community.
Violence towards and harassment of returnees and members of minorities by private individuals were reported.
▭ In February, a Bosnian Croat 78-year-old returnee was beaten to death in Bugojno. Three men were convicted of the murder.
▭ In May an elderly returnee was murdered in her home on the outskirts of Sanski Most. A suspect was reportedly arrested by local police.
The lack of jobs was a major obstacle to sustainable returns. Generally scarce employment opportunities reflected the weak economy and difficulties of transition and post-war reconstruction. In addition, returnees faced discrimination on ethnic grounds.

'War on terror'
Six men of Algerian origin, unlawfully transferred in 2002 by the FBiH authorities to US custody, remained in detention in Guantánamo Bay, Cuba. In April, following a complaint by the wife of one of the detainees, Hadj Boudellaa, the Human Rights Commission within the BiH Constitutional Court concluded that the BiH authorities had failed to implement a 2002 decision of the BiH Human Rights Chamber in the case. They had failed to use diplomatic channels to protect the rights of the detainee, provide

him with consular support, and take all necessary steps to ensure he would not be subjected to the death penalty, including by asking the US government for guarantees to that effect.

In June, the Rapporteur appointed by the Committee on Legal Affairs and Human Rights of the Parliamentary Assembly of the Council of Europe to investigate alleged secret detentions and unlawful inter-state transfers of detainees, reported that the six men were "a well documented example of the abduction of European citizens and residents by the American authorities with the active collusion of the authorities of a Council of Europe member state". The report called for a credible diplomatic intervention by the BiH authorities with the US government to secure the rapid repatriation of the detainees.

Accountability of peacekeepers
In January, Italian members of EUFOR, during an operation to arrest war crimes suspect Dragomir Abazović, shot dead his wife, and seriously wounded him and their 11-year-old son. Reportedly, a EUFOR internal investigation found the troops had acted in self-defence and cleared them of any wrongdoing. An investigation by the East Sarajevo District Prosecutor reportedly found indications that the EUFOR troops fired first. The outcomes of both investigations were forwarded to the competent Prosecutor in Italy.

Exclusion from education
Primary school attendance rates for Romani children were low, and extreme poverty remained one of the main causes of the exclusion of Roma from education. Romani language, culture and traditions were not included in a systematic way in school curricula. Insufficient progress was made in the implementation of the 2004 Action Plan on the Educational Needs of Roma and Members of Other National Minorities. A Council for National Minorities of Bosnia and Herzegovina, tasked with overseeing its implementation, was formally created in April, but was not operational by the end of 2006.

Violence against women
In June the UN Committee on the Elimination of Discrimination against Women expressed concern that BiH remained a country of origin, transit and destination in the trafficking in women, and that victims of sexual violence during the 1992-1995 war suffered additional disadvantages as both female heads of households and IDPs.

AI country reports/visits
Reports
- Partners in crime: Europe's role in US renditions (AI Index: EUR 01/008/2006)
- Europe and Central Asia: Summary of Amnesty International's concerns in the region, January-June 2006 (AI Index: EUR 01/017/2006)
- False starts: The exclusion of Romani children from primary education in Bosnia and Herzegovina, Croatia and Slovenia (AI Index: EUR 05/002/2006)

- Appeal to the United Nations Security Council to ensure that the International Criminal Tribunal for the former Yugoslavia fulfils its mandate (AI Index: EUR 05/006/2006)
- Bosnia and Herzegovina: Behind closed gates — ethnic discrimination in employment (AI Index: EUR 63/001/2006)

Visits
An AI delegate visited BiH in January and March.

BRAZIL

FEDERATIVE REPUBLIC OF BRAZIL
Head of state and government: Luiz Inácio Lula da Silva
Death penalty: abolitionist for ordinary crimes
International Criminal Court: ratified

Problems within the public security, prison and judicial systems, including systematic human rights violations, contributed to persistently high levels of criminal violence. The poorest communities bore the brunt of the tens of thousands of gun-related deaths. Well over 1,000 people were killed in confrontations with the police in incidents classified as "resistance followed by death", many in situations suggesting excessive use of force or extrajudicial executions. Torture continued to be widespread and systematic. Access to land continued to be a focus of human rights violations, including forced evictions and violent attacks on rural land activists, anti-dam campaigners, urban squatter movements and Indigenous peoples. Many people continued to work in conditions equivalent to slave or indentured labour. Human rights defenders continued to be subjected to threats and attacks.

Background
President Luiz Inácio Lula da Silva was re-elected for a second (and final) term. His first term was marked by extensive allegations of political corruption across the political spectrum.

Investigations into corruption highlighted direct and indirect links to the erosion of human rights protection. There were extensive reports of misappropriation of public funds at all levels of the executive and legislature, which undermined the authorities' capacity to guarantee fundamental human rights through social services and increased the loss of public faith in state institutions. In particular, there were a number of high profile cases of alleged corruption in Congress. The involvement of state officials in criminal activity resulted in human rights violations and an apparent increase in organized crime across the country. Law enforcement officials were reportedly involved in the drugs trade, selling guns, and smuggling arms, mobile phones and drugs to members of criminal gangs in detention.

President Lula's first term was also marked by targeted social investment coupled with tight fiscal policy. Central to the government's social policy was the family grant (*bolsa família*), under which around 11 million poor families received grants when they sent children to primary school. This combined policy was welcomed in some sectors for bringing economic stability while reportedly achieving some reductions in social inequality. However, other sectors, including social movements, expressed concern at the budget restraints applied to social investment in other areas, namely public security, land reform and indigenous rights, in order to sustain debt payments and the budget surplus.

While the introduction of legislation to criminalize domestic violence and the further development of programmes to combat torture and protect human rights defenders were welcomed, there was a clear reluctance to address a number of issues. Of greatest concern was the area of public security where there was a continued lack of effective political attention. None of the presidential candidates and few candidates for state governor offered genuine long-term solutions to address the tens of thousands of homicides committed across the country each year. Faced with ever higher levels of violence, state and federal leaders continued to seek political advantage by offering reactive and short-term solutions.

Ratification of the Optional Protocol to the UN Convention against Torture was passed by Congress, although reforms to bring Brazil's legislation in line with the Rome Statute of the International Criminal Court were persistently blocked.

Criminal justice system

The criminal justice system continued to deteriorate in the face of long-term negligence by the federal and state governments. Promised reforms were not implemented, resulting in unprepared and under-funded police, judicial and prison systems being forced to deal inadequately with extreme levels of criminal violence. This contributed to systematic human rights violations by law enforcement officials, including excessive use of force, extrajudicial executions, torture and ill-treatment as well as widespread corruption.

Attempts by certain state authorities to define public security problems as a war saw the increasing adoption of military tactics by state police forces. The poorest communities, enjoying least protection from the state, were doubly victimized, suffering the highest concentrations of violent crime and the repressive and discriminatory methods used by the police to combat it.

Human rights violations by police and army

Police officers killed well over 1,000 people. These killings were rarely investigated fully, as they were registered as "resistance followed by death", often pre-empting any thorough investigation. According to official figures, in the first nine months of 2006 Rio de Janeiro police killed 807 people, a slight increase on the previous year, while in São Paulo 528 people were killed by police, more than the total for the whole of 2005. Police and prison guards were themselves vulnerable to attack and many were killed.

In May the state of São Paulo was shaken by violence by criminals and police. Between 12 and 20 May, members of the First Command of the Capital (Primeiro Comando da Capital, PCC), a criminal gang born in the state's prison system, took to the streets in a massive display of organized violence. Allegedly protesting against prison conditions and the transfer of their leaders to a high security prison, they killed over 40 law enforcement officers, burned more than 80 buses, attacked police stations, banks and a metro station, and co-ordinated revolts and hostage-taking in around half of the state's prisons. In response, police reported that they had killed over 100 "suspects".

In several incidents in poor communities across the state of São Paulo, people were killed by masked men in situations suggesting extrajudicial executions or "death-squad" style revenge killings. State authorities only provided details of those killed by the police following a threat of legal action by the Public Prosecutor's office. At the height of the violence, 117 people died in firearms-related incidents in a single day. The PCC launched further attacks, killing a number of prison guards in July. Federal and state government responses to the violence were widely criticized in the media, by public security experts, by police officers and by human rights activists for seeking to take political advantage ahead of elections rather than finding a resolution to the violence.

The state authorities in Rio de Janeiro adopted increasingly militarized tactics in their attempts to combat drug gangs which held sway over most of the city's shanty towns. An armoured troop carrier, colloquially called the "caveirão", was used to police the poorest parts of the city. There were reports of bystanders being killed by military police officers shooting indiscriminately from "caveirões". In March the army deployed troops and tanks on the streets of Rio de Janeiro's shanty towns in an effort to track down stolen guns. Although federal prosecutors challenged the legality of the operation, neither the state nor federal governments questioned the army's decision to take to the streets. However, residents complained of arbitrary, violent and discriminatory treatment by soldiers who were neither trained nor mandated to carry out such operations.

In December Rio de Janeiro state and municipal authorities announced they were investigating reports that up to 92 favelas (shanty towns) had come under the control of paramilitary-style militias. According to reports the militias were made up of active and former police officers working with the support of local politicians and community leaders. Militias were reportedly providing "security" for these communities. However, residents reported the extensive use of violence and the extortion of protection money. Some communities claimed they had suffered violent retaliation from drug factions when members of the militias withdrew from their communities.

There were reports of "death squad"-style killings in the north-eastern states of Bahia, Pernambuco and Sergipe. Two men previously accused of involvement with the "death squad" known as "the Mission" during the 1990s were appointed as Secretary of Public Security and head of the Military Police in the state of Sergipe. Members of the state human rights commission expressed concern at the return of the "death squad" following reports of several killings and enforced disappearances. In one incident in April witnessed by over 50 people, three teenage boys were taken away by members of the elite unit of the military police in the community of Mosqueiro. One of the boys was allegedly tortured until he fainted and later regained consciousness in a wood. The other two boys reportedly disappeared and by the end of the year no trace of them had been found.

⬜ In April, members of the military police in Recife, Pernambuco state, reportedly detained a group of 14 teenagers who were at the carnival. The police reportedly tortured them, took them to a bridge over the Capibaribe river and forced them to jump in. The bodies of two of the boys, aged 15 and 17, were found two days later. An investigation was initiated and five police officers were charged with homicide and torture, but in June one of the boys testifying against the police was shot dead.

Detention system
The detention system strained under the pressure of an ever-increasing prison population and inadequate financial and political investment. There were regular reports of torture and ill-treatment being used for control, punishment and corruption by police officers, prison guards and other detainees. Detention centres suffered from extreme overcrowding and poor sanitary conditions, while prison staff were unsupported and under-trained. There were numerous riots and countless cases of prisoner-on-prisoner violence as many prisons fell under the control of criminal gangs. Belated attempts to break up the gangs saw the further use of "super-max" style prisons, under the Differentiated Disciplinary System (Regime Disciplinar Diferenciado, RDD), previously criticized by both the National Council on Criminal and Penal Policy of the Ministry of Justice and the National Bar Association as contravening human rights protections set out both in the Constitution and under international law.

The breakdown of the prison system was exemplified in São Paulo state by the conditions in the Araraquara prison after riots in May. For several months 1,600 prisoners, including sick and injured, were kept in a yard with space for 160 people while the prison underwent reconstruction.

There were persistent reports of violations against women in detention. AI witnessed conditions in the Colônia Penal Feminina, a women's prison in Recife, which were extremely poor, with women sleeping on the floor and in shower units, limited health facilities and reports of violent treatment by guards. New-born babies were kept in cells with women, some of whom were reportedly ill, with limited health or safety facilities.

Impunity
The extreme slowness and ineffectiveness of the judicial system reinforced impunity for human rights violations. In February the São Paulo State Supreme Court absolved Colonel Ubiratan Guimarães for his role in the 1992 Carandiru prison massacre in which 111 prisoners were killed. By the end of 2006, no other police officer had stood trial for their part in the massacre.

One important victory against the general tide of impunity was the conviction in March of one of the five military police officers accused of killing 29 residents in the Baixada Fluminense district of Rio de Janeiro in 2005.

Land and housing
Access to land and housing was a focal point for extensive human rights violations. According to the Pastoral Land Commission, 25 land activists were killed between January and October, including 16 in the state of Pará. Millions of people suffered extreme social and economic deprivation as a result of being deprived of access to land and housing both in urban and rural areas.

Those fighting for the right to land, including Indigenous peoples, land activists and urban squatter groups, suffered forced evictions, threats and violent attacks. Some were killed. Those seeking access to land were often denied access to justice. In some cases judicial rulings were reported to have been discriminatory, and in others people faced allegedly politically motivated criminal charges.

⬜ In August the Pará state court, a regional court, issued orders threatening a total of 4,000 families with forced evictions, with no alternative provision. A number of the settlements facing eviction were on land that was eligible for expropriation under legislation for agricultural reform as the farms upon which they were situated had been deemed "unproductive" or were illegally located or were found to be using slave or indentured labour. In September, lawyers for the Pastoral Land Commission managed to have some evictions suspended, but many families remained under threat.

There were continued reports of attempts to undermine the work of social activists in the state of Pernambuco, and efforts to criminalize their leaders. In May an association representing military police officers advertised on hoardings throughout Recife accusing members of the landless workers' movement of being lawless and out of control. Ten members of the landless workers' movement were arrested on what were reported to be politically motivated charges.

⬜ Two separate arrest warrants were issued against Jaime Amorim, a leader of the landless worker's movement. The first was for allegedly leading an occupation onto land that a federal government body had ruled should be appropriated. The second followed public disturbances outside the US Consulate during President Bush's visit to Brazil in November 2005. Jaime Amorim was charged several days after the event with disobedience, incitement to a crime and disrespecting authority. He was detained while attending the funerals of two landless activists killed in August. Both arrest warrants were overturned and he was provisionally released.

In the state of Espírito Santo, the Tupiniquim and Guarani Indigenous peoples suffered threats and attacks, as a result of their long-standing campaign for their hereditary lands. The disputed lands were contested by Aracruz Celulose S/A, a leading producer of eucalyptus pulp. Although the federal government's Indigenous Office had recognized the land as appropriate for demarcation, the decision to proceed with the process was stalled.

▭ In January, members of the federal police violently evicted Tupiniquim and Guarani peoples from settlements built on disputed land. Thirteen Indigenous people were injured and two villages were burnt down, following attacks with helicopters, dogs, rubber bullets and tear gas. According to reports, Aracruz Celulose S/A gave logistical support to the federal police during the eviction.

▭ In September, federal prosecutors initiated a successful civil case against Aracruz Celulose S/A for promoting a discrimination campaign against the Tupiniquim and Guarani peoples.

Slave labour
Advances were made in the fight against slave labour. According to the International Labour Organization, 18,000 people had been released since 1995 from debt bondage by members of the federal government's mobile unit. However, the problem was far from eradicated. According to the Pastoral Land Commission, around 8,000 people a year were forced into situations equivalent to slave or indentured labour. Promised reforms to the Constitution to allow for the confiscation of land where slave labour was used remained pending in Congress.

Human rights defenders
Human rights defenders continued to suffer discrimination, threats and attacks. Many human rights groups suffered a backlash in the wake of the violent attacks by the PCC in São Paulo.

Efforts by the government to put in place its national human rights defenders programme led to initial training sessions for state police officers in the state of Pará and preparation for similar training in the states of Pernambuco and Espírito Santo. However, it was reported that the project suffered from serious shortfalls. Members of civil society participating in the project expressed several concerns, most notably the lack of a properly resourced national body to oversee the programme and the continued reluctance of the federal police to provide protection.

The persistent failure of the authorities to bring those responsible for the killings of human rights defenders to justice continued to place them at risk.

▭ Vicente Cañas Costa, a Spanish Jesuit working in defence of Indigenous peoples, was murdered in 1987 in the state of Mato Grosso. Nineteen years later, two of the men suspected of his murder were brought to trial. While human rights groups welcomed the court's recognition that Vicente Cañas Costa had indeed been murdered, failures in the initial investigation reportedly contributed to both men being acquitted.

AI country reports/ visits
Report
- Brazil: "We have come to take your souls" – the caveirão and policing in Rio de Janeiro (AI Index: AMR 19/007/2006)

Visit
AI delegates visited Brazil in May/June.

BULGARIA

REPUBLIC OF BULGARIA
Head of state: Georgi Parvanov
Head of government: Sergey Stanishev
Death penalty: abolitionist for all crimes
International Criminal Court: ratified

Police reportedly targeted people for ill-treatment and excessive force on the basis of their ethnic identity or sexual orientation. The human rights of minorities were not adequately protected, particularly the housing rights of Romani communities threatened with unlawful and summary eviction from their homes. People with mental disabilities faced harsh living conditions and inappropriate care and treatment.

Background
President Georgi Parvanov, head of the Bulgarian Socialist Party, was returned to power in presidential elections in November.

In March, the Council of Europe Commissioner for Human Rights recommended that the government implement reforms of the justice system; make further efforts to eliminate corruption; strengthen the status, selection, training and pay of judges; adopt new Codes of Administrative and Civil Procedure as a priority; and allow detained suspects unrestricted access to legal counsel. Concerns remained about the inappropriate use of firearms by law enforcement officials.

In May, the European Commission recommended that January 2007 be maintained as the date of Bulgaria's accession to the European Union (EU) only if serious deficits were remedied. In September it allowed accession to go ahead, despite continuing concerns about corruption, on condition that the required changes to the Civil Procedure Code, judicial system and Constitution were adopted.

In March parliament amended the Constitution to incorporate the Ombudsperson institution. A new provision also allowed the institution to initiate cases before the Constitutional Court if it considers a law concerning citizens' rights and freedoms to be unconstitutional.

Bulgaria signed the Council of Europe Convention on Action against Trafficking in Human Beings in November.

Ill-treatment and excessive use of force

Representatives of the European Committee for the Prevention of Torture, on a visit to Bulgaria in September, examined the treatment of detainees in the custody of regular and border police; conditions in investigation detention facilities; regimes for prisoners serving life sentences and foreign prisoners; and implementation of legal safeguards on compulsory placements to psychiatric institutions under the Health Act.

Reports of police ill-treatment continued, particularly against members of the Romani community and on the basis of people's sexual orientation.

⬜ In January the Sofia Military Court ordered further investigation in the case of Angel Dimitrov, who died during a police operation in Blagoevgrad in November 2005, after his family opposed a request by the Sofia District Military Prosecutor for criminal proceedings to be halted. The police had used excessive force while arresting Angel Dimitrov, in violation of domestic and international law, the Ombudsperson reported in March.

⬜ In February the European Court of Human Rights found that Bulgaria had violated Zahari Stefanov's rights to life and to be free from torture and arbitrary detention (*Ognyanova and Choban v Bulgaria*). In 1993 the 23-year-old, of Romani origin, died in Kazanluk police station. An official inquiry at the time concluded that he had jumped of his own accord out of a third-floor room where he was being questioned, and that all his injuries were caused by the fall.

⬜ In October, police reportedly used excessive force in quelling fighting involving 400 Roma in Pazardzhik. Officers were accused by Romani people and the regional governor of exceeding their powers by entering homes and damaging property.

⬜ In May the Commission for Protection against Discrimination initiated an investigation in the case of three police officers who allegedly ill-treated a gay man in October 2005 because of his sexual orientation and ethnic origin. The Commission concluded that during his illegal 12-hour detention, the man was denied food and access to his relatives and medical assistance.

Racism and discrimination

In February, non-governmental organizations (NGOs) and private individuals filed a civil lawsuit in Sofia City Court against Volen Siderov, leader of the Attack

(Ataka) party. They alleged that he incited others, through television broadcasts, publications and public statements, to harass and discriminate against people from ethnic, religious and sexual minorities.

In November, the NGO International Helsinki Federation for Human Rights reported a rise in anti-minority rhetoric and discrimination.

The Romani community

In March the Council of Europe Commissioner for Human Rights recommended the government implement its national plan of 2003-2004 for integrating Roma and establishing a co-ordinated policy for all minorities.

Also in March the government approved a national programme for improving Romani housing conditions, but discrimination in housing persisted.

In July, as Bulgaria assumed the presidency of the Decade of Roma Inclusion, a regional intergovernmental initiative to reduce social and economic exclusion and disparities, legal challenges were initiated by Romani communities over instances of discrimination. The cases concerned threats to demolish houses and the refusal by Sofia Municipality to provide public transport in Sofia's largest Roma settlement in the Fakulteta District.

Plans to forcibly evict inhabitants of a number of Romani neighbourhoods in Sofia were suspended after protests by members of the European Parliament. Some of Sofia's district governments continued to threaten forced evictions, and did little if anything to address the extreme poverty and denial of human rights in many Romani communities. A working group was formed by the Sofia Municipality and Romani NGOs to propose solutions. In July, the Ministry of Labour and Social Policy provided funds to purchase caravans as a temporary solution for evicted residents.

⬜ In April some residents demanded the removal of a Romani neighbourhood in Sofia's Zaharna Fabrika district. The mayor of Sofia said the city prosecutor would help the municipality find a legal way to move Romani residents, promising funds for temporary shelters.

⬜ In June the international human rights organizations, the Centre on Housing Rights and Evictions and the European Roma Rights Centre, appealed to the government to stop unlawful evictions in Dobri Zhelyazkov and Batalova vodenitza, Sofia. The district government had ordered 16 Romani families to leave their homes within 10 days or be summarily evicted, although their communities had lived on the land for generations. The authorities did not provide reasonable justification, adequate notice, consultation with those affected, compensation, alternative housing or social support. The municipality finally said that legal owners would be compensated according to the law, and others would be accommodated in freight containers adapted to make them habitable.

The Macedonian minority

The authorities and the judiciary continued to deny the existence of a Macedonian minority in Bulgaria, and insisted that there was no legal obligation to protect it, a policy backed by all political parties represented in parliament.

⬜ In October, the Sofia City Court refused registration to OMO Ilinden PIRIN, a political party representing some members of the Macedonian minority in Bulgaria, despite an October 2005 ruling by the European Court of Human Rights that a previous ban of the party violated rights to freedom of association and assembly. In November the European Parliament Rapporteur on Bulgaria and the Enlargement Commissioner of the European Commission urged the government to register OMO Ilinden PIRIN.

Concerns about mental health care

In March the Council of Europe Commissioner for Human Rights urged the provision of decent living conditions for people with mental disabilities who lived in social care centres and psychiatric hospitals that had not yet been refurbished. He also called for increased funds to feed people confined in institutions, and a system to ensure judicial review of decisions to confine such people.

In June the Bulgarian Helsinki Committee reported that the sanitary facilities in these institutions were still "in the poorest condition", and that the procedures for placements of patients for compulsory and involuntary treatment, provided under the Health Law of January 2005, had not been implemented.

In October, two NGOs, the Mental Disability Advocacy Centre and the Bulgarian Helsinki Committee, filed with the European Court of Human Rights the case of a man they believed was needlessly detained in a psychiatric hospital and given psychiatric medication against his will, despite the recommendations of five psychiatrists that he receive outpatient treatment.

AI country reports/ visits
Report
- Europe and Central Asia: Summary of Amnesty International's concerns in the region, January-June 2006 (AI Index: EUR 01/017/2006)

BURUNDI

REPUBLIC OF BURUNDI
Head of state: Pierre Nkurunziza
Death penalty: retentionist
International Criminal Court: ratified

Continuing human rights abuses marred the hopes engendered by the 2005 elections, which heralded the end of 12 years of civil conflict. Human rights violations by government forces included arbitrary arrests and detentions, torture and ill-treatment and extrajudicial executions. Until a ceasefire agreement in September, the last armed group still engaged in fighting the government continued to commit human rights abuses, including killing civilians suspected of collaborating with government forces. The ruling party increasingly interfered with the executive and the judiciary, and sought to silence criticism in the media, by political opponents and by human rights defenders.

Background

The ruling party, the National Council for the Defence of Democracy-Forces for the Defence of Democracy (Conseil National Pour la Défense de la Démocratie-Forces pour la Défense de la Démocratie, CNDD-FDD), was widely accused of corruption. It undermined the independence of the judiciary, and harassed and intimidated the independent news media, political opponents and human rights defenders.

In August, seven former high-level officials and opposition political leaders were arrested for an alleged coup attempt. Among them were former Vice-President Alphonse-Marie Kadege, and former President Domitien Ndayizeye, who was charged with "threatening state security". There were widespread doubts about whether there had in fact been a coup attempt.

On 6 September, the second Vice-President, Alice Nzomukunda, resigned, citing corruption and political interference by the chairman of the ruling party.

Armed conflict continued throughout the first half of 2006 between the Palipehutu-FNL, known as the FNL (Forces nationales de libération), and government armed forces (Forces de défense nationale, FDN) in the provinces of Bujumbura rural, Bubanza and Cibitoke. On 7 September, the government and FNL signed a ceasefire agreement. However, several sensitive issues remained unresolved, such as the integration of FNL officers within the FDN.

Arbitrary arrests and detentions

The intelligence services, police and army were responsible for numerous arbitrary and illegal arrests and detentions. To justify arbitrary arrests and detentions, the authorities cited national security and accused detainees of involvement with the FNL, but it appeared that many people were arrested and detained illegally.

More than 1,000 people living in the province of Bujumbura-mairie and surrounding provinces had by April been detained for several months without being brought before a judge. Only 34 of them were prosecuted by the public prosecutor.

Arbitrary and illegal arrests by local authorities were also reported in other provinces, including Ngozi.

On 20 April a teacher at Don Bosco secondary school in Ngozi was reportedly beaten, handcuffed and taken by police to the local cell in Kiremba. He was unlawfully detained without being brought before a judge for a few days. He was accused of having stolen firewood from the forest belonging to the local administration.

Extrajudicial executions

Throughout 2006, the intelligence services and the army were involved in extrajudicial executions of civilians.

Between May and August, about 30 people in the province of Muyinga were arbitrarily arrested by government armed forces, in conjunction with the intelligence service and local administration. According to local sources, at least 16 were executed and their bodies dumped in rivers. Three state agents were arrested in connection with the killings, including the head of the intelligence service in Muyinga. However, the authorities failed to arrest senior officials who reportedly gave the execution orders, despite issuing arrest warrants.

On 4 August, in the commune of Kinama, Bujumbura-mairie, four people were arrested on suspicion of being FNL members by police officers and a former CNDD-FDD fighter reportedly working on behalf of intelligence services. On 14 August, this former fighter took the four detainees away in a vehicle. The following day, their bullet-ridden bodies were found by local residents. The former CNDD-FDD fighter was detained in Mpimba prison, but several witnesses reported seeing him at large in Bujumbura.

Torture and ill-treatment

The government failed to define torture in the country's laws and to align the Penal Procedure Code and the Penal Code with international human rights standards.

Allegations of torture and ill-treatment by the intelligence services, the police and other military and security forces were documented throughout 2006.

On 23 January, Matrenus Ciragira and his family were attacked at night by people armed with shotguns and wearing police uniforms, in the commune of Ruhororo, Ngozi province. During the attack, his wife was raped in front of their children. No investigation was carried out.

Former Vice-President Alphonse-Marie Kadege was allegedly kicked repeatedly on his body by police officers in an interrogation room on 2 August.

On 26 June, in the zone of Mivo, Ngozi commune, two staff members of the non-governmental organization (NGO) Population Services International involved in an AIDS awareness programme were arrested and reportedly tortured by two policemen. By the end of 2006, no investigation had taken place.

Freedom of expression under attack

The relationship between the authorities and the independent media was tense and confrontational. State agents and the ruling party repeatedly threatened journalists.

On 17 April, after a press conference called by the CNDD-FDD parliamentarian Mathias Basabose, in Kinindo, Bujumbura, 30 journalists were summoned by the police to hand in their tapes and recording equipment so that the information could be checked. The journalists refused to comply with the orders and were prevented from leaving the premises. Other journalists turned up to report this incident. Several were reportedly beaten by police officers with gun butts and truncheons.

On 3 September Hussein Radjabu, the CNDD-FDD chairman, delivered a speech to thousands of supporters in which he threatened journalists if they continued to criticize the CNDD-FDD and the government.

Also on 3 September, the CNDD-FDD website published a photograph of Gabriel Nikundana, the news editor of Isanganiro radio station, saying that he had fled to Kenya. When it became clear that this story was false, another article was published on the website on 5 September, linking Gabriel Nikundana to the alleged coup attempt and describing him as "extremist".

Prisoners of conscience

Throughout 2006, human rights defenders faced harassment, and some were arbitrarily detained for peacefully expressing opinions.

On 5 May, Térence Nahimana, director of an NGO, Cercle d'initiative pour une vision commune (CIVIC), wrote a letter to the President saying that the government was deliberately delaying peace negotiations with the FNL. He was arrested on 9 May by the national intelligence service. He was released after three hours of questioning, but the following day he was arrested again. On 15 May, he was formally charged with "threatening state security" and detained in Mpimba prison.

On 16 August, Gabriel Rufyiri, president of an NGO, Observatoire de lutte contre la corruption et les malversations économiques (OLUCOME), was arbitrarily arrested. He was illegally detained for alleging that members of the government and the ruling party were involved in corruption. His organization had exposed the alleged improper sale of the presidential plane and irregularities in government contracts.

Violence against women

Women of all ages were subjected to sexual violence, including rape, in both rural and urban communities. Despite the end of the hostilities in most of the country, local human rights organizations reported a very high incidence of rape cases.

The state's response was characterized by inaction, and the criminal justice system provided scant protection. The police and judiciary often dismissed rape cases and failed to investigate them unless the victim was a young child or they were put under pressure by local human rights organizations.

◻ V N, a 27-year-old woman living in the commune of Kamenge, was raped by two men who broke into her house on 21 February. The men beat, gagged and raped V N and her sister. Neither the local administration nor the police carried out any investigation. Subsequently, V N was rejected by her community.

Human rights abuses by the FNL

Throughout the first half of 2006, the FNL threatened and intimidated the civilian population of Bujumbura rural, Bubanza and Cibitoke, often demanding shelter, food and water. They also killed low-level government officials and civilians suspected of collaborating with government armed forces.

◻ On 16 January, Amélie Bapfumukeko, a council member in Nakibuye, Kanyosha commune, was abducted and killed by alleged FNL combatants. Her body was found the next day about 500 metres from her house. She was accused by local FNL members of collaborating with the government armed forces.

Administration of justice

The justice system continued to suffer from lack of resources and inadequate training. Furthermore, government authorities and CNDD-FDD members reportedly influenced judicial decisions improperly.

◻ On 16 February, a teacher at Gashikanwa secondary school (Ngozi province), who was also a CNDD-FDD member, was arrested by police on suspicion of having raped five of his pupils. Once his arrest became known, the public prosecutor in charge of the investigation received threatening phone calls from members of the security services and CNDD-FDD parliamentarians demanding the teacher's release. The public prosecutor eventually released him, and there were no further investigations into the rapes either by the police or the public prosecutor's office.

Mechanisms to combat impunity

The authorities sent mixed messages during the year about their willingness to tackle the issue of impunity effectively.

On 3 January the President decreed that political prisoners should be granted "provisional immunity", in accordance with clauses in the Arusha peace agreement of 2000. A few days later, the Minister of Justice announced the provisional release of 673 political prisoners. By the end of March more than 3,200 prisoners had been released. However, this decision was not followed by any concrete and targeted measures to combat impunity.

In early February the government issued a memorandum in order to commence talks with the UN on setting up a truth and reconciliation commission and a special chamber to investigate crimes committed in Burundi and bring those responsible to justice. At the end of February, a UN mission arrived in Bujumbura to prepare for negotiations on these mechanisms.

Although this meeting was significant, the government's memorandum contained proposals which could hinder efforts to overcome impunity. For example, it proposed a "procedure of reconciliation" which could prevent or limit the investigation and prosecution of crimes under international law. Subsequent progress was very slow.

On 18 June in Dar es-Salaam, Tanzania, the government and FNL signed an agreement of principles towards lasting peace, security and stability in Burundi. It stated that the truth and reconciliation commission (not yet established) would be renamed the "Truth, Pardon and Reconciliation Commission". Its mandate would be to establish the facts surrounding "the dark period of Burundi history" and various protagonists' responsibilities, with a view to achieving forgiveness and national reconciliation.

Death penalty

After the release of 3,200 political prisoners, 218 prisoners remained under sentence of death. The last executions, of seven civilians, took place in 1997, but courts continued to pass death sentences.

Refugees and internally displaced people

In February, the number of Rwandan refugees in Burundi reached 20,000. By the end of 2006, about 16,000 had been repatriated by the UN refugee agency UNHCR to Rwanda. Between January and December, about 32,000 Burundian refugees returned to Burundi with UNHCR assistance. In June, UNHCR changed its policy from facilitation to promotion of the repatriation.

At the end of 2006, more than 100,000 people still lived in internally displaced people's camps, mainly in the northern and eastern provinces.

AI country reports/ visits
Reports
- Burundi: Provisional immunity does nothing to end impunity (AI Index: AFR 16/001/2006)
- Burundi: Towards what reconciliation? (AI Index: AFR 16/003/2006)
- Burundi: Journalists and human rights monitors under attack (AI Index: AFR 16/004/2006)
- Burundi: Detention measures abused (AI Index: AFR 16/011/2006)
- Burundi: From Itaba to Gatumba – an imperative need for justice (AI Index: AFR 16/014/2006)
- Burundi: Briefing to the Committee against Torture (AI Index: AFR 16/016/2006)

Visits
AI delegates visited Burundi to research violence against women and the demobilization, disarmament and reintegration process in February. AI delegates also attended a workshop with human rights defenders.

CAMBODIA

KINGDOM OF CAMBODIA
Head of state: King Norodom Sihamoni
Head of government: Hun Sen
Death penalty: abolitionist for all crimes
International Criminal Court: ratified

The land crisis continued unabated; over 10,000 urban poor were forcibly evicted from their homes and thousands of rural dwellers lost their lands and livelihoods in land disputes. The authorities continued to use the courts in an effort to curtail peaceful criticism. Restrictions on freedom of assembly were maintained.

Background

A government-led crackdown on peaceful critics ended in February with a deal between the Prime Minister and some adversaries, leading to the release of several prisoners of conscience, among them opposition parliamentarian Cheam Channy. The opposition leader, Sam Rainsy, returned from exile after he received a royal pardon.

The government's junior coalition partner, the National United Front for an Independent, Neutral, Peaceful and Cooperative Cambodia (FUNCINPEC), faced crisis as Prime Minister Hun Sen of the ruling Cambodian People's Party (CPP) stepped up pressure against party president Prince Norodom Ranariddh and his followers. Some 75 senior FUNCINPEC officials were dismissed from the government and the National Assembly, culminating in an extraordinary FUNCINPEC congress on 18 October in which Keo Puth Raksmey became the new party president. In November Prince Ranariddh launched the Norodom Ranariddh Party by joining and taking the lead of the small ultra-nationalist Khmer Front Party.

The UN High Commissioner for Human Rights visited Cambodia in May and concluded that the strengthening of the judicial branch of governance was crucially important for the consolidation of democracy under the rule of law.

Land and housing

Land concessions and other opaque land deals between business interests and the authorities continued. In a series of forced evictions in June and July around 10,000 urban poor in Phnom Penh lost their homes to well-connected businessmen without adequate consultation, compensation or legal protection.
▭ At dawn on 6 June several hundred security officials armed with rifles, tear gas and electric batons began the forced eviction of Sambok Chab village in central Phnom Penh. Around 5,000 villagers were forced into vans and taken to a relocation site some 20 kilometres from the city centre, an area which lacked clean water, electricity, health clinics and schools. The lack of basic amenities at the relocation site led to increased prevalence of diarrhoea, skin infections, malnutrition and respiratory infections, particularly among children and the elderly.

The forced eviction impoverished an already poor community by depriving them of their land and livelihoods. It took place despite the call two weeks earlier by the UN Special Rapporteur on adequate housing and the UN Secretary-General's Special Representative on human rights defenders for an end to the evictions and immediate action to ensure that these families had access to adequate housing consistent with Cambodia's human rights obligations.

On 29 June, armed forces began the forcible eviction of 168 families living next to Phnom Penh's Preah Monivong Hospital. Houses were demolished and the residents, some of whom had lived on the land since 1988, were resettled some 30km from the city without basic facilities.

In both instances police cordoned off the area of eviction, preventing journalists and human rights workers from monitoring events.

Local human rights defenders were targeted by law enforcement agencies in connection with forced evictions and land disputes both in urban and rural areas. At least 15 land rights activists were detained during the year.

Legal system

Long-awaited reform including laws governing the judiciary and criminal justice system did not take place. The anti-corruption law, which had been set as a top priority in the concluding statement of the annual donors' meeting in March, was not passed. Instead a new anti-corruption body under the powerful Council of Ministers was established by the government in August, comprising senior officials of the ruling party.

A Law on the Status of Parliamentarians was passed in August, which limits freedom of expression for parliamentarians. An anti-adultery law imposing custodial sentences was voted through the following month, and a law introducing compulsory military service — in sharp contrast to government pledges to reduce the armed forces — was passed by the National Assembly in October.

In his address to the UN Human Rights Council on 26 September, the UN Special Representative of the Secretary-General for human rights in Cambodia said that the government had used prosecutors and judges, while pretending to uphold their independence, to intimidate or punish critics. He stated that the government had applied the law selectively and that its supporters had enjoyed immunities from the civil and criminal process for blatant breaches of the law.
▭ Born Samnang and Sok Samoeun, who were sentenced in August 2005 to 20 years' imprisonment for the murder of trade union leader Chea Vichea following an unfair trial, remained in prison. After significant domestic and international pressure calling for their release following testimony from a new witness, an appeals hearing was announced for 6 October. As one of the judges did not appear in court the hearing was postponed.

Freedom of speech and assembly

The widely used and controversial criminal defamation law was reformed in May, with the custodial sentence removed. Several high-profile cases were suspended. Subsequently the law against disinformation, which has a maximum prison sentence of three years, was used in a number of cases to silence or intimidate critics, including several journalists.

Death threats were received by two local journalists, Soy Sopheap of the CTN television channel and You Saravuth of *Sralanh Khmer* newspaper, after they reported alleged corruption by military and government-linked individuals. You Saravuth was forced to flee abroad.

Restrictions introduced in early 2003 on the right to assembly continued. Requests for permission to hold demonstrations were regularly refused by the authorities, while demonstrations and protests were often broken up by force.

The Extraordinary Chambers

The Extraordinary Chambers in the Courts of Cambodia were established on the outskirts of Phnom Penh to prosecute suspected perpetrators of gross human rights violations during the Khmer Rouge period (1975-1979). Due to disagreements between national and international judges, a plenary session of the Chambers failed to adopt the tribunal's internal rules which are required to launch investigations and prosecutions. There was renewed criticism of the lack of transparency in the recruitment of Cambodian judges; some were on the ruling party's central committee and others lacked basic legal training.

Former Khmer Rouge leader Ta Mok, one of two detainees scheduled to face prosecution by the Extraordinary Chambers, died on 21 July, never having been tried for his alleged role in crimes against humanity.

AI country reports/ visits
Report
- Cambodia: The murder of trade unionist Chea Vichea — Still no justice (AI Index: ASA 23/008/2006)
Visit
An AI delegation visited Cambodia in March.

CAMEROON

REPUBLIC OF CAMEROON
Head of state: Paul Biya
Head of government: Ephraim Inoni
Death penalty: retentionist
International Criminal Court: signed

Nine men and four women were convicted for practising homosexuality. Scores of people were tortured by members of the security forces. Courts convicted some officials of involvement in killings. At least two students were killed and many others detained during clashes with government forces. Several journalists were briefly detained or beaten. Secessionist political activists were arrested and detained.

Background

Nigeria formally handed the disputed oil-rich Bakassi Peninsula to Cameroon in August and withdrew its troops. Several thousand Nigerian nationals left the peninsula for mainland Nigeria. The handover implemented an October 2002 decision of the International Court of Justice.

More than 80 members of the Kedjom Keku community in Northwest province accused of involvement in the killing of their former traditional chief were arrested between January and March. Many were reportedly beaten at the time of their arrest. Former chief Simon Vugah, who was deposed in 2004, was killed after he returned to Kedjom Keku to reclaim his position. Those detained included Simon Vugah's successor, Benjamin Vubangsi, who was released with about 60 others in September. At least 25 people were held without trial in connection with the killing at the end of 2006.

A power struggle within the Social Democratic Front (SDF) opposition party culminated in the killing in May of Grégoire Diboulé, a supporter of Bernard Muna, leader of a faction opposed to SDF chairman, John Fru Ndi. More than 20 members of the SDF were arrested and charged with involvement in the murder. They were still awaiting trial at the end of the year. John Fru Ndi was charged with complicity to murder and assault but was not detained.

At least 400 people were rendered homeless in November when the government demolished their houses in the Etetak district of the capital, Yaoundé. The government claimed that the houses had been built without authorization, but provided no alternative accommodation or compensation.

Several senior managers of state companies accused of embezzlement were arrested after the government launched an anti-corruption campaign in January. Those detained included Siyam Siwé, a former director general of the Autonomous Port of Douala, and Barthélemy Kamdem, the company's assistant financial director. Others being investigated for embezzlement were members of parliament whose immunity was withdrawn in October.

Convicted for practising homosexuality

Patrick Yousse-Djaudio and another gay man were reportedly sentenced in February to one year's imprisonment for practising homosexuality. In March, four young women were arrested for allegedly engaging in lesbian activities. They were released in June after a court in Douala sentenced them to a three-year suspended prison sentence and a fine.

Two minors arrested in May 2005 with nine others accused of practising homosexuality were released in February without trial. The remaining nine were tried in June. Two were acquitted and seven were sentenced to 10 months' imprisonment then released because of the time already spent in custody. One of these, Alim Mongoche, died of an illness soon after his release.

Twelve young women students were expelled in March from a college on account of being lesbian. They were not able to join any other college.

Threats to freedom of expression

Several journalists were detained or assaulted because of their work. The authorities were not known to have taken any action against those responsible for assaults.
▭ Duke Atangana Etotogo, director of *L'Afrique centrale* newspaper, was arrested on 3 September by members of the military security service after the newspaper published an article critical of the army. He was released without charge on 8 September.
▭ Patient Ebwele of *Radio Equinoxe* was beaten and detained for four hours in April by gendarmes in Akwa-Nord district of Douala.
▭ Eric Motomu, editor of *The Chronicle* newspaper, was assaulted in April by SDF supporters in Bamenda who accused him of publishing articles critical of their leader, John Fru Ndi.

Ten convicted for political killing

In April, a court convicted former chief and member of parliament Doh Gah Gwanyin and nine others of involvement in the death of John Kohtem, an SDF leader beaten to death in August 2004. They were sentenced to 15 years' imprisonment but Doh Gah Gwanyin was released on bail pending his application to appeal. Two of the accused were acquitted.

Student unrest culminates in deaths

In April, several university student leaders in Yaoundé received suspended prison sentences for their role in clashes between students and members of the security forces in November 2005.

At least eight Buea university students were arrested in March during a demonstration in support of independence for Anglophone Cameroon. They were released without charge after several days.

At least two Buea university students were shot dead on 29 November by the security forces during violent demonstrations over alleged corruption and discrimination against Anglophone students. The authorities did not hold any formal investigation into the killings.

Torture and ill-treatment

Torture by members of the security forces continued to be reported.
▭ Serges Ondobo died in April, reportedly as a result of being beaten in police custody in Yaoundé when he protested against the arrest of a fellow trader. The authorities are not known to have taken any action against the policemen responsible.

More than 100 people were reportedly beaten in late October after they were arrested by members of the Rapid Intervention Brigade (Brigade d'intervention rapide, BIR) in and around Maroua, the capital of Extreme North province. The victims were detained for several days at Salack, where many of them were stripped naked, blindfolded and beaten, then held in a cell with water on its floor. The victims included Hamidou Ndjidda, Aziz Dikanza and Ismael Balo Amadou.

The trial by the Douala military tribunal of several gendarmes and a manager implicated in the death of Emmanuel Moutombi, who died in February 2005, ended in March. The manager was found not guilty of involvement in torture but was fined 25,000 CFA Francs (approximately US$50) for slapping Emmanuel Moutombi. A gendarmerie commander was sentenced to 10 months' imprisonment, while three gendarmes convicted of causing the death were sentenced to eight, nine and 10 years' imprisonment. The tribunal ordered the state to pay 44 million CFA Francs (approximately US$88,000) to the victim's family.

Southern Cameroons National Council

As in previous years, members of the Anglophone separatist movement, the Southern Cameroons National Council (SCNC), were arrested and briefly detained.

At least 40 SCNC members were arrested in January while holding a meeting in Buea. They were released without charge after several days. A further 29 were arrested in March and detained for several days in Buea.

More than 60 SCNC members were arrested in Bamenda on 24 April and released without charge on 1 May. When SCNC leaders, including Humphrey Prince Mbiglo, tried to hold a press conference on 7 May to protest, they were among 20 SCNC members who were detained for several days. Fidelis Chinkwo, Emmanuel Emi, Priscilla Khan, Elvis Bandzeka and Cletus Che were arrested in Bamenda on 16 September and released several days later without charge.

Anglophone prisoners

Anglophone prisoners serving long prison sentences for involvement in politically motivated violent activities were transferred in May from Kondengui prison in Yaoundé to their home provinces. Eight were transferred to Bamenda in Northwest province and the ninth, Roland Tatah, was transferred to Buea central prison in Southwest province. One of the nine, Philip Tete, died from an illness in November.

AI country reports/ visits
Visit
The authorities did not respond to AI's request to visit Cameroon.

CANADA

CANADA
Head of state: Queen Elizabeth II, represented by Governor General Michaëlle Jean
Head of government: Stephen Harper (replaced Paul Martin in January)
Death penalty: abolitionist for all crimes
International Criminal Court: ratified

There were concerns about violations of the rights of Indigenous peoples, including discrimination and violence against Indigenous women and girls. Counter-terrorism laws and practices were inconsistent with human rights standards.

The rights of Indigenous peoples

There was no comprehensive national strategy to address continuing discrimination and violence against Indigenous women. The policies and practices of police forces in response to such violence were inconsistent.

There was no progress in resolving the long-standing land dispute with the Lubicon Cree in Alberta, despite calls by the UN Human Rights Committee on Canada in 1990 and 2005 to make every effort to resolve the issue.

There were concerns that the approach to child protection for Indigenous children was discriminatory, both in the levels of funding provided and in the disproportionately high levels of Indigenous children taken into care.

Women's human rights

In September there was a substantial cut in the budget of Status of Women Canada, the federal government agency responsible for promoting gender equality. New restrictions barred advocacy activities by organizations receiving funding from the agency.

There was no progress in implementing recommendations made by a 1996 public inquiry, a 2003 Canadian Human Rights Commission report, and the UN Human Rights Committee in 2005 that there be an independent agency established to receive complaints from women prisoners held in federal detention facilities.

Police abuses

Concerns about excessive use of force involving taser guns continued. In August, Jason Doan died in Red Deer, Alberta, after being subdued by police using a taser, bringing the number of such deaths to 15 since April 2003.

Security and human rights

Three Muslim men subject to security certificates issued under the Immigration and Refugee Protection Act remained in detention and two others were under strict bail conditions. The men faced a serious risk of torture if deported. Appeals to the Supreme Court of Canada in three of the cases were pending at the end of the year.

In September and December, two reports from a public inquiry into Canada's role in the case of Maher Arar were released. He had been deported to Syria in 2002 where he was detained without charge for a year and tortured. The first report cleared Maher Arar, recommended compensation and proposed numerous reforms. In December, the government announced an inquiry into the cases of three other dual Canadian nationals tortured abroad: Abdullah Almalki, Ahmad Abou El-Maati and Muyyed Nureddin.

In October, the preventative and investigative hearing provisions of the 2001 Anti-Terrorism Act were renewed for five years.

Canadian forces in Afghanistan transferred detainees to Afghan officials in circumstances where there was a serious risk of torture and ill-treatment.

Refugee protection

The new government refused to implement the provisions of the 2001 Immigration and Refugee Protection Act establishing a Refugee Appeal Division.

A legal challenge was lodged to the Canada/USA "safe third country" agreement. Under the agreement most refugee claimants arriving in Canada via the USA were required to make their refugee claims in the USA, where there were concerns that some faced human rights violations. The court hearing was expected to begin in February 2007.

Immigration laws failed to provide an absolute ban on deporting individuals to countries where they faced a serious risk of torture. In October, a Federal Court judge ruled that "exceptional circumstances" did not exist to justify the deportation of Mahmoud Jaballah to Egypt, where he was at risk of being tortured.

CENTRAL AFRICAN REPUBLIC

CENTRAL AFRICAN REPUBLIC
Head of state: François Bozizé
Head of government: Elie Dote
Death penalty: abolitionist in practice
International Criminal Court: ratified

Government forces reportedly killed scores of unarmed civilians in response to unrest in the north of the country, displacing tens of thousands of people. The authorities took no action against members of the security forces suspected of responsibility for unlawful killings and other human rights violations. Dozens of suspected political opponents of the government were arrested and unlawfully detained in harsh conditions. About 25 were tried, most of whom were acquitted. Fourteen were not released after their acquittal but detained for a further two weeks.

Background

Violence and insecurity escalated in the north of the country. On 29 January, an armed group attacked the security forces in the town of Paoua, Ouham-Pende province. At least 80 civilians, many of them unarmed, were killed by government forces during a counter-attack. About 7,000 people fled to neighbouring Chad, while an estimated 50,000 more were internally displaced, with little or no access to humanitarian assistance.

Attacks by armed groups persisted throughout the year. In June, UN sources reported that 33 people had been killed in a rebel attack on an army camp in the north.

Government forces continued to be supported by French and Chadian troops, and by members of a peacekeeping force backed by the Monetary and Economic Community of Central Africa (Communauté économique et monétaire d'Afrique centrale, CEMAC). CEMAC peacekeepers received material help from the European Union.

In August former President Ange-Félix Patassé and three other former politicians were tried in their absence on charges of fraud and embezzling public funds. They were convicted of fraud and sentenced to up to 20 years' imprisonment. Ange-Félix Patassé's former economic advisor, Simon Kouloumba, was acquitted and released. He had been awaiting trial since 2003.

Impunity

The authorities failed to take action against members of the security forces who reportedly killed and injured dozens of unarmed civilians in Ouham-Pende and Ouham provinces in late January and February. Government forces, particularly members of the Republican Guard, reportedly targeted unarmed civilians, including boys as young as 10. At least 17 students from Paoua college were reported to have been extrajudicially executed by members of the Republican Guard.

▢ At least 80 people were reportedly killed by regular government forces in Paoua in January and February. The victims included Florent Djembert, Vincent Bozoukon and William Béré. Four unidentified bodies were reportedly burned in the local gendarmerie compound. No investigation into the deaths was reported.

▢ A former member of the Republican Guard, who had allegedly killed several people but was released without charge after being arrested in 2005, continued to threaten human rights defenders before he was killed by insurgents in May. In January he reportedly threatened Maka Ghossokoto, director of *Le Citoyen* newspaper, Nganatouwa Goungaye Wanfiyo, a lawyer, and Adolphe Ngouyombo, a human rights activist.

There was no progress by the government in bringing to justice those responsible for serious human rights abuses, including hundreds of rapes, during conflict in late 2002 and early 2003. The International Criminal Court (ICC) continued to conduct a preliminary analysis of crimes committed during the period, following a referral of the situation by the government in 2005. At the end of the year, the ICC had not announced whether or not it would launch a full investigation.

Political arrests, detentions and trials

Several dozen people were arrested between February and April 2006 and accused of supporting armed groups seeking to overthrow President François Bozizé's government. Many were members of former President Ange-Félix Patassé's Movement for the Liberation of the Central African People (Mouvement de libération du peuple centrafricain), or came from the same Kaba ethnic group.

They were held for weeks or months without charge and without access to their families, lawyers and doctors. In May and June, about 25 were charged with endangering the internal security of the state and related offences.

▢ Lydie Florence Ndouba, an official at the Ministry of Internal Affairs, was arrested on 28 February, apparently because she was the sister of two prominent politicians critical of the government. She was held without charge until 11 May, when she was charged with endangering the security of the state. At her trial in August she told the Criminal Court that she had been ill-treated in custody. She was acquitted.

▢ Pascal Ngakoutou Beninga, a teacher at Bangui University, reported that he was taken to a wood and threatened with death by members of the Republican Guard on 25 March. He was accused of having provided accommodation to armed men and of possessing weapons. Members of the security forces searched his house but reportedly found nothing incriminating.

In August and September, about 25 detainees were tried by the Criminal Court in Bangui. Approximately 20 were acquitted.

▢ Of 16 people tried for endangering the internal security of the state and related charges, 15 were acquitted and one convicted on a lesser charge on 12 September. However, 14 were not released but taken from Ngaragba prison on 13 September by members of the Republican Guard to Bossembélé prison in Ombella-Mpoko province. Members of the Central African Republic Bar Association went on strike in protest, and the government was widely criticized. On 25 September, the detainees were returned to Bangui and released.

At the end of 2006, at least 20 detainees were still held, accused of having connections with armed groups. It was unclear whether all of them had been formally charged.

Detention conditions

AI delegates visited several detention centres in Bangui, including Ngaragba prison, Bimbo prison and the National Gendarmerie's Research and Investigation

Department (Section de recherche et d'investigation, SRI). They found that conditions were so harsh as to be life-threatening.

In most prisons and detention centres, detainees received no food other than that brought by friends or relatives. Many complained of not having enough to eat or suffering from malnutrition. Cells were overcrowded and insanitary.

Detainees suffering ill-health were denied access to medical care. Minors were held together with adults, and unconvicted detainees were held with convicted prisoners. According to reports, in detention centres outside Bangui men and women were generally held together in even worse conditions.

AI country reports/ visits
Report
· Central African Republic: Government tramples on the basic rights of detainees (AI Index: AFR 19/007/2006)
Visit
AI delegates visited the Central African Republic in May.

CHAD

REPUBLIC OF CHAD
Head of state: Idriss Déby
Head of government: Pascal Yaodimnadji
Death penalty: retentionist
International Criminal Court: ratified

Clashes between the security forces and armed opposition groups intensified from April onwards. The Janjawid, an armed Sudanese militia group, crossed the border into eastern Chad, attacking villages, killing civilians and forcibly displacing tens of thousands. Women suffered grave human rights abuses, including rape, during these attacks. At least two people were extrajudicially executed by the security forces, one of whom was tortured before being killed. Human rights defenders and journalists continued to be at risk of detention, unfair trial and imprisonment.

Background
President Idriss Déby's administration continued to be threatened by armed conflict. Armed groups, including the United Front for Change (Front uni pour le changement, FUC), the Rally of Democratic Forces (Rassemblement des forces démocratiques, RAFD) and the Union of Forces for Democracy and Development (Union des forces pour la démocratie et le développement, UFDD), carried out military operations throughout 2006 in the north and east of the country. Armed clashes between the security forces and armed opposition groups intensified from April onwards along the eastern border with Sudan and the Chadian authorities accused Sudan of backing the attackers. In April, the FUC launched attacks in the east and southeast, reaching the capital city, N'Djaména; scores of soldiers and members of armed groups were reportedly killed. The FUC failed to conquer N'Djaména and dozens of its members were arrested. In October, several towns, including Goz Beida, were occupied for more than 24 hours by the UFDD. In November, the UFDD and the RAFD attacked several towns in the east and occupied the towns of Abéché and Guerreda for more than 24 hours. In December, the FUC and the Chadian authorities signed a peace deal in Libya. Under the provision of the accord, the FUC forces would be integrated into the Chadian army.

In order to combat the armed groups, the Chadian authorities withdrew government troops from the eastern border with Sudan, leaving civilians to face larger and more prolonged attacks by the Janjawid.

In January, the National Assembly passed a law extending its own term in office by over a year. Legislative elections which should have taken place in 2006 were postponed until 2007. Despite calls from the African Union and national human rights organizations to postpone the presidential elections, President Idriss Déby was elected in May to serve a third five-year term in a poll boycotted by opposition parties.

In November, the government declared a state of emergency in some regions including Chari Baguirmi, Borkou Ennedi Tibesti and N'Djaména. It created a committee to censor all public and private newspapers and radio stations, in order to prevent the publication or broadcast of information liable to jeopardize public order, national unity, territorial integrity or respect for the republic's institutions.

Also in November, Chad ratified the Rome Statute of the International Criminal Court.

Unlawful killings
The conflict in Sudan spilled over into Chad. The Janjawid extended its activities into eastern Chad, mainly in the Dar Sila department, and attacked a diverse range of ethnic groups identified as "African" rather than Arab. Members of communities such as the Dajo, Mobeh and Masalit left the border area as a result of Janjawid incursions. Hundreds of people, particularly members of the Dajo ethnic group, were killed by the Janjawid throughout 2006, and more than 80,000 people were forcibly displaced. Many remained in Chad as internally displaced persons, but at least 15,000, cut off from a safer escape route, fled into Darfur, despite the continuing conflict and disruption there. The refugees who fled into Darfur had virtually no access to humanitarian assistance. The internally displaced within Chad congregated in informal camps where they often remained at risk of further attacks.

Janjawid attacks on communities in eastern Chad, which began in 2003, initially consisted of frequent, small-scale raids aimed primarily at stealing cattle, which were generally kept at some distance from the villages. People guarding the cattle were often killed if they resisted the better-armed Janjawid, but the villages themselves were not attacked. However, as these incursions became more frequent, the Janjawid began to attack, burn and loot villages, sometimes repeatedly over a period of several days or months, until most of the inhabitants had been killed or forced to flee.

⌷ In March, the Janjawid launched a large-scale attack near N'Djaména village, a few kilometres from Modaina, in which 72 people were killed.

⌷ In October, the Janjawid used incendiary weapons during attacks on Djimeze Djarma village. Seventeen people, including Adam Oumar, Ahmed Haroon and a 90-year-old woman, Hawa Rashadiya, were killed.

⌷ In November, the village of Djorlo was attacked on three sides simultaneously. The Janjawid fired on the outskirts of the village before advancing. Forty people including Yahyah Omar, aged 75, and Sabil Awat, aged 60, were killed. In addition, three babies who were still breastfeeding, including Adam Haroon, were burned alive in their homes and one old crippled man, unable to flee, was also burned alive.

⌷ The village of Koloy was attacked several times between September and November. During these attacks, more than 100 people were killed, including Adam Abdelkerim, Ibrahim Said, Mahamat Abakar and an 85-year-old woman, Hawa Issa.

Violence against women

The widespread insecurity in eastern Chad had particularly severe consequences for women, who suffered grave human rights abuses, including rape, during attacks on villages. Sexual violence often continued after the women were displaced. Women also suffered extreme hardship associated with displacement and the deaths of their male relatives.

⌷ In October, seven women were abducted in Djimeze Djarma and held for 20 days by their attackers. They were beaten with whips and sticks throughout this period. The women did not identify their attackers as members of the Janjawid.

⌷ During an attack on the village of Djorlo in November, the Janjawid raped seven women who had taken refuge in a mosque. According to an eye-witness, the women were captured and beaten, then thrown to the ground. The attackers pinned the women to the ground, tore off their clothes and raped them.

Detention without trial

In May, at least 10 people were arrested in Guité on the suspicion of links with armed groups. Two were released without charge after two days and the others after 15 days.

Dozens of military officers and soldiers, including Adil Ousmane and Colonel Abakar Gawi, were arrested in April shortly after an attack by an armed group on N'Djaména. Some were released, but seven high-ranking officers remained in detention at the end of the year. The reasons for their arrest remained unclear, and no charges were brought against them. The authorities refused to grant the detainees access to their families and lawyers and would not reveal where or on what grounds they were held.

Extrajudicial executions

At least two people were extrajudicially executed by the security forces.

⌷ In May, soldiers in three separate vehicles arrived in Guité and arrested several people. One person was asked to produce his identity card and told to lie down on the ground. Soldiers stamped on him, then one soldier shot him dead at close range.

⌷ In April, Commander Idriss Mahamat Idriss was arrested while riding in a military vehicle. His body, showing signs of gunshot wounds, was found in the morgue a few days later.

Human rights defenders

Human rights defenders and journalists continued to be at risk of detention, unfair trial and imprisonment in violation of their right to freedom of expression. Two human rights defenders were illegally detained and threatened.

Following the decision to censor the press, the Association of Privately Owned Press Editors suspended the publication of five affiliated newspapers: *N'Djaména Bi-hebdo, Notre Temps, le Temps, Sarh Tribune* and *le Messager*.

⌷ In April, René Dillah Yombirin, a public radio journalist and French service correspondent for the BBC, was attacked by several soldiers while he was interviewing residents in the Moursal area shortly after the attack on N'Djaména. He was taken to an unknown destination before being released a few hours later.

⌷ In April, Mingar Monodji, a member of the Chadian Human Rights League, was arrested and detained by soldiers for three days in an unknown location. At the end of the third day, they abandoned him by the side of a road. During his detention, Mingar Monodji was beaten regularly by soldiers who accused him and other human rights activists of being mercenaries opposed to President Déby.

⌷ In May, Tchanguiz Vathankha, director of *Radio Brakoss*, a community radio station, and president of the Chad Union of Privately Owned Radio Stations, was arrested and held without charge for eight days. He was arrested after his organization issued a statement calling for the postponement of the May presidential election.

⌷ In October, Evariste Ngaralbaye, a journalist for the privately owned weekly, *Notre Temps*, was arrested and detained for four days. He was charged with defamation and damage to the reputation and morale of the gendarmerie. Shortly before his arrest, he had published a critical article on the conflict in eastern Chad.

Chad-Cameroon pipeline

In April, Chad threatened to shut down the Chad-Cameroon pipeline if the World Bank refused to release assets frozen in January after the Chadian government amended the Revenue Management Law governing the proceeds of the pipeline project. The government sought to divert pipeline revenues, originally reserved for health and education spending and poverty reduction, to fighting the armed rebellion against President Déby. An interim accord was reached in April, and in July relations were fully normalized after a memorandum of understanding was signed between the Chadian government and the World Bank.

In August, following a tax dispute, the activities of US and Malaysian companies sponsoring the pipeline were suspended. They resumed in October, following an accord reached with the Chadian government.

AI country reports/ visits
Reports
- Chad/Sudan: Thousands displaced by attacks from Sudan (AI Index: AFR 20/005/2006)
- Chad: "We don't want to die before Hissène Habré is brought to trial" (AI Index: AFR 20/002/2006)
- Chad: Testimonies from eastern Chad (AI Index: AFR 20/007/2006)
- Chad: Des militaires détenus depuis plus de cinq mois (AI Index: AFR 20/010/2006)
- Chad: Civilians left unprotected as brutal Janjawid attacks reach 150 kilometres inside Chad (AI Index: AFR 20/013/2006)
Visits
AI delegates visited Chad in May/June and in November/December to carry out research and hold talks with the authorities.

CHILE

REPUBLIC OF CHILE
Head of state and government: Michelle Bachelet (replaced Ricardo Lagos in March)
Death penalty: abolitionist for ordinary crimes
International Criminal Court: signed

Mapuche Indigenous people were harassed and ill-treated by the police. Student demonstrations were dispersed by the security forces, allegedly with excessive use of force. Harsh prison conditions and ill-treatment of detainees were reported. A resolution by the Inter-American Court of Human Rights highlighted the need to annul the Amnesty Law.

Background
In January Michelle Bachelet became the first woman president of Chile. She took office in March pledging to advance social equality and the promotion and protection of fundamental rights, to promote a National Programme of Human Rights and to take the

legal and judicial steps necessary to secure truth and justice for past human rights violations.

In May, the Chilean Supreme Court released former Peruvian President Alberto Fujimori on bail pending a decision on whether to extradite him to Peru where he was accused of corruption and human rights violations. By the end of the year, no decision had been reached and he remained in Chile under an arraignment order which prevented him from leaving the country.

In December, Augusto Pinochet, who governed Chile between 1973 and 1990 following a coup, died in Santiago. Under his government gross human rights violations considered crimes against humanity were committed. At the time of his death he was facing charges in Chilean courts in relation to a financial inquiry (the Riggs case) and four human rights cases — the Prats case, Villa Grimaldi, Operation Colombo and the Caravan of Death — in which thousands of people were subjected to torture, extrajudicial executions and enforced disappearance. He never attended any judicial hearings in any Chilean court.

Indigenous people
There were reports of ill-treatment of members of the Mapuche Indigenous group. In May, a number of Mapuche detainees staged hunger strikes in protest at the unfair application of anti-terrorist laws.

In July, uniformed police officers (carabineros) raided the Indigenous Mapuche community of Temucuicui in Ercilla, Malleco Province. The police claimed that they were searching for stolen animals, but the community denied that stolen animals were being held on community land. Police reportedly fired tear gas, rubber bullets and live ammunition at members of the community, who were unarmed. Several people were injured and a number of homes destroyed. Children were affected by the tear gas and several escaped to nearby hills. Women and children were ill-treated. The community had been subjected to similar police actions earlier in the year. At the end of the year, no investigation was known to have been initiated into the July raid.

In December, police reportedly fired on Temucuicui Mapuche individuals who were collecting their salaries in the city of Ercilla, IX Region. Up to six civilians were believed to have been injured, including a number of children.

Demonstrations
Secondary-school students demonstrated and went on strike in May, June and October to demand a complete overhaul of the education system and the end of disparities between public and private schools. There were clashes with the police and hundreds of people were briefly detained. There were reports of excessive use of force by police against student demonstrators and journalists.

Prison conditions
There were reports of harsh conditions, overcrowding, lack of medical attention, ill-treatment and corruption by prison guards. The case of 80 detainees in Santiago

Prison who were forced to sleep in the open was considered by the Santiago Appeals Court in June. A protection request was submitted on behalf of these men by lawyers working for the Paternitas Foundation, a non-governmental organization.

Amnesty Law
In September the Inter-American Court of Human Rights ruled that the application of the amnesty provisions of the 1978 Amnesty Law were not admissible and such provisions could not be applied to crimes against humanity. The judgment related to the case of Luis Alfredo Almonacid Arellano who was arrested and shot by police in September 1973. By the end of the year President Bachelet had made no decision on whether the Amnesty Law should be annulled, repealed or amended by new legislation which would limit its application.

AI country reports/visits
Reports
- Peru/Chile: 20,000 signatures collected as a result of the international campaign on the Fujimori case (AI Index: AMR 46/008/2006)
- Chile: Medical Concern (AI Index: AMR 22/002/2006)
- Chile: Death of Pinochet is not the end of the story (AI Index: AMR 22/004/2006)

CHINA

PEOPLE'S REPUBLIC OF CHINA
Head of state: Hu Jintao
Head of government: Wen Jiabao
Death penalty: retentionist
International Criminal Court: not ratified

An increased number of lawyers and journalists were harassed, detained, and jailed. Thousands of people who pursued their faith outside officially sanctioned churches were subjected to harassment and many to detention and imprisonment. Thousands of people were sentenced to death or executed. Migrants from rural areas were deprived of basic rights. Severe repression of Uighurs in the Xinjiang Uighur Autonomous Region continued, and freedom of expression and religion continued to be severely restricted in Tibet and among Tibetans elsewhere.

International community
Before China's election to the new UN Human Rights Council, it made a number of human rights-related pledges, including ratification of the International Covenant on Civil and Political Rights and active co-operation with the UN on human rights. Chinese companies continued to export arms to countries where they were likely to be used for serious human rights abuses, including Sudan and Myanmar.

Human rights defenders
The government crackdown on lawyers and housing rights activists intensified. Many human rights defenders were subjected to lengthy periods of arbitrary detention without charge, as well as harassment by the police or by local gangs apparently condoned by the police. Many lived under near constant surveillance or house arrest and members of their families were increasingly targeted. New regulations restricted the ability of lawyers to represent groups of victims and to participate in collective petitions.

⌷ Gao Zhisheng, an outspoken human rights lawyer, had his law practice suspended in November 2005. He was detained in August 2006 and remained in incommunicado detention at an unknown location until his trial in December 2006. In October he was formally arrested on charges of "inciting subversion", and in December he was sentenced to three years' imprisonment, suspended for five years.

Journalists and Internet users
The government's crackdown on journalists, writers, and Internet users intensified. Numerous popular newspapers and journals were shut down. Hundreds of international websites remained blocked and thousands of Chinese websites were shut down. Dozens of journalists were detained for reporting on sensitive issues.

The government strengthened systems for blocking, filtering, and monitoring the flow of information. New regulations came into effect requiring foreign news agencies to gain approval from China's official news agency in order to publish any news. Many foreign journalists were detained for short periods.

Discrimination against rural migrants
Rural migrant workers in China's cities faced wide-ranging discrimination. Despite official commitment to resolve the problem, millions of migrant workers were still owed back pay. The vast majority were excluded from urban health insurance schemes and could not afford private health care. Access to public education remained tenuous for millions of migrant children, in contrast to other urban residents. An estimated 20 million migrant children were unable to live with their parents in the cities in part because of insecure schooling.

⌷ Beijing municipal authorities closed dozens of migrant schools in September, affecting thousands of migrant children. While authorities claimed to have targeted unregistered and sub-standard schools, onerous demands made it nearly impossible for migrant schools to be registered. Some school staff believed the closures were aimed at reducing the migrant population in Beijing ahead of the 2008 Olympics.

Violence and discrimination against women

Violence and discrimination against women remained severe. The disadvantaged economic and social status of women and girls was evident in employment, health care and education. Women were laid off in larger numbers than men from failing state enterprises. Women accounted for 60 per cent of rural labourers and had fewer non-agricultural opportunities than men. The absence of gender-sensitive anti-HIV/AIDS policies contributed to a significant rise in female HIV/AIDS cases in 2006. Only 43 per cent of girls in rural areas completed education above lower middle school, compared with 61 per cent of boys.

Despite strengthened laws and government efforts to combat human trafficking, it remained pervasive, with an estimated 90 per cent of cases being women and children trafficked for sexual exploitation.

▭ Chen Guangcheng, a blind, self-trained lawyer, was sentenced in August to a prison term of four years and three months on charges of "damaging public property and gathering people to stop traffic". He had been arbitrarily confined to his home since September 2005 in connection with his advocacy on behalf of women undergoing forced abortions in Shandong Province. On appeal, the guilty verdict was overturned and the case sent back to the lower court for retrial, but the lower court upheld the original sentence.

Repression of spiritual and religious groups

The government continued to crack down on religious observance outside officially sanctioned channels. Thousands of members of underground protestant "house churches" and unofficial Catholic churches were detained, many of whom were ill-treated or tortured in detention. Members of the Falun Gong spiritual movement were detained and assigned to administrative detention for their beliefs, and continued to be at high risk of torture or ill-treatment.

▭ Bu Dongwei, a Falun Gong practitioner, was assigned to two and a half years' Re-education through Labour in June for "activities relating to a banned organization" after police discovered Falun Gong literature at his home. He had been working for a US aid organization when he was detained.

▭ Pastor Zhang Rongliang, an underground church leader who had been repeatedly detained and imprisoned since 1976, was sentenced in June to seven and a half years' imprisonment on charges of illegally crossing the border and fraudulently obtaining a passport.

Death penalty

The death penalty continued to be used extensively to punish around 68 crimes, including economic and non-violent crimes. Based on public reports, AI estimated that at least 1,010 people were executed and 2,790 sentenced to death during 2006, although the true figures were believed to be much higher.

The National People's Congress passed a law reinstating a final review of all death penalty cases by the Supreme People's Court from 2007. Commentators believed this would lead to a reduction in miscarriages of justice and use of the death penalty.

Executions by lethal injection rose, facilitating the extraction of organs from executed prisoners, a lucrative business. In November a deputy minister announced that the majority of transplanted organs came from executed prisoners. In July new regulations banned the buying and selling of organs and required written consent from donors for organ removal.

▭ Xu Shuangfu, the leader of an unofficial Protestant group called "Three Grades of Servants", was executed along with 11 others in November after being convicted of murdering 20 members of another group, "Eastern Lightning", in 2003-4. Xu Shuangfu reportedly claimed that he had confessed under torture during police interrogation and that the torture had included beatings with heavy chains and sticks, electric shocks to the toes, fingers and genitals and forced injection of hot pepper, gasoline and ginger into the nose. Both the first instance and appeal courts reportedly refused to allow his lawyers to introduce these allegations as evidence in his defence.

Torture, arbitrary detention and unfair trials

Torture and ill-treatment remained widespread. Common methods included kicking, beating, electric shocks, suspension by the arms, shackling in painful positions, cigarette burns, and sleep and food deprivation. In November a senior official admitted that at least 30 wrongful convictions handed down each year resulted from the use of torture, with the true number likely being higher. There was no progress in efforts to reform the Re-education through Labour system of administrative detention without charge or trial. Hundreds of thousands of people were believed to be held in Re-education through Labour facilities across China and were at risk of torture and ill-treatment. In May 2006, the Beijing city authorities announced their intention to extend their use of Re-education through Labour as a way to control "offending behaviour" and to clean up the city's image ahead of the Olympics.

▭ Ye Guozhu was sentenced to four years' imprisonment in 2004 for his opposition to forced evictions in Beijing associated with construction for the Olympic games. It emerged during 2006 that Ye had been tortured while in detention. He was reportedly suspended from the ceiling by the arms and beaten repeatedly by police in Dongcheng district detention centre, Beijing, and also reportedly tortured in another prison in the second half of 2005.

Uighurs in the Xinjiang Uighur Autonomous Region

Government authorities in Xinjiang continued to severely repress the Uighur community and to deny their human rights, including freedom of religion and access to education. An increased number of Uighurs were extradited to China from Central Asia, reflecting growing pressure by China on governments in the region. Seventeen Uighurs remained in detention in Guantánamo Bay.

◻ The family of exiled former prisoner of conscience Rebiya Kadeer continued to be targeted by the Chinese authorities. On 26 November her son Ablikim Abdiriyim, detained in Xinjiang awaiting trial on charges of "subversion" and tax evasion, was seen being carried out of Tianshan District Detention Centre, apparently in need of medical attention. On 27 November her sons Alim and Kahar Abdiriyim were fined heavily and Alim sentenced to seven years' imprisonment on charges of tax evasion.

◻ Husein Celil, a Canadian citizen who fled China in the 1990s as a refugee, was arrested in Uzbekistan and extradited to China in June. He was reportedly accused of "terrorism" and denied access to family or consular representatives.

Tibetans

Tibetans in the Tibet Autonomous Region and other areas experienced severe restrictions on their rights to freedom of religious belief, expression and association, and discrimination in employment. Many were detained or imprisoned for observing their religion or expressing opinions, including Tibetan Buddhist monks and nuns. Excessive use of force against Tibetans seeking to flee repression in Tibet continued. In September witnesses saw Chinese border patrol guards shooting at a group of Tibetans attempting to reach Nepal. At least one child was confirmed killed.

◻ Woeser, a leading Tibetan intellectual, had her weblog shut down several times after she raised questions about China's role in Tibet.

◻ Sonam Gyalpo, a former monk, was sentenced to 12 years' imprisonment in mid-2006 for "endangering state security" after the authorities found videos of the Dalai Lama and other "incriminating materials" in his house. His family learned of his trial and sentencing when they tried to visit him in detention.

North Korean refugees

Approximately 100,000 North Koreans were reportedly hiding in China. The authorities arrested and deported an estimated 150-300 each week without ever referring cases to UNHCR, the UN refugee agency. They also reportedly implemented a system of rewards for turning in North Koreans and heavy fines for supporting them. In September a new crackdown was reported on North Koreans residing illegally in China.

Abuse of North Korean women in China was widely reported, including cases of systematic rape and prostitution. North Korean women were reportedly sold as brides to Chinese men for between US$880 and US$1,890. Some women knew they were being sold into marriage but did not know how harsh conditions in China would be. Others were lured across the border by marriage brokers posing as merchants.

Hong Kong Special Administrative Region

All 14 South Koreans charged with "unlawful assembly" after protesting outside World Trade Organization meetings in December 2005 were acquitted in early 2006, sparking renewed calls for an independent inquiry into the actions of the police during the protests.

The UN Human Rights Committee and the UN Committee on the Elimination of Discrimination against Women reviewed the human rights situation in Hong Kong in March and August respectively. Both made several recommendations for reform.

In September, the Hong Kong Court of Appeal upheld a lower court ruling that laws providing a higher age of consent for sexual relations for gay men than for heterosexuals were discriminatory. The authorities announced that they would not appeal the case further.

Asylum-seekers continued to be refused entry without adequate consideration of their claims. Others were detained for over-staying their visas or other immigration offences. Despite lobbying from human rights and social welfare groups, the authorities confirmed that there were no plans to extend the UN Refugee Convention to Hong Kong. The authorities began to offer limited welfare assistance to asylum-seekers after UNHCR ceased its funding in May, but this was reportedly insufficient to meet basic needs.

AI country reports/ visits
Reports
- People's Republic of China: Abolishing "Re-education through Labour" and other forms of administrative detention – An opportunity to bring the law into line with the International Covenant on Civil and Political Rights (AI Index: ASA 17/016/2006)
- People's Republic of China: Sustaining conflict and human rights abuses – The flow of arms accelerates (AI Index: ASA 17/030/2006)
- People's Republic of China: The Olympics count-down – failing to keep human rights promises (AI Index: ASA 17/046/2006)
- Undermining freedom of expression in China: the role of Yahoo!, Microsoft and Google (AI Index: POL 30/026/2006)

Visits
AI representatives attended several human rights-related meetings in Beijing and Shenzhen.

COLOMBIA

REPUBLIC OF COLOMBIA
Head of state and government: Álvaro Uribe Vélez
Death penalty: abolitionist for all crimes
International Criminal Court: ratified

Serious human rights abuses remained at high levels, especially in rural areas, despite continued reductions in certain types of violence associated with Colombia's long-running internal armed conflict, in particular kidnappings and killings. All parties to the conflict – the security forces and army-backed paramilitaries as well as guerrilla groups, mainly the Revolutionary Armed Forces of Colombia (Fuerzas Armadas Revolucionarias de Colombia, FARC) and the smaller National Liberation Army (Ejército de Liberación Nacional, ELN) – continued to abuse human rights and breach international humanitarian law. They were responsible for war crimes and crimes against humanity. There was a fall in the number of people newly displaced by the conflict, but the large number of displaced people remained a concern. There were further attacks on trade unionists and human rights defenders, mainly by paramilitary groups. Extrajudicial executions by members of the security forces, and selective killings of civilians and kidnappings by guerrilla forces continued to be reported.

Background

President Álvaro Uribe Vélez won a second term of office in elections held in May. Congressional elections were held in March, with President Uribe's allies winning a majority of seats in both houses.

Speculation that the government and the FARC were about to agree an exchange of FARC prisoners for hostages held by the guerrilla group were dashed after President Uribe blamed the FARC for detonating an explosive device on 19 October inside the Nueva Granada Military University in Bogotá; at least 20 people were injured in the blast. The ELN and government representatives held a fourth round of preliminary peace talks in October in Cuba.

By the end of the year, the government reported that more than 30,000 paramilitaries had laid down their arms in a controversial government-sponsored demobilization process. In July, the Constitutional Court ruled that key parts of the Justice and Peace Law – designed to regulate the demobilization process and criticized by human rights organizations – were unconstitutional. In September, the government issued a decree to implement the Justice and Peace Law. Although it had been amended in the light of some of the criticisms levelled by the Court, concerns remained that the Law would exacerbate impunity and deny victims their right to truth, justice and reparation. Despite the supposed demobilization, there was strong evidence that paramilitary groups continued to operate and to commit human rights violations with the acquiescence of or in collusion with the security forces. In November, three legislators were arrested for their alleged links to paramilitaries. Several other legislators and political figures were also reportedly under investigation by the Supreme Court of Justice at the end of the year.

Abuses by paramilitary groups continue despite supposed demobilization

The Organization of American States Mission to Support the Peace Process in Colombia published a report in August. This stated that some demobilized paramilitaries had regrouped as criminal gangs, that others had failed to demobilize, and that new paramilitary groups had emerged. Paramilitaries continued to commit human rights violations in areas where they had supposedly demobilized. More than 3,000 killings and enforced disappearances of civilians were attributed to paramilitary groups since they declared a "ceasefire" in 2002.

On 11 February, demobilized paramilitaries belonging to the Bloque Noroccidente allegedly killed six peasant farmers in Sabanalarga Municipality, Antioquia Department.

Application of the Justice and Peace Law

In September the government promulgated Decree 3391 which revived some of the more controversial elements of the Justice and Peace Law.

Of particular concern was the inclusion of "rural reinsertion" programmes by which the government will finance agro-industrial projects which bring together peasant farmers, displaced people and demobilized paramilitaries. This could result in peasant and displaced communities working alongside those who forced them off their lands and committed human rights violations against them and lead to the legalization of ownership of lands taken by paramilitaries by force. Decree 3391 also failed to adopt measures that would identify and bring to justice third parties, including members of the security forces and politicians, who have supported paramilitary groups, both logistically and financially.

The Justice and Peace Law, which still failed to meet international standards on truth, justice and reparation, was to be applied only to around 2,600 of the more than 30,000 paramilitaries who had reportedly demobilized. The vast majority of paramilitaries had benefited from de facto amnesties under Decree 128 of 2003. On 6 December, the paramilitaries announced they were withdrawing from the "peace process". This followed the government's decision, taken on 1 December, to transfer 59 supposedly demobilized paramilitary leaders from low-security accommodation in a former holiday camp in La Ceja, Antioquia Department, to the high-security prison of Itagüí in the same Department. The government claimed that the paramilitaries had ordered several killings from La Ceja. On 19 December, Salvatore Mancuso became the first high-ranking leader of the paramilitaries to testify before the Office of the Attorney General's Justice and Peace Unit. The Unit was set up under the Justice and Peace Law to investigate human rights abuses committed by those wishing to qualify for the procedural benefits granted by the Law.

Collusion between paramilitaries and state officials

Scandals involving links between paramilitaries and high-ranking members of state institutions threatened to further undermine confidence in the rule of law.

◻ In November, the Office of the Procurator General accused the former director of the Civilian Intelligence Department (Departamento de Administración de Seguridad, DAS) of having links with paramilitary groups. The allegations stemmed from claims, published in the media in April by another DAS official, that the DAS had provided a list of 24 trade union leaders to the paramilitary group Bloque Norte. Several individuals named on the list were killed, others were threatened, while some were reportedly the subject of arbitrary judicial proceedings.

◻ On 9 November, the Supreme Court of Justice ordered the arrest of three congressmen from Sucre Department, Álvaro García Romero, Jairo Merlano and Erik Morris Taboada, for their alleged links to paramilitary groups and, in the case of Álvaro García Romero, for allegedly ordering the massacre by paramilitaries of some 15 peasant farmers in Macayepo, Bolívar Department in 2000. Later in the month the Supreme Court ordered that a further six congressmen answer charges over their alleged links to paramilitary groups.

Press reports in November suggested that the Office of the Attorney General was reviewing more than 100 cases of alleged collusion between paramilitaries and state officials, including political figures, members of the public and judicial administration, and the security forces. In November, the Office of the Procurator General also announced the creation of a special unit to investigate alleged links between public employees and paramilitaries.

Paramilitary groups continued to commit human rights violations in collusion with, or with the acquiescence of, members of the security forces.

◻ On 4 February, community leader Alirio Sepúlveda Jaimes was killed close to a police station in Saravena Municipality, Arauca Department. The gunman, thought to be a paramilitary, was reportedly linked to the local army battalion. Alirio Sepúlveda was one of around 40 social and human rights activists detained by the authorities in Saravena in 2002.

Exhumations of mass graves

More than 80 mass graves were found containing the remains of some 200 people killed by paramilitary groups over the course of the conflict. The Justice and Peace Unit claimed the remains of some 3,000 victims of enforced disappearance were still to be located, although this was thought to be a substantial underestimate. Concerns were raised that some of the exhumations may have been undertaken in a manner which jeopardized forensic evidence and that remains in official custody were being stored in precarious

conditions. There were also concerns regarding the lack of positive identification of remains and appropriate forensic analysis of the evidence. Paramilitaries had reportedly removed remains from some mass graves.

Impunity

Impunity remained a serious problem, and the military justice system continued to deal with human rights cases involving military personnel despite the 1997 ruling of the Constitutional Court that such cases must be investigated by the civilian justice system. However, some cases were transferred to the civilian justice system. Among them was the killing by soldiers of 10 members of the judicial police (the DIJIN), together with a police informer and a civilian, in Jamundí, Valle del Cauca Department, on 22 May. The Office of the Attorney General charged 15 members of the army for their alleged role in the killings, which were reported to have been carried out at the behest of drug traffickers with links to paramilitary groups. Judicial investigators involved in the case were reportedly threatened.

The Inter-American Court of Human Rights issued rulings on emblematic cases of impunity involving massacres carried out by paramilitary groups allegedly with the collusion or acquiescence of the security forces. These included the Pueblo Bello massacre of 1990 in which 43 civilians were killed or forcibly disappeared, and the La Granja and El Aro massacres of 1996 and 1997, in which 19 people were killed. In both cases, the Court held the Colombian state partly responsible and ordered it to make reparations to the victims and their families.

The security forces

There were continued allegations of extrajudicial executions carried out by the security forces.

◻ On 19 September, army soldiers reportedly killed community and labour activist Alejandro Uribe Chacón in Morales Municipality, Bolívar Department.

◻ On 14 April, peasant farmer Adrián Cárdenas Marín was reportedly detained by army troops in Argelia Municipality, Antioquia Department. On 15 April, the army reported that Adrián Cárdenas had been killed in combat a short distance from the town of Argelia.

A number of human rights cases involving the army received national media coverage.

◻ On 25 January, 21 soldiers were reportedly tortured, including sexually, by their superiors in an initiation ceremony at a military training facility in Piedras, Tolima Department. The case was being investigated by the civilian justice system at the end of the year.

◻ The Office of the Procurator General began an investigation into the alleged role of army personnel in a number of bomb plots in Bogotá in July and August, including a car bomb which killed one civilian and injured 19 soldiers on 31 July and which the authorities had attributed to the FARC.

The security forces, including the Mobile Anti-Riot Squad (Escuadrón Móvil Anti-Disturbios, ESMAD) were alleged to have used excessive force during mass demonstrations by peasant farmers and Afro-descendant and Indigenous protesters on 15 and 16 May in Cauca and Nariño Departments. At least one demonstrator died and 50 were injured, including several members of the security forces and a 12-year-old child.

⬭ On 8 March, ESMAD agents reportedly injured several students at the National University in Bogotá when they dispersed a student demonstration. During the demonstration students threw stones at police. One student, Oscar Leonardo Salas, reportedly died on 9 March after sustaining head injuries from a projectile allegedly fired by the ESMAD.

Guerrilla groups

The FARC and ELN continued to commit serious and repeated breaches of international humanitarian law, including hostage-taking and the killing of civilians.

⬭ On 9 October, the bodies were found of four peasant farmers who had been kidnapped by the ELN in Fortul Municipality, Arauca Department. Between March and August, the FARC and ELN allegedly killed more than 20 civilians in Arauca Department.

⬭ On 27 February, FARC guerrillas allegedly killed eight municipal councillors in Rivera Municipality, Huila Department, while they were attending a council meeting.

⬭ On 25 February, the FARC allegedly attacked a bus in Caquetá Department in which at least nine civilians were killed, including two children.

The FARC also allegedly carried out disproportionate and indiscriminate attacks which resulted in the deaths of numerous civilians.

⬭ On 6 March, an attack using explosive devices killed three civilians, including a 76-year-old woman and an eight-year-old boy in San Vicente del Caguán Municipality, Caquetá Department. The government attributed the attack to the FARC.

The FARC and ELN continued to forcibly recruit minors and landmines placed by guerrilla groups continued to kill and maim civilians.

⬭ On 2 August, landmines, allegedly placed by the FARC, killed six civilians working on a government coca eradication programme and five police officers, in La Macarena Municipality, Meta Department.

Trade unionists, human rights defenders and other activists

Human rights, social and community activists continued to be targeted, mainly by paramilitary groups and the security forces, but also by guerrilla groups. More than 70 trade union members were killed in 2006.

⬭ In September, the FARC allegedly tortured and killed Fabián Trellez Moreno, a community leader and legal representative of the Boca de Bebará Local Community Council in Medio Atrato Municipality, Chocó Department.

⬭ In May, in the run-up to the presidential elections, trade unionists, left-wing party activists, human rights and peace non-governmental organizations (NGOs) and university students and staff received e-mail death threats, reportedly from groups claiming to be new paramilitary structures.

⬭ On 2 January, the body of trade unionist Carlos Arciniegas Niño was discovered in Puerto Wilches

Municipality, Santander Department. He had been missing since 30 December 2005. His body reportedly showed signs of torture. The killing was attributed to the paramilitary Bloque Central Bolívar (BCB). On 31 August, the BCB allegedly sent a written death threat to the CUT trade union confederation (Central Unitaria de Trabajadores) in Bucaramanga, Santander Department, despite the fact that the BCB had supposedly demobilized by 1 March.

Civilian communities at risk

Afro-descendant, Indigenous and peasant farmer communities, as well as civilians living in areas of intense military conflict, continued to be at particular risk of attack by all parties to the conflict. More than 770 civilians were killed or forcibly disappeared during the first half of the year. More than 219,000 people were forcibly displaced in 2006, compared with 310,000 in 2005. More than 45 members of Indigenous communities were killed in the first half of 2006.

⬭ On 9 August, unknown gunmen killed five members of the A'wa Indigenous community in Barbacoas Municipality, Nariño Department.

⬭ On 5 and 6 March, the FARC allegedly killed Juan Ramírez Villamizar, the former Indigenous governor of the resguardo (reservation) of Makaguán de Caño Claro, Arauca Department, and his wife Luz Miriam Farías, a schoolteacher in the resguardo's school.

Members of "peace communities" and "humanitarian zones", and of other communities which continued to publicly assert their right not to be drawn into the conflict, were threatened and killed.

⬭ On 16 August, paramilitaries reportedly approached inhabitants of the Curvaradó River Basin area of Chocó Department, and informed them that paramilitaries were planning to kill Enrique Petro, a member of the Afro-descendant Curvaradó Humanitarian Zone. In March, members of the armed forces had reportedly accused Enrique Petro of being linked with guerrillas. The paramilitaries also stated that they were preparing to kill other members of the Curvaradó Humanitarian Zone.

⬭ The body of Nelly Johana Durango, a member of the Peace Community of San José de Apartadó, Antioquia Department, was identified on 15 March by a family member in Tierra Alta, Córdoba Department. Witnesses claimed that she had been taken from her home by the army on 4 March. The army claimed she was a guerrilla killed in combat. More than 160 peace community members have been killed since 1997, mostly by paramilitary groups and the security forces, but also by guerrilla groups.

Kidnappings

Kidnappings continued to fall, from 800 in 2005 to 687 in 2006. Guerrilla groups, mainly the FARC, were responsible for most conflict-related kidnappings, accounting for some 200 kidnappings. Ten were attributed to paramilitary groups and 267 to common criminals. About 200 kidnappings could not be attributed.

⬭ On 26 June in Antioquia Department, the FARC allegedly kidnapped Camilo Mejía Restrepo, his wife

Rosario Restrepo, their son and a nephew. In their efforts to flee from the authorities, the kidnappers were alleged to have killed Camilo Mejía and injured the nephew.

◻ On 7 June, the ELN allegedly kidnapped Javier Francisco Castro in Yondó Municipality, Antioquia Department. The ELN reportedly accused him of having links with the security forces. No information was received by the end of the year as to whether he had been released.

◻ On 27 April, armed men killed Liliana Gaviria Trujillo, sister of former President César Gaviria Trujillo, and her bodyguard, Fernando Vélez Rengifo, in Dosquebradas, Risaralda Department, in what appeared to be a botched kidnap attempt. The authorities claimed the kidnapping was ordered by the FARC.

Violence against women
Combatants continued to kill, sexually abuse, kidnap and threaten women and girls.

◻ On 22 October, 10 army soldiers allegedly entered the home of a woman in Puerto Lleras Municipality, Meta Department. Subsequently, four of the soldiers reportedly raped her in front of her three-year-old son. The woman was reportedly threatened after she reported the rape to the authorities.

◻ On 9 April, a guerrilla member allegedly raped a woman in Fortul Municipality, Arauca Department.

◻ On 21 March, paramilitaries reportedly raped and killed Yamile Agudelo Peñaloza of the Popular Women's Organization (Organización Femenina Popular), in Barrancabermeja, Santander Department. Her body was found the next day.

US military aid
In 2006, US assistance to Colombia amounted to an estimated US$728 million, approximately 80 per cent of which was military and police assistance. In June, the US Congress put a hold on US$29 million because of concerns with the US administration's failure to consult adequately with Congress regarding the certification process. Under the certification process, 25 per cent of aid is dependent on progress by the Colombian government and state authorities on certain human rights indicators. Despite Congress' decision, the funds were released by the State Department. However, the State Department subsequently agreed to meet with the Congress and representatives of the US human rights community to discuss concerns about the certification consultation process and recommendations for improving it. Some US$17 million went to support the demobilization process with some US$5 million going to the Justice and Peace Unit. Human rights conditions for the release of such funding were maintained.

Office of the UN High Commissioner for Human Rights
Despite reported efforts by the Colombian government to weaken the mandate of the Office in Colombia of the UN High Commissioner for Human Rights (UNHCHR), especially in relation to its monitoring role, the government and the UNHCHR announced in September that the full mandate would be extended for a further 12

months. The latest report on Colombia of the UNHCHR, published in January, urged the government to implement UN human rights recommendations and to adopt the long-promised national human rights action plan and increase protection for human rights defenders. It called on the parties to the conflict to respect the right to life and to refrain from indiscriminate attacks, kidnappings, recruitment of child soldiers, and sexual violence. The report also recommended that legislation on the demobilization of members of illegal armed groups be made consistent with human rights principles including the right of victims to truth, justice and reparation. The High Commissioner presented the report to the second regular session of the UN Human Rights Council on 28 September.

AI country visits/reports
Reports
- Colombia: Reporting, campaigning and serving without fear – The rights of journalists, election candidates and elected officials (AI Index: AMR 23/001/2006)
- Colombia: Open letter to the presidential candidates (AI Index: AMR 23/013/2006)
- Colombia: Fear and intimidation – The dangers of human rights work (AI Index: AMR 23/033/2006)

Visits
AI delegates visited the country in February, March and October.

CONGO
(REPUBLIC OF)

REPUBLIC OF CONGO
Head of state: Denis Sassou-Nguesso
Head of government: Isidore Mvouba
Death penalty: abolitionist in practice
International Criminal Court: ratified

At least 12 men arrested in early 2005 continued to be detained without trial. Two human rights defenders were arrested and their trial on charges of abuse of trust concluded in December. Three asylum-seekers from the Democratic Republic of the Congo (DRC) were still detained without charge or trial after nearly three years. There were allegations of torture and ill-treatment of detainees.

Background
The National Resistance Council (Conseil national de résistance, CNR) retained its arms and bases in the Pool region in the south, despite a 2003 peace agreement,

and reports continued of looting and lawlessness by its combatants.

In January, President Sassou-Nguesso became chair of the African Union Assembly of Heads of State and Government.

Political detainees

Former army Colonel Serge André Mpassi and at least 11 other members or former members of the security forces, arrested in early 2005, remained in detention without trial. A further 13 political detainees arrested at the same time had been released provisionally by the start of 2006. Some of the 25 were charged in 2005 with involvement in the theft of military weapons, and all were charged with plotting to overthrow the government. In March the prosecutor of the Brazzaville High Court reportedly told the remaining detainees that an examining magistrate had concluded they had no case to answer. However, by the end of 2006, the authorities had not withdrawn the charges or released the remaining detainees.

By the end of 2006, there had still been no investigation into allegations that Army Sergeant Francis Ngolo Ngapene was tortured at a military airbase in Pointe-Noire shortly after his arrest in February 2005, sustaining injuries that included a broken arm. He remained in Brazzaville's Central Prison.

Detention and prosecution of human rights defenders

Human rights defenders Brice Mackosso and Christian Mounzéo were detained on 7 April. The two men, co-ordinators of an anti-corruption coalition of civil society groups known as Publish What You Pay, appeared to have been detained because of their human rights work, which included investigating and denouncing embezzlement of oil revenues by government officials. They were held at the central prison in Pointe-Noire. After the arrests, police searched their offices and homes without a warrant, seizing documents and other property. The two men were provisionally released on 28 April to await trial on charges of breach of trust, complicity in breach of trust and forgery. A pre-trial judge decided that the breach of trust charges should be dropped, because there was no evidence of misappropriation of funds, but the trial judge ruled that the case should continue on the basis of the original charges. The defence challenged this decision but the prosecution succeeded in reintroducing the charges. After numerous delays, the trial concluded in December with the original charges intact. On 27 December the High Court in Pointe-Noire convicted them and gave them a suspended one-year prison sentence and a fine. They appealed against conviction and sentence. Christian Mounzéo was briefly detained in November on his return from a trip to Europe where, according to the Congolese authorities, he defamed President Sassou-Nguesso.

Torture and ill-treatment

Political detainees and criminal suspects were allegedly tortured and ill-treated.

Four men arrested in May on suspicion of involvement in trafficking arms were allegedly beaten repeatedly by members of the police unit responsible for their detention. One of them, Aymar Mouity, was reportedly suspended by his feet from the ceiling. The four were held in the Moukondo detention centre in Brazzaville, in a cramped and dark cell, which reportedly left them with damaged eyesight. The men were still held without charge or trial at the end of 2006.

Detention and deportation of asylum-seekers

Three former members of the DRC security forces seeking asylum in the Republic of Congo continued to be held without charge or trial at the headquarters of the military intelligence service. Germain Ndabamenya Etikilome, Médard Mabwaka Egbonde and Bosch Ndala Umba had been arrested in March 2004 on the basis of a security agreement between the DRC and the Republic of Congo to crack down on each others' opponents. However, the Republic of Congo authorities reportedly believed the men were DRC spies.

In October, two people who had escaped from prison in the DRC and another asylum-seeker were arrested in Brazzaville and deported to the DRC. One of the two escaped prisoners, Césaire Muzima Mwenyezi, had been serving a life sentence with 18 other former asylum-seekers deported from Brazzaville to the DRC in 2001. They had been convicted of involvement in the January 2001 assassination of then President Laurent Désiré Kabila.

There was no progress in bringing to justice those responsible for the enforced disappearance in mid-1999 of more than 350 refugees who were returning from the DRC.

AI country reports/visits
Report
- Republic of Congo: Political detainees in legal limbo (AI Index: AFR 22/003/2006)

CÔTE D'IVOIRE

REPUBLIC OF CÔTE D'IVOIRE
Head of state: Laurent Gbagbo
Head of government: Charles Konan Banny
Death penalty: abolitionist for all crimes
International Criminal Court: signed

Intense diplomatic efforts, notably by the UN and the African Union (AU), did not prevent further human rights abuses by both government security forces and the New Forces (Forces Nouvelles), the coalition of armed groups in control of the north since September 2002. Women were targeted with impunity by both sides, a situation aggravated by the lack of a functioning justice system. Supporters of President Laurent Gbagbo continued to incite violence against Dioulas, a generic term for anyone with a Muslim family name originating from the north of Côte d'Ivoire or other countries in the sub-region. Hate speech also continued to fuel ethnic clashes in the west of the country. There were violent demonstrations targeted at UN peacekeeping forces, but the presence of about 12,000 peacekeepers prevented a resumption of hostilities. Freedom of expression came under attack from both sides.

Background
Despite intense political pressure from the international community, the conditions required for a presidential election scheduled for October were not met. The election was postponed for a second time, primarily because of disagreements between supporters of President Laurent Gbagbo and opposition parties. The President and his supporters demanded the immediate disarmament of the New Forces, while the opposition insisted on a programme to issue identity documents ahead of the election.

Supporters of President Laurent Gbagbo criticized the presence of French and UN peacekeeping forces, repeatedly demanding their departure.

In January, there were anti-UN demonstrations organized by Young Patriots (Jeunes Patriotes), a loosely defined movement supporting President Gbagbo. UN peacekeepers responded on one occasion, prompting allegations of excessive use of force.

In August, following a scandal surrounding toxic waste dumped in Abidjan (the economic capital), the government resigned. However, when a new government was formed, only two ministries had changed hands.

In October, the UN decided to extend Laurent Gbagbo's mandate for an additional 12 months and to expand Prime Minister Charles Konan Banny's powers. At the end of the year efforts to implement the UN decision were being resisted by President Gbagbo and his supporters.

Violence against women
Serious human rights abuses against women and girls continued to be reported in the government-controlled part of the country, encouraged by an atmosphere of impunity.

In March, a 14-year-old girl was raped in Abidjan by a member of the Command Centre for Security Operations (Centre de Commandement des Opérations de Sécurité, CECOS). A complaint was lodged on her behalf before the military tribunal, but the investigation led to no legal proceedings.

In the part of the country controlled by the New Forces, perpetrators of rape also benefited from virtually total impunity.

In May, a 10-year-old girl was raped by the director of a radio station in Man. Officials close to the New Forces intimidated medical personnel, preventing them from issuing a medical certificate confirming the rape.

Alleged excessive use of force by UN forces
In January, anti-UN demonstrations erupted after a decision by the International Working Group – the international mediation group on Côte d'Ivoire – not to extend the mandates of National Assembly members. Demonstrators demanded the departure of the UN Operation in Côte d'Ivoire (UNOCI) and attacked UN vehicles and buildings while the security forces reportedly stood by passively.

In Guiglo, following demonstrations in front of the UN military compound, UN peacekeepers opened fire on demonstrators, killing five people and wounding at least 20. Peacekeepers maintained that they acted in self-defence, while supporters of President Gbagbo claimed that the UN forces had fired at unarmed demonstrators. The UN opened an internal inquiry into the incident whose findings had not been made public by the end of 2006.

UN sanctions and embargos
The UN imposed sanctions on individuals responsible for inciting hatred and grave human rights violations.

In February, the UN Security Council imposed targeted sanctions on two leaders of the Young Patriots, Charles Blé Goudé and Eugene Djué, for their role during the January anti-UN demonstrations. It also imposed sanctions on Fofié Kouakou, a New Forces commander, for recruiting child soldiers, imposing forced labour and gross human rights violations by forces under his control.

In October, a report drafted by a UN Group of Experts concluded that Ivorian rough diamonds were being exported in violation of the UN embargo imposed in December 2005.

Demobilization at a standstill
Despite international pressure, notably from UNOCI, the repeatedly postponed disarmament, demobilization and reintegration (DDR) programme remained deadlocked because of disagreement over the timetable. Supporters of President Gbagbo wanted DDR to begin immediately, while the opposition refused to disarm until a programme to issue identity documents

ahead of presidential elections had been implemented. This impasse seemed to have been overcome in mid-May when the two parties agreed on the simultaneous launch of the identification and DDR programmes. By June, both the National Armed Forces of Côte d'Ivoire (Forces Armées Nationales de Côte d'Ivoire, FANCI) and the New Forces had reportedly regrouped some 12,000 combatants each. However, by August, the UNOCI had collected only a limited number of arms from pro-government militias in the west when the New Forces declared that they would suspend disarmament due to obstacles in the identification process. By the end of 2006, no further progress on the implementation of the DDR program had been reported.

Human rights violations by security forces

The security forces were responsible for arbitrary arrests, torture and extrajudicial executions of detainees suspected of supporting the New Forces.

In January, in Abidjan, members of the CECOS arrested Dioulas and nationals of neighbouring countries and accused them of financing the rebels. Some detainees were reportedly tortured and at least one, Diallo Ouatreni, died as a result.

Several cases of arbitrary arrest, ill-treatment and torture were reported in the context of widespread extortion at check points and during inspections of identity documents. Dioulas and nationals of neighbouring countries were reportedly targeted.

In February, Moustapha Tounkara and Arthur Vincent, two young mobile phone salesmen, were arrested in Abidjan by members of the CECOS. Their bodies were found the next day, riddled with bullets.

Abuses by the New Forces

Members and supporters of the New Forces were responsible for human rights abuses, including arbitrary detention, torture and ill-treatment. A climate of impunity prevailed due to the absence of a functioning judicial system in the north.

In January, Khalil Coulibaly, Fane Zakaria and Yeo Ibrahime, a former member of the New Forces, were arrested in Korhogo by elements of the New Forces. An eyewitness saw them in detention, but they then disappeared.

In August, at least 15 militants of a new party, the National Union of Ivorians for Renewal (Union nationale des Ivoiriens du renouveau, UNIR), led by Ibrahim Coulibaly, were reported to have been arbitrarily arrested by New Forces in Seguela, in the northwest, and accused of destabilizing the region. Those arrested were reportedly wearing T-shirts in the colours of their party. They were released one week later.

The New Forces also extorted money from civilians on a large scale, severely limiting freedom of movement by requiring villagers to pay a "tax" in order to enter or leave their villages.

Ethnic clashes in the west

In the west, antagonism between the indigenous population and farmers from other regions or from neighbouring countries, including Burkina Faso, continued to provoke conflict over land ownership and ethnic clashes. Xenophobic rhetoric employed by politicians and the news media aggravated the hostility.

In March, intercommunal clashes occurred in several villages including Gohouo, Zagna, Baïbly and Doekpe alongside the zone controlled by French soldiers and UNOCI. Clashes broke out after members of the indigenous Guéré ethnic group attempted to repossess plantations occupied by Burkinabè planters. A number of people were killed and thousands displaced.

Freedom of expression under attack

Journalists and media organizations were harassed and attacked by the security forces and by pro-government militias, notably during the January anti-UN demonstrations.

In January, Young Patriots attempted to set fire to a car in which journalists of the newspaper *24 Heures* were travelling on their way to a meeting of the International Working Group.

In November, members of the security forces entered the premises of state-owned Ivorian Radio and Television (Radio-télévision ivoirienne, RTI) by force and prevented a statement by Prime Minister Charles Konan Banny from being rebroadcast. The Director-General and the management board of RTI were dismissed by presidential decree.

Freedom of expression was also limited in the area held by the New Forces. In Bouaké, the New Forces' stronghold, certain programmes on national radio and television continued to be banned.

In February, an independent journalist was beaten and forced to crawl 40 metres while being sprayed with water inside the General Secretariat of the New Forces in Bouaké.

AI country reports/ visits
Reports
- Côte d'Ivoire: Provide protection to journalists! (AI Index: AFR 31/002/2006)
- Côte d'Ivoire: Clashes between peacekeeping forces and civilians — lessons for the future (AI Index: AFR 31/005/2006)

Visit
In April, an AI delegation visited Côte d'Ivoire to investigate reports of human rights abuses during the January 2006 anti-UN demonstrations and the alleged use of excessive force by UNOCI peacekeeping forces.

CROATIA

REPUBLIC OF CROATIA
Head of state: Stjepan Mesić
Head of government: Ivo Sanader
Death penalty: abolitionist for all crimes
International Criminal Court: ratified

The legacy of the 1991-95 war continued to overshadow human rights. Impunity for war crimes remained widespread and the Croatian judicial system failed to adequately address wartime human rights violations, regardless of the ethnicity of the victims or of the perpetrators. Minorities suffered discrimination. Of at least 300,000 Croatian Serbs displaced by the conflict, approximately 125,000 were officially registered as having returned home.

Background
The first phase of Croatia's accession to the European Union (EU) – the screening by the EU and Croatia of the body of EU common rights and obligations binding member states that candidate countries must accept – was completed in October.

In June parliament amended the Criminal Code to remove imprisonment as a punishment for libel. Although libel remained a criminal offence punishable by a fine, failure to pay the fine would no longer result in imprisonment.

War crimes and crimes against humanity
International prosecutions
In March, Milan Babić committed suicide in the Detention Unit of the International Criminal Tribunal for the former Yugoslavia (Tribunal). Sentenced by the Tribunal in June 2004 to 13 years' imprisonment for crimes committed against the non-Serb population, he was detained at the Tribunal as a witness in the trial of Milan Martić, charged with war crimes and crimes against humanity for his wartime leadership role in areas under Croatian Serb control.

In April the Tribunal declared Vladimir Kovačević, a former commander in the Yugoslav People's Army, unfit to stand trial on mental health grounds. He faced trial for war crimes during an attack on the Croatian city of Dubrovnik, including murder, cruel treatment and attacks on civilians.

In March the Tribunal fined Ivica Marijačić, former editor in chief of the Croatian newspaper *Hrvatski list*, and Markica Rebić, former head of the Croatian security service, for contempt of court. In 2004 they had disclosed the identity of a protected witness in a closed session in 1997 of the trial of former Croatian army General Tihomir Blaškić. In September the Tribunal also fined Josip Jović, former editor in chief of the Croatian daily newspaper, *Slobodna Dalmacija*, for contempt of court on similiar charges. The newspaper had published articles in 2000 about testimony by Croatian President Mesić in a closed session of the trial of Tihomir Blaškić.

In October the Appeal Chamber of the Tribunal confirmed the joining of the cases of Ante Gotovina, Ivan Čermak and Mladen Markač, three former Croatian army commanders charged with crimes against humanity and war crimes against Croatian Serbs, including persecutions, deportation and forcible transfers, and murder. Also in October, the Trial Chamber refused requests by the Republic of Croatia to be allowed to appear as *amicus curiae* (adviser to the court on points of law) in this and another case against six Bosnian Croat former military and political leaders.

Domestic prosecutions
Most war crimes trials before local courts were of Croatian Serb defendants, who were often not present before the court. Despite some steps to investigate and prosecute war crimes against Croatian Serbs, widespread impunity continued for crimes allegedly committed by Croatian army and police officers.

☐ The retrial at the Split County Court of eight former members of the Croatian Military Police accused of torturing and murdering non-Croat detainees in Split's Lora military prison in 1992 ended in convictions in March. Four of the accused were tried in their absence, and remained at large at the end of 2006. In an initial trial in 2002, all had been acquitted; the acquittals were subsequently overturned by the Supreme Court.

☐ In May parliament lifted the immunity from prosecution of Branimir Glavaš, formerly a local leader in the Osijek region of the ruling Croatian Democratic Union, in connection with an investigation into war crimes against Croatian Serb civilians, including murders. The Supreme Court transferred proceedings from Osijek to Zagreb on the grounds that pressure on witnesses in Osijek could hamper their impartial conduct. In December the investigation was suspended when the health of Branimir Glavaš deteriorated following a hunger strike.

☐ In June the trial started at the Osijek County Court of two suspects charged with war crimes, including murders, against Croatian Serbs in and around Osijek.

☐ In October, six former members of a military formation were arrested on suspicion of murdering Croatian Serb civilians in Osijek in 1991-92. Following the arrests, the Osijek County Court ordered investigation of the role of Branimir Glavaš in these crimes.

☐ In December an indictment was issued by the Zagreb County Court in the case of Rahim Ademi and Mirko Norac, transferred by the Tribunal to Croatia in November 2005. Reportedly, the delay in issuing the indictment was owing to difficulties in incorporating the charges in the Tribunal indictment in an indictment compatible with Croatian law. Former Croatian army commanders, the two were charged by the Tribunal with war crimes against Croatian Serbs during military operations in 1993.

Right to return
At least 300,000 Croatian Serbs left Croatia or were displaced during the 1991-95 war, of whom only some 125,000 are officially registered as having returned, a figure widely considered to be an overestimate.

Croatian Serbs faced discrimination in employment and in realizing other economic and social rights. Many, especially those who formerly lived in urban areas, could not return because they had lost their tenancy rights to socially-owned apartments.

In March the European Court of Human Rights determined that it did not have jurisdiction to rule in a case, *Blečić v. Croatia*, in which the applicant's occupancy rights to her flat in Zadar during the war had been terminated. The case illustrated the adverse human rights consequences of discriminatory terminations of occupancy rights.

In August the government announced plans to make 4,000 flats available to former tenancy rights holders. However, the plan will not be completed until 2011 and occupants will not be able to purchase the flats at a substantially reduced price, unlike the mostly ethnic Croat occupants who have previously been able to purchase the flats where they lived.

Harassment of Croatian Serbs by private individuals included racist graffiti, threats and damage to property.

In April an explosive device was thrown into the orchard of a Croatian Serb returnee in the village of Gaj, near Gospić. The police identified a suspect but the Gospić Public Prosecutor reportedly did not pursue the case for lack of evidence.

In July four houses of Croatian Serbs in the village of Biljane Donje, near Zadar, were stoned and surrounding vegetation set on fire. The incident was condemned by the government and President. Four men were arrested shortly after, and were charged in connection with the attack.

Violence against women

Reported incidence of domestic violence remained high. In June a 25-year-old woman was killed by her husband, who then committed suicide, while she was visiting her child who had been placed in a home for children in Zagreb. Before being murdered, she had reportedly asked the relevant authorities to assist her and protect her from her violent husband. In August the non-governmental organization Autonomous Women's House Zagreb filed a complaint against employees of local social welfare authorities and two local judges for their failure to act to protect the woman.

Lack of access to education for Romani children

Member of Romani communities lacked full access to primary education, especially in areas not covered by government and other programmes to promote the inclusion of Roma.

Although "Roma only" classes were increasingly rare, Romani children still experienced discriminatory treatment because of teachers' negative stereotyping and low expectations. Romani children with little or no command of the Croatian language faced extreme difficulties when they started school. The languages spoken by Roma in Croatia were virtually absent from schools, unlike other minority languages.

AI country reports/ visits
Reports
- Europe and Central Asia: Summary of Amnesty International's concerns in the region, January-June 2006 (AI Index: EUR 01/017/2006)
- False starts: The exclusion of Romani children from primary education in Bosnia and Herzegovina, Croatia and Slovenia (AI Index: EUR 05/002/2006)

Visit
An AI delegate visited Croatia in March.

CUBA

REPUBLIC OF CUBA
Head of state and government: Raúl Castro Ruz (provisionally replaced Fidel Castro Ruz in July)
Death penalty: retentionist
International Criminal Court: not ratified

Freedom of expression, association and movement continued to be severely restricted. At least 69 prisoners of conscience remained imprisoned for their political opinions. Political dissidents, independent journalists and human rights activists continued to be harassed, intimidated and detained, some without charge or trial. Cubans continued to feel the negative impact of the US embargo.

Background
During 2006 Cuba secured a place on the UN Human Rights Council and assumed the presidency of the Non-Aligned Movement during its XIV Summit in Havana in September.

In July, Fidel Castro underwent surgery and for the first time since 1959 transferred his responsibilities to other senior officials, including his brother, Raúl Castro Ruz. Political opposition parties and activities were not tolerated.

Political relations with the USA remained tense despite economic exports of agricultural products to Cuba exceeding US$500 million. The US Commission for Assistance to a Free Cuba issued an update of its previous report in July. The European Union did not reintroduce sanctions lifted in 2005 despite continued concerns over the human rights situation in Cuba.

The US government set up a law enforcement task force to track down and prosecute those who circumvent restrictions on travelling and commercial exchanges with Cuba. In November, for the 15th consecutive year, the UN General Assembly passed a resolution calling on the USA to end its embargo on Cuba.

The government continued to deny the UN Special Rapporteur on the human rights situation in Cuba access to the country. AI and other independent human rights organizations were also not allowed to visit.

Prisoners of conscience

At the end of the year, 69 prisoners of conscience continued to be held for their non-violent political views or activities. Twelve others continued to serve their sentences outside prison because of health concerns. No releases of prisoners of conscience were reported during the year.

⬚ Orlando Zapata Tamayo was sentenced to three years in 2003 on charges of showing "contempt to the figure of Fidel Castro", "public disorder" and "resistance". In November 2005 he was reportedly sentenced to an additional 15 years for "contempt" and "resistance" in prison. In May 2006, he was again tried on the same charges and sentenced to an additional seven-year term. He was serving a prison sentence of 25 years and six months.

Detention without charge or trial

Scores of people continued to be held without charge on suspicion of counter-revolutionary activities or on unclear charges. Their legal status remained unclear at the end of the year.

⬚ Prisoner of conscience Oscar Mariano González Pérez, an independent journalist who was arrested in July 2005 as he was about to take part in a demonstration in front of the French embassy, remained in detention without charge or trial.

Freedom of expression and association

Severe restrictions on freedom of expression and association persisted. All print and broadcast media remained under state control. There was a rise in the harassment and intimidation of independent journalists and librarians. People suspected of links with dissident groups or involved in promoting human rights were arrested and detained. There was an increase in arrests on charges of "pre-criminal dangerousness". Access to the Internet remained severely limited outside governmental offices and educational institutions. Journalist Guillermo Fariñas staged a seven-month hunger strike to obtain access to the Internet, without success.

⬚ Armando Betancourt Reina, a freelance journalist, was arrested on 23 May as he took notes and photographs of evictions from a house in the city of Camagüey. He was charged with public disorder. Armando Betancourt was reportedly held incommunicado for a week at the police station before being transferred to Cerámica Roja prison in Camagüey on 6 June. He was awaiting trial at the end of the year.

Harassment and intimidation of dissidents and activists

There was an increase in the public harassment and intimidation of human rights activists and political dissidents by quasi-official groups in so-called acts of repudiation.

⬚ Juan Carlos González Leiva, President of the Cuban Foundation for Human Rights, was reportedly the target of several "acts of repudiation" – involving government supporters reportedly acting with the collusion of the authorities – at his home in the city of Ciego de Avila. He and his family were repeatedly threatened by demonstrators. Juan Carlos González Leiva, who is blind, was arrested in March 2002 for "disrespect", "public disorder", "resistance" and "disobedience" and spent two years in prison without trial. In April 2004 he was sentenced to four years' imprisonment, to be served at his home.

AI country reports/ visits

Reports

- Cuba: Fundamental freedoms still under attack (AI Index: AMR 25/001/2006)
- Cuba: Fear for safety/Fear of torture/intimidation/ harassment – Miguel Valdés Tamayo and Juan Carlos González Leiva (AI Index: AMR 25/002/2006)

Visits

AI last visited Cuba in 1988 and has not been allowed into the country since.

CYPRUS

REPUBLIC OF CYPRUS
Head of state and government: Tassos Papadopoulos
Death penalty: abolitionist for all crimes
International Criminal Court: ratified

Police officers were caught on camera brutally beating two unarmed and handcuffed men. Migrants and asylum-seekers protested at poor detention conditions and lack of welfare provision. Turkish Cypriot students and their teacher were attacked in school by members of a nationalist youth organization. The government failed to implement national action plans to combat domestic violence and the trafficking of women for the purposes of sexual exploitation. The murders of two women by their partners in October and December spurred public discussion about violence against women. The authorities failed to conduct an independent, thorough and impartial investigation into the death of a 26-year-old recruit on national service.

Police ill-treatment

The new Independent Authority, established in April to investigate complaints against the police, assumed its duties by May. The Independent Authority lacked the necessary resources to thoroughly investigate all complaints received, including those about incidents that occurred before it became operational.

In April video footage was made public of police officers ill-treating Marcos Papageorgiou and Yiannos Nicolaou, both aged 27, in the early hours of 20 December 2005. The two men were reportedly dragged from their cars and handcuffed by plain-clothes officers after they refused to comply with search orders and asked to examine officers' identity cards. A search found no evidence of drug dealing. The two men were allegedly punched and kicked intermittently for about an hour by around five officers from special immediate response and traffic units while another eight officers from the same units and the regular police mocked the suspects. Subsequently charged at a police station with resisting arrest and assaulting the police, Marcos Papageorgiou was then admitted to hospital for treatment for cranial and arm fractures, and Yiannos Nicolaou, who also had a fractured arm, was detained overnight without treatment. Their trial was pending. By the end of December, 11 officers were awaiting trial on a number of charges, including torture.

Detention of foreign nationals

On 4 May detainees held in wing 10 of the Central Prison in Nicosia, which is especially reserved for failed asylum-seekers, protested about the duration of their detention — sometimes for over a year — for residing or working without authorization in the country. Some were sentenced to prison terms by the courts, but most were held in administrative detention. Following the prison protest, groups of asylum-seekers held demonstrations in Nicosia between 8 and 19 May. They said they were denied the right to work and access to health and social benefits while their asylum applications were being processed. According to media reports, of an estimated 12,000 asylum-seekers in Cyprus in May, only 300 had a right to work and only 350 received government support.

Official information was not available about the numbers of failed asylum-seekers in prison and migrants detained in police stations around the country, or the lengths of such detentions. No steps were known to have been taken to ensure that the rights of asylum-seekers were protected while their claims were being examined.

Migrants were unlawfully detained in Limassol.
A Sri Lankan national was detained for two and a half months, even though her sentence for working without proper authorization, imposed by a court in March, had been six weeks' imprisonment.
A Filipina national was arrested in April for working without authorization in a location other than the one her employer had stated on the permit. She had filed a complaint for breach of contract because she had been forced to work at the second location.

Violence against women

The government planned to set up a shelter for victims of trafficking and domestic violence, but within Nicosia central prison. Yet it failed to fulfil funding pledges to allow a local non-governmental organization, Apanemi, to continue operating a shelter for victims of domestic violence, the organization reported in November. Apanemi also criticized the authorities for not providing effective protection for victims of domestic violence or adequate access to justice for foreigners who had been raped, and for failing to produce national action plans on domestic violence or the trafficking of women.

Public debate on violence against women followed the murders of two women by their partners in October and December. Two other women were also murdered by their partners between August and October. According to statistics on domestic violence reported in the press in November in the context of this debate, 18 per cent of murders from 1980 to 2005 resulted from domestic violence, and nearly all of the victims were women.

In May the UN Committee on the Elimination of Discrimination against Women expressed concern at the lack of training for the judiciary on gender issues; the inadequacy of research and data on the extent and causes of violence against women; the persistence of trafficking and sexual exploitation of women; and discrimination against women migrants, especially regarding contracts, working conditions, and access to justice.

Racist violence

On 22 November about 20 students from different high schools in Nicosia, wearing hoods, caps and scarves over their faces, attacked a group of Turkish Cypriot students and their Turkish Cypriot teacher with wooden sticks during a class at the English School, a mixed secondary school. The attack was widely condemned, and by the next day the police had identified and questioned the perpetrators, all of whom were minors apart from an 18-year-old, who was charged. The youths claimed to represent the organization National Voice of Greek-Spirited Youths, which stated on 27 November that membership had been withdrawn from those that had been members. Police investigations were continuing at the end of 2006.

Dispute over army death

In October, an inquest opened into the death in September 2005 of Athanasios Nicolaou, a military service recruit aged 26. The police investigation had concluded that his death was suicide, a finding his family disputed. The family believed his death was related to bullying that he had experienced in his unit. The police investigation had not adhered to international standards of independence, thoroughness and impartiality, failing to examine crucial evidence properly. The inquest had not concluded by the end of 2006.

AI country reports/ visits
Reports
- Europe and Central Asia: Summary of Amnesty International's concerns in the region, January-June 2006 (AI Index: EUR 01/017/2006)
- Cyprus: Police brutality must not go unpunished (AI Index: EUR 17/001/2006)

CZECH REPUBLIC

CZECH REPUBLIC
Head of state: Václav Klaus
Head of government: Mirek Topolánek (replaced Jiří Paroubek in August)
Death penalty: abolitionist for all crimes
International Criminal Court: signed

The Romani minority faced severe discrimination in housing, education, health care and employment. Roma and other vulnerable groups were reportedly subjected to police ill-treatment and to racist attacks by private individuals. The European Court of Human Rights ruled that the use of anonymous witnesses breached the right to a fair trial.

Background
The Civic Democratic Party won inconclusive elections to the Chamber of Deputies in June. Mirek Topolánek was appointed to head a minority government. An offer to resign his post after a vote of no confidence in the Chamber in October was declined by President Klaus.

On 26 January, the Senate returned an anti-discrimination bill to the Chamber of Deputies. The Senate opposed the introduction of affirmative action to assist disadvantaged groups, and considered the bill too vague. The proposed law was intended to fulfil obligations following the Czech Republic's accession to the European Union in 2004. Approval of the bill was pending.

On 10 July, the Czech Republic ratified the Optional Protocol to the UN Convention against Torture.

Discrimination against Roma
Roma face discrimination in access to housing, education and employment, according to the final report on the human rights situation of the Roma, Sinti and Travellers in Europe by the Commissioner for Human Rights of the Council of Europe, published in February. The report found that Romani children were unjustifiably placed in special schools for children with mental disabilities, and recommended mechanisms to enable women who had been sterilized without informed consent to obtain compensation.

The number of Roma in low-standard housing has risen over the last 10 years, according to a report by the Ministry of Labour and Social Affairs in August. The study found no comprehensive government programme combating social deprivation.

▢ In October, the Chief of Police apologized for the misuse of police powers in the town of Bohumin on 4-6 October 2005. Private security guards hired by the municipality had prevented independent observers from entering a hostel where several hundred residents, many of them Roma, were being targeted for expulsion by the municipality.

Concerns that Romani children were being taught in segregated classes in primary schools and were over-represented in special schools were highlighted by the European Monitoring Centre on Racism and Xenophobia in a report on Roma and Travellers in public education in May. While recognizing improvements, such as the government's decision in January to collect anonymous data on the Roma community, the report pointed to the need for more active state policies.

▢ On 7 February the European Court of Human Rights rejected a complaint of discrimination in education brought by 18 Romani people from Ostrava who had been placed in special elementary schools for children with learning difficulties. The Court concluded that the Czech Republic had not breached the prohibition on discrimination and the right to education in the European Convention on Human Rights and the related Protocol. The Court said that it could assess only individual complaints, not their social context. An appeal against the ruling was pending before the Great Chamber of the Court.

Forced sterilization of women
In May the government criticized a recommendation in the last Ombudsman's report in 2005 that a law be introduced to provide compensation for women who were sterilized without their consent. The recommendation was not implemented.

The UN Committee on the Elimination of Discrimination against Women in August urged the government to implement the Ombudsman's recommendations. It called for a legal definition of informed, free and qualified consent; mandatory training of medical professionals and social workers on patients' rights; and measures to enable victims of involuntary or coercive sterilization to obtain compensation. The Committee commended the adoption of a national action plan to promote gender equality and new employment legislation prohibiting discrimination and sexual harassment, but urged stronger efforts to overcome persistent and discriminatory stereotypes of women.

The European Roma Rights Centre and two local human rights groups, the League of Human Rights and Life Together, in a report in August, concluded that legal protection against discrimination was insufficient and that women remained vulnerable to serious human rights abuses.

▢ An appeal lodged in December 2005 was still pending in the case of Helena Ferenčiková, who was sterilized in 2001. In November 2005, a court found that Vitkovice hospital had violated her personal rights but refused to award financial compensation on the grounds that the three-year statute of limitation had expired.

Police ill-treatment
Reports continued of police ill-treatment of vulnerable groups, particularly Roma. An independent body was still not available to investigate complaints of police abuses.

▢ A police officer severely beat Kateřina Jacques, a Green Party electoral candidate and senior government human rights official, at a demonstration against the far-right National Resistance Movement in Prague on 1 May. The officer allegedly threw her to the ground, kicked her, beat her with a truncheon and continued to assault her at the police station where she was taken for questioning in handcuffs. After an internal investigation, the Chief of Police acknowledged that the police action against Kateřina Jacques was inappropriate. The Prime Minister said the officer's intervention was "inexcusable" and he should leave the police. The officer was reportedly dismissed. Charges against him were withdrawn in November on the grounds that the arrest had followed police regulations. Kateřina Jacques lodged an appeal against the withdrawal of the charges.

On 30 June, two municipal policemen were alleged to have detained a young Romani man in Brno, driven him to the outskirts, beaten him, put an unloaded gun in his mouth and pulled the trigger. They reportedly suspected him of attacking and robbing the son of one of the officers and other schoolchildren. In November, they were convicted of beating and torturing the man, and given a suspended two-year prison sentence and banned from serving as police officers for five years. Both lodged appeals.

Racially motivated attacks on Roma
Roma were often the target of racially motivated attacks, and penalties handed down by the courts did not reflect the seriousness of the crimes or the racist motives of the assailants.

On 17 May, three young members of the National Resistance Movement broke into a block of flats in Neratovice, banging on the doors of Romani residents and threatening to kill them. Police detained the men on the spot.

On 31 August, three young men had their sentences for an attack on a Romani couple in Jeseník increased by the regional appeals court in Olomouc. Two were given prison terms of three years and three months and three years respectively, and the third received a suspended three-year prison sentence. A public outcry had greeted the original suspended sentences on all three, passed by the district court in Jeseník in January 2004.

A two-year suspended sentence on a soldier convicted of beating a Romani man, imposed by the Regional Court in Plzeň in September, was met with protests by five Romani organizations.

Fair trial rights denied
On 28 February the European Court of Human Rights found the Czech government had violated the right to fair trial by allowing witnesses to remain anonymous in breach of cross-examination requirements under the European Convention on Human Rights. In response to an appeal lodged on behalf of Hasan Krasniki on 2 September 1999, the Court found that, while the use of anonymous witnesses could be compatible with the Convention, in this case it was not. The reliability of anonymous witnesses should be tested and the conviction should not rely exclusively or determinedly on anonymous statements. Czech law has since been amended.

Same sex partnership
In March a law was passed that allowed same-sex couples to register their partnership after the Chamber of Deputies overrode a veto by President Klaus. The law accorded some of the same rights and obligations as married couples have, including the rights to raise children, to inherit property and to information on the health of the partner, and the mutual obligation to pay maintenance. It did not provide the right to adopt children.

AI country reports/visits
Report
- Europe and Central Asia: Summary of Amnesty International's concerns in the region, January-June 2006 (AI Index: EUR 01/017/2006)
Visits
AI representatives visited the Czech Republic in March and September.

DEMOCRATIC REPUBLIC OF THE CONGO

DEMOCRATIC REPUBLIC OF THE CONGO
Head of state and government: Joseph Kabila
Death penalty: retentionist
International Criminal Court: ratified

The Democratic Republic of the Congo (DRC) remained unstable, and several regions of the country suffered widespread insecurity and ethnic tensions. Sporadic conflict continued in most eastern provinces. Extrajudicial executions and other unlawful killings, arbitrary arrests, unlawful detentions, acts of torture or ill-treatment, and life-threatening prison conditions continued on a daily basis. Decades of neglect, poor governance and mismanagement of resources, compounded in the east by war, left essential services and infrastructure, including the justice, health and education sectors, in a state of near-collapse.

Background
Presidential and legislative elections held in July and October offered some hope that the fragile peace might be strengthened, but several armed factions remained suspicious of or openly hostile to the peace process.

The election period was marked by numerous human rights violations including enforced disappearances, arbitrary arrests, ethnic violence, excessive use of force by the security forces to break up political protests, and restrictions on freedom of expression and assembly. The announcement of the results of the first round of presidential elections on 20 August triggered street battles in the capital, Kinshasa, between soldiers loyal to transitional President Joseph Kabila and supporters of Vice-President Jean-Pierre Bemba, in which 23 people were killed.

More than 1.6 million people were internally displaced, while 410,000 were living as refugees in neighbouring countries. The volatile security situation continued to limit humanitarian access to many areas of eastern DRC. Security in the east and in Kinshasa remained dependent to a large extent on the overstretched UN peacekeeping force, MONUC, which comprised around 17,000 personnel at the year's end. MONUC was reinforced by a European Union military rapid reaction force (EUFor) which was deployed in Kinshasa for the period of the elections and was withdrawn by the end of the year.

Despite a UN arms embargo, small arms continued to proliferate. The government was itself accused of a major violation of the embargo in July, for failing to notify the UN of the import of a shipment of tanks, armoured personnel carriers and quantities of ammunition through the port of Matadi.

Security sector reform

One of the transitional government's major priorities was to dismantle the myriad armed forces in the country. This process, which began in 2004, involved disarming all former government soldiers and armed group fighters and offering them demobilization or enrolment into the unified national army, the Armed Forces of the Democratic Republic of the Congo (Forces Armées de la République Démocratique du Congo, FARDC). However, both the army integration process and the national disarmament, demobilization and reintegration (DDR) programmes suffered delays, serious logistical, technical and management difficulties, and a lack of full political support. As a result, the programmes were still only partly complete by the end of the year. Other areas of security sector reform, including the integration of the national police force, remained behind schedule and largely unimplemented.

The army integration programme had serious shortcomings, failing to tackle parallel chains of command and to exclude alleged perpetrators of grave human rights abuses from FARDC ranks. It did not include training for all FARDC soldiers in international humanitarian and human rights law. The devastation of the socio-economic and humanitarian environment posed a huge challenge to efforts to reintegrate former fighters into civilian life. Many former combatants remained without promised government financial support or community-based employment projects for long periods after demobilization. Disgruntled former fighters were a threat to security in many areas of the country.

Unlawful killings

FARDC forces were responsible for the majority of violations of human rights and international humanitarian law reported during 2006, including unlawful killings, rapes, acts of torture, enforced disappearances, illegal detentions and looting. FARDC units failed to protect civilians from attack by armed groups. Poor living conditions for troops and inadequate payment of salaries contributed to FARDC ill-discipline.

Congolese armed groups opposed to the peace process and to integration in the FARDC were also responsible for numerous grave human rights abuses in the provinces of North- and South-Kivu, Katanga and Orientale (Ituri). The human rights abuses, some of which appeared to be ethnically motivated, included rapes, unlawful killings and torture. Some appeared to be war crimes. Foreign armed groups, including the Democratic Forces for the Liberation of Rwanda (Forces Démocratiques de Libération du Rwanda, FDLR), and other Burundian and Ugandan armed groups also continued to be active on Congolese territory and to commit serious abuses.

In January, soldiers of an FARDC integrated brigade shot dead seven people, including two infants, at a church in the village of Nyata in the district of Ituri.

In January, forces of Laurent Nkunda's armed group, opposed to the government and composed mainly of Kinyarwanda-speaking fighters, launched attacks against government forces and civilian centres in North-Kivu province. They allegedly committed numerous unlawful killings and raped scores of women from non- Kinyarwanda-speaking communities.

In August, FDLR forces ambushed, killed and robbed four civilians in Kahuzi-Biega, South-Kivu. A number of abductions of women and girls by FDLR combatants were also reported.

Child soldiers

Several thousand children were either still associated with armed forces or armed groups or had not entered the DDR programme and were not accounted for. In areas of eastern DRC where insecurity persisted, children continued to be recruited, including some who had only recently been demobilized. Some children were forcibly recruited and others were forced to rejoin armed groups because the government had not provided them with meaningful support once returned to their communities. The majority of children released and reunited with their communities were poorly supported and protected on their return to civilian life, and were not given adequate educational or vocational opportunities. There was no mechanism to ensure their protection once returned to their communities and many children remained at risk of being recruited again.

In June, six former child soldiers who were being reunified with their families by an international non-governmental organization were abducted in Kabalekasha, North-Kivu, by heavily armed fighters. They were taken to a military camp where they were held in a pit in the ground. A pregnant woman accompanying the children was beaten. They were later released, but three of the children were subsequently targeted once more by fighters and badly beaten.

Violence against women and girls

Rape of women and girls by government security forces or armed groups remained widespread in all areas of the DRC. Few women had access to adequate medical treatment for consequent injuries or illnesses. Women and girls who had been raped also suffered widespread social discrimination and rejection by their families and communities.

Thousands of girl child soldiers who should have entered the national DDR programme were not accounted for. Many had been forcibly recruited and used as sex slaves by adult fighters. Many commanders and fighters resisted releasing the girls, considering them as their sexual possessions. Other girls, fearing further discrimination and social exclusion, avoided entry into the DDR programme. There was no systematic government effort to trace these missing girls or to offer them appropriate demobilization and reintegration support.

◻ In August, agents of the Congolese National Police (Police Nationale Congolaise, PNC), reportedly raped 37 women and girls from the village of Bolongo-Loka, Equateur province, and subjected other villagers to acts of ill-treatment and torture. The military authorities later arrested nine individuals, including seven PNC agents. They had not been brought to trial by the year's end.

Torture and ill-treatment

Acts of torture and ill-treatment, committed by government security services and armed groups, were routinely reported across the country. Arbitrary arrests, illegal detention, including incommunicado and secret detention (sometimes amounting to enforced disappearance) and prolonged detention without trial remained commonplace. Extremely harsh conditions were reported in most detention centres and prisons, in many cases amounting to cruel, inhuman or degrading treatment.

◻ In August, 84 people, mainly fishermen but including women and children, from N'galiema commune in Kinshasa were detained by members of the Republican Guard , a military force under the command of President Joseph Kabila. They were accused of being "rebels" loyal to Joseph Kabila's electoral rival, Jean-Pierre Bemba. They were forced to strip naked and subjected to sustained beatings. A number of them were reportedly tortured in other ways. They were then placed in a confined cell and held for 48 hours without food. They were later released without charge.

Attacks on human rights defenders

Human rights defenders continued to receive anonymous death threats and were routinely harassed by the authorities.

◻ In April, Hubert Tshiswaka, director of Action against Impunity for Human Rights (Action contre l'impunité pour les droits humains, ACIDH) in Lubumbashi, Katanga province, was threatened with death. The perpetrators were reportedly representatives of the Union of Congolese Nationalists and Federalists (Union nationale des fédéralistes du Congo, UNAFEC) a political party led by the then Minister of Justice. The threats followed ACIDH public statements urging voters to elect politicians based on their human rights record and calling for the dissolution of violent youth wings of political parties.

Impunity

Some perpetrators of human rights abuses were brought to justice. However, impunity persisted in the majority of cases and the government awarded certain armed group leaders command positions in the FARDC, despite well-founded allegations against them of serious human rights abuses. These included Peter Karim and Mathieu Ngodjolo, commanders of two Ituri armed groups who were appointed as colonels in the FARDC in October. Their forces were granted so-called amnesties.

Rehabilitation and reform of the DRC's civilian judicial system, enabling it to investigate past and present human rights abuses in a competent, independent and impartial manner, remained very slow.

◻ In April, seven FARDC soldiers were sentenced to life imprisonment on charges of crimes against humanity, including the rape of 119 women in Equateur province in December 2003.

◻ In August Yves Panga Mandro Kahwa, leader of an armed group in Ituri, was sentenced to 20 years' imprisonment for crimes against humanity.

Another armed group leader, Kyungu Mutanga, known as Gédéon, leader of a mayi-mayi armed group in northern Katanga province, surrendered to the authorities in May after committing atrocities, including unlawful killings, rape and torture, in the region. By the end of the year he had not been charged or tried.

Unfair trials and death sentences

Unfair trials continued to take place and death sentences continued to be passed, the vast majority by military tribunals. No state executions were reported, although at least one summary execution by the military was recorded.

◻ In June, after an unfair and summary trial, a military tribunal in Kinshasa imposed long prison sentences on evangelical church leader Pasteur Fernando Kutino, his colleague, Pasteur Timothée Bompere Mboo, and a third man, Junior Nganda. The arrests and trials appeared to be politically motivated.

International justice

In March, Thomas Lubanga Dyilo, leader of an Ituri armed group, the Union of Congolese Patriots (Union des Patriotes Congolais, UPC), was arrested and transferred to the International Criminal Court (ICC) in The Hague. Thomas Lubanga was formally charged in August with committing war crimes, namely the recruitment and use in hostilities of children aged under 15. Pre-trial hearings to confirm the charges against him began on 8 November. Thomas Lubanga was the first person to be arrested by the ICC.

AI country reports/ visits
Reports
- Democratic Republic of the Congo (DRC): Kinshasa must meet its responsibility to protect civilians (AI Index: AFR 62/003/2006)
- Open letter to DRC parliamentarians on legislation implementing the Rome Statute (AI Index: AFR 62/004/2006)
- Democratic Republic of the Congo: Time to end threats against human rights defenders (AI Index: AFR 62/006/2006)
- Democratic Republic of the Congo: International Criminal Court's first arrest must be followed by others throughout the country (AI Index: AFR 62/008/2006)
- Democratic Republic of the Congo: Acts of political repression on the increase (AI Index: AFR 62/014/2006)
- Democratic Republic of the Congo: Elections are a chance to embrace human rights reform (AI Index: AFR 62/015/2006)
- Democratic Republic of the Congo: Children at war – creating hope for their future (AI Index: AFR 62/017/2006)

Visits
In February and March, AI delegates visited various provinces in eastern DRC and Kinshasa.

DENMARK

KINGDOM OF DENMARK
Head of state: Queen Margrethe II
Head of government: Anders Fogh Rasmussen
Death penalty: abolitionist for all crimes
International Criminal Court: ratified

Concern mounted over worsening intolerance and xenophobia against refugees, asylum-seekers, minorities in general and Muslims in particular. The scope and breadth of new legislation with the stated aim of countering terrorism gave rise to concern about its impact on fundamental human rights.

Discrimination
In its report on Denmark, published in May, the European Commission against Racism and Intolerance (ECRI) expressed deep concern at worsening intolerance and xenophobia against refugees, asylum-seekers, minorities in general and Muslims in particular. ECRI noted with concern legislative provisions disproportionately restricting the ability of members of ethnic minorities to acquire Danish citizenship, to benefit from family reunification, and to access social protection. ECRI also highlighted an atmosphere of impunity, created by the low rate of prosecutions for incitement to racial hatred despite, among other things, inflammatory statements by some politicians and the media.

In October the UN Committee on the Elimination of Racial Discrimination expressed a number of concerns after a periodic review of Denmark. These included the refusal of the Public Prosecutor to instigate proceedings in some cases, despite an increasing number of racially motivated offences and hate speech complaints, including in connection with the publication of cartoons that many Muslims found profoundly insulting. It also raised concern about the fact that asylum-seekers could not lodge appeals in the courts against decisions by the Refugee Board and that asylum-seekers and their children were sometimes housed for several years in asylum centres. It also highlighted asylum-seekers' limited involvement in social, professional, educational and cultural activities outside the centres and the reduction of social benefits for those newly arrived in Denmark, a policy which reportedly created marginalization and poverty.

Violence against women
In August, reviewing Denmark's sixth periodic report, the Committee on the Elimination of Discrimination against Women expressed concern about the extent of violence against women and girls; trafficking of women and girls; and the length of the "reflection period" which meant that after 30 days trafficked women would ordinarily be deported to their country of origin. The Committee also highlighted the vulnerability of foreign married women who had been granted temporary residence permits on the grounds of marriage and who risked expulsion if they left the marital home because of violence by their husbands.

In December, the government announced an extension of the "reflection period" to 100 days.

Terrorism legislation
In June new legislation with the stated aim of countering terrorism came into force. The scope and breadth of these provisions gave rise to concern that previously legitimate political activities may be deemed unlawful. Judicial oversight of police access to private and confidential information was weakened.

Solitary confinement
In December legislation further reducing the time limits for solitary confinement of prisoners was adopted. However, it failed to introduce, even for under-18s, a mandatory maximum duration in cases concerning homicide, drug-related crime or security offences. There were reductions in the use of solitary confinement against under-18s for other offences.

Freedom of expression
In December, three investigative journalists were acquitted of all charges in connection with the publication of classified information about Iraq and the

extent of the government's knowledge, in the run-up to the Iraq war, about the existence of weapons of mass destruction in Iraq. The prosecuting authorities stated that they did not intend to appeal against the acquittals.

Policing

There were reports that police used excessive force in dealing with three separate demonstrations against evictions in Copenhagen.

In September, the mother of 21-year-old Jens Arne Ørskov filed a civil action against the police and the Ministry of Justice in connection with her son's death in police custody in June 2002. The regional state prosecutor concluded he died from the combined effects of intense physical activity with an intake of alcohol and cannabis. However, Danish as well as international medical experts disputed the official cause of death, stating instead that he died from asphyxiation after being forced to lie on his stomach and having pressure applied to his back while handcuffed. Nonetheless, the prosecuting authorities decided not to press charges or take disciplinary action against the police officers involved. The case was scheduled to be heard in October 2007.

AI country reports/ visits
Report
• Denmark: Jens Arne Ørskov's death in custody – A mother's quest for justice (AI Index: EUR 18/001/2006)

DOMINICAN REPUBLIC

DOMINICAN REPUBLIC
Head of state and government: Leonel Fernández Reyna
Death penalty: abolitionist for all crimes
International Criminal Court: ratified

There were further mass expulsions of Haitians and Dominico-Haitians (Dominican of Haitian descent), some of whom were reportedly ill-treated. There were reports of unlawful killings by the security forces. Domestic violence remained a serious concern.

Discrimination against Haitians and Dominico-Haitians
Expulsions
There were continued mass illegal expulsions of Haitian migrant workers and Dominico-Haitians, many of whom were rounded up by officials simply because they were black. There were reports of ill-treatment by migration officials and security forces.

▭ Eight-year-old Francisca José was among five children rounded up by migration officers on 4 January in the capital Santo Domingo. She was allegedly hit twice, causing her to bleed from the mouth. She was held overnight at a detention centre until a local human rights organization managed to secure her release by proving her Dominican nationality.

▭ Scores of people were injured in September when an overcrowded bus from the Dominican Department of Migration carrying 120 alleged irregular Haitian immigrants crashed into a river in Elías Piñas province en route to the border. Some of those being deported reportedly had valid documentation permitting them to work in the country. Many of the injured reportedly did not receive medical attention before being expelled to Haiti.

Access to nationality
The Dominican authorities failed to comply with the September 2005 ruling from the Inter-American Court of Human Rights in the case of two Dominico-Haitian girls who had been denied Dominican nationality. The Court had called for the girls to receive compensation and for the Dominican authorities to implement the necessary measures to grant nationality to the thousands of other Dominicans and their children who had been denied it.

Assaults
There were reports of violent indiscriminate attacks against Haitians. Human rights organizations claimed that killings of Haitians were not investigated by the authorities.

▭ Two Haitian nationals, Edison Odio and Jako Medina, were reportedly set alight by a mob on 7 March in the community of Yabonico in Las Matas de Farfán in apparent revenge for the murder of the local mayor. Jako Medina subsequently died of his injuries. AI was unaware of any proceedings initiated by the authorities to bring those responsible to justice.

People smuggling
The bodies of 24 Haitians were found on 11 January near the border town of Dabajón in the north of the country. They had apparently suffocated to death as they were being illegally transported in a truck to find work in the Dominican Republic. The bodies were reportedly thrown from the back of the truck which contained more than 60 people. Four Dominican nationals, including two members of the military, were on trial at the end of 2006 in relation to the incident.

Unlawful killings by security forces
According to official figures 204 people were killed in shoot-outs with police between January and August, down from 345 for the same period in 2005. However, concerns remained that a number of these fatal shootings may have been unlawful. Fifty-seven members of the security forces were killed during the same period.

Twenty-two-year-old Elvin Amable Rodríguez, a spokesman for the left-wing organization Broad Popular Front for Struggle (Frente Amplio de Lucha Popular) was fatally shot in the head twice by police on 26 September in the town of Navarrete. Police claimed he died in a shoot-out. Two officers were in pre-trial detention at the end of the year.

On 9 July members of the Dominican armed forces reportedly opened fire on a group of Haitian nationals as they tried to cross the border near the town of Dajabón. One of the group was allegedly shot in the back and subsequently died in hospital.

Violence against women
According to government statistics, in the first six months of the year 43 women were killed by their partners or former partners. In April alone 1,800 incidents of domestic violence were reported to the authorities.

Right to health
Despite receiving sufficient international funding, nearly 70 per cent of all people requiring antiretroviral treatment in the Dominican Republic did not receive it. Those most at risk were the poor and marginalized, including the Haitian migrant population and Dominico-Haitians, who faced significant obstacles in gaining access to treatment and care. There were reports of employees being tested for HIV without their consent or as a condition of their employment.

Human rights defenders
Human rights defenders continued to be intimidated and harassed.

Teolé Yeolé García, a Dominico-Haitian rights activist, was illegally deported from Santo Domingo to Haiti on 2 February. He was detained while trying to intervene on behalf of fellow Dominicans who were being illegally rounded up to be deported.

Adonis Polanco, an HIV/AIDS activist, received anonymous death threats, apparently because of his outspoken criticism of the government's failure to provide adequate treatment for people living with HIV/AIDS in his local community in the town of Boca Chica.

AI country reports/ visits
Reports
- Dominican Republic: Open letter from Amnesty International to the President of the Dominican Republic regarding the rights of Haitian migrant workers and their descendants (AI Index: AMR 27/001/2006)
- "I am not ashamed!": HIV/AIDS and human rights in the Dominican Republic and Guyana (AI Index: AMR 01/002/2006)
Visits
AI delegates visited the Dominican Republic in January and June.

ECUADOR

REPUBLIC OF ECUADOR
Head of state and government: Alfredo Palacio
Death penalty: abolitionist for all crimes
International Criminal Court: ratified

Social unrest continued. There were reports that the security forces used excessive force against demonstrators. Infant and maternal mortality rates remained high and domestic violence continued to be a concern. There were reports of torture and ill-treatment and prison conditions remained harsh. Nearly 100 killings were reported on the Colombian border.

Background
Rafael Correa was elected President in November on a platform of constitutional, economic and social reform. He was due to take office in January 2007.

Former President Lucio Gutiérrez was acquitted of charges including corruption and undermining the security of the state and released.

Three magistrates of the new Supreme Court, appointed during the interim government of Alfredo Palacio, were dismissed in November following allegations of corruption.

Protests
Social unrest and protests against economic policies and the impact of extractive companies on the livelihood of communities continued throughout the year. Scores of demonstrators were reportedly injured and there were allegations of excessive use of force by the police and military.

During 2006 several provinces were placed under a state of emergency for periods of at least 60 days in response to the unrest. Under emergency legislation, freedoms of expression, movement and association were suspended and the security forces were empowered to search homes without judicial warrants.

Human rights defenders
Human rights defenders, community leaders and environmentalists who criticized government policies and the impact of extractive companies continued to be threatened and intimidated. Some faced unsubstantiated charges against them.

The legal team representing Indigenous communities suing a multinational oil company for failing to clean up the pollution caused by drilling in Sucumbíos province from 1964 to 1992, was repeatedly threatened. No investigation was opened and no victim received protection, despite precautionary measures ordered by the Inter-American Commission on Human Rights.

Right to health
Infant and maternal mortality remained high. Poor women and children continued to be denied access to

maternity and infant health services free of charge, as guaranteed under 1994 legislation. The government reportedly failed to ensure that clear and accessible information reached poor women.

Women's human rights

Domestic violence remained a concern. The number of complaints filed in the 30 women and family police stations reportedly increased in 2006. According to the Women's Defence Office, this was partly due to the promotion of the 1995 Law Against Violence Against Women And The Family, and improved training for law enforcement officials in responding to violence against women.

Torture and ill-treatment

In February the UN Working Group on Arbitrary Detention expressed concern that ill-treatment and torture to extract confessions or punish suspects were common in police stations.

Police and military officers charged with human rights violations continued to be tried by police or military courts which were neither independent nor impartial. In the vast majority of cases, those responsible for violations were not held to account. ⬦ At the end of the year, 20 police officers sentenced to prison terms ranging from two to 16 years for the enforced disappearance of Elías López Pita in 2000 remained at liberty.

Prison conditions

From April to June emergency legislation was imposed in the overcrowded prison system following security problems inside prisons and a strike by prison personnel demanding improved funding. The government announced an investment of US$8million in infrastructure to improve prison conditions.

In September the Constitutional Court confirmed its 2003 ruling that an article of the Code of Penal Procedure which denied suspects detained while awaiting sentencing the right to be conditionally released was unconstitutional. Reportedly between 5,000 and 7,000 inmates out of a total prison population of 14,000 were waiting to be sentenced.

Rights of ethnic minorities

The UN Special Rapporteur on the situation of human rights and fundamental freedoms of Indigenous people expressed concern at the limited access of Indigenous peoples to health and education, and the negative impact of extractive activities on their environment and living conditions. The Special Rapporteur raised concerns at the failure to fulfil constitutional guarantees to Indigenous peoples to be consulted on extractive projects in their territories. There were allegations of human rights violations involving armed forces personnel employed to guarantee the security of extractive companies.

Killings on the Colombia border

Reports of incursions by Colombian military and armed groups in Ecuadorian territory continued. Since the implementation in 2000 of the US-backed military aid package known as Plan Colombia, human rights organizations have documented over 700 killings, nearly 100 of them in 2006, in Sucumbíos province. In many cases the victims including civilian men, women and children were alleged to be criminal suspects; some showed signs of torture. According to witnesses, police and military officers were implicated in some of the killings. The vast majority of cases were not reported by the relatives of the victims or investigated by the authorities for fear of reprisals. There were reports of threats against witnesses, prosecutors, police officers, governors and other local officials.

AI country reports/visits
Visit
An AI delegation visited Ecuador in October.

EGYPT

ARAB REPUBLIC OF EGYPT
Head of state: Muhammad Hosni Mubarak
Head of government: Ahmed Nazif
Death penalty: retentionist
International Criminal Court: signed

At least 18 people were killed and more than 100 injured in bomb attacks in Dahab (southern Sinai) in April. Peaceful protesters calling for independence for the judiciary and political reform were violently dispersed by police. Hundreds of members of the banned Muslim Brothers organization were arrested and scores were held awaiting trial at the end of the year. Thousands of suspected supporters of banned Islamist groups, including possible prisoners of conscience, remained in detention under emergency legislation without charge or trial; some had been held for more than a decade. Torture and ill-treatment in detention continued to be systematic. In the majority of torture cases, the perpetrators were not brought to justice. At least three people were sentenced to death; four others were executed.

Background

Despite calls for the state of emergency to be lifted, it was renewed in April for two years. The state of emergency, in force continuously since 1981, facilitated human rights violations including prolonged detention without charge, torture and ill-treatment, undue restrictions on freedom of speech, association and assembly, and unfair trials before military courts and (Emergency) Supreme State Security Courts. The government set up a committee in

March to prepare a new anti-terrorism law to replace the emergency legislation.

In February parliament voted to delay for two years local elections scheduled for April. The government said the delay would allow time for the drafting of a new law to strengthen the powers of local council administration, but critics said it would make it more difficult for potential independent candidates for the presidency to meet new conditions of registration introduced in 2005.

In May, the Court of Cassation confirmed the five-year prison sentence imposed on Ayman Nour, leader of the al-Ghad party, who had come a distant second in presidential elections in September 2005. There were concerns that his prosecution and trial were politically motivated.

There were sporadic outbreaks of sectarian violence between Muslims and Christians. In April, three days of religious violence in Alexandria resulted in at least three deaths and dozens of injuries.

Egypt and the European Union failed to agree on implementation of an association agreement that came into force in 2004 in the context of the European Neighbourhood Policy. Negotiations reportedly foundered mainly on differences over human rights in Egypt and over what the agreement should say with regard to nuclear weapons in the Middle East.

In December, the Supreme Administrative Court overturned an earlier decision by an Administrative Court in April 2006 which recognized the right of Egypt's Baha'is to be certified as Baha'is on official documentation. This followed an appeal by the Ministry of Interior. The decision of the Supreme Administrative Court meant that Baha'is must register themselves as Muslims, Christians or Jews if they wish to obtain official documents such as birth and death certificates and identity cards.

Violations in the 'war on terror'

Despite increasing evidence to the contrary, the authorities continued to deny their involvement in the torture and secret detention of people detained as part of the "war on terror", despite the Prime Minister's acknowledgement in 2005 that some 60 suspects had been returned to Egypt from US custody. The UN Special Rapporteur on promotion and protection of human rights while countering terrorism sought to visit the country to assess Egypt's human rights record in the "war on terror", but did not obtain a positive response from the Egyptian authorities.

Following the bomb blasts in Dahab, the security forces killed at least 13 alleged suspects between April and August. A police officer was also reportedly killed and two others wounded during clashes in northern Sinai. Hundreds of people were arrested, accused of having links with what the security forces claimed was a new terrorist group called Unity and Holy War (Tawhid wal Jihad). Scores more were arrested in the north of Cairo in September for alleged links with al-Qa'ida. Some of those cleared of terrorism-related charges by the courts continued to be held under administrative detention orders.

◻ In April, Osama Mostafa Hassan Nasr (known as Abu Omar) was brought before the public prosecutor. This was the first time since his abduction from Italy in February 2003 that he was allowed to have a lawyer present during interrogation. He described his abduction in Italy and unlawful return to Egypt. He said he was tortured while held in secret detention in Egypt and that methods included alternating extremes of temperature and electric shocks to the genitals. There was no indication that the allegations were the subject of any investigation by the Egyptian authorities. In November, the Italian prosecutor investigating Abu Omar's abduction received an 11-page undated handwritten letter from Abu Omar which had been smuggled out of Istiqbal Tora Prison. This gave details of his torture and described the inhumane conditions to which he remained exposed in detention. In 2005 the Italian authorities had issued warrants for the arrest of 22 agents of the US Central Intelligence Agency in connection with the abduction.

◻ The trial of 13 suspects in connection with bombings in Taba and Nuweiba in October 2004 continued before the (Emergency) Supreme State Security Court. Allegations by the accused that their confessions had been extracted under torture were dismissed by the court, which sentenced Muhammed Gayiz Sabbah, Usama 'Abd al-Ghani al-Nakhlawi and Yunis Muhammed Abu Gareer to death. Two other defendants were sentenced to life imprisonment and eight others received prison sentences ranging from five to 15 years.

Administrative detention

Emergency legislation allowing for indefinite detention without charge continued to be used. Some detainees had been held for more than a decade, despite orders for their release by the courts. The non-governmental Egyptian Organization for Human Rights estimated that as many as 20,000 people remained in detention without charge or trial, with many held in appalling conditions. The Ministry of Interior denied this and said there were no more than 4,000 detainees, but did not provide further details. Many detainees were reported to be ill due to poor food and hygiene, severe overcrowding and a lack of adequate medical care.

In August, non-governmental organizations (NGOs) and human rights activists created the Egyptian Network for the Defence of Detainees to train lawyers on issues of administrative detention in Egypt and to mobilize civil society on this issue.

◻ In June the trial opened of 14 people charged in connection with the Cairo bombings of April and May 2005. However, hundreds of people arrested following the bombings reportedly remained in administrative detention, despite having obtained release orders from the courts. Most were believed to be neighbours or acquaintances of those standing trial or to have used the same mosques for prayer. In August 2006, scores of them went on hunger strike in protest at their continued detention. Some women relatives of detainees were summoned to the State Security Intelligence office in Shubra al-Kheima, north of Cairo, and detained for two days, during which they were insulted and threatened with electric shocks.

Torture and ill-treatment

Torture of both political detainees and criminal suspects remained common and systematic, and reportedly led to several deaths in custody. Frequently reported methods included beatings, electric shocks, prolonged suspension by the wrists and ankles in contorted positions, death threats and sexual abuse.

⊡ Pro-reform activists Mohammed al-Sharqawi and Karim al-Sha'ir were arrested following demonstrations in April and May and released on 22 May. Both men were rearrested following a demonstration on 25 May. They were beaten in the street and taken to Qasr Nil police station where they were tortured. Mohammed al-Sharqawi was reportedly sexually abused by those who detained him. Both men were released in July.

There were persistent reports of criminal suspects being tortured during interrogation at police stations.

⊡ Emad al-Kabir, a 21-year-old taxi driver from Bulaq Dakrur in Giza Governorate, was arrested in January after intervening to stop an argument between police officers and his cousin. While in detention at Bulaq Dakrur Police Station, he was slapped and hit with a stick on his hands and legs. He was accused of "resisting the authorities" and presented before the Public Prosecutor, who ordered his release on bail. However, he was instead returned to the police station, held overnight and tortured, including being raped with a stick. One of the police officers filmed the rape using a mobile phone camera and threatened Emad al-Kabir that this would be circulated by video in his neighbourhood to cause him public humiliation and intimidate others. In November, the video, which had reportedly circulated widely in the Bulaq Dakrur neighbourhood and among taxi drivers, was posted on the Internet. It provoked strong protests from human rights organizations and was widely publicized in the media, leading the Public Prosecutor in December to order the arrest of two police officers who were then referred to the South Cairo Criminal Court for trial.

Emad al-Kabir's case, however, was exceptional. Although several police officers were tried during the year for torturing other prisoners, torture allegations were rarely investigated and prosecutions of alleged perpetrators were the exception.

Threat to judicial independence

In June a new law regulating the judiciary was passed by parliament. Despite some positive provisions, such as restrictions on ministerial powers, pro-reform judges as well as opposition parliamentarians allied to the Muslim Brothers criticized the law for failing to guarantee the independence of the judiciary. In July the UN Special Rapporteur on the independence of judges and lawyers expressed concern about the new law, noting the lack of clear criteria for the selection and appointment of judges, and the absence of basic fair trial guarantees in the disciplinary procedures for judges.

Two senior judges, Mahmoud Mekki and Hisham Bastawisi, Vice-Presidents of the Court of Cassation, were made to face a disciplinary board that convened at the High Court Building in Cairo in May after they called publicly for an inquiry into alleged electoral fraud during the 2005 parliamentary elections. The case, which resulted in Mahmoud Mekki being cleared and an official reprimand for Hisham Bastawisi, provoked widespread concern and public protests and demonstrations by opposition political parties, pro-reform groups and trade unionists in support of the two judges. These protests were violently dispersed by the riot police and more than 500 demonstrators, mostly Muslim Brothers, were arrested. They included Essam al-Aryan, Mohammed Morsy and Maged Hassan, all prominent members of the Muslim Brothers. Most were released after a short time.

Freedom of expression, association and assembly

The rights to freedom of expression, association and assembly continued to be restricted. Some NGOs faced obstacles registering and obtaining legal status. Journalists continued to be threatened, harassed and imprisoned because of their work.

⊡ Tal'at Sadat, nephew of the assassinated former President Mohamed Anwar Sadat, was sentenced to one year's imprisonment with labour and a fine in October for defaming the armed forces and spreading false rumours. He had given a series of media interviews in which he alleged that senior army officers had been implicated in the killing of the former president by Islamist soldiers in 1981. He also suggested that President Hosni Mubarak – then Vice-President – had been involved. Although a civilian, he was tried and convicted by a military court, after being stripped of his parliamentary immunity.

In July, a controversial press law was passed by parliament according to which press freedom continued to be restricted. Certain publishing offences, such as insulting public officials, continued to carry custodial sentences. Independent and opposition newspapers withheld publication for a day in protest at the new law and hundreds of media workers protested outside the National Assembly.

⊡ Ibrahim Eissa, chief editor of the opposition newspaper *al-Dostour*, Sahar Zaki, a journalist on the newspaper, and Saied Mohamed Abdullah were sentenced in June to one year's imprisonment and a fine for insulting the President and spreading false rumours. The charges related to articles in April reporting a lawsuit by Saied Mohamed Abdullah against the President and senior officials in the ruling National Democratic Party. The case was still before the Court of Appeal at the end of the year.

Death penalty

Death sentences continued to be imposed. Three people convicted of terrorism-related offences were sentenced to death after an unfair trial. At least four other people were executed.

⊡ Brothers Ezzat and Hamdi Ali Hanafi were executed in June. They had been sentenced to death by the

(Emergency) Supreme State Security Court in September 2005 for armed resistance to a raid by the security forces searching for unspecified drugs. The Court's procedures violated basic principles for fair trial, including the right to appeal before a higher tribunal.

Refugees and migrants

On 3 January the authorities announced that they would forcibly return up to 650 detained Sudanese nationals to Sudan. The detainees, who included refugees, asylum-seekers and migrants, had been arrested after police violently broke up a peaceful demonstration outside the UNHCR office in Cairo on 30 December 2005, killing at least 27 Sudanese nationals and injuring dozens of others. The authorities subsequently released the detainees and said they would not return them to Sudan. However, they did not initiate any investigation into the killings.

In August, Egypt submitted its report for consideration by the Committee on the Rights of All Migrant Workers and Members of Their Families. This report was due in 2004.

AI country reports/ visits
Reports

- Egypt: Fear of forcible return/fear of torture and ill-treatment – Up to 650 Sudanese nationals (AI Index: MDE 12/001/2006)
- Egypt: Amnesty International calls for inquiry into killings and opposes threatened collective expulsions of Sudanese protesters (AI Index: MDE 12/002/2006)
- Egypt: Amnesty International condemns attack against civilians in Dahab (AI Index: MDE 12/006/2006)
- Egypt: Disciplinary action against judges a challenge to judicial independence (AI Index: MDE 12/007/2006)
- Egypt: Amnesty International concerned about the Egyptian security repression against peaceful protesters in Cairo (AI Index: MDE 12/009/2006)
- Egypt: Violent attacks and arrests of peaceful protesters must stop (AI Index: MDE 12/010/2006)
- Egypt: Abusive emergency powers should not be entrenched in new anti-terrorism law (AI Index: MDE 12/014/2006)

Visits
AI delegates visited Cairo in July and December to attend conferences and in September an AI delegation, headed by the Secretary-General, had meetings in Cairo with the Secretary-General of the League of Arab States and with the Minister of Interior and other Egyptian government officials.

EL SALVADOR

REPUBLIC OF EL SALVADOR
Head of state and government: Elías Antonio Saca
Death penalty: abolitionist for ordinary crimes
International Criminal Court: not ratified

Impunity for past human rights violations, including enforced disappearances, persisted. Reports of violence against women continued, but investigations remained inadequate. There were threats against human rights defenders and political activists.

Background
The public security situation continued to cause concern. Various government initiatives to tackle criminal violence did not bring improvements in the security situation. The Human Rights Procurator expressed concern at the possible re-emergence of death squads. Human rights and civil society organizations protested that anti-terrorism legislation passed in September was ill-defined and put human rights at risk, including freedom of assembly and expression.

Enforced disappearance of children
In September the Inter-American Court of Human Rights ruled that the state of El Salvador had only partially fulfilled or failed to fulfil the majority of the Court's recommendations from its 2005 ruling, including providing an effective and timely investigation into the enforced disappearance of three-year-old Ernestina and seven-year-old Erlinda Serrano Cruz in June 1982 during a military operation in Chalatenango. The Court ruled that the state had yet to determine the whereabouts of the girls, investigate and bring those responsible to justice and, among other things, had not yet set up a National Search Commission to trace disappeared children.

At the end of the year, two other cases of children who were victims of enforced disappearance during the armed conflict were being studied by the Inter-American Court of Human Rights and a decision regarding the responsibility of the state in the enforced disappearances was pending.

Violence against women
According to the Institute of Forensic Medicine, 286 women were killed between January and August 2006. Despite four years of campaigning by women's rights organizations, the Attorney General's Office had yet to establish a special prosecutor or division to address the killings of women. Very little progress was made in investigating cases of women who had been killed and in some cases raped in previous years.

Human rights defenders
Individuals and organizations working to defend human rights were threatened and harassed.

Members of the Among Friends Association, including the organization's director, William Hernández, received death threats and were reportedly under surveillance in an attempt to halt the organization's work on behalf of lesbian, gay, bisexual and transgender people. On 1 June, William Hernández was threatened at gunpoint outside the organization's office in San Salvador, soon after the police officer assigned to protect him had left for the day. Two days before this attack, the office was broken into. Windows were broken, files were searched, and threats were written on pieces of paper and left in the office. No valuable office equipment was stolen, but a number of the organization's planning documents were taken. Although in all cases the incidents were reported to the authorities, investigations proved superficial, and no one had been brought to justice by the end of 2006.

Death squads

There was increasing concern among civil society organizations at the possible re-emergence of death squads which had been active during the 1980-1991 armed conflict.

Francisco Antonio Manzanares and Juana Monjarás de Manzanares were murdered in their home on 2 July. Their daughter, Marina Manzanares, a long-standing politicial activist for the main opposition party, the Farabundo Martí National Liberation Front, and radio broadcaster, had received death threats prior to the murders, as had her mother. Marina Manzanares' brother, Francisco Manzanares, also a political activist, was killed in 1996. No one had been brought to justice for these murders by the end of 2006.

EQUATORIAL GUINEA

REPUBLIC OF EQUATORIAL GUINEA
Head of state: Teodoro Obiang Nguema Mbasogo
Head of government: Ricardo Mangue Obama Nfube
(replaced Miguel Abia Biteo Borico in August)
Death penalty: retentionist
International Criminal Court: not ratified

There were fewer reports of political arrests than in previous years. Prisoners of conscience and political detainees arrested in 2003 and 2004 continued to be held without charge or trial, although about 40 were released in June. One person died in police custody reportedly as a result of torture. One execution was carried out. Prison conditions improved slightly. Families were forcibly evicted from their homes.

Background

In January the navy seized a boat carrying military supplies when it made an unscheduled call in Malabo and held it for about a month. The boat had been chartered by the UN and was carrying weapons for its peace-keeping mission in the Democratic Republic of the Congo (DRC).

Under the auspices of the UN Secretary-General, President Obiang Nguema and the Gabonese President, Omar Bongo, began talks in February aimed at resolving a 34-year dispute over ownership of the island of Mbañe. However, no agreement was reached by the end of the year.

In July the European Union signed an agreement with the government to assist the country in areas of human rights and democratization. These included legal reform and training for law enforcement and prison officials.

In August the President unexpectedly dismissed the government and appointed a new one led by Prime Minister Ricardo Mangue Obama Nfube, the first member of the Fang ethnic group to be appointed to that position which was previously reserved for members of the Bubi ethnic group. He declared that the fight against corruption was the main priority of the new government.

In September parliament approved a law forbidding torture, which came into force in November.

Arbitrary arrests and detentions

Although there were fewer arrests of political opponents than in previous years, 14 prisoners of conscience continued to be held, including one held without charge or trial since 2003. Five people "extradited" from Libreville, Gabon, in 2004 appeared to be prisoners of conscience. They were provisionally charged with terrorism and rebellion in May, but the charges were not formalized and they were not tried. Four remained in prison at the end of 2006 while one was released in a presidential pardon in June.

Members of the Convergence for Social Democracy (Convergencia para la Democracia Social, CPDS) and other political activists were arrested and briefly detained, mainly in towns on the mainland, although some were arrested in Malabo. They were often prevented from holding meetings even when they had official permission. None was charged with any offence.

In April, a government official and several police officers entered the CPDS office in the town of Rebola, Bioko Island, and arrested Carlos Oná Boriesa, Carmelo Iridi and about eight others. They were having a meeting which the authorities claimed was illegal. Carlos Oná Boriesa and Carmelo Iridi were taken to the police station in the nearby town of Baney and reportedly flogged. Each was subjected to 50 lashes. All were released without charge by the end of the day.

In October, police officers in Bata arrested four members of the banned Progress Party of Equatorial Guinea (Partido del Progreso de Guinea Ecuatorial). They were arrested at home without warrants and at least one, Filemón Ondó, was hit when he was arrested and again two weeks later when being interrogated. The four were taken to Bata Central Police Station where they were threatened with torture. About three weeks later they were transferred to Bata Public Prison. They were released without charge in mid-November. José Antonio Nguema, one of the detainees, had been arrested in June 2004 and held without charge or trial until June 2006.

Several people, including some CPDS members, were reportedly arrested in districts of the mainland for refusing to clear roads without payment. They included Antonio Eusebio Edu, a 75-year-old member of the CPDS in Nsok-Nsomo, who was arrested and briefly detained in May.

Death in detention
One person was known to have died in police custody, apparently as a result of torture. The authorities, however, claimed that he had committed suicide.

In August, José Meviane Ngua was arrested in Kogo, on the border with Gabon, following a domestic dispute. He was reportedly drunk and resisted arrest. That night two police officers carried him out of Kogo police station and took him to the local hospital where he was declared dead on arrival. The police claimed that he had committed suicide. However, hospital personnel stated that he had bruises in his neck and marks on his back consistent with beating. No autopsy was carried out. The next day a police commission came from Bata to investigate but left without having interviewed the family or hospital personnel. No officers were known to have been prosecuted in this case.

Death penalty
Fernando Esono Nzeng, who had been convicted of murder and sentenced to death in early 2004, was publicly executed in April in Evinayong, on the mainland, after the Supreme Court turned down an appeal.

Prisoner releases
On his birthday in June, President Obiang Nguema "pardoned" 40 prisoners. They included 15 prisoners of conscience convicted of plotting to overthrow the government in an unfair trial in June 2002. They also included about 20 political detainees held without charge or trial since their arrest in 2004 who appeared to be prisoners of conscience. A South African national convicted in November 2004 in an unfair trial of attempting to overthrow the government was released on humanitarian grounds.

Weja Chicampo, a leader of the Movement for the Self-Determination of Bioko Island (Movimiento para la autodeterminación de la isla de Bioko, MAIB), had been held without charge or trial since his arrest in March 2004. Following his pardon, he was expelled from the country, despite being an Equatorial Guinean national. Without informing him or his family, several security officers took him from Black Beach prison, drove him to the airport and put him on a plane bound for Spain, where he was granted asylum.

Forced evictions
The combination of pressure on land, government programmes to rehabilitate major cities and infrastructure, and lack of security of tenure led to several mass forced evictions, carried out without consultation, compensation or due process. Hundreds of homes were destroyed in Malabo, and hundreds more families were at risk of forced eviction in Malabo and Bata.

In July, the Prime Minister and other civilian officials, armed soldiers and police officers arrived in Atepa and Camaremy communities in the Banapa neighbourhood of Malabo. They forcibly evicted some 300 families and demolished their homes. Soldiers hit residents who resisted and one man, Santiago Obama, was arrested and briefly detained. He was subsequently released uncharged.

Prison conditions
There was some improvement in prison conditions, particularly in Black Beach prison following the opening of a new block in late 2005. However, four South African prisoners held there since 2004 remained permanently handcuffed and shackled. The provision of food and medicines remained inadequate, although ill prisoners were seen by doctors. The International Committee of the Red Cross continued to visit prisons periodically.

Human rights defenders
The order suspending lawyer and human rights defender Fabian Nsue Nguema from the Bar Association, which was arbitrarily imposed in June 2005, was lifted in July.

AI country reports/ visits
Statements
- Equatorial Guinea: Prisoners of conscience released (AI Index: AFR 24/002/2006)
- Equatorial Guinea: 300 families evicted and homeless (AI Index: AFR 24/006/2006)

ERITREA

ERITREA
Head of state and government: Issayas Afewerki
Death penalty: retentionist
International Criminal Court: signed

Several thousand prisoners of conscience were detained incommunicado without charge or trial. Some former government leaders were held in a secret place of detention. The whereabouts of many political or religious prisoners, including journalists, were not known. Many were in effect victims of enforced disappearance. An army general remained held after 14 years, and three religious prisoners were still held after 12 years. Many detainees were tortured. Prison conditions, including being held in underground cells or metal shipping containers, amounted to cruel, inhuman and degrading treatment. Virtually no medical treatment was provided.

Background
Two thirds of the population were dependent on international emergency food aid. The government expelled several international NGOs delivering humanitarian assistance. Donors continued emergency humanitarian assistance but most had long suspended development aid because of the government's failure to implement both the constitutional process of democratization and international human rights treaties it had ratified.

As in previous years, human rights defenders were not allowed to operate and independent civil society organizations and unregistered faith groups were prohibited. The only political party allowed was the ruling People's Front for Democracy and Justice (PFDJ), formerly the Eritrean People's Liberation Front (EPLF). No dissent was tolerated.

The UN Security Council extended until January 2007 the UN Mission in Ethiopia and Eritrea (UNMEE) but criticized the stalemate in the negotiations over the border. Eritrea continued to demand that Ethiopia implement the International Boundary Commission's judgement following the 1998-2000 armed conflict and refused any negotiation on border demarcation. The UN Security Council criticized Eritrea's increasing restrictions on UNMEE's movements in the temporary security zone it administers on the Eritrean side of the border, and the arrests of several UNMEE personnel during 2006. It also criticized the incommunicado detention without charge or trial of an international UNMEE staff member, held for some weeks on reportedly false charges of trafficking.

The government continued to host armed Ethiopian and Sudanese opposition groups. It sent military assistance and weapons to the Union of Islamic Courts in Somalia, according to a UN panel monitoring violations of the Somalia arms embargo. It faced the threat of armed opposition from the Sudan-based Eritrean Democratic Alliance, which Ethiopia also supported.

Religious persecution
Minority faith groups such as the Jehovah's Witnesses and over 35 evangelical Christian churches remained banned, their places of worship shut down and religious gatherings prohibited. Only the four main faiths in Eritrea were allowed to function — the Eritrean Orthodox Church, the Catholic Church, the Lutheran (Mekane Yesus) Church and Islam. Dissenting groups within them were also repressed as were those who opposed government authority over them. Patriarch Antonios, head of the Eritrean Orthodox Church, was stripped of his powers in mid-2005 and has been held under house arrest since then for protesting at the 2004 detention of three Orthodox priests and secret prison sentences imposed on them.

Dozens of members of these banned churches were arrested during the year for worshipping at their homes, at weddings, or when proclaiming their faith to others. They were taken to police stations, security prisons or army camps, and often tortured or threatened to make them sign a statement as a condition of release that they would cease practising their faith. They were held incommunicado and illegally, without being brought before a court or charged with any offence. National service conscripts were also punished if they practised their faith.

An estimated 2,000 members of minority evangelical churches, including some 20 pastors, remained in detention in harsh conditions. They included children and women. At least 237 people were arrested during 2006, fewer than in 2005, possibly because of the vigorous international criticism of religious persecution. Most prisoners were held in remote army camps in underground cells or metal shipping containers. None had been allowed access to their families since their arrest. The pastors were mostly held together in Karchele security prison in Asmara.

Helen Berhane, a well-known gospel singer in the evangelical Rema Church, was released in November after being detained in Mai Serwa army camp where she had been held since May 2004. The previous month she had been taken to hospital in Asmara in extremely poor health after being tortured again.

Three Jehovah's Witnesses remained held incommunicado at Sawa military camp near the Sudan border since 1994, when the government stripped all Jehovah's Witnesses of basic citizens' rights for refusing to bear arms or perform military service. Jehovah's Witnesses were arrested during the year, bringing to 27 the number held without charge or trial.

Prisoners of conscience and political prisoners
Eleven former government ministers and former EPLF leaders remained in indefinite secret detention without charge or trial as prisoners of conscience following the September 2001 crackdown on dissent. Their whereabouts in detention had never been disclosed by the government or confirmed by other

sources. There were fears for their safety after new claims in 2006 that General Ogba Abraha and possibly others held secretly with them had died in detention in the intervening years through illness and denial of adequate medical treatment. The government did not reply to appeals to clarify their fate or whereabouts or allow independent access to them. They had in effect become victims of enforced disappearance. They included former Vice-President Mahmoud Ahmed Sheriffo and his former wife Aster Fissehatsion, and former Foreign Ministers Haile Woldetensae and Petros Solomon.

Hundreds of other prisoners of conscience arrested at the same time or later, who were alleged to have opposed the government, remained in detention incommunicado and without charge or trial. The whereabouts of many of them were not known. Several asylum-seekers forcibly returned from Malta in 2002 and Libya in 2003 were still detained.

☐ Aster Yohannes, Petros Solomon's wife and a former PFDJ central committee member, remained in incommunicado detention since 2003 when she returned from the USA to be with her children, whom she has not been allowed to see.

Journalists
Nine journalists working for the state media were detained in November. One was released but by the end of 2006 eight continued to be held without charge or trial in the capital, Asmara.

Ten journalists working in the private media arrested in the 2001 crackdown on dissent and one working in the state media arrested in 2002 were still detained incommunicado without charge or trial. Some were held in the Karchele security prison in Asmara but the whereabouts of the others were not known. All private media remained banned since 2001.

Military conscription
National service, comprising military service and development service such as road-building and construction work, remained compulsory and extended indefinitely for all men aged between 18 and 40, although women were reportedly allowed to leave at the age of 27. Conscript reserve duties extended to the age of 50 and former EPLF veterans were also subject to recall. Some conscripts were permitted to perform their service in civilian government employment but under military conditions.

The internationally recognized right of conscientious objection was denied. This applied particularly to Jehovah's Witnesses who refused military service (though not development service) on faith grounds.

The authorities instituted harsh measures to counter the widespread evasion of military service and desertion by thousands of conscripts. Police searches and round-ups were carried out, and hundreds of parents suspected of involvement with their children's evasion or desertion were detained, some possibly indefinitely. They were released only on payment of a large financial bond for the missing conscript to surrender.

Rule of law
The few functioning courts failed to protect the constitutional rights not to be tortured or arbitrarily detained. Special Courts handed down prison sentences in secret summary trials for corruption and political offences where the accused had no right to legal defence representation or appeal. Secret administrative security committees reportedly imposed prison sentences without any semblance of trial.

Military courts were not functioning. Military conscripts accused of a military offence such as desertion, attempted desertion or being absent without permission were arbitrarily imprisoned or punished with torture, or possibly executed in the most serious cases, on the order of their military commander.

Torture and ill-treatment
Suspected government opponents and alleged supporters of exile opposition groups were tortured in security or military custody. Religious prisoners were tortured to force them to abandon their faith. Torture was also a long-established punishment for civilian prisoners held in army or security custody and conscripts accused of military offences. Methods included being tied in painful positions for hours or days, particularly that known as "helicopter", and beatings.

Religious and political prisoners were held in harsh conditions amounting to cruel, inhuman and degrading treatment. Many were held in metal shipping containers which were overcrowded, lacked sanitary facilities and were subject to extreme temperatures. Medical treatment was virtually non-existent and prisoners were only taken to hospital when they were almost dying. General Bitwoded Abraha, detained almost continually since 1992 in Karchele security prison in Asmara, suffered mental illness for years due to poor prison conditions but has received no medical or psychiatric treatment. Aster Yohannes was also in poor health in the same prison without adequate medical treatment.

AI country reports/visits
Statements
- Eritrea: Independence Day call for a year of urgent human rights improvements (AI Index: AFR 64/004/2006)
- Eritrea: Five years on, members of parliament and journalists remain in secret detention without trial (AI Index: AFR 64/009/2006)

ESTONIA

REPUBLIC OF ESTONIA
Head of state: Toomas Hendrik Ilves (replaced Arnold Rüütel in October)
Head of government: Andrus Ansip
Death penalty: abolitionist for all crimes
International Criminal Court: ratified

Mass statelessness and discrimination against ethnic minorities continued to be of serious concern. The UN Committee on the Elimination of Racial Discrimination expressed concern about Estonia's anti-discrimination laws and its current definition of what constitutes a minority. Police failed to provide adequate protection for participants in a Gay Pride march in Tallinn.

Statelessness

Around 130,000 people living in Estonia remained without citizenship and as a result faced discriminatory practices, particularly in the fields of educational, labour and cultural rights. For example, stateless residents were not allowed to work in certain parts of the public sector, and had only limited rights in terms of movement outside the country.

Stateless residents generally held either temporary or permanent residence permits. In April, Estonia introduced the category of long-term resident which, among other things, reduced restrictions on the right to live and work in other European Union member states. All permanent residents automatically qualify as long-term residents. However, in June 2007 a new language requirement was set to be introduced whereby long-term residency would only be granted to those who had achieved the required level in Estonian.

Minority rights

Discriminatory practices, including barriers to employment, continued towards the country's linguistic minority, affecting some 430,000 people, approximately 30 per cent of the population.

In August, the UN Committee on the Elimination of Racial Discrimination adopted its Concluding Observations on Estonia. The Committee recommended that the definition of what constitutes a minority set out in the Law on Cultural Autonomy of National Minorities should be amended to include non-citizens, including stateless people with long-term residence. The Committee further recommended that Estonia enact anti-discrimination legislation in accordance with the UN Convention against Racism. The Committee also suggested that Estonia consider providing free Estonian language courses to all those applying for citizenship.

Lesbian, gay, bisexual and transgender rights

In August, participants in a Gay Pride march in Tallinn were attacked by more than a dozen counter-demonstrators. More than 10 participants in the march were injured and one person was hospitalized with head injuries. The counter-demonstrators, who reportedly defined themselves as Estonian nationalists, physically and verbally attacked marchers, spat on them and threw stones and eggs. Law enforcement officials failed to intervene to prevent the attacks by the counter-demonstrators; the authorities had not provided sufficient resources to police the march adequately.

International treaties

Estonia ratified the Optional Protocol to the UN Convention against Torture.

AI country reports/ visits

Reports
- Estonia: The right to freedom of peaceful assembly must be protected (AI Index: EUR 51/001/2006)
- Linguistic minorities in Estonia: Discrimination must end (AI Index: EUR 51/002/2006)

Visits
AI delegates visited Estonia in March and August.

ETHIOPIA

FEDERAL DEMOCRATIC REPUBLIC OF ETHIOPIA
Head of state: Girma Wolde-Giorgis
Head of government: Meles Zenawi
Death penalty: retentionist
International Criminal Court: not ratified

There were a number of political trials of opposition party leaders, journalists and human rights defenders. A parliamentary commission reported that the security forces did not use excessive force when they killed 193 demonstrators in 2005, but defecting commission leaders said there had been excessive use of force but that their findings had been changed by the government. Scores of people were detained and some reportedly tortured for opposition activities. Civilians were detained and some were tortured or killed in the armed conflicts in the Oromia and Somali regions, and also in Gambella region. Thousands of political detainees arrested in late 2005 were released but several thousand others still remained in detention without charge or trial. The "genocide" trial of the former Dergue government (1974-1991) ended in December after 12 years with convictions of 33 members in court and

25 others in their absence, including former President Mengistu Hailemariam. Several death sentences were passed by courts but there were no executions.

Background
Five million people were dependent on emergency food aid, especially in the drought-affected Somali region.

The government continued to face armed opposition from the Oromo Liberation Front (OLF) and Ogaden National Liberation Front (ONLF), both based in Eritrea. Ethiopia supported the armed Sudan-based Eritrean Democratic Alliance (EDA).

Ethiopia sent military assistance to Somalia's Transitional Federal Government (TFG), contravening a UN arms embargo, to support it against the forces of the "Islamic Courts", which captured the capital, Mogadishu, in June and extended control over most of central and southern Somalia. In October, Ethiopia increased military assistance to the TFG after the Council of Somali Islamic Courts (COSIC) declared jihad (holy war) against Ethiopia. After increasing clashes with COSIC forces, the large Ethiopian force defeated COSIC in several days of fighting in December, and took control of Mogadishu. It placed the TFG force in power and pursued fleeing COSIC fighters to southwestern Somalia.

The UN Security Council extended until January 2007 the UN Mission in Ethiopia and Eritrea (UNMEE) but criticized the stalemate in negotiations over the contested border. Ethiopia said it accepted the International Boundary Commission's judgment following the 1998-2000 armed conflict, but refused to implement it.

The National Human Rights Commission, legally established in 2004, held a first workshop for non-governmental organizations (NGOs) in mid-2006. It had not started operating by the end of the year.

Political trials
Following the disputed May 2005 elections and mass arrests of opposition party activists, leaders of the Coalition for Unity and Democracy (CUD), journalists and civil society activists were brought to trial in May. They faced charges including treason, outrage against the Constitution and other capital charges. The 76 defendants included Hailu Shawel, the CUD president, Berhanu Negga, an economics professor, and Mesfin Woldemariam, a retired geography professor. In addition, 34 prominent Ethiopians in exile were charged in their absence. Five Voice of America radio journalists who were US citizens were among nine defendants discharged before the trial started.

All but three defendants refused to defend themselves on the ground that they did not expect a fair trial. The trial had not concluded by the end of 2006. AI considered they were prisoners of conscience and sent a trial observer in October.

Four other CUD-related trials on similar charges were not completed at the end of the year. In the trial of Kifle Tigeneh, an elected member of parliament, and 32

other people, some defendants complained in court that they had been tortured to make false confessions. Berhane Mogese, a lawyer, was on trial with 22 others.

A separate trial of Mesfin Woldemariam and Berhanu Negga continued. They were accused of instigating violence during demonstrations at Addis Ababa University in 2000.

Journalists
Fourteen independent press journalists arrested in November 2005 were tried with the CUD leaders. Kifle Mulat, president of the Ethiopian Free Press Journalists Association, was charged in his absence and sought asylum abroad. Two other journalists, Solomon Aregawi and Goshu Moges, were tried in separate capital cases.

All private newspapers which had criticized the government in connection with the elections remained shut down. Many journalists fled the country.

⊡ Frezer Negash, a reporter for a US-based website, was arrested in February when three months pregnant, but released on bail two weeks later.

At least four journalists were charged under the Press Law in connection with alleged offences committed some years previously.

⊡ In March, Abraham Gebrekidan of Politika magazine was jailed for a year for allegedly publishing false information.

A new Press Law, proposed by the government in 2003 to replace the 1992 Press Law, was still under debate. Combined with provisions in the new Criminal Code of May 2005, it could lead to further legal restrictions on the freedom of the media and imprisonment of journalists.

Human rights defenders
Among defendants in the CUD trial were four human rights defenders: Professor Mesfin Woldemariam, former president of the Ethiopian Human Rights Council; Daniel Bekelle, a lawyer and staff member of ActionAid; Netsanet Demissie, chair of the Organization for Social Justice in Ethiopia; and Kassahun Kebede, an Ethiopian Teachers Association (ETA) official.

Two ETA officials were arrested in October without explanation but released on bail after some days. Three other officials were arrested in December and allegedly tortured. The ETA, Ethiopia's longest-established trade union, continued to contest court actions by the Ministry of Justice to ban it and replace it by a pro-government organization bearing the same name.

Political arrests
Dozens of people were arrested in Addis Ababa in late 2006 for possession of a book secretly written in prison by Berhanu Negga or a calendar containing images of the CUD prisoners and calling for civil disobedience.

⊡ Yealemzawde Bekelle, a lawyer working for the European Commission in Addis Ababa, was arrested in October, reportedly after being named by a tortured prisoner. She was released on bail after eight days' incommunicado detention.

Several thousand opposition supporters detained in different parts of the country after the November 2005 demonstration were released on bail after some weeks or months in detention without charge. However, some thousands were believed to be still detained without charge or trial during 2006.

Detentions and killings in the regions

In the Oromia region, there were large-scale arrests in different areas during anti-government demonstrations, particularly by school and college students. Some protesters called for the release of Diribi Demissie, a Mecha Tulema Association community leader on trial since 2004. He and his co-defendants were charged with supporting the OLF, but AI considered them prisoners of conscience. Hundreds of Oromo people detained in November 2005 were reportedly still held during 2006 without charge or trial, as well as others detained in previous years for alleged OLF connections.

Numerous people accused of ONLF connections were reportedly detained in the Somali region, and many political prisoners arrested in previous years were still held without charge or trial. Extrajudicial executions were also reported.

In Gambela region in the southwest, there were scores of arrests of members of the Anuak ethnic group. Hundreds of people arrested during mass killings in Gambela town in December 2003 were still detained without charge or trial.

Some 60 peaceful demonstrators belonging to the Sidama ethnic group in the southern region were arrested in Awassa and other southern towns in March. They were all released on bail by May.

Commission of inquiry

In March parliament established a Commission of Inquiry to investigate the killings during the 2005 demonstrations. The Commission, headed by a judge, took evidence from the public and NGOs and interviewed CUD leaders in prison. In July, the Commission's chairperson fled the country and his replacement did the same in September. They alleged that the Prime Minister had instructed them to change their finding — that the security forces had committed excessive force — which they were not willing to do.

In November the report presented to parliament stated that the Commission had found no evidence of excessive use of force by the security forces. The list of people killed numbered 193, including six police officers, far more than the 78 reported by police. The Commission found that 765 people, including 99 women and several children, had been wounded, almost four times the police figure.

Victims had been shot by army or police bullets, some in the back while escaping and others possibly targeted by snipers. At least 17 people imprisoned earlier in Kaliti prison, mostly on remand for ordinary criminal offences but also some political prisoners, were shot dead in their cells at the same time on suspicion of supporting the demonstrations and trying to escape.

Torture and ill-treatment

Torture was reported by methods including electric shocks and beatings on the feet while tied upside down. The victims were political prisoners, particularly those detained on suspicion of supporting armed political groups such as the OLF and ONLF.

Alemayehu Fantu, an engineer and supermarket owner in Addis Ababa, was reportedly tortured in October to make him admit to publishing or distributing the CUD calendar, and to name others. He was taken to court with visible injuries, which the judges did not investigate, but released on bail on November.

Several of the CUD leaders held in Kaliti prison in Addis Ababa were at first denied medical treatment for illnesses contracted as a result of harsh and unhygienic prison conditions. Professor Mesfin Woldemariam, aged 76, was refused physiotherapy for back and leg complaints. There were fears for his health as a result of his hunger strikes in December 2005 and February 2006. He recovered quickly, however, after being treated in hospital for pneumonia in September. There were serious delays in provision of medical treatment for Hailu Shawel for eye surgery, and Berhanu Negga for a heart complaint.

Serkalem Fasil, a journalist who was seven months pregnant, was taken to hospital to give birth, but denied intensive care treatment for her baby son. She was returned to prison soon after the birth, taking the baby with her.

Four prisoners of conscience were moved as punishment to the Central Prison (Karchele), which was in the process of demolition. CUD leaders Muluneh Eyuel and Amanuel Araya and journalists Eskinder Negga and Sissay Agena were kept for over two months in dark underground cells in solitary confinement.

Dergue trial

The trial of members of the 1974 military government known as the Dergue ended in December after 12 years. Of the 72 people originally charged, 33 had been in custody since 1991, 14 others had died in custody and 25 were tried in their absence, including former President Mengistu Hailemariam, who had asylum in Zimbabwe. All were found guilty of capital offences including genocide and mass killings, with sentencing due in 2007. The long series of other trials of officials of the former government for killings during the "Red Terror" campaign against "anti-revolutionaries" in 1977-79 was nearly completed. Many defendants were jailed for long periods (which most had already served, leading to their release) and several death sentences were imposed. Many convictions went to appeal.

Violence against women

According to Ethiopian women's organizations, violence against women through domestic violence, rape and harmful traditional practices, including female genital mutilation and early marriage, remained widespread. Female genital mutilation was prevalent among many ethnic groups of different faiths in remote rural areas and abductions of girls were associated with early marriages.

Death penalty

Ten death sentences for ordinary crimes were commuted by presidential clemency in September. Several other death sentences for alleged politically related violent crimes were still in force. There were no executions.

AI country reports/ visits
Report
· Ethiopia: Prisoners of conscience on trial for treason — opposition party leaders, human rights defenders and journalists (AI Index: AFR 25/013/2006)
Visit
An AI observer attended the CUD trial in October.

FINLAND

REPUBLIC OF FINLAND
Head of state: Tarja Halonen
Head of government: Matti Vanhanen
Death penalty: abolitionist for all crimes
International Criminal Court: ratified

Conscientious objectors to military service were imprisoned.

Conscientious objection to military service

The length of the civilian alternative to military service remained punitive and discriminatory. Conscientious objectors were obliged to perform 395 days of civilian service, 215 days longer than military service. In October a Ministry of Labour working group proposed shortening the civilian service and recognizing conscientious objection in times of war or other public emergency.

◻ AI considered 11 imprisoned conscientious objectors to military service to be prisoners of conscience. Most served sentences of 197 days for refusing to perform alternative civilian service.

Violence against women

In January the Minister of Social Affairs and Health admitted to AI the need for increased co-ordination among government ministries and for the creation of an action plan on preventing violence against women. No such plan had been produced by the end of 2006.

An updated AI survey in May found that Finnish municipalities lacked the political will, co-ordination, expertise and resources to eradicate violence against women, although a few were doing pioneering work.

An official study in December found that 43.5 per cent of women in Finland were victims of physical or sexual violence or threats of violence by men.

Trafficking in human beings

Under the 2005 national action plan against trafficking, a detailed system for aiding and protecting victims of trafficking was devised, but funding remained uncertain. A special residence permit for victims of trafficking was created under the Aliens Act, but the granting of permits to victims was ordinarily conditional on their co-operation with the authorities.

Finland ratified the UN Protocol to Prevent, Suppress and Punish Trafficking in Persons Especially Women and Children, and signed the Council of Europe Convention on Action against Trafficking in Human Beings.

Asylum

Accelerated asylum-determination procedures under the Aliens Act allowed too short a time for claims to be considered thoroughly and for asylum-seekers to exhaust all avenues of appeal.

An increasing number of people were granted temporary residence permits, resulting in a corresponding increase in the number denied the right to work or family reunification, and allowed only restricted access to education and social and health care.

Unfair residence permit procedures

Residence permits were denied solely on the basis of information from the security police withheld from the applicant. However, in June, Kuopio Administrative Court quashed a refusal to grant a residence permit because the immigration authorities had refused to disclose to the applicant information provided by the security police, denying him a fair hearing. An appeal by the authorities to the Supreme Administrative Court was pending.

◻ In January, Pakistani national Qari Muzaffar Iqbal Naeemi was granted asylum. In 2002 his request for a renewal of his residence permit had been denied. In 2003 his deportation had been ordered on the basis of information that remained undisclosed.

FRANCE

FRENCH REPUBLIC
Head of state: Jacques Chirac
Head of government: Dominique de Villepin
Death penalty: abolitionist for all crimes
International Criminal Court: ratified

Reports of police misconduct, including ill-treatment, continued. Ethnic minorities, migrants and asylum-seekers were particularly vulnerable to such abuse. A new immigration law restricted the rights of migrants. Racist, anti-Semitic and Islamophobic attacks continued. Six former Guantánamo Bay detainees went on trial for terrorism-related charges, but the case was suspended.

Police ill-treatment and impunity

Incidents of abuse by police officers continued to be reported. The National Commission on Ethics and Security (Commission Nationale de Déontologie de la Sécurité, CNDS) reported in April that complaints of police misconduct in 2005 had risen by 10 per cent over the previous year, particularly in relation to minors, asylum-seekers and migrants. The internal police disciplinary body reported a 14.5 per cent increase in the number of sanctions issued against police officers in 2005 compared with 2004.

On 17 August Albertine Sow, who was six months pregnant, was violently handled and punched by police when she asked what was happening during a violent arrest of two young men in Paris. A relative of the young men also tried to intervene. The situation deteriorated and both the relative and Albertine Sow were hit by police batons on the head and ribs. Albertine Sow lodged a complaint with the disciplinary body of the Paris police on 19 August, supported by numerous witnesses. The same weekend, a judicial proceeding was opened into the incident alleging a group assault on the police.

Following his intervention in the violent arrest of a stranger in Montpellier, Brice Petit was convicted in 2005 of defamation for insulting a police officer, but acquitted of other charges. In March 2006 the Court of Appeal in Montpellier confirmed his acquittal. The same month, a complaint Brice Petit had lodged against the police for their violent treatment of him during arrest was closed without action.

Violence against women

Violence against women remained widespread, with official data indicating that on average one woman died every four days as a result of violence by her partner. More than half of the women killed had been the victims of domestic violence on previous occasions. It was reported that almost one in 10 women in France suffered domestic violence. Other hidden but persistent forms of gender-based violence included forced marriage, and the trafficking of women for the purpose of prostitution.

Despite measures taken by the state towards improving its response to the issue of domestic violence, co-ordination and resources remained inadequate. The procedures for women trying to get access to justice were slow and complex. Foreign women faced specific additional difficulties, including social isolation and a fear of losing residence rights.

Asylum and immigration

The government proposed further restrictions on the rights of asylum-seekers, even though the number of asylum applications in 2006 fell by 40 per cent compared with the previous year.

Albania, Macedonia, Madagascar, Niger and Tanzania were added to the list of 12 "safe" countries from which asylum-seekers are dealt with under a fast-track procedure with reduced protection and no social support. Appeals lodged under this system do not lead to the suspension of expulsion proceedings. Following criticism from non-governmental organizations (NGOs), including AI, the government abandoned moves to reduce from one month to 15 days the time allowed to appeal against a rejected asylum application.

A new immigration law, under which irregular migrants will no longer benefit from automatic regularization of status after 10 years' residency in France, was passed in July despite strong popular opposition. Regularization will now take place on a case-by-case basis. Family reunification applications will be allowed after 18 months (previously one year) and applicants must demonstrate sufficient financial means to support family members wishing to join them. For migrants entering France specifically to work, different forms of residence permits will be granted according to the length of contract and level of professional skill in order to support the programme of "selective immigration". A special three-year permit will be created for "highly qualified" immigrants. In other cases, residence permits will be limited to the duration of the holder's work contract. As loss of employment would lead to the risk of expulsion, some migrants will face heightened risk of exploitative working conditions. Foreign residents convicted of "rebellion" (resisting arrest) may have their 10-year residence permit replaced with a one-year permit, renewable annually. The offence of "rebellion" is extremely broad and is commonly cited in controversial arrests or as a counter-charge to accusations of police misconduct.

Expulsions of illegal immigrants continued, totalling some 24,000 by the end of the year. In June the Minister of the Interior offered financial assistance to families fulfilling certain criteria, such as having children in school, to return voluntarily to their country of origin and a review of their migration status if they declined such aid.

On 28 September, three police officers appeared before the Magistrates' Court in Bobigny charged with involuntary manslaughter for the death in January 2003 of Getu Hagos Mariame, an Ethiopian national whose asylum application had been rejected. He died in hospital after being forcibly restrained by police officers accompanying his expulsion. The officers allegedly used such force that they blocked the arterial blood flow to his brain. The officers were suspended from duty for 10 months but were later readmitted to the border patrol police. In November, the senior officer involved was convicted of involuntary homicide and given a six-month suspended sentence. The other two officers involved were acquitted.

Racism and discrimination

Racist, anti-Semitic and Islamophobic attacks continued to be a problem. In March the National Consultative Human Rights Commission (CNCDH) reported a 38 per cent decrease in racist threats and attacks during the previous year, although a national survey revealed an increase in racist attitudes. Mosques were vandalized in Carcassonne and Quimper at the beginning of Ramadan.

In February a young Jewish man, Ilan Halimi, was kidnapped in Paris by a gang and held for ransom for three weeks before being tortured to death. The suspected gang leader said they had chosen Ilan Halimi because he was Jewish and therefore assumed to be rich. The event sparked protests involving tens of thousands of demonstrators in Paris and across the country. Anti-Semitic attacks followed the demonstrations.

Poor prison conditions

Prison conditions remained poor. A report by the Council of Europe Commissioner for Human Rights strongly criticized conditions inside prisons and noted chronic overcrowding. The Minister of Justice stated in July that the prison population had reached almost 60,000, although the number of prisoners held in pre-trial detention had significantly fallen.

Restriction on freedom of expression

On 12 October parliament adopted a bill that would make it a crime to contest that the massacres of Armenians in the Ottoman Empire in 1915 constituted genocide. The new crime would be punishable by up to five years' imprisonment and a fine. The bill was awaiting approval by the Senate and the President.

'War on terror' concerns

Guantánamo Bay detainees

Six former detainees at the US military base in Guantánamo Bay went on trial in France for alleged "criminal conspiracy in relation to a terrorist enterprise". The six, all French nationals, were captured in Afghanistan in 2001 and transferred to Guantánamo Bay. In 2004 and 2005 they were released to France, where they subsequently spent an average of 18 months in remand detention. The men had been interviewed in Guantánamo Bay in 2002 by French secret service agents. Although the information gathered was not presented at the trial in France, the men's lawyers said that it had triggered the judicial investigation. The court, which had been due to deliver its judgment in September, asked for further investigations, including the questioning of high-

ranking officials from the secret services and Ministry of Foreign Affairs. A new trial was due to start in May 2007.

Rendition flights

A report of AI's investigations into secret rendition flights by the USA in the "war on terror", published in April, contained information on six flights suspected to have landed or made stopovers at French airports. The information cast further doubt on claims by the French authorities that they had been unaware of such flights. A preliminary inquiry on this matter was opened following a complaint lodged by two NGOs in December 2005, but the public prosecutor closed the inquiry in August, saying that it was not possible to gather information on the identity of passengers of the flights in question.

Anti-terrorism law

Law 2006-64, which was passed in January, gives custodial judges the authority to order up to two additional 24-hour extensions of police custody in terrorism cases – in addition to the two 24-hour extensions already permitted – where there is believed to be a serious risk of an imminent terrorist attack or where international co-operation is necessary to the investigation. The new law means that a detainee may be held for six days before appearing before a judge. Suspects have access to a lawyer after 72 hours, 96 hours and 120 hours.

Death penalty

In January, following a 2005 decision by the Constitutional Council that France's ratification of the International Covenant on Civil and Political Rights required a constitutional reform, President Jacques Chirac announced his intention to amend the Constitution to reflect the prohibition of the death penalty in all circumstances. Such a measure would also enable France to become party to the Covenant's Second Optional Protocol, aimed at total abolition of the death penalty.

AI country reports/visits

Reports

- France: Violence against women – a matter for the state (AI Index: EUR 21/001/2006)
- Europe and Central Asia: Summary of Amnesty International's concerns in the region, January-June 2006 (AI Index: EUR 01/017/2006)

GAMBIA

REPUBLIC OF THE GAMBIA
Head of state and government: Yahya Jammeh
Death penalty: abolitionist in practice
International Criminal Court: ratified

More than 70 civilians and members of the military, including prisoners of conscience, were unlawfully detained after an alleged coup attempt in late March. Several journalists and editors were also unlawfully detained for many weeks. At least 12 detainees were reportedly tortured. Trials of suspected coup plotters were continuing in military and civilian courts at the end of the year. Five people who allegedly escaped may have been extrajudicially executed. Repression of the right to freedom of expression intensified.

Background
In September President Jammeh won presidential elections.

Unlawful detentions and torture
After an alleged coup attempt in late March, more than 70 people were unlawfully detained for longer than the 72 hours allowed by Gambian law. Among those held by the National Intelligence Agency (NIA) were prisoners of conscience, lawyers, journalists, editors, civilians, military and security personnel, and politicians.

On 27 March suspects reportedly dressed in military uniform appeared on national television "confessing" to involvement in a coup attempt.

Some of the detainees were held incommunicado for several weeks at the NIA headquarters and the Mile 2 prison, where at least 12 were allegedly tortured or ill-treated. The number of those still held at the end of 2006 was not clear.

▭ Mariam Denton, a lawyer and prisoner of conscience, was detained on 6 April and unlawfully held in Mile 2 prison for over three months. Although her lawyers' application for access was granted by the High Court on 25 April, the prison authorities denied access until after 10 May. She was released without charge on 25 July after a failed attempt by the prosecutor to have her charged with concealment of treason.

At least 12 detainees were allegedly tortured. Some reportedly had their heads covered with plastic bags or were held under water for long periods. Others were reportedly burned with cigarettes or severely beaten.

Trials after alleged coup attempt
Preliminary hearings began in the High Court in Banjul on 10 May for 15 defendants detained in relation to the coup attempt. Charges, including treason and concealment of treason, all of which are capital and non-bailable offences, were made public in late May. One defendant was reportedly released on

8 December. Two other detainees were charged with ancillary crimes, one of whom reportedly had the charges against him dropped in November and was released. On 28 July it was reported that another seven detainees, including Abdoulie Kujabi, a former Director General of the NIA, had been charged with conspiracy to commit treason. Their trial had not started by the end of 2006 and one of them was reportedly released on 8 December.

On 18 July, several defence lawyers reportedly withdrew from one case, citing concerns about the independence of the judge. Some detainees were denied access to their lawyers. At least four military defendants in the treason trial were transferred to a court martial, where their statements suggested that confessions had been obtained under duress or torture.

Suspected extrajudicial executions
The authorities alleged that former NIA Director General Daba Marena and four soldiers – Ebou Lowe, Alieu Cessay, Alpha Bah and Malafi Corr – escaped during a prison transfer around 4 April. There were fears that they had in fact been extrajudicially executed or become victims of enforced disappearance. No independent investigation into the alleged escape had been initiated by the end of the year.

Freedom of expression
At least nine Gambian and foreign journalists and editors were detained, and some were reportedly tortured. Harassment and threats against journalists, editors and media critical of the government intensified.

▭ On 28 March, Musa Saidykhan, editor of *The Independent*, and Madi Ceesay, managing director, were arrested and the newspaper's premises were closed. The two men were held incommunicado at the NIA headquarters until 20 April, when they were released without charge and without an official reason for their detention. The newspaper remained closed at the end of the year.

▭ On 10 April, Lamin Fatty, a reporter with *The Independent,* was detained at the NIA headquarters in connection with the coup attempt. He was held incommunicado for over two months. In May, he was charged with publishing false information. His trial was continuing at the end of the year.

▭ On 25 May the online *Freedom Newspaper* had its web-site hacked into, and a list of over 300 names of alleged "informers" was published in a pro-government newspaper. At least four journalists were subsequently arrested but were released without charge. One journalist was held incommunicado at the NIA headquarters for almost five months before being released without charge.

Impunity
There were no official investigations into past human rights violations. The government did not bring to justice those responsible for the assassination of journalist Deyda Hydara in December 2004.

Statement
· Gambia: Alleged coup plot must not be used as excuse to violate citizens' human rights (AI Index: AFR 27/004/2006)

GEORGIA

GEORGIA
Head of state: Mikheil Saakashvili
Head of government: Zurab Noghaideli
Death penalty: abolitionist for all crimes
International Criminal Court: ratified

Pre-trial and convicted prisoners were reportedly ill-treated on several occasions, and excessive force was reportedly used in prison disturbances in which at least eight detainees died and many more were wounded, including special forces officers. Police officers continued to enjoy impunity in dozens of cases in which torture, ill-treatment and excessive use of force have been alleged. The authorities failed to protect women from domestic violence or bring its perpetrators to justice. A new law on domestic violence was a positive step, although it postponed the setting up of urgently needed temporary shelters for women and children. The internationally unrecognized breakaway areas of Abkhazia and South Ossetia retained the death penalty. Civil society activists in South Ossetia risked harassment because of contacts with Georgian activists.

Torture, ill-treatment and excessive force
The government's two-year Plan of Action against Torture, which expired in December 2005, was not extended although many recommendations by a range of international human rights bodies remained unimplemented. These included recommendations made by the UN Special Rapporteur on torture and other cruel, inhuman and degrading treatment or punishment, the UN Committee against Torture, and the European Committee for the Prevention of Torture and Inhuman and Degrading Treatment or Punishment.

In a positive move in April, parliament removed any time limit on the period in which charges could be brought for the crimes of torture, threat of torture, and inhuman and degrading treatment.

Investigations were opened into allegations of police torture or ill-treatment in dozens of cases. Five officers were sentenced to prison terms of between three and seven years. Investigations were allegedly not thorough or impartial in at least some cases.

In January officers of the Interior Ministry severely beat and otherwise ill-treated Sandro Girgvliani and his friend Levan Bukhaidze on the outskirts of Tbilisi. Levan Bukhaidze was abandoned and managed to get back to the city. Sandro Girgvliani died as a result of injuries he sustained and was found near a local cemetery the next day. In July, four officers were sentenced to prison terms for causing his death. However, no impartial investigation was opened into allegations that those who killed Sandro Girgvliani had acted on the orders of senior officials of the Interior Ministry, it was reported.

In May the UN Committee against Torture called on the authorities to introduce regular monitoring by an independent oversight body of human rights violations by police and prison personnel; to strengthen investigative capacity to ensure allegations of torture or other ill-treatment were investigated promptly and thoroughly; and to promptly inform all detainees of their rights to counsel and to be examined by a medical doctor of their own choice. The Committee also recommended legislation on reparation for victims of abuse and in the meantime practical measures to provide redress, fair and adequate compensation, and rehabilitation.

Investigation-isolation facilities and prisons
In several instances, ill-treatment and excessive force were allegedly used against inmates of investigation-isolation facilities and prisons. However, only in the case of disturbances in Tbilisi in March was there an official investigation, which did not start until June and had not made its results public by the end of 2006.

On 27 March special police and prison forces entered the Investigation-Isolation Prison No. 5 in Tbilisi to suppress an allegedly orchestrated armed riot and attempted break-out. The operation left at least seven inmates dead and many others wounded, including special forces officers. The same day President Mikheil Saakashvili and senior officials denied allegations that excessive force had been used. Unofficial reports suggested that the special forces had been sent in to suppress a spontaneous protest over abuses of prison hospital inmates by a senior prison official and special forces during the night of 26 to 27 March. It was also alleged that they did not attempt non-violent means to establish control, but immediately fired automatic weapons and rubber bullets and beat detainees with truncheons. Many of the injured reportedly did not receive adequate medical treatment. In some cases, doctors only obtained access to detainees following interventions by the Ombudsman.

Violence against women in the family
Violence against women by their partners and former partners included verbal and psychological abuse, physical and sexual violence, and killings. Most frequently, women were beaten, hit and kicked, but they were also burned with cigarettes, had their heads bashed against walls, or were raped.

The authorities did not gather comprehensive statistics on domestic violence. A study by the non-governmental Caucasus Women's Research and

Consulting Network reported that 5.2 per cent of women had experienced frequent physical abuse by their partner, adding to the data produced by UN Population Fund studies in Georgia in 1999 and 2005 which found that 5 per cent of women reported physical abuse.

Among obstacles to eradicating domestic violence were the widespread impunity enjoyed by its perpetrators, and insufficient measures and services to protect victims such as temporary shelters and adequate, safe housing. The authorities also failed to ensure a functioning cross-referral system between health workers, crisis centres, legal aid centres, and law enforcement authorities, or to provide mandatory government training programmes for police, procurators, judges and medical staff.

The adoption by parliament in May of a new law on domestic violence was an important step in meeting the government's obligations to prevent abuses and protect survivors. The law introduced a definition of domestic violence in domestic legislation, and a legal basis for issuing protection and restraint orders. However, implementation of the provision for temporary shelters for victims of domestic violence was postponed until 2008. Also, a plan outlining measures and activities necessary to implement the law, which should have been approved within four months of the law's publication, had not been approved by the end of 2006.

In August the UN Committee on the Elimination of Discrimination against Women was concerned that the provision of the new domestic violence law to set up shelters for women and children had been postponed, that there was a lack of official data on domestic violence, and that domestic violence may still be considered a private matter. The Committee urged that a national action plan to combat domestic violence be completed and implemented, and recommended that a properly resourced mechanism be given the necessary powers to promote gender equality and monitor its practical realization. It also recommended strengthening the protection of victims; data collection, research and evaluation of measures taken; training; and public awareness raising.

Abkhazia and South Ossetia
Freedom of expression at risk
In June the mother of civil society activist Alan Dzhusoity was dismissed from her job as head mistress of a school in Tskhinval/Tskhinvali, South Ossetia, in an apparent attempt by the authorities of South Ossetia to put pressure on her son to end his contacts with Georgian civil society organizations. Several days later, Alan Dzhusoity and fellow activists Alan Parastaev and Timur Tskhovrebov, in a television discussion in Tbilisi, called for an independent South Ossetia, peace and dialogue between South Ossetians and Georgians, and acknowledgement by Georgia that the South Ossetian population had a right to self-determination. Eduard Kokoity, the de facto President of South Ossetia, subsequently summoned civil society activists and warned them against contact with Georgians.

Death penalty
South Ossetia continued a moratorium on death sentences and executions. Abkhazia had a moratorium on executions only. Two prisoners were on death row in Abkhazia. Reportedly, at least 16 people had been sentenced to death in Abkhazia since the early 1990s.

In June the Parliamentary Assembly of the Council of Europe (PACE), in recommendations on the death penalty in Council of Europe member and observer states, stated that the death penalty should be abolished in Abkhazia and South Ossetia, and that all death sentences in Abkhazia should be immediately commuted to bring an end to the state of uncertainty suffered by prisoners on death row for years.

AI country reports/ visits
Reports
- Europe and Central Asia: Summary of Amnesty International's concerns in the region, January-June 2006 (AI Index: EUR 01/017/2006)
- Commonwealth of Independent States: Positive trend on the abolition of the death penalty but more needs to be done (AI Index: EUR 04/003/2006)
- Georgia: Briefing to the Committee against Torture (AI Index: EUR 56/005/2006)
- Georgia: Thousands suffering in silence – Violence against women in the family (AI Index: EUR 56/009/2006)

Visits
In January AI delegates met senior government officials and key policy makers in Georgia to discuss torture and other ill-treatment. In April an AI delegate conducted a research visit.

lence – Violence against women in the family (AI Index: EUR 56/009/2006)Violen

GERMANY

FEDERAL REPUBLIC OF GERMANY
Head of state: Horst Köhler
Head of government: Angela Merkel
Death penalty: abolitionist for all crimes
International Criminal Court: ratified

Germany was implicated in abuses linked to the US-led "war on terror". Asylum laws left refugees whose status had been withdrawn vulnerable to deportation to unsafe countries.

Background
In September Germany signed the Optional Protocol to the Convention against Torture and Other Cruel, Inhuman or Degrading Treatment or Punishment.

Renditions

The authorities failed to hold anyone responsible for Germany's involvement in the USA's programme of secret detentions and renditions – the unlawful transfer of people between states outside of any judicial process.

▭ In May, a parliamentary committee of inquiry decided to investigate the case of German citizen Muhammad Zammar. He was apprehended in Morocco in December 2001, allegedly by Moroccan security services, and subsequently transferred to Syria, reportedly on a US Central Intelligence Agency (CIA) plane. He was reportedly tortured in the Palestine Branch (Far' Falastin) of Military Intelligence in Damascus, the Syrian capital. In November 2002, a delegation of German intelligence and law enforcement officials interrogated Muhammad Zammar in Syria for three days. Even though he was detained without access to family, a lawyer or German embassy officials, the delegation did nothing to help him and failed to inform the German embassy or his family about his situation. In October 2006 Muhammad Zammar was apparently charged by Syria's Supreme State Security Court, including with offences related to membership of the outlawed Muslim Brotherhood. If convicted, he could face the death penalty. At the end of 2006 he was reportedly held in Sednaya prison on the outskirts of Damascus. Germany had not held to account anyone responsible, directly or indirectly, for any human rights violations suffered by Muhammad Zammar.

▭ In May the same parliamentary committee of inquiry began looking into the case of Khaled el-Masri, a German citizen who was detained in Macedonia in December 2003, handed to US officials, and later secretly flown to Afghanistan via Iraq. In Afghanistan, he said he was beaten and given insufficient food. He was interrogated repeatedly by US agents and by a uniformed German-speaking man. In May 2004 he was released and returned to Germany via Albania. On 1 June the German Federal Intelligence Service declared that one of its staff members had been told about Khaled el-Masri's detention in December 2003, but had failed to report it.

Torture and other ill-treatment

In relation to alleged terrorist suspects, Germany failed to respect the prohibition on torture and other ill-treatment.

▭ In August, after negotiations between the government and the US authorities, German-born Turkish citizen Murat Kurnaz was released from US detention at Guantánamo Bay, Cuba. Classified government documents leaked in March showed that the USA had offered to release Murat Kurnaz in 2002, but Germany had proposed that he be sent to Turkey even though there was no evidence that he had committed a crime. Following his release, Murat Kurnaz said that while held earlier in US detention in Kandahar, Afghanistan, German soldiers banged his head on the ground. The prosecutor's office in Tübingen started an investigation into this allegation.

German soldiers who helped guard the prison in Kandahar confirmed that there had been a German-speaking detainee there.

▭ In November the German Federal Court of Justice found Moroccan citizen Mounir el-Motassadeq guilty of being an accessory to murder on 246 counts in connection with the attacks on the World Trade Center in New York on 11 September 2001. He was sentenced to seven years' imprisonment. In June 2005, the Hamburg Supreme Court had ruled that evidence possibly obtained under torture or cruel, inhuman or degrading treatment was admissible in the retrial, a ruling that breached international law.

Universal jurisdiction

In March, the German Attorney General decided not to prosecute the former Uzbekistani Minister of Internal Affairs Zokir Almatov, who was reportedly one of the commanders of the security forces responsible for a mass killing in the Uzbekistani city of Andizhan in May 2005. Zokir Almatov had already fled Germany, where he had been receiving medical treatment, after he was alerted to an attempt to persuade the federal prosecutor to open a criminal investigation against him under Germany's Code of Crimes against International Law. This law allows courts to exercise universal jurisdiction in cases of alleged crimes against humanity, war crimes or genocide, irrespective of where they were committed or the nationality of the accused and the victims.

In November a criminal complaint was filed against the US former Secretary of Defense Donald Rumsfeld and other high-ranking US officials for alleged crimes under international law committed in Iraq and at Guantánamo Bay. The complaint was based on the Code of Crimes against International Law.

Refugees at risk

The Federal Agency for Migration and Refugees continued to withdraw refugee status from individuals, particularly those from Afghanistan and Iraq, even though they would not be safe if returned. After refugee status was withdrawn, the residence permits of the individuals concerned were often cancelled, putting them at risk of deportation to their country of origin. In November the Interior Minister declared that people could be deported to northern Iraq.

The government proposed new asylum legislation that did not fully conform to international refugee laws and standards as well as European Union directives. For example, individuals would not be properly protected against religious persecution. The proposal also failed to resolve the issue of the approximately 200,000 people with "leave to remain" status, among whom were people whose asylum claims had been rejected but who had not been deported for humanitarian reasons. Their continued stay in Germany was decided on a monthly basis and they had restricted access to the labour market. The proposal would give these people a two-year residence permit provided that they had found employment by the end of September 2007.

Police accountability

🗁 In November, the Regional Court of Dessau refused, on grounds of insufficient evidence, to open proceedings against two policemen allegedly involved in the death of Sierra Leonean citizen Oury Jalloh, who died in 2005 after being burned alive in a police cell. He had been chained to his bed allegedly because he had resisted arrest. Preliminary investigations by the State Attorney concluded that the fire alarm in Oury Jalloh's cell had been switched off during the incident.

AI country reports/ visits
Report
· Partners in crime: Europe's role in US renditions
  (AI Index: EUR 01/008/2006)

were taken towards abolition and death sentences continued to be handed down. No executions were carried out.

The National Reconciliation Commission
In October the government began paying reparations to some 2,000 Ghanaians who had suffered human rights abuses under former governments. The reparation payments were recommended by the National Reconciliation Commission, which was formed in 2002 to address human rights violations committed under various governments since Ghana gained independence in 1957.

GHANA

REPUBLIC OF GHANA
Head of state and government: John Agyekum Kufuor
Death penalty: abolitionist in practice
International Criminal Court: ratified

The government began paying reparations to victims of human rights violations under previous governments. The death penalty continued to be handed down in cases of murder and for treason. Violence and discrimination against women remained prevalent.

Violence against women
Women continued to be victims of domestic violence and female genital mutilation.

The Domestic Violence Bill was the subject of Parliamentary debate, during which a clause that would criminalize marital rape was dropped. The Bill had not become law by the end of the year.

Forced evictions
Forced evictions and internal displacement, particularly of marginalized people, continued to occur.

🗁 Hundreds of residents from the Dudzorme Island (in the Digya National Park) were forcibly evicted in late March and early April. Those evicted were not provided with alternative housing or with compensation. On 8 April, some of those evicted were reportedly forced into an overloaded ferry, which subsequently capsized, leaving around 30 people dead according to official sources, and many others unaccounted for.

Death penalty
Despite statements by government officials that the death penalty should be abolished, no concrete steps

GREECE

HELLENIC REPUBLIC
Head of state: Karolos Papoulias
Head of government: Constantinos Karamanlis
Death penalty: abolitionist for all crimes
International Criminal Court: ratified

Two agents of the intelligence service were charged in connection with the alleged abduction of seven people in the context of the "war on terror". Migrants suffered ill-treatment, and there were concerns about forcible return. Migrant children were held in detention on at least two occasions. A draft law aimed at bringing the country's asylum procedure in line with international standards was being finalized but had not been passed by the end of the year. Conscientious objectors continued to face persecution. Women victims of domestic violence or trafficking and forced prostitution were not granted the necessary protection.

Abductions and incommunicado detention in the 'war on terror'
In May, two agents of the Hellenic Intelligence Service were charged in connection with the alleged abductions of one Indian and six Pakistani nationals in Athens in July 2005. No evidence came to light in the cases of six other agents initially suspected of involvement in the abductions. The eight agents were the subject of further investigations. The abductions appeared to have taken place in the context of international investigations into the London bombings of July 2005. The government originally stated that its intelligence service and other agencies had not been involved. In November, Javed Aslam, a Pakistani national, who had complained to the prosecutor on behalf of his co-nationals, was arrested by Greek police and was held in Korydallos prison awaiting deportation, after an arrest warrant was issued by the

Pakistani authorities, charging him with illegal migration and smuggling of human beings.

Treatment of migrants and refugees
The government failed to allow asylum-seekers access to the country and continued to return them to their country of origin, without legal aid or access to asylum procedures.

In September, 118 people who had been shipwrecked on the island of Crete two weeks earlier were expelled to Egypt, without being given access to lawyers and AI representatives who had requested to meet them.

In September, 40 people trying to reach the island of Chios by boat were intercepted by Greek coastguards who allegedly took them on board after their boat had sunk, handcuffed them, took them towards Turkey and forced them into the water. The bodies of six people were found on the Turkish coast, 31 were rescued by the Turkish authorities, and three were reported missing. The Greek authorities denied the allegations.

Detention conditions reportedly amounted to ill-treatment. The detention of minors was also reported.

It was reported that six minors were among refugees and migrants being held at the detention centre on the island of Chios. There were also reports of overcrowding and lack of toilet facilities at the centre.

Five minors were detained in the city of Volos for 45 days before being transferred to Athens where they were detained for a second time.

There were also reports of ill-treatment of migrants and asylum-seekers.

Forty migrants, including minors, who were attempting to board ships bound for Italy from the port of Patras were reportedly detained at the Patras Port Security Office and some were beaten.

Conscientious objection to military service
The majority of the conscientious objectors who were expected to benefit from the law on military service refused to resubmit their applications in protest against the punitive length of civilian service. In October, an application for conscientious objector status was rejected because the grounds for the application were not religious.

In May Lazaros Petromelidis was handed a five-month suspended prison sentence by the Athens Appeals Court. He appealed against the sentence.

In June the Athens Military Appeals Court ruled on the cases of two conscientious objectors accused of disobedience. Boris Sotiriadis was acquitted and Giorgos Koutsomanolakis was convicted and handed a 10-month suspended prison term.

In October the Athens Military Appeals Court decreased Giorgos Monastiriotis' 40-month prison sentence for desertion to 24 months, with three years' suspension. He was convicted after refusing to follow his unit to Iraq.

Domestic violence
In October parliament adopted a law combating domestic violence, placing the emphasis on the

preservation of the family unit rather than on the rights of the victims, who in the vast majority of cases are women. Under the law, judicial arbitration would be at the initiation of the prosecutor rather than at the victim's request, a definite time frame for immediate implementation of restraining orders was lacking, and budgetary provisions to ensure the implementation of the law had not been allocated by the end of the year.

Trafficking in human beings
In February Albania and Greece signed an agreement on the protection of Albanian children being trafficked into Greece. By the end of the year, the agreement had yet to be ratified by the parliament. The agreement set out procedures for the provision of food, shelter, and medical and psychosocial support; the appointment of temporary guardians; arrangements for voluntary return; the integration process upon their return; and the prohibition of detention and criminal prosecution of children.

The agreement did not, however, specify conditions on voluntary return of children, including the process of determining whether the return was indeed voluntary. Nor did it specify provisions for the protection of children during the criminal investigation process or for cases of children trafficked by their parents.

In April a Bulgarian woman was detained on the island of Rhodes for illegal entry, and two men who had arranged her transfer from Crete to Rhodes were charged with trafficking and pimping. The woman reported that after she was detained, a police officer took her to his house where he raped her, and when she was taken to the police station she was raped by another officer. A criminal investigation was opened, the two officers were charged with rape, and the guard on duty at the police station at the time and the police station commander were both charged with neglect of duty.

There were concerns that victims of trafficking were required to testify against their traffickers before being given protection.

Freedom of expression
In July the European Court of Human Rights ruled unanimously that Greece had violated Article 9 of the European Convention on Human Rights in the case of Mehmet Agga, an elected but unofficial Mufti in the prefecture of Xanthi, who had been convicted in 1997 by a domestic court for usurping the function of a minister of a "known religion" under Article 175 of the Criminal Code.

Update: The killing of Marinos Christopoulos
In November, Giorgos Tylianakis, the police officer who had killed a 22-year-old Romani man, Marinos Christopoulos in October 2001, was sentenced to 10 years and three months' imprisonment by the Court of Appeals.

AI country reports/ visits
Report
· Greece: High time to comply fully with European standards on conscientious objection (AI Index: EUR 25/003/2006)

Visits
AI delegates visited Greece in July and September. In September, the Secretary General of AI met senior government figures.

GRENADA

GRENADA
Head of state: Queen Elizabeth II, represented by Daniel Williams
Head of government: Keith Mitchell
Death penalty: abolitionist in practice
International Criminal Court: not ratified

The 'Grenada 17'
In June the Truth and Reconciliation Commission presented its report to Parliament. According to reports, the Commission called for "an appropriate opportunity for the 'Grenada 17' to access existing or established courts... which would studiously ensure the process of fair trial." The "Grenada 17" were convicted in 1986 following unfair trials of the murder of Prime Minister Maurice Bishop and others in 1983. During the trial the defendants alleged that some of the statements used in evidence against them had been obtained under torture and there were serious concerns about the possible bias of judicial officials and jurors involved in the case. The Commission also called for efforts to be made to find the bodies of those who died during the coup and US invasion and to pay compensation to their families. The government had failed to take any steps to implement the Commission's recommendations by the end of the year.

In December the UK Judicial Committee of the Privy Council, Grenada's highest court of appeal, heard a constitutional motion presented by the 13 members of the "Grenada 17" who remained in prison challenging the constitutionality and fairness of their detention. A decision was expected in early 2007. Three of the "Grenada 17" – Andy Mitchell, Vincent Joseph and Cosmos Richardson – were released in December after completing 20 years in prison. Their sentences had been reduced to 20 years for good behaviour. Phyllis Coard had been released in 2000 for health reasons.

GUATEMALA

REPUBLIC OF GUATEMALA
Head of state and government: Óscar Berger Perdomo
Death penalty: retentionist
International Criminal Court: not ratified

Threats, attacks and intimidation against human rights defenders, in particular those focusing on economic, social and cultural rights, intensified. Large numbers of women continued to be killed, with few successful prosecutions of the perpetrators. There was some progress in bringing to justice some of those responsible for human rights violations committed during the internal armed conflict.

Background
There were continued high levels of crime, affecting all sectors of society.

Various groups protested against different government economic policies. February saw protests against the Central America Free Trade Agreement. In June, doctors protested against under-investment in health services and infrastructure. Some rural Indigenous communities continued to oppose mining activities in their areas.

In February, the Office of the UN High Commissioner for Human Rights in Guatemala issued its first report. Among other recommendations it called for more investment to prevent human rights violations and protect human rights.

Constitutional guarantees were suspended twice during the year in certain rural areas as combined army and police forces searched for alleged weapons caches and crops producing illegal drugs. Civil society groups protested against the manner of the searches and accused them of being politically motivated, as communities in the targeted areas had protested against government policies.

In October, a Mexican court authorized the extradition of former President Alfonso Portillo, who left the presidency in January 2004, to face charges of corruption. An appeal was lodged.

In December the government signed an agreement with the UN to establish the International Commission Against Impunity in Guatemala. The Commission would support the Public Prosecutor's Office in prosecuting the activities of illegal security forces and clandestine security organizations. The agreement was not submitted to Congress for ratification by the end of the year.

Violence against women
At least 580 women were killed, according to police records. According to the Public Prosecutor's Office, during 2006, six people were sentenced for such killings, which often involved sexual violence.

In June, the UN Committee on the Elimination of Discrimination against Women expressed concern at the disappearances, rape, torture and murders of women and the engrained culture of impunity for such crimes. In September, Congress approved the creation of a new National Institute of Forensic Sciences which would unify the forensic services of different government bodies. A law which considered sexual relations with a female minor a crime only if the girl was "honest" remained in force.

☐ In February, the body of Silvia Patricia Madrid, a 25-year-old sex-worker, was found semi-naked on a road on the outskirts of Guatemala City. She had been strangled and her body showed signs of sexual violence. The authorities did not collect evidence from the alleged murder scene.

Economic, social and cultural rights
According to the UN, over 30 per cent of the population lived on less than US$2 a day. Inequality persisted in the country. A disproportionately high number of those with low incomes and limited access to healthcare and education were women, Indigenous people and rural dwellers.

Evictions in rural areas continued, with 29 reported to have been carried out. In July the UN Committee against Torture called for the government to prevent the use of excessive force, provide specific training for police officers, and ensure that complaints concerning forced evictions were thoroughly investigated.

☐ In April, approximately 400 people of the San José La Mocá farm, Department of Alta Verapaz, were forcibly evicted. The community had been in dispute with the farm's owner over alleged unpaid wages. They were forced onto a nearby road, with no access to clean water, food or shelter. In July, one member of the community was killed and 38 wounded in further violence related to the eviction.

Threats, intimidation and impunity
During a visit in May, the UN High Commissioner for Human Rights stated that there had been no significant progress in combating impunity or eliminating clandestine groups. More than half of the reported 278 attacks on human rights activists and organizations were against those focusing on economic, social and cultural rights, including labour rights, the rights of Indigenous peoples and housing rights.

In June a Spanish judge and prosecutor, investigating a case of alleged genocide, visited the country to interview witnesses and suspects. The two officials were prevented from pursuing the case, but in July the judge issued international arrest warrants for the five accused, including former President General Efraín Ríos Montt.

☐ In July, Erwin Orrego, a member of the Emergency Front of Market Sellers of Guatemala, was kidnapped and threatened with execution, allegedly by police officers. He was released after human rights organizations alerted the media and authorities.

Death penalty
A proposal to abolish the death penalty was rejected after the relevant commission in Congress returned an unfavourable verdict. Two new proposals to establish a system for allowing pardons of those sentenced to death progressed through Congress. In 2005 the Inter-American Court of Human Rights (IACHR) had ruled that the lack of possibility of a pardon meant that the death sentences could not be carried out.

Nine prisoners had their death sentences commuted to 50-year prison terms after judgments by the IACHR relating to the definition of crimes for which the death penalty could be applied. Twenty-one prisoners remained under sentence of death. No death sentences were passed during the year and no executions took place.

AI country reports/ visits
Reports
- Guatemala: Land of injustice? (AI Index: AMR 34/003/2006)
- Guatemala: A summary of Amnesty International's concerns with regard to the Guatemalan Government's implementation of the United Nations Convention against Torture and Other Cruel, Inhuman and Degrading Treatment or Punishment (AI Index: AMR 34/013/2006)
- Guatemala: Human rights defenders at risk (AI Index: AMR 34/016/2006)
- Guatemala: No protection, no justice – killings of women (an update) (AI Index: AMR 34/019/2006)AMR
Visit
An AI delegation visited in March to conduct research.

GUINEA

REPUBLIC OF GUINEA
Head of state: Lansana Conté
Head of government: Cellou Dalein Diallo, until April
Death penalty: retentionist
International Criminal Court: ratified

In February and in June, the security forces used excessive force against civilian demonstrators, resulting in multiple deaths and injuries. Torture and ill-treatment of protestors and of detainees were reported. Seven military personnel remained held without trial. Nine people were sentenced to death.

Background
In April, a few hours after a major cabinet reshuffle by Prime Minister Cellou Dalein Diallo was announced, a decree suspending him for "serious wrongdoing" was read on national radio and television. Guinea's ailing president, Lansana Conté, gave no further information and the post of prime minister was abolished by decree in May.

Excessive use of force

On at least three occasions in February and in June, the security forces used excessive force against demonstrators and students. The security forces reportedly used tear gas, beat students with police batons and fired live ammunition. No independent investigation was launched into the resulting deaths.

In February, at least two people were killed and several injured in Gueckedou, in the southeast, when police clashed with demonstrators protesting at the appointment of a mayor belonging to the Progress and Unity Party (Parti de l'unité et du progrès, PUP), the ruling party. Opposition parties accused officials of fraud during the December local elections.

In June, unarmed students demonstrated in major cities including Labé and Conakry after learning that their exams would not be supervised because of a nationwide strike over price rises for basic commodities. In clashes with security forces, more than 10 students were killed. The Minister of Internal Affairs put the official death toll at 11. According to hospital sources, 18 people were killed and more than 80 injured.

UN Secretary-General Kofi Annan and the African Union President Alpha Oumar Konaré expressed concern that the security forces had used excessive force against unarmed demonstrators. However, despite national and international pressure, no independent inquiry appeared to have been opened.

Torture and ill-treatment

There were consistent reports of beatings and other ill-treatment of demonstrators during the protest marches in February and June. Dozens of demonstrators were injured during attempts by the security forces to disperse them.

A military officer arrested in 2005 was tortured and ill-treated on Kassa Island. He was locked in a tiny cell nicknamed "Vietnam", less than a cubic metre in size. Unable to stand or extend his legs, he was forced to crouch for 72 hours and given nothing but breadcrumbs to eat. He was later taken aboard a small inflatable boat, bound, thrown into the water and dragged by his hands at speed for half an hour.

Detention without trial

Seven soldiers and military officers, including Naroumba Kante, Djan Foula Kamara and Mamady Condé, held since 2003 on suspicion of plotting to overthrow President Conté, were still detained in Conakry Central Prison. They had not been charged by the end of 2006. The detainees' families wrote to the authorities requesting visitation rights and a prompt, fair trial. They received no reply.

Releases of military officers

Between March and July, four military officers, including Mamy Pé and Kabinet Kaba, were released without charge. They had been arrested following an attempt to assassinate President Conté in January 2005. They were held on Kassa Island, where access to detainees is extremely difficult.

Death penalty

In September, the Assize court sentenced nine people to death for the murder of a local politician in May. No executions were reported.

GUINEA-BISSAU

REPUBLIC OF GUINEA-BISSAU
Head of state: João Bernardo "Nino" Vieira
Head of government: Aristides Gomes
Death penalty: abolitionist for all crimes
International Criminal Court: signed

Dire economic and social conditions continued to threaten political stability. Tens of thousands of people faced hunger in the south while fighting in the northern border area displaced thousands of families. There were restrictions on freedom of expression.

Background

The country remained one of the poorest in the world. In October a United Nations Development Programme report indicated that two in three people lived in abject poverty and that one in four children died before reaching the age of five.

There were frequent strikes throughout the year by teachers, health workers and others over non-payment of salaries. In September the police violently dispersed a demonstration by striking workers.

In September, a bill prohibiting the practice of female genital mutilation was tabled in the People's National Assembly. However, it was not enacted by the end of the year.

Conflict and forced displacement

In March, the army clashed with a faction of the Senegalese separatist group Democratic Forces of Casamance Movement (Mouvement des forces démocratiques de Casamance, MFDC), in the north, along the border with Senegal. About 20,000 people, mostly women and children, were internally displaced following attacks on the town of São Domingos and surrounding villages. More than 2,000 took refuge across the border in Senegal.

The MFDC reportedly laid landmines including along the main road. Eleven people died and 12 others were injured when a bus carrying people fleeing the fighting hit an explosive device. There were also unconfirmed reports of deliberate killings by the MFDC.

Fundamental freedoms

Freedom of expression came under attack. Journalists and politicians were threatened for reporting the fighting along the northern border and for criticizing the authorities. At least four politicians were reportedly arrested and briefly detained. On several occasions in March armed soldiers entered a hotel in São Domingos where international journalists were lodged, apparently seeking to arrest a foreign correspondent.

◻ Marcelino Simões Lopes Cabral, a former minister of defence, was arrested at home in Bissau and detained for a few days in April for allegedly helping the leader of the MFDC. No charges were brought against him. He had been arrested before, in 2003, for criticizing the government of the day.

◻ In August, two soldiers, Commodore Mohamed Laminé Sanhá and Lieutenant-Colonel Almane Alam Camará, were arrested for allegedly plotting to kill the Chief of the General Staff of the Armed Forces. They were released uncharged after three days. They had been arrested on several occasions before since 2000, and on each occasion were released uncharged after spending several months in prison.

Food shortages

Tens of thousands of people in the south faced hunger following the failure of the 2005 rice crop owing to the build up of salt in rice paddies, compounded by irregular rainfall. In addition the price of cashew nuts, the country's main export, fell. In May the government launched an appeal for aid which began to arrive in September. However, despite the government's price fixing, most of the population could no longer afford to buy rice.

GUYANA

REPUBLIC OF GUYANA
Head of state: Bharrat Jagdeo
Head of government: Samuel Hinds
Death penalty: retentionist
International Criminal Court: ratified

There were attacks on freedom of expression. Marginalized communities had difficulty in accessing treatment for HIV/AIDS. Twenty-three people were on death row. Death sentences continued to be passed. No executions were reported.

Background

The People's Progressive Party (PPP) was returned to office for a fourth consecutive term following peaceful general elections in August. The murder in April of Satyadeow Sawh, the PPP Agriculture Minister, had created fears of a recurrence of political violence between supporters of the mainly Indo-Guyanese PPP and the opposition People's National Congress (PNC), which is principally Afro-Guyanese.

Freedom of expression

Five newspaper employees and an opposition journalist were killed.

◻ Five employees of the newspaper *Kaieteur News* were shot execution-style on 8 August at the newspaper's printing plant. The motive for the killings was unclear, although the owner of the newspaper had allegedly received threats over the coverage of a series of rapes in the capital, Georgetown. Three men were charged with the killings.

◻ Ronald Waddell, a journalist, radio talk show host and former candidate for the PNC, was shot outside his home in a Georgetown suburb on 30 January. According to eyewitness reports, two men shot him repeatedly as he was getting into his car. He died later in hospital. No one had been charged with the murder by the end of 2006.

People living with HIV/AIDS

Despite positive steps to ensure the right to health, stigma and discrimination towards HIV/AIDS remained a barrier to the successful implementation of treatment. The Indigenous Amerindian population had particularly limited access to HIV/AIDS-related health care and information. Men who have sexual relations with other men were criminalized and discriminated against, which restricted their access to HIV/AIDS prevention, treatment and care. There were reports of people being dismissed from their jobs on the basis of their HIV status. Violations of the rights to privacy and confidentiality contributed to the spread of the disease by discouraging people from seeking an HIV test or treatment.

AI country reports/visits
Report
- "I am not ashamed!": HIV/AIDS and human rights in the Dominican Republic and Guyana
  (AI Index: AMR 01/002/2006)

Visit
AI delegates visited Guyana in January.

HAITI

REPUBLIC OF HAITI
Head of state: René Garcia Préval (replaced Boniface Alexandre in May)
Head of government: Jacques-Edouard Alexis (replaced Gérard Latortue in May)
Death penalty: abolitionist for all crimes
International Criminal Court: signed

Presidential, local and legislative elections were held in February and December, signalling a return to democratic rule. Slow progress was made in building security, justice and respect for human rights after two years of transitional government and UN presence. However, armed violence in the forms of unlawful killings and kidnappings by illegal armed groups remained at critical levels in the capital throughout 2006. Clashes between security forces, including UN peacekeeping forces, and armed groups continued sporadically. Members of the police suspected of criminal activities and human rights violations were not brought to justice. Violence against women persisted. Hundreds of people remained in prison without charge or trial.

Background

After two years of transitional government, marked by widespread human rights violations and insecurity, René Garcia Préval was elected in February and the country regained political stability. Presidential and legislative elections were held in relative calm after being postponed four times. In December, local elections concluded the electoral process with few violent incidents reported.

The international community remained concerned about the humanitarian situation and continued to mobilize resources to improve security, government capacity, and the dire economic condition of millions of Haitians. The human rights situation was also of concern despite the presence of the UN Stabilization Mission in Haiti (MINUSTAH) since 2004. The 8,000-strong UN mission, mandated to secure the country, came under increasing criticism as it showed little success in stopping armed violence and promoting and protecting human rights. The government's disarmament, demobilization and reintegration programme was criticized by members of parliament as it gave priority to dialogue with illegal armed groups. Some parliamentarians proposed the reintroduction of the death penalty as a means to deter armed violence. The UN Secretary-General visited Haiti in August and the UN High Commissioner for Human Rights visited in October.

The government remained unable to ensure the economic, social and cultural rights of its population with 60 per cent of its 8.5 million people living on less than US$1 a day. Serious food shortages, difficulties in access to safe drinking water, and the highest prevalence of HIV/AIDS in the region aggravated the humanitarian situation. Migration and trafficking of people into the Dominican Republic continued unabated and the Haitian authorities failed to enforce border and migration controls. They also failed to assist migrant workers deported back to Haiti.

The proliferation of small arms continued to fuel armed violence and human rights abuses. The government supported the proposal for an international arms trade treaty at the UN General Assembly.

Violence against women

Women and girls continued to be tortured, raped and killed by illegal armed groups and by individuals. No significant progress was made in investigating and prosecuting those responsible. On 1 September, hundreds of women survivors of rape and other forms of sexual violence marched in Port-au-Prince and called on the government to take necessary measures to prevent all forms of violence and discrimination against women. The demonstrators also called on illegal armed groups to stop committing rape.

◻ On 22 November, the body of Fara Natacha Dessources, aged 20, was found bearing clear marks of torture and several gunshot wounds. She had been kidnapped a week earlier in La Plaine, in the northeast suburbs of Port-au-Prince by armed individuals.

Human rights defenders

Human rights defenders continued to face harassment and intimidation.

There were fears for the safety of members of AUMOHD (Association des Universitaires Motivés pour un Haïti de Droit) after its president, Evel Fanfan, received death threats. AUMOHD was defending the rights of survivors of armed violence and promoting a peaceful conflict resolution process between rival gangs in Grand Ravine, a deprived neighbourhood of Port-au-Prince.

◻ Bruner Esterne, the co-ordinator of the Grand Ravine Community Council for Human Rights, was shot dead by three unknown individuals in September. He was a survivor and witness of the 20 August 2005 attack led by police officials and members of the illegal armed group Small Machetes Army (Lame Ti Manchet) at a football stadium in Martissant, where at least nine people were killed and dozens wounded. He was working closely with AUMOHD.

Unlawful killings

Unlawful and indiscriminate killings by illegal armed groups continued. Most of the perpetrators of these crimes continue to enjoy total impunity.

◻ On 7 July, the illegal armed group Small Machetes Army attacked residents of Grand Ravine, killing at least 24 people including four women and four children. Dozens of houses were looted and burned down, leading to forced displacement of survivors and other residents in fear of further attacks.

Prisoners of conscience, political prisoners

The administration of justice continued to fall short of international standards of due process and fairness as thousands of people remained imprisoned without charge or trial. Less than one fifth of the nearly 4,500 prisoners had been sentenced. However, key political prisoners from the transitional government of 2004-6 were released.

▭ Catholic priest Gérard Jean-Juste was conditionally released in January on medical grounds. He had been held since July 2005 without charges or trial. He was allowed to leave the country to seek medical treatment in the USA. AI declared him a prisoner of conscience after he was illegally arrested on fabricated charges.

▭ Annette Auguste, a Lavalas grass-roots activist and folk singer arrested in May 2004, was finally brought to trial and acquitted on 15 August. Prosecutors put forward no evidence against her.

▭ Former Prime Minister Yvon Neptune was released in July after spending more than two years in detention without trial.

Harsh prison conditions

Harsh prison conditions continued to be the norm throughout the country. Overcrowding, inadequate food and medical neglect resulted in dire conditions at most prisons. Inmates relied on family members to fulfil their basic needs including food. At least 50 prisoners escaped from the National Penitentiary in Port-au-Prince in July and December.

Impunity

The justice system continued to suffer from lack of resources, corruption and inadequate training for personnel, preventing the effective investigation and prosecution of previous human rights violations.

▭ On 9 March, seven police officers arrested for involvement in the killings at the Martissant stadium in August 2005 were released by the investigating magistrate in charge of the case. No members of the Small Machetes Army were arrested despite continuous threats against witnesses and survivors of the August 2005 and July 2006 attacks.

Disarmament

After ineffectual attempts during the two-year transitional government, a National Commission for Disarmament, Demobilization and Reintegration (CNDDR) was finally established in September with the assistance of MINUSTAH. Dozens of armed group members joined the DDR programme, but violence continued at an alarming level.

AI country reports/visits
Reports
- Haiti: The call for tough arms controls — voices from Haiti (AI Index: AMR 36/001/2006)
- Open letter to the president of the Republic of Haiti (AI Index: AMR 36/011/2006)

HONDURAS

REPUBLIC OF HONDURAS
Head of state and government: Manuel Zelaya Rosales (replaced Ricardo Maduro in January)
Death penalty: abolitionist for all crimes
International Criminal Court: ratified

Individuals and organizations involved in defending the human rights of Indigenous and rural communities continued to be attacked and intimidated. High levels of violence against women, children and young people persisted, with little effective government response.

Background

Manuel Zelaya Rosales of the Liberal Party assumed the presidency in January. In April, the Central America Free Trade Agreement, which includes the USA, the Dominican Republic and other Central American states, came into effect in Honduras.

There were mass protests by Indigenous and environmental groups against the government's mining policies which they claimed were carried out without proper consultation and posed a threat to the environment and to the health of people living in mining areas.

Honduras ratified the Optional Protocol to the Convention against Torture in May.

According to UN figures, as of June 2006 nearly half of the population lived below the poverty line and 20 per cent survived on US$1 or less a day.

Economic, social and cultural rights

Organizations and individuals involved in the defence of human rights in the context of land disputes were subjected to threats and intimidation. In most cases the authorities failed to bring the perpetrators to justice.

▭ In June, Jessica García, a leader of the Afro-descendant Garifuna community in the village of San Juan Tela, Atlántida department, northern Honduras, was allegedly threatened and forced at gunpoint to sign over land belonging to the community to a company who reportedly planned to build a tourist resort.

▭ In July, the Supreme Court acquitted brothers Leonardo and Marcelino Miranda. They had been convicted of a murder committed in 2001 following a politically motivated trial. The real reasons for their detention were believed to be their role as Indigenous community leaders and their efforts to obtain official recognition of communal land titles. Complaints by the brothers of threats and torture had not been investigated by the end of the year.

Violence against women

In November, the head of the Public Prosecutor's Office Special Unit for Women's Affairs voiced her concern at increasing levels of violence against women. During the year around 150 women were killed. Women's human rights organizations highlighted the high levels of killings and domestic violence and the poor record of state institutions in addressing gender-based violence.

Children and young people

According to local human rights organizations more than 400 children and young people were killed during the year. In the majority of cases, those responsible were not brought to justice.

In September the Inter-American Court of Human Rights found that the authorities had failed to investigate and bring to justice those responsible for the extrajudicial executions of four young people by police officers in 1995, even after witnesses had identified the police officers involved. Moreover, the Court ordered Honduras to establish a training programme for police, judicial and Public Prosecutor's Office officials and prison staff about the special protection that the state should afford children and young people.

AI country reports/ visits
Report
- Honduras: Human rights defenders at risk – Montaña Verde prisoners of conscience (AI Index: AMR 37/001/2006)

HUNGARY

REPUBLIC OF HUNGARY
Head of state: László Sólyom
Head of government: Ferenc Gyurcsány
Death penalty: abolitionist for all crimes
International Criminal Court: ratified

The police reportedly used excessive force and ill-treated protesters and detainees. Discrimination continued to deprive the Romani community of a range of rights, including the right of full access to education. Legal measures adopted to combat violence against women allowed for the use of restraint orders on abusers only where criminal proceedings had started.

Background
Parliamentary elections in April returned the Hungarian Socialist Party to power in coalition with the Alliance of Free Democrats. Police and protesters clashed between 17 and 20 September after it was

revealed that the Prime Minister had admitted in May that he had lied during the election campaign. There was further violence on 23 October at the commemoration of the start of the 1956 uprising.

Excessive use of force and ill-treatment
Police officers reportedly used excessive force on peaceful demonstrations that later turned violent in the capital, Budapest, during the night of 20 to 21 September and again on 23 October. Rubber bullets, water cannon and tear gas were said to have been used indiscriminately and without warning against both peaceful and violent protesters. Police officers were reportedly masked and not wearing badges of identification, such as identity numbers. There were also allegations that police beat protesters taken into custody, held under-18s together with adult detainees, and fabricated some of the charges. Some detainees were denied immediate access to a lawyer, including during questioning.

On 24 October, Budapest chief of police Péter Gergényi was reported as saying that police "acted lawfully, professionally and proportionately". On 27 October, the European Commission requested an explanation from the Hungarian authorities on the alleged excessive use of force. In November the Prime Minister set up a committee "to explore the social, economical and political causes which led to the riots and the response thereto". The committee would not deal with individual complaints.

In June, reporting on its visit in 2004, the European Committee for the Prevention of Torture noted concerns about detainees' rights of access to a lawyer from the very outset of their detention. It called for a fully fledged and properly funded legal aid system for those in police custody unable to pay for a lawyer, and for a guarantee that detainees can be examined, if they so wish, by a doctor from outside the police service.

Discrimination against Roma
Members of the Romani community continued to face discrimination in education, housing and employment.

In March, the Council of Europe Commissioner for Human Rights called for measures to be developed that would help Roma obtain decent housing, would firmly punish discriminatory or anti-Roma behaviour, and stop the over-representation of Romani children in special classes or home education.

In March the UN Committee on the Rights of the Child made public its Concluding Observation following review of Hungary's second periodic report under the UN Children's Convention. The Committee expressed concerns about the prevalence of discriminatory and xenophobic attitudes, in particular towards the Romani population. The Committee noted that Romani children were especially stigmatized, excluded and impoverished in relation to the rest of the population because of their ethnicity. Such discrimination was most notable in housing, jobs and access to health, adoption and educational services. The Committee expressed concern at the arbitrary segregation of Romani children in special institutions or classes.

Access to preschools is reportedly limited in regions with predominantly Romani populations and high levels of poverty.

◻ In June the Debrecen Appeals Court found that the Miskolc municipality, by integrating seven schools without simultaneously redefining their catchment areas, had perpetuated the segregation of Romani children, violating their right to equality of treatment. It was ruling on an appeal by the non-governmental organization Chance for Children Foundation against the county court dismissal in November 2005 of a lawsuit alleging citywide segregation of Romani school children by the local council of Miskolc.

Violence against women

In June the UN Committee on the Elimination of Discrimination against Women made available Hungary's sixth periodic report on measures taken to implement the UN Women's Convention. These included the Act on Equal Treatment and the Promotion of Equal Opportunities, in force since 2003, and new powers under the Criminal Procedure Code to issue restraint orders against the perpetrators of family violence, which came into force in July. However, women's and human rights organizations continued to criticize restrictions that allow restraint orders to be issued only when a criminal prosecution has been initiated.

Forced sterilization

In August the Committee found Hungary in violation of the UN Women's Convention for its failure to protect the reproductive rights of a Romani woman sterilized without her consent in 2001. It recommended that domestic legislation be brought in line with the principle of informed consent in cases of sterilization and with international human rights and medical standards. Provisions allowing physicians to carry out sterilizations without following specified procedures "when it seems to be appropriate in given circumstances" should be repealed.

AI country reports/ visits

Reports
- Hungary: Reports of excessive use of force by the police (AI Index: EUR 27/001/2006)
- Europe and Central Asia: Summary of Amnesty International's concerns in the region, January-June 2006 (AI Index: EUR 01/017/2006)

Visits
AI delegates visited Hungary in April and September.

INDIA

REPUBLIC OF INDIA
Head of state: APJ Abdul Kalam
Head of government: Manmohan Singh
Death penalty: retentionist
International Criminal Court: not ratified

Perpetrators of past human rights violations continued to enjoy impunity. Concerns grew over protection of economic, social and cultural rights of already marginalized communities. Human rights violations were reported in several states where security legislation was used to facilitate arbitrary detention and torture. A new anti-terror law, in place of the repealed Prevention of Terrorism Act (POTA), was being considered in the aftermath of multiple bombings in Mumbai and elsewhere. The Armed Forces Special Powers Act (AFSPA), long criticized for widespread abuses in the north-east, was not repealed. Justice and rehabilitation continued to evade most victims of the 2002 Gujarat communal violence. Human rights legislation was amended undermining the powers of the National Human Rights Commission (NHRC). New laws to prevent violence against women and guarantee rural employment and right to information had not been fully implemented by the end of the year. Socially and economically marginalized groups such as *adivasis, dalits,* marginal/ landless farmers and the urban poor continued to face systemic discrimination and loss of resource base and livelihood because of development projects.

Background

An agreement reached with the USA in March gave India access to strategic nuclear material and equipment for civilian purposes, and signalled closer Indo-US ties.

Hundreds of people were killed in bomb attacks during the year, including 21 in the north Indian city of Varanasi in March, more than 200 in multiple bombings in Mumbai in July, and 37 in Malegaon, Maharashtra state, in September. Concern about such attacks continued to dominate peace talks between India and Pakistan, which made little progress. The two countries agreed to set up an "anti-terror mechanism", the details of which were not spelled out. Little progress was made in continuing dialogue over Kashmir, Nagaland and Assam.

Rising Maoist activity in some states added to security and human rights concerns. Several states, including Orissa and West Bengal, witnessed protests by people whose livelihoods were threatened by ongoing and proposed fast-tracked development projects. High suicide rates by debt-ridden farmers were recorded in some states, including Maharashtra, Andhra Pradesh and Kerala.

Following renewed fighting in Sri Lanka, around 10,000 Tamil refugees fled the island by sea and arrived in Tamil Nadu, already home to over 100,000 refugees; about 50,000 of the refugees were reportedly in camps with inadequate facilities.

Security legislation

India continued to play no direct role in the US-led "war on terror". However, demands for new anti-terror legislation in place of the repealed POTA grew after the bombings in Mumbai and Malegaon.

Following the bomb attacks, hundreds of people, mostly Muslims, were arbitrarily detained for short periods in Maharashtra. Sixteen people were charged under the state Control of Organised Crime Act. Local courts acquitted three of the 16 for lack of evidence.

Implementation of security legislation led to human rights violations in several states. An official panel report acknowledged widespread abuses of the AFSPA in the north-east but drew criticism for ignoring impunity issues and recommending use of the Unlawful Activities Prevention Act. Protests demanded repeal of the AFSPA.

At least 400 people remained in jail under the repealed POTA and several continued to face special trials whose proceedings fail to meet fair trial standards. The few convictions related to serious and high-profile cases. Official committees reviewed a majority of pending cases. However, the review process was questioned, with Gujarat and other states rejecting the committees' key recommendation to drop POTA charges.

Jammu and Kashmir

Politically motivated violence slightly decreased, but torture, deaths in custody, enforced disappearances and extrajudicial executions continued to be reported. Some six deaths in custody, 38 enforced disappearances including several juveniles, and 22 extrajudicial killings were reported in 2006. Identity-based attacks by Islamist fighters continued.

▭ In May, 35 Hindus were killed in Doda and Udhampur districts. Government officials accused Lashkar-e-Taiba, a Pakistan-based armed Islamist group, of carrying out the killings to derail the peace process.

▭ In October, 17-year-old Muhammad Maqbool Dar of Pakherpora died in custody after he was questioned by the Rashtriya Rifles, an army counter-insurgency force. A magistrates' inquiry and an internal army inquiry were ordered.

Impunity for human rights violations by state agents continued, although in a few cases criminal action was initiated after years of delay.

▭ In April, the Central Bureau of Investigation (CBI) indicted five army officers for the extrajudicial killing of five villagers at Pathribal in March 2000. The officers were charged with fabricating evidence to support their claim that the men were foreign fighters killed in an "encounter" with security forces. The officers had earlier claimed that the men had killed 35 Sikhs at Chittisinghpora four days before the "encounter". When local villagers protested in Brakpora that the five men were innocent villagers, the army opened fire,

killing 10 protesters. An inquiry into the Pathribal incident stalled when it was found that DNA samples had been tampered with.

A new report indicated that some 10,000 people had been victims of enforced disappearance since 1989. The Association of the Parents of Disappeared People reported that the authorities failed to provide information to the families of the victims about their whereabouts. Outstanding concerns over the existing powers of the state Human Rights Commission were heightened in August when its chairperson resigned over the "non-serious" attitude of the state government towards human rights violations.

Impunity

Little progress was made in cases relating to the 1984 anti-Sikh riots in Delhi which followed the assassination of Prime Minister Indira Gandhi by two of her Sikh bodyguards and led to a massacre of nearly 3,000 Sikhs. In 2005 the United Progressive Alliance (UPA) government promised to reopen the latest of many inquiries following the forced resignations of two leaders of the ruling Congress party, which heads the UPA. A judicial commission had concluded that there was credible evidence of involvement in the attacks against the two leaders who resigned.

In Punjab, a majority of police officers responsible for serious human rights violations during civil unrest between 1984 and 1994 continued to evade justice. In response to 2,097 reported cases of human rights violations during this period, the NHRC ordered Punjab state to provide compensation in 1,051 cases concerning people who died in police custody and appointed a commissioner to decide on compensation for 814 additional cases. CBI findings on these deaths in custody were not made public and the NHRC did not actively pursue with the judiciary the outstanding issues of impunity.

2002 Gujarat violence

Justice continued to evade most victims and survivors of the 2002 violence in Gujarat in which thousands of Muslims were attacked and more than 2,000 were killed. Rehabilitation continued to be slow. Members of the Muslim minority in Gujarat reportedly faced difficulties in accessing housing to rent and public resources. An official panel concluded that over 5,000 displaced families lived in "sub-human" conditions.

There continued to be few successful prosecutions relating to the violence. However, 1,594 cases closed by the state police were reopened on the orders of the Supreme Court and 41 police officials were being prosecuted for their alleged role.

New evidence on the riots emerged, in the form of details of mobile phone calls made between those leading the attacks and politicians belonging to the then ruling Bharatiya Janata Party (BJP), a Hindu nationalist party. The judicial commission appointed in 2002 by Gujarat's state government to investigate the attacks had not completed its work by the end of the year.

The Gujarat High Court set aside the Union government order appointing another commission to investigate the cause of the 2002 Godhra train fire which killed 59 Hindu pilgrims. The Court said there was no need for a second commission into the fire, which triggered attacks on Muslims and the subsequent violence.

Six key cases relating to killings and sexual assault of Muslim women in which complainants had sought transfer to courts outside Gujarat were still pending before the Supreme Court at the end of the year.

⌐ In March, a Mumbai court sentenced nine people to life imprisonment and acquitted eight others after a retrial in the Best Bakery case, relating to the massacre during the 2002 violence of 14 people in Vadodara city. In 2003, a local court had acquitted all the accused, but the Supreme Court transferred the case to Mumbai. The Mumbai court later convicted Zahira Shaikh, and another female relative of the victims, of perjury after they "turned hostile" and retracted their statements, reportedly under pressure.

The UPA government's draft bill to prevent communal violence was still pending before parliament. It had been introduced in 2005 following widespread criticism of the BJP-led government for failing to halt the Gujarat violence. Meanwhile, two other states ruled by the BJP — Rajasthan and Chhattisgarh — passed laws criminalizing religious conversion in certain circumstances, inviting criticism that they were acting against freedom of choice of religion.

Chhattisgarh

There was rising violence in the Dantewada area between Maoists and members of the anti-Maoist Salwa Judum, a militia widely believed to be sponsored by the Chhattisgarh state government. Civilians were routinely targeted by both sides and 45,000 *adivasis* were forced to live in special camps putting them at increased risk of violence. The Chhattisgarh authorities enacted legislation banning media coverage of certain human rights violations.

⌐ On 28 February, suspected Maoists set off a landmine blowing up a truck; 26 people were killed and 30 injured.

Economic, social and cultural rights

Around 300 million people remained in poverty despite implementation of new legislation guaranteeing minimum annual employment for the rural poor. New legislation on the right to information, seen as a means to empower the poor, was not fully implemented; the Union government and state governments were reluctant to disclose crucial information about their decision-making processes.

Concerns grew over protection of economic, social and cultural rights of already-marginalized communities (including *adivasis*) amidst fears of unchecked exploitation of their resource base by the government and businesses. Several states witnessed periodic protests against acquisition of land and other resources for mining, irrigation, power and urban infrastructure purposes. Such developments were associated with forced evictions, harassment, arbitrary detentions, excessive police force and denial of access to justice.

⌐ In January, 11 *adivasis* were killed when police fired into demonstrators protesting against the displacement that would be caused by the proposed Tata Steel project in Orissa.

⌐ In April, police used excessive force against activists staging a protest fast in Delhi against displacement caused by the Narmada dam project; some protesters were detained.

⌐ In July and September/October, activists protesting against the Uttar Pradesh government's decision to acquire farmland for the Reliance gas project faced police harassment and detention.

Bhopal

Twenty-two years after the Union Carbide Corporation (UCC) pesticide plant in Bhopal leaked toxic gases that devastated countless lives and the environment, survivors continued to struggle for adequate compensation, medical aid and rehabilitation. After a sustained campaign, including a survivors' march from Bhopal to Delhi in April, the government agreed to clean up toxic waste, provide safe drinking water and set up a commission for rehabilitation of the victims. However, there was little progress on the ground on these initiatives by the end of 2006. In August, monsoon rains caused flooding in areas around the UCC plant, raising fears of contamination of groundwater. UCC and Dow Chemicals (which took over UCC in 2001) continued to reiterate that they had no responsibility for the gas leak or its consequences.

Violence against women

Legislation passed in 2005 to ensure comprehensive protection of women from all forms of domestic violence, including dowry deaths, sexual assault and acid attacks, came into effect in October. It was yet to be fully implemented by states.

Traditional preference for boys continued to lead to abortions of female foetuses, despite the ban on pre-natal sex determination since 1993. Only a few people were convicted of violating the ban, a fact criticized by the Supreme Court. Protests were staged in Punjab and Rajasthan over the slow pace of investigation into such cases.

Many of the abuses suffered by Muslim women in Gujarat in 2002 fell outside the definition of rape in national law. This continued to hamper victims' quest for justice.

Two Supreme Court directives offered advances for victims of rape. The Court directed that lack of medical evidence would no longer be grounds for discounting testimony, and that the identity of victims should remain confidential in court judgments.

Death penalty

At least 40 people were sentenced to death in 2006; no executions took place. Comprehensive information on the number of people on death row was not available.

Anxiety rose over the fate of clemency petitions after the Supreme Court ruled that it could review executive decisions on such petitions. The ruling followed fierce debate triggered by the clemency petition submitted on behalf of Mohammed Afzal, who was sentenced to death on charges relating to the armed attack on India's parliament in December 2001.

Other issues

There were concerns that amendments to the Protection of Human Rights Act, 1993, would weaken the operating framework of the NHRC which already had no mandate to investigate abuses by armed forces and complaints more than a year old. The amendments also allow for transfer of cases from the NHRC to state-level commissions which continued to be starved of resources; 11 of the 28 states had yet to set up such commissions and five of those operating had no chairpersons.

AI country reports/ visits

Statements

- India: Amnesty International condemns multiple bomb attacks in Mumbai (AI Index: ASA 20/017/2006)
- India: Continuing concern over the safety of civilians, including *adivasis*, caught in escalating conflict in Chhattisgarh (AI Index: ASA 20/018/2006)
- India: Concerns with Protection of Human Rights Act (AI Index: ASA 20/019/2006)
- India: Amnesty International condemns multiple bomb attacks in Malegaon, Maharashtra (AI Index: ASA 20/025/2006)
- India: Continued detention two years after the repeal of POTA (AI Index: ASA 20/026/2006)
- India: The Armed Forces Special Powers Act (AFSPA) Review Committee takes one step forward and two backwards (AI Index: ASA 20/031/2006)

Visits

AI's Secretary General and other delegates visited India in February and met government officials and civil society organizations. AI delegates also met officials and activists in May, July and December.

INDONESIA

REPUBLIC OF INDONESIA
Head of state and government: Susilo Bambang Yudhoyono
Death penalty: retentionist
International Criminal Court: not ratified

Perpetrators of human rights violations continued to enjoy impunity for violations which occurred in Nanggroe Aceh Darussalam (NAD) and Papua. In Papua, cases of extrajudicial executions, torture and excessive use of force were reported. Across the country, ill-treatment or torture in detention facilities and police lock-ups continued to be widely reported. Three people were executed in September, sparking increased debate about the death penalty. At least 13 people were sentenced to death. Freedom of expression remained under threat with at least eight people prosecuted for peacefully expressing opinions.

Background

In May, Indonesia's ratification of the International Covenant on Civil and Political Rights and the International Covenant on Economic, Social and Cultural Rights came into force, but legislation had not been enacted by the end of 2006 to incorporate the treaties' provisions into domestic law.

In June Indonesia was elected to the UN Human Rights Council and it promised to ratify the Rome Statute of the International Criminal Court by 2008.

Minority religious groups and church buildings continued to be attacked. In Sulawesi, sporadic religious violence occurred throughout the year.

In July, a long-awaited Witness Protection Act (Law 13/2006) was passed, establishing a witness and victim protection agency, among other positive developments. However, non-governmental organizations (NGOs) protested that incomplete definitions rendered the Law's protections inadequate.

Impunity

In October, the Supreme Court overturned the conviction of Pollycarpus Budihari Priyanto for the murder of human rights defender Munir, who was poisoned on a flight to the Netherlands in 2004. No-one has been held to account for this crime.

The majority of human rights violations by the security forces were not investigated, and impunity for past violations persisted. The Attorney General's Office (AGO) failed to act on two cases in which the National Human Rights Commission (Komnas HAM) had submitted evidence in 2004 that crimes against humanity had been committed by the security forces.

In March, Eurico Guterres — a Timorese militiaman sentenced to 10 years' imprisonment for crimes against humanity committed in Timor-Leste in 1999 — was jailed after the Supreme Court upheld his 2002 conviction. He is the only person found responsible for the 1999 crimes by the ad hoc Human Rights Court to have had his conviction upheld.

The Commission of Truth and Friendship established jointly by Indonesia and Timor-Leste to document crimes committed in Timor-Leste in 1999 and to promote reconciliation began its work. Provisions in its mandate included the ability to recommend amnesty for perpetrators of gross human rights violations.

In December the Constitutional Court annulled Law 27/2004 which mandated an Indonesian Commission of Truth and Reconciliation. Rights activists had challenged provisions allowing amnesty for perpetrators of severe human rights violations and limiting victims' ability to obtain compensation. However, the Court ruled that the whole law should be repealed as it was "illogical", some articles violated the Constitution, and the annulment of individual articles would render the rest of the law unenforceable. The annulment of the law left victims of past human rights violations without a compensation mechanism.

Torture and ill-treatment
Torture and ill-treatment of detainees and prisoners continued to be widespread.

☐ Twenty-three men were reportedly ill-treated during police interrogation to make them "confess" to involvement in violence during a demonstration in Jayapura, Papua, in March. Before their trial in May, 16 of the defendants were reportedly kicked by police officers and beaten around the head and body with rifle butts and rubber batons to make them admit their guilt in court. Those who refused to acknowledge the charges were allegedly beaten and kicked by police when they returned to detention.

Prison conditions fell short of minimum international standards. Detainees lacked access to adequate bedding, health services, adequate food, clean water and hygiene products. They were subjected to physical and sexual violence and suffered from severe overcrowding. Juveniles were sometimes held together with adults, and women detainees were sometimes guarded by male guards.

Death penalty
At least three people were executed by firing-squad during 2006 – Fabianus Tibo, Dominggus da Silva and Marinus Riwu from Sulawesi. Their case heightened debate on the death penalty. There were concerns that their trial had been unfair and two of the three men were allegedly ill-treated before being executed.

There were announcements during 2006 that 19 further prisoners would be executed, including three men convicted of involvement in the 2002 Bali bombings. However, none of these were executed by the end of the year.

At least 92 people were known to be under sentence of death at the end of 2006.

Discrimination and violence against women
In May, the National Commission on Violence Against Women criticized the lack of gender-sensitive provisions in the draft revision of the Criminal Procedure Code (KUHAP). The draft lacks sufficient provisions for the investigation and prosecution of crimes of sexual or gender-based violence and fails to address the particular needs of women in custody.

In August, the government issued a circular banning doctors and nurses from practising "female circumcision" (female genital mutilation). However, those who continued the practice would face no punishment.

Plans to pass into law a controversial pornography bill that would penalize women who wore short skirts or refused to cover certain parts of their body were ongoing at the end of the year.

The increasing application of Shariah bylaws by local governments appeared to disproportionately affect women. In February, a woman was sentenced to three days in jail after a judge ruled, after an unfair trial, that she was a sex worker because she was out on the street alone at night wearing make-up. In Tangerang municipality alone, there were at least 15 other cases in 2006 of women being arrested for similar offences — one 63-year-old woman was arrested while buying fruit.

Women domestic workers, who are excluded from the national Manpower Act, were subjected to violations of labour rights and to physical, sexual and psychological abuse. In June, the Ministry of Manpower prepared draft legislation on domestic workers but it did not regulate many basic workers' rights such as maximum hours of work and the minimum wage, or the special needs of women.

Nanggroe Aceh Darussalam
The security situation in Nanggroe Aceh Darussalam (NAD) remained stable despite sporadic clashes.

The Aceh Governance Bill, passed by Parliament in July, provided for a Human Rights Court to be established for NAD to try perpetrators of future violations. However, it contained no provisions to bring to justice perpetrators of past human rights violations.

In September, local organizations submitted information to Komnas HAM about mass graves excavated in NAD since the signing of a peace agreement in August 2005. The organizations urged Komnas HAM to conduct thorough investigations and to prevent further excavations from taking place without the presence of the necessary medical and legal experts.

In December, the first local elections were held in NAD in the presence of the European Union-led Aceh Monitoring Mission, which extended its stay until 15 December.

Throughout the year concerns were expressed over the increased use of Shariah law in NAD, and its adverse effects on women. Women complained that they were disproportionately targeted by Vice and Virtue patrols and were harassed for minor infractions and sometimes for no apparent reason. Reports indicated that at least 23 people were caned for gambling, adultery, selling and consuming alcoholic drinks, and theft.

Papua

There were reports of extrajudicial executions, torture and ill-treatment, excessive use of force during demonstrations and harassment of human rights defenders.

In at least six incidents civilians were shot at by the security forces.

In January, a child was shot dead and at least two people were injured after security forces opened fire in the village of Waghete. Accounts of the incident by the police and by victims and witnesses differed widely. Many observers feared that the incident was in reprisal for the high-profile actions of 43 people from the Waghete region who sought asylum in Australia in January.

In March, five members of the security forces were killed in Abepura after clashes with protesters demanding the closure of the gold and copper mine, PT Freeport. Security forces used tear gas and fired rubber bullets at the crowd. At least six civilians – and possibly many more – were injured, including one passer-by. Twenty-three people were prosecuted in connection with the violence. By the end of 2006, at least 21 men had been sentenced after unfair trials to between four and 15 years' imprisonment. All the detainees were reportedly ill-treated in police detention. Lawyers and human rights defenders involved with the trials were subjected to intimidation and received death threats.

Severe restrictions continued to bar nearly all foreign journalists and NGOs from operating in Papua. Officials claimed that foreign organizations were divisive, although access to Papua was granted to at least one international media team, albeit restricted and closely monitored.

Freedom of expression

At least eight prisoners of conscience were sentenced to prison terms during 2006 and eight others sentenced in previous years remained in jail. They included peaceful political activists, union leaders, religious practitioners and students.

In February and March, six union leaders – Robin Kimbi, Masri Sebayang, Suyahman, Safrudin, Akhen Pane and Sruhas Towo – were sentenced to prison terms of between 14 months and two years, apparently because of legitimate trade union activities. The men were arrested following a strike and demonstration at a palm oil plantation owned by the company Musim Mas, in Riau province, in September 2005. The strike followed the company's refusal to negotiate with the union, SP Kahutindo, over issues including the implementation of minimum labour standards under national legislation. Four of the men – Suyahman, Safrudin, Akhen Pane and Sruhas Towo – were released in November.

In December the Constitutional Court repealed as unconstitutional Articles 134, 136 and 137 of the Criminal Code, which punished "insulting the President or Vice-President" with up to six years' imprisonment. These articles had long been used to inhibit free speech and to imprison activists.

Security legislation

In April, the police declared that around 200 people had been arrested since anti-terrorism operations began after the 2002 Bali bombing. At least 56 people were arrested under anti-terrorism legislation during 2006, and a further 24 people previously arrested were convicted. Despite declarations made in February by the government and lawmakers that anti-terrorism legislation (Law 16/2003) would be revised, there was no visible progress during the year.

Reports that terrorist suspects were subjected to ill-treatment by police officials during interrogations continued. In April, police shot dead two terrorist suspects during a raid in Wonosobo, Central Java.

Economic, social and cultural rights

Large-scale evictions were carried out with inadequate consultation, little or no compensation and excessive use of force.

In January, two large-scale forced evictions occurred in east Jakarta, reportedly leaving over 600 families homeless, without suitable compensation or alternative housing. The series of forced evictions related to the expansion of the East-Jakarta-Cikarang railroad.

In May, exploratory drilling in east Java by the oil and gas company Lapindo Brantas triggered a vast flow of hot, noxious mud which had not been stemmed by the end of the year. The mudflow displaced around 10,000 people, engulfing entire villages, cultivated areas and infrastructure. In areas close to the mudflow more than 1,000 people were hospitalized with breathing difficulties and there were fears of water pollution.

Lapindo Brantas offered to pay an extrajudicial stipend of around US$35 a month to those displaced, and reportedly set aside 6.9 billion Rupiah (US$750,000) to cover future agricultural losses. Those affected protested that the compensation was inadequate. In September the President decreed that Lapindo Brantas should pay 1.5 trillion Rupiah (US$163 million) to repair state infrastructure. He ordered that nearly 3,000 families be permanently relocated and provided with jobs and financial compensation. However, the government was not explicit on other rights, including the rights to adequate housing and water.

At the end of the year, hundreds of thousands of people were still without shelter as a result of the 27 May earthquake in Yogyakarta, which killed 5,900 people and displaced 1.5 million.

AI country reports/ visits
Report
- Indonesia: Comments on the draft revised Criminal Procedure Code (AI Index: ASA 21/005/2006)
Visits
In February and March, AI delegates visited Java to conduct research on women domestic workers in Indonesia. AI delegates also visited Indonesia in July and September.

IRAN

ISLAMIC REPUBLIC OF IRAN
Head of state: Leader of the Islamic Republic of Iran:
Ayatollah Sayed 'Ali Khamenei
Head of government: President: Dr Mahmoud
Ahmadinejad
Death penalty: retentionist
International Criminal Court: signed

The human rights situation deteriorated, with civil society facing increasing restrictions on fundamental freedoms of expression and association. Scores of political prisoners, including prisoners of conscience, continued to serve prison sentences imposed following unfair trials in previous years. Thousands more arrests were made in 2006, mostly during or following demonstrations. Human rights defenders, including journalists, students and lawyers, were among those detained arbitrarily without access to family or legal representation. Torture, especially during periods of pre-trial detention, remained commonplace. At least 177 people were executed, at least four of whom were under 18 at the time of the alleged offence, including one who was under 18 at the time of execution. Two people were reportedly stoned to death. Sentences of flogging, amputation and eye-gouging continued to be passed. The true numbers of those executed or subjected to corporal punishment were probably considerably higher than those reported.

Background
The rift between Iran and the international community over the government's insistence on maintaining its nuclear enrichment programme continued to widen. In March, the International Atomic Energy Agency referred Iran to the UN Security Council. In December the Security Council agreed on a programme of sanctions against Iran following Iran's failure to meet an August deadline to suspend the programme. Iran continued to accuse foreign governments of fomenting unrest in border areas, and in turn was accused of involvement in the worsening security situation in Iraq. In February the US government sought an extra US$75 million to "support democracy" in Iran. President Ahmadinejad continued to make statements threatening to the State of Israel and questioning the Holocaust. The European Union-Iran human rights dialogue remained suspended.

Local elections and elections to the Assembly of Experts, which oversees the appointment of the Supreme Leader, were held in December. The Council of Guardians, which reviews laws and policies to ensure that they uphold Islamic tenets and the Constitution, excluded all but 164 Assembly of Experts candidates, including at least 12 women who registered, on the basis of discriminatory selection procedures. The results of both elections were generally seen as a setback to the government of President Ahmadinejad.

The authorities faced armed opposition from Kurdish and Baluchi groups.

In December, the UN General Assembly passed a resolution condemning the human rights situation in Iran. Iran failed to set a date for visits by any UN Human Rights mechanisms despite having issued a standing invitation in 2002.

Repression of minorities
Ethnic and religious minorities remained subject to discriminatory laws and practices which continued to be a source of social and political unrest.
Arabs
Arabs continued to complain of discrimination, including in access to resources, as well as forced evictions. In October, the Council of Guardians approved a bill allocating 2 per cent of Iran's oil revenues to Khuzestan province, home to many of Iran's Arabs.

Scores of Arabs were detained during the year. At least 36 were sentenced to death or received lengthy prison terms after conviction in unfair trials of involvement in causing bomb explosions in Ahvaz and Tehran in 2005. Five were executed including Mehdi Nawaseri and Mohammad Ali Sawari who were executed in public in February following the broadcast of their televised "confessions".

◻ At least five women were detained, some along with their children, between February and April, in circumstances which suggested that they may have been held in order to force their husbands to give themselves up or make confessions. Four women and two children were believed to be still held at the end of the year.

◻ Seven lawyers defending some of those accused in connection with the bombings were summoned to appear before the Ahvaz Revolutionary Prosecutor in October on charges of "acting against state security". The summons was issued in connection with a letter they had sent to the Head of the Revolutionary Court in Ahvaz complaining about deficiencies in the trial of their clients.
Azerbaijanis
In May, widespread demonstrations took place in mainly Azerbaijani north-western towns and cities in protest at the publication of a cartoon offensive to Azerbaijanis in the state-run *Iran* newspaper. Hundreds, if not thousands, were arrested and scores reportedly killed by the security forces, although official sources downplayed the scale of arrests and killings. Further arrests occurred, many around events and dates significant to the Azerbaijani community such as the Babek Castle gathering in Kalayber in June, and a boycott of the start of the new academic year over linguistic rights for the Azerbaijani community.

◻ Prisoner of conscience Abbas Lisani was detained in June for over three months for his participation in the demonstrations in Ardabil against the cartoon. In September, he was sentenced to 16 months' imprisonment and 50 lashes on charges including "disturbing state security". At the end of October, five days after submitting an appeal, he was redetained, and his family was later informed that his sentence had been increased to 18 months' imprisonment with an additional three years of enforced internal exile. He stated his unconditional opposition to the use of violence. By the end of the year he faced two further prison sentences imposed for his attendance at the 2003 and 2005 Babek Castle gatherings.

Kurds
In February, clashes between Kurdish demonstrators and the security forces in Maku and other towns reportedly led to at least nine deaths and scores, if not hundreds, of arrests. In March, Kurdish Majles deputies wrote to the President demanding an investigation into the killings and calling for those responsible to be brought to justice. An investigation was reportedly set up, but its findings were not known by the end of the year. Some of those detained later reportedly received prison terms of between three and eight months.

▢ Mohammad Sadeq Kabudvand, the Head of the Human Rights Organization of Kurdistan and editor of the banned weekly newspaper *Payam-e Mardom*, had his 18-month suspended prison sentence for "publishing lies and articles aimed at creating racial and tribal tension and discord" increased on appeal to one year's actual imprisonment. Although summoned to prison in September, he remained at liberty at the end of the year, pending an appeal to the Supreme Court. Other *Payam-e Mardom* journalists were also brought to trial.

Baluchis
In March a Baluchi armed group, *Jondallah*, killed 22 Iranian officials and took at least seven hostage, in Sistan-Baluchistan province. Following the incident, scores, possibly hundreds, of people were arrested; many were reportedly taken to unknown locations. In the months following the attacks, the number of executions announced in Baluchi areas increased dramatically. Dozens were reported to have been executed by the end of the year.

Religious minorities
Members of Iran's religious minorities were detained or harassed on account of their faith.

In February over 1,000 Nematollahi Sufis peacefully protesting against an order to evacuate their place of worship in Qom were arrested. Hundreds were injured by members of the security forces and members of organized pro-government groups. In May, 52 Sufis, including two lawyers representing the group, were sentenced to one year's imprisonment, flogging and a fine, and the lawyers were banned from practising law. In August, Grand Ayatollah Fazel Lankarani issued a religious edict designating Sufism as "null and void".

Several evangelical Christians, mostly converts from Islam, were detained, apparently in connection with their religious activities.

▢ In September, Fereshteh Dibaj and her husband, Reza Montazemi, were detained for nine days before being released on bail. Fereshteh Dibaj is the youngest daughter of convert Mehdi Dibaj who was murdered in 1994 shortly after being released from prison where he had been held for nine years for "apostasy".

Sixty-five Baha'is were detained during 2006 and five remained held at the end of the year. In March Mehran Kawsari was released early from his three-year prison sentence imposed in connection with an open letter sent to the then President in November 2004.

In March, the UN Special Rapporteur on Freedom of Religion or Belief expressed concern about an October 2005 letter instructing various government agencies to identify, and collect information about, Baha'is in Iran.

Human rights defenders
Human rights defenders faced deepening restrictions on their work and remained at risk of reprisals. In January, the Ministry of the Interior was reported to be preparing measures to restrict the activities of non-governmental organizations that allegedly received finance from "problematic internal and external sources aimed at overthrowing the system". Students, who remained a politically active section of society, were frequently targeted for reprisals, including arbitrary arrest and denial of the right to study in the new academic year.

▢ In August, the Ministry of the Interior banned activities by the Centre for Defenders of Human Rights (CDHR), run by Nobel Peace Prize Laureate Shirin Ebadi and other leading lawyers, stating that it did not have a permit. In September, the Ministry of the Interior said a permit would be issued "if changes were made to the [centre's] mission statement".

▢ Abdolfattah Soltani, a lawyer and co-founder of the CDHR, was released on bail in March. He was later sentenced to five years' imprisonment for "disclosing confidential documents" and "propaganda against the system". The sentence was under appeal at the end of the year.

▢ Prisoner of conscience Akbar Ganji, a journalist who implicated government officials in the murder of intellectuals and journalists in the 1990s, was released in March after completing his six-year prison sentence.

Torture and cruel, inhuman and degrading punishments
Torture remained common in many prisons and detention centres, particularly in the investigative stage of pre-trial detention when detainees are denied access to a lawyer for indefinite periods. At least seven people reportedly died in custody, some in circumstances where torture, ill-treatment or denial of medical care may have been contributory factors.

▢ Political prisoners Akbar Mohammadi and Valiollah Feyz Mahdavi died in July and September respectively after going on hunger strike to protest at their continued detention.

▢ Fourteen-year-old Mohammad Reza Evezpoor, an Iranian Azerbaijani, was arrested in April after writing "I am a Turk" on a wall. He was reportedly tortured during his three days in detention, including by being suspended by his feet for 24 hours and denied food and water. He was beaten again when rearrested in September.

At least two amputations were carried out and one person was sentenced to eye-gouging. Flogging remained a common punishment.

◻ Leyla Mafi received a flogging of 99 lashes in February before being released from prison into a women's rehabilitation centre. Forced into prostitution as an eight-year-old and raped repeatedly, she was arrested in early 2004 and charged with "acts contrary to chastity" for which she was sentenced to flogging followed by death. Following international pressure, her death sentence was overturned.

Impunity

Victims of human rights violations and their families continued to lack redress.

◻ A re-examination, ordered in 2001, of the cases of Ministry of Intelligence officials accused of the 1998 "serial murders", remained incomplete. Nasser Zarafshan, lawyer for the families of some of the victims, continued to serve a five-year prison sentence following his conviction on politically motivated charges.

Death penalty

At least 177 people were executed in 2006, including one minor and at least three others who were under 18 at the time of the alleged offence. Death sentences were imposed for a variety of crimes including drug smuggling, armed robbery, murder, political violence and sexual offences. Following domestic and international protests, the death sentences of some women and of some prisoners aged under 18 at the time of the alleged offence were suspended or lifted; some were sentenced to death again after a retrial. Two people were reportedly stoned to death despite a moratorium on stoning announced by the judiciary in 2002. Others remained under sentence of stoning to death. In September, Iranian human rights defenders launched a campaign to save nine women and two men sentenced to death by stoning and to abolish stoning in law. By the end of the year the stoning sentences of at least three of the 11 had been quashed.

Freedom of expression and association

Freedom of expression and association was increasingly curtailed. Internet access was increasingly restricted and monitored. Journalists and webloggers were detained and sentenced to prison or flogging and at least 11 newspapers were closed down. Relatives of detainees or of those sought by the authorities remained at risk of harassment or intimidation. Independent trade unionists faced reprisals and some academics, such as Ramin Jahanbegloo, were detained or dismissed from their posts.

◻ Up to 1,000 members of the independent, but banned, Sherkat-e Vahed Bus Company Union were arrested in January after striking to demand recognition of their union and to protest at the detention of the union's head Mansour Ossanlu. All were later released, but dozens were still forbidden from returning to their jobs at the end of the year. Mansour Ossanlu was released on bail in August after being held for over seven months in connection with his trade union activities, but was redetained for one month in November, reportedly after attending meetings organized by the International Labour Organization.

Women's rights

Demonstrations in Tehran in March and June demanding an end to discrimination in law against women were broken up harshly by the security forces. Some protesters were injured.

◻ Former Majles deputy Sayed Ali Akbar Mousavi-Kho'ini was arrested at the June demonstration and held for over four months before his release on bail in October. He reported that he had been tortured in detention.

In August, women's rights activists launched a campaign to gather a million signatures to a petition demanding equal rights for women.

AI country reports/visits
Reports
- Iran: Human rights defender at risk — appeal case: Abdolfattah Soltani (AI Index: MDE 13/009/2006)
- Iran: New government fails to address dire human rights situation (AI Index: MDE 13/010/2006)
- Iran: Defending minority rights — the Ahwazi Arabs (AI Index: MDE 13/056/2006)

IRAQ

REPUBLIC OF IRAQ
Head of state: Jalal Talabani
Head of government: Nuri al-Maliki (replaced Ibrahim al-Ja'afari in May)
Death penalty: retentionist
International Criminal Court: not ratified

Tens of thousands of civilians were killed or injured in daily and widespread violence that continued to escalate throughout 2006. Many of the killings were the result of deliberate attacks by Sunni and Shi'a armed groups as the conflict took on an increasingly sectarian nature. Iraqi security forces committed widespread human rights violations, including killings of civilians and torture and other ill-treatment of detainees, and were suspected of involvement in sectarian killings. Soldiers belonging to the US-led Multinational Force (MNF) also committed human rights violations, and some were prosecuted on charges including the killing, rape or inhumane treatment of civilians. The MNF held thousands of people in arbitrary detention without charge or trial. Members of Iraq's most vulnerable groups, including minorities and women, continued to be targeted for abuses. The violence caused many thousands of people to be displaced from their homes, as neighbourhoods in Baghdad and some other centres were increasingly affected by rising sectarianism; hundreds of thousands of Iraqis fled the country and sought refuge abroad. The first trial of officials from the pre-2003 Iraqi government resulted in death sentences for former President Saddam Hussain and two of his co-defendants after an unfair trial. Scores of other people were sentenced to death, including after unfair trials. At least 65 women and men, including Saddam Hussain, were executed.

Background

A permanent Iraqi government took office on 22 May, some three years after the invasion of Iraq by a US-led coalition. Elections in December 2005 for the 275-member Council of Representatives ushered in a new parliament with a four-year term, but it took several months for the parties to agree on the composition of the new government. The main Shi'a alliance, the United Iraqi Alliance, held the largest number of seats, and Nuri al-Maliki of the Shi'a Da'wa Party became Prime Minister.

Hopes that the appointment of a new, popularly elected government would bring peace and stability were dashed virtually from the outset, and the year was marked by unrelenting, spiralling and increasingly sectarian violence. According to the UN Assistance Mission for Iraq (UNAMI), some 34,452 people were killed during 2006 and thousands of others were injured, adding to the toll of victims of violent deaths since the March 2003 invasion. An independent estimate published in September in the UK medical journal *The Lancet* suggested that more than 600,000 people had suffered violent deaths since March 2003; the US-led coalition and the Iraqi authorities said this was an over-estimate, but did not themselves provide accurate data.

Conditions in Baghdad and other centres became increasingly desperate as bombs were detonated in markets, other gathering places and near queues of people seeking recruitment to the police or other paid work. Added to this, groups of armed men carried out mass abductions from communities they targeted apparently for sectarian reasons; sometimes their victims were released, but in many cases they were found murdered and mutilated, their bodies dumped in the streets. As the economy continued to founder and amid a proliferation of weapons, kidnapping for ransom by criminal gangs became common.

As casualties among US and UK forces continued to mount, these forces sought to hand over frontline duties to newly recruited and trained Iraqi government forces. In the south, UK forces moved out of Muthanna province in July to be replaced by Iraqi government forces, and Iraqi troops took on a greater role alongside US forces in central Iraq. At the end of the year, however, US President George Bush appeared ready to commit thousands of additional US troops in a new effort to buttress Iraqi government forces and overcome the insurgency.

Sectarian violence and attacks by armed groups

Sectarian and political violence escalated throughout the year. Members of different armed groups, including Ba'athists, Sunni and Shi'a extremists and others, targeted civilians for deliberate killings, abductions and other abuses. Iraqi security forces linked to some of the armed groups were accused of involvement in sectarian killings. Many bodies of the victims bore marks of torture and were dumped on streets.

On 22 February, armed groups bombed the al-Askari mosque, a prominent Shi'a shrine, in the city of Samarra. No one was killed, but the mosque and its golden dome were seriously damaged. In the immediate aftermath, Sunni and Shi'a clerics and mosques were attacked, and random mortar shootings and bomb attacks reportedly claimed many lives. Thereafter, sectarian violence and sectarian "cleansing" intensified and continued throughout the year. Thousands of civilians were driven from their homes in mixed neighbourhoods in Baghdad. Both Sunni and Shi'a armed groups were responsible for the "cleansing" drive.

People were also targeted because of their ethnic identity. Palestinian residents of Iraq were among those particularly at risk. In the three weeks following the bombing of the al-Askari mosque, at least 12 Palestinians were killed, and attacks on their residential areas by unidentified assailants continued throughout the year.

⌐ On 17 July, more than 40 people were killed at a mostly Shi'a market in Mahmoudiya, south of Baghdad.

A group called Supporters of the Sunni People posted a message on the Internet taking responsibility for this and other attacks targeting Shi'a Muslims. The following day in the town of Kufa, a suicide bomber detonated a van packed with explosives at a market outside the golden-domed mosque, a Shi'a shrine, after luring labourers with job offers. At least 59 Shi'a Muslims were killed and more than 130 injured.

⌷ On 14 October, dozens of Sunnis were reportedly killed in the town of Balad; some were shot dead, others bore signs of torture. The killings were apparently in retaliation for the deaths the previous day of 17 Shi'a workers, whose beheaded bodies were reportedly found in al-Dulyiyah, a predominantly Sunni town, north of Baghdad.

Non-Muslim religious minorities were frequently targeted for attack because of their faith. Many were killed, including religious leaders. The attacks prompted thousands of members of these communities to seek safety abroad.

⌷ On 10 October, Raad Mutar Falih al-Othmani, a jeweller and trainee religious leader from the Mandaean community, was reportedly shot dead in his house in al-Suwayra by unknown assailants.

⌷ The decapitated body of Father Boulos Iskandar, a priest from the Syriac Orthodox Church, was found in Mosul on 11 October, a week after he was kidnapped. The kidnappers had allegedly demanded that the priest's church denounce controversial public remarks on Islam made by Pope Benedict XVI in September.

There were reports of people being harassed, threatened or killed because of their actual or perceived sexual orientation.

By the end of the year, more than 400,000 people had fled their homes for other locations within Iraq, most because of the sectarian violence. UNHCR, the UN refugee agency, estimated that the number of Iraqis living as refugees in neighbouring countries, mainly Syria and Jordan, had swelled to 1.8 million.

Violations by Iraqi security forces

Iraqi security forces under the control of the Interior Ministry reportedly committed widespread human rights violations, including involvement in killings of civilians and torture and other ill-treatment of detainees. They reportedly maintained close links with two Shi'a armed groups, the Mahdi Army and the Badr Brigades, from whose ranks many were said to have been recruited, and were accused of supporting or acquiescing in abuses committed by these groups. The security forces were also alleged to have been involved in "death squad"-style killings.

⌷ In October, an entire police brigade was suspended pending investigations into its involvement in the abduction of 26 Sunni factory workers in October, at least 10 of whom were later found dead.

Torture and other ill-treatment of detainees by Interior Ministry security forces was reported.

⌷ On 30 May, a joint Iraqi-MNF team inspected Site 4 detention centre in Baghdad, where 1,431 detainees were held under the control of the Interior Ministry. The inspection found that detainees had been systematically abused, in some cases amounting to torture, and were being held in unsafe, overcrowded and unhealthy conditions. In November, the Interior Minister announced that arrest warrants for 57 employees, including a police general, had been issued in connection with the abuses.

No findings were made public of investigations launched in 2005 into alleged human rights violations in an Interior Ministry detention centre in the al-Jadiriyah district of Baghdad. US military forces had raided the detention centre and reportedly found at least 168 detainees in appalling conditions, many of whom had allegedly been tortured.

Violations by US-led Multinational Force

There were frequent allegations that US forces committed human rights violations against Iraqi civilians, including unlawful killings. In some cases, investigations were launched. Charges were brought against several US and UK military personnel, including for human rights violations in previous years. In cases where investigations were concluded without any prosecutions, no detailed findings were published.

⌷ In December, four US soldiers were charged with unpremeditated murder and faced trial before a military court. The charges related to the deaths of 24 men, women and children in Haditha, north of Baghdad, on 19 November 2005. Four other US soldiers were charged with attempting to cover up the incident.

⌷ In November, a US soldier pleaded guilty before a military court to raping and killing Abeer Qasim Hamza, a 14-year-old girl, and murdering three of her relatives in Mahmoudiya in March. He was sentenced to life imprisonment. Three other soldiers faced charges of rape and murder in the same case, as well as arson for burning the girl's body to destroy evidence. A fifth soldier, who had already been discharged from the army on mental health grounds when the charges arose, pleaded not guilty in a civilian federal court.

⌷ A court martial of seven UK soldiers began in September. One soldier pleaded guilty to inhumane treatment. The six others pleaded not guilty to charges relating to the death of Baha Dawud Salim al-Maliki, also known as Baha Mousa, a hotel receptionist, who died in British custody in Basra in 2003, and the ill-treatment of other detainees. Baha Mousa and the other detainees were arrested in September 2003 and taken to a detention centre where they were allegedly beaten and otherwise abused.

Thousands of people were held by the MNF without charge or trial and without the right to challenge the lawfulness of their detention. Many were released without explanation after months or years in detention, and thousands continued to be held without any effective remedy. Detainees in US custody had their detention initially reviewed by a magistrate and thereafter every six months by a non-judicial body. MNF forces also detained people standing trial before Iraqi courts.

In December, more than 14,500 detainees were being held by US forces, mainly in Camp Cropper, near

Baghdad, and Camp Bucca, near Basra. Increased capacity at Camp Cropper enabled the US authorities to transfer detainees out of Camp Fort Suse and Abu Ghraib prison and hand both facilities to the Iraqi authorities in September. At the end of the year UK forces were holding approximately 100 detainees in Iraq.

Targeting of professionals and human rights defenders

Many professionals and human rights defenders were targeted for abuses in connection with their work.

Several judges and lawyers were killed or threatened, especially those involved in terrorism-related cases. Several lawyers refused to defend those accused of terrorism to avoid being targeted.

◻ A M, a Palestinian lawyer resident in Iraq, fled the country in October after allegedly escaping an attempt on his life and being threatened. His clients included people accused of terrorism-related offences.

More than 60 journalists and media workers were reportedly killed in Iraq in 2006.

◻ Masked gunmen killed 11 people and wounded two at the Baghdad office of the satellite TV channel al-Sha'abiya in October.

◻ On 22 February Atwar Bahgat, a correspondent with the TV channel al-'Arabiya, and her colleagues Khaled Mahmoud al-Falahi and 'Adnan Khairallah were kidnapped. Their bodies were found the next day near Samarra.

Academics, teachers and members of the medical profession were kidnapped for ransom. This prompted many other professionals to flee Iraq.

Violence against women

The situation of women continued to deteriorate. There was increased violence against women, including abductions, rapes and "honour killings" by male relatives. Politically active women, those who did not follow a strict dress code, and women human rights defenders were increasingly at risk of abuses, including by armed groups and religious extremists.

◻ On 29 July, unidentified assailants shot dead Salah Abdel-Kader, a lawyer in Baghdad who acted in cases of "honour killings" and custody battles. A note was reportedly found near his body accusing him of not following Islamic law.

Trial of Saddam Hussain and others

The first trial before the Supreme Iraqi Criminal Tribunal (SICT) concluded in July. Former President Saddam Hussain and seven other former officials were tried for human rights violations in connection with the killing of 148 people from the largely Shi'a village of al-Dujail following an attempted assassination of Saddam Hussain in 1982.

Saddam Hussain, his half brother and former head of the intelligence service Barzan al-Tikriti, as well as Awad al-Bandar, former head of the Revolutionary Court, were sentenced to death in November. Their death sentences were upheld by the Appeals Chamber on 26 December and four days later Saddam Hussain was executed.

Political interference undermined the independence and impartiality of the SICT, causing the first presiding judge to resign and blocking the appointment of another. The court failed to take adequate measures to ensure the protection of witnesses and defence lawyers, three of whom were assassinated during the trial. Saddam Hussain was denied access to legal counsel for the first year after his arrest, and complaints by his lawyers throughout the trial relating to the proceedings appeared to have been inadequately addressed by the tribunal. The appeal process was conducted in haste and failed to rectify any of the flaws of the trial; the appeals chamber instructed the SICT to reconsider the life sentence imposed on former Vice-President Taha Yassin Ramadan because it considered it too lenient.

A second trial before the SICT began on 21 August to consider allegations that Saddam Hussain and six others were responsible for mass killings and enforced disappearances of members of Iraq's Kurdish minority in 1988 in the so-called Anfal Campaign. In September the presiding judge was forced to step down following accusations of bias by the Iraqi government. Following his replacement, the trial continued but had not concluded by the end of the year; it was expected to continue against the other accused following the execution of Saddam Hussain.

Death penalty

Scores of people were sentenced to death and at least 65 men and women were executed. The authorities reported three execution sessions in Baghdad, each involving the hanging of more than a dozen people. At the end of the year, about 170 men and women reportedly remained on death row.

In May the Court of Cassation confirmed the death sentences imposed on Shihab Ahmad Khalaf and Abdullah Hana Hermaz Kelanah, who had been found guilty of leading the activities of a terrorist organization in November 2005. Although both men confessed, at least one of them, Shihab Ahmad Khalaf, said he had done so under duress. The judge allegedly refused to launch an investigation into his allegations of torture. At the end of 2006 no further information was available.

Northern Iraq

The largely autonomous Kurdish region was much more stable than the rest of the country in 2006, although some human rights violations were reported. The two dominant parties, the Kurdistan Democratic Party (KDP) and the Patriotic Union of Kurdistan (PUK), agreed to form a unified government for the region, the Kurdish Regional Government, which was announced in May.

◻ Security forces opened fire at protesters in the towns of Darbandikhan and Kalar on 7 and 9 August respectively, reportedly killing two people. In other towns where demonstrations took place, scores of people were reportedly detained, among them nine local journalists. Demonstrators had taken to the streets to protest against fuel shortages and to call for improved public services.

Several people were believed to be held incommunicado, and there were reports that the Kurdish authorities ran secret detention centres.

🗀 Three Turkish nationals, members of the Turkey-based non-governmental Association for the Rights of Freedom of Thought and Education, were detained in June at or near the Turkish-Iraqi border crossing of Habur/Ibrahim Halil near Zakho in Iraq. At the end of the year, Metin Demir, Mustafa Egilli and Hasip Yokus remained in detention in Arbil in Northern Iraq without having been charged or tried.

The first executions in the Kurdish-controlled region of Northern Iraq since 1992 took place on 21 September, when 11 people were executed after being convicted of killings and kidnappings.

AI country reports/ visits
Reports
- Beyond Abu Ghraib – detention and torture in Iraq (AI Index: MDE 14/001/2006)
- Iraq: Amnesty International greatly concerned by rising toll of civilian killings, including for discriminatory motives (AI Index: MDE 14/030/2006)
- Iraq: Amnesty International alarmed at rise in executions (AI Index: MDE 14/033/2006)
- Iraq: Amnesty International deplores death sentences in Saddam Hussain trial (AI Index: MDE 14/037/2006)
- Iraq: One year on, still no justice for torture victims (AI Index: MDE 14/038/2006)
- Iraq: Amnesty International deplores execution of Saddam Hussain (AI Index: MDE 14/043/2006)

IRELAND

IRELAND
Head of state: Mary McAleese
Head of government: Bertie Ahern
Death penalty: abolitionist for all crimes
International Criminal Court: ratified

Judicial inquiries into police misconduct criticized the National Police Service (An Garda Síochána). There was concern at Ireland's record in upholding the human rights of children.

Policing
The judicial inquiry into the April 2000 fatal shooting of John Carthy by police published its report in July. It severely criticized police systems, management and training in dealing with mental health emergencies in the community and the use of lethal force. It identified a series of command failures by police scene commanders, including that insufficient precautions were taken to avoid or minimize the risk to life. It also found that John Carthy "was probably subjected to physical abuse while under interrogation" while in custody on a separate occasion in September 1998, and that investigations into this matter were inadequate.

The judicial inquiry into complaints against members of the police Donegal Division published its third, fourth and fifth reports in August. It highlighted gross abuses of powers and fabrication of evidence; abuse of search warrants under the Offences against the State Act; specific misbehaviour by individual police officers; and "staggering" indiscipline and insubordination. Among other things, it found that police officers conspired to invent a story to ensure the acquittal of another officer facing a criminal charge.

The Police Ombudsman Commission, empowered to investigate complaints against members of the police, including cases involving deaths or serious injury during police operations, had not come into operation. As a result, the ineffective Police Complaints Board continued to deal with complaints.

🗀 At the end of the year, the inquest into the death of Terence Wheelock remained adjourned. He died in 2005 in hospital after being found unconscious in a police cell.

'War on terror'
In June, Ireland was one of the states identified in Senator Marty's report for the Parliamentary Assembly of the Council of Europe as responsible for passive collusion in the US-led programme of secret detentions and renditions (illegal transfer of people between states outside of any judicial process). There was concern that the government had not satisfactorily investigated allegations that Shannon airport may have been used by foreign aircraft in the transfer of detainees by the USA or its agents.

Also in June a civilian aircraft landed at Shannon airport en route from Kuwait to the USA carrying a US Marine in US military custody without the required consent of the Irish government. This gave rise to concern that aircraft registered as private, yet used for state functions, availed themselves of entitlements for overflight and landing without prior authorization or notification.

International Criminal Court

The International Criminal Court Act 2006 was enacted in October, establishing domestic jurisdiction over crimes under the Rome Statute of the International Criminal Court. However, the Act appeared to prohibit domestic jurisdiction over conduct that occurred before its entry into force.

Places of detention

Gary Douch was killed in August by another prisoner in Mountjoy Prison, Dublin. There was concern about the absence of a statutory mechanism for independent and effective investigations into prison-related complaints, including deaths in custody.

The Inspector of Prisons and Places of Detention's annual report, published in August, noted prison overcrowding, limited occupational and educational activities, and inadequate prisoner complaints procedures.

The Prisons Bill 2006, published in November, proposed placing the Office of the Inspector of Prisons on a statutory footing, as repeatedly called for by the European Committee for the Prevention of Torture. However, the Bill failed to provide investigation of or adjudication on individual prisoner complaints as functions of the Inspector.

In November, the Irish Human Rights Commission advised that law and practice in the determination of life sentences was incompatible with the European Convention on Human Rights, and that the Parole Board should be placed on a statutory footing and charged with determining applications for temporary release.

Children

In September, reviewing Ireland's periodic report, the UN Committee on the Rights of the Child noted the failure of the authorities to implement fully its previous recommendations on the adoption of a child rights-based approach in policies and practices. Among other things, the Committee expressed concern about the lack of incorporation of the UN Children's Convention into domestic law; limitations in the mandate of the Ombudsman for Children in investigations related to children in prison and police stations; racism and xenophobia faced by children from ethnic minority communities; the lack of privacy protection for children prosecuted in higher courts; the fact that corporal punishment was not prohibited; the lowering of the age of criminal responsibility to 10 years for serious crimes; the lack of separate detention facilities for children aged 16 and 17; the lack of recognition of the Traveller community as an ethnic group; and child poverty.

Residential facilities

State-run or funded residential facilities for children in care and unaccompanied asylum-seeking children lacked an inspection system.

In November a government-commissioned review of deaths between 2002 and 2005 at the Leas Cross Nursing Home for the elderly was published. It found that the care provided to residents was deficient on many levels, consistent with institutional abuse. It concluded that deficiencies in care at Leas Cross were likely to be replicated in other institutions throughout Ireland owing to a lack of structure, funding, standards, and oversight. It criticized the absence of systematic monitoring of deaths in nursing homes.

Treatment of people with intellectual disabilities

Inappropriately, adult inpatient mental health units continued to admit children. The establishment of an independent inspectorate for residential care facilities for adults with intellectual disabilities was delayed.

Asylum-seekers and victims of trafficking

Guidance for legislative proposals to consolidate and reform immigration legislation, and establish a single protection procedure was published in September. It gave rise to concerns, including a lack of clarity in distinguishing between refugee protection and subsidiary forms of protections; failure to address the lack of transparency and inconsistent decision-making in the present appeal mechanism; failure to address the continued inappropriate housing of immigration detainees in prisons; and the absence of specific protection measures for victims of trafficking. Likewise, the Criminal Law (Trafficking in Persons and Sexual Offences) Bill 2006 published in July failed to provide for the latter.

Discrimination

In his July report, the UN Co-ordinator on Follow-up of the Committee on the Elimination of Racial Discrimination urged the Irish government to engage in dialogue with the Traveller community regarding the identification of Travellers as an ethnic group.

Women

A National Women's Strategy to address gender inequality had still not been published by the end of the year. Non-governmental organizations providing crisis and support services to women experiencing gender-based violence continued to be under-funded.

Arms trade

In August, Irish-made components were reportedly exported to the USA for incorporation into attack helicopters supplied to Israel.

Despite a government announcement in August that it would legislate on arms export controls, by the end of the year no proposals had been published.

ISRAEL AND THE OCCUPIED TERRITORIES

STATE OF ISRAEL
Head of state: Moshe Katzav
Head of government: Ehud Olmert (replaced Ariel Sharon in April)
Death penalty: abolitionist for ordinary crimes
International Criminal Court: signed but declared intention not to ratify

Increased violence between Israelis and Palestinians resulted in a threefold increase in killings of Palestinians by Israeli forces. The number of Israelis killed by Palestinian armed groups diminished by half. More than 650 Palestinians, including some 120 children, and 27 Israelis were killed. Israeli forces carried out air and artillery bombardments in the Gaza Strip, and Israel continued to expand illegal settlements and to build a 700-km fence/wall on Palestinian land in the Occupied Territories. Military blockades and increased restrictions imposed by Israel on the movement of Palestinians and the confiscation by Israel of Palestinian customs duties caused a significant deterioration in living conditions for Palestinian inhabitants in the Occupied Territories, with poverty, food aid dependency, health problems and unemployment reaching crisis levels. Israeli soldiers and settlers committed serious human rights abuses, including unlawful killings, against Palestinians, mostly with impunity. Thousands of Palestinians were arrested by Israeli forces throughout the Occupied Territories on suspicion of security offences and hundreds were held in administrative detention. Israeli conscientious objectors continued to be imprisoned for refusing to serve in the army. In a 34-day war against Hizbullah in Lebanon in July-August, Israeli forces committed serious violations of international humanitarian law, including war crimes. Israeli bombardments killed nearly 1,200 people, and destroyed or damaged tens of thousands of homes and other civilian infrastructure. Israeli forces also littered south Lebanon with around a million unexploded cluster bombs which continued to kill and maim civilians after the conflict.

Background

Ehud Olmert became Prime Minister in April having exercised the powers of the office from January when Prime Minister Ariel Sharon suffered a severe stroke. Ahead of the March legislative elections, Prime Minister Ehud Olmert announced his intention to implement unilaterally a "convergence" plan, under which Israel would annex Palestinian land west of the 700-km fence/wall being built by Israel in the occupied West Bank, including East Jerusalem, and retain control of the Jordan Valley and the West Bank border with Jordan. According to this plan, Israel would annex some 12 per cent of the occupied West Bank, including the locations of all the main Israeli settlements, where more than 80 per cent of Israeli settlers reside.

Relations between the Israeli government and the Palestinian Authority (PA) deteriorated after the Islamic Resistance Movement (Hamas) won the parliamentary elections in the Occupied Territories in January. The Israeli government had no official relations with the Hamas administration, although it maintained relations with PA President Mahmoud Abbas and his Fatah party.

Hizbullah-Israel war

In the 34-day war which broke out on 12 July, after Hizbullah's military wing crossed into Israel and attacked an Israeli patrol, killing three Israeli soldiers and capturing two others. Israeli forces carried out air and artillery bombardments, killing nearly 1,200 people in Lebanon, including hundreds of children. Israeli forces also destroyed tens of thousands of homes and commercial properties, mostly in south Lebanon and in the suburbs of Beirut; and targeted and damaged main roads and bridges throughout the country. Hizbullah missiles fired into Israel caused the deaths of 43 civilians and damaged hundreds of buildings.

In the course of the conflict Israeli forces committed serious violations of international human rights and humanitarian law, including war crimes. In particular, Israeli forces carried out indiscriminate and disproportionate attacks on a large scale. Israeli forces also appear to have carried out direct attacks on civilian infrastructure intended to inflict a form of collective punishment on Lebanon's people, in order to induce them and the Lebanese government to turn against Hizbullah, as well as to cause harm to Hizbullah's military capability.

At least six Lebanese nationals, most of them known or suspected Hizbullah fighters, remained detained in Israeli prisons at the end of the year, while Hizbullah did not disclose the fate or condition of the two Israeli soldiers it had captured. Indirect negotiations for a prisoner exchange were reportedly ongoing between the two sides. Israel suspended access by the International Committee of the Red Cross (ICRC) to the prisoners it held after Hizbullah refused to grant such access to the two Israeli soldiers.

In the final days of the war, after the terms of the ceasefire had been agreed, Israeli forces launched hundreds of thousands of cluster bombs containing up to 4 million bomblets into south Lebanon. The million or so unexploded bomblets that were left continued to kill and maim civilians long after the end of the war. Some 200 people, including tens of children, had been killed or injured by these bomblets and newly laid mines by the end of the year. Despite repeated requests, Israel did not provide detailed maps of the exact locations where its forces launched cluster bombs to the UN bodies mandated to clear unexploded ordnance.

Killings of Palestinians

Israeli forces carried out frequent air and artillery bombardments against the Gaza Strip, often into densely populated refugee camps and residential areas. Some 650 Palestinians, half of them unarmed civilians and including some 120 children, were killed by Israeli forces. This toll was a threefold increase compared with 2005. On 27 June the Israeli army launched operation "Summer Rains" following an attack two days earlier by members of Palestinian armed groups on a military post inside Israel in which two Israeli soldiers were killed and a third – Corporal Gilad Shalit – was captured. Israeli attacks escalated dramatically after the capture of Gilad Shalit, although the preceding months had also been marked by killings of Palestinians and Israeli air and artillery bombardments in the Gaza Strip and the West Bank.

On 9 June, seven members of the Ghalia family – five children and their parents – were killed and some 30 other civilians were injured when Israeli forces fired several artillery shells at a beach in the north of the Gaza Strip. The beach was crowded with Palestinian families enjoying the first weekend of the school holidays. The Israeli army denied responsibility for the killings but failed to substantiate their claim.

In the early morning of 8 November, 18 members of the Athamna family were killed and dozens of other civilians were injured when a volley of artillery shells struck a densely populated neighbourhood of Beit Hanoun, in the north of the Gaza Strip. The victims, eight of them children, were killed in their sleep or while fleeing the shelling, which lasted for around 30 minutes and during which some 12 shells landed in the area. The Israeli authorities expressed regret for the killings, saying that the houses were mistakenly struck due to a technical failure, but rejected calls for an international investigation. The attack came in the wake of a six-day Israeli army raid in Beit Hanoun code-named "Autumn Clouds", during which Israeli forces killed some 70 Palestinians, at least half of them unarmed civilians and including several children and two ambulance emergency service volunteers. The raid also injured some 200 others, including scores of children.

Most Palestinians were killed in the Gaza Strip, although scores were also killed in the West Bank.

Eight-year-old Akaber 'Abd al-Rahman 'Ezzat Zayed was shot dead by Israeli special forces who opened fire on the car in which she was travelling to hospital with her uncle, who was seriously injured in the attack. The incident took place on 17 March in Yamun village, near the northern West Bank town of Jenin.

On 19 December, 14-year-old Dua'a Nasser 'Abdelkader was shot dead by Israeli soldiers as she approached the fence/wall with a friend near Fara'un, a village in the north of the West Bank.

Israeli forces continued to assassinate wanted Palestinians, killing and wounding bystanders in the process.

Nine members of the Abu Salmiya family were killed when an Israeli F16 fighter jet bombed their home at 2.30am on 12 July. According to the Israeli army, a senior leader of Hamas' armed wing was in the house at the time of the strike but survived. However, the strike wiped out an entire family: the owner of the house, Nabil Abu Salmiya, a Hamas political leader and university lecturer; his wife Salwa; and seven of their children all aged under 18. Dozens of neighbours were also injured and several other houses were damaged in the strike.

Attacks by Palestinian armed groups

Killings of Israelis by Palestinian armed groups continued but decreased to half the previous year's figure and to the lowest level since the beginning of the intifada in 2000. In total, 21 Israeli civilians, including a child, and six soldiers were killed in Palestinian attacks in Israel and the Occupied Territories.

Eleven Israeli civilians were killed and 68 others were injured in a suicide bomb attack claimed by the armed wing of Islamic Jihad on 17 April in Tel Aviv's old bus station.

One of two suicide bombings, on 30 March, killed four Israeli civilians, one of them aged 16, near the entrance of the Israeli settlement of Kedumim, in the northern West Bank.

There was a significant increase in the launching of homemade "Qassam" rockets by Palestinian armed groups from the Gaza Strip into the south of Israel. In most cases these indiscriminate rockets caused no casualties, but two Israeli civilians, Fatima Slutzker and Yaakuv Yaakobov, were killed in separate rocket attacks on Sderot in November and several others were injured.

Attacks by Israeli settlers

Israeli settlers in the West Bank repeatedly attacked Palestinians and their property, as well as international peace activists and human rights defenders who sought to document their attacks on Palestinians. Some of the attacks occurred during the olive harvest season, in October and November, when Palestinian farmers attempted to go to their fields close to Israeli settlements and which Israeli settlers sought to prevent them accessing. In June the Israeli Supreme Court issued a ruling instructing the army and police to protect Palestinian farmers seeking to work their land from attacks by settlers. The incidence of such attacks decreased, but several more were carried out, some in the presence of Israeli security forces who failed to intervene.

In the evening of 25 March a group of Israeli settlers assaulted 'Abderrahman Shinneran as he slept in his tent with his wife and three children in Susia in the southern Hebron Hills. When his brother 'Aziz went to his rescue he too was assaulted and injured.

On 18 November, Tove Johansson, a 19-year-old Swedish human rights defender, was assaulted by

Israeli settlers as she accompanied Palestinian school children through an Israeli army checkpoint near the Tel Rumeida Israeli settlement in the West Bank city of Hebron. She was struck with a broken bottle and sustained facial injuries. Israeli soldiers at a nearby checkpoint took no action to stop the attack or apprehend the perpetrators.

Impunity and the administration of justice
In December the Supreme Court rejected a discriminatory law enacted the previous year that denies Palestinian victims compensation for abuses suffered at the hands of Israeli forces. However, impunity remained widespread for Israeli soldiers and settlers responsible for unlawful killings, ill-treatment and other abuses of human rights of Palestinians and attacks against their property. Investigations and prosecutions relating to such abuses were rare and usually only occurred when the abuses were exposed by human rights organizations and the media. By contrast, the Israeli authorities took a range of measures against Palestinians suspected of direct or indirect involvement in attacks against Israelis, including measures such as assassinations, physical abuse and collective punishment that violate international law. Palestinians convicted of involvement in attacks against Israelis were usually sentenced to life imprisonment by Israeli military courts, whereas in the exceptional cases in which Israelis were convicted of killing or abusing Palestinians, Israeli courts imposed lenient sentences.

Thousands of Palestinians, including scores of children, were detained by Israeli forces. Many were arrested during Israeli army operations in the Gaza Strip. The majority of those arrested were released uncharged, but hundreds were accused of security offences. Those detained included dozens of Hamas government ministers and parliamentarians, who were arrested after Palestinian gunmen captured an Israeli soldier in June, apparently to exert pressure for the soldier's release.

Trials of Palestinians before military courts often did not meet international fair trial standards, with allegations of torture and other ill-treatment of detainees inadequately investigated. Hundreds of Palestinians were held in administrative detention without charge or trial; more than 700 were being held at the end of the year. Family visits to some 10,000 Palestinian prisoners were severely restricted as many of their relatives were denied visiting permits.

Imprisonment of conscientious objectors
Several Israelis, both men and women, who refused to serve in the army because they opposed Israel's occupation of the Occupied Territories, were imprisoned for up to four months. They were prisoners of conscience.
- Uri Natan, aged 18, served eight consecutive prison sentences totalling five months for refusing to be drafted because of his conscientious objection to Israel's military occupation of the Occupied Territories.

Violations of economic and social rights
Israel continued to expand illegal Israeli settlements and stepped up construction of a 700-km fence/wall, 80 per cent of which runs inside the occupied West Bank, including in and around East Jerusalem. Large areas of Palestinian land were seized and utilized for this purpose. The fence/wall and more than 500 Israeli army checkpoints and blockades throughout the West Bank increasingly confined Palestinians to restricted areas and denied them freedom of movement between towns and villages within the Occupied Territories. Many Palestinians were cut off from their farmland, their main source of livelihood, or could not freely access their workplaces, education, health facilities and other services.

Further discriminatory measures were put in place to enforce the system of segregated roads and checkpoints for Israelis and Palestinians. In November the Israeli army issued an order prohibiting Israelis from using their vehicles to transport Palestinians in the West Bank, where many roads or stretches of road are prohibited to Palestinians and reserved for use by Israelis – mainly the 450,000 Israeli settlers who live in the West Bank. In the Gaza Strip, the Rafah crossing to Egypt, the only entry and exit point for the 1.5 million Palestinian residents, was kept completely or partially closed by the Israeli authorities for most of the year. The passage of goods was similarly restricted by the Israeli authorities' frequent and prolonged closures of the Karni merchandise crossing, the only one they permit.

The damaging impact of the prolonged blockades and movement restrictions was compounded by the Israeli authorities' confiscation of tax duties due to the PA – some US$50 million a month, equivalent to half of the PA's administration budget. As a result, humanitarian conditions in the Occupied Territories deteriorated to an unprecedented level, marked by a rise in extreme poverty, food aid dependency, high unemployment, malnutrition and other health problems among the Palestinian population.

The destruction of Palestinian infrastructure by Israeli forces caused long-term damage and additional humanitarian challenges. In June the Israeli bombardment of the Gaza Strip's only power plant, which supplied electricity to half of the area's inhabitants, as well as Israel's destruction of bridges, roads, and water and sewage networks, caused the population to be without electricity for most of the day throughout the hottest months of the year and interfered with water supplies. Israeli forces also bombed and destroyed several PA ministries in the Gaza Strip and other buildings housing charities and institutions reportedly linked to Hamas. These attacks destroyed or damaged scores of residential properties, rendering hundreds of Palestinians homeless.

Other Palestinians were made homeless when Israeli forces bulldozed their houses in the West Bank, including in the East Jerusalem area, on the grounds that they had been built without licences which the Israeli authorities require but make it impossible in those areas for Palestinians to obtain. The same reason was invoked to destroy tens of homes of Israeli Arab Bedouins in unrecognized Bedouin villages in the south of Israel, which the Israeli authorities intend to uproot.

AI country reports/ visits
Reports
- Israel/Occupied Territories: Briefing to the UN Committee on the Elimination of Racial Discrimination (AI Index: MDE 15/002/2006)
- Israel/Lebanon: Out of all proportion — civilians bear the brunt of the war (AI Index: MDE 02/033/2006)
- Israel/Lebanon: Israel and Hizbullah must spare civilians — Obligations under International Humanitarian Law of the Parties to the Conflict in Israel and Lebanon (AI Index: MDE 15/070/2006)
- Israel/Lebanon: Deliberate destruction or "collateral damage"? — Israeli attacks on civilian infrastructure (AI Index: MDE 18/007/2006)
- Israel and the Occupied Territories: Road to nowhere (AI Index: MDE 15/093/2006)

Visits
AI delegations visited Israel and the Occupied Territories in April, May, August, September, November and December. In December AI's Secretary General headed a delegation that visited Israel and the Occupied Territories and held meetings with the Israeli and PA governments. She expressed concern about the deteriorating human rights situation and urged them to take concrete measures to end impunity and address continuing human rights abuses. AI also called for investigations and reparations for victims of violations during the Hizbullah-Israel war.

ITALY

ITALIAN REPUBLIC
Head of state: Giorgio Napolitano (replaced Carlo Azeglio Ciampi in May)
Head of government: Romano Prodi (replaced Silvio Berlusconi in May)
Death penalty: abolitionist for all crimes
International Criminal Court: ratified

Italy lacked a comprehensive asylum law. The government failed to forward extradition requests for 26 US citizens to the USA in the Abu Omar rendition case. Several migrants were given an expulsion order and some were sent back to their countries of origin based on counter-terrorism laws in place since 2005. No specific crime of torture was provided for in Italian law.

Migration
Italy still lacked a specific and comprehensive law on asylum, and retained the Bossi-Fini law on migration which included provisions that contravened human rights laws and standards.
Detention and expulsions of migrant minors
Migrant minors continued to be routinely detained upon arrival at the maritime border in Italy, in contravention of international human rights and refugee law. The right of detained minors to be kept separate from adults who are not members of the same family was in many cases not respected. Minors were often not given legal aid or information about their rights and were in some cases at risk of being forcibly returned to their countries of origin due to inaccurate age assessment. In some cases unaccompanied minors also faced body searches, inspections and confiscation of belongings. Some minors were not granted prompt access to asylum procedures, while others were considered as asylum-seekers without their knowledge and received residence permits which they did not understand.

⌕ In January, three brothers of Somali origin who were minors were sent back to Ghana, from where they had arrived only the previous day, reportedly carrying false passports. During their detention at Malpensa Airport in Milan they were reportedly not asked their age or nationality, nor informed about the possibility of applying for asylum and not allowed to contact their relatives in Europe. The three eventually fled to Côte d'Ivoire.
Corruption and abuses in detention centres
Conditions in many detention centres continued to be problematic. There were reports of guards taking bribes to supply migrants with overpriced goods and complaints of poor legal, medical and psychological assistance.

⌕ In October it was reported that groups of migrants escaped from the Caltanissetta detention centre in Sicily after bribing guards. The Ministry of the Interior and the Caltanissetta public prosecutor began investigations into abuses and crime at the same centre.

Access to migrant detention centres
Following a declaration by the Minister of the Interior that AI should be allowed access to migrants' detention centres, procedures were initiated to authorize such access. Access had previously been denied to AI and other non-governmental organizations.

Co-operation with Libya
High-level discussions with the Libyan authorities began regarding joint actions aimed at stemming migration to Italy and included promises by the Italian authorities of financial support to Libya to build detention centres for migrants, and by Libya to patrol its southern borders. This undertaking was given despite the fact that Libya had not ratified the UN Refugee Convention and its Protocol, and had not established national asylum procedures.

Counter-terrorism measures
Abu Omar abduction and rendition
Preliminary judicial investigations were concluded in the case of Abu Omar, an Egyptian citizen with an Italian residence permit, who was abducted from a street in Milan in 2003 as part of the USA's programme of secret detentions and renditions – the unlawful transfer of people between states outside of any judicial process. Abu Omar was flown by the USA to Egypt, where he was reportedly tortured in detention. The abduction was reported to have been carried out by US Central Intelligence Agency (CIA) agents and members of the Italian military and security service agency, Servizio per le Informazioni e la Sicurezza Militare (SISMI). Although the Minister of Justice gave permission for Italian magistrates to interview suspects in the USA, by the end of 2006 the Ministry had not forwarded extradition requests to the US authorities. By the end of the year a total of 26 arrest warrants for alleged US operatives had been issued, including one for the head of the CIA office in Italy at the time of the abduction. Arrest warrants were also issued for two SISMI agents.

In December, prosecutors asked a judge to indict the 26 US operatives and nine Italian citizens, including the head of SISMI at the time of the abduction.

Summary expulsions
Several migrants were given expulsion orders and some were sent back to their countries of origin based on counter-terrorism legislation (Law 155/05, the so-called "Pisanu Law") in place since 2005. No judicial control was carried out on whether those expelled were involved in criminal activities, whether the expulsion itself was legal, or whether subjects of the expulsion orders risked human rights abuses in their countries of origin. Those expelled during the year included nationals from Egypt, Morocco, Syria and Tunisia.

▭ One man was summarily expelled to Syria despite having a residence permit to remain legally in Italy. He was reportedly detained for several days by the Syrian authorities before being released.

The Pisanu Law allowed expulsion orders of both regular and irregular migrants to be decided and implemented based on "well-grounded reasons to believe that his/her stay in the territory could favour in any manner terrorist organizations and activities". The law did not require the person deported to have been convicted of or charged with a crime connected to terrorism and did not provide for judicial confirmation or authorization of the decision and of its implementation. The law provided for a judicial appeal against the decision, but not for suspension of the actual deportation pending the appeal. The expulsion procedure lacked effective protection from *refoulement* for people who could be at risk of persecution or other serious human rights violations once in the country of origin. In November, the European Court of Human Rights suspended the deportation of three people about to be expelled based on the Pisanu Law. The Court based its decision on the risks they would run in their countries of origin if expelled, including the risk of torture and ill-treatment.

The Italian Constitutional Court was investigating whether some provisions of the Pisanu Law violated the right to judicial remedy, the right to defence, and the right to fair trial.

During the second half of the year, evidence emerged regarding a governmental list of migrants to be expelled on suspicion of involvement in terrorism. At least one of the persons expelled in 2006 based on the counter-terrorism law was on the list.

Police concerns
Italy still failed to make torture, as defined in the UN Convention against Torture, a specific crime within its penal code. There was no independent police complaints and accountability body. Policing operations were not in line with the European Code of Police Ethics, for example in the requirement for officers to display prominently some form of identification, such as a service number, to ensure they could be held accountable.

▭ An investigation continued into a December 2005 operation in Val di Susa when several hundred law enforcement officers attempted to remove around 100 people demonstrating against a high-speed rail link. Demonstrators were reportedly assaulted and beaten, many while sleeping.

Updates: policing of 2001 demonstrations
Trials of police officers continued in relation to policing operations around the mass demonstrations in Naples in March 2001 and during the G8 Summit in Genoa in July 2001.

▭ In November a Genoa court declared that it would not reopen investigations into the death of Carlo Giuliani, a young man fatally shot by a law enforcement official during the 2001 demonstrations in the city. Calls to reopen investigations had been prompted by the emergence of potential new evidence.

International scrutiny
In April, the UN Human Rights Committee adopted its Concluding Observations on Italy after reviewing the

state's periodic report. The Committee recommended among other things that Italy establish an independent national human rights institution, in accordance with the UN Paris Principles. It also recommended that efforts be increased to ensure that prompt and impartial investigations were carried out into allegations of ill-treatment by law enforcement officers.

The Committee further recommended that the maximum period during which a person may be held in custody following arrest on a criminal charge be reduced, even in exceptional circumstances, to less than the current five days and that the detainee be given access to independent legal advice immediately. It also recommended that Italy ensure that the judiciary remain independent of the executive power, and that judicial reform not jeopardize this independence.

AI country reports/ visits
Reports
- Italy: Invisible children – The human rights of migrant and asylum-seeking minors detained upon arrival at the maritime border in Italy (AI Index: EUR 30/001/2006)
- Italy: Five years after the G8 Genoa policing operations – Italian authorities must take concrete action to prevent and prosecute police brutality in all circumstances (AI Index: EUR 30/005/2006)
- Italy: Abu Omar – Italian authorities must cooperate fully with all investigations (AI Index: EUR 30/006/2006)

JAMAICA

JAMAICA
Head of state: Queen Elizabeth II, represented by Kenneth Hall (replaced Howard Cooke in February)
Head of government: Portia Simpson Miller (replaced Percival James Patterson in March)
Death penalty: retentionist
International Criminal Court: signed

Widespread sexual violence, including rape, continued during 2006, posing severe health risks for women and girls. Murder rates declined but were still among the highest in the world. Already high levels of killings by the police rose over the previous year's total. Impunity continued to be the norm for such abuses.

Background
In February Portia Simpson Miller was elected as president of the ruling People's National Party (PNP) and in March she became the country's first female Prime Minister. Corruption allegations emerged in October when the opposition revealed that the PNP had received a donation of 31 million Jamaican dollars from a company selling Nigerian crude oil to the international market for Jamaica.

Sexual violence against women and girls
Sexual violence continued throughout the country, resulting in severe health risks for women and girls. Sexual harassment and assault by strangers, friends, family, acquaintances and lovers was widespread but the authorities failed adequately to investigate and punish the perpetrators. Rates of HIV infection among women and girls continued to rise and people living with HIV faced systematic discrimination.

The discussions aimed at reforming the Offences Against the Person Act and the Incest Punishment Act, ongoing since 1995 and 2000 respectively, re-started in a parliamentarian joint committee on 6 December. Proposed amendments to both acts would offer greater legal protection to women and children, including making marital rape a criminal offence and increasing punishments for perpetrators of sexual violence. The Centre for Investigations of Sexual Offences and Child Abuse was improved and given further powers to investigate these crimes.

▱ Early in 2006 a 13-year-old girl was repeatedly sexually assaulted by three teenagers in the back of a van. The assault was allegedly supervised and tape-recorded by a 46-year-old former deacon of a local church. The teenagers and the former deacon were charged with indecent assault and carnal abuse, but in November the charges were dropped by the public prosecutor's office and replaced with trafficking in human beings. The accused were released on bail pending trial, which had not started by the end of the year.

📁 Enid Gordon was raped by two men when she was 15 years old. Two men were arrested, charged and released on bail. In October 2005, a week before she was due to testify against the men, Enid Gordon was found strangled in the place where she had been raped a year earlier. Two suspects were arrested and forensic evidence taken, but the results of the investigation were still pending.

Crime and insecurity

Homicide rates in Jamaica remained high, although numbers decreased in 2006. A total of 1,355 murders were committed during the year according to official figures, a decrease since 2005 of more than 20 per cent.

Small arms were widely available, exacerbating already high levels of violence. In October Jamaica voted in favour of a UN resolution to start working towards an Arms Trade Treaty.

Gang warfare was prevalent. Gangs were sometimes the perpetrators of violence in communities, although were sometimes perceived as the protectors of those communities due to distrust of the police. Gang leaders were known to demand adolescent girls from their families for sexual exploitation and assault.

Unlawful killings

Reports of police brutality continued. At least 138 people were allegedly killed by police during the year. Impunity for police abuses and a complete lack of accountability in the security and justice systems remained the norm.

📁 Glenroy McDermoth, a police officer from the Jamaican Constabulary Force, was sentenced to life imprisonment in February for shooting in the back and killing Michael Dorsett in 2000. This was the first conviction of a police officer for murder committed while on duty since October 1999.

Death penalty

No executions took place during 2006. The last was in 1988. The 1993 Privy Council ruling that sentences on death row prisoners must be carried out within five years or be commuted remained in force. Some calls were made by high-ranking government officials to renew hangings. Seven prisoners were held on death row.

AI country reports/ visits
Report
• Jamaica: Sexual violence against women and girls in Jamaica – "Just a little sex" (AI Index: AMR 38/002/2006)
Visit
AI delegates visited Jamaica in December to meet government officials and non-governmental organizations concerning violence against women.

JAPAN

JAPAN
Head of government: Abe Shinzo (replaced Koizumi Junichiro in September)
Death penalty status: retentionist
International Criminal Court: not ratified

Four people were executed in December, ending a 15-month unofficial moratorium on executions. Amendments to immigration law introduced fast-track procedures to deport "possible terrorists" that breached international human rights standards. The issue of reparations to the victims of Japan's system of sexual slavery during World War II remained unresolved.

Background

Prime Minister Koizumi Junichiro stepped down in September after five years in office and was succeeded by his Cabinet Secretary, Abe Shinzo.

A nuclear test by North Korea in October intensified public debate in Japan on whether to revise Article 9 of the Constitution which defines Japan as pacifist. In July all Japanese troops were withdrawn from Iraq.

The Legal Committee of the Diet (parliament) discussed a Bill that would criminalize any discussion about committing a criminal offence. It was feared that vague and broad terms contained in the law would restrict freedom of speech.

In August, the government announced that Japan would accede to the Rome Statute of the International Criminal Court in July 2007.

Death penalty

As a result of Justice Minister Seiken Sugiura's commitment not to sign execution orders while in office, no executions were carried out between 16 September 2005 and 25 December 2006. Following his replacement as Justice Minister by Jinen Nagase, a supporter of the death penalty, the moratorium was ended and on 25 December, four people were executed in secret by hanging – Hidaka Hiroaki in Hiroshima, Fukuoka Michio in Osaka, and Akiyama Yoshimitsu, aged 77, and Fujinami Yoshio, aged 75, in Tokyo.

At the end of 2006, 94 prisoners remained on death row. Executions are typically held in secret and prisoners are either not warned of their impending execution or are notified only on the morning of the day of execution.

Refugees and immigration

The number of asylum-seekers increased to more than 900, although the number of people recognized as refugees fell to 26. Lawyers, most of them Tokyo-based, faced difficulties in gaining access to asylum-seekers at detention facilities, especially when their clients were detained in immigration facilities far from Tokyo.

Amendments were introduced to the Immigration and Refugee Recognition Law that introduced fingerprinting and photographing of all visitors to Japan. They also brought in fast-track procedures to deport anyone deemed by the Justice Minister as a "possible terrorist", which had the potential to undermine the principle of *non-refoulement*.

Some people with valid passports who applied for asylum on arrival in Japan were reported to have been detained indefinitely at hotels near airports of entry if they were deemed likely to abscond. They were not guaranteed the right to communicate with the outside world, or to have access to adequate medical treatment and food. In addition, they did not always have prompt access to a lawyer or advice about their rights in a language they understood. As a result, they did not have adequate recourse to a judicial process.

◻ More than 30 asylum-seekers, including two 16-year-old Kurdish minors, were detained for about 40 days in July-August at a hotel near Narita airport soon after they sought asylum. All were charged for their accommodation at the hotel.

Reparations for violence against women

Survivors of Japan's system of sexual slavery before and during World War II continued to be denied full reparations. Japanese courts have repeatedly thrown out lawsuits seeking compensation, and the government continued to argue that compensation claims were settled by post-war treaty arrangements.

◻ In August the Tokyo District Court refused to award damages to eight Chinese women who were victims of Japan's sexual slavery system, even though it acknowledged that the women had been kidnapped, held against their will and raped as teenagers.

Substitute prison system (*daiyo-kangoku*)

The *daiyo-kangoku* system of pre-trial detention continued to allow police to hold suspects in police cells without charge for up to 23 days, a practice that facilitates the extraction of "confessions" under duress. Under the *daiyo-kangoku* system, suspects are solely under the control of the police; there are no rules or regulations regarding the duration of interrogation; lawyers' access to clients during questioning is restricted; and there is no electronic recording of interviews by police.

During 2006 amendments to legislation concerning *daiyo-kangoku* were introduced, giving the *daiyo-kangoku* system legal status for the first time. The amendments provide for detainees to be informed of some of their rights and for lawyers to be appointed, but only after charges have been brought. Detainees are usually charged only after they have "confessed". AI had long campaigned for abolition of the *daiyo-kangoku* system rather than its reform.

AI country reports/visits

Report
- "Will this day be my last?": The death penalty in Japan (AI Index: ASA 22/006/2006)

Visit
AI delegates visited Japan in February.

JORDAN

HASHEMITE KINGDOM OF JORDAN
Head of state: King Abdullah II bin al-Hussein
Head of government: Ma'arouf Bakhit
Death penalty: retentionist
International criminal court: ratified

Tens of people were arrested for political reasons, including on suspicion of terrorism, and many were reportedly detained incommunicado. Some were tried by the State Security Court (SSC), whose procedures fell far short of international fair trial standards, and sentenced to prison terms or, in some cases, to death, despite alleging in court that they had been tortured. There were new reports of torture and ill-treatment of prisoners and at least four suspicious deaths in custody. Freedom of expression continued to be restricted. Women were subject to legal and other discrimination and inadequately protected against domestic violence, and there were allegations of abuses against migrant workers. At least 42 people were sentenced to death and at least four were executed.

Background

A Memorandum of Understanding between the UK and Jordan, allowing for the involuntary return of terror suspects from the UK to Jordan, remained in place. No one had been returned to Jordan under it by the end of the year.

In May, Jordan became a member of the UN Human Rights Council.

In October, 129 prisoners, most, but not all of whom had been convicted, were released under a Royal Pardon. Another 266 detainees, held without charge or trial under the Law on Crime Prevention, were released at the same time.

In December, the King called upon the government to give due attention to reports on human rights violations in the country, issued by the government-funded National Centre for Human Rights.

Abuses in the context of the 'war on terror'

The Prevention of Terrorism bill became law in November despite concerns expressed domestically and internationally that it did not conform to international human rights law and standards. The new law's definition of "terrorist acts" was too broad and could be used to criminalize membership of political opposition groups or other peaceful activities.

Reports persisted that al-Jafr prison in south-east Jordan was being, or had been, used in co-ordination with US intelligence agencies for the secret detention of people suspected by the US authorities of possessing information about terrorism. The Jordanian government denied this. The prison was closed in December, however, on the orders of the King, who called for an improvement in prison conditions. The UN Special

Rapporteur on torture visited Jordan in June 2006 and described al-Jafr prison as "a punishment centre, where detainees are routinely beaten, and subjected to corporal punishment, amounting to torture".

A report by the Council of Europe, published in June, accused Jordan of having a prominent role in the transfer, detention and torture of foreign nationals under the US government's renditions policy.

Tens of people were detained for political reasons, many for suspected involvement in terrorism. Many were held incommunicado by the General Intelligence Department (GID), the main security service responsible for the arrest, detention and interrogation of political suspects, during which they may have been subjected to torture or ill-treatment. At least 34 political cases were heard by the SSC, during 18 of which the defendants withdrew "confessions" they had made in pre-trial detention, saying they had been extracted under torture. The SSC was not known to have investigated these allegations adequately.

▢ Four men, including Yazin Muhammad al-Haliq, Usama Abu Hazeem and Muhammad 'Arabiat, were sentenced to death by the SSC in March for allegedly planning terrorist attacks and possessing illegal explosives. The sentences were then reduced to 10 years' imprisonment. The court reportedly disregarded the defendants' allegations that they had been forced to sign "confessions" they were not permitted to see, under torture, including prolonged beatings with sticks to their bodies and soles of their feet, burning with cigarettes, sleep deprivation, as well as threats and verbal abuse. At the end of 2006, their case was pending appeal before the Court of Cassation.

▢ Sheikh Abu Muhammad al-Maqdisi continued to be detained, reportedly in solitary confinement in the GID detention centre in Amman. Although he was apparently charged days after his arrest in July 2005 with conspiracy to commit terrorist acts, and reportedly denied legal counsel, he had not been brought to trial by the end of the year. His arrest followed a media interview on "resistance" to US involvement in Iraq.

Torture and ill-treatment
In June, the UN Special Rapporteur on torture carried out a fact-finding mission to Jordan at the invitation of the government, and reported that torture was systematically practised by the GID and the Criminal Investigation Department. He called on the Jordanian authorities to ensure that all torture allegations were properly investigated, for the use of torture to be made a criminal offence in accordance with international standards and for appropriate penalties to be imposed on those convicted of torture.

There were persistent reports that Islamist prisoners were subject to ill-treatment in Jordanian prisons, including Qafqafa, Swaqa and Jweideh prisons. Reports included beatings by prison staff, prolonged solitary confinement, denial of fresh air and exposure to hot temperatures. There were reportedly at least four suspicious deaths in custody.

In October, the Minister of the Interior announced the establishment of a Human Rights Department within the Ministry, whose responsibilities would include improving prison facilities.

▢ On 13 April, armed anti-terrorist police reportedly raided cells occupied by Islamist prisoners at Qafqafa prison. Inmates and their families said the operation's intent was to remove two inmates. The authorities said they were searching for drugs and weapons. One inmate, Khaled Fawzi 'Ali Bishtawi, died, reportedly from gunshot wounds. His case was referred to the National Institute of Forensic Medicine to establish the cause of death. The results were not made public and no one was known to have been held to account for his death.

Death penalty
At least 42 people were sentenced to death, including 17 who were tried in their absence. Of these, 14 had sentences immediately commuted to prison terms. At least four prisoners were executed.

▢ Salem Sa'ad Bin Sweid and Yasser Fathi Ibrahim Freihat were hanged at Swaqa prison on 11 March. The SSC sentenced them to death in 2004 for involvement in the killing of US diplomat Laurence Foley in Amman in 2002. They alleged in court that they had been tortured to make them "confess". No investigation into these allegations is known to have been held.

Draft amendments to legislation concerning the death penalty remained pending before Parliament. The amendments would reduce the number of capital offences and replace the death penalty with life imprisonment for crimes such as possession of weapons or explosives and drug-related offences.

Freedom of expression and association
There were new violations of the rights to freedom of expression and association. The Public Assemblies Law was invoked to deny permission for some demonstrations, including those in opposition to Israel. Several people were arrested, apparently after exercising their right to freedom of expression. Some of these were arrested for criticizing the king and "inciting sectarian or racial strife".

▢ Journalists Jihad al-Moumani and Hashim al-Khalidi were both sentenced by the Amman Penal Court to two months' imprisonment for insulting religious sentiment after republishing cartoons depicting the Prophet Muhammad. At the end of 2006, they were on bail pending appeal.

▢ In September, the King pardoned Members of Parliament Muhammad Abu Faris and 'Ali Abu Sukkar after they were sentenced to prison terms by the SSC for "harming national unity" and "inciting sectarian or racial strife". They had expressed condolences to the family of the leader of al-Qa'ida in Iraq, Abu Mus'ab al-Zarqawi, a Jordanian national, after he was killed by US forces. One of them reportedly described Abu Mus'ab al-Zarqawi as a "martyr".

Discrimination and violence against women
Temporary amendments to legislation concerning women remained pending before Parliament. These

amendments would give women the right to divorce without their husband's consent and establish penalties for perpetrators of family killings.

Article 98 of the Penal Code continued to be used as a defence in cases where men killed their female relatives. The Article allows for reduced sentences where the killing is deemed to be committed in a "fit of rage" caused by unlawful or dangerous acts on the part of the victim. In March, after Article 98 was invoked, the Criminal Court passed a sentence of only one year's imprisonment against a man convicted of killing his daughter.

According to official records, 12 women and two men were victims of family killings during the year.

Migrant workers

In May 2006, the US National Labor Committee reported that migrant workers' rights were being abused in more than 25 Jordanian textile factories that supply US retailers, stating that employers confiscated the passports of tens of thousands of foreign workers and trapped them "in involuntary servitude". The Committee alleged that the abuses included rape, beatings with sticks and belts and that some employees were made to work more than 100 hours each week and some were denied wages for half a year. Shortly after, the Minister for Labour published a report accepting that there was evidence of abuses in "some factories" including unpaid overtime but denied many of the Committee's findings, including its allegations of physical abuse.

Refugees

Nearly 200 Iranian Kurdish refugees who had fled Iraq's al-Tash camp in January 2005 continued to reside in Iraq close to the Jordanian border, after being denied entry to Jordan in contravention of international refugee law. They were housed in tents and subsisted on supplies brought or donated by passing travellers. In March, more than 100 Palestinians who had lived as refugees in Iraq were also denied entry to Jordan, and spent several weeks at the border before they were resettled in Syria. Some 63 other Palestinian refugees who had been confined for three years to a refugee camp near Ruweished after they fled to Jordan, were resettled in Canada in October. Others, however, remained confined to the camp.

AI country reports/visits
Report
• Jordan: "Your confessions are ready for you to sign" – Detention and torture of political suspects (AI Index: MDE 16/005/2006)
Visits
AI delegates made several visits to Jordan in 2006.

KAZAKSTAN

REPUBLIC OF KAZAKSTAN
Head of state: Nursultan Nazarbaev
Head of government: Danial Akhmedov
Death penalty: retentionist
International Criminal Court: not ratified

Asylum-seekers and refugees from China and Uzbekistan continued to be at risk of detention and forcible return. At least three men were forcibly returned to China. A jailed opposition leader was released. A defendant on trial for the murder of a prominent opposition party leader was sentenced to death after what appeared to be an unfair trial.

Background

In December the Organization for Security and Co-operation in Europe decided to postpone the decision on Kazakstan's bid for the 2009 chairmanship of the organization until December 2007. In October the Commission of the European Union had said that Kazakstan needed to do more to improve respect for human rights.

Freedom of assembly

In February police reportedly broke up an unauthorized demonstration in Almaty organized by opposition parties following the murder of Altinbek Sarsenbaev, leader of the opposition True Bright Path (Naghiz Ak Zhol) party. The organizers of the demonstration were subsequently brought before a court and sentenced to fines and 15 days' administrative detention.

Forcible return

Despite better co-operation between the government and UNHCR, the UN refugee agency, Kazakstan continued to disregard its obligations under international law. Refugees were not effectively protected and continued to be at risk of forcible return to China and Uzbekistan where they were subjected to serious human rights violations.

▭ In November UNHCR expressed serious concern for the safety of a Uighur asylum-seeker, whose fate and whereabouts were unknown since his release from detention in October. A court in Almaty had quashed the criminal charges on which he had been detained in June. UNHCR feared that he might have been forcibly deported.

▭ Two Uighur men originally from China's Xinjiang Uighur Autonomous Region (XUAR) – 35-year-old Yusuf Kadir Tohti (also known as Erdagan) and 30-year-old Abdukadir Sidik – were held in incommunicado detention in China after they were forcibly returned from Kazakstan in May. The Chinese authorities reportedly accused Yusuf Kadir Tohti of "separatism" and asked for his extradition. Abdukadir Sidik had fled the XUAR in 1999 after publicly protesting against the Chinese authorities' policy on minorities. According to a letter written by Abdukadir Sidik from prison before he was forcibly returned, he was interrogated and threatened by Chinese police officers while in detention in Kazakstan.

⎯ In January the authorities denied that they had detained nine Uzbekistani nationals , including four registered asylum-seekers, in 2005. Instead they claimed that the men had been detained by Uzbekistani law enforcement officers on Uzbekistani territory. However, according to reliable sources, the nine were detained in the city of Shymkent, in the south of Kazakstan, on 24 and 27 November, and held incommunicado until their forcible return to Uzbekistan on 29 November 2005. According to reports, only two of the returned men were initially given access to lawyers in Uzbekistan; the others were held incommunicado. Two were subsequently sentenced to six years in prison following a closed trial in Tashkent, Uzbekistan, in April 2006. Rukhiddin Fakhruddinov, a former independent imam (religious leader) of a mosque in Tashkent, was sentenced to 17 years in prison in September by a court in Tashkent after a closed trial.

⎯ In August the authorities released Uzbekistani national Gabdurafikh Temirbaev into the care of the UNHCR, and allowed him and his family to be permanently resettled to a third country. Gabdurafikh Temirbaev had reportedly been in Kazakstan since 1999, when he fled persecution for his religious beliefs in Uzbekistan. He was detained by officers from the security services in June 2006, reportedly following an extradition request from Uzbekistan. Gabdurafikh Temirbaev had been recognized as a refugee by the UNHCR in June after a thorough status determination procedure.

Fair trial concerns

⎯ In January Galimzhan Zhakianov, one of the leaders of the former opposition Democratic Choice of Kazakstan party, was released on parole following an appeal hearing. He had been sentenced to seven years' imprisonment in 2002 for "abuse of office" and financial crimes, but the real reason for his imprisonment appeared to be his peaceful opposition activities.

⎯ In February the bodies of Altinbek Sarsenbaev, a former information minister and ambassador to Russia, his bodyguard and driver were discovered on the outskirts of Almaty. They had been shot in the back with their hands tied behind them. Altinbek Sarsenbaev had resigned his position to join the opposition Naghiz Ak Jol party in 2003. Opposition leaders alleged that the murder was politically motivated because Altinbek Sarsenbaev had been very outspoken, particularly on official corruption.

In June, Yerzhan Utembaev, the main defendant in the trial for the murder of Altinbek Sarsenbaev, retracted his confession in court. Yerzhan Utembaev, the former head of the Senate's secretariat, claimed that he had been put under severe psychological pressure in pre-trial detention to admit to ordering and organizing the murder. Another defendant, Rustam Ibrahimov, a former member of an elite special unit of the security

services, who was accused of carrying out the murder, stated in court that the charges against him had been fabricated and that he had been coerced into signing a confession. There was concern that the defendants had been presumed guilty from the moment of their detention on 22 February. On 1 March President Nursultan Nazarbaev told a joint session of parliament that Yerzhan Utembaev had already confessed to law enforcement officers and that he had received a personal letter from Yerzhan Utembaev in which the latter admitted his guilt. Opposition groups and relatives of Altinbek Sarsenbaev claimed that the defendants were "scapegoats" and that the trial was a "farce".

In August Rustam Ibrahimov was sentenced to death. Yerzhan Utembaev was sentenced to 20 years in prison. In December the Criminal Chamber of the Supreme Court began a review of these verdicts and of those of eight other defendants also sentenced in August.

AI country reports/ visits
Reports
- Europe and Central Asia: Summary of Amnesty International's concerns in the region, January-June 2006 (AI Index: EUR 01/017/2006)
- Commonwealth of Independent States: Positive trend on the abolition of the death penalty but more needs to be done (AI Index: EUR 04/003/2006)

Visit
AI delegates visited Kazakstan in October.

KENYA

REPUBLIC OF KENYA
Head of state and government: Mwai Kibaki
Death penalty: abolitionist in practice
International Criminal Court: ratified

The government intensified its intimidation and harassment of journalists and human rights defenders. Impunity for abuses by police was reinforced as the authorities failed to investigate allegations of police brutality. Violence against women and girls, including rape and domestic violence, remained a serious concern, although a new law was passed outlawing sexual offences.

Background
The government of Mwai Kibaki faced widespread criticism over the involvement of several senior

ministers in two corruption scandals. The Vice-President and two cabinet members were among 30 people summoned by the Kenya Anti-Corruption Commission (KACC) in connection with the Anglo Leasing scandal, in which large sums of government money were paid for equipment that was never provided. However, the Attorney General, Amos Wako, decided not to prosecute the 15 suspects indicted by the KACC.

The report of an inquiry into the Goldenberg scandal, which involved the loss of $1 billion in false gold and diamond exports in the 1990s, was published in February. It recommended corruption charges against businessman Kamlesh Patni, education minister George Saitoti, former President Daniel Arap Moi and several others. In March five people, including Kamlesh Patni, were charged. In August a panel of three High Court judges ruled that George Saitoti, who had resigned, had no case to answer.

Attacks on media freedom
There was increased intimidation and harassment of media workers and journalists by the authorities.

☐ In March, armed police, acting on government orders, raided the offices and presses of the Standard group, a leading media company, and the studios of KTN television. They set fire to the 2 March edition of the *Standard*, damaged equipment at both sites and confiscated computers. The raid provoked widespread protests both nationally and internationally. Three *Standard* journalists had been arrested before the raid and charged with producing "alarming" articles for reporting that the President had held secret talks with a political opponent. The Standard group filed a complaint against the Internal Security Minister and the Police Commissioner in connection with the raid, and a Parliamentary Committee held hearings to investigate it. In September the charges against the three journalists were dropped.

☐ Clifford Derrick Otieno, who filed a private prosecution alleging assault by First Lady Lucy Kibaki, the wife of President Kibaki, in May 2005, was repeatedly threatened and harassed. He was forced to leave the country in January, but his family continued to be threatened. His case against Lucy Kibaki was terminated by the Chief Magistrate. In November, following repeated postponements, the Constitutional Court dismissed his appeal challenging the termination.

☐ In May, two journalists working for the Citizen television channel were reportedly assaulted by police after they had attempted to photograph officers allegedly trying to extract bribes.

A draft bill — the Media Council of Kenya Bill 2006 — proposed a statutory media council in place of the existing voluntary council. The bill was criticized on the grounds that it proposed imposing restrictions on the work of journalists through an annual licensing system, allowed for political interference through the composition of its appointments board, and limited the right of appeal against the proposed council's decisions. By the end of 2006 the bill had not been passed by parliament.

Harassment of human rights defenders
The government sought to undermine and obstruct the work of human rights defenders. Non-governmental organizations accused the government of using the KACC and the Kenya Revenue Authority to intimidate its critics.

☐ In September, the Chairman of the Kenya National Commission of Human Rights, Maina Kiai, was summoned by the KACC for an investigation into allegations of abuse of office. The allegations against Maina Kiai, an outspoken critic of the government, included issues related to his relocation allowance and the manner in which auditors were selected. Forty civil society organizations came to his defence, stating that the investigation was politically motivated and part of a wider plan by the government to harass and intimidate human rights defenders.

Impunity
The authorities failed to investigate allegations of human rights violations by police, including reports of torture and unlawful killings. Provincial Commissioner Hassan Noor Hassan reportedly issued "shoot-to-kill" orders to police in Nakuru district in October, following a spate of ethnic clashes.

☐ Despite a request for information by the Special Representative of the UN Secretary-General for Human Rights Defenders, there was no news of an investigation into allegations of ill-treatment made by Ojiayo Samson and Mithika Mwenda, both human rights activists. The two men were beaten by police officers in July 2005 after being arrested during a demonstration and continued to face criminal charges.

☐ There was still no investigation into the deaths of Paul Limera, aged 14, Hillary Ochieng, aged 17, Vincent Otieno, aged 15, George Ogada and Paul Mwela, who were shot by police officers during a demonstration in 2005.

In October the Justice Minister, Martha Karua, announced the creation of a new body to receive public complaints about police excesses and hold the police accountable.

☐ A group of former Mau Mau insurgents launched a suit against the UK government in October, seeking compensation for human rights abuses including rape, beatings and other torture committed during the rebellion for independence in the 1950s. According to the Kenya Human Rights Commission, tens of thousands of people were tortured by the British authorities at the time.

Violence against women and girls
Women continued to face widespread violence, and violence against girls reportedly increased. Most sexual violence against girls was reportedly committed by family members or close family friends.

☐ In March, 10 schoolgirls were raped during a demonstration in the town of Nyeri. Five local boys were later arrested, but no prosecution was reported.

The government passed the Sexual Offences Act 2006 in May. The new act imposed minimum sentences for different crimes; defined rape, defilement and other sexual offences; and proscribed the use of previous sexual experience or conduct as evidence against the victim. However, the act did not recognize marital rape, provided a restrictive definition of rape and did not criminalize forced female genital mutilation.

Forced evictions
Tens of thousands of residents were forcibly evicted from forest areas and informal settlements. Evictions were characterized by violence, the destruction of houses and property, and inadequate resettlement and compensation provisions. Notice was sometimes, but not always, given.

The government pledged to develop national guidelines on evictions, and in May set up an inter-ministerial task force to finalize them, but no draft had been issued by the end of the year.

▢ In March, 3,000 families were evicted from Kipkurere Forest in the Rift Valley. Settlements were burned, and property and food stocks destroyed.

▢ In June, 8,000 people were evicted from Emborut Forest, in the Rift Valley. Houses, schools and churches were burned down.

▢ More than 600 families were left without shelter after Komora slum in Nairobi was destroyed in September to make way for a private development. Residents complained that they had nowhere to go, that they had been given only 10 minutes to clear their homes, and that the iron sheets they had used for their dwellings were destroyed.

Protection of refugees and asylum-seekers
Tens of thousands of new Somali refugees crossed the border into Kenya, joining the 160,000 refugees — mostly from Somalia — already living in camps around the town of Dadaab in the east of the country. By late October, an estimated 34,000 had arrived, fleeing increased violence in southern and central Somalia.

At Kakuma camp, near the Sudanese border, there were reports of rising tensions between refugees and members of the local Turkana ethnic group. Four people were killed in clashes and attacks on the camp in August. Refugees who had been repatriated to southern Sudan returned to Kakuma camp in May, reportedly because of insecurity in southern Sudan.

Kenya, Rwanda and UNHCR, the UN refugee agency, signed an agreement in March on the voluntary return of about 3,000 Rwandan refugees.

Death penalty
Despite the government's commitment to abolishing the death penalty, expressed to the UN Commission on Human Rights in March 2005, there were no significant movements in that direction in 2006. Death sentences continued to be imposed; however, no executions have been carried out since 1986.

AI country reports/ visits
Statement
• Kenya: A Joint Appeal to African Ministers on urban housing (AI Index: AFR 32/002/2006)
Visit
An AI delegation visited Kenya in September/October.

KOREA
(DEMOCRATIC PEOPLE'S REPUBLIC OF)

DEMOCRATIC PEOPLE'S REPUBLIC OF KOREA
Head of state: Kim Jong-il
Head of government: Pak Pong-ju
Death penalty: retentionist
International Criminal Court: not ratified

Systemic violations of human rights, including the rights to life and to food, continued. The rights to freedom of movement, expression and association were severely curtailed. Access by independent monitors continued to be restricted. There were many reports of enforced disappearances among families of North Koreans who left the country or were forcibly returned. Despite some changes in the criminal law, the political and sometimes arbitrary use of imprisonment, torture and capital punishment continued.

Background
In July the Democratic People's Republic of Korea (North Korea) conducted missile tests followed by an unprecedented nuclear test in October.

Following the missile tests, the UN Security Council adopted Resolution 1695 voicing disapproval. After the nuclear test, in October, the Security Council unanimously adopted Resolution 1718 demanding that North Korea eliminate all its nuclear weapons and imposing weapons and financial sanctions. Both resolutions called on North Korea to return unconditionally to the stalled six-party talks on its nuclear programme. Resolution 1718 invoked Chapter VII of the UN Charter, which sets out the Security Council's powers to maintain peace, but stopped short of the threat of force if North Korea did not comply. In December, six-nation talks (involving North Korea, South Korea, Japan, the USA, Russia and China) on resolving the North Korean nuclear crisis resumed in Beijing after 13 months, but ended in stalemate.

In November, the Third Committee of the UN General Assembly adopted its second resolution condemning North Korea's record on human rights.

Severe floods left several thousand people killed or missing in July and October.

Worsening food crisis
The UN Special Rapporteur on the right to food announced in October that 12 per cent of the population suffered from severe hunger. Agricultural output was expected to be substantially lower than the previous year following the floods.

In May, the World Food Programme (WFP) was reported to be implementing a two-year plan requiring 150,000 metric tons of grain for 1.9 million North Koreans "most in need — especially women and children". As of October, the WFP had reportedly received only 8 per cent of the US$102 million required.

North Koreans in Asia

Approximately 100,000 North Koreans were reportedly hiding in China, living in constant fear of deportation. An estimated 150-300 North Koreans were forcibly repatriated from China every week. Most North Korean women in China reportedly faced abuses, including systematic rape and prostitution.

There were mass arrests of 175 North Koreans in Bangkok, Thailand, in August, followed by the arrests of 86 in October and a further 50 in November. Over 500 North Koreans were reportedly detained by Thai authorities. Nearly 10,000 North Koreans were reportedly settled in South Korea.

Enforced disappearances

Hundreds of North Koreans forcibly returned from China were unaccounted for. Several families of North Koreans who left the country without permission disappeared. They were believed to be victims of enforced disappearance, as the North Korean authorities punished whole families for being associated with someone deemed hostile to the regime ("guilt-by-assocation").

◻ Lee Kwang-soo arrived in South Korea by boat in March with his wife, two children and a friend. In August he discovered that 19 members of his and his friend's families in North Korea had gone missing between March and early August 2006.

North Koreans settled in South Korea have been abducted from the China border by North Korean security forces. The North Korean authorities have also abducted nationals of other countries, including South Korea, Japan, Thailand and Lebanon.

Denial of access

Despite repeated requests, the government continued to deny access to independent human rights monitors, including the UN Special Rapporteur on the situation of human rights in the Democratic People's Republic of Korea (DPRK) and the UN Special Rapporteur on the right to food.

The UN relief agencies were reportedly permitted to visit only 29 of the 213 regions. Following government demands to reduce its staff, the WFP cut its international staff from 46 to 10 and reduced the number of monitoring visits. Five of the WFP's regional offices, from which its inspectors monitored distribution of food aid, were closed. These reductions increased concerns about lack of transparency in food aid distribution.

Freedom of expression

Opposition of any kind was not tolerated. Any person who expressed an opinion contrary to the position of the ruling Korean Workers' Party reportedly faced severe punishment and so did their families in many cases. The domestic news media continued to be strictly censored and access to international media broadcasts remained severely restricted. In October, the NGO Reporters Sans Frontieres listed North Korea as the worst violator of press freedom.

Any unauthorized assembly or association was regarded as a "collective disturbance", liable to punishment. Religious freedom, although guaranteed by the Constitution, was in practice sharply curtailed. People involved in public and private religious activities faced imprisonment, torture and execution.

Death penalty

Executions were by hanging or firing-squad. There were reports of executions of political opponents in political prisons and of people charged with economic crimes, such as stealing food.

◻ Son Jong-nam was reportedly sentenced to be executed on charges of betraying his country, sharing information with South Korea and receiving financial assistance from his brother, a North Korean settled in South Korea since 2002. In April 2006, according to UN sources, he was imprisoned in the basement of the National Security Agency in Pyongyang and was "practically dead" as a result of torture. Son Jong-nam had left North Korea in 1997 with his wife, son and brother and had become a Christian – deemed to be a serious crime in North Korea. He was forcibly returned by Chinese authorities to North Korea in 2001 and imprisoned for three years in the Hamgyung-buk do prison camp. He was released in May 2004 and met his brother in China before returning to North Korea. The North Korean authorities learned that he had met his brother and arrested him in January 2006. He was believed to be alive at the end of 2006.

Prison conditions

Prisoners, particularly political prisoners, reportedly suffered appalling conditions, in a wide range of detention centres and prisons.

North Koreans forcibly returned from China faced torture or ill-treatment and up to three years' imprisonment. Their punishments depended on their age, gender and experiences. Women and children were generally sentenced to two weeks in a detention centre, although longer sentences of several months in labour camps were also common. The consequences of repatriation were reportedly most severe for pregnant women, who suffered forced abortions in poor medical conditions. People who confessed to meeting South Koreans or missionaries were punished particularly harshly. Summary executions and long sentences of hard labour were still enforced, although the authorities often released prisoners close to death, who died shortly after their release.

KOREA
(REPUBLIC OF)

REPUBLIC OF KOREA
Head of state: Roh Moo-hyun
Head of government: Han Myeong-sook (replaced Han Duck-soo in April, who replaced Lee Hae-chan in March)
Death penalty: retentionist
International Criminal Court: ratified

A draft bill to abolish the death penalty was discussed by the National Assembly for the first time, but no progress was made towards a final vote. More than two years after a law to regulate the employment of migrants was enacted, migrant workers continued to have limited protection against discrimination or abuse, including few possibilities of obtaining redress. In August, at least 189,000 irregular migrant workers faced detention and deportation. At least one prisoner of conscience was still imprisoned under the National Security Law. At least 936 conscientious objectors were in prison for refusing to do military service.

Background
Food aid to North Korea, suspended following a missile test in July, was resumed after floods in August. However, following a nuclear test by North Korea in October, food aid was again halted.

In an unprecedented move, South Korea supported a resolution on human rights in North Korea passed by the UN General Assembly in November. Foreign Minister Ban Ki-moon was appointed as UN Secretary-General, to take up the post in January 2007.

Death penalty
There were no executions. At least two prisoners were sentenced to death. At least 63 prisoners were under sentence of death at the end of 2006.

A bill to abolish the death penalty was discussed by a National Assembly committee in February and before a public hearing in April. However, it was not put before the National Assembly as the committee did not vote on it.

In February, the Ministry of Justice announced that it was conducting in-depth research into the death penalty in response to public pressure for abolition. However, the findings had not been made public by the end of 2006.

Abuses against migrant workers
In August official figures recorded some 360,000 migrant workers, who included at least 189,000 irregular migrant workers. The 2003 Act Concerning the Employment Permit for Migrant Workers failed to provide adequate safeguards against discrimination and abuse. Many migrant workers continued to be at risk of verbal and physical abuse in the workplace, subjected to racial discrimination and not paid regularly. Most received less pay than Korean workers for the same work, did not receive severance pay, were exposed to poor working conditions, and remained at increased risk of industrial accidents.

A National Human Rights Commission of Korea study reported in January that 20 per cent of detained migrant workers were beaten and nearly 40 per cent verbally abused. More than one-third alleged being stripped naked and searched, and 5.2 per cent alleged being subjected to sexual abuse by immigration officers during body searches following arrest. Some 15 per cent reportedly suffered injuries. Women, who constitute roughly one-third of all migrant workers in Korea, were particularly vulnerable to exploitation, including sexual violence. Some arrests were carried out without appropriate documentation, such as arrest warrants or detention order papers.

Conscientious objectors
At least 936 conscientious objectors, mostly Jehovah's Witnesses, were in prison following convictions in 2005 and 2006 for refusing compulsory military service.

📁 20-year-old Ahn Jae-kwang was detained in January, the first conscientious objector to be detained since the National Human Rights Commission recognized the right of conscientious objection and recommended a system of alternative service in December 2005. The Seoul West District Court issued an arrest warrant on the grounds that pre-trial detention for offences punishable by imprisonment was the norm, even though the criminal procedure law provided for pre-trial imprisonment only where there was a possibility of destruction of evidence or flight by the suspect.

In April the Ministry of National Defence announced the establishment of a policy group to consider alternative civilian service.

National Security Law
The government did not amend or repeal the 1948 National Security Law.

📁 Cheon Wook-yong remained in prison under the National Security Law. Arrested in November 2004 on his return to South Korea, he was sentenced to three and a half years in prison for allegedly releasing national secrets and assisting an anti-government organization. Cheon Wook-yong had visited North Korea, crossing from China in August 2004. He was captured and interrogated by the North Korean Defence Department. He was then sent back to China where he was detained for 13 days on suspicion of illegal border transgression. He was arrested and detained under vaguely worded articles of the National Security Law that allowed his conviction despite a lack of evidence that he had threatened national security.

Evictions
In February residents of Daechuri village in Pyongtaek, Gyeonggi Province, mostly farmers aged in their 60s and 70s, started resisting evictions aimed at expanding a US army base. They said that money offered was insufficient to buy equivalent land elsewhere or compensate for loss of livelihoods. Thousands of security personnel and

hundreds of private contractors destroyed farmers' houses. Farmers and activists were injured in protests, and some were briefly detained. The security forces imposed severe restrictions on the movement of some 40 families still living in Pyongtaek. A consultation carried out before the eviction reportedly was a sham and did not reflect the farmers' concerns.

☐ Kim Ji-tae, a farmers' leader, was sentenced to two years' imprisonment in November after being convicted on a charge of obstructing public officials engaged in performing their duties. AI considered him a prisoner of conscience, convicted for protesting peacefully and in order to curtail farmers' rights to protest and protect their livelihood. He was released pending appeal.

AI country reports/ visits
Reports
- South Korea: Key arguments against use of the death penalty (AI Index: ASA 25/005/2006)
- South Korea: "Migrant workers are also human beings" (AI Index: ASA 25/007/2006)
Visits
AI delegates visited South Korea in February, August and December.

KUWAIT

STATE OF KUWAIT
Head of state: al-Shaikh Sabah al-Ahmad al-Sabah (replaced Shaikh Saad al-Abdullah al-Sabah in January, who replaced al-Shaikh Jaber al-Ahmad al-Sabah earlier in January)
Head of government: al-Shaikh Nasser Mohammad al-Ahmad al-Sabah (replaced al-Shaikh Sabah al-Ahmad al-Sabah in February)
Death penalty: retentionist
International Criminal Court: signed

Women participated in National Assembly elections for the first time. Five former Guantánamo Bay detainees were acquitted and other "security detainees" began appeals against their convictions. Migrant workers faced a wide range of abuses. At least 10 people were executed for murder and drug smuggling. At least six others were under sentence of death. There were reports of torture and ill-treatment in detention.

Background
The Emir dissolved the National Assembly in May following a dispute by parliamentarians over electoral reform. Parliamentary elections, scheduled for 2007, were held in June. A majority of elected seats were won by opposition MPs, and in July the Assembly approved an electoral reform bill designed to reduce electoral corruption and reduce the number of constituencies from 25 to five.

Women's rights
The parliamentary elections allowed women to exercise their newly acquired political rights in national elections for the first time. Earlier in the year, a municipal council by-election saw women in Salmiya district participating in a local election for the first time.

'War on terror'
In September, two Kuwaiti nationals, Abdullah Kamel al-Kandari and Omar Rajab Amin, were returned to Kuwait from US detention in Guantánamo Bay, Cuba, and were believed to be detained pending trial on terrorism-related charges.

In May, the Criminal Court acquitted five Kuwaiti nationals, Abdulaziz al-Shimmari, Adel al-Zamel, Mohammad al-Deehani, Saad al-Azmi and Abdullah al-Ajmi, who had been returned from Guantánamo Bay in November 2005, of the charges of "belonging to al-Qa'ida" and "committing an act of aggression against a friendly foreign nation, thus endangering Kuwait's foreign relations". During the trial the men protested their innocence, and said that they had confessed under torture by US interrogators in Guantánamo Bay to being members of al-Qa'ida and the Taleban.

In December, the Court of Cassation quashed former Guantánamo Bay detainee Nasser Najd al-Mutairi's five-year prison sentence for belonging to al-Qa'ida, seeking to take up arms against a friendly state and possessing weapons. He had been acquitted of the charges by a lower court in June 2005, but the Appeals Court overturned the verdict in November 2005.

In September, the Appeals Court reopened the trial of some 28 of 37 individuals who had been tried the previous year on terrorism-related charges, including membership of the Peninsula Lions Brigade, a group allegedly linked to al-Qa'ida. In November, the death sentences against four defendants were upheld, and the death sentences that had been imposed on two others were commuted to life imprisonment.

Migrant workers
There were new reports of abuses against migrant workers. In May the authorities opened an investigation into a complaint filed by the Indian Embassy which alleged that 60 Indian nationals had faced abuses by an unidentified company, including non-payment of salaries, forced overtime without pay, and denial of medical facilities.

In July, a new law intended to curtail abuses against domestic migrant workers came into effect, requiring contracts stipulating working conditions for domestic workers to be signed by the government's domestic labour office, the sponsor and the worker.

Freedom of expression and association

In May, the 15 founders of the Ummah Party were acquitted of breaching laws on the press and public gatherings. One individual was fined for "circulating publications without prior authorization".

In May, the Constitutional Court revoked restrictions in force since 1979 on public gatherings.

In March, a new press law gave power to license and suspend publications to the courts. It failed to repeal provisions that allowed for the imprisonment of journalists.

KYRGYZSTAN

KYRGYZ REPUBLIC
Head of state: Kurmanbek Bakiev
Head of government: Feliks Kulov
Death penalty: abolitionist in practice
International Criminal Court: signed

Five Uzbekistani men were forcibly returned to Uzbekistan. The Uzbekistani security forces continued to pursue refugees and asylum-seekers in Kyrgyzstan, in some cases in joint counter-terrorism operations with the authorities in Kyrgyzstan. At least five Uzbekistani asylum-seekers were reportedly subjected to enforced disappearance. Widespread torture and ill-treatment in temporary police detention centres was reported. Human rights activists were harassed for taking up cases of violence against women in police custody.

Background

Demonstrators protested at corruption and accused the state of collusion with organized crime. Edil Baisalov, leader of a human rights organization and member of the For Reforms opposition coalition, was attacked by an unidentified assailant in April, days after he had helped organize a demonstration protesting at the election of Rysbek Akmatbaev, a suspected criminal leader, to his late brother's parliamentary seat. Rysbek Akmatbaev was later killed by unidentified gunmen in May.

Following tensions between parliament and government over constitutional reform, protesters at a week-long For Reforms demonstration in Bishkek in November called for the resignation of the President and Prime Minister. A new Constitution drafted by both sides was adopted by parliament and signed into law in November.

Death penalty

The new Constitution abolished the death penalty. Repeal of death penalty provisions in the criminal code was still pending at the end of 2006. A 1998 moratorium on executions was extended.

Deaths in suspicious circumstances

There were no investigations into the circumstances surrounding killings by the security forces during counter-terrorism operations.

▭ Five people were killed during a July counter-terrorism operation in Jalalabad by the security police (SNB). The SNB alleged they were members of the Islamic Movement of Uzbekistan (IMU) armed opposition group and the Islamic Hizb-ut-Tahrir political party, both banned.

▭ Independent Kyrgyzstani imam Muhammadrafik Kamalov from Kara-Suu was shot and killed by security forces in August. Killed with him were two suspected IMU members accused of an armed raid on the border with Tajikistan in May in which at least a dozen security officers and armed men died. In October three men were sentenced to death for their part in the raid. The SNB initially accused imam Kamalov of being an IMU member, and then suggested that he could have been used as a human shield. His death and burial sparked peaceful demonstrations in Kara-Suu.

▭ In September an Uzbekistani national suspected of being an IMU leader was reportedly shot and fatally wounded by SNB officers when he refused to surrender. SNB sources said his wounds were not fatal and that he had died of heart failure in hospital. The SNB had linked him to the May border incident and to the death of imam Kamalov.

Refugees from Uzbekistan at risk

Of more than 500 asylum-seekers who fled Andizhan in Uzbekistan in May 2005 when security forces fired on mainly unarmed demonstrators, killing hundreds of people, five were extradited to Uzbekistan, many were detained, and a number appeared to have been subjected to enforced disappearance.

▭ In August the authorities extradited four refugees and one asylum-seeker to Uzbekistan without giving advance notice to UNHCR, the UN refugee agency. The four refugees, detained in Kyrgyzstan since June 2005, had been recognized as refugees by UNHCR, but lost appeals against the Kyrgyzstani authorities' decision not to recognize their refugee status in June. Uzbekistani asylum-seeker Faez Tadzhikalilov, detained since September 2005, was still awaiting the outcome of a government review of his asylum application when he was extradited. In Uzbekistan, the five were reportedly held incommunicado and charged in November with the murder in May 2005 of the Andizhan city prosecutor.

Uzbekistani nationals in hiding in Kyrgyzstan were reportedly among hundreds of people arbitrarily detained by Kyrgyzstani and Uzbekistani security forces.

▭ Gulmira Maksudova was arrested in July and charged with terrorism and counterfeiting documents. She is a daughter of Akram Yuldashev, the alleged leader of the Akramia opposition group imprisoned since 1998, who has been accused of masterminding the Andizhan events from prison. In September, Osh regional court acquitted her and ordered her release after it found no evidence of terrorism.

In August, UNHCR and human rights organizations expressed concern at the apparent enforced disappearance of Uzbekistani refugees and asylum-seekers in south Kyrgyzstan. At least two were subsequently reported to be in pre-trial detention in Andizhan in Uzbekistan.

□ UNHCR said Kyrgyzstani officials had failed to respond to inquiries about the enforced disappearance of at least five named Uzbekistani refugees, among them a secular democratic opposition activist reportedly abducted in July by Uzbekistani security services. Because the safety of the refugees could not be guaranteed in Osh, UNHCR moved all registered refugees to Bishkek with a view to resettling them permanently in a third country.

Excessive force and torture

In August special troops were sent in to a temporary detention facility in Jalalabad after riots reportedly broke out following a violent altercation between an inmate and a guard. Officials subsequently admitted that officers had kicked, punched and beaten detainees with batons. Detainees told human rights activists that they had been beaten by up to seven officers while handcuffed and made to wear gas masks with the air supply turned off. They said beatings and torture were routine in the severely overcrowded facility, and that they had no bedding, sanitation or exercise and inadequate ventilation. No officers responsible for torture or other ill-treatment were brought to justice.

□ According to detainees, in July a senior official at the facility severely beat a female detainee with mental problems to force her to reveal her husband's whereabouts. Her husband, a suspected IMU member, gave himself up to prevent further ill-treatment of his wife. Reportedly, the woman subsequently had a miscarriage, and was transferred to a psychiatric hospital.

In June, two human rights organizations, Spravedlivost (Justice) and Vozdukh (Breath of Air), complained of harassment by regional law enforcement officers after they took up the cases of two women allegedly tortured in police custody.

□ In January a pregnant witness in a theft case was reportedly hit and threatened and called a prostitute while being questioned by a Department of Internal Affairs officer. The woman was subsequently hospitalized for 10 days for a threatened miscarriage. She complained to the regional prosecutor's office, but no action was taken. When Spravedlivost publicized her allegations in February, the officer filed a criminal suit for defamation against both. The defamation trial, which started in June, was postponed when the witness became ill. She had been insulted and threatened in court by the officer's supporters. The trial resumed in November.

□ In June, Internal Affairs officers reportedly beat a woman arrested at her home in Bazar-Kurgan. Her family were denied access to her in detention. Detained twice before, in 2003 and 2005, she had previously alleged torture, including repeated rape, in custody. Azimzhan Askarov, an activist with the Vozdukh human rights organization which took up her case, was reportedly threatened with criminal defamation charges by an officer accused by the woman of beating her and inserting needles under her fingernails in 2005. The district prosecutor said that Azimzhan Askarov's articles incited social, racial or ethnic hatred and that his office would in future censor them before publication. In July the woman was sentenced to five years in prison for theft, subsequently suspended on appeal. She and her family were reported to be under pressure from Internal Affairs officers to withdraw the torture allegations. An appeal to the Supreme Court was pending at the end of 2006.

AI country reports/visits
Reports
· Europe and Central Asia: Summary of Amnesty International's concerns in the region, January-June 2006 (AI Index: EUR 01/017/2006)
· Commonwealth of Independent States: Positive trend on the abolition of the death penalty but more needs to be done (AI Index: EUR 04/003/2006)
Visit
AI delegates visited Kyrgyzstan in November.

LAOS

LAO PEOPLE'S DEMOCRATIC REPUBLIC
Head of state: President Choummaly Sayasone (replaced Khamtay Siphandone in June)
Head of government: Bouasone Bouphavanh (replaced Bounyang Vorachit in June)
Death penalty: retentionist
International Criminal Court: not ratified

Continued restrictions on freedom of expression and association were a source of concern. Lack of access by independent human rights monitors hampered an exact appraisal of the situation. At least two people were sentenced to death; no one was known to have been executed. The situation for groups of ethnic Hmong hiding in the jungle remained grave and led to a steady stream of people taking refuge in neighbouring Thailand.

Background
In March the Eighth Congress of the Lao People's Revolutionary Party (LPRP) adopted the new five-year Socio-Economic Development Plan for 2006-2010, outlining the government's policy direction. Choummaly Sayasone was elected as new party leader. In June he was formally appointed President and Bouasone Bouphavanh became the new Prime Minister.

The government's controversial resettlement policy continued, ostensibly to reduce poverty. People in the rural highlands, largely ethnic minorities, were moved to more accessible areas in or closer to the lowlands, while their traditional slash and burn cultivation methods were targeted for eradication. The policy, partly implemented by force, threats and intimidation, had devastating consequences for certain communities, who experienced loss of livelihoods, increased food insecurity and health problems.

Criticism surrounding the Nam Theun 2 hydropower dam continued, as around 600 families living within the future dam perimeter were resettled in new villages. The Nam Theun 2 Power Company, as well as the Asian Development Bank, the World Bank and other lenders to the project, described arrangements as satisfactory while critics warned that compensation to those affected was erratic and insufficient.

In February, the government declared Laos free of opium poppies after a six-year eradication campaign. Although the statement was welcomed by the international community, caution was raised over the risk of increased poverty for former opium farmers unless they were sufficiently supported to develop alternative sources of income.

The government failed to ratify the International Covenants on Civil and Political Rights and on Economic, Social and Cultural Rights, both of which were signed in December 2000.

Hmong in hiding
Groups of ethnic Hmong living in jungle areas continued to be at risk of attacks, hardship and disease. These were remnants of an anti-communist resistance from the 1960s and were living in extreme poverty while hiding from the authorities, particularly the military.

Throughout the year violent onslaughts were reported from the provinces of Bolikhamsai, Luang Prabang, Vientiane and Xieng Khouang as government troops intensified operations.

On 6 April, government troops launched an attack against a Hmong group foraging for food some 20 kilometres from the tourist town of Vang Vieng, killing at least 26 people, mostly women and children. Government authorities denied the attack.

Hundreds of people hiding in the same area emerged from the jungle in late October seeking to reintegrate into mainstream society. A small group fled to neighbouring Thailand to seek protection against alleged persecution. Their fate was unknown.

In August, the government publicly conceded for the first time in many years that there was a refugee flow of ethnic Hmong Laotians into Thailand, where some 7,000 Lao Hmong lived in an informal refugee camp in Phetchabun province. Some 400 recognized refugees and asylum-seekers, including children, were arrested and detained under Thai migration legislation, and were at risk of deportation. In November a group of 53 was forcibly returned from Thailand to Laos.

A group of 27 Hmong, including 22 children, who were forcibly returned to Laos from Thailand in December 2005, remained in incommunicado detention at the end of the year. There was no official confirmation of their whereabouts.

Political imprisonment
The number of political prisoners remained unknown as access to prisons by independent monitors was limited and there was no source of independent information about prisoners in general. Prison conditions were commonly reported to be harsh.

Thao Moua and Pa Fue Khang, ethnic Hmong men who assisted two European journalists attempting a clandestine visit to Hmong groups in hiding in 2003, remained imprisoned. The two men, who had acted as guides and porters, were sentenced to prison terms of 12 and 15 years in June 2003 for obstructing justice and possession of weapons and drugs after an unfair trial.

Four prisoners of conscience remained in Samkhe prison. They included Thongpaseuth Keuakoun and Seng-aloun Phengphanh, members of the Lao Students' Movement for Democracy who were arrested in October 1999 after attempting to hold a peaceful demonstration in Vientiane.

Death penalty
Laos retained the death penalty for a wide range of offences and sentenced at least two people to death, both for drugs-related offences. There were no reports of executions.

AI country reports/ visits
Reports
- Laos: Massacre of unarmed Hmong women and children (AI Index: ASA 26/002/2006)
- Laos: Fear for safety/torture/ill-treatment/arbitrary detention (AI Index: ASA 26/005/2006)

LATVIA

REPUBLIC OF LATVIA
Head of state: Vaira Vike-Freiberga
Head of government: Aigars Kalvītis
Death penalty: abolitionist for ordinary crimes
International Criminal Court: ratified

Lesbian, gay, bisexual and transgender (LGBT) people continued to face discrimination. A Gay Pride march in the capital Riga was banned on security grounds following alleged threats against the marchers. Citizenship requirements were made stricter.

Statelessness
More than 400,000 people continued to live in Latvia without citizenship. The vast majority were citizens of the former Soviet Union who were living in Latvia at the time of the break-up of the Soviet Union. In order to obtain citizenship, non-citizens must pass a number of tests, for example on the Latvian Constitution and language. On 8 August, the Latvian parliament introduced amendments to existing citizenship laws which stipulate that those who fail the Latvian language exam three times are no longer eligible for citizenship. The amendments also extended the time applicants must wait to resubmit their citizenship applications from three to six months. Statelessness implies, among other things, restrictions to trans-border movement and restrictions on political rights.

In June, the Latvian Parliament rejected an amendment to the law which would have eased requirements on non-citizens wanting to obtain the European Union (EU) Long-Term Resident status. Current regulations require non-citizens to demonstrate Latvian language skills and to have permanent residence permits in order to be eligible for EU Long-Term Resident status.

European Court of Human Rights
In June, the European Court of Human Rights concluded that Latvia had violated Natella Kaftailova's rights to respect for private and family life. Natella Kaftailova, who is of Georgian origin, had lived in Latvia since 1984 and became stateless after the break-up of the Soviet Union in 1991. She failed to apply for permanent resident status in Latvia by the final deadline of August 1992 and in January 1995 she was served with a deportation order, asking her and her then 10-year-old daughter to leave the country. The Court concluded that during her time in Latvia, Natella Kaftailova had formed and developed personal, social and economic relationships, which constituted the private life of any human being. It also found that the Latvian authorities' refusal to grant her the right to reside lawfully and permanently in Latvia represented an interference with her private life which could not be considered "necessary in a democratic society".

Minority rights
On 17 November, the Parliamentary Assembly of the Council of Europe (PACE) issued a resolution on national minorities in Latvia. PACE invited the Latvian authorities to review the existing difference in rights between citizens and non-citizens with a view to abolishing those that are not justified or strictly necessary. PACE also invited the Latvian authorities to amend legislation so as to make it possible to use the minority language in relations between national minorities and the administrative authorities in areas where they live in substantial numbers, as well as to implement the Framework Convention for the Protection of National Minorities in good faith and to consider withdrawing the two declarations recorded in the instrument of ratification.

Lesbian, gay, bisexual and transgender rights
On 19 July, Riga City Council banned the Riga Pride 2006 march because of alleged threats of violence against participants. Three days later, people attending a church service held in support of Riga Pride 2006 were attacked by a large group of people who threw eggs and excrement at them. Seven people were eventually sentenced to pay small fines for taking part in the attacks.

A Member of the European Parliament and members of national parliaments from around Europe were among those attacked by a group of up to 100 people as they tried to leave a press conference organized by Riga Pride 2006 at a hotel in central Riga in July. The organizers had requested police protection well in advance. Despite this, no significant police presence materialized until several hours after the start of the attack.

In September, following international pressure, including from other EU member states, Parliament passed an amendment to the Latvian Labour Law which explicitly bans discrimination on the grounds of sexual orientation.

AI country visits/ reports
Report
- Poland and Latvia: Lesbian, gay, bisexual and transgender rights in Poland and Latvia (AI Index: EUR 01/019/2006)

LEBANON

LEBANESE REPUBLIC
Head of state: Emile Lahoud
Head of government: Fouad Siniora
Death penalty: retentionist
International Criminal Court: not ratified

In a 34-day war in July-August between Hizbullah and Israel, about 1,200 Lebanese people were killed, hundreds of them children, and around one million were displaced by Israeli attacks. The attacks also destroyed tens of thousands of homes and much civilian infrastructure in Lebanon. At least 20 people were killed and scores injured by Israeli cluster munitions that remained after the conflict. Hizbullah launched missiles into Israel, causing the deaths of 43 civilians and damaging hundreds of buildings. The UN inquiry into the assassination of former Prime Minister Rafiq al-Hariri continued. Palestinian refugees resident in Lebanon continued to face restrictions, including on access to housing and work, and rights at work. The law continued to discriminate against women and failed to afford them adequate protection against violence.

Background

On 12 July, Hizbullah's military wing (Islamic Resistance) attacked an Israeli patrol inside Israel, killing three Israeli soldiers and capturing two others. A major military confrontation ensued between Israeli and Hizbullah forces. The Lebanese government said that it had no advance warning of the attack by Hizbullah that triggered the conflict, did not condone it and sought a ceasefire from the outset.

Hostilities ended on 14 August, following UN Security Council Resolution 1701, which imposed a ceasefire and enlarged the role of the UN Interim Force in Lebanon (UNIFIL). On 17 August the Lebanese army moved into south Lebanon.

Internal tensions sharpened after the conflict. In November, six government ministers, including all five representatives of the Shi'a community, resigned from the cabinet provoking a political crisis. On 21 November, Industry Minister Pierre Gemayel of the Kataeb (Phalange) Party was killed by unknown assassins. The UN Security Council agreed to a request from Prime Minister Fouad Siniora that the UN International Independent Investigation Commission (UNIIIC) would include the killing among the attacks committed since October 2004 in relation to which it was providing technical assistance to aid the investigations being carried out by the Lebanese authorities. Throughout December, thousands of supporters of Hizbullah, the Free Patriotic Movement (FPM) and allied political parties mounted continuous mass and largely peaceful protests in Beirut calling for a greater role in government.

Hizbullah-Israel war

By the time of the ceasefire on 14 August, Israeli attacks had killed 1,191 people in Lebanon and injured more than 4,400, the overwhelming majority of them civilians. One-third of the civilians killed were children. Some 40 Lebanese soldiers were killed in Israeli strikes, even though the Lebanese army did not participate in the fighting.

Around a million people, a quarter of the country's population, were displaced during the conflict, of whom some 200,000 had not been able to return to their homes by the end of the year.

Much of Lebanon's civilian infrastructure was damaged or destroyed, including tens of thousands of homes, Beirut airport, seaports, major roads, bridges, schools, supermarkets, petrol stations and factories. About 50 schools were destroyed and up to 300 damaged by Israeli bombardments. Many of Lebanon's fishermen, factory workers and agricultural workers lost their livelihoods. A large oil spill caused by Israel's bombing in mid-July of the coastal Jiyye power station presented a long-term threat to the marine life of the region.

Up to one million unexploded cluster bomblets remained in south Lebanon after the conflict, posing a continuing risk to civilians. Some 200 people, including tens of children, had been killed and injured by these bomblets and newly laid mines by the end of the year. The task of clearing unexploded ordnance was made more difficult by the Israeli authorities' failure to provide maps of the exact areas targeted by their forces when using cluster bombs.

Six-year-old 'Abbas Yusef Shibli was playing with three friends near his home in Blida village on 26 August when one of the children tried to pick up what to him looked like a perfume bottle. It exploded, rupturing his colon and gall bladder, and perforating his lung. His three friends were also injured.

Hizbullah fighters reportedly fired nearly 4,000 rockets, some of them armed with ball-bearings, into northern Israel, including into populated areas. The rockets could not be targeted sufficiently accurately to distinguish between military and civilian targets. The rockets caused the deaths of 43 civilians, forced thousands of civilians in northern Israel to be displaced from their homes or to spend long periods in bomb shelters, and damaged buildings. There were also clashes across south Lebanon between Israeli troops and Hizbullah combatants.

Hizbullah did not disclose the fate or condition of the two Israeli soldiers it had captured, while at least six Lebanese nationals, most of them known or suspected Hizbullah fighters, remained detained in Israeli prisons at the end of the year. Indirect negotiations for a prisoner exchange were reportedly ongoing between the two sides. Israel suspended access by the International Committee of the Red Cross (ICRC) to the prisoners it held after Hizbullah refused to grant such access to the two Israeli soldiers.

Both Hizbullah and Israel committed serious violations of international humanitarian law, including war crimes. Hizbullah's rocket attacks on northern Israel amounted to deliberate attacks on civilians and civilian objects, as well as indiscriminate attacks. Its attacks also violated other rules of international humanitarian law, including the prohibition on reprisal attacks on the civilian population

Rafiq al-Hariri investigation

In September, the UNIIIC submitted its fifth interim report on its investigation into the killing of former Prime Minister Rafiq al-Hariri and 22 others in 2005. On 13 November the Cabinet approved a UN draft for an international tribunal to try those suspected of involvement in the killings, but it was unclear whether the absence of the six ministers who resigned invalidated the vote. The decision also required ratification by Parliament and the President.

Enforced disappearances

Despite campaigning by families and non-governmental organizations, the fate of thousands of Lebanese and other nationals who became victims of enforced disappearance between 1975 and 1990 remained unknown.

The identities were confirmed of 15 Lebanese soldiers, whose bodies were among 20 exhumed in Beirut in November 2005. In May, Lebanese Forces leader Samir Gea'gea' said that four Iranians who were kidnapped by his militia in 1982 were killed soon after their seizure. The State Prosecutor stated in June that some 44 bodies exhumed in 'Anjar in December 2005 dated from before the 1950s. The body of French national Michel Seurat who was kidnapped in 1985 was returned to his family in March after reportedly being found during construction work.

Political arrests

On 5 February, there were violent protests at the Danish Embassy in Beirut against the publication in a Danish newspaper of cartoons that offended many Muslims. The Embassy was set alight and at least one person died in the violence. More than 400 people were arrested, including 42 Syrian nationals who were reportedly not present at the protests. The 42 were detained in Barbar Khazen prison in west Beirut, under the control of the Internal Security Forces (ISF). They were held there for five days and denied access to legal counsel. At least two were beaten by ISF interrogators in an apparent attempt to force "confessions" about their involvement in the protests. On 10 February, they were taken before the military court in Beirut, which ordered their release.

On 11-12 February, more than 200 other people arrested in connection with the 5 February protests were reportedly brought before the same court, whose procedures fall short of international standards for fair trials. The outcome of the hearings was not made public.

Torture and other ill-treatment

Torture and other ill-treatment in custody continued to be reported.

▭ Thirteen people arrested between 30 December 2005 and 4 January 2006 on security charges were reported to have been tortured or otherwise ill-treated while detained at the Information Branch of the Internal Security Department and in a special section of Rumieh prison. Alleged methods included beatings with sticks and metal bars, sleep deprivation and threats of death and rape. A number of the men reportedly "confessed" as a result of torture and duress. Three of the men were released in September.

The authorities continued to refuse to allow the ICRC unfettered access to all prisons, especially those operated by the Ministry of Defence where civilians are held. This was despite a presidential decree in 2002 granting the ICRC such access.

Human rights groups criticized a memorandum of understanding signed in late 2005 by the UK and Lebanon in which the Lebanese authorities provided assurances that terrorism suspects returned to Lebanon from the UK would not be treated inhumanely or tortured. The groups argued that such memorandums undermine the absolute prohibition of torture.

Palestinian refugees

Several hundred thousand Palestinian refugees living in Lebanon continued to face wide-ranging restrictions on access to housing, work and rights at work. A law regulating property ownership bans Palestinian refugees from owning property, and the Lebanese authorities prohibit the expansion or renovation of refugee camps.

In June, the UN Committee on the Rights of the Child criticized persistent discrimination faced by Palestinian children in Lebanon. The Committee expressed concern about the harsh social and economic living conditions of Palestinian refugee children in refugee camps and their limited access to public services, including social and health services and education.

Discrimination and violence against women

Women continued to face widespread discrimination in public and private life. Neither the legal system nor the policies and practices of the state provided adequate protection from violence in the family. Discriminatory practices were permitted under personal status laws, nationality laws, and laws in the Penal Code relating to violence in the family.

Human rights defenders

In general, human rights groups operated freely but some human rights defenders were harassed by the authorities.

▭ Muhamad Mugraby, a lawyer and human rights defender, was tried on charges of "slander of the military establishment" for criticizing Lebanon's military court system to members of the European Parliament in 2003. In April, the Military Court of Cassation dropped the charges and ruled that the Permanent Military Court, which had convicted him, did not have jurisdiction in such a case.

AI country reports / visits
Reports
- Lebanon: Limitations on Rights of Palestinian Refugee Children, Briefing to the Committee on the Rights of the Child (AI Index: MDE 18/004/2006)

- Israel/Lebanon: Deliberate destruction or "collateral damage" – Israeli attacks on civilian infrastructure (AI Index: MDE 18/007/2006)
- Israel/Lebanon: Under fire – Hizbullah's attacks on northern Israel (AI Index: MDE 02/025/2006)
- Israel/Lebanon: Out of all proportion – civilians bear the brunt of the war (AI Index: MDE 02/033/2006)
- Israel/Lebanon: Israel and Hizbullah must spare civilians – Obligations under international humanitarian law of the parties to the conflict in Israel and Lebanon (AI Index: MDE 15/070/2006)

Visits

AI delegates visited Lebanon in January, March, July, August, September and December. In December, AI's Secretary General held meetings in Beirut with the President, Prime Minister, Speaker of the National Assembly and other senior government officials, and visited victims and survivors of the recent war in areas of south Lebanon. AI also called for investigations and reparations for victims of violations during the Hizbullah-Israel war.

LIBERIA

REPUBLIC OF LIBERIA
Head of state and government: Ellen Johnson-Sirleaf
Death penalty: abolitionist for all crimes
International Criminal Court: ratified

There were violent incidents over land issues due to ethnic tensions in the north of the country as refugees and internally displaced people returned home. Dissatisfied demobilized former combatants contributed to the violence. Reforms of the police and army progressed, but the process for the reform of the judiciary was extremely slow. Few steps were taken to develop a mechanism to prosecute those suspected of committing war crimes and crimes against humanity during the conflict that ended in 2003. Former President Charles Taylor was handed over to Liberia in March and immediately transferred to the Special Court for Sierra Leone to face trial on charges of war crimes and crimes against humanity committed during the armed conflict in Sierra Leone. The Truth and Reconciliation Commission started operations in June. Violence against women remained widespread. There were several incidents of journalists being harassed by the security forces.

Background

On 16 January Ellen Johnson-Sirleaf, the first woman head of state in Africa, was inaugurated. All political appointments were concluded by the middle of the year, with seven women in cabinet positions. Civil society organizations expressed concern over some appointments, such as that of Kabineh Ja'neh, former political leader of the armed group Liberians United for Reconciliation and Development (LURD), as an associate Justice to the Supreme Court.

The new President took a strong stand against corruption. An audit of the National Transitional Government of Liberia carried out by the Economic Community Of West African States (ECOWAS) was made public in July. Several senior government officials were dismissed after being accused of corruption. The Governance Reform Commission drew up an anti-corruption policy paper which largely focussed on addressing corruption within the government. At least six former members of the National Transitional Government of Liberia were arrested and charged with theft in early December, a move by the government which was publicly condoned by members of civil society.

The government met more than half its targets under a 150-day action plan designed to address some of the most urgent needs of the population. A donors' conference in July demonstrated a commitment to long-term engagement with Liberia.

The resettlement of 314,095 internally displaced people, including 9,732 refugees, which began in March 2004, was completed in April, approximately six months earlier than expected.

In September the mandate of the UN Mission in Liberia (UNMIL) was extended to March 2007. UNMIL released two public reports largely focused on failures in the administration of justice.

By September close to 39,000 former combatants still had not entered reintegration programmes. There were plans to incorporate these into projects sponsored by the United Nations Development Programme (UNDP) Trust Fund.

The unstable security situation in Côte d'Ivoire continued to present a threat to Liberia. There were concerns about the possible movement of armed groups from Côte d'Ivoire to Liberia and the recruitment of former Liberian combatants, including children.

Sanctions

In June the government sent a letter to the UN Security Council highlighting progress made in meeting the criteria for lifting sanctions on diamonds and timber. Also in June, the UN Security Council lifted the embargo on timber, but extended the sanctions on diamonds for a further six months with a review after four months. The UN arms embargo was partially lifted.

The Minister of Justice sought to facilitate the passing of legislation to implement UN Security Council resolutions in Liberian law. Difficulties arose particularly in connection with the freezing of individuals' assets, since several members of parliament were on the asset freeze list. Edwin Snowe, who was subject to a travel ban and asset freeze, was elected as Speaker of the House. Isaac Nyanebo, a former LURD member, became interim Senate President. At the end of 2006, four members of parliament were still on the asset freeze list.

Political violence

Throughout the year demobilized army officers and former security personnel staged protests, some violent, expressing dissatisfaction with severance and pension benefits or reintegration packages. There were several violent incidents when former commanders and demobilized soldiers illegally occupied rubber plantations.

Disputes arose over land during resettlement and reintegration.

◻ Violence erupted in May when residents of Ganta rioted after rumours that members of the Mandingo ethnic group were going to claim land. The government responded by establishing a presidential commission to investigate the cause of the violence.

Rubber plantations

Efforts to regain control of rubber plantations occupied since the end of the conflict by former rebel combatants made some progress. A joint Government/UNMIL task force on rubber plantations took over some plantations, including the Guthrie rubber plantation on 15 August.

In May UNMIL released a report on the rubber plantations expressing concern about an absence of state authority and the rule of law, and about illegal arrests and detentions. UNMIL increased patrolling activities in five rubber plantations, reducing the number of reported human rights abuses against civilians.

Reform process

Army restructuring activities began in January with US assistance. Recruitment activities took place throughout the year and by September approximately 500 of 7,000 people who had applied were recommended for recruitment. In mid-October civil society organizations held a forum on security sector reform to express their concerns.

By September most of the 2,400 Liberian National Police who did not succeed in reaching the second round of recruitment for the new police force had been retired and given severance pay.

Despite significant progress in reforming and restructuring the police, levels of violent crime, often committed by former combatants, remained high. In September the Ministry of Justice publicly called for residents in Monrovia, the capital, to form vigilante groups to protect themselves. This call was condemned by members of civil society who accused the government of abdicating its responsibilities and called for the police to be strengthened.

There were efforts to address the many problems confronting the justice system, including failure to uphold constitutional guarantees, the extrajudicial settlement of criminal cases and interference by the executive. A joint UNMIL/Government of Liberia Rule of Law Task Force strategy paper laying out a reform agenda for the judiciary was reportedly endorsed by the President but not made public. During 2006 UNMIL assisted in the hiring of prosecutors and public defence staff, and training of existing staff. Case load management improved, and public confidence in the justice sector increased to a certain extent. However, there were numerous reports throughout the year of violations of due process.

A Law Reform Commission was proposed to review laws to ensure they meet international standards. A Judicial Inquiry Commission, to set standards for the behaviour of judges, was also proposed.

Transitional justice

Little progress was made in setting up an Independent National Commission on Human Rights (INCHR), provided for in the Comprehensive Peace Agreement that ended the conflict. A selection panel to appoint commissioners, nominated by the Chief Justice in consultation with civil society, started to be appointed.

In February, seven Commissioners were inaugurated to the Truth and Reconciliation Commission (TRC). After a three-month preparatory period, the TRC started work in June and in September its work plan was made public. Nearly 200 people were recruited by the end of September to take witness statements, a process which began on 10 October. However, public hearings due to take place at the end of the year were delayed. On 23 October supporters of former President Charles Taylor appealed to the Supreme Court to stop the TRC from hearing testimony against the former President, stating that it would prejudice his trial at the Special Court for Sierra Leone (see below). Concerns were raised about the safety of witnesses, the role of civil society in the TRC process, and how the TRC should respond to public concerns.

By the end of 2006, the TRC had received approximately US$2.2 million of the estimated US$14 million required.

Charles Taylor

On 17 March President Johnson-Sirleaf made an official request to the Nigerian government for Charles Taylor to be handed over to Liberia. On 25 March the Nigerian President Olusegun Obasanjo officially agreed to the request. Charles Taylor temporarily escaped from his place of refuge in Nigeria but was later arrested. He arrived in Liberia on 29 March, where he was arrested by UNMIL, mandated by UN Security Council Resolution 1622, and immediately transferred to the Special Court for Sierra Leone.

Despite fears that his arrest would provoke violence, in fact there were overall expressions of relief by the Liberian public. The arrest and transfer of Charles Taylor was widely seen as an important step in addressing impunity in West Africa.

Suspected war criminals

Former associates of Charles Taylor were arrested in January and February but later released.

◻ The trial of Dutch national Gus van Kowenhoven, a former associate of Charles Taylor, ended in June. He was convicted of arms trading and sentenced to eight years' imprisonment. However, he was acquitted on charges of war crimes.

🗀 Roy Belfast Jr, also known as CharlesTaylor Jr, son of Charles Taylor, was arrested in the USA in March for passport fraud. He pleaded guilty to the charge. On 6 December, while he was awaiting sentencing, the US Federal Grand Jury indicted him for torture and conspiracy to commit torture, allegedly committed while he was head of the Anti-Terrorist Unit. He was the first person to be charged under the anti-torture statute in the USA since the law was enacted in 1994.

Women's rights
Rape of women and girls continued throughout 2006. Despite the passing of a new law on rape in December 2005, there were repeated failures to implement it. Rape suspects were regularly released on bail. Many rape cases were settled extrajudicially. Concerns that rape cases were not given priority in the courts were repeatedly highlighted by UN and women's rights groups. There was only one successful prosecution for rape during 2006.

UNMIL facilitated a one-week visit to Liberia by the UN Committee on the Elimination of Discrimination against Women to assist the government in meeting its reporting obligations under the UN Women's Convention.

Press freedom
On many occasions throughout the year, government officials, including the President, raised concerns about irresponsible press reporting. Journalists were repeatedly harassed by the Special Security Services (SSS).

🗀 In April journalists from two independent newspapers, the *Inquirer* and the *Informer*, were assaulted by police while covering clashes between police and street vendors in Monrovia.

🗀 In May George Watkins, a reporter with Radio Veritas, was assaulted by SSS agents, allegedly for reporting that the SSS had recruited a former rebel commander.

🗀 In June SSS agents harassed and briefly detained four local journalists at the executive mansion, while they were putting a story together about the dismissal of several senior SSS personnel.

🗀 In October, four policemen in Zwedru, Grand Gedeh County, reportedly flogged a local journalist from a community radio station for criticizing the police service.

🗀 In December reporter Rufus Paul of the *Daily Observer* was assaulted, allegedly on the orders of the Director of the National Archives. The journalist was investigating alleged misappropriation of funds at the National Archives by the Director.

AI country reports/ visits
Reports
· Liberia: Truth, Justice, and Reparation: Memorandum on the Truth and Reconciliation Commission Act (AI Index: AFR 34/005/2006)
· Liberia: Submission to the Truth and Reconciliation Commission (AI Index: AFR 34/006/2006)

· Liberia: A brief guide to the Truth and Reconciliation Commission (AI Index: AFR 34/007/2006)
Visit
AI delegates visited Liberia in May/June to carry out research.

LIBYA

SOCIALIST PEOPLE'S LIBYAN ARAB JAMAHIRIYA
Head of state: Mu'ammar al-Gaddafi
Head of government: al-Baghdadi Ali al-Mahmudi (replaced Shukri Ghanem in March)
Death penalty: retentionist
International Criminal Court: not ratified

Law enforcement officials resorted to excessive use of force, killing at least 12 demonstrators while breaking up a protest and one detainee during a prison disturbance. Over 150 political detainees, including prisoners of conscience, were released following pardons. Freedom of expression and association remained severely restricted. Several Libyans suspected of political activism abroad were arrested or otherwise intimidated when they returned to the country. Five Bulgarian nurses and a Palestinian doctor were sentenced to death by firing squad for a second time. There were continuing concerns about the treatment of migrants, asylum-seekers and refugees. No progress was made towards establishing the fate or whereabouts of victims of enforced disappearances in previous years.

Background
Relations with the USA and European Union countries continued to improve. The USA restored full diplomatic relations in May and later removed Libya from a list of state sponsors of terrorism.

In March, Shukri Ghanem was replaced as prime minister by al-Baghdadi Ali al-Mahmudi. Shukri Ghanem had been promoting a broad programme of reforms, but was opposed by other influential figures.

The authorities announced the creation of new mechanisms to address human rights issues and investigate complaints from citizens about human rights violations, but gave few details of these bodies or how they would operate.

Excessive use of force
Killings of Benghazi demonstrators
At least 12 people were killed and scores injured in February when police opened fire on demonstrators in Benghazi protesting against the publication of cartoons depicting the Prophet Muhammad in a number of

European newspapers and the actions of an Italian government minister who appeared on Italian television wearing a T-shirt showing one of the cartoons. According to official statements, the demonstration by several hundred protestors began peacefully but became violent when a group of demonstrators attacked the Italian Consulate in Benghazi with stones and clashed with police protecting it, who then opened fire with live ammunition. Further demonstrations then took place in Benghazi and other eastern cities, including Tobruk and Darna, in the following days and were also dispersed with excessive force by the security forces, reportedly resulting in at least five more deaths.

The authorities publicly denounced the excessive use of force and dismissed the Secretary of the General People's Committee for Public Security (equivalent to interior minister). In June they reported that the Prosecutor-General's office had undertaken the necessary investigations immediately after being informed of the incident and had charged 10 senior officials with offences such as giving orders for the illegal use of gunfire. However, they were not known to have been tried by the end of the year.

Killings at Abu Salim Prison

In October one prisoner, Hafed Mansur al-Zwai, died and several others were injured when security forces clashed with detainees at Abu Salim Prison in Tripoli. A week later, the Prosecutor-General's office announced that it had opened an investigation but its outcome was not known by the end of the year. Initial reports indicated that the death was caused by a bullet, but the official autopsy stated that it resulted from a blow to the head. The Prosecutor-General's office stated that three other prisoners and eight police officers had required hospital treatment but unofficial sources reported that nine prisoners had been taken to hospital for treatment of bullet wounds and other injuries. The incident occurred after dozens of prisoners were brought back to the prison following the postponement of a trial hearing at a criminal court specializing in terrorism-related crimes. They faced charges of belonging to a banned organization, reportedly the Libyan Islamic Fighting Group, and terrorism-related offences.

The authorities reported in July that an official investigation into killings of up to 1,200 detainees following disturbances at Abu Salim Prison in 1996 was ongoing. However, no information was made available regarding the details of the investigation.

Releases of political prisoners

In January, six political prisoners – Muftah al-Mezeini, Awad al-Urfi, Ahmed Zaed, Musa al-Shaeri, Salah Khazzam and Ahmed al-Khafifi – were released due to ill health. Ahmed al-Khafifi had been convicted by the People's Court and sentenced to life imprisonment for supporting a banned organization. The People's Court, abolished in 2005, was an exceptional court for political cases where the rights of the accused were routinely violated.

In March some 130 political prisoners, including dozens of prisoners of conscience, were released in an amnesty. They included some 85 members of the Libyan Islamic Group (also known as the Muslim Brothers), many of whom had been held since 1998. The Gaddafi Development Foundation (formerly known as the Gaddafi International Foundation for Charitable Associations), headed by Saif al-Islam al-Gaddafi, son of Mu'ammar al-Gaddafi, had concluded that they had neither used nor advocated violence. Sentences imposed on them in 2002 by the People's Court were overturned by the Supreme Court in September 2005, but re-imposed by a lower court in February. Two had been sentenced to death and others to long prison terms. AI considered them to be prisoners of conscience, while the authorities maintained that they had been fairly convicted in a regular criminal court on charges of setting up a banned secret organization with the aim of overthrowing the political system.

Also released was Abdurrazig al-Mansouri, a writer and journalist who had been sentenced to 18 months' imprisonment in 2005 for possessing an unlicensed pistol, although it appeared that the real reason for his imprisonment was his publication of critical articles about politics and human rights in Libya on a news website shortly before his arrest.

Some of the releases appeared to be conditional; the Muslim Brothers, in particular, were reportedly forced to sign pledges that they would not undertake any political activities.

In November some 20 political prisoners of Jordanian, Lebanese, Libyan and Syrian nationality were released. They had been arrested in a group of 52 people in Benghazi in 1990 and accused of attempting to overthrow the government and of propagating subversive ideas from abroad. Some of them said that they had been tortured during incommunicado detention. Those released were among 23 people sentenced to life imprisonment in 1991 by the People's Court.

Restrictions on freedom of expression and association

The rights to freedom of expression and association continued to be severely restricted. In August, Saif al-Islam al-Gaddafi criticized the continuing restrictions, including the lack of press freedom and the domination of the media by four state-owned newspapers, and called publicly for political reform, stating that individuals were imprisoned for no reason. Later that month, however, Mu'ammar al-Gaddafi urged his supporters to "kill enemies" if they asked for political change.

☐ Fathi el-Jahmi remained in detention at an undisclosed location understood to be a special facility of the Internal Security Agency, with visits from his family reportedly permitted only every few months. A prisoner of conscience, he was arrested and detained in March 2004 after he criticized Libya's head of state and called for political reform in international media interviews. According to the authorities, he was being tried on charges related to exchanging information harmful to the national interest with a foreign state, and had access to a lawyer. However, they did not disclose where he was being tried.

Several Libyans suspected of political activism abroad were arrested or otherwise intimidated when they returned to the country, in some cases apparently after receiving official assurances that they would not be arrested.

Idriss Boufayed, a long-standing critic of the government, was arrested and taken into incommunicado detention in early November. The authorities did not disclose to his family the reasons for his arrest or his place of detention. Unconfirmed reports suggested that he was being held under guard in a psychiatric hospital in Tripoli. Idriss Boufayed was recognized as a refugee in Switzerland, but returned to Libya in September, reportedly after receiving assurances from the Libyan embassy that he would not be at risk. He was released at the end of December.

In July the authorities provided details about Mahmoud Boushima and Kamel el-Kailani, who were arrested and detained on their return to Libya from the UK in July 2005. They said that the two men had been charged with belonging to the Libyan Islamic Fighting Group and that Mahmoud Boushima was detained pending an investigation into his case. Kamel el-Kailani was released in April. Both men had reportedly received assurances from the authorities that they would not be arrested on their return.

Death penalty
No executions were reported during the year, but death sentences continued to be passed.

In December, five Bulgarian nurses and a Palestinian doctor were sentenced to death by firing squad for a second time after being convicted of knowingly infecting hundreds of Libyan children with HIV in a hospital in Benghazi in 1998. Confessions which the accused alleged were extracted under torture were used as evidence against them, while defence lawyers were not allowed to bring in international medical experts. The six medics had been in detention since 1999. Previous death sentences against them were overturned by the Supreme Court in 2005.

Rights of migrants, asylum-seekers and refugees
There were continuing concerns about the treatment of migrants, asylum-seekers and refugees. Foreigners arrested on suspicion of being irregular migrants reportedly often suffered abuse in detention, such as beatings, and were collectively deported without access to a lawyer or an assessment of their individual cases. In November, on the occasion of a Euro-African conference on migration and development held in Tripoli, the Libyan authorities announced that they had significantly increased repatriations of migrants. They had deported some 50,000 from the beginning of the year until 6 November, compared with fewer than 5,000 in 2004.

AI country reports/ visits
Statements
- Libya: AI welcomes release of political prisoners (AI Index: MDE 19/002/2006)

- Libya: Investigation needed into prison deaths (AI Index: MDE 19/006/2006)
- Libya: Death sentences for foreign medics must be withdrawn (AI Index: MDE 19/007/2006)

LITHUANIA

REPUBLIC OF LITHUANIA
Head of state: Valdas Adamkus
Head of government: Gediminas Kirkilas (replaced Algirdas Brazauskas in July)
Death penalty: abolitionist for all crimes
International Criminal Court: ratified

Trafficking in women and girls for purposes of sexual exploitation remained a serious problem.

Background
In May, Prime Minister Algirdas Brazauskas resigned after one party pulled out of his coalition government, causing a political crisis. In July, Gediminas Kirkilas formed a new government at the head of a four-party minority coalition.

Trafficking of women and girls
Trafficking of women and girls for purposes of sexual exploitation remained a serious problem. According to statistics from the European Police Office, Europol, well over 1,000 women and girls were trafficked abroad annually from Lithuania, primarily to western European countries. Non-governmental organizations reported that the actual number was much higher. According to the UN Office on Drugs and Crime, Lithuania was one of the four central and south-eastern European countries where women and girls were at highest risk of being trafficked. In addition to being a country of origin for trafficking victims, Lithuania remained a country of transit and destination, primarily for women and girls from Belarus, Ukraine and the Russian Kaliningrad region.

International scrutiny
In February, the European Committee for the Prevention of Torture (CPT) published a report based on findings during a 2004 visit to Lithuania. The CPT reported that it had received several allegations of ill-treatment in detention facilities, supported by medical reports. The CPT also noted that people complaining of ill-treatment could not obtain a forensic medical examination without prior authorization by an investigator or prosecutor, and that the authorities should remedy this.

The CPT stated that conditions in a number of detention facilities were totally unacceptable. It stated that detainees were locked up 24 hours per day in filthy, overcrowded cells, with little or no access to natural light and, in many cases, dim artificial lighting. In some cells, there were no sanitary facilities. Prompt medical screening was not available to people held in police detention centres.

MACEDONIA

THE FORMER YUGOSLAV REPUBLIC OF MACEDONIA
Head of state: Branko Crvenkovski
Head of government: Nikola Gruevski (replaced Vlado Buckovski in August)
Death penalty: abolitionist for all crimes
International Criminal Court: ratified

The International Criminal Tribunal for the former Yugoslavia (Tribunal) did not return cases under its jurisdiction to Macedonia for trial. Parliamentary elections that resulted in a change of government were marred by violence between ethnic Albanian parties. Investigations continued outside Macedonia into allegations that the authorities unlawfully transferred a German national into US custody.

Background
Following elections on 5 July, government passed to a coalition of the Internal Macedonian Revolutionary Organization-Democratic Party for Macedonian National Unity and the Democratic Union for Integration (DUI).

Legal reforms required by the Stabilization and Association Agreement with the European Union (EU) proceeded. In October the EU Commissioner declared it too soon to set a date for negotiations on accession to the EU. The 8 November progress report noted concerns about the independence of the judiciary, widespread corruption, failure to ensure the representation of minorities in public administration, and the situation of Roma despite plans for integration.

In May parliament voted to abolish compulsory military service as part of a government plan to establish a professionalized military in 2007.

Political violence
Political rivalry between the two largest ethnic Albanian parties, the Democratic Party of Albanians (DPA) and the DUI, triggered pre-election violence. The DPA, which won more seats than the DUI, protested at its exclusion from government by blocking roads and holding mass demonstrations. Party leaders alleged that the Ohrid Agreement, which concluded the 2001 internal conflict, had broken down.

Between 15 and 17 June, DPA members allegedly drove a bulldozer into the DUI office in Saraj, two grenades were reportedly thrown at DUI offices in Struga and Saraj, and the DUI office in Tetovo came under attack. On 18 June unidentified gunmen shot at the car of the DPA mayor of Saraj, Imer Selmani; he escaped unharmed. On 23 June, DUI member Abdulhalim Kasami was shot and wounded in front of his house in Tetovo. On 24 June firearms were used in fighting in Rasce between DPA and DUI supporters, and three DUI members were injured. Criminal investigations were opened.

Impunity for war crimes
Former Minister of Internal Affairs Ljube Boshkovski remained in the custody of the Tribunal. He had been indicted in 2005, with Johan Tarchulovski, for command responsibility for an attack on the village of Ljuboten in August 2001 when seven ethnic Albanian men died and over 100 more were detained, tortured and ill-treated. In October, the Chief Prosecutor to the Tribunal announced that four other cases in which the Tribunal had seized primacy but had issued no indictments — including the case of 12 Macedonian citizens abducted by armed ethnic Albanians in 2001 — would be returned in 2007 to the Macedonian authorities for prosecution.

In April the Ministry of Internal Affairs reportedly issued a search warrant to establish the whereabouts of three ethnic Albanians — Sultan Memeti, Hajredin Halimi and Ruzdi Veliu. They were believed to be victims of enforced disappearance, last seen in the custody of the Macedonian authorities during the 2001 internal conflict. In May the Ministry said that an investigation into the enforced disappearance of six further Albanians was under way, but in November could report no progress in any disappearance cases.

'War on terror'
The Parliamentary Assembly of the Council of Europe questioned Macedonia about the involvement of security and intelligence officials in the unlawful arrest, detention and ill-treatment of Khaled el-Masri, a German citizen of Lebanese descent. The Macedonian authorities reportedly held him in a Skopje hotel for 23 days in 2003 before rendering him at Skopje airport to the US authorities, who flew him to Afghanistan. The Macedonian authorities denied involvement, and did not open an investigation into the allegations. The new government failed to acknowledge that any violations had taken place. The European Parliament's Temporary Committee conducted investigations in April, including in meetings with government officials. In June it reported inconsistencies in the account given by the Macedonian authorities.

In March, ethnic Albanians Rajmonda Malečka and her father Bujar Malečka were released from prison on appeal and expelled from Macedonia. Their original sentence of five years' imprisonment on terrorism charges in May 2005 had been confirmed in a retrial at Skopje District Court in November 2005. The Supreme Court had in 2005 stated that the charges were without foundation.

Torture and ill-treatment
In January the Council of Europe Directorate of Legal Affairs reported severe overcrowding in Idrizovo and Skopje prisons. Detainees received inadequate health care and educational activities because of continuing staff shortages. In May the European Committee for the Prevention of Torture and Inhuman or Degrading Treatment or Punishment visited Macedonia.

Also in May the European Court of Human Rights ruled admissible the case of Pejrusan Jasar, a Romani man allegedly ill-treated in police detention in 1998.

A new police law passed in October aimed at ensuring representation of the ethnic Albanian community in the police force. However, it failed to provide an independent mechanism for police accountability, including to investigate allegations of ill-treatment and torture by "Alpha" special police units.

Prisoners of conscience
On 3 March, Zoran Vranishkovski, bishop of the Serbian Orthodox Church in Macedonia in Ohrid and prisoner of conscience since July 2005, was released from the charge of allegedly inciting religious and ethnic hatred, but remained in detention pending trial on further charges.

Journalists were imprisoned for defamation, despite amendments to a law introduced in May which removed criminal penalties for the offence.
🗀 On 21 November journalist Zoran Bozinovski was released from a three-month prison sentence for defamation following domestic and international appeals.

Discrimination
Although minority representation in police and municipal employment was introduced in July under the Ohrid Agreement, DPA members reported continued discrimination against ethnic Albanians.

The UN Committee on the Elimination of Discrimination against Women recommended in February that the government take temporary special measures to address discrimination in education, health care and participating in public life against, in particular, rural, Romani and ethnic Albanian women. In November the UN Committee on Economic, Social and Cultural Rights noted widespread discrimination against Roma, including in obtaining citizenship and personal documents required for social insurance, health care and other benefits, and recommended special measures to address discrimination in employment faced by Roma and other minority women.
🗀 Mass demonstrations by the Romani community followed the disappearance of Trajan Bekirov, a 17-year-old boy last seen being pursued by members of a special police unit on suspicion of theft on 10 May. His body was found in a river on 27 May in a search

organized by relatives. The authorities did not conduct a search or proper investigation, and only provided his parents with the autopsy report after international pressure.

Up to 2,000 Romani refugees from Kosovo, denied refugee status in procedures which often failed to provide individual determinations, remained in Macedonia. The government failed to provide access to education, employment, health care and housing.

Violence against women
In February the UN Committee on the Elimination of Discrimination against Women noted that legislation failed to define discrimination against women or the principle of equality of men and women. A law to this effect was introduced in May. The Committee was also concerned at the prevalence of violence against women, including domestic violence, and the persistence of trafficking in women and girls, including an increase in internal trafficking, despite a National Programme to Combat Human Trafficking and Illegal Migration.

AI country reports/ visits
Reports
- Partners in crime: Europe's role in US renditions (AI Index: EUR 01/008/2006)
- Europe and Central Asia: Summary of Amnesty International's concerns in the region, January-June 2006 (AI Index: EUR 01/017/2006)

Visit
AI delegates visited Macedonia in November.

MALAWI

THE REPUBLIC OF MALAWI
Head of state and government: Bingu wa Mutharika
Death penalty: abolitionist in practice
International Criminal Court: ratified

Nearly a million people needed food aid in 2006. Freedom of expression continued to be threatened, with a number of media workers charged with criminal libel. Torture and ill-treatment by police and life-threatening prison conditions were reported.

Background
Moves to impeach the President were formally ended in January. The Vice-President, Cassim Chilumpa, a member of the President's former party, the United Democratic Front, was arrested for treason in April and remained under house arrest at the end of 2006.

Former President Bakili Muluzi was briefly detained in July on allegations of corruption. On the same day the director of the Anti-Corruption Bureau was suspended by the President for allegedly not following appropriate procedures when he ordered the arrest of the former President. The charges against Bakili Muluzi were withdrawn.

Poverty
Malawi's recovery from a devastating drought in 2005 brought some relief to the rural poor. However, more than 900,000 people remained reliant on food aid – a drop from 4.8 million people in need of food aid in 2005. Production on small-scale farms was also affected by the high incidence of HIV and AIDS. Approximately 14 per cent of the population has contracted the virus.

Press freedom
Freedom of expression continued to be threatened, particularly in the first half of the year, when the government brought charges of criminal libel against a number of media workers.

▭ In May, Robert Jamieson, editor-in-chief of the *Chronicle* newspaper, sub-editor Dickson Kashoti and reporter Arnold Mlelemba were arrested on criminal libel charges for alleging that Malawi's former Attorney General was implicated in the sale of a stolen laptop. The three were provisionally released.

▭ Jika Nkolokosa, general manager of Blantyre Newspapers Limited, and Maxwell Ng'ambi, a journalist, were charged with criminal libel for reporting that the Minister of Health was implicated in improper accounting. The charges against Jika Nkolokosa were dropped but Maxwell Ng'ambi was convicted and fined.

Policing
Torture and ill-treatment of suspects in custody remained a major concern. In June the Malawi Human Rights Commission raised concerns about abuse and torture at Lilongwe, Kawale, Lingadzi and Kanengo Police Stations.

▭ Miyonda Mundiwa, a suspected car thief, had his leg cut when police officers hit him with a machete during questioning at Lilongwe Police Station in April.

Prisons
Large numbers of prisoners died in custody. More than 280 deaths were recorded, an average of 23 prisoners per month per 10,000 prisoners. This was a sharp increase from 14 deaths per month recorded in 2005. Most of the deaths were linked to inadequate diet.

MALAYSIA

MALAYSIA
Head of state: Raja Tuanku Syed Sirajuddin
Head of government: Abdullah Ahmad Badawi
Death penalty: retentionist
International Criminal Court: not ratified

The year ended without the government fulfilling its pledge to establish an independent police complaints commission. At least 80 men accused of links to Islamist extremist groups were held without charge or trial under the Internal Security Act (ISA). Freedom of expression, association and assembly continued to be constrained by restrictive laws. People suspected of being irregular migrants or asylum-seekers were harassed and detained in harsh conditions pending deportation. Hundreds of people, mostly alleged irregular migrants, were imprisoned or caned after unfair trials. Death sentences continued to be passed and four executions were carried out.

Police reform
Non-governmental organizations continued to press the government to create an Independent Police Complaints and Misconduct Commission (IPCMC). In 2005 a Royal Commission of Inquiry into the police had recommended a wide range of reforms, including the establishment of an IPCMC by May 2006. Draft legislation to establish an IPCMC remained under consideration by the Attorney General at the end of the year. A range of other reform recommendations, including repeal or review of laws allowing for detention without trial or requiring police permits for public assemblies, were not implemented.

Police brutality

There were continued reports of excessive use of force by police officers during peaceful demonstrations. In March and May police armed with shields violently dispersed a series of peaceful protests in Kuala Lumpur against fuel prices, with batons and water cannon. Several people were reported seriously injured and dozens arrested. All were subsequently released.

There was still concern over the effectiveness of safeguards to ensure the safety and wellbeing of detainees in police custody. At least five people, including one woman, were reported to have died in custody during the year.

Detention without trial

The ISA, which allows for detention without trial for periods of up to two years, renewable indefinitely, continued to be applied and also used as a threat. At least 80 men accused of membership of or links to Islamist extremist groups remained in detention at the end of the year. At least 20 detention orders were renewed, and the reasons were not made public.

In May, 11 people were arrested under the ISA in Sabah for alleged involvement in an Islamist group known as Darul Islam Sabah.

In October, at least 17 alleged members of Jemaah Islamiyah and the Malaysia Militant Group (Kumpulan Militan Malaysia) were released, but remained under orders restricting their freedom of movement.

At least 700 criminal suspects remained in detention under the Emergency (Public Order and Prevention of Crime) Ordinance (EO), which allows for indefinite detention without trial. Many were detained under the EO because the police did not have sufficient evidence to charge them. In October, the Federal Court ruled that the lawfulness of EO detentions by police could not be challenged in the courts once the Minister of Internal Security had issued a detention order.

Migrant workers, refugees and asylum-seekers

Refugees, asylum-seekers and migrant workers remained vulnerable to arrest, detention in poor conditions and deportation under the Immigration Act. Migrant workers were subjected to psychological and physical abuse by agencies and employers, and were often denied equal access to benefits and protections guaranteed to Malaysian workers, including maternity provisions, limited working hours and holidays.

Excessive use of force and ill-treatment were reported during repeated raids and mass arrests, mostly conducted by members of the volunteer civilian armed corps RELA (Ikatan Relawan Rakyat Malaysia), of suspected irregular migrant workers. Hundreds were whipped after being found guilty of immigration offences.

In February, the bodies of five migrant workers who allegedly fled a RELA raid were found in a lake in Selayang, near Kuala Lumpur. Witnesses reported that at least one body bore signs of ill-treatment.

Freedom of expression and association

There was continued criticism of the Printing Presses and Publication Act which allows the authorities to refuse, revoke or suspend printing permits.

During the year, two newspaper editors were forced to resign following their newspapers' coverage of police abuses, and four newspapers were suspended after publishing drawings of the Prophet Muhammad, first published in a Danish newspaper in 2005 and judged offensive.

In May the opposition People's Justice Party (Parti Keadilan Rakyat) protested at the refusal to grant a printing permit for the party's official paper.

Two opposition parties, the Malaysian Dayak Congress and the Socialist Party of Malaysia (Parti Sosialis Malaysia), were denied registration under the Societies Act.

Death penalty and corporal punishment

In March the Malaysian Bar Council passed a resolution calling for the abolition of the death penalty and a moratorium on all executions.

Death sentences, however, continued to be passed during 2006, mostly as a mandatory punishment for certain drug-related offences. Four executions for armed treason were carried out. The authorities continued not to disclose regular statistics on capital punishment.

In May, Parliament passed a water privatization bill, which also extended the death penalty to cover serious cases of water contamination.

Caning, a cruel, inhuman or degrading punishment, was also carried out.

AI country reports/visits
Report
- Malaysia: Amnesty International's campaign to stop torture and ill-treatment in the 'war on terror' (AI Index: ASA 28/003/2006)

Visits
Amnesty International delegates met government officials in March, and local civil society groups in June to discuss progress in the implementation of police reform.

MALDIVES

REPUBLIC OF MALDIVES
Head of state and government: Maumoon Abdul
Gayoom
Death penalty: abolitionist in practice
International Criminal Court: not ratified

Political freedom continued to be undermined by the
slow pace of constitutional reforms. More than 100
people were arbitrarily arrested ahead of public
rallies. Scores of them were believed to be prisoners
of conscience. At least six political prisoners were
sentenced to terms of imprisonment. Police
reportedly used unnecessary force while detaining
political activists who offered no resistance. Torture
and other ill-treatment continued in custody. Several
long-serving prisoners of conscience were released.

Background
In March, President Maumoon Abdul Gayoom
announced the government's Roadmap for the Reform
Agenda Ushering In a Modern Democracy. It promised a
new constitution by June 2007 and the first multi-party
elections in October 2008.

In September, the Maldives acceded to the
International Covenant on Civil and Political Rights
(ICCPR), the Optional Protocol to the ICCPR, and the
International Covenant on Economic, Social and
Cultural Rights.

Resistance from conservative elements within the
government and disruptive moves from the opposition
threatened to derail political and judicial reforms.

Freedom of expression
Scores of government critics were accused of breaking
the law while peacefully expressing their views or
attending rallies.

Member of Parliament Ahmed Shafeeq was briefly
detained in April for attending a peaceful rally in
Malé. He was reportedly severely beaten at the time
of arrest and admitted to hospital. No investigation
was carried out.

More than 100 people were detained in advance of
a planned anti-government protest scheduled for
10 November in Malé. The riot police also prevented
people from leaving the islands for the demonstration.
A boat full of opposition supporters was allegedly
raided by the police and all passengers detained. Scores
of detainees were held for weeks without charge, while
at least 22 were released after being charged with
apparently unsubstantiated, politically motivated
criminal offences.

Intense pressure on the media to refrain from
publishing articles critical of the government
continued. Journalists ignoring this pressure were
harassed, detained or charged with criminal offences.

Aminath Najeeb, editor of the *Minivan* newspaper,
received a summons in May to appear before the

criminal court, apparently as part of the government's
attempt to close *Minivan*. Before the summons, she was
harassed by masked men circling her house.

Mohamed Yooshau, Imran Zahir and Ibrahim Manik
were detained for weeks at various times during the
year. Abdulla Saeed (Fahala) was sentenced to 20 years'
imprisonment for carrying drugs which were believed
to have been planted on him by the police after his
arrest.

Unfair trials and prisoners of conscience
Courts continued to sentence political activists to
terms of imprisonment.

Ahmed Abbas, a political cartoonist, designer of
Maldivian banknotes and prominent critic of the
government, was sentenced in November to six
months' imprisonment without knowing he was being
tried. His conviction related to his remarks in a
newspaper in August 2005. He only found out about his
conviction by chance, when checking the government's
website. Fearing ill-treatment, he sought sanctuary in
the UN building in Malé but had to leave after
government pressure. He was then detained by the
police and transferred to the prison island of Maafushi.
He was believed to be a prisoner of conscience.

Several prisoners of conscience were released.
Ahmed Ibrahim Didi and Naushad Waheed were
released in February and Jennifer Latheef was released
in August. Chairperson of the Maldivian Democratic
Party, Mohamed Nasheed, was released in September.

Torture and other ill-treatment
Police tortured and otherwise ill-treated detainees
arrested while taking part in peaceful demonstrations.

Sixteen-year-old Moosa Afaau was reportedly
grabbed around his neck by a plain-clothed officer in
February while watching a street rally. He was
reportedly dragged to the ground, his trousers were
pulled down and he was hit with a baton on his thighs
and genitals. He was then taken to a police station, tied
to a chair and punched in the face every time he fell
asleep. No one has been held accountable.

AI reports/ visits
Report
· Maldives: Renewed repressive measures against the
  opposition (AI Index: ASA 29/010/2006)

MALI

REPUBLIC OF MALI
Head of state: Amadou Toumani Touré
Head of government: Ousmane Issoufi Maïga
Death penalty: abolitionist in practice
International Criminal Court: ratified

Freedom of expression came under attack with journalists arrested, imprisoned and fined. Two death sentences were handed down, despite a bill before the National Assembly to abolish the death penalty.

Background

In May, members of the Tuareg ethnic group attacked and occupied military camps in the region of Kidal and Menaka town. The attackers, led by a former member of a Tuareg armed group who joined the army following a 1992 peace agreement, withdrew from the camps a day later, after stealing weapons and equipment. Their demands included greater government support for the development and autonomy of regions populated by Tuaregs. In July, an accord was reached between the armed groups and the government. The Tuaregs abandoned their claims for autonomy and the government pledged to increase development efforts in the northern regions, particularly in Kidal.

Attacks on freedom of expression

In August, six staff members of Radio Kayira, including Amadou Nanko Mariko, managing director of the Koutiala radio station, Sidi Traoré and Mohamed Diakité, were arrested in Niono for broadcasting without a licence. They were later charged with opposing the authority of the state and sentenced to one-month prison terms and a fine. They lodged an appeal. The Radio Kayira network belongs to a political party represented in the government, African Solidarity for Democracy and Independence (Solidarité africaine pour la démocratie et l'indépendance, SADI).

Death penalty

In March, Zoumana Diarra and M'Pié Diarra were sentenced to death by the Bamako Assize Court for criminal offences including murder and poisoning. No executions have taken place in Mali during the last decade. A private member's bill on the abolition of the death penalty was presented to the National Assembly in April, but had not been voted on by the end of the year.

MALTA

REPUBLIC OF MALTA
Head of state: Edward Fenech-Adami
Head of government: Lawrence Gonzi
Death penalty: abolitionist for all crimes
International Criminal Court: ratified

Journalists, human rights activists and others were subjected to arson attacks for speaking out against racism. Irregular migrants continued to be subject to a policy of automatic detention. Conditions in migrant detention centres were harsh and insanitary, and came in for criticism by the European Union (EU).

Racism

Overt racism continued to increase. The non-governmental coalition, the European Network Against Racism (ENAR), noted that debate in the news media and on the Internet was increasingly hostile towards immigrants and that racist attacks and hate speech were on the rise.

Arson attacks targeted individuals or organizations that actively worked to protect the human rights of migrants and refugees or denounced racist and discriminatory attitudes and actions in Maltese society. Racist speech and attacks appeared to find increasing legitimacy within Maltese society.

⌂ In early March the house of a poet was set on fire in an arson attack just a few days after he launched a book of poetry promoting tolerance and refugee rights.

⌂ On 13 March, seven cars belonging to the Catholic Church's Jesuit Community were destroyed by fire at night, shortly before publication of the Report on Racism and Xenophobia in Malta by the European Monitoring Centre on Racism and Xenophobia (EUMC). The Jesuit Community is EUMC's partner in Malta. On 11 April a car belonging to a lawyer working with the Jesuit Refugee Service was set alight and destroyed.

⌂ On 3 May the editor of the weekly *Malta Today* newspaper had his house torched by arsonists. He had published an editorial on racism and immigration shortly before the attack.

⌂ On 13 May the home of a journalist from the daily newspaper, *The Malta Independent*, who had denounced the extreme right and written about racism and immigration, was attacked. In the early hours, arsonists leaned five burning tyres filled with petrol against her back door. Smashed glass and petrol were spread on the road in front of the house, in an apparent attempt to prevent her family escaping or to block help arriving.

Migrants and asylum-seekers

Malta maintained its automatic detention policy for irregular migrants. On arrival they are held in closed detention centres for up to 18 months and later transferred to open centres. The policy clearly violates international human rights laws and standards. Migrants were detained without first having a proper medical screening, potentially putting the health of other detainees and detention centre staff at risk. Non-governmental organizations and journalists were still not allowed access to migrant detention centres.

Four administrative detention centres for asylum-seekers and migrants were in deplorable condition and failed to meet legally binding international standards, the EU Committee on Civil Liberties, Justice and Home Affairs reported in March. A delegation of the Committee, visiting four detention centres, found that the Hal-Safi detention centre "was like a cage", without sheets on the beds, broken and dirty mattresses, and no heating. Hygiene conditions were intolerable, with broken showers, no hot water, and toilets without doors and in a state of disrepair. At the Hal-Far centre, delegates found high levels of mosquitoes and rat infestation, and appalling conditions in bathrooms. Some residents who had fled the Darfur region of Sudan said their asylum applications had been rejected on the grounds that "they could have moved to safer areas of the country". At the Lyster Barracks centre, there were only two functioning toilets for more than 100 people, no provision of sanitary towels for women, and no area outside for fresh air and exercise, the Committee reported.

Domestic violence

The Domestic Violence Act came into force in February, and the Commission on Domestic Violence created under the Act was set up in March. The Commission's responsibilities and competencies include awareness-raising; developing and outlining strategies to identify problems of domestic violence so as to offer better protection to victims; suggesting areas for research; educating the general public; and identifying training for professional groups. The Commission is required to publish an annual report.

MAURITANIA

ISLAMIC REPUBLIC OF MAURITANIA
Head of state: Colonel Ely Ould Mohamed Vall
Head of government: Sidi Mohamed Ould Boubacar
Death penalty: abolitionist in practice
International Criminal Court: not ratified

At least 15 people were arbitrarily arrested and accused of belonging to a terrorist organization, including several possible prisoners of conscience. Although eight prisoners held since 2005 were provisionally released, others remained detained without charge. There were reports of torture in detention. Slavery and forced labour continued to be practised.

Background

In April, Colonel Ely Ould Vall, President of the Military Council for Justice and Democracy, stated that deposed President Maaouyia Ould Sid' Ahmed Taya would be allowed to return to Mauritania, but would be banned from participating in forthcoming elections. In June, a new Constitution was approved by referendum, reducing the presidential mandate to five years, with a limit of two terms. Article 99 clearly condemns any constitutional reform aimed at maintaining a president in power. The reforms were due to become effective with the presidential election scheduled for March 2007. This election would return the country, ruled by a military junta since a bloodless coup in August 2005, to civilian rule.

In November, the Coalition of Forces for Democratic Change (Coalition des forces pour le changement démocratique, CFCD), a coalition of former opposition parties, expressed its satisfaction with measures taken by the government to guarantee transparency during legislative elections.

In May, a National Commission on Human Rights was set up and was given the task of evaluating detention conditions, following a prison breakout in Nouakchott in April which led to a clampdown by the authorities.

In June, a new law lessened censorship of newspapers by the Ministry of the Interior, reduced the sentences for press crimes, and foresaw the creation of private television and radio. In October, six members of a new institution responsible for regulating the media were named.

Provisional releases

In July, eight people charged with belonging to an unauthorized organization and putting the country at risk of foreign reprisals were provisionally released. They had been arrested in 2005 along with 13 others, including Abdallahi Ould Eminou and two Algerian nationals. Three detainees escaped from Nouakchott Central Prison in April. Several were reportedly tortured in custody.

Possible prisoners of conscience

At least 15 people were arbitrarily arrested and accused of links to al-Qa'ida or other terrorist organizations. Some may have been prisoners of conscience. Several were held for up to a few days and then released uncharged. However, the majority were charged with endangering the security of the state and criminal conspiracy. They had not been brought to trial by the end of 2006.

🗀 In June, two military officers, Abderahamane Ould Lekwar and Mohamed Ould Lagdaf, and three civilians including former ambassador Mohamed Ould Mohamed Aly and Mohamed Salek Ould El Hadj Moktar, President of Democrats without Borders, were arrested. They were charged with criminal conspiracy, endangering state security and conspiring against the constitution. All were close to former President Taya.

🗀 In July, eight people, including Med Lemine Ould Jiddi and Taher Ould Abdel Jelil, were arrested and charged with terrorist acts, training abroad to commit terrorist acts in Mauritania and belonging to an unauthorized association. Four were provisionally released and four remained in detention.

Slavery

Although President Vall committed to abolishing all forms of slavery in Mauritania, forced labour and slavery reportedly continued to be practised. Estimates of the number of people held in slavery varied widely. In June, at least eight people were released from slavery in the Adrar region 450km north of Nouakchott, while others reportedly remained in captivity in the region of Tagant, 400km north-east of Nouakchott.

MEXICO

UNITED MEXICAN STATES
Head of state and government: Felipe Calderón Hinojosa (replaced Vicente Fox Quesada in December)
Death penalty: abolitionist for all crimes
International Criminal Court: ratified

Felipe Calderón of the National Action Party (Partido de Acción Nacional, PAN) was elected president in controversial elections. President Vicente Fox completed his mandate without fulfilling the administration's commitment to end human rights violations and impunity, which remained widespread. The Federal Congress once again failed to approve reforms to the Constitution and the public security and criminal justice systems to improve the protection of human rights. There were continuing reports of torture, arbitrary detention, excessive use of force and unfair judicial proceedings, particularly at state level. Serious human rights violations were reported in Oaxaca State in the context of a protracted political crisis. Violence against women remained endemic in many states and the campaign for justice for the women of Ciudad Juárez and Chihuahua City continued. Several journalists were killed. Human rights defenders and political opponents in some states remained at risk of harassment or unfounded criminal prosecutions. Measures to prosecute those responsible for systematic human rights violations in previous decades failed. Indigenous peoples in several states continued to face discrimination including in access to basic services, such as health care and education.

Background

High levels of violent crime and public insecurity continued to be major public concerns. In November several armed opposition groups reportedly claimed responsibility for the detonation of three explosive devices in Mexico City. Central American and Mexican migrants seeking to cross the border to the USA could face increased threats to their safety with the proposed extension of the border wall by the US government.

Elections and their aftermath

The fairness of the national elections and the narrow margin of the PAN victory were challenged by the second-placed candidate, Andrés Manuel López Obrador, of the Democratic Revolutionary Party (Partido de la Revolución Democrática, PRD). After several weeks of major street protests by PRD supporters demanding a full recount of votes, the Federal Electoral Tribunal ruled there were only sufficient grounds for a partial recount of ballot boxes. In September the Tribunal confirmed Felipe Calderón as President. Andrés Manuel López Obrador and his supporters refused to accept the results and in November set up a "parallel" government. On

1 December, Felipe Calderón was sworn in as President, without making any clear commitment to strengthen the protection of human rights. The appointment of the Governor of Jalisco State as federal Interior Minister raised concern owing to his failure to prevent or punish serious human rights violations committed in Jalisco during his governorship.

International human rights mechanisms and reform

The Mexican government appeared before six UN thematic committees to assess its compliance with treaty obligations. These included the UN Children's Convention, the UN Convention against Racism, the International Covenant on Economic, Social and Cultural Rights, the UN Women's Convention, the Convention against Torture and the Migrant Workers' Convention. The respective committees made a series of recommendations. The government of President Fox played a positive role in UN reform to strengthen human rights protection. Mexico took over the presidency of the new UN Human Rights Council.

There was little progress on government human rights initiatives. The implementation of the National Human Rights Programme remained inadequate. The federal judiciary published the results of its consultation on reform of the judicial system. With the exception of some reforms to the juvenile justice system, there were virtually no advances in introducing proposed constitutional and legal reforms to ensure the protection of human rights in the public security and criminal justice system.

Oaxaca crisis

In June, state police used excessive force against striking teachers occupying Oaxaca city centre and bringing it to a standstill. The Popular Assembly of the People of Oaxaca (Asamblea Popular del Pueblo de Oaxaca, APPO) was formed to support the teachers and demand the resignation of the governor. Its supporters occupied official buildings and TV and radio stations. State police, often wearing civilian clothes, reportedly shot at APPO supporters, resulting in the deaths of at least two and injuries to many others. APPO supporters established barricades blocking city streets. During the crisis, state police reportedly arbitrarily arrested, held incommunicado and tortured several teachers and APPO supporters before filing charges on the basis of allegedly fabricated evidence.

At the end of October, municipal and state police reportedly attacked several barricades set up by APPO supporters, leading to the deaths of three civilians and injuries to many others. Some 4,500 Federal Preventive Police (Policía Federal Preventiva, PFP) entered the city using tear gas, batons and water cannons. Some protesters responded with violence and scores were arrested. Many were reportedly beaten and threatened by the PFP once in custody. At least 19 PFP officials were reportedly injured. In November, after clashes with police, more than 140 people were arrested, many of whom were reportedly not involved in violence. Scores were reportedly beaten and denied access to family, medical attention and legal advice. More than 90 remained in custody at the end of the year.

In early November teachers returned to work, but some faced threats and detention. In December, scores of APPO leaders and supporters were subject to warrants issued during the protests, some allegedly on the basis of fabricated evidence. There was concern that those involved in peaceful protest would be detained and be subject to unfair judicial proceedings. During the crisis, more than 17 civilians were reportedly killed and scores of others injured. Federal and state authorities failed to effectively investigate allegations of serious human rights violations by the end of the year.

▭ On 27 October, US reporter Bradley Roland Will was shot and killed on a barricade while filming a clash between protesters and armed gunmen, later identified as local governing party officials. Two officials were detained, but later released without charge after state authorities concluded APPO supporters were responsible. There was serious concern about impartiality of the official investigation.

▭ On 29 October Jorge Alberto López Bernal died as a result of being struck by a tear gas canister reportedly fired by the PFP. Federal authorities did not conduct criminal investigations into this or other reports of human rights violations allegedly committed by PFP agents.

Excessive force – public security

High levels of violent crime, often related to drug trafficking, undermined public security in many parts of the country. Massive policing operations against protesters led to serious violations of human rights.

▭ In April, federal and state police evicted striking miners blocking access to the Lázaro Cárdenas steel plant in Michoacán State. Violent clashes ensued in which José Luis Castillo Zúñiga and Héctor Álvarez Gómez were shot and killed by police and 54 other people were injured, including police officers. In October the National Human Rights Commission found that federal and state police had acted illegally and had used excessive force, and called for a criminal investigation. The authorities refused to comply with the recommendation.

▭ On 3 May, Mexico State Police clashed with demonstrators in Texcoco resulting in a major state and federal police operation in the neighbouring town of San Salvador Atenco where a number of police were reportedly held hostage. Police used tear gas, batons and firearms against members of the community, detaining 211 people over the two days, many of whom were repeatedly beaten and tortured while being transported to the state prison. Twenty-six people remained in custody at the end of the year accused of kidnapping, despite serious concerns about the reliability of evidence presented against several of them and the fairness of judicial proceedings. Even Magdalena García Durán, who won a federal injunction against her unfair detention, remained in custody. A number of state police officers were under investigation for assault at the end of the year.

Violence against women and Ciudad Juárez

Violence against women and gender discrimination remained widespread throughout Mexico. The Special Federal Congressional Commission on Feminicide produced a major report on murders of women in 10 states. The report highlighted the consistent failure of state governments to compile reliable information on gender-based violence or to put in place effective measures for its prevention and punishment. A federal law strengthening the right of women to live free from violence was passed. In February a Special Federal Prosecutor's Office for Crimes of Violence against Women was established.

There were continued reports of murders of women in Ciudad Juárez and the City of Chihuahua. The Chihuahua state authorities introduced some improvements in response to new killings. However, they failed to prosecute many previous cases or hold to account any officials implicated in the original botched investigations. The Federal Attorney General's Office concluded its investigation into past cases, but failed to acknowledge the scale of gender-based violence in Ciudad Juárez over 13 years, leading to criticism that it was seeking to downplay the murders and abductions of women in the city.

In June, after two and half years in custody, David Meza Argueta was acquitted of the murder of Nayra Azucena Cervantes in Chihuahua City in 2003. The basis of the case against him was a confession reportedly extracted under torture by Chihuahua judicial police. David Meza filed a complaint of torture against state officials. Two state judicial police were reportedly expelled from the force for using torture during their investigations.

In May, during the police operation in San Salvador Atenco, Mexico State, 47 women were detained and transported to prison. At least 26 women reported to the National Human Rights Commission that they had been sexually assaulted or raped by state police officers during the journey to prison. At the end of the year, the local state-led investigation had resulted in only minor charges against one of the officials involved.

Arbitrary detention, torture and unfair judicial procedures

Arbitrary detention, ill-treatment, torture and violations of due process rights of criminal suspects remained common. Courts continued to overlook reports of such abuses. Access to legal counsel was often denied in the early stages of detention and state-appointed lawyers frequently failed to guarantee the right to effective defence. The poorest and most disadvantaged detainees, such as Indigenous peoples, were often denied minimum fair trial standards.

In May, two Indigenous men, Aureliano Álvarez Gómez and Tiburcio Gómez Pérez, were detained in connection with an alleged kidnapping in the municipality of Huitiupán, Chiapas State. No arrest warrant was produced and they were reportedly severely beaten during interrogation by state judicial police. The two men were denied legal assistance and were not charged, but held by judicial order (arraigo)

for more than 50 days in a secure house run by the State Prosecutor's Office. Lawyers from a local human rights organization were denied access to the men for four days and when they were able to visit them were unable to talk in private or document the visible signs of their injuries. In June the two men were charged and remanded in Amate prison where they were tortured by other inmates, reportedly with the consent of prison authorities. No investigation into the two men's treatment was known to have been initiated by the end of the year.

On 4 May, José Gregorio Arnulfo Pacheco was repeatedly beaten and kicked by state police officers at his home in San Salvador Atenco. He was subsequently diagnosed with fractured ribs, a fractured trachea, cranial fissures and severe bruising. He was released from custody at the end of July after the judge recognized his physical incapacity to have committed the alleged offences. The outcome of the Public Prosecutor's Office appeal against his release was awaited at the end of the year.

Journalists and human rights defenders

Ten journalists were murdered and many others received threats, reportedly in reprisal for their work. Those investigating organized crime networks were at particular risk. Investigations conducted by a Special Federal Prosecutor failed to result in prosecutions of any of those responsible. There were continued reports of intimidation and judicial harassment of human rights defenders in a number of states.

In September the National Supreme Court broadened an investigation into the misuse of the criminal justice system which led to the prosecution of journalist and women's rights defender Lydia Cacho on defamation charges in December 2005. The investigation was continuing at the end of the year.

In January Martín Barrios of the Labour Rights Commission of Tehuacán Valley (Comisión de Derechos Humanos y Laborales del Valle de Tehuacán) in Tehuacán, Puebla State, was released following national and international concern at his continued detention after unfounded blackmail charges against him were dropped. A month later, he and other members of the Labour Rights Commission were reportedly warned that their lives were at risk because of their human rights work.

Impunity for past abuses

As widely expected, the Special Federal Prosecutor's Office (FEMOSPP), established to secure justice for grave human rights violations committed during Mexico's "dirty war" (1960s-1980s), failed to deliver results. The military reportedly continued to show limited co-operation and the FEMOSPP did not challenge military jurisdiction, which has repeatedly assured impunity for military officials accused of serious human rights violations. Nevertheless, the Fox government stated that the work of the FEMOSPP was complete and ordered its closure in November.

In February, a draft report compiled by the historical truth unit of the FEMOSPP was leaked to an Internet website. It identified more than 700 cases of enforced disappearance, more than 100 extrajudicial executions and more than 2,000 cases of torture committed by the armed forces and security agencies during the "dirty war". In the final days of the administration, a weakened version of the report was officially circulated on the Internet, but the government failed to endorse it, publicize its findings or ensure victims and their relatives would have access to truth, justice or reparations.

◻ In November, a federal court determined on appeal that the statute of limitations had not expired on the genocide charges faced by former President, Luis Echeverría, in connection with the 1968 Tlatelolco Square massacre.

◻ In May, the prosecution of Miguel Nazar Haro, former head of the Federal Directorate of Security, and other former security officials accused of the 1976 enforced disappearance of Jesús Piedra Ibarra, was halted. In September, a judge ordered the end of Miguel Nazar Haro's house arrest as the other case against him for human rights violations committed during the 1970s collapsed.

Economic, social and cultural rights

The UN Committee on economic, social and cultural rights noted that, despite the government's efforts, 40 million people continued to live in poverty, particularly Indigenous communities and other socially disadvantaged groups.

◻ Indigenous and peasant farming communities threatened with eviction by the proposed construction of the Parota dam in Guerrero State, despite a successful legal challenge freezing its construction, continued to face intimidation.

AI country reports/ visits
Reports
- Mexico: Human rights — an unavoidable duty for candidates (AI Index: AMR 41/019/2006)
- Mexico: "How can a life be worth so little?" — Unlawful killings and impunity in the city of Reynosa (AI Index: AMR 41/027/2006)
- Mexico: Violence against women and justice denied in Mexico State (AI Index: AMR 41/028/2006)
Visits
AI delegates visited Mexico in June and November.

MOLDOVA

REPUBLIC OF MOLDOVA
Head of state: Vladimir Voronin
Head of government: Vasile Tarlev
Death penalty: abolitionist for all crimes
International Criminal Court: signed

Torture and ill-treatment were widespread and conditions in pre-trial detention were poor. A number of treaties protecting women's rights were ratified, but men, women and children continued to be trafficked for forcible sexual and other exploitation and measures to protect women against domestic violence were inadequate. Constitutional changes to abolish the death penalty were made. Freedom of expression was restricted and opposition politicians were targeted.

Torture and ill-treatment

In its report published in February, following a visit in 2004, the European Committee for the Prevention of Torture (CPT) found that torture and ill-treatment was still widespread in Moldova and that important safeguards for the prevention of torture were not observed.

The European Court of Human Rights ruled in three cases that Moldova had violated Article 3 of the European Convention on Human Rights. In one of these, the Court decided that the General Prosecutor's Office had failed to conduct an effective investigation into the torture allegations of Mihai Corsacov and, by refusing to open a case against the police officers concerned, had deprived him of an effective remedy against the ill-treatment he had suffered during his arrest in 1998. Reports of widespread torture and ill-treatment continued during the year.

◻ Vitalii Colibaba was arrested in Chişinău on 21 April, accused of injuring a policeman during a brawl. He was allegedly suspended from a crowbar and beaten on the head and neck by three police officers until he lost consciousness. Vitalii Colibaba was not granted access to a lawyer until six days after his arrest, and was allegedly beaten as a punishment when the lawyer wrote a complaint to the Prosecutor's office. A forensic examination carried out in the presence of the three officers who had allegedly tortured him found no evidence of ill-treatment. Vitalii Colibaba was released on bail in May and charges against him were still pending at the end of the year.

◻ On 18 January, the Prosecutor's office turned down a request to start criminal proceedings against police officers suspected of torturing Sergei Gurgurov in Rîscani district in Chişinău in October 2005, after he was detained in connection with the theft of a mobile phone. In April 2006, Sergei Gurgurov was again detained for violating his bail conditions, although his lawyer had explained that he was unable to attend the police station because he was undergoing medical treatment for injuries sustained when he was tortured. On 12 May, the Chişinău appeal court ruled that his detention had been illegal.

Harassment of lawyers

In June, lawyers Ana Ursachi and Roman Zadoinov, who had worked closely with AI on the cases of Vitalii Colibaba and Sergei Gurgurov, were informed that they would face criminal prosecution for spreading false information about human rights violations in Moldova and damaging the country's international image. In a letter to the Bar Association, the Prosecutor General's Office stated that the two lawyers could face prosecution under Article 335 of the Criminal Code for "misuse of official position" which carries a maximum prison sentence of five years.

Inhumane conditions in pre-trial detention centres

Reporting on its 2004 visit, the CPT described conditions in places of detention run by the Ministry of the Interior as "disastrous" and stated that in many cases the conditions amounted to inhuman or degrading treatment.

During the year AI expressed concern at conditions in the cells at the police Commissariat in Orhei. Located in the basement, they were intended to hold four detainees, but reportedly there were usually seven or more. Ventilation was poor and cells were infested with fleas and lice. Many detainees suffered from skin diseases but were rarely given access to a doctor. Toilet facilities amounted to a bucket for use in the cell in full view of others. Detainees were reportedly forced to sleep in turns, on a brick platform and without blankets, sheets or a mattress.

Violence against women

On 28 February, Moldova ratified the Optional Protocol to the UN Convention on the Elimination of All Forms of Discrimination against Women, and on 19 May it ratified the Council of Europe's Convention against Trafficking in Human Beings, the first country to do so. In February a draft law on preventing and combating violence in the family was presented to parliament. It did not provide adequate measures to protect victims or prosecute perpetrators.

In August, the UN Committee on the Elimination of Discrimination against Women considered Moldova's second and third periodic reports. It expressed concern at the level of domestic violence against women and the increasing trend of trafficking in young women and girls, and the lack of protection for victims. The Committee recommended that the draft law on preventing and combating domestic violence should be passed with some amendments.

Freedom of expression

There was concern about the apparent lack of respect by the Moldovan authorities for freedom of expression.

On 28 April, the Mayor of Chişinău refused an application by the non-governmental organization (NGO) GenderDoc-M, to hold a Gay Pride rally in Chişinău on the grounds that religious groups had announced that they would organize protest actions if the rally went ahead.

The Mayor's office in Chişinău refused permission for a demonstration demanding the erection of a statue in honour of a Romanian writer. Despite the fact that the NGO Hyde Park had been granted permission on appeal, police detained all the demonstrators for 40 hours in poor conditions in Buiucani district police station, without access to a lawyer, before releasing them and charging them with participating in an unsanctioned meeting, resisting the police, and insulting police officers. Audio recordings made on a mobile phone during the arrest did not provide evidence of such resistance. All charges were subsequently dropped.

On 4 October, the Mayor of Chişinău refused permission for AI Moldova to hold a rally against the death penalty in front of the Belarus and US embassies on 10 October. On 15 November the Supreme Court declared the Mayor's actions to be unlawful.

Opposition politicians prosecuted

Some opposition politicians appeared to be targeted for their political views.

Gheorghe Străisteanu, a former member of parliament, founder of the first private television company in Moldova and a well-known critic of government attacks on media freedoms, was detained on 21 August and charged with threatening to murder Mihai Mistreţ, the Mayor of Ţigăneşti, in connection with a local council decision to cancel the lease on land he was renting. On two occasions cups of chlorine bleach were thrown into his cell, causing him to faint. He was released under house arrest on 28 November. Gheorghe Străisteanu had previously been detained in 2005 and charged with a series of large-scale thefts from cars.

Abolition of the death penalty

On 29 June the Moldovan parliament voted unanimously to amend Clause 3 of Article 24 of the Constitution, which provided for the death penalty in exceptional cases, thus abolishing the death penalty in law. On 29 July parliament ratified Protocol 13 to the European Convention on Human Rights and the Second Optional Protocol to the International Covenant on Civil and Political Rights, aiming at the abolition of the death penalty. Parliament had voted to abolish the death penalty in 1995, with all pending death sentences commuted the following year and provisions for this punishment removed from the criminal code.

Self-proclaimed Dnestr Moldavian Republic

On 17 September the internationally unrecognized Dnestr Moldavian Republic (DMR) voted in favour of continuing the region's de facto independence from Moldova and for eventual union with the Russian Federation. Tudor Petrov-Popa and Andrei Ivanţoc remained in detention in Tiraspol, despite a July 2004 judgement by the European Court of Human Rights which found their detention to be arbitrary and in breach of the European Convention on Human Rights. They were members of the "Tiraspol Six", sentenced to prison terms in 1993 for "terrorist acts", including the murder of two DMR officials. The four men convicted with them were released in 1994, 2001 and 2004. On 10 May the Committee of Ministers of the Council of Europe adopted a fourth interim resolution in the case, asking for execution of the judgement of the European Court of Human Rights. The resolution asked Moldova to continue its efforts to secure the release of the two men and requested the Russian Federation to comply with the judgement.

AI country reports/ visits
Reports
- Europe and Central Asia: Summary of concerns in the region, January-June 2006 (AI Index: EUR 01/017/2006)
- Commonwealth of Independent States: Positive trend on the abolition of the death penalty but more needs to be done (AI Index: EUR 04/003/2006)

MONGOLIA

MONGOLIA
Head of state: Nambaryn Enkhbayar
Head of government: Miyegombiin Enkhbold (replaced Tsakhiagiin Elbegdorj in January)
Death penalty: retentionist
International Criminal Court: ratified

Secrecy surrounded the application of the death penalty. Detainees in pre-trial detention centres and police stations and those facing the death penalty were at risk of torture and ill-treatment.

Background
In January, the government headed by Tsakhiagiin Elbegdorj resigned. Corruption was prevalent and institutionalized. Mongolia ratified the UN Convention against Corruption in January and in July passed the Mongolian Anti-Corruption Law which came into force in November.

Death penalty
Executions were carried out in secret and there were no official statistics of death sentences. Detention periods of over 24 months along with the continuous use of hand and foot cuffs were reported.

Torture and ill-treatment
Torture and ill-treatment appeared to be systematic in police stations and pre-trial detention centres. There

was widespread impunity for law enforcement officials, and compensation and rehabilitation were not available to torture victims.

Detention conditions were harsh and overcrowding was typical. Prisoners were at risk of tuberculosis and faced extremes of heat and cold. Six prisoners whose death sentences were commuted served special 30-year "isolation sentences", separated from other prisoners and denied visits from families and lawyers.

There was a lack of light and fresh air and high levels of humidity and air pollution at the Gants Khudag detention centre. Prisoners suffered damaged eyesight and other health problems.

⌂ One detainee went blind after spending 300 days in Gants Khudag detention centre. He applied for compensation for damage to his eyesight resulting from his detention conditions and for compensation for his ill-treatment by prison officers. Both applications were unsuccessful.

Forced evictions
⌂ In August a number of informal "Ninja" miners were arrested and evicted for trespassing on the Ar Naimgan site of the Altan Dornod mining company. Police and military units arrested everyone without local identity cards, including women and children, and held them for over 24 hours in the police detention centre in Ogoomor soum. Over 10,000 "Ninja" miners were forcibly put on trucks and taken to isolated rural areas with no infrastructure and without access to food, water or medical services.

Environmental damage
No compensation or other reparation was offered to herdsmen who were forced to leave their land as a result of damage to their livestock and lands associated with the mining industry's use of chemical toxins. There were high levels of mercury and sodium cyanide in the Zaamar and Boroo mining areas in Toev, Selenge and Ovorkhangai provinces and much livestock was poisoned by these and other toxins.

Onggi River, which passes through Omnogovi, Ovorkhangai and Dundgovi provinces and covers a distance of 435km, dried out after 30 mining licences were granted for extraction and prospecting in the headwaters. The disappearance of the river left at least 57,000 people in the region short of drinking water. More than 80,000 cattle had to be moved to other provinces, costing each family over one million togrog (US$880).

Restriction of freedom of expression
Freedom of expression remained severely restricted. During the year, more than 40 journalists were threatened or attacked, or were harassed or investigated by the authorities. The local news media were controlled by the authorities; they were often threatened and discriminated against if they criticized the authorities. Ten journalists were reportedly arrested and their cameras and other equipment destroyed during demonstrations.

⌂ In July, B Tsevegmid, a journalist with Nomin TV, was beaten in Orkhon Aimag by unidentified people who had reportedly asked her to stop broadcasting. There was reportedly no proper investigation by the police.

◻ In April, D Arvin, a Member of Parliament, illegally removed from public distribution a newspaper containing a negative article about her. She claimed her political status authorized the action.

MONTENEGRO

MONTENEGRO
Head of state: Filip Vujanović
Head of government: Željko Šturanović, replaced Milo Djukanović in November
Death penalty: abolitionist for all crimes
International Criminal court: ratified

Montenegro declared independence from Serbia and Montenegro and was recognized as a UN member state in June. Some progress was made towards overcoming impunity for war crimes and political killings. Torture and ill-treatment by law enforcement officers were widespread.

Background
In a referendum held on 21 May, 55.4 per cent of voters were in favour of independence. Montenegro declared independence on 3 June and on 28 June was recognized as a UN member state. New defence and foreign ministers were appointed.

Negotations began in September with the European Union (EU) on the EU Stabilization and Association Agreement.

In June Montenegro formally requested membership of the Council of Europe, but a decision was delayed pending the introduction of a new constitution.

In August compulsory military service was abolished by decision of the President.

Parliamentary elections in September resulted in victory for the pro-independence government coalition led by Prime Minister Milo Djukanović, who resigned in November.

Impunity for war crimes
Progress was made in tackling impunity for crimes committed during the wars of the 1990s. On 18 May the Serbian Supreme Court confirmed the verdict handed down by Belgrade District Court in May 2005, which had convicted four members of the Bosnian Serb paramilitary group, the Avengers (Osvetnici), for the abduction and murder of 16 Montenegrin members of the Bosniak ethnic group in October 1992.

In February six former police officers were indicted for the enforced disappearance of some 83 Bosniak civilians, apparently "deported" from Montenegro to territory under Bosnian Serb control in the Republic of Bosnia and Herzegovina in 1992. Investigative proceedings did not open until September. The state prosecutor rescinded an earlier decision to stop civil cases in which relatives and survivors of enforced disappearance had petitioned the authorities for reparations.

◻ In June Podgorica District Court acknowledged that Sanin Krdžalija had been unlawfully deported to Foča in 1992. His mother and daughter were awarded damages for the emotional pain caused by his death, but their application for reparations for suffering caused by the failure of the authorities to investigate his enforced disappearance was dismissed. Courts similarly dismissed applications in five other cases.

Torture and ill-treatment
In May, following a 2005 visit to Serbia and Montenegro, the European Committee for the Prevention of Torture reported that it had received numerous allegations of torture and ill-treatment of detainees by police officers. The majority of cases reportedly occurred at the time of arrest or during the first hours of detention at police stations, apparently to extract confessions.

Abuses reported included a mock execution in which a gun was placed in a detainee's mouth. Baseball bats and garden tools associated with reports of ill-treatment were found in Bar and Budva police stations.

◻ On 9 September, 17 men of ethnic Albanian origin, including three US citizens, were arrested and reportedly racially abused, ill-treated and, in some cases, tortured by police officers, during arrest, in court and at Podgorica police station. The men were transferred to Spuž prison on 12 September and 14 of them remained in detention at the end of the year. On 7 December, 18 men, including five US citizens, were indicted for conspiracy, "terrorism" and armed insurrection. An internal investigation was opened into complaints of ill-treatment by the police lodged on behalf of seven of the men.

Suspected political killings
In August, 10 suspects were indicted in connection with the murder in August 2005 of Slavoljub Šćekić, former chief of the Montenegrin police.

In December Damir Mandić was acquitted of being an accomplice to the murder in 2004 of Duško Jovanović, editor of the newspaper *Dan*.

On 24 October, Srdjan Vojičić, a driver, was killed during an attack on author Jevrem Brković.

Denial of rights to displaced people
Some 16,545 Roma and Serbs displaced from Kosovo in 1999 remained in Montenegro. They had previously been denied access to civil, political, economic and social rights by being refused civil registration.

Violence against women
The authorities took over the funding of a shelter for victims of trafficking in January.

A draft law on Protection from Violence in the Family failed to include measures to criminalize people who violate court protection orders. Non-governmental organizations called for a co-ordination body to be established to ensure the effective application of the law.

AI country reports/ visits
Report
- Montenegro: The right to redress and reparation for the families of the "disappeared" (AI Index: EUR 66/001/2006)

MOROCCO/ WESTERN SAHARA

KINGDOM OF MOROCCO
Head of state: King Mohamed VI
Head of government: Driss Jettou
Death penalty: abolitionist in practice
International Criminal Court: signed

The government began considering recommendations made by the Equity and Reconciliation Commission in 2005, but key follow-up steps had not been undertaken by the end of 2006. Eight Sahrawi human rights defenders imprisoned in 2005 were released, but two others were detained amid continuing protests against Moroccan rule in Western Sahara. Some 200 suspected Islamist activists were arrested and charged, and in some cases convicted, many on the basis of a vague definition of terrorism. Two were sentenced to death. Over 500 members of the unauthorized Islamist group, Al-Adl wal-Ihsan (Justice and Charity), were charged with offences such as belonging to an unauthorized association after the group launched a recruitment campaign. Unlawful expulsions of refugees, asylum-seekers and migrants continued, during which some were allegedly sexually abused by security force personnel.

Background
A 5,000-strong community police unit created in 2004, the Urban Security Groups, was disbanded in October after accusations of brutality, particularly when breaking up demonstrations and making arrests. Beatings by its officers allegedly caused the deaths of several people, including Hamdi Lembarki and Adel Zayati in 2005 and Abdelghafour Haddad in 2006.

The deadlock in attempts to resolve the dispute between Morocco and the Polisario Front over Western Sahara continued to form the backdrop of demonstrations by Sahrawis against Moroccan administration of the territory. The Polisario Front calls for an independent state in Western Sahara and runs a self-proclaimed government-in-exile in refugee camps in south-western Algeria.

Equity and Reconciliation Commission
In January, King Mohamed VI gave a speech to mark the publication of the final report of the Equity and Reconciliation Commission, which in November 2005 finished its investigations into grave human rights violations committed between 1956 and 1999, particularly cases of enforced disappearance and arbitrary detention. He expressed his sympathy for the victims of the violations, but stopped short of offering an apology.

The King instructed the national human rights institution, the Human Rights Advisory Board, to follow up the work of the Commission. In June, Prime Minister Driss Jettou set up joint working committees comprising government officials and former members of the Commission to examine the Commission's recommendations, particularly on reparations and institutional and legal reforms. The Board began informing victims and their families of the results of research into 742 cases of enforced disappearance that it said it had resolved. It continued the Commission's research into 66 unresolved cases. The Board said that a detailed list of the enforced disappearance cases examined by the Commission would be published in mid-2006, but this had not happened by the end of the year. No progress was made on providing victims with effective access to justice and holding accountable individual perpetrators, issues not addressed by the Commission.

Arrests and trials of Sahrawis
Eight Sahrawi human rights defenders imprisoned in 2005 for involvement in protests against the Moroccan administration of Western Sahara were released following royal pardons in March and April. Some 70 others arrested during or after demonstrations in the territory in 2005 and 2006 and charged with violent conduct were also freed. In February the Justice Ministry stated that the human rights defenders had been imprisoned for their involvement in criminal acts, not for their views. However, AI considered them likely to be prisoners of conscience, targeted for exposing abuses by Moroccan security forces and publicly advocating self-determination for the Sahrawi people.

Demonstrations by Sahrawis against Moroccan rule continued into 2006. Hundreds of people were reportedly arrested. The vast majority were released after questioning by the police. Some 20 were later convicted and sentenced to up to six years in prison for inciting or participating in violence. At least 10 demonstrators alleged that they were tortured or ill-treated during questioning in police custody. Sahrawi human rights activists continued to be the subject of intimidation by the security forces.

◻ Brahim Sabbar, Secretary-General of the Sahrawi Association of Victims of Grave Human Rights Violations Committed by the Moroccan State, was sentenced after an unfair trial to two years' imprisonment in June for assaulting and disobeying a police officer. In May, his association had published a report detailing dozens of recent allegations of arbitrary arrest and torture or ill-treatment. Brahim Sabbar and his colleague Ahmed Sbai were awaiting another trial on separate charges that included belonging to an unauthorized association and inciting violent protests. Both were possible prisoners of conscience.

A mission of the Office of the UN High Commissioner for Human Rights visited Western Sahara in May. Its leaked confidential report concluded that the human rights situation there was of serious concern, and that Sahrawi people were denied their right to self-determination and were severely restricted from exercising other rights, including the rights to express their views, create associations and hold assemblies.

Abuses in the 'war on terror'
Some 200 suspected Islamist activists, including at least nine members of the police and military, were arrested and charged with offences that included preparing terrorist activities, belonging to terrorist groups and undermining state security. Two were tried and sentenced to death, while at least 50 received prison terms of up to 30 years on the basis of a broad and unspecific definition of terrorism.

Some 300 suspected Islamist prisoners, many sentenced on terrorist charges following bomb attacks in Casablanca in May 2003, staged a month long hunger strike in May to demand their release or a judicial review of their trials. Many had been convicted after trials that breached international fair trial standards. Dozens of them alleged that they had been tortured in previous years during questioning by the security forces.

Four Moroccan nationals were transferred from US custody in Guantánamo Bay, Cuba, to Morocco in February and October. Three were tried and convicted in November. One of them was sentenced to five years' imprisonment for setting up a "criminal gang", among other charges, and was held in custody. The other two received three-year prison sentences for forging official documents, but remained at liberty pending appeals. The fourth returnee faced charges of belonging to a terrorist organization, among other offences. Five other former Guantánamo detainees, who were returned to Morocco in 2004, were on trial on similar charges. The authorities categorically denied foreign media reports that the USA planned to build a secret detention centre in Morocco.

Arrests and trials of Al-Adl wal-Ihsan activists
Over 3,000 members of Al-Adl wal-Ihsan were reportedly questioned by the police after the group launched a recruitment campaign in April, with members opening their homes to the public to present the group's literature. The vast majority were released without charge after questioning. Over 500 were reportedly charged with offences that included participating in unauthorized meetings or assemblies, and belonging to an unauthorized association.

◻ The house of one of the group's leaders, Mohamed Abbadi, was sealed after the authorities accused him of holding illegal meetings there. In October, he and three other members of the group were sentenced to one year in prison for breaking the seals, but remained at liberty pending appeal.

Other members were prosecuted and sentenced to suspended prison sentences or fines, or were awaiting trial at the end of the year.

◻ A trial against the group's spokesperson, Nadia Yassine, was ongoing at the end of the year. In a 2005 interview with the newspaper *Al Ousbouiya Al Jadida* she said that she believed that the monarchy was not appropriate for Morocco. She was charged, along with two journalists from the newspaper, with defamation of the monarchy.

Refugees and migrants
In July, three migrants died as they tried to scale the fence between Morocco and the Spanish enclave of Melilla. One fell onto the Spanish side of the border, reportedly dying from gunshot wounds. The other two died after reportedly falling from the fence into Moroccan territory. Witnesses alleged that Moroccan security forces shot in the direction of the migrants. No results were announced of the official investigations into the 2005 deaths of migrants at the borders with the Spanish enclaves of Ceuta and Melilla.

Thousands of people suspected of being irregular migrants, including minors, were arrested by the Moroccan authorities and expelled to Algeria and, to a lesser extent, Mauritania. They reportedly included dozens of refugees or asylum-seekers. Those arrested were generally expelled shortly after their arrest, without the chance to appeal against the decision to deport them or to examine the grounds on which the decision was taken, despite these rights being guaranteed by Moroccan law. They were often left without adequate food and water. One of a group of 53 migrants expelled to the border between Western Sahara and Mauritania by the Moroccan authorities and left without food or water was reported in August to have died of dehydration.

◻ In late December hundreds of foreign nationals were arrested and expelled to the border with Algeria following raids in several cities. At least 10 recognized refugees and 60 asylum-seekers registered with the UNHCR, the UN refugee agency, in Rabat were reportedly among them. Several deportees alleged that they had been subjected to sexual abuse or robbed by security force personnel in Algeria and Morocco.

Women's rights
The Justice Ministry said in June that Morocco planned to lift reservations it had made when ratifying the Convention on the Elimination of All Forms of Discrimination Against Women.

The UN Committee on Economic, Social and Cultural Rights examined Morocco's record on these rights in May. It welcomed recent legislative reforms to improve the status of women, but expressed concern that Moroccan legislation still contained "some discriminatory provisions, particularly with regard to inheritance and criminal matters". It acknowledged Morocco's efforts to combat domestic violence, but noted with concern that the Criminal Code contained no specific provision making domestic violence a punishable offence.

Polisario camps
A mission of the Office of the UN High Commissioner for Human Rights visited the refugee camps in Tindouf in south-western Algeria in May. Its leaked confidential report recommended closer monitoring of the human rights situation in the camps.

Those responsible for human rights abuses in the camps in previous years continued to enjoy impunity. The Polisario Front took no steps to address this legacy.

AI country reports/visits
Report
- Spain/Morocco: Failure to protect the rights of migrants – Ceuta and Melilla one year on (AI Index: EUR 41/009/2006)

Visit
An AI delegate visited Morocco in July to participate in a conference on transitional justice in Rabat and to meet local human rights organizations.

MOZAMBIQUE

REPUBLIC OF MOZAMBIQUE
Head of state: Armando Guebuza
Head of government: Luisa Diogo
Death penalty: abolitionist for all crimes
International Criminal Court: signed

There were reports of extrajudicial executions of prisoners and criminal suspects by the police. Ten police officers were sentenced to between three and 10 years' imprisonment for carrying out extrajudicial executions. Clashes between the ruling and main opposition parties resulted in eight people being injured and the arrest of at least five members of the Mozambique National Resistance (Resistencia Nacional Moçambicana, Renamo). Restrictions on freedom of the press remained and three journalists were unlawfully held in detention for a week.

Background
Mozambique ratified the African Union Convention on Preventing and Combating Corruption and the UN Convention against Transnational Organized Crime and its three protocols: the Protocol against the Illicit Manufacturing of and Trafficking in Firearms, Their Parts and Components and Ammunition; the Protocol to Prevent, Suppress and Punish Trafficking in Persons, Especially Women and Children; and the Protocol against the Smuggling of Migrants by Land, Sea and Air.

Efforts to combat crime continued to be hindered by the deaths of police officers from AIDS-related illnesses. In March the police authorities reportedly began to demand HIV tests from potential new recruits, in contravention of the country's Constitution. To mitigate the shortage and the difficulties in recruiting new officers, the authorities decided to start recruiting new officers from the Armed Forces training centres.

A fund to help the fight against HIV/AIDS was set up by the government and seven funding agencies, aiming at providing anti-retroviral drugs to 50,000 people. Statistics put the rate of HIV infection at 16.1 per cent of the 15 to 49-year age group.

Incidents of domestic violence increased, with 3,000 cases reported between May and October.

Unlawful killings
There were several reports of unlawful killings and other human rights violations by police officers and a member of the Presidential Guard. However, most of the incidents were not investigated and only a few officers were arrested or demoted. None had been tried by the end of the year. Some police officers were prosecuted for human rights violations committed in previous years.

In May, police officers shot dead several prisoners as they tried to escape from Maputo Central Prison by climbing over the prison walls. Eyewitnesses reported that police officers clubbed and shot at the escaping prisoners and killed some after they were recaptured. Following the escape, the Maputo Central Prison temporarily banned visits from relatives and human rights organizations. However the Mozambican Human Rights League (Liga Moçambicana dos Direitos Humanos) was eventually given access to the prison and stated that three prisoners were killed during the break-out and at least 10 were seriously injured. Those who were captured after the attempted breakout were reportedly put in disciplinary cells and tortured. By October the situation in the prison had reportedly returned to normal with prisoners being allowed to receive visitors.

▢ In January, a police officer shot dead 21-year-old Julêncio Gove when he went to the rescue of a woman who was being beaten by another police officer in a street in Matola, Maputo province. After shooting him, the officer reportedly kicked the body several times. The police officer was subsequently arrested following several demonstrations by local people. However, he was not known to have been tried by the end of the year.

▢ A member of the Presidential Guard shot dead Abdul Monteiro in June after he accidentally damaged a car belonging to the Office of the President. Three members of the Presidential Guard chased Abdul Monteiro and shot at the tyres of his car, bringing it to a halt. After he surrendered, the officers reportedly shot him in the leg, beat him and then shot him dead. An investigation was started and one of the officers was arrested. He had not been brought to justice by the end of the year.

Ten police officers charged in 2005 with assault and extrajudicial execution of suspected criminals, extortion and theft, were sentenced in October to between three and 10 years' imprisonment in Manica province. Two of the officers were sentenced in their absence, as they had absconded, while three were acquitted and one died before the end of the trial.

Political violence

In May, eight people were seriously injured in clashes between supporters of the ruling Front for the Liberation of Mozambique (Frente da Libertação de Moçambique, Frelimo) and Renamo members in Inhangoma, Tete province, during the visit of Renamo's Secretary General to the area. Five Renamo members were subsequently arrested and reportedly convicted for excessive self-defence. However, the convicted men were reportedly not even present when the incident occurred. They were sentenced to between eight and 20 months' imprisonment.

The 20 Renamo members arrested in September 2005 following violence over alleged election rigging in the town of Mocímboa da Praia, Cabo Delgado province, were released pending trial in October 2006. The trial had still not taken place by the end of the year.

MYANMAR

UNION OF MYANMAR
Head of state: Senior General Than Shwe
Head of government: General Soe Win
Death penalty: abolitionist in practice
International Criminal Court: not ratified

The human rights situation deteriorated during the year, as the authorities stepped up repression against both armed and peaceful political opposition throughout the country. The UN Security Council placed Myanmar on its formal agenda. Widespread and systematic violations of international human rights and humanitarian law, amounting to possible crimes against humanity, were committed in the course of military activities in Kayin State and Bago Division. As the authorities continued with plans to draft a new Constitution, activists were pressured into resigning from political parties. Scores of arrests continued throughout the year of people engaged in peaceful political activities or other non-violent exercise of the right to freedom of expression and association. At the year end most senior opposition figures were imprisoned or administratively detained, among more than 1,185 political prisoners held in deteriorating prison conditions. At least two people were sentenced to death.

Background
The National Convention to draft principles for a new Constitution concluded a session in January and reconvened in October, without the National League for Democracy (NLD), the main opposition party. Legislation criminalizing adverse comment on the Constitution remained in place, while delegates were restricted from open discussion. The authorities announced that most decisions on the draft Constitution's principles had been made, including on areas relating to the role of the military and on citizens' rights and duties.

International developments
The UN Security Council placed Myanmar on its formal agenda in September. The UN General Assembly adopted a resolution and the UN Human Rights Council extended the mandate of the Special Rapporteur, who continued to be denied access to the country. The UN Under-Secretary-General for Political Affairs visited Myanmar in May and November.

Members of the Association of South East Asian Nations (ASEAN) expressed dissatisfaction with the slow pace of reforms in Myanmar and renewed calls for the release of political prisoners. The International Labour Organization (ILO) expressed grave concern at the lack of progress by the authorities on forced labour. The European Commission initiated a new humanitarian aid programme to treat HIV/AIDS, tuberculosis and malaria.

Crimes against humanity

Military operations against the Karen National Union (KNU) in eastern Kayin (Karen) State and neighbouring districts increased. More than 16,000 were displaced by the conflict. Villagers reported widespread and systematic commission of acts constituting violations of international humanitarian and human rights law on a scale that amounted to crimes against humanity. Destruction of houses and crops, enforced disappearances, forced labour, torture and extrajudicial killings of Karen civilians increased. Many villagers faced food shortages after the authorities banned them from leaving their village to farm or buy food. The use of land mines by both the armed wing of the Karen National Union and the *tatmadaw* (Myanmar army) also increased. Other violations included acts of collective punishment, such as prolonged closures and other movement restrictions, the burning of whole villages and the reported killing in February in northern Kayin state of a village headman and other civilians. In other areas skirmishes took place between the Shan State Army–South and the army, with the loss of civilian life.

Forced labour

The widespread practice of forced labour was reported throughout the year in Kayin, Mon, Rakhine and Kachin states, and in Bago Division. Prisoners were reported to have increasingly been required to act as porters for the military, and to have been subjected to torture and other forms of ill-treatment. A number of prisoner porters attempting to escape were reportedly killed. The ILO expressed concern that the authorities' continued threats of legal action against people making "false" complaints of forced labour presented a significant obstacle to joint co-operation in addressing the issue. In response to specific requests by the ILO, by the end of the year the authorities had released two people imprisoned in connection with the legal filing of reports of forced labour and dropped prosecutions of others. A six-month moratorium on the prosecution of those making complaints about forced labour was promised in July.

Political imprisonment

Political trials were conducted according to laws which criminalized the peaceful exercise of human rights and in proceedings which did not meet international fair trial standards. Arrests took place without warrants and defendants were denied the right to legal counsel or counsel of their choice. Detainees were held incommunicado for lengthy periods.

▢ Former student leaders and prisoners of conscience Htay Kywe, Ko Ko Gyi, Paw U Tun, Min Zeya and Pyone Cho were detained in late September and held incommunicado until the end of the year. The authorities stated that this was to "prevent insurgency".

▢ U Aung Thein, 77, a member of the NLD's Central Committee, was arrested with three others in April; all four were sentenced in July to 20 years' imprisonment. U Aung Thein was said to have "confessed" to possessing a satellite telephone used to speak to NLD leaders outside the country.

▢ Win Ko, an NLD member from Bago Division, was reported to have been sentenced to three years' imprisonment in October for collecting signatures calling for the release of detained political leaders. He was charged with selling illegal lottery tickets.

▢ Refugees Chit Thein Tun and Maung Maung Oo were abducted from India to Myanmar by an unknown armed group. They were handed over to the Myanmar authorities and tortured while held incommunicado. They were sentenced to death in a secret trial on charges of exploding a bomb on the Myanmar-India border.

Prisoners of conscience and senior NLD leaders Daw Aung San Suu Kyi, U Tin Oo, Daw May Win Myint, and Dr Than Nyein, all held without charge or trial, had their detention extended by the maximum term of one year. The latter two have been held since October 1997, and were detained beyond the expiry of their seven-year prison sentence. Daw Aung San Suu Kyi was held in increasing isolation and permitted only infrequent visits by her doctor.

Releases

A number of releases took place during 2006.

▢ Two human rights defenders, lawyer U Aye Myint and Su Su Nwe, imprisoned in October 2005 for seven years and 18 months respectively in connection with reporting forced labour and land confiscation by the local authorities, were released in June and July.

▢ U Shwe Ohn, a senior Shan political figure and writer in his 80s, was released from house arrest after the expiry of his detention order in February.

▢ At least two members of the KNU detained since the early 1980s, who were in poor health, were released in September and October.

Prison conditions

Already poor prison conditions deteriorated during the year. The authorities imposed new restrictions on the quantity of food that prisoners were able to receive from relatives, and reduced the budget for food granted to prison authorities. Medical shortages in prisons were reported. Visits by the International Committee of the Red Cross (ICRC) were suspended in January after the ICRC refused to accede to conditions that they be accompanied by members of government affiliated agencies. Partly as a result of poor prison conditions, many prisoners of conscience were in poor health including Dr Than Nyein, a doctor and NLD MP-elect, suffering from liver disease and other complaints.

Torture and other ill-treatment

Torture and other forms of ill-treatment during interrogation and pre-trial detention were frequently reported. Torture in prison was believed to have increased. Attempts by relatives to seek redress were met with official resistance, harassment and pressure to withdraw complaints.

▢ Ko Thet Naing Oo, a former political prisoner, was severely beaten by police and fire brigade officers in Yangon in March and died the same day.

Deaths in custody

At least six political prisoners died in prison. Torture, poor diet and inadequate medical treatment were believed to have contributed to their deaths. Many had been held in prisons distant from their families, depriving them of necessary food and medicine.

□ Thet Win Aung, 35, a student activist and prisoner of conscience, died in Mandalay Prison in October. He had been tortured on arrest in 1998, and was serving a 59-year prison sentence. He had suffered numerous health complaints in prison, including malaria and mental illness, and had been held for protracted periods in solitary confinement.

Freedom of expression, peaceful assembly and association

Legislation restricting the peaceful exercise of the right to freedom of expression, peaceful assembly and association continued to be rigorously enforced. Access to the Internet remained restricted. The government blocked many websites and placed periodic blocks on free internet e-mail services.

From April members and supporters of both the NLD and the Shan Nationalities League for Democracy were subjected to threats and harassment. Meetings were disrupted, and the state-run press regularly denounced and threatened the NLD, accusing it of plotting to incite unrest in the country. By the end of the year hundreds of NLD members were reported by the official press to have resigned.

AI country reports/ visits
Statements

- Myanmar: Human rights violations continue in the name of national security (AI Index: ASA 16/002/2006)
- Myanmar: The UN Security Council must act (AI Index: ASA 16/007/2006)
- Myanmar: Ko Thet Win Aung, prisoner of conscience, dies in prison (AI Index ASA 16/015/2006)

NAMIBIA

REPUBLIC OF NAMIBIA
Head of state and government: Hifikepunye Pohamba
Death penalty: abolitionist for all crimes
International Criminal Court: ratified

Civil society organizations expressed alarm at the high level of violence against women and children. The ruling South West African Peoples' Organisation (SWAPO) party refused to discuss abuses committed at its camps before independence. Little progress was made concerning an investigation into several mass graves near the Angolan border. Suspects detained in connection with a separatist attack in the Caprivi region in 1999 spent their seventh year in jail as their trial entered its third year.

Background

A cabinet committee appointed to deal with mass graves from the 1966-89 liberation war had not taken a decision on the matter by end of 2006. An opposition call to debate the imprisonment and torture of hundreds of SWAPO members in SWAPO camps in Angola before independence was rejected by the ruling party in October. SWAPO used its parliamentary majority to dismiss the Congress of Democrats' motion before it could be debated, claiming that such a discussion could undermine the policy of national reconciliation.

Violence against women and children

In October the Legal Assistance Centre (LAC) released figures showing that the number of reported rapes more than doubled between independence in 1990 and 2005. Civil society organizations termed the high level of child rapes a "national emergency" and called for increased education and reform of the police and justice system.

Freedom of expression

The UN Special Rapporteur on the promotion and protection of the right to freedom of opinion and expression wrote to the government in August requesting clarity about threatening remarks made by the President of SWAPO and Namibia's former President Sam Nujoma in reaction to demands for compensation from former combatants. Human rights activists attending a SWAPO rally in Katutura on 30 July reported that the former President had made death threats against two female war veterans – Ruusa Malulu, chairperson of the National Committee on the Welfare of Ex-Combatants, and Lapaka Ueyulu, a radio announcer.

Action on corruption

The government established an Anti-Corruption Commission in February. Despite criticisms that it was under-resourced, the Commission started to make arrests and several cases involving lower to middle ranking government officials were before the courts.

Caprivi detainees

The trial of 119 people charged with involvement in the 1999 separatist attacks in the Caprivi region entered its third year. Most of the accused had been detained for seven years. Police officers accused of torturing suspects detained in the wake of the attacks had not been subject to any formal charges or disciplinary action.

In September the government outlawed the United Democratic Party, which supports secession for the Caprivi region. The party is the political wing of the Caprivi Liberation Army, which launched the attack on the town of Katima Mulilo in the north-eastern region in 1999.

Access to AIDS treatment

In December 2006 President Pohamba told a World AIDS Day gathering that 22,000 AIDS patients were receiving anti-retroviral drugs, while about 50,000 Namibians were estimated to be in need of anti-retroviral treatment.

NEPAL

NEPAL
Head of state: King Gyanendra Bir Bikram Shah Dev
Head of government: Girija Prasad Koirala (replaced King Gyanendra Bir Bikram Shah Dev in April)
Death penalty: abolitionist for all crimes
International Criminal Court: not ratified

The political transition, cessation of hostilities and relaunching of a peace process following popular protests in April led to major improvements in the human rights situation and raised expectations that long-standing issues, such as caste-, ethnic- and gender-based discrimination, would be addressed. The new coalition government and the armed opposition Communist Party of Nepal (CPN) (Maoist) pledged their commitment to human rights in a series of agreements, culminating in the Comprehensive Peace Agreement signed in November. Key challenges remained, including holding both parties to their promises and ensuring accountability for past human rights violations and abuses.

Background

The year began with growing opposition to the rule of King Gyanendra, who seized executive authority in February 2005 and imposed increasingly severe restrictions on freedoms of assembly, association and expression. More than 3,000 people were detained between mid-January and mid-February for involvement in political demonstrations, including senior political leaders and prominent peace activists. Police used excessive force against demonstrators and ill-treated activists in custody.

A renewed protest movement gathered strength in April, known as the People's Movement (Jana Andolan). The demonstrations, initiated by the coalition of major political parties known as the Seven Party Alliance (SPA), eventually included a broad cross-section of the population and also had the backing of the CPN (Maoist).

The royal government again imposed undue restrictions on freedoms of assembly and expression and the security forces used excessive force in efforts to suppress the protests. The security forces used batons, live and rubber bullets and tear gas canisters, fired at close range, to control the crowds, resulting in the deaths of at least 18 people and injuries to more than 4,000. Hundreds of peaceful political and civil society activists were among those arrested.

On 24 April, King Gyanendra announced the reinstatement of the House of Representatives. Nepali Congress leader Girija Prasad Koirala was appointed Prime Minister, heading an SPA coalition government. Within days, the House convened for the first time since 2002 and endorsed a proposal to hold elections for a constituent assembly to rewrite the country's 1990 Constitution and decide the fate of the monarchy.

The CPN (Maoist) announced a three-month ceasefire on 26 April. The SPA government reciprocated with an indefinite ceasefire on 3 May. Negotiations, starting on 26 May, resulted in a series of agreements that paved the way for the Comprehensive Peace Agreement signed on 21 November. The Peace Agreement ended Nepal's decade-long armed conflict and included provisions on political, social and economic transformation. It committed both parties to the establishment of an interim government, including representatives from the CPN (Maoist), and to constituent assembly elections by mid-June 2007.

An agreement in late November established procedures to ensure that CPN (Maoist) combatants would be confined to temporary camps and lock their weapons under UN supervision while the Nepal Army would remain in barracks and store an equal number of arms.

Both parties requested the UN to provide assistance in election observation and continued human rights monitoring.

Peace process and human rights

All the agreements signed in the course of the talks included human rights commitments. However, many of the pledges were vaguely worded and few had been fully implemented by the end of the year.

In May the SPA government and the CPN (Maoist) agreed a Code of Conduct for the ceasefire. By mid-November, the National Monitoring Committee established to oversee compliance said it had found violations of the Code of Conduct in 913 cases out of 1,425 complaints, but no further action was taken and the Committee was dissolved at the end of that month.

The role of Nepal's National Human Rights Commission (NHRC) remained unclear. The NHRC's reputation for independence was damaged in 2005, when new Commissioners were appointed by the King. In July, the Chairperson and Commissioners resigned; new appointments had not been made by the year's end.

The Peace Agreement signed on 21 November contained significant human rights commitments, including an end to impunity for human rights abuses and guarantees of the rights to food, health and education. It provided for a Truth and Reconciliation Commission to investigate "serious violations of human rights and crimes against humanity" committed during the armed conflict and a National Peace and Rehabilitation Commission to provide assistance to conflict victims. The Peace Agreement also included pledges to publicize the whereabouts of victims of enforced disappearances within 60 days and to create an environment conducive to the return of internally displaced people.

Marginalized groups were under-represented in the peace process. Neither the SPA government nor the CPN (Maoist) leadership included women in their peace talk teams. The 31-member National Monitoring Committee included only two women, and a six-member, all-male Interim Constitution Drafting Committee was expanded to include four women and a Dalit representative only after widespread protests.

Abuses by the CPN (Maoist)

Despite the CPN (Maoist)'s public commitments to respect international human rights standards, there were continuing reports of unlawful killings, abductions, torture and ill-treatment, extortion, threats and harassment by members of the CPN (Maoist). Investigations by the Office of the High Commissioner for Human Rights (OHCHR) in Nepal found that many of the abuses were committed in the context of the "law enforcement" activities of the CPN (Maoist) and its "people's courts". In November, the CPN (Maoist) pledged to dissolve the "people's government" and "people's courts" on the day the interim parliament was formed.

There were reports of ongoing child recruitment after the ceasefire, particularly in the days and weeks preceding the Peace Agreement. Under the Peace Agreement, both parties pledged not to use children aged 18 or below in military activities and to provide assistance for their rehabilitation.

Abuses by other armed groups

Other armed groups, in particular the anti-Maoist "village defence forces" and the Terai Janatantrik Mukti Morcha (TJMM), were responsible for human rights abuses, including unlawful killings and abductions. In July, the CPN (Maoist) declared "war" against the TJMM, a splinter group advocating self-determination for the Madhesi people of the southern Terai region. By the year's end, there had been no systematic effort to disarm the village defence forces, which had gained strength in 2005 with the support of the security forces.

Human rights violations by the security forces

The security forces were responsible for unlawful killings, enforced disappearances, arbitrary arrests and detentions, and the widespread use of torture, including rape, in the context of the decade-long conflict. The army regularly resorted to indiscriminate or disproportionate attacks in its battles with the CPN (Maoist), resulting in the deaths of civilians and damage to homes, schools and other civilian objects.

Throughout 2005 and early 2006, the King increasingly used the security forces to control peaceful political opposition. The Nepal Police (NP), Armed Police Force (APF) and the Royal Nepalese Army (renamed the Nepal Army in May) were deployed to curb political demonstrations in early 2006 and were all responsible for the use of excessive force, according to OHCHR investigations. The NP and APF arbitrarily detained thousands of people during the demonstrations.

With the cessation of hostilities in May, conflict-related violations ended almost completely. The Army Bill adopted by the parliament in September contained provisions to bring the army under civilian control but did not adequately address concerns regarding jurisdiction for violations of human rights and humanitarian law committed by the military.

Accountability

Measures to address past violations and abuses were inadequate.

In May, the SPA government appointed a Commission of Inquiry chaired by a former Supreme Court judge to investigate human rights violations committed in the context of suppressing the People's Movement. The Commission delivered its report to the SPA government in November but its findings were not made public. The Commission reportedly recommended action against more than 200 people, including King Gyanendra, senior ministers and security officials. The SPA government formed a committee to study the report.

In early June, the Home Ministry established a one-person Disappearances Committee without the capacity to investigate the hundreds of unresolved cases of enforced disappearance.

Authorities were reluctant to proceed with criminal investigations into past human rights violations, even when presented with detailed reports by local human rights defenders and the OHCHR. Neither the security forces nor the CPN (Maoist) took concrete steps to strengthen accountability within their ranks.

Women's rights

Violence against women was not widely recognized as a human rights issue. Gender-based violence was under-reported, partly due to fear of retaliation and to the scarcity of shelter and other support services. Widows and single women were particularly at risk of violence and harassment.

Many women human rights defenders believed that the political transition presented an opportunity to secure more equitable representation in government and press for legal reform. Lawyers estimated that there were at least 118 discriminatory provisions contained in 54 different laws, including the 1990 Constitution.

Internally displaced people
Between 100,000 and 250,000 people were displaced during the conflict. Following the cessation of hostilities in May, some internally displaced people (IDPs) began to return to their communities, but prevailing security concerns discouraged large-scale returns. Despite the repeated commitments of both parties to ensure the safe return of IDPs, there were no comprehensive policies to provide necessary assistance and protection.

Bhutanese refugees
Toward the end of 2006, there were moves to resolve the plight of around 106,000 Bhutanese refugees living in camps in south-eastern Nepal after their forced expulsion from Bhutan in the early 1990s. The SPA government attempted to reopen talks with the government of Bhutan, suspended since 2003. In October, the USA offered to resettle up to 60,000 refugees and other countries said they would provide resettlement. Refugees were reportedly divided about the offers, with some fearing that accepting resettlement would end all hopes for repatriation to Bhutan and legitimize "ethnic cleansing".

AI country reports/ visits
Visits
AI delegates visited Nepal in February, March and December.

NETHERLANDS

KINGDOM OF THE NETHERLANDS
Head of state: Queen Beatrix
Head of government: Jan Peter Balkenende
Death penalty: abolitionist for all crimes
International Criminal Court: ratified

New legislation increased the length of time people charged with terrorism offences could be detained pending trial. Reports of ill-treatment of Iraqi detainees by military personnel in 2003, which disclosed war crimes allegations, emerged.

War crimes allegations
After allegations emerged that Dutch Military Intelligence personnel had ill-treated several detainees in Al-Muthana province in Iraq in 2003, the Minister of Defence confirmed in November that an independent committee would examine the interrogation methods used by the Military Intelligence and Security Services in Iraq at that time, including the use of ski goggles, loud music or noise, and water. The Ministry of Defence subsequently confirmed that these methods had been used.

It also emerged that, as early as November 2003, the Royal Military and Border Police had investigated the treatment of suspects by the Military Intelligence and Security Services, and that the prosecuting authorities concluded in 2004 that no offence had been committed. No information about the allegations or investigations had previously been provided to Parliament or the public.

The standing Review Committee on the Intelligence and Security Services announced a separate investigation.

Imprisonment following *refoulement*
In June, Syrian national 'Abd al-Rahman al-Musa was sentenced to death for membership of the Muslim Brotherhood after an unfair trial before the Syrian Supreme State Security Court. The Dutch authorities had failed to prevent his expulsion from the USA to Syria via the Netherlands in January 2005, or to allow him to exercise his right to file an asylum application despite warnings about his safety. His death sentence was immediately commuted to 12 years' imprisonment. He was reportedly held incommunicado for most of his detention, but was eventually allowed some family visits. AI considered him a prisoner of conscience, held solely for his non-violent beliefs. In May the UN Working Group on Arbitrary Detention found his detention to be arbitrary, given "the gravity of the violation of the right to a fair trial".

Terrorism
New legislation with the stated aim of countering terrorism was officially published in November, but had not entered into force by the end of 2006. It provided

for an increase in the maximum period of pre-trial detention for people charged with terrorism offences, from 104 days ⟶ a further period of up to two years, and for the prosecution not to be obliged to fully disclose evidence during this further period. Under the legislation, the detainee would have the right to periodically challenge both the detention and the decision not to disclose evidence.

In September, the government proposed measures that would make it easier to withdraw residence permits from non-nationals convicted of any crime. This could increase the number of those designated as "undesirable aliens". Non-nationals thus designated could be deported, banned from re-entry for up to 10 years, or imprisoned for up to six months if they remain in the country. If suspected of terrorism, they could be designated on the basis of secret intelligence withheld from them and their lawyers.

Deaths and detentions of migrants

Migrant children continued to be detained in accordance with unchanged government policy, although the numbers appeared to decline following nationwide protests.

In September the independent Dutch Safety Board reported on its investigation into the October 2005 fire in a temporary detention centre at Amsterdam's Schiphol airport in which 11 irregular migrants died and 15 other people were injured. The Board confirmed earlier concerns about unsafe detention conditions and found that safety recommendations had not been fully implemented, that guards lacked training and intervened inappropriately, and that other detention centres had similar deficiencies. It concluded that "there would have been fewer or no casualties if fire safety was taken more seriously by the government authorities responsible". Following publication of the report, the Ministers of Justice and Housing resigned. Their successors announced reorganization of government departments, strengthened fire safety regulations, and offered to discuss compensation for the victims. The criminal investigation into the cause of the fire continued. In April the Board criticized the Minister of Immigration for the expulsion of survivors and other witnesses before they could be interviewed. Shortly before publication of its report, most survivors still in the country were granted residence permits.

AI country reports/visits
Statement
- The Netherlands: Concerns about Schiphol fire need urgent follow up (AI Index: EUR 35/001/2006)

NEW ZEALAND

NEW ZEALAND
Head of state: Queen Elizabeth II, represented by Anand Satyanand (replaced Silvia Cartwright in August)
Head of government: Helen Clark
Death penalty status: abolitionist for all crimes
International Criminal Court: ratified

A refugee released by the Supreme Court from nearly two years' detention was still under threat of deportation on the basis of a secret security assessment. A taskforce on violence against women proposed reforms including some within the criminal justice system.

'War on terror'
The fate of Algerian refugee Ahmed Zaoui continued to hang in the balance pending review of a security assessment alleging he was a risk to New Zealand security. A senior member of Algeria's Islamic Salvation Front (*Front islamique du salut*, FIS) party, he claimed asylum on his arrival in New Zealand in December 2002, and was recognized as a refugee in August 2003. He was subsequently detained for 23 months – 10 in solitary confinement – under a security risk certificate issued by the Director of Security on the basis of intelligence information to which neither he nor his counsel have access. His appeal against the security risk certificate filed in March 2003 had still not been heard at the end of 2006.

Violence against women
In July a joint taskforce on violence against women made up of representatives from government, non-governmental agencies and the judiciary released its first report. The taskforce noted that the victims of extreme family violence in New Zealand are predominantly women and children, and launched a programme of action. Its aims included: a nationwide campaign to change attitudes to violence; changes in the justice sector to meet the needs of victims, offenders and family members; and a review of deaths resulting from family violence to gain greater understanding of how to strengthen prevention systems.

Other concerns
In September the police began a year-long trial of the Taser stun-gun despite concerns expressed by AI, other human rights groups and the Mental Health Commission.

By the end of 2006 the government had not announced steps to implement the Action Plan for Human Rights it commissioned in 2002 and formally received in March 2005.

NICARAGUA

REPUBLIC OF NICARAGUA
Head of state and government: Enrique Bolaños
Death penalty: abolitionist for all crimes
International Criminal Court: not ratified

Increasing levels of sexual and domestic violence were reported. Former agricultural workers suffering health problems as a result of the use of pesticide continued to protest at their treatment.

Background
In April, the Central America Free Trade Agreement, which includes the USA, the Dominican Republic and other Central American states, came into effect.

In October, the National Assembly approved a bill which outlawed all forms of abortion. Previously abortions had been permitted in cases where the woman's life was at risk. The President signed the bill into law in November.

Presidential and legistlative elections were held in November. The candidate of the Sandinista National Liberation Front, Daniel Ortega, won. He was due to assume the presidency in January 2007.

Violence against women
In a report submitted to the Inter-American Commission on Human Rights, national women's organizations raised concerns about increasing levels of violence against women. The inadequate response of the authorities remained a serious concern.

Economic, social and cultural rights
Poverty remained widespread with 80 per cent of the population living on less than US$2 a day, according to a 2006 report by the UN Development Programme (UNDP).

Former agricultural workers suffering health problems caused by exposure to the pesticide Nemagón protested against alleged irregularities and corruption in the way compensation had been paid to them. According to local non-governmental organizations, more than 1,383 people had died of Nemagón-related illnesses between 2003 and 2006.

Indigenous peoples
In June, Indigenous peoples complained publicly to the Inter-American Commission on Human Rights that the government was continuing to violate their rights. They alleged that Indigenous communal lands remained improperly demarcated and that the government continued to promote unregulated logging and award licences for the exploitation of natural resources without the informed consultation of Indigenous peoples living in the affected areas.

Lesbian, gay, bisexual and transgender people
The media reported homophobic comments made by the President in March. He was alleged to have ordered that a list of all members of his government "suspected" of being part of the "gay-lesbian world" be compiled so that he could dismiss them before leaving office in January 2007. Nicaragua continued to criminalize gay and lesbian relationships.

NIGER

REPUBLIC OF THE NIGER
Head of state: Mamadou Tandja
Head of government: Amadou Hama
Death penalty: abolitionist in practice
International Criminal Court: ratified

A military court sentenced more than 100 soldiers to prison terms for mutiny. Freedom of expression came under frequent attack.

Background
A coalition of workers' unions and civil society organizations, the Fairness/Equality Coalition against the High Cost of Living, organized national strikes in June and July to protest at government economic policies that increased the cost of basic utilities such as water and electricity. Talks between the government and the Coalition began but produced no outcome by the end of 2006.

Trials of military personnel
In March and in October, a military court tried more than 170 soldiers accused of staging a mutiny in August 2002 and convicted more than 100. The defendants were not permitted to choose their lawyers. One soldier was sentenced to nine years' imprisonment for attempted murder, but most were freed, having already served four years in pre-trial detention.

Freedom of expression under attack
Throughout 2006, the authorities arrested journalists covering cases of government mismanagement or other political issues. Several were sentenced to prison terms.

In September, publisher Mamane Abou and journalist Oumarou Keita of the weekly Le Républicain were sentenced to 18 months' imprisonment on charges of spreading false news and defaming the state after publishing an article accusing the Prime Minister of seeking favour with Iran. They were released on appeal in November.

Threat of mass expulsion
In October, the government announced it would expel some 100,000 Arab pastoralists from the south-east to Chad, reportedly because of rising tensions with

Indigenous communities. Following international protests, the government announced that it would instead relocate the Mahamid Arabs to more fertile pastoral regions.

AI country reports/ visits
Report
- Niger: Prisoners of conscience (AI Index: AFR 43/001/2006)

NIGERIA

FEDERAL REPUBLIC OF NIGERIA
Head of state and government: Olusegun Obasanjo
Death penalty: retentionist
International Criminal Court: ratified

Politically motivated violence increased ahead of elections scheduled for 2007. Several candidates for political office were attacked during primary elections and at least four were reported to have been killed. The security forces in the Niger Delta committed human rights violations with impunity. Violence against women, including rape by state employees, remained widespread. Human rights defenders and journalists continued to face intimidation and unlawful detention. Death sentences continued to be handed down.

Background
A proposed Constitutional amendment that would have allowed President Obasanjo to remain in office for a third term was defeated in May. However, media speculation that the President was still intent on securing a third term remained widespread.

Primary elections ahead of the 2007 elections took place amid heightened political violence. Investigations by the Economic and Financial Crimes Commission (EFCC) of 31 of Nigeria's 36 state governors and the impeachment of four state governors exacerbated political tensions. Two impeachments were overturned by the courts in December. In September Vice-President Atiku Abubakar, who opposed the third term amendment, was suspended from the ruling party because of allegations of corruption. He later confirmed he would stand for the presidency in 2007 as a candidate for the opposition Action Congress party. In December President Obasanjo instituted proceedings to replace Atiku Abubakar as Vice-President, a process which could leave him open to arrest. Atiku Abubakar instituted a legal challenge to his removal as Vice-President.

In March Liberian President Ellen Johnson-Sirleaf asked the Nigerian government to hand over former Liberian President Charles Taylor to face trial at the Special Court for Sierra Leone. Charles Taylor subsequently escaped but was recaptured by Nigerian security forces, and on 29 March was surrendered to the Special Court.

In June the Inspector General of Police inaugurated human rights desks in police stations in Lagos. However, according to human rights defenders, these mechanisms, where they existed, lacked adequate resources and were inefficient.

Death penalty
Approximately 500 prisoners were estimated to be on death row. No executions were reported. However, at least 18 death sentences were handed down during 2006.

In a report published in January, the UN Special Rapporteur on extrajudicial, summary or arbitrary executions (who visited Nigeria in 2005) highlighted three main concerns related to the death penalty. He noted widespread procedural irregularities, including the use of torture by the police to extract confessions and a lack of legal representation in capital cases. He criticized death row conditions as atrocious and stated that the average 20-year stay on death row was unacceptable. He also criticized the imposition of death by stoning for adultery or sodomy in 12 states, in contravention of Nigerian and international law.

On 1 October, 107 death row inmates reportedly had their sentences commuted to life imprisonment as part of the country's Independence Day celebrations.

Oil, injustice and violence
Human rights violations by the security forces were a frequent occurrence in the Niger Delta. Violations included extrajudicial executions, torture and destruction of homes.

2006 saw a rise in attacks on oil installations by militants in the Niger Delta. Dozens of oil workers were kidnapped. A newly emerged group—the Movement for the Emancipation of the Niger Delta (MEND)—claimed responsibility for several kidnappings as well as attacks that resulted in the deaths of more than 10 members of the security forces. The attacks in the Niger Delta resulted in oil production dropping by approximately 25 per cent.

Armed groups in the Delta were reported to be forging links with politicians ahead of elections in April 2007, leading to fears of increased violence. Local non-governmental organizations reported that dozens of people died during political violence and several primary elections were postponed as a consequence of violence.

No action was known to have been taken to bring to justice members of the security forces suspected of being responsible for grave human rights violations in Odioma in February 2005, when a raid by members of the Joint Task Force resulted in at least 17 people being killed and acts of torture, including rape of women. The report of the Judicial Commission of Inquiry established in the aftermath of the Odioma incident was not made public. Members of the security forces reportedly remained in Odioma and further human rights violations were reported in February. No subsequent reports of violations were received.

The report of the Judicial Commission of Inquiry into an incident on 4 February 2005, during which soldiers fired on protesters at Chevron's Escravos oil terminal killing one man and injuring at least 30 others, had not been made public by the end of 2006.

Extrajudicial executions

Extrajudicial executions by members of the police and security forces continued to be widespread. These included civilians being killed by police during routine road checks or for refusing to pay a bribe, shootings of suspected armed robbers on arrest, and extrajudicial executions of detainees. Despite the alarming number of such killings, the government took very little action to address the problem.

In August, 12 suspected armed robbers, including a boy under the age of 18, were reportedly extrajudicially executed by police in Abia State. The victims had been arrested during a raid in which four other suspects were killed. On 10 August Abia police displayed the suspects to journalists and other spectators. An eyewitness stated that some of the suspects appeared to have gunshot wounds. On 11 August the dead bodies of the 12 suspects were seen dumped outside the morgue at a government hospital, reportedly taken there by police. No action was taken to investigate the deaths or bring the perpetrators to justice.

Political violence

There was widespread violence linked to state and federal elections due to be held in April 2007, including political assassinations and violent clashes between supporters of different candidates during the primary elections, particularly within the ruling People's Democratic Party (PDP). The government failed to take effective action to deal with the violence or to address the role of politicians in fomenting it. Police investigations and arrests following some assassinations and political violence were criticized as politically tainted.

In August the Inspector General of Police was reported in the independent media as saying that politicians were recruiting students to engage in political violence. In the same month the Commissioner of Police of Ebonyi State claimed that a number of political candidates had reportedly started to train "thugs" in preparation for the elections. The Commissioner warned all candidates for political office to cease such activities, but no further action was reported. There were similar allegations that politicians were endorsing and encouraging political violence in several states during 2006.

On 27 July Chief Funsho Williams of the PDP, candidate for Governor in Lagos State, was killed at his home. The Inspector General of Police stated that 244 suspects were arrested in connection with his murder, including his political associates, personal aides and four policemen. By the end of the year, 209 suspects had been released for lack of evidence, while 35 remained in police custody. The specific charges against those who remained in detention were unclear.

On 14 August Dr Ayo Daramola, a candidate for Governor in Ekiti State, was fatally stabbed at his home. Police arrested eight people in connection with the murder, including an aide to the former Ekiti State Governor, Ayo Fayose, who was impeached in October in connection with an unrelated matter. One other suspect was reportedly shot evading arrest.

Violence against women

Violence against women, including domestic violence and sexual violence by state officials and private individuals, remained pervasive. Underlying factors included the entrenched culture of impunity for human rights violations committed by the police and security forces, and the authorities' consistent failure to exercise due diligence in preventing and addressing sexual violence by both state and non-state actors.

In August a Bill to incorporate the UN Women's Convention in domestic law was presented to the Senate. No further progress was made by the end of the year. The Domestic Violence and Other Related Matters Bill, which was debated by the Lagos House of Assembly, had not become law by the end of the year.

In December the Federal Government announced the introduction of a Bill on reform of discriminatory laws against women and a Bill on elimination of violence from society, which would cover all forms of violence including domestic violence.

Prisoner releases, pre-trial detention

In January the Federal Government announced an initiative aimed at speeding up the trial or unconditional release of up to 25,000 inmates out of a prison population estimated by the government at 45,000. However, no tangible results were seen by the end of the year. In November the government announced a case-by-case review of the prison population. Again, no action was evident by the end of the year.

An estimated two-thirds of all people held in prisons were awaiting trial, and the average pre-trial detention period was estimated to be at least five years, with many people detained for 10 years or more without going to trial.

Impunity

A Judicial Commission of Inquiry established to investigate the killing by police of five Igbo traders and one woman in June 2005 submitted its report to the government in August 2005. The report was published by a civic organization, the CLEEN Foundation. Eight police officers were charged with murder. The trial had not concluded by the end of the year. On 14 August the Abuja High Court granted bail to two of the accused, a Deputy Commissioner of Police and a constable.

Journalists and human rights defenders

Human rights defenders and journalists critical of the government, and in particular of President Obasanjo, continued to face intimidation and harassment.

In June Bukhari Bello was dismissed as Executive Secretary of the Nigerian National Human Rights Commission, four years before the expiry of his contract.

The termination of his tenure appeared to have been related to his comments on the repression of the media by security agencies and his criticism of the government.

⌷ On 8 November the managing editor of *The News* newspaper, Babafemi Ojudu, was detained overnight in Abuja reportedly on the orders of the Inspector General of Police. He was not formally charged, but was questioned about an allegation by a murder suspect that he had tried to generate false allegations about an impeached state governor.

⌷ On 22 December the head of the editorial board of the privately owned *Thisday* newspaper, Godwin Agbroko, was found shot to death in Lagos in suspicious circumstances.

Forced evictions

Several incidents of forced evictions were reported as well as frequent threats of forced eviction. Nigeria was named one of the three worst violators of housing rights by the Centre on Housing Rights and Evictions.

Development under the Abuja Master Plan resulted in several incidents of forced evictions. In November the Minister of the Federal Capital Territory reportedly stated that some 80 per cent of the houses demolished in Abuja city centre and its environs did not qualify for compensation because they had been built illegally.

Bill outlawing same-sex relationships

In January the Minister of Justice presented to the Federal Executive Council a Bill outlawing same-sex marriages, involvement in same-sex marriages and same-sex relationships in public or in private. The draft bill provided five years' imprisonment for any person involved in a same-sex marriage or who aided or abetted such a union. The draft bill also prohibited the registration of gay organizations. The Bill was presented to the Senate in April. No further progress on the bill had been made by the end of the year.

AI country reports/ visits

Reports
- Nigeria: Rape – the silent weapon (AI Index: AFR 44/020/2006)
- Nigeria: Oil, poverty and violence (AI Index: AFR 44/017/2006)
- Nigeria: Government interference with the independence of the National Human Rights Commission (AI Index: AFR 44/012/2006)
- Nigeria: Same Sex Bill negates Nigeria's obligations to fundamental human rights (AI Index: AFR 44/013/2006)
- Nigeria: AI statement for the public hearing on the domestic violence and related matters bill (AI Index: AFR 44/010/2006)
- Nigeria: Open Letter to President Obasanjo (AI Index: AFR 44/008/2006)
- Nigeria: Making the destitute homeless – forced evictions in Makoko, Lagos State (AI Index: AFR 44/001/2006)

Visits
AI delegates visited Nigeria in January/February and in November/December.

OMAN

SULTANATE OF OMAN
Head of state and government: Sultan Qaboos bin Said
Death penalty: retentionist
International Criminal Court: signed

Important improvements were made to the labour law but these did not apply to domestic workers, who were mostly foreign migrants and who continued to be subject to exploitation and abuse by employers. A possible prisoner of conscience was released after completing her prison sentence. At least one prisoner remained under sentence of death.

Background

In August activists were banned from staging a peaceful children's demonstration outside the UNICEF Office in Muscat against Israeli attacks on Lebanon.

In September, Oman signed a free trade agreement with the USA.

Political trials

It emerged during 2006 that at least 18 military officers had been tried in June 2005 reportedly accused of involvement in a conspiracy to overthrow the government. They were convicted and received prison sentences ranging from three to 25 years following a trial before a military court, but all were released following a royal pardon in July 2005. Some 31 civilians had been tried separately before the State Security Court (SSC) in May 2005 on charges of threatening national security, but they too were pardoned and released.

Human rights activist released

Human rights activist and former member of parliament Taiba al-Mawali was released from prison on 31 January after serving a six-month sentence. She was arrested in June 2005 and prosecuted for sending messages by mobile phone and the Internet in which she criticized the trial of 31 men before the SSC in May 2005. She received an 18-month prison term, reduced to six months on appeal. Taiba al-Mawali was a possible prisoner of conscience.

Employment rights

Amendments to the 2003 Labour Law, introduced in July by decree 74/2006, established legal rights to form trade unions, engage in collective bargaining and carry out union duties free from official pressure or interference. It also prohibited forced or coerced labour. However, domestic workers, many of whom were foreign migrants and women, were not covered by the law.

Women's rights

Oman acceded to the UN Women's Convention in February and the authorities later announced that a committee had been established to promote its implementation. However, women continued to be subject to discrimination both in national law and in practice, notably in terms of personal status, employment and participation in public life.

The UN Special Rapporteur on trafficking in persons, especially women and children, visited Oman in November. In her initial findings, the Special Rapporteur expressed concern about reports of ill-treatment and abuse of domestic workers by employers, including sleep deprivation, withholding payment of salaries, restrictions on movement and denial of access to basic communications including use of the telephone. The Special Rapporteur also found that women from Central and East Asian countries had been trafficked into Oman for prostitution.

Death penalty

At least one prisoner, Zuhair Islam Abdul Haq, a Bangladeshi national convicted of murder in 2004, was believed to be under sentence of death.

PAKISTAN

ISLAMIC REPUBLIC OF PAKISTAN
Head of state: Pervez Musharraf
Head of government: Shaukat Aziz
Death penalty: retentionist
International Criminal Court: not ratified

Scores of people suffered arbitrary detention and enforced disappearance. Victims included terror suspects, Baloch and Sindhi nationalists, and journalists. Unlawful killings were carried out with impunity. The blasphemy laws were used to persecute members of religious minorities. "Honour" killings continued to be reported. Tribal and religious councils unlawfully exercised judicial functions and enforced cruel, inhuman and degrading punishments. At least 446 people were sentenced to death. The number of executions reported, 82, including one juvenile, was a steep increase from the previous year.

Background

While the confrontation between the army and nationalist activists intensified in Balochistan province, in the tribal areas the government agreed a peace pact with tribal elders and local Taleban. The September agreement apparently allowed tribal fighters to find shelter and to set up quasi-governmental structures, collect taxes, impose their "penal code" and exercise quasi-judicial functions.

Some people were publicly executed by vigilante groups seeking to impose their own interpretation of Islamic norms. More than 100 people were killed in the tribal areas, apparently for co-operating with the government. Many decapitated bodies were found with notes warning others not to support the government.

The dialogue with India faltered when Indian police accused Pakistan of involvement in bomb blasts in Mumbai, and Pakistan accused India of supporting Baloch nationalists. It resumed towards the end of the year.

Arbitrary detention/ enforced disappearances

Scores of people suspected of links to terrorist groups, Baloch or Sindhi activists, and journalists were arbitrarily detained and subjected to enforced disappearance. State agents denied knowledge of whereabouts to relatives and when questioned in court during habeas corpus hearings. Those released reported being tortured and ill-treated.

⌒ Abdur Rahim Muslim Dost, an Afghan settled in Pakistan, and his brother were released in April 2005 from Guantánamo Bay after more than three years' detention. In September, he was arrested again in Peshawar, apparently in connection with a book recording the brothers' experiences. Habeas corpus hearings were repeatedly adjourned. In December state agencies denied holding him. His fate and whereabouts remained unknown at the end of the year.

⌒ Munir Mengal, director of the first independent Baloch-language TV channel, launched in Dubai, was arrested by intelligence agency officials on 4 April at Karachi airport. His fate and whereabouts remained unknown. Relatives were told by immigration officials that he had been taken away by Inter Services Intelligence personnel. Police refused to register a complaint. During hearings of his habeas corpus petition in July, the Sindh High Court was told by the Ministry of Defence that none of its agencies was holding him and that the Ministry had only administrative, not operational, control over these agencies and therefore could not enforce compliance with court orders.

Excessive use of force and unlawful killings

Impunity for unlawful killings of criminal suspects and political opponents of the government contributed to their increase.

⌒ In June, the body of Hayatullah Khan was found shot dead in North Waziristan. He was abducted in December 2005 after disseminating photographic evidence that a drone attack had been carried out by US forces, thereby contradicting official accounts. Officials had told relatives on several occasions that he would soon be released. The reports of two official inquiries were submitted to government but not made public.

⌒ In January between 13 and 18 people were reportedly unlawfully killed by missiles fired from US drones in the tribal areas, and in October at least 82 people died in a similar attack. In both attacks children were reportedly killed. State officials described the victims as "militants" but had made no attempts to arrest them or to stop their activities. In October, officials claimed that Pakistani helicopters alone had carried out the attack, despite eyewitnesses describing bomb explosions 20 minutes before the helicopters arrived. No investigation was carried out.

Failure to protect minorities
At least 44 registered cases of blasphemy were reported during 2006. Blasphemy cases took years to conclude. The accused were rarely released on bail and were often ill-treated in detention.

▢ Ranjha Masih was acquitted of blasphemy in November by the Lahore High Court for lack of evidence. He was sentenced to life imprisonment in 2003 after being arrested during the funeral in 1998 of a Catholic bishop who committed suicide to protest at the targeting of Christians.

Violence against women
"Honour" killings, domestic violence including maiming and harmful traditional practises continued at a high level. Jirgas, councils of elders, which the Sindh High Court had banned in 2004, continued to "sentence" girls and women to cruel punishments.

▢ In Mardan and Swabi districts, 60 girls and women were handed over to their families' opponents to settle conflicts and as compensation for murder in three months in mid-2006.

In November, parliament passed an amendment to the Hadood Laws which continued to criminalize heterosexual consensual sex outside marriage, but provided that complaints of sex outside marriage should be investigated by a court to establish admissibility before formal charges are laid. Under the Zina Ordinance, police had frequently arrested couples deemed not lawfully married by their relatives and charged them with fornication. The new law also banned charging a woman with fornication if she had complained of being raped but was unable to prove absence of consent.

A presidential ordinance to allow bail for women undergoing trial for all offences except murder, corruption and terrorism was introduced. Some 1,300 women held on fornication charges were released on bail.

Children's rights
The appeal against the Lahore High Court judgement of December 2004 which declared the Juvenile Justice System Ordinance (JJSO) unconstitutional, remained pending. The temporarily reinstated JJSO continued to be poorly implemented as many areas remained without parole officers and the number of juvenile courts remained insufficient and in some areas there were none. Juveniles continued to be tried with adults.

Death penalty
Some 446 people were sentenced to death, mostly for murder. Eighty-two people were executed, mostly in Punjab province.

▢ Mutabar Khan, believed to be 16 at the time of an alleged murder in 1996, was executed in Peshawar Central Prison in June 2006. He did not benefit from the Presidential Commutation Order of 2001, which overturned the death sentences of all juveniles then on death row, as he could not prove his age. The family of the murder victim had earlier agreed to pardon him in return for compensation, but later retracted the pardon.

▢ In November, President Musharraf commuted the death sentence of Mirza Tahir Hussain after his execution date had been postponed several times. He had been sentenced to death in 1998 for murder and robbery. Different courts had reached divergent judgements in this case, ranging from acquittal to the death penalty.

Earthquake relief
International relief agencies said that many reconstruction programmes faced funding deficits and delays due to administrative difficulties and lack of information about victims' needs. The earthquake in October 2005 killed almost 73,000 people and rendered more than 3.5 million homeless.

AI country reports/visits
Reports
- Pakistan: Unlawful executions in the tribal areas (AI Index: ASA 33/013/2006)
- Pakistan: Human rights ignored in the "war on terror" (AI Index: ASA 33/036/2006)
- Pakistan: Working to stop human rights violations in the "war on terror" (AI Index: ASA 33/051/2006)
Visits
AI delegates attended the World Social Forum in March, and held a workshop on enforced disappearances jointly with the non-governmental Human Rights Commission of Pakistan in Islamabad in September. The government denied responsibility for widespread enforced disappearances documented by AI; President Musharraf described the report as "nonsense" to which he did not wish to respond.

PALESTINIAN AUTHORITY

President: Mahmoud Abbas
Prime Minister: Isma'il Haniyeh (replaced Ahmad Quray in March)
Death penalty: retentionist

Palestinians in the Occupied Palestinian Territories (OPT) suffered wide-ranging human rights abuses and humanitarian conditions deteriorated significantly due to military and punitive economic actions by Israel, cuts in international aid and growing violence between rival Palestinian political factions. Killings of Palestinians by Israeli forces increased threefold compared to the previous year, totalling more than 650; some of the victims were militants engaged in violence against Israel, but half were unarmed civilians. Palestinian armed groups carried out further attacks on Israelis, killing 27 Israelis, half the previous year's figure, of whom 21 were civilians. Inter-factional violence between rival Palestinian security forces and armed groups increased; some 150 people were killed in gun battles and attacks, including scores of civilian bystanders. Abductions of Palestinians and foreign nationals, notably journalists and aid workers, were frequent. Foreigners were promptly released unharmed, whereas some Palestinians were killed or ill-treated. Impunity remained widespread, with law enforcement and the administration of justice virtually paralysed by inter-factional confrontations.

Background
Inter-factional tensions increased after President Mahmoud Abbas' Fatah party, which had ruled the Palestinian Authority (PA) since its establishment more than a decade earlier, was defeated by the Islamic Resistance Movement (Hamas) in parliamentary elections in January. Hamas formed a government, headed by Prime Minister Isma'il Haniyeh, in March. Armed confrontations between rival security forces and armed groups increased as repeated attempts to form a coalition government of national unity failed. In December President Abbas announced his intention to call presidential and parliamentary elections, sparking a new wave of inter-factional fighting.

Following the establishment of a government led by Hamas, which refused to recognize the state of Israel, the Israeli government began confiscating tax duties due to the PA, and key Western donors ceased direct aid to the PA government on the grounds that they considered Hamas a "terrorist organization". This created a deepening crisis in the Palestinian economy, exacerbated by frequent Israeli military attacks on Palestinian infrastructure and a blockade imposed by Israel on the OPT. The Gaza Strip bore the brunt of the Israeli bombardments and blockade. At the same time, Palestinian armed groups increased their firing of homemade "Qassam" rockets from the Gaza Strip into the south of Israel, notably in the second half of the year.

Deteriorating economic and social conditions
Conditions for Palestinians in the OPT deteriorated throughout the year. Their economic situation was hit hard by Israel's confiscation of import tax duties that it collects on behalf of the PA, half the entire PA government budget; the cut in aid to the PA government by international donors, notably the European Union (EU) and the USA; and banking sanctions imposed by Israel, which prevented the transfer of funds to the Hamas administration. The measures left the PA government, the largest employer in the OPT, unable to pay salaries or deliver health, education and other key services to three and a half million Palestinians living under Israeli occupation in the West Bank and Gaza Strip.

The international community took no measures to require Israel, as the occupying power, to meet its obligation under international law to ensure the basic humanitarian needs of the Palestinian population. The EU established a Temporary International Mechanism (TIM) in an effort to reduce the humanitarian crisis. However, by the end of the year it was still not fully operational and did not prevent further deterioration of the already overstretched health sector, which could not cope with a growing number of patients. The increased demand was caused by the numerous casualties of Israeli military attacks and the patients who were prevented from seeking treatment abroad by the continuing Israeli blockade on the Gaza Strip.

Education and other crucial public services were similarly affected by the lack of funds, particularly when the PA was unable to pay the salaries of more than 150,000 public sector workers for several months. In September teachers joined other public sector workers striking to protest against the non-payment of their salaries. The education of hundreds of thousands of children was disrupted as a result. In December UN aid agencies launched a US$450 million emergency appeal in response to the growing needs of the Palestinian population.

Destruction of Palestinian infrastructure by Israeli forces caused long-term damage and a further worsening of living conditions. In June, Israeli forces bombed and badly damaged the Gaza Strip's only power plant, which supplied electricity to half of its 1.5 million inhabitants and left them without electricity for most of the day throughout the hottest months of the year, and often without water that is extracted and distributed using electricity. Israeli forces also bombed bridges, roads, and water and sewage networks. Hundreds of Palestinians were made homeless as scores of buildings were destroyed and damaged by Israeli air strikes and artillery shelling in the Gaza Strip. Other homes were demolished by Israeli bulldozers in the West Bank, including in the East Jerusalem area.

Conflict

Palestinian armed groups launched a growing number of "Qassam" rockets from the Gaza Strip into the south of Israel. These indiscriminate rockets killed two Israeli civilians and injured several others, and caused widespread alarm, although most resulted in no casualties.

The main Palestinian parties, notably Fatah and Hamas, restated their 2005 commitment to refrain from killing Israelis – known as the *tahadiyeh* (quiet) – but continued to carry out attacks on Israelis together with other groups. However, the number of Israelis killed in such attacks decreased to half the previous year's figure and to the lowest level since the beginning of the intifada in 2000. In total, 21 Israeli civilians, including a child, and six soldiers were killed in Palestinian attacks. The deadliest attack was a suicide bombing claimed by the armed wing of Islamic Jihad on 17 April, which killed 11 civilians and injured 68 others in Tel Aviv. A second suicide attack killed four Israeli settlers, including a 16-year-old child, near the Israeli settlement of Kedumim, in the northern West Bank, on 30 March. The al-Aqsa Martyrs' Brigades, Islamic Jihad and the Popular Resistance Committees (PRC) claimed responsibility for most attacks. In June the armed wing of Hamas and the PRC claimed responsibility for an attack on an Israeli military base near the Gaza Strip in which two soldiers were killed and a third was captured. Hamas announced that the soldier, Corporal Gilad Shalit, would only be freed in exchange for the release of some of the 10,000 Palestinians in Israeli jails. Negotiations were reportedly ongoing but no exchange of prisoners had been agreed by the end of the year.

Killings of Palestinians by Israeli forces increased threefold compared to the previous years (see Israel and the Occupied Territories entry). Some 650 Palestinians, half of them unarmed civilians and including about 120 children, were killed in Israeli air strikes, artillery shelling and reckless shooting into densely populated refugee camps and residential areas. Israeli forces bombed and destroyed several PA government ministries and other buildings, housing charities and institutions linked to Hamas. Israeli attacks escalated dramatically after the capture of Gilad Shalit in June. Most of the Israeli attacks targeted the Gaza Strip, although scores of Palestinians were also killed in towns and villages throughout the West Bank.

Unlawful killings, lawlessness and impunity

Security forces loyal to the previous PA Fatah administration and the al-Aqsa Martyrs' Brigades and other armed groups linked to Fatah challenged the authority of the new Hamas administration, which set up a new security force made up of its loyalists. Armed confrontations between rival security forces and armed groups were particularly frequent in the Gaza Strip, where family feuds and common law crimes often were intertwined with political violence. Bystanders were frequently caught in the crossfire and scores were killed and injured amid growing lawlessness.

◻ Ten-year old Ousama Ba'lousha and his two brothers, Ahmad and Salam, aged seven and four, were shot dead in Gaza City on their way to school on 11 December, when gunmen opened fire at the car in which they were travelling. The boys' father, a high-ranking officer in the PA intelligence services, had reportedly survived an assassination attempt some months earlier. Fatah and Hamas blamed each other for the killings of the children but the perpetrators were not brought to justice.

The proliferation of unlicensed weapons helped fuel the violence and insecurity. PA law enforcement and judicial authorities were unable or unwilling to carry out their duties. Victims of abuses were denied justice and redress, while the perpetrators of abuses were not held to account. In the West Bank, the Israeli army continued in practice to prevent PA security forces from operating in many areas ostensibly under the jurisdiction of the PA. The economic crisis and the government's inability to pay civil servants and others employed directly by the PA, including members of the security forces, led to strikes and demonstrations, some of which developed into riots such as in June and September when security officials stormed the parliament and ministries, destroying public property.

Abductions and other unlawful killings

Scores of Palestinians and some 20 foreign journalists and aid workers were abducted by Palestinian armed groups, mostly in the Gaza Strip. All the foreign nationals were released unharmed, mostly within hours, but two journalists were held for two weeks in August. The captors usually demanded jobs or political concessions from the PA in exchange for the release of their foreign hostages. Abductions of Palestinians took place in the context of confrontations between rival armed groups, security forces and feuding families, but little information was known about the identities of the victims or the demands made for their release. Most were released, but several were killed, including some who their captors accused of "collaborating" with Israeli security services. Killings of alleged "collaborators" were claimed by or were believed to have been carried out by the al-Aqsa Martyrs' Brigades and other Fatah splinter groups.

Violence against women

Women continued to suffer from the negative impact of the occupation and conflict, including the destruction of homes, increased poverty and movement restrictions that further restricted their access to health services and education. While there were increased demands on women as carers and providers, the deteriorating situation contributed to increased family and societal violence. At least four women were killed by male relatives in "honour" crimes in the Gaza Strip.

◻ In August, Faiza 'Id Abu Sawawin was shot dead in the Gaza Strip, reportedly by a member of her family, for reasons of "family honour". It could not be confirmed whether the man who killed her was detained.

AI country reports/ visits

Reports
- Israel/Occupied Territories: Briefing to the UN Committee on the Elimination of Racial Discrimination (AI Index: MDE 15/002/2006)
- Israel and the Occupied Territories: Road to nowhere (AI Index: MDE 15/093/2006)

Visits
AI delegates visited areas under the jurisdiction of the PA in April, May, June, November and December. In April, they met Prime Minister Haniyeh and other PA government officials and submitted a memorandum detailing AI's concerns and recommending measures to improve human rights in the PA. In December the organization's Secretary General headed a delegation that visited the West Bank and Gaza Strip. She met the PA President and representatives of the Hamas-led government and expressed concern about the deteriorating human rights situation and increasing lawlessness, and called for an end to impunity in the areas under the PA jurisdiction.

PAPUA NEW GUINEA

PAPUA NEW GUINEA
Head of state: Queen Elizabeth II, represented by Paulias Matane
Head of government: Michael Somare
Death penalty: abolitionist in practice
International Criminal Court: not ratified

There were high levels of violent crime across the country. The police continued to enjoy impunity for human rights violations. There was endemic violence against women and children.

Law and order
There were high levels of violent crime across the country. Land disputes, riots and violence between communities were common. At least 70 people were believed to have died in 2006 in the long-running feud between the Ulga and Kulga tribes in the Nebilyer region of the Western Highlands.

A state of emergency, which was declared in August in the Southern Highlands, remained in place at the end of the year.

In Bougainville, former combatants who had remained outside the peace process rearmed, contributing to the high level of gun crime on the island.

A report by the National Gun Committee recommending reforms to combat the proliferation of illegal firearms had still not been tabled to Parliament one year after its submission to the government.

There were major changes in the leadership of the police force. There was little public confidence in the ability of the police to fight crime. The police complained of limited resources; however, they often appeared to actively avoid involvement in sensitive local cases for fear of reprisals. Poor data collection by the police, or incompetent prosecution, particularly in cases of violence against women, often undermined efforts to deliver justice, and many cases were dismissed by the courts following inadequate or delayed investigations.

Violations by the police
There were persistent reports of police brutality against detainees, including rape and other forms of torture. In the absence of clear and systematic accountability mechanisms, officers accused of violence were rarely investigated or prosecuted.

The government was not known to have responded to a request by the UN Special Rapporteur on torture to visit the country made at the beginning of the year.

▢ Although two police officers were charged in January for the shooting of unarmed schoolboys in Enga province in October 2005, the police had not sent the cases to the public prosecutor by the end of the year.

▢ By the end of the year, none of the officers accused of involvement in the rape and other ill-treatment of women and girls arrested during a raid on Three Mile Guest House in Port Moresby in March 2004 had faced prosecution.

Violence against women
Violence in the home and community affected the majority of women in the country. Women human rights activists undertook essential work offering counselling, shelters and legal advice to survivors of violence, with little or no support from the government.

Increases in sexual crimes were reported in at least three provinces. Port Moresby, Lae and settlements around other cities were the worst affected.

In a high-profile case in January, a provincial governor was sentenced to 12 years' imprisonment for rape. However, few incidents of violence against women were reported or investigated, and the perpetrators were rarely punished.

Women continued to suffer widespread "sorcery-related" abuses. In Chimbu province alone, approximately 150 were believed to be killed each year for allegedly practicing witchcraft.

The government initiated some measures to address the HIV/AIDS epidemic. However, impunity and social attitudes surrounding violence against women fuelled the spread of the disease.

Death penalty
In April, the new Minister for Justice ruled out a return to executions and said that he would work towards abolishing the death penalty.

Three men who had been under sentence of death since 1997 had their sentences commuted to life imprisonment after the appeal court found that the trial judge had mistakenly assumed he was required by law to impose the death penalty.

AI country reports/ visits
Reports
- Papua New Guinea: Violence against women – not inevitable, never acceptable! (AI Index: ASA 34/002/2006)
- Papua New Guinea: Women human rights defenders in action (AI Index: ASA 34/004/2006)
Visit
An AI delegation visited Port Moresby in September.

PARAGUAY

REPUBLIC OF PARAGUAY
Head of state and government: Nicanor Duarte Frutos
Death penalty: abolitionist for all crimes
International Criminal Court: ratified

Journalists were reportedly subjected to threats and attacks during the first half of the year. There were reports of armed civilian patrols operating in the north of the country. One community leader was killed. Prison conditions were poor.

Economic, social and cultural rights
Peasants continued to be evicted from their land which was then given to landowners for the monoculture of soya bean crops. Indigenous people, women, children and the elderly suffered ill-health, malnutrition and hunger.

In August, former President Alfredo Stroessner died in exile in Brazil. Requests for his extradition were unsuccessful and he was never brought to trial for the many human rights violations committed during his rule, including in the context of Operation Condor, a joint plan by Southern Cone military governments in the 1970s and 1980s to eliminate opponents.

Threats and attacks against journalists
Journalists were subjected to threats and attacks because of their investigative work on politics, drugs and the environment.

In February, Enrique Ramón Galeano, a radio journalist, disappeared after being seen in a police station in Azotey in the city of Horqueta. After receiving death threats, he was placed under police protection in 2005. The prosecutor who had been investigating Enrique Ramón Galeano's whereabouts expressed concern for her own safety.

Prison conditions
Prisons were reportedly overcrowded and conditions harsh, sometimes amounting to cruel, inhuman or degrading treatment. In Tacumbú prison in the capital, Asunción, 40 inmates with mental illness reportedly had no access to medicines or medical care, no mattress or bedding and lived in unsanitary conditions. A prosecutor filed a legal petition for medical assistance on their behalf.

Armed civilian patrols
In July, two community leaders were attacked by members of the Neighbourhood Security Commission (Comisión Vecinal de Seguridad), a government-sponsored armed civilian patrol group, in the city of San José del Norte, San Pedro department. Luis Martínez, who was shot more than 30 times, was killed and Zacarías Vega was wounded. The attack appeared to be linked to the men's work raising awareness of peasants' rights, their campaigning against the excessive use of agricultural pesticides, and their opposition to the use of firearms by civilian patrols in the area. Luis Martínez's family and Daniel Romero, another community leader, and his family received death threats after they pressed for an investigation into the shooting. An official investigation was launched into the shooting, but there was no news of any progress at the end of the year.

UN Special Rapporteur on torture
In November, following a visit to Paraguay, the UN Special Rapporteur on torture criticized severe prison overcrowding and the lack of basic human rights for prisoners, including health care and the provision of clothing, food and mattresses. He also stated that detainees in police stations were widely subjected to torture during the first few days in custody. He expressed concern that torture was not criminalized in the military criminal code and at allegations of beatings and degrading treatment of conscripts. He stressed the need to investigate effectively all suspected cases of torture and bring perpetrators to justice, eradicate corruption, and increase the use of non-custodial measures.

AI country reports/ visits
Statements
- Paraguay: Fear for safety/death threats (AI Index: AMR 45/001/2006)
- Paraguay: The search for truth and justice continues (AI Index: AMR 45/002/2006)

PERU

REPUBLIC OF PERU
Head of state and government: Alan García (replaced Alejandro Toledo Manrique in July)
Death penalty: abolitionist for ordinary crimes
International Criminal Court: ratified

Discrimination in the provision of maternal and infant health care to marginalized communities continued. Human rights defenders were threatened and intimidated. Some progress was made in bringing the perpetrators of human rights violations in previous years to justice. There were fears that the death penalty could be extended.

Background
Newly elected President Alan García promised to implement austerity plans, including wage cuts for government officials and civil servants, and to increase expenditure to improve the living conditions of those in poverty. However, he did not commit himself to implement the National Human Rights Plan which was agreed by the government at the end of 2005.

Independent candidates won the majority of votes in the November regional and municipal elections.

The Constitutional Court ruled that some articles of the new legislation on the military and police justice system were unconstitutional because they violated principles of independence and impartiality. In December, Congress passed legislation allowing the military justice system to remain in force until June 2007.

The state of emergency declared in 2003 in various provinces in the departments of Ayacucho, Huancavelica, Cusco and Junín, remained in place. There were reports that the armed group Shining Path (Sendero Luminoso) continued to be active in these areas.

Two leaders of Shining Path, Abimael Guzmán and Elena Iparraguirre, were sentenced in a civilian court to life imprisonment. Nine other high-ranking members of Shining Path were also sentenced to between 25 and 35 years' imprisonment. Two others were acquitted. All had previously been tried and convicted by military courts which were neither independent nor impartial.

Right to health
Hundreds of women and children from marginalized communities continued to die unnecessarily because of discrimination in the provision of maternal and infant health care. Despite the development of state health insurance for those on lower incomes, the scheme was not reaching many women and children from poor communities.

Maternal and child mortality rates remained among the highest in the region. In the rural areas the likelihood of dying from maternity-related causes was twice as high as in urban areas, and considerable differences persisted between urban and rural areas in access to medical care.

Human rights defenders
Human rights defenders, including victims of human rights violations and their relatives, witnesses, prosecutors and forensic experts, continued to be threatened and intimidated because of their activities. Threats were rarely investigated and none of the perpetrators were brought to justice.

Congress passed legislation which required non-governmental organizations seeking international funding to be supervised by government authorities who would assess whether their work complied with national development policies. There were concerns that this could restrict the work and independence of human rights defenders.

Environmental concerns
Scores of demonstrators were injured and one was shot dead during violent clashes with the police and security personnel of the Yanacocha gold mining project in Cajamarca Province. The demonstrators had blocked a road to protest against the environmental impact of El Azufre dry dock which was under construction by the project. Following this incident members of the non-governmental organization supporting the communities who opposed the gold mining project, Training and Intervention Group for Sustainable Development (Grupo de Formación e Intervención para el Desarrollo Sostenible, GRUFIDES), were repeatedly threatened and intimidated. One of those protesting against the project, environmentalist Edmundo Becerra Corina, was shot dead in Yanacanchilla, Cajamarca Province. He had reportedly received several death threats because of his opposition to the expansion of the mining company's activities to San Cirilo hills. The attack took place days before his meeting with the Ministry of Energy and Mines.

Death penalty
At the end of the year Congress was considering four draft bills, three of which would extend the scope of the death penalty to offences including the rape of children and of people with physical or mental disabilities, and the fourth draft bill would regulate the enforcement of the death penalty in cases of terrorism. Two of the bills also proposed the withdrawal of Peru from the American Convention on Human Rights, which prohibits the extension of the death penalty. At present the Constitution allows for the death penalty for treason in time of war and terrorism. No one had been sentenced to death since the current Constitution came into force in 1993.

Justice and impunity
Four police officers were sentenced to prison terms of between 15 and 16 years for the enforced disappearance of student Ernesto Castillo Páez in Lima in 1990. They were the first ever members of the security forces to be convicted of enforced disappearance.

The investigation and prosecution of the 47 cases of past human rights violations documented by the Truth and Reconciliation Commission made slow progress. According to the Ombudsman's Office, only two new cases went to trial in 2006, bringing the number of cases in the judicial system to 24. The rest of the 47 cases remained at the investigation stage at the end of the year.

The armed forces continued to refuse to co-operate with civilian courts trying and investigating military officers accused of past human rights violations.

Legislation was passed to grant legal aid to military officers accused of past human rights violations. No legal aid was granted to victims of violations and their relatives, despite reports that nearly 70 per cent of victims had no access to legal representation.

Congress passed the Regulation of the Comprehensive Reparation Plan to provide redress to victims of human rights violations during the 20-year armed conflict. The National Council of Reparations, responsible for creating an official registry of victims, was established in October.

Ollanta Humala, runner-up in the presidential elections, was charged with offences including murder and enforced disappearance committed when he was a captain at a military base in San Martín department, northern Peru, between 1991 and 1992. The investigation had not concluded by the end of the year.

For the third time, the Special Attorney's Office on Forced Disappearance, Extrajudicial Execution and Exhumations of Mass Graves closed the investigation into the alleged responsibility of President Alan García, former members of his cabinet and top-ranking military officers in the killing of at least 118 inmates by navy officers during a riot in 1986 at the El Fronton prison in Lima. Human rights organizations representing the victims' relatives and some of the survivors appealed against the decision. The appeal remained pending at the end of the year.

Inter-governmental organizations
The Committee against Torture expressed concern at continuing complaints of torture against the police, the military and prison officials, as well as allegations of reprisals, intimidation and threats against those who reported these violations. The Committee urged Peru to guarantee prompt, impartial and thorough investigations in the civilian criminal justice system.

The Committee on the Rights of the Child expressed concern about high levels of poverty and urged Peru to take action to ensure universal access to basic goods and services, including housing and clean drinking water, paying special attention to remote and rural areas.

AI country reports/visits
Report
- Peru: Poor and excluded women – Denial of the right to maternal and child health (AI Index: AMR 46/004/2006)

Visit
AI delegates attended the III National Conference on the Right to Health in Lima in July.

PHILIPPINES

REPUBLIC OF THE PHILIPPINES
Head of state and government: Gloria Macapagal Arroyo
Death penalty: abolitionist for all crimes
International Criminal Court: signed

A one-week State of Emergency was declared in response to alleged coup conspiracies. Rights of peaceful assembly were restricted and rebellion charges filed against prominent leftist politicians and others. Political killings of leftist activists continued as the government declared "all-out war" on communist rebels. A police task force and Commission of Inquiry established to investigate the killings resulted in only a limited number of arrests and prosecutions. Arbitrary arrests and enforced disappearances were reported in the context of counter-insurgency operations. Peace talks between the government and Muslim separatists in Mindanao continued. All death sentences were commuted and Congress passed a law abolishing capital punishment. Armed groups were reportedly responsible for abuses, including unlawful killings.

Alleged coup plots
In February, President Gloria Arroyo declared a week-long State of Emergency in response to alleged coup conspiracies involving members of the mainstream opposition in "tactical alliance" with rightists, communist rebels, leftist politicians and members of the military.

Police enforced a ban on public assemblies and raided a newspaper office, threatening to shut down media outlets that failed to follow "responsible" reporting guidelines.

Scores of people were arrested or threatened with arrest, particularly members of legal leftist political parties which were accused by government and military officials of links with the Communist Party of the Philippines (CPP) and its armed wing, the New People's Army (NPA). Dozens were arrested and charged with "rebellion" in the period following the alleged coup plot, including critics of the government.
□ In February, Crispin Beltran, Congress Representative for the Anakpawis (Toiling Masses) party, was detained on a warrant of arrest for rebellion. After the validity of the warrant and a subsequent charge of "incitement to sedition" were challenged by lawyers, he was further charged with rebellion. He had not been tried by the end of 2006.
□ Police sought to arrest five other leftist Congress Representatives on suspicion of rebellion. Afforded Congressional protective custody from arrest, they remained in the Congressional compound for over two months as prosecutors conducted preliminary investigations. The charges were dismissed by a court in May but further rebellion charges were filed against the five Representatives and over 45 other leftist suspects. All remained under threat of arrest at the end of 2006.

Political killings and counter-insurgency

A long-standing peace process between the government and the National Democratic Front (NDF), representing the CPP-NPA, appeared to be abandoned as the government declared a new offensive against communist rebels.

Armed attacks continued on members of legal leftist political parties, including Bayan Muna (People First) and Anakpawis. Reports of the number of such victims of alleged political killings ranged from 61 to at least 96 during the year. Most were killed by unidentified armed men on motorcycles. In some cases, those attacked had reportedly been under surveillance by people linked to the security forces or had received death threats.

▭ Rafael Markus Bangit, an Indigenous people's leader and Bayan Muna provincial co-ordinator, was shot dead in Isabela province (northern Luzon) by two masked gunmen. He was about to re-board a bus, while travelling with his son. He had earlier told colleagues that he believed he was under surveillance.

Amid reports of ineffective investigations, and with witnesses and relatives of the victims too frightened to co-operate with the police, perpetrators were rarely brought to justice. In May the authorities set up a special police investigative task force. However, only a limited number of people were arrested and few cases were filed in court by the end of the year, and no one was held accountable for cases stretching back to 2001. President Arroyo in August established a Commission of Inquiry, headed by former Supreme Court Justice José Melo, to investigate the killings and make recommendations for remedial action, including appropriate prosecutions and legislative proposals.

As military operations intensified, there were reports nationwide of arbitrary detentions, extrajudicial executions, enforced disappearances, torture and harassment of civilians suspected of being CPP-NPA supporters.

▭ In February, Audie Lucero, a 19-year-old youth activist with the leftist Kilusan para sa Pambansang Demokrasya (Movement for National Democracy), disappeared after being questioned by soldiers and police at a hospital in Balanga City (Bataan, Luzon) about a wounded friend he had helped bring for medical attention. His body was found in a field the next day. The military reported that the wounded man was a rebel.

▭ Also in February police arrested 10 youths aged between 19 and 24 and a 15-year-old girl, who had been hitchhiking in Benguet Province on their way to a music festival at the resort of Sagada. Most reported being beaten, suffocated with plastic bags and drenched with gasoline to force them to admit involvement in an NPA attack on a military detachment. The 11 were charged with robbery and homicide, and remained in detention until December.

Abolition of the death penalty

In April, President Arroyo announced the commutation of all death sentences. At least 1,230 prisoners had been sentenced to death since 1994. Death sentences were replaced with life imprisonment without the possibility of parole.

Congress voted in favour of a Bill to repeal the death penalty law, and the President signed it in June. In 1987 the Philippines had become the first Asian country to abolish the death penalty for all crimes. However capital punishment was reintroduced in 1994, and seven prisoners were subsequently executed by lethal injection.

Mindanao peace process

Peace negotiations between the government and the separatist Moro Islamic Liberation Front (MILF) continued to make progress, albeit slowly. Disagreements continued over ancestral domain land claims and the amount of territory to be included in an expanded Muslim autonomous region as part of a peace settlement.

A ceasefire agreement was periodically broken by clashes between MILF and government forces. Sporadic bomb attacks on civilian targets were allegedly perpetrated by Islamists, some reportedly linked to the MILF. MILF leaders denied links with Jemaah Islamiyah, a regional network accused of involvement in violent or terrorist activity, or with Abu Sayaff, a Philippine Muslim separatist group responsible for kidnappings and killings of civilians.

In October the Senate amended an Anti-Terrorism Bill, including by reducing the time suspects could be detained without judicial authority, and by withdrawing clauses extending law enforcement powers to the military.

AI country reports/ visits
Reports
- Philippines: Political killings, human rights and the peace process (AI Index: ASA 35/006/2006)
- Philippines: Towards ensuring justice and ending political killings (AI Index: ASA 35/010/2006)
Visits
AI delegates visited the Philippines in February during the State of Emergency and in December.

POLAND

REPUBLIC OF POLAND
Head of state: Lech Kaczyński
Head of government: Jarosław Kaczyński (replaced Kazimierz Marcinkiewicz in July)
Death penalty: abolitionist for all crimes
International Criminal Court: ratified

Lesbian, gay, bisexual and transgender (LGBT) people were subjected to discrimination and intolerance. Allegations that Poland had allowed secret detention centres on its territory as part of the US-led "war on terror" were not satisfactorily resolved during investigations by the Council of Europe and the European Parliament. Chechens granted refugee and "tolerated stay" status had difficulties in accessing education services and social benefits. President Lech Kaczyński and a number of other prominent officials called for restoration of the death penalty.

Background
In a minority government since parliamentary elections in September 2005, the Law and Justice Party (PiS), formed a coalition government in May with the League of Polish Families (LPR) and the Self-Defence (Samoobrona) party. After a political crisis in September, Samoobrona was expelled from the government, but later readmitted when PiS faced losing early parliamentary elections.

Discrimination on grounds of sexual orientation
Openly homophobic statements made by politicians and officials, including the encouragement of violence against peaceful demonstrators, worsened the climate of discrimination and intimidation.
☐ Wojciech Wierzejski, LPR Vice-President and member of parliament, in May encouraged the use of force against participants in the annual Equality March in Warsaw in June. He reportedly said, "If deviants begin to demonstrate, they should be hit with batons".
☐ In May the Deputy Minister of Education said that an international project organized by LGBT rights groups and financially supported by the European Commission would lead to the "depravity of young people", and that such groups should not receive funding. In September a project submitted by one LGBT organization to the National Agency of Youth Programme was rejected by the Ministry of Education on the grounds that it "aimed to propagate homosexual behaviour".
☐ In June the Minister of Education dismissed the director of the National In-Service Teacher Training Centre for having books that encouraged teachers to organize meetings with LGBT organizations. The only book that met the description was an anti-discrimination handbook by the Council of Europe, which subsequently expressed concern at the "homophobia...and homophobic behaviours" within the government. The Centre's new director said in October that "homosexual practices lead to drama, emptiness and degeneracy".

Demonstrators from the LGBT community and other activists were reportedly attacked by counter-demonstrators and unable to exercise their right to peaceful assembly because of police failures.
☐ In April, despite the presence of the police, more than 1,000 participants of a Tolerance March in Kraków were reportedly harassed and intimidated by members of a right-wing grouping, the All Polish Youth, who held a counter-demonstration, the Tradition March.

Court rulings clarified the legality of the Equality March in Warsaw arranged for 10 June, which the City Council of Warsaw finally authorized on 1 June. Owing to threats from counter-demonstrators, the march organizers agreed a different route with the Council and the police provided sufficient forces to guarantee security. The march went ahead without major incidents.
☐ In January the Constitutional Court confirmed a Warsaw court ruling of September 2005 that the banning of the Equality March in Warsaw in June 2005 by the then Mayor Lech Kaczyński was unlawful, and declared that demonstrators need only inform city officials that a public demonstration would be taking place.
☐ In May the Supreme Administrative Court in Warsaw upheld the decision of the Regional Administrative Court in Poznań, in the case of an LGBT march banned in November 2005, that the threat from a counter-demonstration could not be grounds for banning the demonstration.

Secret detention centres and renditions
In March the Secretary-General of the Council of Europe released his opinion on alleged secret detention centres in member states set up as part of the USA's programme of secret detentions and "renditions" – the illegal transfer of people between states outside of any judicial process. He expressed concern at Poland's inadequate response to questions of whether officials had been involved in the detentions or renditions.

In June the Rapporteur on secret detentions of the Parliamentary Assembly of the Council of Europe (PACE) reported on the global "spider's web" of detentions and transfers by the US Central Intelligence Agency (CIA) and alleged collusion by 14 Council of Europe states. He reported that the Polish authorities were unable, despite repeated requests, to provide information from national aviation records to confirm CIA-connected flights into Poland.

In November a Temporary Committee of the European Parliament, looking into allegations of illegal CIA activity in Europe, deplored Poland's lack of co-operation and failure to establish a special inquiry committee or an independent parliamentary investigation.

Refugees
The majority of asylum seekers from Chechnya in the Russian Federation were denied refugee status, in violation of the 1951 Refugee Geneva Convention, and were granted "tolerated stay" permits only.

UNHCR, the UN refugee agency, reported in May that almost half of school-age children seeking asylum did not attend school at all. People with only "tolerated stay" permits were denied the social assistance given to asylum-seekers and the integration package provided for refugees.

The number of asylum-seekers sent back to Poland from other European Union (EU) states increased following application of the so-called Dublin II Regulation, which establishes criteria and mechanisms for determining which EU state will examine an asylum application.

International scrutiny

In March, reporting on its last visit in 2004, the European Committee for the Prevention of Torture made recommendations to the government on the treatment of detainees. It urged police officers to be informed on a regular and frequent basis that physically or verbally ill-treating detainees was unacceptable and would be severely punished; that only strictly necessary force should be used during arrests; and that there was no justification for striking detainees once they were brought under control. The Committee called on the authorities to ensure that judges and prosecutors who heard a complaint of police ill-treatment from any person before them should immediately request a forensic medical examination. The Committee expressed concern that Poland had not implemented recommendations on police detention facilities for children made during its previous visit in 2000.

Death penalty

President Kaczyński called for the restoration of the death penalty in Poland and throughout Europe in a Polish public radio broadcast on 28 July, saying: "Countries that give up this penalty award an unimaginable advantage to the criminal over his victim, the advantage of life over death." In August the LPR announced a campaign for Europe-wide restoration of the death penalty and for a referendum on its reintroduction in Poland. Wojciech Wierzejski called the EU's ban on the death penalty "anachronistic."

In response, the European Commission said that the death penalty was "not compatible with European values." The President of the PACE wrote in an open letter to President Kaczyński that "its reintroduction... would be a direct attack on our common values, which are founded on respect for the basic human dignity of every person."

AI country reports/ visits

Reports
- Poland and Latvia: Lesbian, gay, bisexual and transgender rights in Poland and Latvia (AI Index: EUR 01/019/2006)
- Poland goes backwards: No to the restoration of the death penalty (AI Index: EUR 37/002/2006)

Visits

AI delegates visited Poland in May and June.

PORTUGAL

PORTUGUESE REPUBLIC
Head of state: Aníbal António Cavaco Silva (replaced Jorge Fernando Branco de Sampaio in March)
Head of government: José Sócrates Carvalho Pinto de Sousa
Death penalty: abolitionist for all crimes
International Criminal Court: ratified

Incidents of police ill-treatment and fatal shootings continued to be reported. Training in the use of firearms by police officers remained inadequate. Overcrowding, poor hygiene and lack of resources in prisons increased concerns about substandard conditions. Reform of the penal code to extend the definition of domestic violence to include unmarried and same-sex couples was proposed in April. Violence in the home remained pervasive. Insufficient resources hampered efforts by the national Commission for Equality and against Racial Discrimination to deal with continuing incidents of racism.

Fatal shootings

At least six people died as a result of lethal force by police during 2006, again raising long-standing concerns about the possibly unnecessary or disproportionate use of force. Police trade union leaders have blamed inadequate training for such killings. Officers also lacked sufficient guidelines on use of weapons.

On 3 October, one man was killed and another gravely injured during a police chase of a car carrying four young men in Porto. A police officer fired five shots at the vehicle, allegedly aiming for the tyres but killing one occupant and injuring another. After the vehicle came to a halt, the survivors, including the seriously injured man, were reportedly assaulted by the police although they had surrendered themselves. The case was under investigation by the Homicide Brigade of the Porto Judicial Police. The General Inspectorate of Internal Administration also opened an inquiry. The driver of the vehicle was charged with disobeying police orders and dangerous driving.

Overcrowded prisons

According to the Directorate General of Prison Services in May, 70 per cent of prisons were operating over their intended capacity and three of them – Portimão, Angra do Heroísmo and Guimarães – at more than double the designated number of prisoners. Overcrowding reduced the resources available for each prisoner and exacerbated poor hygiene conditions and the transmission of infectious diseases. Of a total of 91 prisoners' deaths in 2006, 74 were from illness, 14 were suicides and three were recorded as homicide.

In June Minister of Justice Alberto Costa announced government plans to close 22 prisons and enlarge others, increasing total capacity from 12,000 to 14,500 places. Most of the prisons were scheduled to close over the next three years, raising concerns about the impact on conditions in remaining prisons.

Violence against women

Of all violent incidents reported to the Portuguese Association of Victim Support, 86 per cent related to domestic violence. Many were not reported to the police. Under-reporting hampered justice in individual cases and also impeded efforts to tackle domestic violence across society by hiding its full extent and nature. Thirty-nine women died as a result of domestic violence between November 2005 and November 2006.

Reforms to the penal code proposed in April included defining domestic violence to include ill-treatment between unmarried, same-sex and former couples, as well as abuse between parents and children. If the violence takes place within the family home, this will be considered an aggravating factor.

Racism

Incidents of racist discrimination continued to be reported nationwide. The Commission for Equality and Against Racial Discrimination reported that in the previous six years it had received 190 complaints. Of these, only two had resulted in a fine and 60 cases were still pending. Insufficient resources resulted in cases taking two or three years to resolve, and many were shelved for lack of evidence, contributing to impunity for acts of racism.

Rights of migrants

An immigration law passed in August included measures to provide residence permits to victims of trafficking. However, such permits would be available only to those who collaborated with the police, risking undue pressure being brought on victims at risk of reprisals.

AI country reports/ visits

Report
- Europe and Central Asia: Summary of Amnesty International's concerns in the region, January-June 2006 (AI Index: EUR 01/017/2006)

PUERTO RICO

COMMONWEALTH OF PUERTO RICO
Head of state: George W Bush
Head of government: Aníbal Aceveda-Vilá
Death penalty: abolitionist for all crimes

Update: killing in suspicious circumstances

An investigation by the US Justice Department's Office of Inspector General (OIG) into the fatal shooting of independence activist Filiberto Ojeda Ríos in September 2005 cleared the Federal Bureau of Investigation (FBI) of wrongdoing. The report found no violation of policy when an FBI officer fired the fatal shot after seeing Ojeda Ríos at a window with a gun, some 90 minutes after an initial exchange of gunfire after police had surrounded the house. However, in its report, published in September, the inquiry was critical of many aspects of the planning and execution of the operation, including the decision not to allow an FBI crisis negotiating team to send a negotiator, and directions given by FBI headquarters not to allow officers into the house until the following day. The OIG inquiry was based mainly on FBI testimony as others had declined to provide testimony.

Excessive use of force

In February, the FBI was alleged to have used excessive force against a group of journalists covering a news event in which police were raiding the house of a political activist. Journalists were allegedly assaulted and sprayed with pepper spray. A civil lawsuit against the FBI was pending at the end of the year.

QATAR

STATE OF QATAR
Head of state: Shaikh Hamad bin Khalifa al-Thani
Head of government: Shaikh Abdullah bin Khalifa al-Thani
Death penalty: retentionist
International Criminal Court: not ratified

At least 2,000 people continued to be deprived of their Qatari nationality. A woman who had been confined to her family home against her will since 2003 was allowed to leave the country. At least 21 prisoners were under sentence of death but no executions were reported.

Abuses in the 'war on terror'

Some 17 detainees, including several foreign nationals, were released during the year after being held for prolonged periods by the security forces. Some had been held since 2005. At least one other was tried and convicted.

⊏ Fahad al-Mansouri, who had been detained without charge or trial since his arrest in November 2005, was reported to have been tried in connection with "belonging to a secret organization" and sentenced to 10 years' imprisonment.

⊏ Hamid 'Aladdin Shahadeh, a Jordanian national, was released without charge in October. Arrested in March 2005, he had reportedly been held in the State Security prison in the industrial area of Doha.

Political prisoners

At least 31 prisoners sentenced for allegedly plotting to overthrow the government in 1996 remained in prison. They had been convicted after an unfair trial in 1999. Allegations that they were tortured or ill-treated in pre-trial detention were never adequately investigated. Eighteen remained under sentence of death and at least 13 others were serving prison terms.

Torture and ill-treatment

The UN Committee against Torture examined Qatar's implementation of the Convention against Torture in May. The Committee welcomed Qatar's report but expressed concern that Qatari legislation fails to define torture in accordance with international standards and that arrest and detention procedures placed suspects at increased risk of torture, particularly the lack of access to a lawyer or independent doctor or any requirement that the authorities notify a detainee's relatives of the arrest.

Deprival of nationality

At least 2,000 people, many of them members of the al-Ghufran branch of the al-Murra tribe, continued to be denied Qatari nationality by the authorities. They were formally deprived of Qatari nationality in 2004 and 2005 on the grounds that they held Saudi Arabian nationality, although they denied this. In March, the authorities announced that they were carrying out a review of such cases and by the end of the year some 4,000 others were believed to have had their nationality reinstated. In at least some cases, however, Qatari authorities were alleged to have amended individuals' birth records to state that they were born in Saudi Arabia, so rendering them ineligible to participate in elections in Qatar.

'Abdullah Hussein 'Ali Ahmed al-Malki was believed not to have had his Qatari nationality restored by the end of the year. His nationality was revoked soon after he criticized the Qatari authorities in comments broadcast on the al-Jazeera satellite television station in May 2005.

Violence against women

The UN Special Rapporteur on trafficking in persons, especially in women and children, visited Qatar in November and expressed concern about the number of migrant workers who were victims of human trafficking. The Special Rapporteur recommended that the Qatari authorities implement international obligations related to human trafficking, create an office of National Coordinator on Human Trafficking, and take steps to introduce mechanisms which would ensure that victims of trafficking were properly identified and treated.

Hamda Fahad Jassem al-Thani, a member of Qatar's ruling family who had been confined to her home against her will since November 2003, was injured in June when she sought to escape. She was admitted to hospital after intervention by the Qatari Human Rights Committee. In October, she was permitted to leave Qatar and rejoin her husband in Egypt.

Death penalty

Eighteen people convicted of involvement in a coup attempt in 1996 remained under sentence of death. Three new death sentences were imposed in February, on two Nepalese and one Indian national convicted of murder. No executions were reported.

AI country reports/ visits

Report

- Qatar: Briefing to the Committee against Torture (AI Index: MDE 22/002/2006)

ROMANIA

ROMANIA
Head of state: Traian Băsescu
Head of government: Călin Popescu-Tăriceanu
Death penalty: abolitionist for all crimes
International Criminal Court: ratified

Roma continued to face intolerance and discrimination. Allegations of ill-treatment by law enforcement officials continued. Women remained at risk of trafficking and domestic violence. Concerns remained about patients in mental health institutions. The Council of Europe and the European Parliament expressed concern at Romania's lack of willingness to engage in a thorough investigation into allegations of collusion with the US-led programme of renditions and secret detention centres.

Background

In September the European Commission (EC) allowed Romania's accession to the European Union (EU) to go ahead in January 2007, despite continuing concerns about the transparency and efficiency of the judicial process and about the impartiality and effectiveness of investigations into allegations of high-level corruption.

In August, Romania ratified the Council of Europe's Convention on Action against Trafficking in Human Beings.

Unlike the previous year, the authorities did not oppose a parade called the Gayfest, organized by the lesbian, gay, bisexual and transgender community, from going ahead in May in the capital, Bucharest. However, police had to intervene to protect marchers from counter-demonstrators who threw eggs, stones and plastic bottles.

Discrimination

In its report on Romania, published in February, the European Commission against Racism and Intolerance expressed concern at the lack of knowledge about and the failure to implement anti-discrimination legislation. The Roma community continued to be discriminated against in all areas including employment, education and housing.

A law to prevent and punish all forms of discrimination was amended in June to meet the requirements of the EU's racial equality directive. However, by the end of the year Parliament had yet to approve a draft law on the protection of ethnic minorities.

The Romani community

In January, the National Council for Combating Discrimination ruled that an anti-Roma speech made by Corneliu Vadim Tudor, leader of the Greater Romania Party (Partidul România Mare), was in breach of Romanian anti-discrimination law. The speech referred to an incident in 1993 in the village of Hădăreni during which three Romani men were killed and 18 Romani houses were destroyed. No sanctions were initiated against him owing to parliamentary immunity.

The authorities failed to implement the July 2005 judgement by the European Court of Human Rights in the Hădăreni case. The community development strategy, initiated by the government in accordance with its obligations arising from the friendly settlement in the case, was reportedly shelved. The legal suits concerning the damages due to the victims of the attacks were still pending in national courts. A significant number of the perpetrators of the attacks, including law enforcement officials, remained unpunished.

In November, the National Council for Combating Discrimination fined several members of the New Right (Noua Dreaptă) organization for publishing a number of articles on the New Right website containing degrading, humiliating and offensive material about the Romani community. The Roma Centre for Social Intervention and Studies (Centrul Romilor pentru Intervenție Socială și Studii) lodged a formal complaint against the New Right and against its leader, Tudor Ionescu; a decision was still pending at the end of the year.

Evictions

In October, the Tulcea municipality forcibly evicted 25 Romani families, around 110 people, from a building that they had occupied for the previous seven years. Some Roma accepted the offer by the municipality of rooms in two ruined buildings with no access to electricity, hot water and sanitation and only limited access to drinking water, located in an enclave inside the Tulcea industrial port. After their relocation, the children stopped going to school because of distance and their parents' fear for their safety.

The rest of the people evicted remained sleeping outside the building. The local authorities had only offered to move them to mobile housing located outside Tulcea, also in a heavily industrialized area. The authorities acknowledged these structures offered very limited shelter since they could not be connected to any utilities. Court proceedings challenging the legality of the evictions, which were brought by the European Roma Rights Centre and other Roma non-governmental organizations (NGOs), were continuing at the year's end.

Penal code amendments

In June, international and domestic NGOs expressed their concern regarding amendments to the Penal Procedure Code. These allow prosecutors to intercept electronic mail and tap phones for up to 96 hours before informing a judge and to undermine client-lawyer confidentiality through phone tapping.

Police concerns

In August, five Romani individuals reported that they had been subjected to physical abuse during a joint operation by Bontida village police and Cluj county gendarmerie. Two of the Roma were minors who were allegedly prevented from contacting their parents while held at the police station. Both the police and gendarmerie denied any abuses. A complaint lodged by the men was still pending at the end of the year.

In September, violent clashes between police and members of the Romani community in Reghin, Apalina district, reportedly resulted in injuries to two policemen and 36 Romani women, men and children. The incident reportedly began when a police officer alleged that he had been assaulted by two Romani men. Shortly afterwards, a violent altercation broke out after plain-clothes police officers and masked Special Forces police officers arrived at the Apalina district, reportedly to serve two subpoenas. The police claimed they were attacked by several Roma using rocks, metal bars and pitchforks. The Roma claimed that Special Forces officers provoked the violence by using excessive force, including by firing rubber bullets and tear gas. The initial police investigation cleared the officers of any wrongdoing. In November, following a visit by two members of the European Parliament, the General Police Inspectorate opened a preliminary investigation into the incident. The investigation was continuing at the end of the year.

Violence against women

In June, the UN Committee on the Elimination of Discrimination against Women published its concluding comments on Romania's sixth periodic report. It urged the authorities to enhance the effective enforcement of its domestic violence legislation and to ensure that all women who are victims of violence have access to immediate means of redress and protection, including protection orders, and access to a sufficient number of state-funded safe shelters and legal aid. It also called on the authorities to increase their efforts to prevent human trafficking by addressing its root causes, in particular women's economic insecurity.

Mental health care

In May an international human rights and advocacy organization, Mental Disability Rights International (MDRI), published a report on the rights of children with disabilities in Romania. In spite of government claims that the placement of babies in institutions had ended, MDRI found children, many of them unidentified, languishing in poorly staffed medical facilities. Some children were found in adult psychiatric facilities, tied down with bed sheets, their arms and legs twisted and left to atrophy.

In January, the European Committee for the Prevention of Torture published its report on a visit to Romania in 2004. This raised concerns about the death of many patients, due to malnutrition or hypothermia, at Poiana Mare psychiatric hospital, an establishment already strongly criticized in the past in respect of the patients' living conditions, in particular food and heating.

▭ Following the deaths of 17 people at the Poiana Mare psychiatric hospital in 2004, and domestic and international pressure relating to the case, the Ministry of Health announced the decision to close down the hospital in November 2005. In February 2006 the Ministry of Justice closed down the ward for high security patients and transferred them to another institution. However, at the end of the year, 413 patients remained in Poiana Mare.

Secret detention centres and renditions

In June, the Parliamentary Assembly of the Council of Europe's Rapporteur on secret detentions reported on a global "spider's web" of detentions and transfers by the US Central Intelligence Agency (CIA) and alleged collusion by 14 Council of Europe member states. He found that the Romanian authorities showed a lack of transparency and genuine willingness to co-operate with the investigation into whether the USA had secret detention centres in Romania.

In November, members of the European Parliament's Temporary Committee on allegations of illegal CIA activity in Europe said that more investigation of the CIA's possible actions in Romania was needed. It criticized Romania's inquiry report as superficial and expressed concern about the lack of control by Romanian authorities over US activities in military bases in Romania.

AI country reports/ visits
Report
- Europe and Central Asia: Summary of Amnesty International's concerns in the region, January-June 2006 (AI Index: EUR 01/017/2006)

RUSSIAN FEDERATION

RUSSIAN FEDERATION
Head of state: Vladimir Putin
Head of government: Mikhail Fradkov
Death penalty: abolitionist in practice
International Criminal Court: signed

Human rights defenders and independent civil society came under increasing pressure. The authorities clamped down on the peaceful exercise of the rights to freedom of expression and assembly. Journalists were intimidated and attacked and one, Anna Politkovskaya, was killed. The authorities failed adequately to tackle racism and discrimination against people because of their ethnic identity or sexual orientation. Racist and homophobic attacks, some of them fatal, continued. Violence against women in the family was widespread and the state failed to provide adequate protection for women at risk. Police frequently circumvented safeguards designed to protect detainees against torture. Extrajudicial executions, enforced disappearances and abductions, torture including in unofficial detention centres, and arbitrary detentions continued in the North Caucasus region, in particular in Chechnya. In Chechnya, impunity remained the norm for those who committed human rights abuses, and people seeking justice faced intimidation and death threats. The European Court of Human Rights ruled that Russia had violated the rights to life, to liberty and security, to respect for private and family life and to an effective remedy, and to the prohibition of torture. The government failed to co-operate fully with international human rights mechanisms against torture.

Background

Opposition parties protested at amendments to electoral laws that removed the requirement of a minimum voter turn-out to validate election results. A new Federal Law on Counteracting Terrorism adopted in March set out no explicit safeguards for individuals detained in counter-terrorism operations, and allowed the armed forces to conduct such operations outside the territory of the Russian Federation. Growing nationalist sentiment raised fears of increasing xenophobia in the run-up to elections in 2007. A new immigration policy restricted foreign street traders from working in Russian retail street markets from January 2007.

In May, President Vladimir Putin announced a drive against pervasive corruption among officials. The cost of corruption to the country was US$240 billion a year, as much as the federal budget, the office of the General Procurator said in November. The authorities exercised tight control over the media, in particular television.

There were a number of apparent contract killings of businessmen, officials and politicians. Russia's chairing of the G8 group of major industrial states, and of the Council of Europe Committee of Ministers from May, increased international scrutiny of the government's human rights record.

Violence and instability in the North Caucasus continued. In June, Chechen separatist leader Abdul-Khalim Sadulaev was killed in Argun, Chechnya, in fighting with police and security forces. Shamil Basaev, the Chechen opposition leader who claimed responsibility for the Beslan school siege, North Ossetia, in September 2004 and other war crimes in the Chechen conflict, was killed in July in an explosion.

Restrictions on dissent

Limits on freedom of expression and assembly came into force in April under amendments to three federal laws – on closed administrative-territorial entities, on public organizations and on non-commercial organizations – and regulations specifying reporting requirements for civil society organizations. Ostensibly aimed at improving the regulation of non-governmental organizations (NGOs), in practice new powers to scrutinize the funding and activities of Russian and foreign civil society organizations were legally imprecise, allowed arbitrary implementation and disproportionate penalties, and diverted resources from substantive programmes.

Amendments in July to the 2002 law on "extremist activity" broadened the definition of "extremism", criminalized public justification of terrorism and slander of government officials, and threatened to restrict and punish the activities of civil society organizations and other government critics.

Attacks on journalists

Journalists were intimidated, faced with groundless criminal proceedings and attacked. Human rights defenders were subjected to administrative harassment and some received anonymous death threats.

◻ Russian journalist and human rights defender Anna Politkovskaya was shot dead on 7 October at the block of flats where she lived in Moscow, in all likelihood because of her work as a journalist. Her courageous coverage of the conflict and human rights situation in Chechnya since 1999 for *Novaia Gazeta* (New Newspaper) had won her numerous awards, and she had also written extensively about violence in the army, state corruption and police brutality. She had been subjected to intimidation and harassment by the Russian and Chechen authorities because of her outspoken criticism. A vigil in her memory on 16 October in Nazran, Ingushetia, was broken up violently. At least five human rights activists were detained by police and charged with administrative offences. Four were cleared, but the vigil organizer was fined.

◻ On 3 February, Stanislav Dmitrievskii was sentenced to a suspended two-year prison term and four years' probation for inciting "race hate" after he published articles by Chechen separatist leaders that advocated

neither racism nor violence. The NGO he led, the Russian-Chechen Friendship Society, was ordered by a court to close in November. The decision was motivated in part by Stanislav Dmitrievskii's conviction, applying a new NGO law forbidding individuals convicted of an "extremist" crime from heading an NGO.

Demonstrations

Many bans on demonstrations did not appear to be legitimate or proportionate restrictions of freedom of assembly. Peaceful protesters were detained despite informing the authorities of their intention to demonstrate as required in law.

◻ Anti-globalization protesters were detained on their journey to St Petersburg in the run-up to the G8 summit in July, apparently sometimes on spurious grounds.

◻ In April officers of a special police unit (OMON) reportedly used excessive force to disperse over 500 men, women and children protesting at alleged corruption by local authorities in Dagestan. Murad Nagmetov was killed and at least two other demonstrators were seriously injured after police reportedly fired tear gas canisters directly into the crowd without warning. The local procuracy opened investigations.

Conflict in the North Caucasus

Extrajudicial executions, enforced disappearances and abductions, arbitrary detention and torture, including in unofficial places of detention, were reported in the government's counter-terrorism operation in the North Caucasus, particularly in Chechnya and Ingushetia. Individuals who sought justice in the Russian courts or before the European Court of Human Rights faced intimidation from officials. Defence lawyers were also harassed.

The conflict, sometimes characterized as an insurgency, continued in Chechnya despite efforts to restore normalcy, including through large-scale reconstruction projects. Federal forces and Chechen police and security forces fought Chechen armed opposition groups, and federal forces shelled mountainous areas in the south. In turn, Chechen armed groups attacked police officers and convoys of federal forces, and planted car bombs. The presence of numerous paramilitary forces, their arbitrary actions and their lack of accountability made it difficult to determine the identity of those responsible for serious human rights violations.

International agencies estimated 180,000 people were still internally displaced within Chechnya by the conflict. Of these around 37,000 were registered as living in temporary accommodation, where conditions were reportedly poor. In April, Ramzan Kadyrov, Prime Minister of Chechnya, said the centres were "a nest of criminality, drug addiction and prostitution" and demanded their closure. Reportedly, five centres housing 4,500 people were closed, and individuals were removed from lists of inhabitants in other centres, although no alternative accommodation was available.

◻ Bulat Chilaev and Aslan Israilov were believed to have been subjected to enforced disappearance by

Chechen or Russian federal forces. About 10 eyewitnesses saw them being bundled into a car by armed masked men in uniform in Chechnya on 9 April. A military identity tag was later found near the spot. Their whereabouts remained unknown. Bulat Chilaev was a driver for the NGO, Grazhdanskoe Sodeistvie (Civic Assistance), whose work includes medical support for the displaced and others affected by the armed conflict.

In Ingushetia, armed groups reportedly assassinated officials, also killing their relatives including children, passers-by and guards. Arbitrary detentions, one extrajudicial execution and torture in police custody were reported. Serious violations including torture were also reported in North Ossetia and Dagestan. There were nearly 25,000 people displaced by the Chechen conflict in Ingushetia and Dagestan at the end of 2006.

International scrutiny
In May, for Russia's election to the UN Human Rights Council, the government pledged active co-operation with UN human rights bodies and highlighted the scheduling of a visit by the UN Special Rapporteur on torture for 2006. However, in October the Special Rapporteur postponed his visit, set to focus on the North Caucasus, because the Russian authorities had said the standard conditions of such visits – in particular, arriving unannounced at places of detention and interviewing detainees in private – contravened Russian law. The Special Rapporteur had been asking to visit Chechnya since 2000.

Council of Europe
In January the Parliamentary Assembly of the Council of Europe adopted a strongly worded resolution on Chechnya. It condemned ineffectual investigations and resulting impunity for human rights violations; reprisals against applicants to the European Court of Human Rights; the complete failure of harsh security measures to restore law and order, and resulting desperation, violence and instability. It urged the Committee of Ministers of the Council of Europe to "confront its responsibilities in the face of one of the most serious human rights issues in any of the Council of Europe's member states".

In May NGOs urged Russia to fulfil commitments made on accession to the Council of Europe a decade earlier, including to address impunity in Chechnya.

In May, a delegation visiting Chechnya from the European Committee for the Prevention of Torture was denied immediate access to the village of Tsenteroi, where unofficial detention facilities were reportedly located.

Russia failed to ratify Protocol 6 to the European Convention on Human Rights which provides for abolition of the death penalty in times of peace, despite its commitment to do so by February 1999. In November the State Duma (parliament) postponed to 2010 the introduction of jury trials in Chechnya, the one remaining region without a jury system. This had the effect of extending the current moratorium on the death penalty, introduced in 1999 when death sentences were banned until the jury system had been introduced everywhere.

UN Committee against Torture
Among concerns of the UN Committee against Torture in November were the absence of a definition of torture in the Criminal Code that reflected the definition in the UN Convention against Torture; laws and practices that obstructed detainees' access to lawyers and relatives; numerous and consistent allegations of torture and other ill-treatment or punishment by law enforcement personnel, including in police custody; failures in investigations into allegations of torture and ill-treatment; violent hazing of recruits in the military and reprisals against complainants; trafficking of women and children; and lack of safeguards against forcible returns. The Committee's concerns on Chechnya included reliable reports of unofficial places of detention, enforced disappearances and abductions, and torture.

Torture
Torture was used in police custody across the country. Safeguards against torture – such as notifying relatives of arrest, and rights to legal counsel and to medical examination by a doctor of choice – were circumvented by police officers focused on obtaining "confessions". The Procuracy routinely failed to ensure effective investigation of torture allegations or remedy against torture. There was no fully effective, independent and nationally enforced mechanism for unannounced visits to places of detention. Convicted prisoners were reportedly beaten in a number of colonies, including in Perm and Sverdlovsk Regions, according to reports.

In January the European Court of Human Rights ruled that the Russian authorities had subjected Aleksei Mikheev to torture in police detention in September 1998, and had denied him access to legal remedies. The Court found the government had violated the prohibition of torture and the right to an effective remedy.

In April, Aslan Umakhanov's lawyer was not informed when he was transferred from the pre-trial detention centre in Ekaterinburg back to police custody for questioning in connection with a criminal investigation. Police investigators allegedly beat him severely and subjected him to electric shocks to force him to "confess". The authorities refused to open a criminal investigation into his alleged torture, despite a medical certificate attesting to his injuries.

Former Guantánamo detainees
In Kabardino-Balkaria, Rasul Kudaev remained in detention amid concerns about his health. A former Guantánamo detainee, in 2004 he was transferred from US to Russian custody, detained for around four months, then released. He was arrested in Kabardino-Balkaria and charged with terrorism-related offences after the October 2005 attack on the capital, Nalchik. His state-appointed lawyer, removed from the case in November 2005 after she complained officially that he had been tortured in police custody, was not reinstated despite appeals to the courts.

Forcible return
In some cases, orders to extradite individuals to Uzbekistan where they risked being subjected to

torture were overturned by Russian courts or their implementation was stayed in accordance with Russia's obligations under international human rights and refugee law. However, the Russian authorities forcibly returned at least one person to Uzbekistan in violation of its international obligations.

◻ The Russian authorities opened a criminal investigation in October into the deportation of Rustam Muminov to Uzbekistan. He had been deported that month although the Moscow City Court had yet to rule on his appeal against his deportation order and he had informed Russian officials that he wished to apply for asylum. The European Court of Human Rights had issued a request to stay the deportation just prior to his removal.

Lesbian, gay, bisexual and transgender rights

Lesbian, gay, bisexual and transgender (LGBT) people were subjected to violent attacks while attending LGBT clubs in Moscow. The police were criticized for not providing sufficient protection.

◻ In Moscow, a Gay Pride march was banned in May. Mayor Yuri Luzhkov and Russian Orthodox and Muslim leaders publicly criticized the planned march and made homophobic statements, and a Moscow court upheld the ban. LGBT demonstrators instead laid flowers at the tomb of the Unknown Soldier by the Kremlin and joined an authorized demonstration near Moscow city hall. At both sites, counter-demonstrators hurled homophobic abuse and attacked some individual protesters. The police reportedly failed to provide protection or to differentiate between peaceful and violent protesters, detaining individuals from both groups. A number of LGBT activists and journalists were injured.

Racism, xenophobia and intolerance

The authorities failed to provide protection or to investigate effectively many racially motivated attacks, including murders. A small rise in prosecutions of race hate crimes and local initiatives such as increased policing were inadequate to address the scale of the problem, and there was no comprehensive programme to combat racist and xenophobic ideas and ideologies.

◻ Liana Sisoko, a nine-year-old girl of Russian and Malian origin, was seriously injured when she was stabbed on 25 March by two youths near the lift in her block of flats in St Petersburg. The attackers reportedly painted a swastika and the words "skinheads...we did it" near the scene of the attack.

◻ A Romani man and an ethnic Russian woman were killed in an apparently racist attack by 20 youths armed with metal bars and spades who attacked a Romani family and the woman, a visitor, in the Volgograd Region on 13 April. Others were seriously injured.

◻ Seven defendants were convicted of "hooliganism" in March for their roles in the fatal attack on a nine-year-old Tajik girl, Khursheda Sultonova, in February 2004. They were sentenced to between 18 months' and five and a half years' imprisonment. The only defendant charged with racially motivated murder was acquitted on that count.

Discriminatory policing

NGOs Jurix and the Open Society Justice Initiative released research demonstrating that Moscow police disproportionately stopped and searched non-Slavs. After relations worsened between Russia and Georgia in September and October, hundreds of Georgian nationals were deported for allegedly violating immigration rules or being involved in crime. Individuals were held pending deportation in reportedly insanitary conditions and without water or food. Two Georgian nationals died awaiting deportation, allegedly due to the poor conditions and inadequate medical attention.

Violence against women

No measures under Russian law specifically addressed violence against women in the family, and government support for crisis centres and hotlines was totally inadequate. In November the UN Committee against Torture expressed concern about the reports of prevalent domestic violence and the lack of sufficient shelters for women. The Committee recommended the Russian authorities should ensure protection of women by adopting specific legislative and other measures to address domestic violence, providing for protection of victims, access to medical, social and legal services and temporary accommodation and for perpetrators to be held accountable.

◻ One of the few government-supported shelters for women in the Russian Federation, in Petrozavodsk, Republic of Karelia, was closed.

Fair trial concerns

Prisoners served sentences after trials that failed to meet international fair trial standards, and in which their lawyers considered the charges to be politically motivated.

◻ Former YUKOS oil company head Mikhail Khodorkovskii and associate Platon Lebedev, serving nine-year prison sentences following convictions in 2005 for fraud and tax evasion, were denied the right to serve their sentences in or near their home areas. Mikhail Khodorkovskii was unlawfully held in a punishment cell for two weeks in January for having a copy of publicly available government decrees on prisoner conduct. He was also held in a punishment cell for a week in March for drinking tea in an unauthorized place.

◻ Mikhail Trepashkin, a lawyer and former security services officer, was denied adequate medical treatment for chronic bronchial asthma. He was serving a four-year sentence in a prison colony imposed by a military court in 2005 following conviction on charges including divulging state secrets. He was reportedly placed in an unheated, unventilated punishment cell by the prison administration in an attempt to make him withdraw complaints about the fairness of his trial and his treatment.

AI country reports/ visits
Reports
· Commonwealth of Independent States: Positive trend on the abolition of the death penalty but more needs to be done (AI Index: EUR 04/003/2006)

- Russian Federation: Rasul Kudaev (AI Index: EUR 46/003/2006)
- Russian Federation: Amnesty International's concerns and recommendations in the case of Mikhail Trepashkin (AI Index: EUR 46/012/2006)
- Russian Federation: Preliminary briefing to the UN Committee against Torture (AI Index: EUR 46/014/2006)
- Russian Federation: Violent racism out of control (AI Index: EUR 46/022/2006)
- Russian Federation: Supplementary briefing to the UN Committee against Torture (AI Index: EUR 46/039/2006)
- Russian Federation: Russian Chechen Friendship Society closed under new NGO law (AI Index: EUR 46/048/2006)
- Russian Federation: Torture and forced "confessions" in detention (AI Index: EUR 46/056/2006)

Visits

AI delegates visited the Russian Federation in April, June, July and December. In July, AI's Secretary General met the President together with other heads of global civil society organizations.

RWANDA

REPUBLIC OF RWANDA
Head of state: Paul Kagame
Head of government: Bernard Makuza
Death penalty: retentionist
International Criminal Court: not ratified

The government maintained tight control over all sections of civil society, whose work was conducted in a climate of fear and suspicion. Trials continued of people suspected of involvement in the 1994 genocide. There were concerns about the fairness of some of the trials. Several thousand detainees were held in long-term detention without trial in harsh conditions. Six hundred people remained on death row.

Background

The international community continued to depict post-genocide Rwanda as a success story. However, the authorities failed to provide basic health care and education to communities which were excluded from local governance. Cross- and inter-ethnic tensions persisted in the country.

In November, diplomatic tensions between Kigali and Paris reached crisis point after a French judge issued international arrest warrants for nine close aides of Rwandan President Paul Kagame.

Independent journalists under attack

Journalists were subjected to intimidation, harassment and violence. The authorities failed to conduct independent and impartial investigations into attacks or threats against journalists. The authorities repeatedly denied that there were restrictions on freedom of expression in Rwanda, accusing independent journalists of "unprofessionalism".

▭ Bonaventure Bizumuremyi, the news editor of *Umuco*, reportedly had his home in Kigali ransacked in January by four men armed with clubs and knives. Before this attack, *Umuco* had criticized the ruling party for ineptitude and for allegedly controlling the judiciary.

The judicial system remained compromised and regularly enforced laws that curtailed free expression.

▭ In August, the High Court upheld a suspended sentence of one year in prison and a fine imposed on Charles Kabonero, editor of *Umuseso*, for "public insult". In 2004, *Umuseso* had questioned the integrity of the parliamentary Deputy Speaker, Denis Polisi.

Human rights defenders

In June 2006, the National Commission for Human Rights released its 2005 annual report in Kinyarwanda. According to national newspapers, this report, which was supported by some Rwandan human rights organizations, showed a 95 per cent improvement in the human rights situation since 2004.

However, some human rights defenders said that their work was under intense scrutiny by the authorities, that freedom of expression remained severely controlled since the 2004 clampdown on human rights organizations, and that self-censorship was widespread.

At the end of 2006, parliament was working on a new bill to strengthen government control over the activities and publications of non-governmental organizations.

Genocide trials

Trials continued under the gacaca system – a community-based system of tribunals established in 2002 to try people suspected of crimes during the 1994 genocide. Concerns about the fairness of the gacaca system included a perceived lack of impartiality and reports that defendants were not allowed to defend themselves either during the information retrieval process prior to the trial or during the trial itself. In addition, the information-retrieval phase was reportedly controlled by grass-roots authorities (nyumbakumi) although the law assigned responsibility to the gacaca judges themselves.

Poorly qualified, ill-trained and corrupt gacaca judges in certain districts fuelled widespread distrust of the gacaca system.

▭ In Munyaga (Rwamagana district, East province) a judge reportedly visited people who had been summoned for questioning and asked them for money in return for an acquittal. In the same district, two people were sentenced to 30 years' imprisonment, despite doubts over their involvement in the genocide.

According to reports from local authorities and genocide survivors' associations, in the East province some genocide survivors were subject to intimidation, harassment and assault before testifying before a gacaca court.

In November, at Rukumberi (Ngoma district, East province) Frédéric Musarira, a genocide survivor, was allegedly killed by a man who had recently been released from prison after confessing his involvement in the genocide. In retaliation, genocide survivors in the area reportedly killed at least eight people.

Rwandans fled the gacaca system to neighbouring countries throughout 2006. Some were afraid that the tribunals would expose their involvement in the genocide. Others fled out of fear of false accusations.

Approximately 20,000 Rwandan asylum-seekers fled from southern Rwanda to Burundi early in the year, according to the UN refugee agency UNHCR. The common issues forcing them to flee were persecution by local authorities, drought conditions and gacaca court summonses.

In July, further groups of Rwandans fled from the East province to avoid the gacaca system, including 40 people from Munyaga, Rwamagana district, who entered Uganda.

Pre-trial detention
Several thousand detainees remained incarcerated on a long-term basis without trial. Approximately 48,000 detainees were awaiting trial for alleged participation in the genocide.

☐ Dominique Makeli, a former journalist for Radio Rwanda, remained in detention without trial after almost 12 years. The charges against him have repeatedly changed. The authorities' latest accusation was that in 1994 he had incited genocide in a programme for Radio Rwanda in 1994.

☐ Two Catholic nuns, Sisters Bénédicte Mukanyangezi and Bernadette Mukarusine, remained in detention without trial after more than 12 years.

Prison conditions
Approximately 69,000 people were reportedly held in prisons during 2006. All prisons were overpopulated with the exception of Mpanga Prison. For example, Gitarama prison reportedly held 7,477 detainees although its official capacity was 3,000.

Detention conditions remained extremely harsh and amounted to cruel, inhuman or degrading treatment. Underground cells were reported to exist in some prisons and detention centres.

☐ At least 50 people were reportedly held in harsh and insanitary conditions in an underground cellar in Gitarama prison for more than a year. These prisoners were seldom allowed to go outside.

Death penalty
Six hundred prisoners remained on death row. The last execution was carried out in 1998. In October, the political bureau of the ruling party strongly recommended abolishing the death penalty. The continued existence of the death penalty constituted

one of the main obstacles preventing the transfer to Rwanda's national jurisdiction of detainees held by the International Criminal Tribunal for Rwanda (ICTR) or indicted genocide suspects living abroad.

Investigations of genocide and war crimes
The Commission of Inquiry set up in April 2005 to investigate the alleged role of the French military in the genocide started work in April 2006. Rwandan officials stated that, depending on the Commission findings, they might lodge a complaint against French military personnel before the International Criminal Court.

In May, the Rwandan Prosecutor General compiled a new list of 93 genocide suspects said to be living abroad. Concerns were raised over the accuracy of this list, as some of those named had apparently died, or were not in the named country. Few foreign governments initiated judicial proceedings against alleged Rwandan genocide suspects residing, sometimes under false identities, in their countries.

In November, a French judge investigating the shooting down of former President Habyarimana's plane in 1994 issued international arrest warrants for nine high-ranking Rwandan officials. He also requested that the ICTR issue an indictment for President Paul Kagame's arrest for his involvement.

The investigation by a Spanish judge into the murder of Spanish nationals and other crimes committed between 1990 and 2002 in Rwanda was reportedly completed. The investigation focused on the direct involvement of 69 members of the Rwandan Patriotic Front (RPF), some of whom were high-ranking figures in the military.

International Criminal Tribunal for Rwanda
Trials of prominent genocide suspects continued before the ICTR, which held 56 detainees at the end of 2006. Nine trials, involving multiple and single defendants, were ongoing. Seven cases were concluded in 2006. Two detainees were acquitted and the others were sentenced to terms of imprisonment. One case was pending appeal. Eighteen suspects indicted by the ICTR were still at large.

The ICTR was mandated by the UN Security Council to complete all trials by the end of 2008. It ceased to issue indictments for individuals suspected of involvement in genocide, war crimes and crimes against humanity in Rwanda.

Since its inception, the ICTR has tried only members and supporters of the government in place in April 1994. It did not fully implement its mandate by investigating all war crimes and crimes against humanity committed in 1994, notably those committed by the RPF.

Update: enforced disappearances
Augustin Cyiza, a prominent member of civil society, was reportedly a victim of enforced disappearance in 2003 during the run-up to elections. Rwandan officials denied knowledge of his whereabouts in 2005, but sources claimed he had been abducted and killed.

Léonard Hitimana, a member of the Transitional National Assembly, disappeared in April 2003. In April 2006, the President of the National Commission for

Human Rights stated that the investigation into his case was confidential, and that results would be released in due course. The fate of Léonard Hitimana remained unknown.

Political prisoners

Pasteur Bizimungu, former President of Rwanda, and Charles Ntakirutinka were sentenced to 15 and 10 years' imprisonment respectively in 2005 on charges of inciting civil disobedience, associating with criminal elements and embezzlement of state funds. Both men had, prior to their arrest, launched a new political party, the Democratic Party for Renewal (Parti Démocratique de Renouveau, PDR-Ubuyanja). Many human rights observers considered that their prosecution was an attempt to eliminate political opposition. They were held at the Central Prison, Kigali.

AI country reports/ visits
Statements
- Rwanda: Freedom of expression under attack (AI Index: AFR 47/002/2006)
- Rwanda: Reports of extrajudicial executions in Mulindi military detention centre must be independently investigated (AI Index: AFR 47/004/2006)
- Rwanda: Appeal to the UN Security Council to ensure that the mandate of the International Criminal Tribunal for Rwanda is fulfilled (AI Index: IOR 40/045/2006)

Visit
AI delegates visited Rwanda in October.

SAUDI ARABIA

KINGDOM OF SAUDI ARABIA
Head of state and government: King Abdullah Bin 'Abdul 'Aziz Al-Saud
Death penalty: retentionist
International Criminal Court: not ratified

The government continued with reform initiatives but these had little impact in improving human rights. There were new violations linked to the "war on terror" and further clashes between security forces and members of armed groups. Scores of people suspected of belonging to or supporting such armed groups were reported to have been arrested but the authorities did not divulge their identities or other information about them, and it was unclear whether any were charged and brought to trial. Peaceful critics of the government were subjected to prolonged detention without charge or trial. There were allegations of torture, and

floggings continued to be imposed by the courts. Violence against women was prevalent and migrant workers suffered discrimination and abuse. At least 39 people were executed.

Background

Saudi Arabia was elected to a seat on the new UN Human Rights Council in May.

About 2,000 demonstrators in various cities protested against the Israeli bombardment of Lebanon in July and August. Several people were arrested but all were believed to have been released without charge.

Some of 300 members of the Ismaili Shi'a community were briefly arrested in September when they held a protest in Nijran against the continuing detention of other Ismailis, who had been detained in connection with demonstrations and clashes in April 2000. Following this, some of the remaining Ismaili prisoners were released, but others were still believed to be held at the end of 2006.

Abuses in the context of the 'war on terror'

The government continued to pursue its stated policy of fighting terrorism, often paying little regard to international law.

Clashes between security forces and armed groups continued in various parts of the country, including Abqiq, Riyadh and Jeddah. At least five men on the government's list of suspected al-Qa'ida militants were reportedly killed in a rest house in February during clashes with security forces in al-Yarmuk district, Riyadh.

The Minister of Interior announced in April that a State Security Court would be introduced to investigate and try alleged terror suspects and supporters of terrorism but it was not clear whether this had been established by the end of 2006. In June the King said that those who handed themselves in to the authorities would benefit from an amnesty and be pardoned for their actions.

Scores of people suspected of links to al-Qa'ida were arrested. At least 100, including foreign nationals, were reportedly arrested in March, June and August alone in Mecca, Madinah and Riyadh.

The authorities did not disclose the names, legal status or other details of those arrested in 2006 and in previous years, and it was not known whether any of them were charged or brought to trial.

▭ Fouad Hakim, who was reportedly arrested in December 2004 for suspected links to an "extremist organization", was believed to have been detained without charge or trial, and without access to a lawyer until he was released from al-Ruwais prison, Jeddah, in November.

▭ Muhiddin Mugne Haji Mascat, a Somali national, was detained in al-Ha'ir prison in Riyadh. A doctor, he was arrested in November 2005 for allegedly providing medical treatment to a security suspect. He was released without charge in April.

▭ Two men arrested in November 2005 — Abdel Hakim Mohammed Jellaini, a British national arrested while on a business trip to Mecca and accused of giving financial assistance to an "extremist organization", and

Abdullah Hassan, a Libyan national — were released without charge in July. However, their passports were withheld and they were not permitted to leave Saudi Arabia. Abdel Hakim Mohammed Jellaini had reportedly been beaten and denied food during part of his detention.

The Minister of Interior reportedly announced in April that thousands of detainees had been released, including 700 men linked to al-Qa'ida who the authorities had "involved in a programme aimed at correcting their extremist views". He did not disclose when or over what period these releases had occurred.

Guantánamo Bay detainees

At least two dozen Saudi Arabian nationals and an ethnic Uighur who had been detained by US forces in Guantánamo Bay, Cuba, were repatriated to Saudi Arabia in May and June. They were detained upon arrival and held at al-Ha'ir prison. There were fears that Siddeq Ahmad Siddeq Nour Turkistani, the Uighur, would be at risk of torture or execution if he were to be removed to China; he was still believed to be in Saudi Arabia at the end of 2006. The Saudi Arabian authorities said that the Investigation and Public Prosecution Commission would review the cases of the returned detainees, and at least 12 of them were released in May and August. Some were said to have been released for lack of evidence of any offence; others were sentenced to one-year prison terms for document forgery.

Political prisoners and possible prisoners of conscience

Critics of the government were subjected to detention without charge or trial, often for prolonged periods, before being tried or released.

☐ Dr Shaim al-Hamazani, Jamal al-Qosseibi, Hamad al-Salihi and 'Abdullah al-Magidi were tried in September, having reportedly been detained without charge or access to lawyers at al-Ha'ir prison for almost two years. They were arrested in 2004 after they called for political and judicial reform and the release of political prisoners. They were sentenced to prison terms of between one and a half and three and a half years. Dr Shaim al-Hamazani was released in October, having completed the requisite period in prison, but continued to be banned from travelling abroad.

☐ Hind Sa'id Bin Zu'air was detained in August, together with her 10-month-old baby, and held for a week before being released uncharged, apparently because her father, Dr Sa'id Bin Zu'air, has been critical of government policies pursued in the context of the "war on terror".

☐ Twenty men, who were among 250 people reportedly arrested for attending a private social gathering in al-'Ashamia area in Jizan in August, appeared to be prisoners of conscience detained solely for their actual or perceived sexual orientation. They continued to be detained without charge or trial at the end of the year; others held at the same time were released uncharged.

☐ A possible prisoner of conscience, Kamil 'Abbas al-

Ahmad, was released in September from the General Intelligence Office (al-Mabahith al-'Amma) in al-Dammam. He had been detained since August 2003 for undisclosed reasons, apparently connected to his Shi'a religious beliefs.

Freedom of expression

Despite greater press freedom in recent years, writers and journalists who called for reform were subject to short-term arrests, travel bans or censorship. Some also faced harassment by private individuals aligned to conservative sectors of society.

☐ In February the daily *Shams* newspaper was suspended for six weeks after it re-published the cartoons of the Prophet Muhammad as part of its campaign to urge actions against the cartoons.

☐ In March Mohsen al-Awaji was reportedly arrested after he published articles on the Internet criticizing the authorities and calling for an end to censorship of websites. He was released without charge after eight days.

☐ Hamza al-Muzaini, an academic who allegedly criticized a cleric in an article, was fined in May by the Ministry of Information. He was physically attacked and branded an "infidel" in September by a group of young men as he gave a speech on reform of the school curriculum.

☐ In October a court dismissed a case against Raja al-Sanei', author of a book about the lives of young Saudi Arabian women. She had been accused of defaming Saudi Arabian society and misinterpreting verses of the Qur'an. The Ministry of Culture and Information did not permit her book or some 20 others to be featured at the Riyadh International Book Fair, because they were considered defamatory to Saudi Arabia and Islam.

Scores of people, including pro-reform figures, were subjected to travel bans after their release from detention. Dr Matrouk al-Falih and Muhammad Sa'eed Tayyeb, who were arrested in 2004 for calling for reform, reportedly remained subject to restrictions on their freedom of expression and movement imposed when they were released in August 2005, and March 2004, respectively. Muhammad Sa'eed Tayyeb was reportedly required to sign a statement at the time of his release that he would not again call for political reform.

☐ Sa'ad Bin Sa'id Bin Zu'air and his brother, Mubarak Bin Sa'id Bin Zu'air, and their father, Dr Sa'id Bin Zu'air, were reportedly subject to censorship and banned from travelling. Sa'ad Bin Sa'id Bin Zu'air was also detained without charge or trial from June to August, during which he was held incommunicado in 'Ulaisha prison, Riyadh, after he was interviewed on the satellite TV station, Al-Jazeera.

Women's rights

Women continued to face pervasive discrimination, in particular severe restrictions on their freedom of movement. Domestic violence remained widespread; the Saudi Arabian Human Rights Society reported that it had received reports of hundreds of cases of domestic violence. In May it was reported that King

Abdullah had ordered that a new court be established which would specialize in hearing domestic violence cases, but it was not clear how far this had progressed by the end of the year.

Women activists continued to lobby for their rights. Following her release, Wajeha Al-Huwaider, who was briefly arrested in August 2005 for carrying a placard urging King Abdullah to grant more rights to women, vowed to carry on her activities.

In February the Shura (Consultative Council) rejected a private member's bill to lift the ban on women driving motor vehicles. In June the authorities appointed six women as consultants to the Shura to advise on issues affecting women.

The Ministry of Labour's plans to increase the number of Saudi Arabian women in employment suffered a setback. It postponed the implementation of a decision that only women could be employed in lingerie shops after shop owners proved unable to comply.

Forced removal
Abulgasim Ahmed Abulgasim, a political opponent of the Sudanese government and member of an armed political group in Darfur, was arrested by Saudi Arabian security forces on 26 September at his home in Jeddah where he had lived for over 20 years. He was apparently arrested because of a speech he gave at the Sudanese Embassy in which he criticized the Sudanese government. He was deported to Sudan, where he was arrested immediately and held incommunicado, on 28 September.

Migrant workers
Migrant workers were subject to abuses by state authorities and by private employers. Abuses by state authorities included detention without charge or trial, and abuses by employers included physical and psychological ill-treatment and non-payment of salaries.

◻ Isma'il 'Abdul Sattar, a Pakistani national, reportedly remained in detention without charge or trial at al-Ruwais prison, Jeddah, having been arrested 10 years previously following a police raid on the company where he worked.

◻ Nour Miyati, an Indonesian domestic worker, who was severely injured by her employer and then sentenced to 79 lashes by a court in Riyadh for accusing him of abuse, had her sentence overturned on appeal.

Torture and ill-treatment
There were reports of torture in custody. Sentences of flogging, a form of cruel, inhuman and degrading punishment which may amount to torture, continued to be routinely imposed by the courts. Those sentenced to floggings included young men and children accused by the Committee for the Prevention of Vice and Promotion of Virtue of harassing women. The government was reported in May to have instructed the Committee to refer cases of harassment of women to the prosecuting authorities.

◻ Ma'idh Al-Saleem was released in November following a pardon by the King. He was reported to have been arrested in 2001, aged 16, and to have been

tortured for several days until he "confessed" to making "verbal comments contrary to Shar'ia". He was sentenced to death but this was later reduced on appeal to 14 years' imprisonment and 4,000 lashes, to which he was subjected in repeated sessions of 50 lashes at a time.

◻ Nabil Al-Randan was reported to have fled Saudi Arabia when, in April, the Court of Cassation upheld a sentence of 90 lashes for "immoral behaviour" after he appointed two women to work in a restaurant he owned.

◻ Puthen Veetil Abdul Latheef Noushad, an Indian national who was sentenced to have an eye removed in December 2005, was pardoned by the man he was said to have partially blinded in a dispute and released on 5 April.

Death penalty
At least 39 people were executed. The authorities did not disclose the number of people sentenced to death. Many defendants complained that they were not represented by lawyers and were not informed of the progress of their trial.

◻ Suliamon Olyfemi, a Nigerian, remained under sentence of death. He had been convicted of murder after a trial in 2004 which was conducted in Arabic, a language which he did not understand, without the assistance of an interpreter. He was reportedly tortured or ill-treated in pre-trial detention and denied access to legal representation or adequate consular assistance.

◻ Majda Mostafa Mahir, a Moroccan national who was sentenced to death after an unfair trial in 1997, and whose death sentence was annulled after the victim's family requested a revocation of the sentence, was released on 12 November and returned to Morocco. In April, the Secretary of the Crown Prince had reportedly visited her in Briman prison, Jeddah.

◻ Hadi Sa'eed Al-Muteef, who was sentenced to death for making "verbal comments contrary to Shar'ia" in 2001, had his sentence commuted to a prison term. He was reportedly denied access to a lawyer, and not informed of proceedings against him or appeal processes.

Saudi Arabia assured the UN Committee on the Rights of the Child in January that it had not carried out any executions of child offenders since the Convention on the Rights of the Child came into force in Saudi Arabia in 1996. However, child offenders continued to be sentenced to death.

◻ Five teenagers were reported in August to have been sentenced to death by a lower court in Madinah, in connection with the murder of a 10-year-old boy in 2004.

AI country reports/ visits
Statement
· Saudi Arabia: Government must take urgent action to abolish the death penalty for child offenders (AI Index: MDE 23/001/2006)

SENEGAL

REPUBLIC OF SENEGAL
Head of state: Abdoulaye Wade
Head of government: Macky Sall
Death penalty: abolitionist for all crimes
International Criminal Court: ratified

Sporadic fighting resumed in the southern Casamance region and an intervention by the army of Guinea-Bissau led thousands of people to flee. Leaders and supporters of opposition parties were harassed and threats to freedom of expression continued. Hundreds of migrants and asylum-seekers were arrested while trying to reach Europe. A draft law permitting Hissène Habré to be tried in Senegal was adopted.

Background
In February, talks between the government and the Democratic Forces of Casamance Movement (Mouvement des forces démocratiques de Casamance, MFDC), an armed group seeking independence for the region, were again postponed because of violent clashes between rival MFDC factions.

Political tension between supporters of President Wade and opposition leaders intensified in the run-up to a presidential election scheduled for February 2007. Opposition parties protested against a constitutional amendment adopted in November abolishing the minimum percentage of votes required for a President to be elected. Tension escalated after the arrest of Jean-Paul Dias, leader of the Gaïndé Centrist Block (Bloc des centristes gaïndé, BCG). He was accused of insulting the head of state and calling on opposition leaders not to respond to court or police summonses. His son, Barthélémy Dias, was arrested on similar charges in August. Both were sentenced to prison terms. Jean-Paul Dias was provisionally released in September on health grounds while his son benefited from a presidential pardon in November.

Harassment of political opponents
In February, former Prime Minister Idrissa Seck was released after seven months in jail after most of the charges against him – including threatening state security and embezzlement – were dropped. Nevertheless, some of his supporters continued to be harassed and some were arrested on charges of complicity in money laundering.

Arrests and repatriation of migrants
Thousands of migrants and asylum-seekers, mostly sub-Saharan Africans, continued to transit through Senegal. Many sought to reach the Canary Islands (Spain) and hundreds were arrested by Senegalese security forces. Coastal surveillance was reinforced after an agreement in August between Senegal and Spain to implement joint security measures to curb the flow of clandestine migrants. In September and October, more than 90 Pakistani migrants, including at least one minor, were arrested, charged with attempted illegal immigration and repatriated.

Fighting in Casamance
The resumption of fighting in Casamance led to the displacement of more than 8,000 people in the border region, of whom some 6,000 fled to neighbouring Guinea-Bissau and 2,000 deeper into Senegal. In April forces of the Guinea-Bissau army entered Senegalese territory to attack the base of the MFDC faction led by Salif Sadio, claiming that he was a major obstacle to peace in Casamance and was threatening the security of neighbouring countries. Many people fled their homes at this time. However, Salif Sadio remained at large and his forces reportedly retreated into northern Casamance. In August, another wave of more than 6,000 people fled to neighbouring Gambia following clashes between rival MFDC factions in northern Casamance.

Freedom of expression
Threats to freedom of expression continued, targeting journalists and writers critical of the government. Customs officers were reportedly disciplined for allowing several books published in France and written by Senegalese authors, including Abdou Latif Coulibaly, to enter Senegal. As a result, other books were blocked at customs and could not be distributed in Senegal.
In January, six staff members of the private radio station, Sud FM, who had been briefly detained in October 2005 after an interview with Salif Sadio, were acquitted after charges of "complicity in endangering the security of state" were dropped.

Hissène Habré
Progress was made in the fight against impunity. In July, the African Union (AU) Assembly of Heads of State and Government required Senegal to try Hissène Habré, Chad's former President, who had been living in Senegal since he was ousted from power in 1990. This decision followed Senegal's request that the AU indicate who had jurisdiction to try Hissène Habré. He has been subject since 2005 to an extradition request and international arrest warrant issued by a Belgian judge for torture and other crimes committed during his rule from 1982 to 1990. In November Senegal's Council of Ministers adopted a draft law to permit Hissène Habré to be tried. In December, the government set up a working group to be in charge of organizing Hissène Habré's trial.

SERBIA

REPUBLIC OF SERBIA
Head of state: Boris Tadić
Head of government: Vojislav Koštunica
Death penalty: abolitionist for all crimes
International Criminal Court: ratified

Serbia's failure to arrest and transfer indicted suspects to the International Criminal Tribunal for the former Yugoslavia (Tribunal) led to the suspension of talks on a Stabilization and Association Agreement with the European Union (EU). Low-ranking officials were brought to justice in domestic war crimes trials. Discrimination continued against Romani and other minorities, especially in Kosovo.

Political developments

On 2 May the EU suspended negotiations on the Stabilization and Association Agreement after the authorities in Serbia and Montenegro failed to arrest suspects indicted by the Tribunal – in particular Bosnian Serb General Ratko Mladić. Negotiations remained suspended. On 14 December Serbia was admitted to NATO's Partnership for Peace.

Following an independence referendum on 21 May, Montenegro seceded from the state of Serbia and Montenegro. The Council of Europe continued to separately monitor Serbia's compliance with conditions agreed on accession.

Just over 50 per cent of voters in a referendum in October favoured the new Serbian Constitution, which restated that Kosovo and Metohija were part of Serbian territory. The Albanian minority in southern Serbia boycotted the referendum, and ethnic Albanians in Kosovo were not eligible to vote.

Final status of Kosovo

Following the failure to reach agreement between the Serbian and Kosovo authorities in talks from February to October, in November the UN Special Envoy for Kosovo – with the agreement of the UN Secretary-General – postponed a decision on the final status of Kosovo until after Serbian elections in January 2007. Kosovo remained part of Serbia and was administered by the UN Interim Administration Mission in Kosovo (UNMIK).

On 10 March, UNMIK began to transfer government responsibilities to the Provisional Institutions of Self-Government in Kosovo. On 1 June the Special Representative to the UN Secretary-General in Kosovo (SRSG) announced that UNMIK had begun preparations to leave Kosovo. The EU began preparing for UNMIK's handover to an EU Crisis Management Operation.

Impunity for war crimes

Former Serbian President Slobodan Milošević died following a heart attack at the Tribunal Detention Unit on 11 March. He had been on trial before the Tribunal for war crimes and crimes against humanity in Kosovo and Croatia, and for genocide, war crimes and crimes against humanity in Bosnia and Herzegovina.

The Tribunal further restricted the conditions under which former Kosovo Prime Minister Ramush Haradinaj could engage in domestic politics. Indicted for crimes against humanity and war crimes on 24 February 2005, he had been provisionally released from the Tribunal in June 2005. He was re-elected leader of the Alliance for the Future of Kosovo on 20 May 2006.

In June, Carla del Ponte, Chief Prosecutor to the Tribunal, reported to the UN Security Council that Serbia's co-operation with the Tribunal remained "difficult and frustrating", although there were improvements in access to archives and documents. She expressed serious concerns at the lack of co-operation by UNMIK.

▢ On 21 June indictments were joined of charges of war crimes in Kosovo against six senior Serbian political, police and military officials. Proceedings started in July.

▢ On 27 February the International Court of Justice opened public hearings on genocide charges filed by Bosnia and Herzegovina against Serbia and Montenegro.

▢ On 17 November the Tribunal transferred to Serbia the indictment against Vladimir Kovačević, charged with six counts of war crimes in connection with the bombing of Dubrovnik in Croatia.

Serbia
Domestic war crimes trials

Progress was made in bringing Serbs suspected of war crimes to justice in domestic proceedings at the special War Crimes Chamber of the Belgrade District Court, although the Supreme Court continued to overturn war crimes verdicts and send cases back for retrial.

▢ The trial continued of five former members of the paramilitary unit known as the Scorpions. They were charged with war crimes, together with three others, for the killing of six Bosniak civilians in 1995 at Godinjske bare near Trnovo in Bosnia and Herzegovina.

▢ On 30 January, Milan Bulić was sentenced to eight years' imprisonment for involvement in war crimes against Croatian civilians in 1991 at Ovčara in Croatia. Fourteen other defendants had been convicted and sentenced in December 2005.

▢ In March, at the request of the SRSG, an Interpol warrant requested by Serbia, for the arrest on suspicion of war crimes of Kosovo Prime Minister Agim Çeku, former Kosovo Liberation Army (KLA) chief of staff and commander of the Kosova Protection Corps, was withdrawn.

▢ In April the SRSG unsuccessfully challenged the Serbian court's jurisdiction in the case of Anton Lekaj, a former KLA soldier. On 18 September the court sentenced him to 13 years' imprisonment for war crimes, including the rape of a Romani girl in Kosovo and the murder of three Romani men.

Enforced disappearances

Human rights groups in February called for a parliamentary inquiry into an alleged official cover-up of the transfer from Kosovo to Serbia of the bodies of ethnic Albanians killed in 1999. Some were hidden in mass graves, others allegedly burned at the Mačkatica smelting plant. On 30 June the last of the bodies of more than 700 ethnic Albanians exhumed from mass graves were returned to Kosovo. Police investigations were opened, according to reports in September, but no indictments were published by the end of 2006.

◻ On 2 October, the trial started at the War Crimes Chamber in Belgrade of eight former police officers — including Radoslav Mitrović, former Kosovo special police commander and Radojko Repanović, police commander in Suva Reka — indicted on 25 April for the murder of 48 ethnic Albanian civilians, all but one from the same family, in Suva Reka in March 1999. Some of their bodies had been exhumed at Batajnica.

◻ On 13 November the trial opened of two former police officers indicted in August for the murder of three Kosovo-Albanian brothers with US nationality.

Torture and ill-treatment
The new Serbian Criminal Code, which entered into force on 1 January, introduced a specific criminal offence of torture.

Numerous detainees alleged torture and other ill-treatment aimed at extracting "confessions", mostly at the time of arrest and during the first hours of detention at police stations, according to a report by the European Committee for the Prevention of Torture published in May. Reported methods included "falaka" (beating on the soles of the feet).

◻ In November police allegedly used excessive force against a prison protest at the government's failure to implement an amnesty law. Lawyers and relatives were reportedly unable to visit some of the 50 prisoners who had been hospitalized or placed in solitary confinement.

Political killings
◻ In May the Serbian Supreme Court ordered the retrial of Milorad Ulemek and former secret police chief Radomir Marković, citing serious violations of procedure. The two men had been convicted of the attempted murder of government minister Vuk Drašković and the murder of four other men, and sentenced to 15 and 10 years' imprisonment respectively, in June 2005.

◻ In November, Aleksandar Simović was arrested for the murder in June of Zoran Vukojević, a witness at a separate trial of Milorad Ulemek and others on charges of murdering former Serbian Prime Minister Zoran Đinđić. Others indicted for the murder of Zoran Đinđić remained at large.

◻ On 10 September municipal election candidate Ruždija Durović was killed in a shooting incident at a polling station in Novi Pazar in the Sandžak region. The killing was believed to be politically motivated. Three others were injured. Two suspects were arrested within 24 hours and remained in detention in November. Four people were injured in November when an explosive device was thrown into the home of a Democratic Action Party official.

Human rights defenders
Prosecutions believed to be malicious and politically motivated were opened in several proceedings against Biljana Kovačević-Vučo, director of the Lawyers Committee for Human Rights, and Humanitarian Law

Centre director Nataša Kandić. The charges included defamation.

Discrimination against minorities
◻ In October, eight football fans were indicted in Čačak for racial abuse of a Zimbabwean player, and 152 Belgrade fans were arrested for racial abuse during a football match against the mainly ethnic Bosniak team from Novi Pazar.

◻ On 6 February Šabac Municipal Court convicted Bogdan Vaslijević of "violating the equality of citizens" for preventing three Romani people from entering a swimming pool on 8 July 2000. He received a suspended three-month prison term.

◻ On 6 March the UN Committee on the Elimination of Racial Discrimination found that Serbia and Montenegro had failed to provide an effective remedy in the case of a Romani man, Dragan Durmić, refused entry to a Belgrade discotheque in March 2000.

Violence against women
Violence against women, including domestic violence and trafficking for the purposes of forced prostitution, remained widespread. On 10 January, the Ministry for Labour, Employment and Social policy published a draft strategy on combating violence against women but failed to consult women's organizations.

Kosovo
An UNMIK regulation in February effectively withdrew the jurisdiction of the Ombudsperson's Office over UNMIK. The Human Rights Advisory Panel, proposed as an alternative mechanism on 23 March, failed to provide an impartial body which would guarantee access to redress and reparations for people whose rights had been violated by UNMIK. It had not been constituted by the end of 2006.

Recommendations to strengthen protection for minorities by the Advisory Committee on the Framework Convention for the Protection of National Minorities, made public in March, were not implemented. The UN Human Rights Committee criticized the lack of human rights protection in Kosovo following consideration of an UNMIK report in July.

In November the European Court of Human Rights considered the admissibility of a case against French members of the NATO-led Kosovo Force (KFOR) brought by the father of a 12-year-old boy killed in May 2000 by an unexploded cluster bomb that the troops had failed to detonate or mark. His younger son was severely injured.

Inter-ethnic violence
Impunity continued for the majority of perpetrators of ethnically motivated attacks. Most attacks involved the stoning of buses carrying Serb passengers by Albanian youths. In some cases, grenades or other explosive devices were thrown at buses or houses, and Orthodox churches were looted and vandalized.

Three predominantly Serbian municipalities declared a "state of emergency" on 2 June following attacks they considered ethnically motivated, and announced a boycott of the UNMIK police and the Kosovo Police Service (KPS). Additional international police were deployed and ethnic Albanian KPS officers withdrawn.

📁 On 1 June, a Serbian youth was shot dead on the road between Zvečan/Zveçan and Zitkovac/Zhitkoc.

📁 On 20 June, a 68-year-old Serbian man who had returned the previous year to Klinë/a was reportedly shot dead in his own house.

📁 In June, two Romani families reportedly left the village of Zhiti/Zitinje after an incident in which an ethnic Albanian was later arrested.

War crimes trials
Impunity for war crimes against Serbs and other minorities continued.

📁 On 11 August former KLA member Selim Krasniqi and two others were convicted before an international panel of judges at Gnjilanë/Gjilan District Court of the abduction and ill-treatment at a KLA camp in 1998 of ethnic Albanians suspected of collaborating with the Serb authorities. They were sentenced to seven years' imprisonment. A visit to Selim Krasniqi in prison by Prime Minister Agim Çeku provoked an outcry.

UNMIK police failed to conduct investigations into outstanding cases of abducted members of minority communities. On 13 October the bodies of 29 Serbs and other non-Albanians exhumed in Kosovo were handed over to the Serbian authorities and to families for burial in Belgrade.

Excessive force by police
📁 On 25 May, 33 women, 20 children and three men required treatment for exposure to tear gas and other injuries after UNMIK police beat people and used tear gas in the village of Krusha e Vogël/Mala Kruša. Women had surrounded a convoy of armoured UNMIK vehicles escorting defence lawyers for Dragoljub Ojdanić, indicted by the Tribunal with responsibility for the murder of over 100 men and boys in the village in 1999. An UNMIK inquiry found that the police had used reasonable force, but acknowledged that the incident could have been avoided with adequate preparation.

On a number of occasions, UNMIK and KPS officers used excessive force in peaceful demonstrations against UNMIK and the Kosovo status talks by members of the non-governmental Vetëvendosje! (Self Determination!) organization.

📁 On 23 August, 15 people were reportedly ill-treated following arrest at Pristina police station. The Acting Ombudsperson asked the prosecutor to open an investigation in the case of one man whose arm and nose were broken and eyes injured.

📁 On 6 December the commander of Peja/Peć KPS and two KPS officers were suspended following a detainee's death in custody.

Discrimination
📁 Most Romani, Ashkali and Egyptian families living on lead-contaminated sites near Mitrovicë/a voluntarily moved to a former military camp at Osterode at the beginning of 2006. Some Roma remained at one site until it was destroyed by fire. There was a lack of meaningful consultation with the communities before relocation and on the rebuilding of their former homes in the Romani neighbourhood of south Mitrovicë/a. Some of the community returned to newly built houses in December.

In February the European Court of Human Rights decided it was not competent to rule on a petition by the communities that their economic and social rights had been violated, on the grounds that UNMIK was not a party to the European Convention on Human Rights.

📁 In early 2006, a senior KPS officer was reportedly removed from his post and other officers given training after a complaint to the UNMIK police commissioner by two gay men. After being assaulted on 31 December 2005 in a village outside Pristina, they had been taken to hospital by KPS officers and asked to file a complaint, but were later subjected to insulting and degrading abuse when their sexual orientation was discovered. Officers told them, incorrectly, that homosexuality was unlawful in Kosovo.

Refugee returns
The rate of return of people displaced by the conflict in Kosovo remained low, although it was reported in June that some 400 Serbs had agreed to return to Babush village near Ferizaj/Uroševac. Those forcibly returned to Kosovo from EU member states were rarely provided with support and assistance by the authorities.

Violence against women
Up to three cases a day of domestic violence were reported by the UNMIK police. The Ministry of Justice and Social Welfare agreed in July to provide funding for the women's shelter in Gjakova/Đakovica, and promised financial support for other shelters.

Trafficking for the purposes of forced prostitution continued to be widespread. Reportedly, 45 criminal proceedings related to trafficking were taking place in July. Little progress was made in implementing the Kosovo Action Plan of Trafficking, published in 2005.

AI country reports/ visits
Reports
- Europe and Central Asia: Summary of Amnesty International's concerns in the region, January-June 2006 (AI Index: EUR 01/017/2006)
- Kosovo/Kosova (Serbia): Human rights protection in post-status Kosovo/Kosova — Amnesty International's recommendations relating to talks on the final status of Kosovo/Kosova (AI Index: EUR 70/008/2006)
- Kosovo (Serbia and Montenegro): United Nations Interim Administration Mission in Kosovo (UNMIK) — Conclusions of the Human Rights Committee, 86th Session, July 2006 (AI Index: EUR 70/011/2006)
- Kosovo (Serbia): The UN in Kosovo — a legacy of impunity (AI Index: EUR 70/015/2006)6)

Visit
AI delegates visited Kosovo in April.

SIERRA LEONE

REPUBLIC OF SIERRA LEONE
Head of state and government: Ahmad Tejan Kabbah
Death penalty: retentionist
International Criminal Court: ratified

The police officially took over internal security at the beginning of the year. Several political opponents of the government were arrested and faced trial. Former Liberian President Charles Taylor was transferred to the Special Court for Sierra Leone in March, and three trials before the Special Court continued. Trials of former combatants were concluded. There was little progress in implementing the recommendations of the Truth and Reconciliation Commission, in strengthening the justice system or in reforming laws that discriminate against women.

Background

The UN peacekeeping office in Sierra Leone (UNAMSIL) was replaced with a peace-building office, the UN Integrated Office in Sierra Leone (UNIOSIL), at the start of the year. UNIOSIL made a slow start to its work due to staffing difficulties. The UN Peacebuilding Commission, an intergovernmental advisory body to co-ordinate the resources of the international community in countries emerging from conflict, chose Sierra Leone as a pilot.

The overall security situation was generally stable and the government took further steps towards assuming responsibility for the maintenance of security. There were, however, some security concerns in areas bordering Guinea. Support for the army from the International Military Advisory and Training Team (IMATT), a retraining body from Britain, the USA, Canada, Bermuda, Australia and France, continued throughout the year.

Sierra Leone remained one of the poorest countries in the world with 70 per cent of the population living on less than US$1 a day and high illiteracy rates. Rates of mortality and disease were at crisis levels due to the inadequacy of the health infrastructure.

Four political parties campaigned ahead of elections scheduled for mid-2007.

Special Court for Sierra Leone

On 29 March Charles Taylor was transferred from Nigeria to Liberia after an official request to the Nigerian government by Liberian President Ellen Johnson-Sirleaf. Upon arriving in Liberia, Charles Taylor was arrested and transferred to the Special Court for Sierra Leone. On 30 March, the Special Court for Sierra Leone made an official request to the Netherlands to host his trial there, citing security issues. There were concerns that political considerations lay behind the move, rather than security.

On 15 June the United Kingdom (UK) agreed to imprison Charles Taylor if he was sentenced to a prison term. On 16 June UN Resolution 1688 was passed, which relocated the trial from Freetown to the premises of the International Criminal Court in The Hague, the Netherlands. On 20 June Charles Taylor was officially transferred to The Hague. The indictment against Charles Taylor was reduced from 17 to 11 counts of war crimes and crimes against humanity. In April Charles Taylor pleaded not guilty. Two pre-trial hearings took place, and the trial was due to start in 2007.

Trials continued before the Special Court for Sierra Leone of those bearing the greatest responsibility for crimes against humanity, war crimes and other serious violations of international law committed in the civil war after 30 November 1996. Charges included murder, mutilation, rape and other forms of sexual violence, sexual slavery, conscription of child soldiers, abductions and forced labour. In December the UN Secretary-General appointed Stephen Rapp, a US national and Chief of Prosecutions at the International Criminal Tribunal for Rwanda, as the new Prosecutor of the Special Court.

Of 11 people indicted, 10 were in custody, but Johnny Paul Koroma, former Chairman of the Armed Forces Revolutionary Council (AFRC), remained at large. Although individually charged, the trials were conducted in three groups. In the Revolutionary United Front (RUF) trial of three men including Issa Sesay, the prosecution closed on 2 August and the defence was due to start in 2007. In the Civil Defence Forces trial of three men including Moinina Fofana, closing arguments began in late November. In the AFRC trial, the defence concluded in December.

Arrests and trials of political opponents

Several suspected political opponents of the government were arrested and tried during the year.
⌂ In January Omrie Golley, former spokesman of the RUF, Mohamed Alpha Bah and David Kai-Tongi were arrested in Freetown. The three were charged with treason, and by the end of the year, after numerous delays, the trial had not been concluded.
⌂ In February Charles Margai, interim leader of the People's Movement for Democratic Change (PMDC), was arrested, prompting peaceful protests by PMDC supporters. His trial was continuing at the end of the year.

Trials of former combatants

The trials of former members of the RUF and AFRC charged with treason, who had been detained in Pademba Road Prison, concluded before the High Court in Freetown. Forty-two were acquitted, three were sentenced to 10 years' imprisonment and 13 received other sentences.

In the trial of 31 members of the West Side Boys, an armed group, 25 were acquitted and six sentenced to life imprisonment.

Press freedom

In February the Minister of Justice announced that he would not pursue charges of manslaughter in the case of Harry Yansaneh, editor of the newspaper *For di People*, who died after being beaten by a group of men in 2005. Human rights defenders called for the extradition from the UK of three men allegedly involved in the assault, who fled to the UK after his death.

◁ In March Sarh Musa Yamba, Editor of the *Concord Times*, was arrested by the Criminal Investigation Department (CID), allegedly on the orders of the Attorney General's office. He was later released without charge.

Reform of the justice sector
There was little progress in the reform of the justice sector. The main challenges included the slow pace of trials and interference with the judiciary by the executive.

After members of civil society lobbied the Law Reform Commission, it announced plans to reform the Constitution to bring it in line with current legislation. It planned to hold a referendum on an amended draft Constitution in July 2007, coinciding with presidential and parliamentary elections.

Violence against women
Women continued to face widespread discrimination and violence, compounded by a lack of access to justice. Little progress was made in reforming proposed laws on marriage, inheritance and sexual offences. Delays in the Law Officer's Department continued and by the end of 2006 draft laws had not yet been presented to Parliament for approval. Legislation on domestic violence remained in the drafting stage. A draft report on the implementation of the UN Women's Convention was delayed until 2007.

In the informal legal sector, chiefs and local court officials often gave rulings and adjudications in cases outside their jurisdiction. The government did little to curtail the practices of chiefs who illegally imposed fines or imprisoned women based on their interpretation of customary law, under which women's status in society is equal to that of a minor.

National Human Rights Commission
By October the five Commissioners chosen by the President for the National Human Rights Commission were approved by Parliament. They were Jamesina King, Yasmin Jusu Sheriff, Edward Sam, Joseph Stanley and Reverend Kanu. The Commission's mandate was to focus on human rights protection and promotion and to serve as a watchdog body.

Truth and Reconciliation Commission
Implementation of the recommendations of the Truth and Reconciliation Commission (TRC), whose report was published in 2004, was minimal. A code of conduct for judges and magistrates was adopted to reduce political interference in the prosecution of corruption cases. During 2006 a TRC task force developed a comprehensive action plan for the government to implement the TRC recommendations and identified a government agency, the National Commission for Social Action, to assist in the process.

Death penalty
Despite efforts by civil society to achieve abolition of the death penalty, a key recommendation of the TRC, 22 people, including five women, remained under sentence of death. Lawyers for Legal Assistance publicized plans to petition the Supreme Court to order the government to abolish the death penalty.

AI country reports/ visits
Reports
- Sierra Leone: Women face human rights abuses in the informal legal sector (AI Index: AFR 51/002/2006)
- Sierra Leone: Special Court for Sierra Leone: Issues for consideration regarding the location of the trial of Charles Taylor (AI Index: AFR 51/005/2006)

Visit
AI delegates visited in May to launch AI's report on abuses of women's rights in the informal legal sector.

SINGAPORE

REPUBLIC OF SINGAPORE
Head of state: S R Nathan
Head of government: Lee Hsien Loong
Death penalty: retentionist
International Criminal Court: not ratified

Freedom of expression and assembly came under increasingly close controls. Men arrested in previous years were held without charge or trial under the Internal Security Act amid fears that they were at risk of ill-treatment. Death sentences were imposed and at least five people were executed. Criminal offenders were sentenced to caning.

Background
The People's Action Party (PAP), which has dominated political life and wider society for nearly half a century, was re-elected for a five-year term in May. The party's stated commitment to building a more open society did not materialize.

Restrictions on free expression and assembly
Civil defamation suits and criminal charges were used or threatened against government critics, human rights activists, Falun Gong practitioners and foreign news media. Tighter restrictions on several major foreign publications were announced in August, enabling the authorities to take punitive measures more easily.

◁ Dr Chee Soon Juan, leader of the opposition Singapore Democratic Party, was declared bankrupt in

February when he was unable to pay damages of 500,000 Singapore dollars (approximately US$306,000) to two PAP leaders when a 2001 defamation suit ended. As a bankrupt, he was barred from seeking election. He was imprisoned for eight days in March for contempt of court after saying publicly that the judiciary lacked independence. In November he was sentenced to a prison term of five weeks for speaking in public without a permit. On his release he faced further criminal charges for speaking in public without a permit and attempting to leave the country without permission. In August the publisher and the editor of the *Far Eastern Economic Review* were sued for defamation in connection with a favourable article about him.

▢ J B Jeyaretnam, former leader of the opposition Workers' Party, unsuccessfully appealed against the bankruptcy imposed on him in 2001 after a series of politically motivated defamation suits. He remained unable to stand for re-election.

▢ Writer Lee Kin Mun was suspended by the state-owned newspaper *Today* following publication of a critical article on Singapore's living costs.

▢ Two Falun Gong practitioners were convicted of holding an illegal protest outside the Chinese Embassy and sentenced in November to prison terms of 15 days and 10 days respectively. Nine practitioners were charged with illegally assembling to distribute leaflets. Jaya Gibson, a British journalist and Falun Gong practitioner, was denied entry to Singapore.

▢ The government restricted both domestic and foreign activism relating to a meeting in Singapore of the World Bank and International Monetary Fund in September, provoking worldwide criticism, including from both institutions.

Detention without charge or trial
Some 34 men remained in detention without charge or trial under the Internal Security Act. The authorities claimed the men were involved in militant Islamist groups and posed a security threat to Singapore. Seven detainees were reportedly released after co-operating with the authorities and responding well to "rehabilitation". In February, Deputy Prime Minister Wong Kan Seng was reported as saying that the treatment of such detainees was not a "tea party" but denied they had been tortured.

Conscientious objectors
At least eight conscientious objectors were imprisoned, and 12 others continued to serve their sentences during 2006. All were members of the banned Jehovah's Witnesses religious group. There were no moves towards offering an alternative to military service.

Death penalty and corporal punishment
At least five people were executed, two in June following conviction for drug trafficking, the others in November after being convicted of murder. Death sentences were handed down to at least five people.

The presence of foreign prisoners on death row raised the international profile of Singapore's high rate of executions. The UN Special Rapporteur on extrajudicial, summary or arbitrary executions expressed concern about executions in Singapore and called for an end to death sentences for drug-related offences, arguing that the mandatory death sentence is a violation of international legal standards. In January the Singapore Law Society said it intended to carry out "an open-minded review of the legal issues" related to the death penalty.

People continued to be sentenced to caning throughout the year, including a 16-year-old boy convicted of theft and judged unsuitable for reformative training.

SLOVAKIA

SLOVAK REPUBLIC
Head of state: Ivan Gašparovič
Head of government: Robert Fico (replaced Mikuláš Dzurinda in July)
Death penalty: abolitionist for all crimes
International Criminal Court: ratified

Roma faced serious discrimination in access to housing, education, employment, health care and other services, as well as persistent prejudice and hostility. Romani pupils were frequently taught in segregated classes or were over-represented in special schools for children with mental disabilities. Women, particularly from the Romani community, were vulnerable to trafficking for the purpose of sexual exploitation.

Background
In parliamentary elections on 17 June, the Direction-Social Democracy (Smer) party won the most votes. To secure a ruling majority, it formed a coalition with the Slovak National Party (SNS) and the People's Party-Movement for a Democratic Slovakia. As both coalition partners, particularly the SNS, were deemed to have promoted ethnic or racial prejudices and hatred, Smer's membership of the Party of European Socialists in the European Parliament was suspended.

On 3 February, the Constitution was amended to increase the powers of the Public Defender of Rights (Ombudsperson), including the right to bring cases before the Constitutional Court when laws and regulations threaten human rights and basic freedoms. Another amendment specified the duty of all public security forces to co-operate with the Public Defender.

Exclusion of Roma
Roma faced discrimination in access to housing, education and employment, according to the final

report on the human rights situation of the Roma, Sinti and Travellers in Europe by the Commissioner for Human Rights of the Council of Europe, published in February. The Commissioner expressed concern that Romani children were unjustifiably placed in special schools. He recommended that the government of Slovakia establish mechanisms to enable women who had been sterilized without informed consent to obtain compensation.

Concerns that Romani children were being taught in segregated classes in primary schools and were over-represented in special schools were expressed by the European Monitoring Centre on Racism and Xenophobia in a report in May on Roma and Travellers in public education.

The Council of Europe Advisory Committee on the Framework Convention for the Protection of National Minorities published its second opinion on Slovakia in June. Although it found improvements in inter-community relations and intercultural understanding, prejudice and intolerance towards certain groups persisted, and hostile attitudes toward the Roma needed to be addressed. The Roma generally faced serious disadvantages, including in education, employment, housing and health care, and their involvement in public affairs was insufficient.

Almost 75 per cent of Romani households depended on aid from the state, municipalities or charitable organizations, according to a UN Development Programme report released in October. The report recommended a public debate in Slovakia on the introduction of temporary affirmative action measures for Roma, and that consideration be given to extending compulsory school attendance from the current age of 15 to 18 years.

In the first reported court case brought under the 2004 Anti-Discrimination Law, on 31 August the District Court of Michalovce ruled that a café in Michalovce had discriminated against three Roma activists from a local non-governmental organization, Nová Cesta, by denying them access in an incident in 2005. However, the court failed to specify the grounds of discrimination.

International scrutiny

In February the European Committee for the Prevention of Torture published a report of its visit to Slovakia in 2005, noting among other things allegations that the police ill-treated detainees at the time of arrest and in custody. The Committee recommended that priority be given to police training, particularly in high-risk situations such as the apprehension and interrogation of suspects, and for measures to enable people who alleged police ill-treatment, or their lawyer or doctor, to request a forensic medical examination.

The Committee also reported that "net beds" were still widely used at the time of its visit in facilities for people with mental illnesses and disabilities. It recommended that comprehensive scientific research be commissioned into the use of "net beds" in psychiatric establishments and alternative methods of managing patient care.

Racially motivated attacks

Members of ethnic minorities continued to be subjected to racist attacks. Police investigations sometimes appeared dilatory or failed to acknowledge the racist motives of the attackers.

On 13 July, three young men, one of them under the age of 18, reportedly attacked three students from Angola near student hostels in Bratislava's Mlynská Dolina district, shouting racist and Nazi slogans. Police were still investigating the alleged attackers at the end of 2006.

Reports of an attack on an ethnic Hungarian girl in Nitra on 25 August provoked an outcry and protests by the Hungarian government. A police investigation concluded that she had fabricated her account. A court ruling on her complaint was pending.

On 9 September, three masked men attacked a Romani family at their home in Sered', injuring a girl and a 57-year-old man. The police detained the perpetrators and confirmed that the attack was racially motivated.

Trafficking of women

In January, the government adopted a National Action Plan to Fight Human Trafficking for 2006-2007, to address the trafficking of women from Slovakia to other countries for the purpose of sexual exploitation and other sexual abuse. Romani women and girls were particularly vulnerable to such crimes.

In September, the police in the Czech Republic detained and brought charges against 16 people for trafficking women from Slovakia and the Czech Republic.

AI country reports/ visits
Report
· Europe and Central Asia: Summary of Amnesty International's concerns in the region, January-June 2006 (AI Index: EUR 01/017/2006)
Visits
AI representatives visited Slovakia in March and September.

SLOVENIA

REPUBLIC OF SLOVENIA
Head of state: Janez Drnovšek
Head of government: Janez Janša
Death penalty: abolitionist for all crimes
International Criminal Court: ratified

There was continued concern about the status of thousands of people whose names were removed from the registry of permanent residents in 1992 (known as the "erased"). Members of Romani communities faced discrimination, including in access to education.

The 'erased'
The authorities failed to resolve the problems relating to the so-called "erased", some 18,305 individuals unlawfully removed from the Slovenian registry of permanent residents in 1992. The "erased" were people from other former Yugoslav republics who had been living in Slovenia but had not acquired Slovenian citizenship after Slovenia became independent. The authorities failed to ensure that the "erased" had full access to economic and social rights, including the right to work and access to health care.

Although the Slovenian Constitutional Court had ruled in 1999 and 2003 that the removal of these individuals from the registry of permanent residents was unlawful, approximately one third of the "erased" still did not have Slovenian citizenship or a permanent residence permit. Many were living in Slovenia "illegally" as foreigners or stateless persons; others were forced to leave the country. Those who managed to obtain Slovenian citizenship or permanent residency – often after years of bureaucratic and legal struggle – continued to suffer from the consequences of their past unregulated status and had no access to full reparation, including compensation.

In June, 11 "erased" people filed an application with the European Court of Human Rights claiming that the "erasure" resulted in violations of their rights, including the right to private and family life, the right to be free from inhuman or degrading treatment or punishment, the right to freedom of movement, and the right to be free from discrimination.

Discrimination against Roma
The authorities failed to fully integrate Romani children in education and tolerated in certain primary schools the creation of special classes for Romani children, where in some cases a reduced curriculum was taught.

The so-called "Bršljin model", used at the Bršljin elementary school in the city of Novo Mesto, provided for the creation of separate groups for pupils who did not perform sufficiently well in certain subjects. These were intended as "catch-up groups" and, at least in theory, would allow for pupils to return to mainstream groups. Teachers in Bršljin admitted that such groups were composed mostly, and sometimes exclusively, of Roma.

Such a model had been criticized by education experts in Slovenia for effectively resulting in the segregation of Roma. It was also criticized by the Council of Europe Commissioner for Human Rights, in a report published in 2006.

In October, approximately 30 members of a Romani family, living in the village of Ambrus, were forced to leave their homes under police escort after having been targeted in ethnically motivated attacks by non-Roma. They were provided temporary accommodation in a reception centre for refugees and subsequently prevented from returning to their homes, which were demolished in December on the grounds that they had been built illegally. The authorities failed to promptly, thoroughly and impartially investigate ethnically motivated attacks with a view to bringing those responsible to justice.

AI country reports/ visits
Reports
- Europe and Central Asia: Summary of Amnesty International's concerns in the region, January-June 2006 (AI Index: EUR 01/017/2006)
- False starts: The exclusion of Romani children from primary education in Slovenia, Croatia and Bosnia and Herzegovina (AI Index: EUR 05/002/2006)
Visit
An AI delegate visited Slovenia in March.

SOMALIA

SOMALI REPUBLIC
Head of state of Transitional Federal Government: Abdullahi Yusuf Ahmed
Head of government of Transitional Federal Government: Ali Mohamed Gedi
Head of Somaliland Republic: Dahir Riyaale Kahin
Death penalty: retentionist
International Criminal Court: not ratified

Thousands of civilians fled in early 2006 as the Islamic Courts fought a warlord coalition in Mogadishu. The Islamic Courts took over Mogadishu in June and most of the south and central areas of Somalia later. Throughout the year, the Transitional Federal Government (TFG) had little control. Conflict between the Islamic Courts and the TFG, supported by the Ethiopian army, broke out in December. The Islamic Courts were defeated and the Ethiopian force entered Mogadishu and placed the TFG in power.

Fighting continued in the south-west of the country. There were arbitrary detentions of journalists in all areas, and unfair political trials in Somaliland and reports of torture. Human rights defenders were at risk in all areas. At least seven people were executed.

Background

Many areas were subject to drought, with humanitarian access impeded by insecurity and threats to staff. International reconstruction aid was delayed due to the absence of a united and effective government in Somalia, 15 years after the state collapsed in 1991. Conditions for 400,000 internally displaced people remained poor. Discrimination and violence against minorities remained widespread, with little protection from government or justice institutions.

Somalia's Foreign Minister ratified 17 African Union (AU) treaties in February, completing Somalia's signing of all 31 AU treaties and conventions, including the African Convention on Human and Peoples' Rights. The TFG, however, had no means to implement them. Steps to create National Human Rights Commissions were taken by the Transitional Federal Parliament and by the authorities in Puntland and Somaliland, but the commissions did not become functional.

Transitional Federal Government

The Transitional Federal Government (TFG), a coalition of clan-based faction leaders which was created from the 2002-4 peace talks held in Kenya, was provisionally based during the year in Baidoa town in the west. Although recognized by the UN and international community, it was unable to extend its control beyond Baidoa or establish itself in the capital, Mogadishu. Other regions were controlled by faction leaders through their clan militias but Puntland Regional State in the north-east had a functioning government, remaining nominally part of Somalia. The TFG opposed the de facto independence of Somaliland in the north-west. In Mogadishu and other southern areas, there was little security for civilians.

In September a suicide bomber in Baidoa failed to assassinate the TFG President but killed 11 men, including his brother and bodyguards.

Islamic Courts

Fighting broke out in Mogadishu in early 2006 between militias of a new Union of Islamic Courts (UIC) and warlords who had formed an "Alliance for Restoration of Peace and Counter-Terrorism", which was reportedly supported clandestinely by the USA. Hundreds of civilians were killed in the crossfire until the UIC captured Mogadishu in June. This brought peace to the capital after many years of violence and extortion by warlords' militias. The UIC reopened the airport and seaport, which had been closed for many years, and promised humanitarian access to international organizations.

In June preliminary negotiations about power-sharing between the TFG and UIC were held in Khartoum and mediated by Sudan under Arab League auspices, in order to avoid a threatened conflict. They agreed to avoid hostilities and establish a joint army and police force.

The UIC created the Council of Somali Islamic Courts (COSIC) to replace the UIC, with an executive committee headed by Sheikh Sharif Sheikh Ahmed. A legislative committee was headed by Hassan Dahir Weys, who was wanted by the USA for alleged involvement in al-Qa'ida operations in Kenya and Tanzania and also reportedly led the UIC militia known as "Shabab" (youth militants). The COSIC extended its control through the central and southern regions, mostly without any fighting, and set up local Islamic courts with militias. In September its forces took over the southern port of Kismayu and began to form regional administrations linked to the Islamic courts in Mogadishu and other areas.

Talks between the COSIC and the TFG in Sudan broke down. Ethiopian troops were called in by the TFG President. In October, the COSIC, which demanded an Islamic state in Somalia and opposed the presence of foreign forces, declared jihad (holy war) against Ethiopia. After increasing clashes with COSIC forces, open conflict broke out in December. After some days, COSIC forces were defeated, some fleeing to the south-west with the Ethiopian army and TFG force in pursuit. In late December Ethiopian troops entered Mogadishu to place the TFG in power.

International community response

The UN, African Union, European Union and League of Arab States supported the continuation of the IGAD (Inter Governmental Authority for Development) peace and reconciliation process. This had led to the formation of the TFG in 2004, and provided for an IGAD-led peace support force (IGASOM). As conflict increased towards the end of the year between the Ethiopian-supported TFG forces and the COSIC, the UN Security Council authorized preparations for the deployment of the IGASOM force. The UN Security Council kept in force the 1992 Somalia international arms embargo, but exempted IGASOM from the embargo. In May and November, the UN arms embargo monitoring group had criticized Ethiopia, Eritrea and other countries for violating the embargo and recommended targeted sanctions.

Somaliland

The self-declared Somaliland Republic continued its demand for international recognition. It received some international development assistance. Its unresolved border dispute with neighbouring Puntland remained a cause of tension. The Somaliland Government on several occasions accused the UIC/COSIC of attempting to destabilize Somaliland.

Justice and rule of law

There was no rule of law or justice system consistent with international standards in the central and southern regions of Somalia. Islamic (Shari'a) courts, which became the basis of the administrative and judicial system in most of the south from mid-2006, did not allow the right to legal defence counsel or meet internationally recognized standards of fair trial. The COSIC imposed increasingly harsh interpretations of Shari'a law regarding morality offences and dress code, including banning musical entertainment. Offenders were arbitrarily flogged and humiliated by militias.

⌷ Sister Leonela Sgorbati, 70, an Italian Catholic humanitarian worker, was killed in Mogadishu in September, reportedly because of her religion. Her Somali bodyguard was also killed. The COSIC condemned the murders and said it had arrested the alleged killer but he was not brought to court.

⌷ Over 100 demonstrators were detained briefly in Kismayu in October by the incoming COSIC forces.

In Somaliland there were several arbitrary detentions and unfair trials.

⌷ Nine people were arrested in Hargeisa in September 2005 after a shoot-out between an Islamist armed group and police. Their trial started in early 2006 but was not completed by the end of the year. Several defendants, including Sheikh Mohamed Sheikh Ismail, alleged that they had been tortured. More than 50 people demonstrating in Hargeisa against the alleged torture were arrested. They were sentenced to one year's imprisonment in summary and unfair trials by an "emergency court" consisting of administration and security officials. They were released by presidential pardon in October 2006.

⌷ Twenty-seven elders of the Ogaden clan from Ethiopia, who had been arrested in 2003 but acquitted of armed conspiracy by the Supreme Court on appeal in 2005, were finally released in late 2006.

Journalists

More than 20 journalists were arrested in different areas, although most were released quickly after interventions by media associations. The National Union of Somali Journalists (NUSOJ), which actively engaged in protecting press freedom and reporting abuses against journalists, was formally recognized by both the TFG and the COSIC. A COSIC proposal to impose heavy restrictions on the media was under discussion in late 2006.

⌷ In June Martin Adler, a Swedish photographer, was killed in Mogadishu at a UIC rally. The UIC condemned the murder but the alleged killer, although reportedly arrested, was not brought to trial.

⌷ In October, three radio journalists were arrested in Baidoa by TFG police for reporting on Ethiopian soldiers in the area. They were released uncharged after some days.

⌷ In early December, Omar Farouk Osman Nur, NUSOJ Secretary General, was arrested by COSIC militias and held incommunicado in a secret prison. He was released uncharged later that day.

Human rights defenders

Somali human rights defenders, most working within well-established national coalitions in Somalia and Somaliland, continued to monitor human rights violations and conduct advocacy with the authorities and general public. At times, many faced severe risks, in particular members of women's organizations.

In Mogadishu in June, talks were held between the UIC and the Civil Society Alliance. A ban on civil society organizations was withdrawn, and UIC representatives agreed to recognize non-governmental organizations and uphold the freedom of the press. However, increasing restrictions on freedom of expression and assembly severely threatened their work.

Women's rights

Several women's rights organizations, grouped in coalitions such as the Coalition of Grassroots Women's Organizations (COGWO) based in Mogadishu, and Nagaad women's coalition in Somaliland, campaigned actively, particularly against female genital mutilation, rape and domestic violence. The UIC, however, refused to meet or recognize women's NGOs.

Refugees and internally displaced people

Tens of thousands of people fled from Mogadishu during the fighting in the first part of the year, and from other areas affected by the advance of UIC forces and fighting in the latter part of the year. Many refugees from the Kismayu area entered Kenya and tens of thousands were displaced inside the country.

Conditions in camps and informal settlements containing 400,000 long-term internally displaced people remained extremely poor, with little international assistance reaching the most vulnerable.

There were hundreds of deaths at sea of people trying to reach Yemen from Puntland in trafficking operations. A Puntland government ban on trafficking in October was widely ignored. In October, 1,370 Ethiopians arrested for trying to reach Yemen were either deported to Ethiopia or allowed to claim asylum.

Death penalty

Despite local campaigns in all areas against the death penalty, death sentences were imposed by Islamic courts in the south and by ordinary courts in Somaliland. According to the Somali Islam-based custom of *diya* (compensation), death sentences were lifted by courts when the murder victim's family accepted compensation from the perpetrator's family.

Three men were publicly executed in Mogadishu and a nearby town by Islamic court militias in June.

⌷ Omar Hussein was publicly executed in Mogadishu in May by the 16-year-old son of a man whose murder he admitted. An Islamic court ordered him to be knifed to death in the same manner as the murder.

In Somaliland there were at least four people executed in 2006. Several others were under sentence of death and awaiting the outcome of appeals or presidential clemency decisions. These included seven men allegedly linked with al-Qa'ida who were convicted in November 2004 of killing three aid workers. Judgement on their appeal to the Supreme Court had not been delivered by the end of 2006.

Statement
· Somalia: Fears for human rights in looming conflict
  (AI Index: AFR 52/004/2006)
Visit
An AI representative attended a regional meeting on
women's rights in Somaliland in November.

SOUTH AFRICA

REPUBLIC OF SOUTH AFRICA
Head of state and government: Thabo Mbeki
Death penalty: abolitionist for all crimes
International Criminal Court: ratified

Torture of detainees by police and misuse of lethal
force continued to be reported. A Commission of
Inquiry found that corruption and maladministration
were institutionalized in South Africa's prisons and
that sexual violence was rife. Asylum-seekers
continued to have difficulty accessing asylum
determination procedures and hundreds of suspected
illegal immigrants were detained beyond the legal
time limit. The remaining 62 death sentences were
replaced with alternative sentences. Although the
number of people receiving anti-retroviral treatment
for HIV/AIDS increased, fewer than half of those
needing it had access. The number of reported rapes
remained high, and legal reforms affecting access to
justice for survivors were further delayed.

Background
Political tensions within the ruling African National
Congress (ANC) and between the ANC and its Alliance
partners were marked at the time of court proceedings
relating to corruption and rape charges against former
Deputy President Jacob Zuma. His supporters accused
the National Directorate of Public Prosecutions (NDPP)
of having a political agenda against Jacob Zuma.

In local government elections in March, the ANC won
a majority in most municipal councils, although the
government's record on delivery of socio-economic
transformation continued to be challenged.

Political violence in KwaZulu Natal led to the deaths
of a number of ANC and Inkatha Freedom Party
candidates.

Business, church and other delegations appealed to
President Mbeki to take effective measures against
high levels of violent crime. The government placed
the investigative arm of the NDPP, known as the
Scorpions, under the political control of the Minister
of Safety and Security.

The Deputy President and Deputy Minister of Health
began a dialogue with civil society organizations on
achieving a more effective response to the HIV/AIDS
pandemic.

Human rights violations by police
Torture and misuse of lethal force against crime
suspects continued to be reported, in a context of high
levels of violent crime and police fatalities.
Corroborated cases involved members of the South
African Police Service (SAPS), particularly from the
Serious and Violent Crime Units (SVCU), torturing
suspects with suffocation and electric shock devices, as
well as kicking and beating suspects. Several detainees
died as a result. Interrogation sessions sometimes took
place in informal locations. Torture equipment was
found on the premises of the Vanderbijlpark SVCU after
a court-ordered search.

▭ Musa Jan Sibiya died at Lydenburg police station in
February after allegedly being assaulted by police. A
state district surgeon reported he died from natural
causes, but an independent postmortem found he had
died from a ruptured bowel caused by a traumatic
perforation.

▭ Msizwe Mkhuthukane died in February at East
London police station after being similarly assaulted.
He was denied urgent medical care in custody. On 1
November five police officers appeared in court on
murder charges.

▭ A security guard, R, and his wife lodged a civil claim
for damages against the police authorities after they
were subjected to electric shock torture at Randburg
police station on 1 May. R was also kicked, slapped and
punched while handcuffed and tied at the ankles, and
subjected to suffocation torture with plastic sheeting.
He was transferred to Roodepoort police station and
denied medical care until he was released uncharged
with his wife on 4 May. The state denied any liability in
response to the legal suit.

Protests continued against poor socio-economic
conditions and forced evictions. Police appeared to
have used excessive force in some cases, including, in
June, against community members from
Maandagshoek, Limpopo, protesting against Anglo-
Platinum use of their land for mining and, in
September, against members of the Durban-based
Shack-Dwellers Association (Abahlali baseMjondolo).

In July the Harrismith Regional Court acquitted three
police officers of all charges arising from the death of
17-year-old Teboho Mkhonza and injuries to scores of
others when police broke up a non-violent
demonstration in August 2004. The court accepted
defence evidence that the boy had died as a result of
negligence by hospital staff. The police had opened fire
without warning using illegal live ammunition. In
October, 13 Harrismith community activists were
acquitted of charges of public violence arising from the
same demonstration.

On 26 July the Director of Public Prosecutions
withdrew charges against 51 members of the Landless
People's Movement who had been on trial since 2004
on charges under the Electoral Act.

Abuse of prisoners

The 3,500-page report of the Jali Commission of Inquiry, appointed by President Mbeki in 2001 to investigate corruption and violence in prisons, was made public in November. Among its findings were that corruption and maladministration were institutionalized and that C-Max Super-Maximum security prison made routine use of solitary confinement and torture. It found that sexual violence was rife, with young, gay and transsexual prisoners most vulnerable, and that warders were implicated in many sexual assaults and in selling sexual favours by incarcerated youths to adult prisoners.

Impunity for abuses was fostered by management failure to institute hearings and follow up on criminal charges. Police investigations were also manipulated by prison staff. An example was the failure to discipline prison warders implicated in a mass assault on prisoners in Ncome prison in January 2003. Despite independent medical corroboration of allegations that prisoners had been beaten, the Department of Correctional Services (DCS) allowed the official investigation to lapse. The Jali Commission recommended charges against named DCS members in relation to this and some other incidents.

On 23 April the Port Elizabeth High Court ordered that prisoners at St Alban's Prison could consult their lawyers in private to prepare a civil claim for assault against the DCS. They had been denied access to lawyers after prison staff allegedly embarked on a mass assault of prisoners in retaliation for the killing of a colleague.

Inhumane prison conditions persisted due to severe overcrowding, with two thirds of prisons holding more than 100 per cent of their capacity.

Refugees and asylum-seekers

The Department of Home Affairs (DHA) initiated new procedures at the Pretoria and Johannesburg Refugee Reception Offices in an effort to improve the management of over 1,000 new applications from asylum-seekers weekly. However, in December the Pretoria High Court ruled, in a case involving seven Zimbabweans, that the procedures were unconstitutional and unlawful, including the practice of issuing only "appointment slips" to applicants, which left them without legal protection against arbitrary arrest, detention and deportation. The "pre-screening" policy had resulted in unlawful rejections of applications. The Court directed the DHA to receive and process applications for asylum in a fair and non-discriminatory manner. The Cape Town High Court made a similar ruling in June.

Hundreds of suspected illegal immigrants detained at Lindela Repatriation Centre (Lindela) were unlawfully held beyond the period allowed under the Immigration Act (30 days or 120 days with a court warrant). In August the Johannesburg High Court ordered the DHA to release 57 Congolese nationals who were facing imminent deportation. The group included at least one recognized refugee, 18 who held asylum-seeker permits and nine with DHA "appointment slips". Forty-four of

them had been held for between 35 days and 16 months. Also in August, at least 10 people with asylum-seeker permits were deported to Burundi.

Private security guards at Lindela appeared to have used excessive force in response to detainees' protests in July and November.

Unlawful transfer

Police and DHA officials handed over Khalid Mehmood Rashid, a national of Pakistan, to Pakistan government agents in November 2005. He was flown out of South Africa on a flight with no number. Twelve months later, he had still not been produced in the Pakistan High Court in response to a habeas corpus petition. By the end of the year the Pretoria High Court had not given a ruling on whether the manner of Khalid Mehmood Rashid's removal from South Africa was unlawful and contrary to the country's international human rights obligations.

Death penalty

The justice authorities completed the process of replacing the remaining 62 death sentences with alternative sentences by July. The Constitutional Court ruled on 30 November that the orders made under its 1995 judgement which found the death penalty to be unconstitutional had now been complied with fully by the government.

People living with HIV/AIDS

UNAIDS reported in December that the HIV epidemic in South Africa continued to grow, with prevalence of HIV among women attending public antenatal clinics 35 per cent higher in 2005 than in 1999. Some 5.4 million people, including a quarter of a million children under 15, were living with HIV. In November the Department of Health reported that 273 accredited facilities were providing anti-retroviral treatment (ART) to 213,828 people, although some 300,000 others still needed access to it. Children's access to paediatric ART was also still limited. On 1 December the Deputy President announced the draft strategic plan for 2007 to 2011.

An application by 15 Durban Westville HIV-positive prisoners and the Treatment Action Campaign for prisoners to have access to ART was granted by the Durban High Court in June. The state appealed against this ruling and failed to implement an urgent interim order. In August the High Court found the state in contempt of court and ordered the original ruling to be implemented, along with other measures to give prisoners access to ART. By the end of November, four more prisons had been accredited to provide ART.

Violence against women and children

Police statistics for the year April 2005 to March 2006 recorded 54,926 reported rapes, a decrease of 0.3 per cent, with 42.7 per cent of them against children under the age of 18.

In June, Parliament resumed discussion on the draft Sexual Offences Bill, which had been held up in the Department of Justice since 2004. Organizations assisting survivors of sexual violence and child sexual abuse remained concerned that the Bill did not adequately protect complainants, especially children, at the investigation and trial stages. The Bill, however, contained an expanded statutory offence of rape applicable to all forms of "sexual penetration" without consent and defined forms of coercion which would indicate lack of consent. The state would be obliged to provide post-exposure prophylaxis to victims exposed to the risk of HIV and to develop a national policy framework to improve implementation of the Bill. It had not been passed by the end of the year.

Investigators, prosecutors and the courts remained restricted by the common-law definition of rape in their response to sexual violence cases. In July the Pretoria High Court upheld a conviction of rape in a magistrate's court against an accused charged with anally penetrating a nine-year-old child, on the grounds that the common-law definition of rape, which is limited to penile penetration of the vagina without consent, was inconsistent with the requirements of constitutional law. However, the High Court ruling was under appeal at the end of the year.

There were fears that the disestablishment of specialist detective units, including the unit responsible for investigating family violence and child sexual abuse, would undermine the effectiveness of police investigations. Community-based organizations produced evidence indicating that police had lost rape investigation dockets through inefficiency or corruption.

The high number of deaths of boys attending traditional circumcision schools — more than 100 in the preceding 10 years — prompted national public hearings by the South African Human Rights Commission (SAHRC) and two other statutory bodies. The hearings, conducted in October, were held in four provinces. The SAHRC also conducted hearings, in September, on school-based violence.

Impunity

There was concern about the legality of prosecution guidelines approved by the Cabinet in 2005 and presented to Parliament in January 2006. The guidelines would give the NDPP the administrative discretion to allow immunity from prosecution for crimes "emanating from the conflicts of the past" for people who failed to apply for or were refused amnesty by the Truth and Reconciliation Commission's Amnesty Committee. While the applicant would have to disclose all the circumstances of the alleged offence, and the NDPP would have to obtain the views of any victims before arriving at a decision, there was no obligation to take into account the victims' views or provision for judicial assessment of the truthfulness of the evidence. The guidelines did not explicitly exclude from consideration for immunity crimes such as torture, crimes against humanity and war crimes.

As of 30 September, the government had paid reparations of R30,000 (approximately US$4,200) to 15,520 individuals identified by the Truth and Reconciliation Commission as eligible because of human rights abuses before May 1994.

Freedom of expression

In October a Commission of Inquiry into allegations of politically motivated interference in the output of the public broadcaster, the SABC, found that certain individuals were being excluded from interviews in news programmes for improper reasons. The Commissioners found that the head of news and current affairs, Dr Snuki Zikalala, had instructed staff not to use certain individuals on grounds which included their opinions on controversial issues, and that he had threatened to discipline some staff if they failed to follow these instructions. The SABC Board, who had appointed Dr Zikalala, did not make the report public. It made a failed attempt to get a High Court order compelling the *Mail & Guardian* newspaper to remove a leaked copy from its website.

AI country reports/visits
Reports
- South Africa: Government must investigate circumstances of "disappeared" Pakistani's transfer (AI Index: AFR 53/001/2006)
- South Africa: Briefing for the Committee against Torture (AI Index: AFR 53/002/2006)

Visits
In October and November AI delegates visited the country for research and held meetings with civil society organizations and the Department of Foreign Affairs. AI representatives attended the UN Committee against Torture hearing on South Africa in November.

SPAIN

KINGDOM OF SPAIN
Head of state: King Juan Carlos I de Borbón
Head of government: José Luis Rodríguez Zapatero
Death penalty: abolitionist for all crimes
International Criminal Court: ratified

The government announced the opening of a dialogue process with ETA following the armed group's declaration of a permanent ceasefire in March, but this ended after a bomb attack in the car park of Madrid Barajas airport on 30 December. One year after the death of 13 migrants at the border points of Ceuta and Melilla there was still no outcome to the investigations. Three more migrants died in a similar incident in July 2006. The number of migrants and asylum-seekers arriving by boat in the Canary Islands in 2006 was almost seven times higher than the total for 2005 and exceeded the total for the previous four years combined. There continued to be reports of torture and ill-treatment by law enforcement officials, with impunity in many cases. The Supreme Court made a landmark ruling on the inadmissibility of evidence proceeding from Guantánamo Bay.

Background

In May 2005 parliament approved the opening of a dialogue between the government and those "who abandon violence". This was followed in March 2006 by the announcement of a "permanent ceasefire" by the Basque armed group Euskadi Ta Askatasuna (ETA). Tensions surrounding the dialogue process increased after an outbreak of violence in the Basque region in September and the theft of some 350 pistols from a French arms depot at the end of October. On 30 December a bomb exploded in the car park at Madrid Barajas airport, killing two people. An hour before the explosion ETA telephoned a warning about the bomb. The government subsequently announced that the dialogue was over.

The Spanish Parliament and the regions of Catalonia, Valencia and Andalucía all approved modifications to their regional statutes of autonomy, granting greater powers of self-government. In July the government presented a bill to parliament relating to the recognition of human rights abuses suffered during the 1936-1939 civil war and the ensuing dictatorship.

Migration and asylum

The situation of migrants and asylum-seekers in Spain remained a matter of grave concern. Undocumented migrants continued to be issued with expulsion orders and left with no means of support or of regularizing their status. Figures available from the Spanish Refugee Aid Commission for the first six months of the year recorded 2,504 asylum requests, of which 2,165 were rejected or declared inadmissible.

Migration routes appeared to change, with over 31,245 asylum-seekers and undocumented migrants from west Africa arriving in the Canary Islands during the year. Regional government authorities used makeshift reception centres to house them, and the severe overcrowding aggravated poor conditions in pre-existing centres. The arrivals included several hundred unaccompanied minors, far exceeding the region's reception capacity for minors and endangering their fundamental rights. Overcrowding in immigration centres led to tension and violence.

The arrival of large numbers of asylum-seekers and migrants in the Canary Islands put extreme pressure on asylum determination procedures there, already identified as inadequate. There were concerns about the restricted access to legal and interpreting assistance and the accelerated returns process. In September, the Public Prosecutor's Office of the Canary Islands began a series of inspections into the conditions in immigration detention centres on the islands, following complaints by police trade unions that they did not comply with basic standards of hygiene due to overcrowding.

Investigations into the deaths of at least 13 migrants in September and October 2005 at the border in Ceuta and Melilla have still not identified or punished those responsible. In July 2006, three more migrants died as they attempted to cross the border at Melilla. Spanish police fired rubber bullets as a warning and the migrants were shot at with live ammunition by Moroccan forces, causing them to fall from the six-metre-high fence. Three days later, the government approved 10.5 million euros in aid to Morocco for border control measures, without tying these to human rights clauses or demanding an explanation for the deaths at the border in 2005 and 2006. Under a pre-existing returns agreement, migrants continued to be sent back to Morocco when it could be proved they had departed from that country. There were insufficient legal and protection guarantees accompanying these measures, putting such migrants at risk of ill-treatment.

Spain was one of the countries participating in a joint sea patrol mission by various European Union (EU) countries and co-ordinated by Frontex, the EU external border control agency. This operation was intended to intercept migrants' boats at sea and return them to the country of origin. This raised serious concerns regarding the respect of fundamental rights such as the right to seek asylum, the right to leave one's own country, and the right not to be returned to a country where one would be at risk of human rights violations.

Police ill-treatment and impunity

There continued to be reports of torture and ill-treatment by law enforcement officers, aggravated by a lack of systematic and independent investigations into such incidents. According to a study published by SOS Racismo, a national anti-racism organization, state law enforcement officers were responsible for one in three reported incidents of racist violence.

In April, Spain ratified the Optional Protocol to the UN Convention against Torture, which it had signed in 2005. Despite this, Spain maintained practices which the UN Special Rapporteur on torture condemned for increasing the risk of ill-treatment and torture, such as the use of incommunicado detention.

◻ In January, police officers were involved in the violent break-up of a traditional street party in the town of Arenys de Mar in Catalonia, in the north-east of the country. The party was interrupted by the Mossos d'Esquadra, a contingent from the Catalonian autonomous police force. According to reports, they used violence in attempting to disperse the gathering, beating people on the head and body with batons, and charging at the group, resulting in injuries to several people. Joan Munich, one of the revellers, received at least one blow to the head and fell to the ground, temporarily losing consciousness. When he regained consciousness he was arrested and later convicted of assaulting a police officer, and given a one-year suspended prison sentence and a fine. Two of his companions were convicted for disobeying a police order and fined. All three appealed but were unsuccessful. Seven other men present at the incident filed complaints against the police but these cases also failed.

In June, a woman was punched in the face by a national police officer when she attempted to intervene in the apparently violent arrest of a stranger outside a bar in Barcelona. According to reports, she was then arrested and taken to the police station, where she was pushed into a cell by four police officers and beaten all over her head and body. As she lay on the cell floor she was kicked in the head while handcuffed behind her back. A police doctor who examined her in detention recorded only minor bruising, but a medical report obtained by the woman after her release noted multiple bruising on her head, face, arms, legs and back. In August she was fined for resisting arrest.

In February, eight of the nine police officers involved in the ill-treatment and death in custody of Juan Martínez Galdeano in July 2005 were suspended from duty. Charges against one of the officers were dropped and the others were charged with serious assault, injury and negligent manslaughter. The Office of the Public Prosecutor of Almería requested a sentence of 10 years' imprisonment for the senior officer present and eight years' imprisonment for the others. According to the autopsy and later medical reports, Juan Martínez Galdeano's death was caused by a combination of the violent beating and restraint techniques used on him by the police officers and an adverse reaction to cocaine that he had consumed.

Violence against women
Violence against women continued to be a serious problem. Eighty-six women died in 2006 as a result of domestic violence, 68 of whom were killed by their partners or former partners.

Since the coming into force of the law on gender-based violence in January 2005, complaints regarding such crimes increased by 18 per cent. However, the new courts dedicated to dealing with such cases had insufficient resources to deal with the number of cases received. More than 20 per cent of the protection orders requested by victims were rejected by the judicial authorities. Rehabilitation programmes for those convicted of domestic violence did not meet demand and 1,700 convicted abusers were waiting for a place on such a programme. There was a continuing lack of crisis centres for victims in many regions.

'War on terror'
In July, the Supreme Court quashed the sentence of Hamed Ahmed, a former Guantánamo Bay detainee, and ordered his immediate release. After returning to Spain from Guantánamo Bay, where he had been a prisoner since 2002, he was convicted by the Spanish National High Court in October 2005 of membership of a terrorist organization and was sentenced to six years' imprisonment. The Supreme Court ruled that Guantánamo Bay constituted a legal limbo without guarantees or control, and therefore all evidence originating from it must be declared completely null and void. As a result, there was no evidence against Hamed Ahmed except his own statement, which the Supreme Court found contained no incriminating evidence.

AI country reports/ visits
Reports
- Spain: More rights, but the obstacles remain (AI Index: EUR 41/006/2006)
- Spain and Morocco: Failure to protect the rights of migrants – Ceuta and Melilla one year on (AI Index: EUR 41/009/2006)
Visit
AI delegates visited the Canary Islands in June to investigate alleged violations of the rights of asylum-seekers and migrants arriving in the islands.

SRI LANKA

DEMOCRATIC SOCIALIST REPUBLIC OF SRI LANKA
Head of state: Mahinda Rajapakse
Head of government: Ratnasiri Wickremanayake
Death penalty: abolitionist in practice
International Criminal Court: not ratified

The human rights situation in Sri Lanka deteriorated dramatically. Unlawful killings, recruitment of child soldiers, abductions, enforced disappearances and other human rights violations and war crimes increased. Civilians were attacked by both sides as fighting escalated between the government and the Liberation Tigers of Tamil Eelam (LTTE). Hundreds of civilians were killed and injured and more than 215,000 people displaced by the end of 2006. Homes, schools and places of worship were destroyed. Although both sides maintained they were adhering to the ceasefire agreement, by mid-2006 it had in effect been abandoned. Emergency regulations, introduced in August 2005, remained in force. A pattern of enforced disappearances in the north and east re-emerged. There were reports of torture in police custody; perpetrators continued to benefit from impunity.

Background
Although the government and LTTE met in February to discuss implementation of the ceasefire agreement, a further meeting scheduled for April did not take place. Further talks in October ended in disagreement over the government closure of the main highway to the Jaffna Peninsula.

In March the UN Special Rapporteur on extrajudicial, summary or arbitrary executions, reporting on a 2005 visit to Sri Lanka, said that freedoms of expression, movement, association and participation were threatened, particularly for Tamil and Muslim civilians.

In May, President Mahinda Rajapakse unilaterally appointed new members of the Human Rights Commission after their predecessors' terms of office had expired. The Commission appeared no longer to comply fully with constitutional and international standards for national human rights institutions.

In May Sri Lanka was elected to the UN Human Rights Council for a two-year term. In support of its candidacy, the government pledged to form a new Human Rights Ministry and introduce a Human Rights Charter.

In May the European Union (EU) listed the LTTE as a terrorist organization, freezing its assets and barring its officials from travel to or within the EU. In response, the LTTE leadership said all EU monitors on the Sri Lanka Monitoring Mission (SLMM) should leave the country by September.

In September the Supreme Court ruled there was no legal basis for the UN Human Rights Committee to hear cases from Sri Lanka. The Court held that Sri Lanka's accession to the First Optional Protocol to the International Covenant on Civil and Political Rights was unconstitutional and illegal as it gave the Committee judicial powers without parliamentary authorization.

International human rights bodies raised concerns about the escalating human rights abuses and violations of international humanitarian law in Sri Lanka at the UN Human Rights Council in September and November.

Rising civilian deaths

Both the UN Secretary-General and the UN Emergency Relief Coordinator expressed concern at the rising civilian casualties in the conflict. The UN estimated that some 3,000 civilians had been killed in conflict-related violence since hostilities had worsened in 2006. The LTTE targeted army personnel and civilians with suicide bombings, claymore mines and grenade attacks.

In April, following a suicide bomb attempt on the life of army chief Lieutenant-General Sarath Fonseka in which 10 people were killed, a major air and artillery offensive was launched on LTTE positions in Trincomalee District, killing at least 12 civilians. After a bomb in Trincomalee town left five people dead, including a child, more than 20 Tamil and Muslim civilians were killed and thousands forcibly displaced in apparent reprisal attacks by members of the Sinhalese community.

The LTTE denied accusations that it was behind a claymore mine attack on a bus in June in which 67 civilians were killed in Kebitigollawe, northern Sri Lanka.

The SLMM found government forces responsible for the killing in August of 17 aid workers from the Action Contre La Faim agency in Muttur, Trincomalee District. A magisterial inquiry had not concluded by the end of 2006. Also in August, 51 young people were estimated killed and 100 injured when the air force bombed a former children's home in Mullaitivu, northern Sri Lanka, claiming it to be an LTTE training centre. Three severely injured girls were detained under emergency regulations, one of whom remained in the custody of the Terrorist Investigation Department in Colombo.

In October a suicide bombing of a navy convoy 170km north-east of Colombo, killed around 100 navy personnel, the largest number of people killed in a suicide bombing in recent years.

The army admitted shelling Kathiraveli, Batticaloa District, in November but accused the LTTE of using civilians as human shields. As many as 40 people were killed and more than 100 wounded when a school sheltering displaced people was hit.

The internally displaced

Over 215,000 people were displaced in the north and east as a result of renewed fighting, and at least 10,000 fled to India. Tens of thousands of people were displaced by a major armed forces offensive in July to seize control of the Mavil Aru waterway in eastern Trincomalee District.

An estimated half a million people had been displaced earlier in the conflict and by the 2004 tsunami. Many of these remained vulnerable to harassment and violence from the LTTE, other armed groups and members of the Sri Lankan security forces.

Displaced people had few employment opportunities and limited health and education services and suffered the effects of alcohol abuse and widespread domestic violence. Most tsunami camps were well-funded and of a reasonable standard, but those for people displaced by the conflict often lacked electricity, transport and proper sanitation. Concerns remained about this disparity of treatment.

Lack of humanitarian access

Humanitarian aid agencies were unable to reach many of those at risk in the north and east. From August, aid supplies to the north were obstructed by the closure of the Jaffna Peninsula road and a sea blockade by the LTTE. Humanitarian and medical workers were threatened, harassed and subject to abductions and attacks, and their work further hampered by new registration requirements.

The UN called on both parties to the conflict to allow humanitarian agencies free and unimpeded access to the affected population, and to provide greater security for aid workers.

Unlawful killings and impunity

The number of unlawful killings dramatically increased. Several hundred extrajudicial killings were reported. They were carried out by forces of the government, the Karuna group, a splinter group of the LTTE reportedly co-operating with government forces, the LTTE and other armed opposition groups.

▭ In January, five students were shot dead at close range, allegedly by the government Special Task Force in Trincomalee town. The only witness prepared to come forward — the father of one of the youths — received death threats.

▭ Unidentified gunmen suspected of links with the armed forces shot and killed Vanniasingham Vigneswaran, a Tamil National Alliance politician, in Trincomalee in April. A member of the same party,

Nadarajah Raviraj, was shot dead in Colombo in November.

☐ In April, eight Sinhalese farmers were hacked to death by suspected LTTE members in Kalyanapura.

☐ The navy denied responsibility for a spate of incidents in May. Details remained unclear but the incidents resulted in casualties and deaths on Kayts Island off the Jaffna Peninsula, which included the deaths of 13 Tamil civilians, among them a four-month-old baby and a four-year-old boy. The area is controlled by the navy.

☐ In August, unidentified gunmen killed Kethesh Loganathan, Deputy Head of the Sri Lanka Peace Secretariat and long-time critic of the LTTE, which were widely believed to be behind the killing.

Child soldiers

At least 50 children a month were recruited as soldiers in the north and east. According to UNICEF, the UN Children's Agency, by mid-2006 there were still 1,545 under-age fighters in LTTE forces.

In June over 100 children were reportedly recruited in government-controlled areas in the east by the Karuna group. In November, a special adviser to the UN Special Representative for Children and Armed Conflict reported that government forces had been actively involved in forcibly recruiting children to the group.

Enforced disappearances

In July presidential directives were re-issued requiring the security forces to issue receipts for arrested persons and inform the Human Rights Commission within 48 hours. The Commission reported 419 enforced disappearances in Jaffna for the first half of 2006. A local non-governmental organization recorded 277 abductions from April to September. Disappearances and abductions were attributed to several forces, including the security forces, the LTTE and the Karuna group.

☐ In January, seven aid workers employed by the Tamil Rehabilitation Organization were abducted by unidentified armed men.

☐ Eight young Tamil men who went missing from a Hindu temple in Manthuvil East, Jaffna District, in May were feared to have been taken away in army vehicles seen in the vicinity.

☐ Father Thiruchchelvan Nihal Jim Brown, a Catholic priest from Allaipiddy, and Wenceslaus Vinces Vimalathas went missing after crossing a navy checkpoint in August on Kayts Island. It was feared they had been taken into custody by navy personnel.

On 4 September President Rajapakse said an international commission of inquiry would investigate abductions, disappearances and extrajudicial killings. On 6 November, however, the government announced the establishment of a national commission with an international observer group.

Torture

There were numerous reports of torture in police custody. According to the non-governmental Asian Commission for Human Rights, two people died in custody in 2006.

Death penalty

A number of high profile murder cases fuelled demands for an end to the moratorium on executions. According to the Director General of Prisons, at least 12 death sentences were passed. Approximately 167 people remained on death row. No executions were reported.

AI country reports/ visits
Reports
· Sri Lanka: A climate of fear in the East (AI Index: ASA 37/001/2006)
· Sri Lanka: Waiting to go home – the plight of the internally displaced (AI Index: ASA 37/004/2006)
· Sri Lanka: Observations on a proposed commission of inquiry and international independent group of eminent persons (AI Index: ASA 37/030/2006)
· Sri Lanka: Establishing a commission of inquiry into serious violations of human rights law and international humanitarian law in Sri Lanka – Amnesty International's recommendations (AI Index: ASA 37/031/2006)
· UN Human Rights Council, Third regular session: Compilation of statements by Amnesty International (including joint statements) (AI Index: IOR 41/034/2006)
Visit
AI delegates met senior government officials in Sri Lanka in September.

SUDAN

REPUBLIC OF SUDAN
Head of state and government: Omar Hassan al-Bashir
Death penalty: retentionist
International Criminal Court: signed

A Darfur Peace Agreement negotiated in Abuja, Nigeria, was signed in May by the government and one faction of the opposition armed groups in Darfur, but conflict, displacement and killings increased. The government failed to disarm the armed militias known as the Janjawid, who continued to attack civilians in Darfur and launched cross-border raids into Chad. Hundreds of civilians were killed in Darfur and Chad, and some 300,000 more were displaced during the year, many of them repeatedly. Displaced people in Darfur and Darfuri refugees in Chad were unable to return to their villages because of the lack of security. In August government forces launched a major offensive in North Darfur and Jebel Marra, which was accompanied by Janjawid raids on villages and continued at the end of 2006. The air force frequently bombed civilians. The African Union Mission in Sudan (AMIS) was unable to stop killings, rapes and displacement of civilians or looting. Government security services arbitrarily detained suspected opponents incommunicado and for prolonged periods. Torture was widespread and in some areas, including Darfur, systematic. Human rights defenders and foreign humanitarian organizations were harassed. Freedom of expression was curtailed. The authorities forcibly evicted displaced people in poor areas of Khartoum and people in the Hamdab area where a dam was being built. Armed opposition groups also carried out human rights abuses.

Background
The 2005 Comprehensive Peace Agreement (CPA) between the government and the Sudan People's Liberation Movement remained in effect, although clashes between tribal or government-supported militias and the Sudan People's Liberation Army (SPLA) continued in some areas. Salva Kiir Mayardit, President of the Government of South Sudan, was appointed First Vice-President of the Government of National Unity (GNU) led by head of state Field Marshal Omar al-Bashir. Thousands of displaced people and refugees returned home to the south, but many remained in refugee camps in neighbouring countries or displaced in Khartoum. The CPA provided for joint commissions, some of which had either not been set up by the end of 2006, including the Human Rights Commission, or were not functioning effectively, such as the National Petroleum Commission.

Southern members of the GNU were not consulted on important issues such as the crisis in Darfur, and complained that the south's share of oil revenues was insufficient. The government of Sudan still rejected the July 2005 report of the Abyei Boundary Commission and took no steps to implement the Abyei Protocol, which provided for shared government in the oil-rich border area of Abyei.

In June the Eastern Sudan Peace Agreement was signed in Asmara, Eritrea, by the Sudanese government and the Eastern Sudan Front, which included the Beja Congress and the Free Lions Movement representing the Rashaida ethnic group. The state of emergency in eastern Sudan was lifted.

Sudan acceded to the two Additional Protocols to the Geneva Conventions. The National Assembly passed the Organization of Humanitarian and Voluntary Work Act in March which placed restrictions on the work of national and international non-governmental organizations (NGOs).

Official commissions of inquiry set up in previous years failed to report their findings including those into the deaths in custody of Popular Congress detainees in September 2004 and the killings of demonstrators in Port Sudan in January 2005.

International scrutiny of Darfur
In March the African Union Peace and Security Council (PSC) called for the transition to a UN force from the AMIS peacekeeping force in Darfur. The effectiveness of AMIS was impeded by lack of equipment and funding, internal organizational problems, and restrictions placed on its activities by the government.

The UN Mission in Sudan (UNMIS), a large UN multidimensional peacekeeping force set up under the CPA, had more than 10,000 troops in the south and in Abyei, Nuba Mountains and Blue Nile in the north. In August the UN Security Council passed Resolution 1706 to send a UN force to protect civilians in Darfur, which the government rejected. An agreement by the PSC in December, to extend the AMIS mandate for six months until June 2007 and move to a strengthened, hybrid African Union/UN force in Darfur, was accepted by the government.

A Panel of Experts, set up under a Security Council resolution to monitor the 2005 arms embargo, reported on several occasions that all sides were breaching it. A Security Council resolution in May ordered a travel ban and assets freeze on four individuals named by the Panel.

There were regular reports to the Security Council by the UN Secretary-General, the human rights component of UNMIS, and the UN Special Rapporteur on the situation of human rights in the Sudan. In September the government ordered the expulsion of the Special Representative of the UN Secretary-General for Sudan, Jan Pronk, after he described government defeats in North Darfur and commented on low army morale in his personal weblog.

In December a Special Session on Darfur of the UN Human Rights Council resolved to send a five-member high-level mission to assess the human rights situation in Darfur.

The Prosecutor of the International Criminal Court visited Khartoum in February and June, but did not visit Darfur or issue any indictments in 2006. He presented six-monthly reports to the UN Security Council. In December he said his Office was seeking to finalize submissions to the judges to be made in February 2007.

Southern Sudan
Clashes continued between the SPLA and government-supported militias, and between rival ethnic groups.
⌲ In Jonglei State scores of civilians were reportedly killed in April and May during clashes between armed groups and direct attacks on villages. Some 30 civilians were killed in Malakal in November in severe fighting between the SPLA and southern militias incorporated in the Sudanese armed forces.

Arbitrary detentions were widespread.
⌲ Charles Locker, Executive Director of the NGO, Manna Sudan, was detained by local authorities in Ikotos in July, and subsequently detained without charge or trial in Torit until September. He appeared to have been detained for criticizing the role of the governor of Eastern Equatoria state and other local government authorities in tribal clashes.

Darfur
A Darfur Peace Agreement (DPA) was signed in May by the government and one faction of the Sudan Liberation Army (SLA) led by Minni Minawi. Other armed opposition groups, including the SLA and the Justice and Equality Movement, refused to sign. Most displaced people opposed the agreement, which was

felt to lack guarantees for safe return and compensation. In demonstrations which turned into riots in many camps for the displaced, there were deaths, including of police officers, and numerous arrests. Some individuals and groups later signed the peace agreement. Under the DPA's terms, Minni Minawi was appointed Senior Assistant to the President. However, a government promise to disarm the Janjawid was broken, as it had been after numerous previous agreements, and none of the agreed commissions was operating by the end of 2006, including the Compensation Commission. Some Janjawid were incorporated into the armed forces or remained in paramilitary units and continued receiving financial and material assistance from the government.

The government took no action to halt cross-border Janjawid attacks against targeted ethnic groups in Chad, which resulted in the deaths of hundreds of civilians and tens of thousands of displacements during the first half of the year. Attacks across the border resumed in October, in which some 500 civilians were unlawfully killed, many more were raped, thousands were driven from their homes, and villages were destroyed (see Chad entry). In total, 100,000 people were displaced by such attacks in Chad.

A number of armed groups which opposed the DPA regrouped as the National Redemption Front in June. After a massive troop build-up in Darfur in August, the government launched an offensive against areas controlled by those groups in North Darfur and Jebel Marra. Government aircraft indiscriminately or directly bombed civilians. Forces of the SLA Minawi faction also attacked civilians. In November, Janjawid killings and forcible displacements of civilians in villages near areas controlled by armed opposition groups increased. Members of armed opposition groups were responsible for attacking humanitarian convoys, abducting aid workers, and reportedly killing and torturing civilians.

☐ In July more than 72 people, including some 11 primary school pupils, were killed during attacks by the SLA Minawi faction, at the time allied with the government, on villages apparently under SLA control in North Darfur. AMIS was accused of failing to answer pleas for help.

☐ The Gereida region was insecure throughout 2006, with scores of villages destroyed in attacks by Janjawid or other armed groups. Some 80,000 people fled the camp for Internally Displaced Persons (IDP) in Gereida after fighting between forces of the SLA Minawi faction and the Justice and Equality Movement in October.

☐ In November at least 50 civilians were killed, including 21 children under 10, when Janjawid attacked eight villages and an IDP camp in Jebel Moon in West Darfur. AMIS forces arrived the day after the attack. The Governor of West Darfur promised an inquiry but no findings had been made public by the end of 2006.

Violence against women

Rapes of women by Janjawid militias in Darfur remained systematic. Most rapes of women took place when they ventured outside IDP camps to collect firewood.

Other women were raped after Janjawid attacks on villages. The perpetrators benefited from almost complete impunity. Authorities routinely took no effective action to investigate women's complaints of rape. At worst, raped women were arrested for adultery.

☐ In May military police travelling by train to Nyala raped six women near Belail IDP Camp. Community leaders reported the rapes to the police, who immediately arrested three men. By the following day they had all been released.

☐ Janjawid accompanying the armed forces offensive in North Darfur in September captured five girls and women aged between 13 and 23 in the village of Tarmakera, south of Kulkul. They were reportedly raped and severely beaten before being released the following day.

Violence against demonstrators

Excessive force was used against many demonstrations opposing government policy.

☐ Peaceful demonstrations against price rises in petrol and sugar in Khartoum on 30 August were put down with tear gas and batons by the police. Sentences of up to two months' imprisonment for public order offences were passed on 80 people.

Freedom of expression

Freedoms of expression and association were curtailed. Journalists were frequently arrested and newspapers censored and seized.

☐ A meeting of national and international NGOs in advance of the African Union summit in Khartoum in January, attended by AI delegates, was raided by National Security agents. Three of the participants were briefly detained.

☐ In February, five members of the non-governmental Sudan Social Development Organization (SUDO) were detained for several hours after they held a training session in human rights monitoring in al-Da'ein University in South Darfur.

☐ Abdallah Abu Obeida, a correspondent for *Al-Ra'y al-'Amm* newspaper, was detained incommunicado for two weeks in October. He was questioned about Darfur before being released without charge.

Human rights defenders were harassed and sometimes detained.

☐ Mossaad Mohammed Ali and Adam Mohammed Sharif, two human rights lawyers, were briefly detained in May. They were working with the non-governmental Amal Centre, which provides legal aid and rehabilitation for torture victims. Adam Mohammed Sharif was freed the following day, but Mossaad Mohammed Ali was held for five days before being released after worldwide protests. They were not charged and no reason was given for their detention.

Detentions

The security forces, in particular the National Security Agency, arbitrarily detained people incommunicado and without charge or trial.

☐ Ali Hussein Mohammed Omar and two other members of the Beja Congress were arrested in March in Kassala, ill-treated and held for 10 weeks in secret locations without being charged and without access to their families or lawyers.

☐ In Khartoum in September scores of Darfuris and others were arrested and held incommunicado without formal charges, allegedly in the context of the murder of Mohammed Taha, editor of *al-Wifaq* newspaper. His killing in September appeared to be politically motivated. Those detained included Abulgasim Ahmed Abulgasim, who had been summarily deported from Saudi Arabia (see Saudia Arabia entry).

Scores of displaced people were detained in May during demonstrations and riots against the DPA in numerous IDP camps in Darfur.

☐ Mohammed Osman Mohammed and two others were arrested after police fired live ammunition at protesters in Otash IDP camp in May. The same day, police used excessive force against scores of demonstrators, including women, as they carried a memorandum of concerns about the DPA to the UN office in Nyala. Scores were arrested and 25 remained in detention awaiting trial at the end of 2006.

Cruel, inhuman or degrading punishments and torture

Cruel, inhuman or degrading punishments such as flogging were imposed for offences including the brewing of alcohol or adultery. Torture continued to be used systematically against certain groups, including students and detainees in Darfur.

☐ In February scores of students from Juba University in Khartoum were beaten with batons by armed police and security services after they gathered to call for the university to be relocated to Juba. Some 51 were detained and, according to reports, taken to secret centres known as "ghost houses" where they were beaten, deprived of food and not allowed access to legal counsel or their families.

☐ Ibrahim Birzi reportedly died as a result of torture and is thought to have been buried secretly. He was one of 13 internally displaced people from Foro Baranga, south of al-Jeneina in Darfur, who were arrested in September, severely beaten with bicycle chains and leather whips, and had their heads submerged under water. They were reportedly suspected of being supporters of the Sudan Liberation Army/Movement (SLA/M).

Trials and death sentences

Appeal courts and criminal courts in Khartoum acquitted political detainees in some trials. However, in the majority of trials, rights of defence were curtailed or absent, and testimony given under duress was accepted as evidence. Dozens of death sentences were passed, usually after unfair trials in which rights of defence, including the right to be represented by counsel, were not respected.

☐ In April the remaining 10 defendants in a trial of Popular Congress members were acquitted after the Special Court in Khartoum North accepted that their confessions were obtained under torture. They had been arrested in September 2004 and charged with an attempted coup.

☐ In a trial before the Khartoum Criminal Court of 137 residents of Soba Aradi, a settlement of mostly displaced people in Khartoum North, 62 detainees were acquitted in June and August for lack of evidence. They were charged in connection with clashes in May 2005, in which 14 police officers and 30 IDPs were killed, over the proposed relocation of the settlement. Seven defendants were sentenced to death in November.

In Darfur, trials before Specialized Criminal Courts set up in 2003 to try crimes such as banditry failed to meet international fair trial standards. In some cases, the courts admitted as evidence confessions reportedly made under duress and later retracted in court.

Trials before the Special Criminal Court on the Events in Darfur (SCCED) have mostly been for ordinary offences unconnected with crimes under international law in Darfur. The Court's inauguration in July 2005 coincided with the opening of the investigation by the International Criminal Court into war crimes and crimes against humanity in Darfur.

☐ In the only case involving attacks on civilians known to have come before the SCCED, three men, including two border guards, were sentenced to up to three years' imprisonment in May for stealing goods in the village of Tama in October 2005. No one was charged in connection with the killing of 28 civilians during the attack.

Forced evictions

There was forced displacement in many areas, including Darfur, parts of the south, and the area of the Meroe dam. The Khartoum municipal authorities continued to forcibly evict internally displaced people who had settled in the Khartoum area, notwithstanding an agreement reached between the Governor of Khartoum State and a Consultative Committee on Re-Planning Affecting IDPs composed of representatives from the UN, other governments and donors. The Governor had promised a moratorium on all relocations until they were better planned and until the new locations met certain minimum standards.

☐ On 16 August, without prior warning, bulldozers began to demolish homes in Dar al-Salam, an IDP settlement 43km south of Khartoum housing some 12,000 IDPs. Many had fled droughts and famine in Darfur in the 1980s. Armed police and Special Forces used violence and tear gas against residents, and carried out arrests. Four people died, including a child, and many were injured.

☐ The building of the Meroe dam on the River Nile will cause the relocation of some 50,000 people. In August, 2,723 households in Amri were given six days to evacuate their homes and reportedly not provided with shelter, food or medical care. Journalists who tried to visit the displaced were briefly detained and sent back to Khartoum.

AI country reports/ visits
Reports
- Chad/Sudan: Sowing the seeds of Darfur – ethnic targeting in Chad by Janjawid militias from Sudan (AI Index: AFR 20/006/2006)

- Sudan: Protecting civilians in Darfur — a briefing for effective peacekeeping (AI Index: AFR 54/024/2006)
- Sudan (Darfur): Korma — yet more attacks on civilians (AI Index: AFR 54/026/2006)
- Sudan: Darfur — threats to humanitarian aid (AI Index: AFR 54/031/2006)
- Sudan: Crying out for safety (AI Index: AFR 54/055/2006)
- Sudan/China: Appeal by Amnesty International to the Chinese government on the occasion of the China-Africa Summit for Development and Cooperation (AI Index: AFR 54/072/2006)
- Sudan: Sudan government's solution — Janjawid unleashed in Darfur (AI Index: AFR 54/078/2006)
- Sudan/Chad: 'No-one to help them' — rape extends from Darfur into Eastern Chad (AI Index: AFR 54/087/2006)

Visits

AI delegates visited Khartoum to attend an NGO meeting during the African Union summit in January. AI was allowed no further visas to visit Sudan.

AI delegates visited Chad in May, July and November to carry out research on Sudan and attacks from Sudan into Chad.

SWAZILAND

KINGDOM OF SWAZILAND
Head of state: King Mswati III
Head of government: Absalom Themba Dlamini
Death penalty: retentionist
International Criminal Court: not ratified

A new Constitution came into force, promising increased human rights protection. Reports of torture, ill-treatment and excessive use of force by members of the police persisted, and there was a lack of redress for the victims. While a third of all adults were living with HIV, less than half those requiring antiretroviral therapy were receiving it. Children's rights were undermined by poverty, HIV/AIDS, sexual violence and discrimination. Women and girls continued to suffer discrimination under the law, and survivors of rape, particularly in rural areas, faced obstacles in access to justice and health care.

Legal and constitutional developments

A new Constitution came into force in February, providing qualified guarantees for civil and political rights.

The legal status of political parties remained uncertain as the King's Proclamation of 1973, under which they were banned, was not repealed. An International Labour Organization (ILO) delegation, visiting the country in June, signed an agreement with the government and "social partners" who undertook to review the impact of the Constitution on rights protected under ILO conventions and recommend repeal of non-compliant statutes. An organization attempting to register as a political party sought a High Court order to clarify its position. A ruling was pending at the end of the year. In November the National Constitutional Assembly, trade union officials and others challenged the validity of the Constitution in the High Court. The case was postponed until 2007 because of a shortage of judges.

Access to legal remedies in human rights cases was limited by the failure of government to ensure an efficient and independent judicial appointment process. By the end of 2006 there was only one permanent judge on the High Court Bench, along with three judges with temporary contracts. The constitutionality of the Judicial Services Commission, which advises the King on judicial appointments, was challenged in the High Court in October. The hearing was postponed until 2007.

The Court of Appeal was reconstituted as the Supreme Court, with two new judicial appointments.

In July the King assented to the Prevention of Corruption Act.

Human rights violations by law enforcement officials

Incidents of torture, suspicious deaths in custody, and use of excessive force by police were reported. Crime suspects as well as members of political organizations were the main victims. Impunity for human rights violations by law enforcement officials was a persistent problem.

🗀 In March the High Court, when granting bail, ordered the government to investigate allegations of torture by 16 defendants charged with treason and other offences in connection with petrol bombings in late 2005. Allegations of suffocation torture, beatings and other ill-treatment had earlier emerged at magistrates' court hearings. Nine defendants were interrogated and allegedly tortured at one police station, Sigodveni. Four defendants also appeared in the High Court with visible injuries sustained while held at Sidwashini prison. Independent forensic medical examinations in March of some defendants confirmed that their injuries were consistent with the allegations. In October the Prime Minister established a commission of inquiry.

🗀 In January Takhona Ngwenya was assaulted at Mbabane police station, where she had gone to make a statement about the theft of a friend's phone. She was punched and kicked all over her body, including her face, and subjected to suffocation torture with a black plastic bag so that she lost consciousness. She required medical treatment. In response to a civil claim for damages, the police denied liability.

🗀 In July Mduduzi Motsa died in custody at Sigodveni police station. The police initially told his relatives that he had died in a motor accident but later said that he had committed suicide in his cell. The police reportedly prevented relatives from attending the official postmortem.

In a number of incidents demonstrators were subjected to excessive force by members of the police Operations Support Services Unit. In September university students attempting to deliver a petition to the Prime Minister's office in Mbabane were beaten with batons and kicked to the ground. In December supporters of the political organization, PUDEMO, were tear-gassed and baton-charged by police in Manzini. PUDEMO member Mphandlana Shongwe, who went to Manzini police station to inquire about arrested demonstrators, was beaten, kicked and knocked against a wall and required hospital treatment for his injuries.

Violations of the right to fair trial

The 16 defendants charged with treason and other offences had not been brought to trial by the end of the year. The High Court had ordered the accused to be released on bail in March on the grounds that the prosecution had not presented a prima facie case against any of them. In November the state's appeal on a technicality against the bail ruling was postponed until 2007.

Children's rights

Children's access to education was limited by the impact of poverty, HIV/AIDS, sexual violence and discrimination on the basis of gender and disability. The number of children orphaned by AIDS was estimated at 70,000 and 10 to 15 per cent of households were headed by children, mostly by girls who were vulnerable to multiple forms of abuse.

Additional training and capacity for the police Domestic Violence, Child Protection and Sexual Offences Unit (DV Unit), the establishment of child friendly interview facilities and the development of Community Child Protection Committees at local level began to improve children's access to justice in cases of abuse.

In September the UN Committee on the Rights of the Child (CRC) expressed concern at the lack of a "systematic and comprehensive" legislative review to bring domestic legislation into line with the Convention on the Rights of the Child. The CRC was also concerned at the lack of protection under the law against early and forced marriage, the position of adolescent girls suffering marginalization and gender stereotyping and their low school completion rates. The CRC criticized the persistence of corporal punishment in the family and in schools, and the provision in the Constitution which permitted "moderate chastisement" of children. The courts continued to impose corporal punishment on under-18-year-old boys.

The government significantly increased its national budget allocation for the education of orphans and vulnerable children, but continuing delays in payments to schools jeopardized the children's access to education. In November the Swaziland National Association of Teachers applied to the High Court for an order to compel the government to make the payments. The case was postponed until 2007 because of the shortage of judges.

Women's rights

The new Constitution provided women for the first time with the right to equal treatment with men, including equal opportunities in the political, economic and social spheres, and provided some protection for women from being compelled to comply with customs against their will.

Women and girls continued to face discrimination under both the civil and customary legal systems. Incidents of forced or early marriage under the practices known as *Kutekwa* and *Kwendziswa* continued to be reported.

The Commissioner of Police reported a 15 per cent increase in cases of rape and abuses of women and children. Survivors of sexual violence, particularly in rural areas, faced continuing obstacles to access to justice and emergency health care due to the lack of co-ordinated and adequately resourced services. The DV Unit took steps to improve police investigation skills and data collection.

The draft Sexual Offences and Domestic Violence Bill, intended to improve the legal framework for investigating and prosecuting crimes of rape and other forms of sexual violence, was still with the Ministry of Justice and Constitutional Affairs at the end of the year.

People living with HIV/AIDS

In December UNAIDS estimated that 33 per cent of adults were living with HIV in 2005. The government reported that among pregnant women attending antenatal clinics there was a slight decline since 2004 in prevalence rates to 39.2 per cent. The prevalence rate for the most affected group, 25 to 29 years, declined from 56 to 48 per cent.

In February some 15,000 of the estimated 36,500 people requiring anti-retroviral therapy (ART) were reported to be receiving it free of charge through public facilities. The Swaziland National AIDS Program took steps to increase access to post-exposure prophylaxis treatment for rape survivors and to prevent transmission of HIV from mother to child. The number of HIV Testing and Counselling Centres increased to 23 from only three in 2002. In June the government released the Second National Multisectoral HIV and AIDS Strategic Plan for prevention and treatment.

In October the World Food Programme expressed concern that patients were abandoning ART. Contributing factors included food shortages, the scarcity and cost of public transport systems, and the cost of other necessary medication for opportunistic infections and side-effects of ART. Organizations of people living with HIV and AIDS called for official structures to work more closely with them in addressing the causes and consequences of the epidemic.

Death penalty

There were no executions and no new death sentences were imposed by the High Court. The new Constitution retained the death penalty but it was no longer a mandatory punishment for certain crimes.

AI country reports/ visits
Reports
- Swaziland: Persistent failure to call police to account (AI Index: AFR 55/001/2006)
- Swaziland: Memorandum to the Government of Swaziland on the Sexual Offences and Domestic Violence Bill (AI Index: AFR 55/003/2006)
Visit
An AI delegation visiting in April held high-level government meetings and consultations with a range of medical, legal and civil society organizations on human rights concerns. It co-hosted with local non-governmental organizations a seminar on improving access to justice and health care for survivors of sexual violence.

SWEDEN

KINGDOM OF SWEDEN
Head of state: King Carl XVI Gustaf
Head of government: Fredrik Reinfeldt (replaced Göran Persson in October)
Death penalty: abolitionist for all crimes
International Criminal Court: ratified

A UN human rights body confirmed that the Swedish authorities were responsible for multiple human rights violations in connection with a summary expulsion to Egypt. The Swedish government reiterated that decisions by UN Committees were not legally binding, and continued to refuse to provide redress, including compensation, to the victims. In March there were major changes in the asylum process.

Update: 'war on terror' deportations
In November the UN Human Rights Committee found that the Swedish authorities' summary expulsion of Mohammed El Zari to Egypt in 2001 breached the prohibition of *refoulement* (involuntary return of anyone to a country where they would be at risk of serious human rights abuses), and that the diplomatic assurances obtained from Egypt in this case were insufficient to eliminate the manifest risk of torture. These findings confirmed the conclusions of the UN Committee against Torture in 2005 in respect of a complaint against Sweden by another Egyptian asylum-seeker, Ahmed Agiza, jointly expelled to Egypt with Mohammed El Zari.

The Human Rights Committee also found that the Swedish authorities were responsible for the ill-treatment at the hands of US agents on Swedish soil immediately before the expulsion; failed to instigate a prompt, independent and impartial investigation into the ill-treatment and bring appropriate charges; and failed to provide an effective, independent review of the decision to expel Mohammed El Zari, despite the real risk of torture in Egypt. The Swedish authorities also breached his right of complaint by immediately expelling him despite advance notification that he would be seeking international interim protection measures in the event of a negative decision on his asylum claim.

The government continued to insist that such decisions by UN Committees were not legally binding, and provided no legal ground for compensation.

Refugees and asylum-seekers
In March a new Aliens Act entered into force, dissolving the Aliens Appeals Board and establishing a right to appeal against negative asylum decisions, among others, to higher courts. Appeals against first instance decisions of the Swedish Migration Board would be lodged with the Migration Courts, whose decisions in turn could be the subject of appeal to the Migration Court of Appeal. The Act also heralded a greater possibility for oral hearings.

However, in many cases, the Migration Courts did not maintain the confidentiality of personal information or details of persecution, including torture. Nor did they always accede to asylum-seekers' requests for closed hearings, giving rise to concerns about personal safety, particularly where rejection of applications could lead to deportations. The Migration Board did not respond to AI's call for asylum-seekers to be informed that confidentiality might not be respected in appeal proceedings.

Sexual orientation and gender-based persecution were introduced as grounds for seeking refugee status. In September the Stockholm Migration Court rejected the appeal of an Iranian asylum-seeker who had sought asylum on the grounds of his sexual orientation. The Court used only one source of country information, a Swedish Ministry for Foreign Affairs report, concluding that he was not at risk of persecution in Iran solely on these grounds, particularly if he concealed his sexual orientation. AI criticized the decision and the Ministry report, arguing that persecution based on sexual orientation was enshrined in law in Iran and could lead to the imposition of the death penalty. In December the Migration Court of Appeal declined to hear an appeal against the lower court's decision, which therefore became final.

The authorities actively sought to deport rejected Eritrean asylum-seekers, despite recommendations to all states by the UNHCR, the UN refugee agency, to refrain from forcible returns to Eritrea.

From September, under a Migration Board decision, all asylum-seekers were to be granted an appointed legal representative, apart from those whose claims would be determined by another European Union member state in accordance with the so-called Dublin Regulation.

Violence against women

In June a Commission established in 2005 to look at municipalities' responsibilities on violence against women made public its recommendations. Several corresponded to issues that had been raised by AI. They included the need to amend the Social Services Act to increase municipalities' responsibilities for improving support and protection for women subjected to violence, among them women with special needs. In June the UN Special Rapporteur on violence against women, on a fact-finding mission to Sweden, highlighted considerable differences in the way municipalities discharged these responsibilities. She called for greater public scrutiny and guidance.

AI country reports/ visits
Reports
- Partners in crime: Europe's role in US renditions (AI Index: EUR 01/008/2006)
- Sweden: The case of Mohammed El Zari and Ahmed Agiza — violations of fundamental human rights by Sweden confirmed (AI Index: EUR 42/001/2006)olations of fundamental human rights by Sweden confirmed (AI Index: EUR 42/001/2006

SWITZERLAND

SWISS CONFEDERATION
Head of state and government: Moritz Leuenberger
Death penalty: abolitionist for all crimes
International Criminal Court: ratified

The rights of asylum-seekers and migrants were further restricted under new legislation. A new law permitted the expulsion of a violent partner from the family home in cases of domestic violence, but migrant women were left at risk of deportation if they ended a relationship with a violent partner. The UN Special Rapporteur on racism found strong evidence of institutional racism within the police.

Changes to migration and asylum law

Under a 2005 asylum law approved by national referendum on 24 September 2006, access to the asylum procedure can be refused to people without national identity documents. The time frame for appeal against a decision to refuse consideration of an asylum case was reduced to five days in many instances, with no state-sponsored legal representation for those who cannot afford a lawyer. Under the new law, irregular migrants can be detained pending expulsion for up to two years while their identity is determined. Minors can be detained for up to one year, in contravention of international standards. In October the chair of the Federal Supreme Court, Dr Giusep Nay, expressed concern that the provisions in law relating to detention were not in line with Switzerland's international legal obligations.

Family reunification measures for migrants from outside the European Union were further restricted under a new migration law passed in September.

Violence against women

Figures released in October by the Federal Office of Statistics indicated that approximately 28 women die each year in Switzerland as a result of domestic violence. On 23 June Parliament amended the civil law permitting the expulsion of the aggressor from the shared home if requested by the victim of domestic violence. However, migrant women living in Switzerland for fewer than five years remained vulnerable to expulsion if they stopped cohabiting with the partner named on their residence permit.

Racism

Following a visit in January, the UN Special Rapporteur on racism noted that racism, xenophobia and discrimination were "trivialized" in political debate in Switzerland. He also observed strong evidence of institutional racism, including within the police. Allegations continued of ill-treatment, excessive use of force and racist abuse by police officers, and of subsequent impunity for the perpetrators.

Extraditions under diplomatic assurances

Three Turkish nationals who applied for asylum or re-examination of an asylum claim in 2006 were arrested in response to an extradition request from Turkey, reportedly to face charges of involvement with armed opposition groups. Despite the risk of an unfair trial if returned to Turkey, the Swiss authorities agreed to the return of two of the applicants on the basis of a diplomatic assurance by the Turkish authorities that they would not be arbitrarily detained, tortured or unfairly tried. Appeals against the decision were pending. The third case was still pending an initial decision at the end of 2006.

SYRIA

SYRIAN ARAB REPUBLIC
Head of state: Bashar al-Assad
Head of government: Muhammad Naji al-'Otri
Death penalty: retentionist
International Criminal Court: signed

Freedom of expression and association continued to be severely restricted. Scores of people were arrested and hundreds remained imprisoned for political reasons, including prisoners of conscience and others sentenced after unfair trials. Discriminatory legislation and practices remained in force against women and the Kurdish minority. Torture and ill-treatment in detention continued to be reported and carried out with impunity. Human rights defenders continued to face arrest, harassment and restrictions on their freedom of movement.

Background

The state of emergency imposed in 1962 remained in force. A UN investigation continued to indicate high-level Syrian involvement in the February 2005 assassination of former Lebanese prime minister Rafiq al-Hariri, which Syria denied.

Syria hosted more than 200,000 Lebanese refugees who fled to the country during the July/August conflict, as well as some 500,000 Iraqi refugees displaced by the continuing conflict in Iraq. There were also some 500,000 Palestinian refugees in Syria and tens of thousands of Syrians remained displaced due to Israel's continuing occupation of the Golan.

A European Union-funded human rights centre was closed down in March, shortly after opening. The Association Agreement between Syria and the European Union, initialled in October 2004 and containing a human rights clause, remained frozen for a further year at the final approval stage. Syria's relations with the USA remained strained.

Releases

Five of the remaining prisoners from the pro-reform movement referred to as the "Damascus Spring" – Riad Seif and Ma'mun al-Homsi, both former parliamentary deputies, Walid al-Bunni, Habib 'Issa and Fawaz Tello – were freed on 18 January, seven months before the expiry of their five-year sentences.

Imprisonment for political reasons

Scores of people were arrested during 2006 for political reasons, including tens of prisoners of conscience. Hundreds of political prisoners, including prisoners of conscience, remained imprisoned. Scores faced trial before the Supreme State Security Court (SSSC), Criminal Court or Military Court, all of which failed to respect international standards for fair trials.

In April, Riad Drar al-Hamood was sentenced by the SSSC to five years' imprisonment on charges of belonging to a "secret organization", "publishing false news" and "inciting sectarian strife". A member of the Committees for Revival of Civil Society, an unauthorized network of people engaging in human rights-related and political discussion, he was arrested in June 2005 after making a speech at the funeral of the prominent Kurdish Islamic scholar, Sheikh Muhammad Ma'shuq al-Khiznawi, who had been abducted and killed. The charge of "inciting sectarian strife" was commonly used against human rights defenders and activists seeking to promote the rights of Syrian Kurds.

Ten of the scores of signatories to the "Beirut-Damascus Declaration" that sought normalization of relations between Syria and Lebanon were arrested between 14 and 18 May. Human rights lawyer Anwar al-Bunni, writer Michel Kilo and Mahmoud 'Issa – who was rearrested in October after being released on bail in September with former prisoner of conscience Khalil Hussein and Suleyman Shummar – remained detained at the end of the year. The five men faced multiple charges including one common charge of insulting the President, government officials or public servants.

There were increased concerns for the health of Dr 'Aref Dalilah, aged 63. He was said to have suffered a stroke in mid-2006 and continued to suffer from diabetes and high blood pressure. He remained imprisoned in a small, isolated cell serving the 10-year sentence imposed on him for his involvement in the 2001 pro-reform movement referred to as the "Damascus Spring".

The trial of former "Damascus Spring" prisoner Kamal al-Labwani, who was arrested in November 2005 on his return to Syria after several months in Europe and the USA during which he peacefully called for democratic reform, continued before the Criminal Court. He was charged with "encouraging foreign aggression against Syria", an offence punishable by life imprisonment. In November he was badly beaten by a criminal prisoner, reportedly at the instigation of the authorities.

Eight young men remained detained incommunicado at the end of 2006 after being arrested between January and March, apparently in connection with their involvement in developing a political discussion group. They were reportedly tortured during their interrogation. They were being tried by the SSSC. Seven of the men were charged with "subjecting Syria to the risk of hostile acts", and all eight with "publishing false news that may offend the dignity of the State".

In August former "Damascus Spring" prisoner of conscience Habib Saleh was sentenced by the military court in Homs to three years' imprisonment for "weakening nationalist sentiments" and "spreading false news". The charges related to articles critical of the Syrian authorities that he had published on the Internet.

Scores of individuals were facing trial for their alleged following of the "Islamist trend". On 14 November the SSSC sentenced 11 men from al-'Otaybe who were arrested in April 2004 to prison terms of six to nine years for membership of a Salafi organization. Some 23 young men from Qatana remained detained following their arrests in July 2004. Members of both groups were reportedly tortured and ill-treated during long periods of incommunicado detention.

⌷ On 20 December, Kurdish activist and secretary of the outlawed Syrian Kurdish Democratic Unity Party, Muhi al-Din Sheikh Aali, was reportedly arrested by Military Intelligence, in Aleppo, northern Syria. At the end of the year he remained in incommunicado detention at an unknown location.

Freedom of expression

Freedom of expression remained strictly controlled.

⌷ Seventeen state employees working in various government ministries were dismissed without explanation but apparently on account of their links to the "Beirut-Damascus Declaration". The dismissals were ordered by Prime Minister Muhammad Naji al-'Otri on 14 June.

⌷ Upon his release in September after serving a six-month sentence imposed by the Military Court for "insulting the President", "harming the dignity of the State" and "inciting sectarian strife", writer Muhammad Ghanem was also reportedly suspended from his employment in the Education Directorate in al-Raqqa.

⌷ Dozens of Syrian Internet news sites were reportedly blocked during 2006, including www.syriaview.net, www.thisissyria.net, www.kurdroj.com, www.shril.info and www.arraee.com.

Torture and ill-treatment

Torture and ill-treatment in custody continued to be reported, and allegations of such ill-treatment were not investigated.

⌷ It was reported in April that Muhammad Shaher Haysa died in custody in Damascus as a result of torture and ill-treatment he was subjected to while detained for six months. He was reportedly arrested on suspicion of involvement in the Jund al-Sham organization.

⌷ 'Ali Sayed al-Shihabi, a former prisoner of conscience for nine years, remained detained at the end of the year following his arrest in August, apparently in relation to articles he had written for the Internet. While held at the Investigation Branch in Damascus he was beaten with sticks on his feet and hands.

⌷ In October, Muhammad Haydar Zammar, a German national of Syrian origin held in secret, incommunicado detention since December 2001 and reportedly tortured, was brought before the SSSC on charges including membership of the outlawed Muslim Brotherhood for which, if convicted, he could face the death penalty.

Violence and discrimination against women

At least 10 women were reportedly killed by close male relatives for alleged reasons of "honour". Perpetrators continued to enjoy near impunity for the crimes on account of inadequate investigations and of provisions in the Penal Code that allow for reduced sentences for killing a female member of the family who is allegedly committing "adultery" or having other "sexual relations". Women's rights activists worked to end discriminatory legislation including in the areas of marriage, divorce, the family, inheritance and nationality, and to achieve greater protection against domestic and other forms of violence.

⌷ In a village near Sweida in July, a teenage woman with learning difficulties was reportedly killed by her brother, following her rape by a relative. A trial was ongoing at the end of the year.

⌷ In March a young woman was reportedly forced to marry the man who had raped her and thereby absolve him of any crime, in accordance with article 508 of the Penal Code.

Discrimination against Kurds

Syrian Kurds continued to suffer from identity-based discrimination, including restrictions on the use of the Kurdish language and culture. Tens of thousands of Syrian Kurds remained effectively stateless and as such continued to be denied equal access to social and economic rights.

⌷ Some 75 Kurds were reportedly released in September following their arrests in March for peacefully celebrating Nowruz (the lunar New Year) in Aleppo. The celebration was violently broken up by the security forces.

⌷ Four teachers were reportedly detained for one month from 4 August for teaching the Kurdish language.

Human rights defenders

Several unauthorized human rights organizations continued to be active, although their members were at risk of arrest, harassment and travel bans.

⌷ Dr 'Ammar Qurabi, media spokesman of the National Organization for Human Rights, was detained for four days in March at Palestine Branch of Military Intelligence in Damascus, then released without charge.

⌷ On 11 July the offices of the Human Rights Association of Syria were attacked, with windows broken and animal faeces smeared on the walls.

⌷ On 27 July Muhannad al-Hasani, head of the Syrian Human Rights Organization, was prevented from travelling to a meeting on organizational systems in Jordan, by order of the security services. In October he was prevented from travelling to Morocco to attend the Euro-Mediterranean Civil Forum.

⌷ In November, Nizar Ristnawi, a founding member of the Arab Organization for Human Rights-Syria, was sentenced by the SSSC to four years' imprisonment for "spreading false news" and "insulting the President". The charges and sentence appeared to be based on his work promoting human rights and democracy. Nizar Ristnawi was arrested in April 2005 and detained incommunicado until August 2005.

UN Working Group on Arbitrary Detention

In May the UN Working Group on Arbitrary Detention determined that the detention of five individuals deported to Syria was arbitrary, given "the gravity of the violation of the right to a fair trial". Muhammad Fa'iq Mustafa was deported from Bulgaria in November 2002 and sentenced to 12 years' imprisonment by the Field Military Court, before being released in November 2005. Ahmet Muhammad Ibrahim was deported from Turkey in March 2005, reportedly tortured, then released in January 2006. Nabil al-Marabh, who was deported to Syria from the USA in January 2004, was sentenced in March by the SSSC to five years' imprisonment for "subjecting Syria to the risk of hostile acts". Both 'Abd al-Rahman al-Musa, who was deported from the USA in January 2005, and Muhammad Osama Sayes, who was deported from the UK in May 2005, were sentenced to death by the SSSC in June for affiliation to the Muslim Brotherhood. The sentences were immediately commuted to 12 years' imprisonment.

Death penalty

The death penalty remained in force for a wide range of offences, but the authorities disclosed little information about its use. At least seven individuals were sentenced to death under Law 49 of 1980 for affiliation with the outlawed Muslim Brotherhood organization, then had the sentences commuted to 12 years' imprisonment.

Impunity/ enforced disappearances

There was increased discussion within civil society over the issue of combating past impunity, particularly with regard to mass human rights abuses committed since the late 1970s. The fate of more than 17,000 people, mostly Islamists, who "disappeared" after they were detained in the late 1970s and early 1980s, and hundreds of Lebanese and Palestinians who were detained in Syria or abducted from Lebanon by Syrian forces or Lebanese and Palestinian militias, remained unknown.

AI country reports/ visits

Visit

In January AI visited Syria for the first time since 1997, and met government officials, lawyers and others, including detainees' families.

TAIWAN

TAIWAN
Head of state: Chen Shui-bian
Head of government: Su Tseng-chang (replaced Frank Hsieh Chang-ting in January)
Death penalty: retentionist

Hundreds of thousands of people participated in political demonstrations for and against President Chen Shui-bian in the wake of corruption allegations against him and his family. Media organizations raised concerns for the safety of journalists covering such protests. Mandatory death sentences were abolished, but the death penalty remained as a discretionary punishment for murder and several other crimes. No executions were carried out during the year, but five people were sentenced to death and between 70 and 100 continued to be held on death row. Some legislative reforms were introduced or proposed aimed at addressing sexual harassment and domestic violence, both of which reportedly remained widespread.

Death penalty

In a break from the past, no executions were carried out during 2006 but around 70-100 prisoners continued to be held on death row, including 23 whose sentences had been confirmed by the Supreme Court. Some measures were introduced aimed at improving conditions of detention on death row. The use of shackles was reduced and legal aid was extended to death row prisoners.

In a response to campaigning by anti-death penalty activists in October, Minister of Justice Shih Mao-lin stated that reliance on the death penalty as a method of crime control was illusory and that his Ministry would push for law revisions to bring about the eventual abolition of the death penalty. However, he signed an execution order for one death row prisoner, Chong De-shu, just weeks later. His execution had not taken place by the end of the year.

The law continued to provide for imposition of the death penalty for numerous crimes by shooting or lethal injection, although so far lethal injection has not been used.

🗁 Liu Bing-lang, Su Chien-ho and Chuang Lin-hsun, known as the "Hsichih Trio", faced their 11th retrial after being convicted of murder. The case was based almost entirely on their confessions which were allegedly extracted through torture at the hands of the police. Chuang Lin-hsun has suffered from mental illness since his time in police custody.

Freedom of expression, association and assembly

Several human rights groups formed a coalition to campaign for reforms to the Assembly and Parade Law, including to provisions requiring police permission to hold a public demonstration. Some journalists were assaulted by demonstrators or the police during political demonstrations both for and against the President.

▢ In May a Taipei court ruled that Lin Bo-yi, a university student charged with violating the Assembly and Parade Law, was not guilty on grounds that he was "making a petition" which did not require a permit from the police in advance. Lin Bo-yi had participated in a peaceful student rally in July 2005 outside the Ministry of Education protesting at high tuition fees. He had cited his constitutional rights to freedom of assembly and association in his defence.

Violence against women
New regulations aimed at preventing sexual harassment took effect in February.

Legislators discussed draft amendments to the Domestic Violence Law, including proposals to clarify that same-sex and unmarried couples are within its scope, but no amendments had been introduced by the end of the year.

AI country reports/visits
Statements
- Amnesty International calls on Taiwan to abolish the death penalty, October 2006 (AI Index: ASA 38/001/2006)
- Taiwan: Imminent execution of Chong De-shu (AI Index: ASA 38/002/2006)

TAJIKISTAN

REPUBLIC OF TAJIKISTAN
Head of state: Imomali Rakhmonov
Head of government: Akil Akilov
Death penalty: retentionist
International Criminal Court: ratified

Widespread and routine torture or other ill-treatment by law enforcement officers continued to be reported. At least one opposition party activist died in custody in suspicious circumstances. Increasing numbers of women were detained for membership of banned Islamic movements or parties.

Background
President Imomali Rakhmonov won a third seven-year term as president following elections in November which the Organization for Security and Co-operation in Europe concluded "lacked genuine choice and meaningful pluralism."

Following international pressure the government allowed access to five independent websites perceived to be critical of the regime and which it had blocked in the run-up to the presidential elections reportedly on security grounds.

Relations with neighbouring Uzbekistan continued to be tense and at least four ethnic Uzbek men were sentenced to long prison terms on charges of espionage.

Torture and ill-treatment
There were continuing reports of unlawful arrests and widespread and routine torture or other ill-treatment by law enforcement officers, several of whom were sentenced to prison terms.

▢ In May, 12 inmates in Kurgan-Tiube prison went on trial for their alleged part in an incident in August 2005 in which some 100 prisoners reportedly cut their veins in protest at cruel, inhuman and degrading conditions of detention and regular ill-treatment. The authorities claimed it was a riot. Relatives of the inmates held a press conference in which they claimed that some of the men had had their plaster casts and bandages removed for their court appearances. The judge reportedly refused to consider the prisoners' injuries and dismissed their allegations of torture.

▢ In November the UN Committee against Torture considered Tajikistan's first report and raised concerns about the "numerous allegations regarding widespread routine use of torture and ill-treatment by investigative personnel, particularly to extract confessions to be used in criminal proceedings." It also reported on "the failure of judges to dismiss or return cases for further investigation in instances where confessions were obtained as a result of torture." It was further concerned about the very small number of officials convicted for acts of torture and other ill-treatment.

Death in custody
▢ Sadullo Marufov, a member of the Islamic Renaissance Party (IRP), died in police custody in May after he was detained for questioning by law enforcement officers in Isfara. Initially the officers claimed that he had committed suicide by jumping from a third floor window. The IRP claimed that an autopsy report indicated that he had been beaten and ill-treated, and alleged that he had been pushed from the window. The general prosecutor's office subsequently announced that following an investigation three officers had been detained.

Detentions and unfair trials
More than 50 alleged members of the banned Islamic opposition party Hizb-ut-Tahrir, including at least 20 women, and 30 alleged members of the Islamic Movement of Uzbekistan were detained. Many were sentenced to long prison terms after unfair trials.

AI country reports/visits
Report
- Commonwealth of Independent States: Positive trend on the abolition of the death penalty but more needs to be done (AI Index: EUR 04/003/2006)

TANZANIA

UNITED REPUBLIC OF TANZANIA
Head of state: Jakaya Kikwete
Head of government: Edward Lowassa
Head of Zanzibar government: Amani Abeid Karume
Death penalty: retentionist
International Criminal Court: ratified

All death sentences were commuted. Journalists were at times harassed or arrested. Several thousand long-settled unregistered migrants were deported. Prison conditions were harsh.

Background
Talks on legal and electoral reform in semi-autonomous Zanzibar continued between the ruling Party of the Revolution (Chama Cha Mapinduzi) and the opposition Civic United Front (CUF) but without much progress.

Freedom of expression and the media
Journalists writing articles criticizing the government were at times harassed, threatened or arrested.
▭ Three journalists of *Rai* newspaper were arrested and charged in July.
▭ In August Richard Mgamba of *The Citizen* newspaper was arrested and threatened with being stripped of his citizenship and expelled from the country on account of an interview he gave in a documentary film about arms trafficking.
▭ Three visiting mainland journalists were briefly arrested in Zanzibar in September.

A previous sedition case against opposition party leader Augustine Mrema and two environmental rights activists, all three of whom were free on bail, was continuing.

Violence against women
Female genital mutilation continued to be illegally practised in many rural areas on the mainland, with rates of over 80 per cent among some ethnic groups. No prosecutions were reported. The World Health Organization reported a high rate of domestic violence in Tanzania, with 30 per cent of victims suffering serious injuries due to severe beatings.

Prison conditions
The government accepted the need to reduce severe overcrowding in prisons but little action was taken. The National Commission for Human Rights and Good Governance inspected mainland prisons and criticized harsh conditions, particularly the holding of juvenile prisoners together with adults. The Commission was still barred by the Zanzibar government from working or opening an office in Zanzibar.

Migrants' rights
The government ordered the deportation of all illegal immigrants who had failed to register or apply for citizenship. Deportations began of several thousand people originating from neighbouring countries such as Rwanda, Burundi, Uganda and Democratic Republic of the Congo who had lived in Tanzania for up to 15 years or longer. There was a much larger number of such people, some of whom were former refugees integrated into rural communities who had never regularized their status.

Death penalty
In August President Kikwete commuted all death sentences on mainland Tanzania to life imprisonment. The total number of commutations was not officially disclosed, but was estimated to be about 400. Many of the prisoners had been on death row for several years. At the end of 2006, no one was under sentence of death in Tanzania, either on the mainland or in Zanzibar.

THAILAND

KINGDOM OF THAILAND
Head of state: King Bhumibol Adulyadej
Head of government: Surayud Chulanont (replaced Thaksin Shinawatra in October)
Death penalty: retentionist
International Criminal Court: signed

After the 19 September military coup, coup leaders abrogated the 1997 Constitution and issued decrees instituting martial law and restricting the rights to freedom of expression, association and assembly. Martial law was lifted in 41 provinces in December but remained in place in 35 border provinces. Violence continued in the mainly Muslim southern provinces. Armed groups bombed, beheaded or shot Muslim and Buddhist civilians, including monks, teachers and members of the security forces. The authorities arbitrarily detained people and failed to investigate human rights abuses. Two human rights defenders were killed and others, particularly in the south, were at risk of intimidation, threats and attacks. Torture and ill-treatment continued to be reported. Almost 900 people remained under sentence of death. No executions were known to have taken place. Migrant workers were not able to exercise their basic labour rights. Hmong asylum-seekers were forcibly returned by the authorities to Laos.

Background
Mass demonstrations in Bangkok protesting against the government of Prime Minister Thaksin Shinawatra began in February, and continued for several months. Protesters condemned alleged widespread financial irregularities

during his administration. Thaksin Shinawatra called for April elections, which were won by his Thai Rak Thai party and boycotted by the major opposition parties. The results were nullified in May by the Constitutional Court and new elections were scheduled to take place in November. In September Thaksin Shinawatra was deposed while abroad by the military-led Council for Democratic Reform (CDR), led by Army Commander-in-Chief Sondhi Boonyaratkalin, in a bloodless coup. The 1997 Constitution was abrogated and an interim one, providing for the drafting of a new constitution, a referendum and elections, was promulgated in October. Four officials of the deposed government were briefly detained in the aftermath of the coup.

In October the CDR appointed General Surayud Chulanont as Interim Prime Minister and renamed itself the Council for National Security, retaining key decision-making powers over government appointments, including the National Legislative Assembly (the interim legislature) and in the constitution drafting process.

In December co-ordinated bomb attacks in Bangkok resulted in the deaths of three people and injuries of 40 others. No one claimed responsibility.

Legal developments

Article 3 of the Interim Constitution provides that "human dignity, rights, liberties, and equality... as well as Thailand's existing international obligations" shall be protected, but does not specify which rights and how they would be protected. The CDR Announcement 10 placed restrictions on the media; some 300 community radio stations were closed and some Internet sites blocked. Announcement 15 prohibited political parties from meeting or conducting other political activities. Announcement 7 banned political gatherings of more than five people. In November the government announced it would lift the ban but it is not clear if this was officially revoked. The security forces did not take any action against demonstrators.

The Emergency Decree, promulgated by the cabinet in July 2005, remained in force in the three mainly Muslim southern provinces. Its provisions included detention without charge or trial for up to 30 days, other forms of administrative detention, and the use of unofficial detention centres.

Conflict in the south

Some 1900 people were killed in the last three years in ongoing violence in the Songkla, Pattani, Yala and Narathiwat Provinces in the south. Drive-by shootings, bombings, and beheadings by armed groups continued throughout the year on an almost daily basis. The armed groups responsible did not identify themselves. The new government announced a major policy shift towards solving the crisis peacefully. However, violence by insurgents continued.

In January the discovery of the bodies of 300 unidentified people in unmarked graves was announced amid allegations that some might be victims of enforced disappearances. According to preliminary forensic statements some had not died of natural causes. Forensic identification of the bodies had not been completed by the end of the year.

In June the National Reconciliation Commission, appointed by the Thaksin Shinawatra government in 2005 to help resolve the crisis in the south, submitted its final report. Recommendations included making the local Bahasa dialect, spoken by Muslims, a working language.

Under provisions of the Emergency Decree, scores of people were detained for 30 days without charge or trial at the Yala Police Training School and in military camps, denied access to lawyers, and some were tortured or otherwise ill-treated during interrogation. In November the authorities announced that they would stop using a "blacklist", which had been used as the basis to arrest people or coerce them to attend residential camps at military facilities for between one and four weeks, in what amounted to arbitrary detention.

In October the government re-established the Southern Border Provinces Administrative Centre, abolished by Thaksin Shinawatra in 2002, to co-ordinate government efforts to quell the violence in the south.

In early November the new Prime Minister, General Surayud Chulanont, publicly apologized for the deaths of 85 Muslims caused by the security forces during the October 2004 demonstrations at Tak Bai police station in Narathiwat Province, in the south of the country. However, no security personnel were brought to justice in connection with the deaths. The Attorney General announced that cases would be dropped against 58 protesters charged with illegal gathering and public disturbance following the demonstrations, and a court ruled that compensation would be provided to the families of the 78 protesters who were crushed to death while being transported in army trucks from the demonstrations. However, they signed an agreement that they would not pursue any other legal forms of redress. A further court case for compensation brought by the families of the other seven victims was pending at the end of the year.

⊟ In October, Muhammad Dunai Tanyeeno, a Narathiwat village leader, who was helping the 2004 Tak Bai victims (see above) seek access to justice, was shot dead after attempting to bring some of the victims to meet the Fourth Army commander.

Abuses by armed groups

In September, five people were killed in a series of bomb explosions in Hat Yai, Songkla Province, by insurgents. In October insurgents beheaded a Burmese migrant worker in Pattani Province and in December they shot dead two teachers and then burned their bodies.

In November, after two local villagers were killed and houses were burned, reportedly by insurgents, over 200 mostly Buddhist civilians from Bannag Sata and Than Tho Districts, Yala Province, sought refuge in a Buddhist temple. Also in November some Buddhist monks in Narathiwat Province suspended their alms rounds in villages because of fear of attacks. Schools in many southern districts were closed for security reasons.

Torture and ill-treatment

In December Charnchai Promthongchai died in custody in Mae Hong Son Province after having reportedly been beaten to death by soldiers.

Impunity

Section 17 of the Emergency Decree provides immunity from criminal and civil liability, as well as from disciplinary measures, for officials acting under the decree. No one was brought to justice for excessive use of force and possible extrajudicial executions when security forces opened fire on armed Muslim groups in April 2004, killing over 100 people. The shootings were in retaliation for an attack by the armed groups on government facilities, in which five members of the security forces were killed. Article 37 of the Interim Constitution provides for legal immunity for the CDR leaders and those ordered by them to "mete out punishment and other administrative acts".

In January a police officer was found guilty of coercing Somchai Neelapaijit, a Muslim human rights lawyer, into his car in March 2004 in Bangkok. Somchai Neelapaijit has not been seen or heard of since. The police officer was sentenced to three years' imprisonment; however, he was released on bail and returned to his job.

The enforced disappearances of more than 20 people since the escalation of violence in the south were not properly investigated by the police. The Justice Ministry announced in November that it would investigate some of the killings of over 2,500 people during the 2003 "drugs war" and call on families of the victims to file cases.

Refugees and migrants

In November, 53 Hmong asylum-seekers were forcibly returned to Laos from Nong Khai Province. Some 7,000 Lao Hmong asylum-seekers remained in a camp in Phetchabun Province in poor conditions. Around 400, including children, were detained in several detention facilities also in poor conditions.

Camps on the Thai-Myanmar border housed some 150,000 refugees. Since 2004 over 24,000 Burmese refugees were resettled in third countries. Some 740,000 Burmese migrant workers renewed their registration permits with the government, but tens of thousands of others worked illegally.

AI country reports/ visits
Report
• Thailand: "If you want peace, work for justice" (AI Index: ASA 39/001/2006)
Visits
AI delegates visited Thailand in July and December.

TIMOR-LESTE

DEMOCRATIC REPUBLIC OF TIMOR-LESTE
Head of state: Kay Rala Xanana Gusmão
Head of government: José Manuel Ramos-Horta (replaced Mari Bim Amude Alkatiri in July)
Death penalty: abolitionist for all crimes
International Criminal Court: ratified

Violence erupted in April and May after around 600 soldiers were dismissed from the army. Up to 38 people died and around 150,000 people were displaced as they fled the fighting. The judiciary and the police remained weak institutions. Impunity continued for human rights violations committed in connection with the independence referendum in 1999.

Background

The UN Office in Timor-Leste had its one-year mission extended from May to August after the violence in April and May. It was replaced by the UN Integrated Mission in Timor-Leste, mandated to foster stability and support national elections in 2007, which included up to 1,608 police personnel within a civilian peacekeeping component.

A new Code of Penal Procedure entered into force in January which reinforced guarantees of suspects' rights.

Violence, killings and displacement

In March, around 600 soldiers, more than a third of the armed forces, were dismissed after protesting over discrimination and poor conditions of work. Violent confrontations between the sacked soldiers and their supporters, the armed forces and the police broke out throughout April and May in the capital, Dili. An estimated 38 people were killed and some 150,000 people displaced. In May an international peacekeeping force composed of troops from Australia, Malaysia, New Zealand and Portugal was deployed.

In October an independent UN Commission of Special Inquiry found the violence was "the expression of deep-rooted problems inherent in fragile state institutions and a weak rule of law." It recommended the prosecution of several people, including two former ministers for unlawful use and movement of weapons, and key rebel leaders, and further investigation into former Prime Minister Mari Alkatiri's alleged role in the illegal arming of civilians.

The government agreed a programme to rebuild the national police force, which disintegrated in Dili in May. Rigorous screening of all existing Dili-based police personnel, as a prerequisite for returning to work, began in September.

Sporadic violence continued throughout 2006, including the burning and stoning of houses. Violence by unidentified groups was reported around camps for the internally displaced. Fighting between gangs resulted in several deaths. At the end of the year, many of the displaced were still living in temporary shelters.

Freedom of expression and assembly

The Law of Assembly and Demonstration, which was adopted in January, contained provisions that could restrict rights of assembly and peaceful demonstration.

A new Criminal Code, planned to enter into force in January, was withdrawn for revision following widespread criticism of provisions restricting freedom of expression. It provided for up to three years' imprisonment for defamation of a public figure.

Past human rights violations

Both the Timorese and Indonesian governments resisted further initiatives to bring to justice all perpetrators of serious crimes in Timor-Leste in 1999. The government failed to consider the report of the national Commission on Reception, Truth and Reconciliation, which the President presented to Parliament in November 2005.

The Truth and Friendship Commission, established jointly by Indonesia and Timor-Leste to document the crimes committed in 1999 and to promote reconciliation, started work. Its mandated ability to recommend amnesty for perpetrators of gross human rights violations had been widely criticized.

In July the UN Secretary-General presented a new report on justice and reconciliation for Timor-Leste. The report was prepared in response to the UN Security Council's request to the UN Secretary-General to review the earlier Commission of Experts' report with "a practically feasible approach" which would take into account the views of the governments of Timor-Leste and Indonesia. It recommended a new UN programme of assistance to include the establishment of an experienced team to complete outstanding investigations into serious crimes committed in 1999 and the strengthening of the national justice system's capacity to prosecute the perpetrators.

TOGO

TOGOLESE REPUBLIC
Head of state : Faure Gnassingbé
Head of government : Yawovi Agboyibo (replaced Edem Kodjo in September)
Death penalty : abolitionist in practice
International Criminal Court : ratified

Despite national and international pressure, impunity persisted, particularly in relation to acts of political violence committed during the 2005 presidential election. Supporters of the opposition continued to be detained without trial. There were reports of torture and ill-treatment of detainees in custody.

Background

In April, the Togolese National Dialogue between the government and opposition parties resumed. It had been interrupted following the death of President Gnassingbé Eyadéma in 2005. In August, 12 years of political deadlock ended with an agreement to create a national unity government to organize parliamentary elections in 2007. The parties agreed to loosen the eligibility conditions for presidential candidates, to revise electoral rolls and to ensure equitable access to the media during campaigns. They also agreed on the need to end impunity and political violence, to establish a commission to investigate politically motivated violence, and to end interference by army and security forces in the political dialogue.

In July, for the first time since being refused entry in 1999, an AI delegation visited Togo.

In September, President Faure Gnassingbé appointed as Prime Minister Yawovi Agboyibo, leader of the Action Committee for Renewal (Comité d'Action pour le Renouveau, CAR), an opposition party. The Union of Forces for Change (Union des Forces de Changement, UFC) refused to participate in the new government.

UN Committee against Torture

In May, the UN Committee against Torture expressed concern about widespread allegations of torture including rape, enforced disappearances, arbitrary arrests and secret detentions, in particular following the April 2005 presidential election. It noted that the perpetrators of such acts appeared to benefit from total impunity. The Committee welcomed a number of positive steps, including a 1998 law prohibiting female genital mutilation and the commitment to modernize the judiciary. The Committee urged Togo to prevent torture or ill-treatment on its territory, specifying that military personnel should not be involved in the arrest or detention of civilians, and to eliminate impunity.

Detention without trial

A number of people detained in 2005 continued to be held without trial in Lomé Central Prison, including suspected critics of the government. Most were reportedly tortured or ill-treated during the first few days of detention.

▢ Gérard Akoumey, a member of the UFC, was arrested in September 2005 and accused of a bomb attack on a post office. However, witnesses did not recognize him and he told the judge that he had been tortured. No action was taken to investigate his allegation of torture. He was charged with being a member of a criminal group.

▢ Kossi Azonledji, a Togolese refugee living in Ghana and a UFC activist, was arrested at his workplace in Ghana in September 2005 by Ghanaian police and handed over to Togolese security forces. He was held for a month in an unknown location, accused of a bomb attack against a post office, detained for two days in Lomé Gendarmerie, then transferred to Lomé Central prison.

Torture, death in custody

There were numerous reports of torture and ill-treatment of detainees.

▢ The family of Yaya Moussa, a salesman who died in police custody after being arrested on 7 May, filed a complaint against the authorities. A relative said that he had been beaten at the time of his arrest. Members of his family were not allowed to visit him and only learned of his death five days later, when told that his body was in the morgue.

Impunity

Despite official commitments to end impunity, no progress was reported in holding anyone to account for past human rights abuses. These included an assault on journalist and human rights defender Dimas Dzikodo, who lodged a complaint after being attacked by unidentified men on his way home from work in October 2005. In March, then Prime Minister Edem Kodjo announced that he had instructed the police and judicial authorities to drop any charges against those allegedly responsible for offences directly linked to the election, with the exception of those suspected of murder. Nevertheless, a number of victims of human rights violations committed during the 2005 presidential election lodged complaints.

Death penalty

In February, the Assize Court of Kara upheld the death sentences on two individuals tried in absentia for offences including murder. No executions were reported. In July, Prime Minister Edem Kodjo told an AI delegation that he was personally opposed to the death penalty, and the Minister of Human Rights said that the government should introduce a bill abolishing the death penalty.

AI country reports/ visits

Report
- Togo: One year on from the April 2005 bloodshed, there is still complete impunity (AI Index: AFR 57/001/2006)

Visit
In July, AI delegates conducted research in Togo and met government officials.

TRINIDAD AND TOBAGO

REPUBLIC OF TRINIDAD AND TOBAGO
Head of state: George Maxwell Richards
Head of government: Patrick Manning
Death penalty: retentionist
International Criminal Court: ratified

Impunity continued in cases of alleged killings by police. There were further reports of abuses by the police. Death sentences continued to be imposed.

Background

The level of violent crime remained high, with 368 murders registered during the year. The conviction rate for murders, including alleged killings by state agents, remained low. The Director of Public Prosecutions and the country's chief magistrate both admitted that intimidation of witnesses was having a severe negative impact on criminal judicial proceedings. In November the Law Association of Trinidad and Tobago expressed its alarm at what it described as the virtual collapse of the criminal justice system, and called for a new witness protection programme and improved forensic investigations.

Unlawful state killings and impunity

There were further reports of unlawful killings by state agents, and a pattern of impunity continued for such killings. In March, Dave Burnett, a police constable, was convicted for the January 2004 murder of Kevin Cato, the first time since the country's independence in 1962 that a police officer had been convicted of a murder committed while on duty. Despite this, there was reportedly little progress in the investigations into 37 other cases of alleged killings by state agents committed since September 2003, and intimidation of witnesses was widely reported.

▢ In November, Kevon Sween was shot dead by police officers who were looking for the perpetrators of a murder committed earlier that day. Police claimed they were fired upon first, but eyewitnesses reportedly claimed that the victim was unarmed and had offered to surrender.

▢ In July, two prison officers were acquitted of the June 2001 murder of Anton Cooper, a detainee in the Golden Grove remand prison. A postmortem certificate had stated that his death was caused by "asphyxia associated with multiple blunt traumatic injuries."

Abuses by the security forces

There were continued reports of torture and ill-treatment by members of the security forces.

▢ In August, Rabindranath Choon, a Hindu cleric's assistant, was reportedly abducted by four police officers, seriously beaten and robbed as he cycled home from a prayer meeting. He was held for several hours and released without charge. The police officers were charged and released on bail awaiting trial.

⌐ In November, nine inmates in Golden Grove prison in the town of Arouca were reportedly shot with rubber bullets by members of the police anti-crime squad who had responded to reports of a prisoner firing a weapon in the remand section. One prisoner reportedly lost his eye in the incident and scores of others were allegedly beaten by members of the police anti-crime squad. Prisoners on remand at the prison had rioted in August in protest at alleged ill-treatment by prison guards, poor prison conditions and delays in judicial proceedings.

Death penalty
At at least two new death sentences were passed.

AI country reports/visits
Reports
- Trinidad and Tobago: End police immunity for unlawful killings and deaths in custody (AI Index: AMR 49/001/2006)
- Trinidad and Tobago: Death sentence for police officer convicted of murder (AI Index: AMR 49/002/2006)

TUNISIA

REPUBLIC OF TUNISIA
Head of state: Zine El 'Abidine Ben 'Ali
Head of government: Mohamed Ghannouchi
Death penalty: abolitionist in practice
International Criminal Court: not ratified

Freedom of expression and association remained severely restricted. At least 12 people were sentenced to lengthy prison terms following unfair trials on terrorism-related charges, while around 50 others were still on trial at the end of the year. Torture and ill-treatment continued to be reported. Hundreds of political prisoners sentenced after unfair trials in previous years, including prisoners of conscience, remained in prison. Many had been held for more than a decade and were reported to be in poor health.

Background
Tunisia's election in May to the newly created UN Human Rights Council drew widespread criticism from human rights groups in view of the government's severe restrictions on fundamental freedoms.

In November, a group of members of parliament called on President Ben 'Ali to stand for re-election in 2009, by which time he will have been in power for 22 years. A referendum in 2002 revised the Tunisian Constitution to allow the President an unlimited number of successive five-year terms.

Some 135 political prisoners were released conditionally, 81 of them in February and the rest in November, following presidential amnesties. Most had been imprisoned for over 14 years because of their membership of the banned Islamist organization, Ennahda (Renaissance), after unfair trials before the Bouchoucha and Bab Saadoun military courts in 1992. Approximately 100 other members of Ennahda remained imprisoned, some reportedly in poor health as a result of harsh prison conditions and torture in pre-trial detention many years before. Some were in urgent need of medical treatment.

In June, the European Parliament adopted a resolution calling for the convening of a European Union-Tunisia Association Council meeting to discuss human rights in Tunisia after the government continued to prevent the Tunisian Human Rights League (Ligue tunisienne pour la défense des droits de l'homme, LTDH), a non-governmental organization, from holding its national congress. The European Union (EU) criticized the Tunisian government further in October after it cancelled an international conference on the right to work in the Euro-Mediterranean Region shortly before it was due to be held in Tunis in September.

In December, shoot-outs in the south of Tunis between the police and alleged members of the Salafist Group for Preaching and Combat (Groupe Salafiste pour la Prédication et le Combat, GSPC), a group allegedly linked to al-Qa'ida, left dozens dead and many others injured, including police officers.

Abuses in the 'war on terror'
The request of the UN Special Rapporteur on the promotion and protection of human rights while countering terrorism to visit Tunisia to assess the government's human rights record in the "war on terror" remained unanswered. The authorities continued to use the controversial 2003 anti-terrorism law to arrest, detain and try alleged terrorist suspects. Those convicted were sentenced to long prison terms. The anti-terrorism law and provisions of the Military Justice Code were also used against Tunisian nationals who were returned to Tunisia against their will by authorities in other countries, including Bosnia and Herzegovina, Bulgaria and Italy. While in the custody of the Tunisian authorities, many were charged with links to terrorist organizations operating outside the country. Some were referred to the military justice system. Access by defence lawyers to their clients was increasingly curtailed in terrorism-related cases.

In June and July scores of alleged terrorist suspects, including alleged members of the GSPC, were arrested and held incommunicado for up to several weeks and reportedly tortured, before being referred to Tunis Criminal Court for trial. They were still detained without trial at the end of the year. Many were transferred to remote prisons, hundreds of kilometres from their families.

☐ Hicham Saadi, who was released in February following a presidential pardon after being sentenced to 12 years' imprisonment on terrorism-related charges in 2004, was rearrested in June and held incommunicado for 25 days and reportedly tortured. He was charged with belonging to the GSPC. In October, he jumped from a window in a failed attempt to escape when he was brought before the examining magistrate in Tunis. He remained in detention awaiting trial at the end of the year.

☐ In September, Badreddine Ferchichi, also known as Abu Malek, was returned to Tunisia from Bosnia and Herzegovina, after the authorities there rejected his application for asylum. He was detained for several days, during which he was allegedly assaulted, before being taken before a military judge on 6 September and charged, under the Military Justice Code, with "serving, in time of peace, in a foreign army or terrorist organization operating abroad." He had fought as a volunteer for Bosnian Muslim forces during the 1992-95 war in the former Yugoslavia. At the end of the year he was awaiting trial before a military court. If convicted, he could face up to 10 years' imprisonment.

☐ Six members of the so-called Zarzis group were released in February. Abdelghaffar Guiza, Omar Chlendi, Hamza Mahroug, Ridha Ben Hajj Ibrahim, Omar Rached and Aymen Mcharek, all originally from the town of Zarzis in the south of Tunisia, were arrested in 2003 and imprisoned on terrorism-related charges in April 2004 after an unfair trial before a criminal court in Tunis. Confessions allegedly extracted under torture while they were held incommunicado in pre-trial detention were used as principal evidence against them.

Freedom of expression

Freedom of expression remained severely curtailed. At least two journalists critical of the government were dismissed by the directors of their newspapers while others continued to work but faced government pressure and judicial proceedings in an attempt to intimidate them.

☐ In April, the Union of Tunisian Journalists (Syndicat des journalistes tunisiens) was prevented from holding a meeting of its executive board, and its members continued to face police harassment and intimidation. Its president, Lotfi Hajji, was briefly detained on at least three separate occasions during the year.

☐ The authorities stepped up harassment of women wearing the hijab (Islamic headscarf). This followed statements by the Ministers of Foreign Affairs and the Interior and the Secretary-General of the ruling political party, the Constitutional Democratic Rally (Rassemblement constitutionnel démocratique), against the rise in the use of the hijab by women and girls, and beards and the *qamis* (knee-length shirts) by men. They called for a strict implementation of decree 108 of 1985 of the Ministry of Education banning women from wearing the hijab at educational institutions and when working in government departments. Some women were reportedly ordered to remove their hijabs before being allowed into schools, universities or workplaces and others were forced to remove them in the street. Some women were reportedly taken to police stations and forced to sign statements in which they committed themselves to stop wearing the hijab.

Human rights activists and organizations

Human rights defenders continued to face harassment and sometimes physical violence. Many, along with their families and friends, were subjected to surveillance by the authorities and their activities were severely restricted. Several non-governmental human rights organizations continued to be denied legal recognition.

☐ The LTDH continued to be prevented from holding its sixth national congress and access to its headquarters in Tunis was barred to all except members of its executive board. Its regional offices also continued to be closed to the public as well as to its elected members. The court case against the executive board was again postponed until January 2007. The authorities contacted the embassies in Tunisia of a number of countries and apparently threatened to sever diplomatic relations should their representatives continue to meet Tunisian human rights defenders. They specifically forbade meetings with members of the LTDH on account of the ongoing legal proceedings against it. Nevertheless, staff of several embassies visited the LTDH headquarters in solidarity.

☐ In October and November, state security officials imposed tight surveillance around the office of the National Council for Liberties in Tunisia (Conseil national pour les libertés en Tunisie, CNLT), a non-governmental organization denied legal registration, effectively preventing access by prisoners' families and former political prisoners. Some who did visit were reportedly arrested when they left, taken to police stations and made to commit in writing that they would not visit the CNLT office again.

☐ In May, Yves Steiner, a member of the Executive Committee of AI Switzerland, was forcibly removed by police officers from a hotel in the town of Sidi Bou Saïd where the annual meeting of AI Tunisia was being held, taken to the airport and expelled from Tunisia. He was roughly treated by officials while being transferred to the airport and his mobile phone was confiscated. The day before, he had criticized human rights violations in Tunisia, including restrictions on freedom of expression and association, in a speech to members of AI Tunisia.

☐ Hichem Osman, then chair of AI Tunisia, was arrested in May at the university where he worked, detained for six hours and questioned about events at the AI Tunisia annual meeting. He was told by the police that the meeting had failed to abide by the statute of AI Tunisia by offering a platform for criticism of the Tunisian government and President. He was officially notified that the section would be dissolved should this reoccur.

Independence of the judiciary

In October, the outgoing head of the European Commission delegation in Tunis publicly criticized the slow pace of political reform and called for better training for judges and lawyers to consolidate the independence of the judiciary.

In May, lawyers organized a number of sit-ins to protest against a new law creating the Higher Institute for Lawyers. They protested that the law was being adopted by the Tunisian Parliament without taking into account the outcome of consultation with the Lawyers' Association, as envisaged in an EU-Tunisia convention on financing the reform of the justice system. The Institute, which would be under the supervision of the Ministries of Justice and Higher Education, would be responsible for training future lawyers, a task so far entrusted to the Lawyers' Association and the Association of Tunisian Judges (Association des magistrats tunisiens, AMT). Lawyers opposed the law on the grounds that it undermined judicial independence. Many lawyers were physically assaulted by police during the sit-ins.

Wassila Kaabi, a judge and member of the executive board of the AMT, was prevented from travelling to Hungary in September to participate in a meeting of the International Union of Judges. Under Tunisian law, judges require the permission of the Secretary of State for Justice to leave the country.

Prisoners of conscience

Critics and opponents of the government continued to be at risk of imprisonment, harassment and intimidation because of the peaceful expression of their views.

Prisoner of conscience Mohammed Abbou went on several hunger strikes to protest against his continued detention and ill-treatment by the authorities at the prison in El-Kef. His wife and children were harassed and intimidated several times by police who were stationed continuously outside their home in Tunis. In November, Mohammed Abbou was taken to El-Kef hospital for tests on his kidneys. In December, his wife Samia, along with Samir Ben Amor, a lawyer, Moncef Marzouki, an opposition leader, and Slim Boukhdir, a journalist, attempted to visit him in prison. They were stopped by police nine times while driving from Tunis to El-Kef, ostensibly to check their identities and the car's registration documents. Later, when they left a restaurant in El-Kef, they were attacked by about 50 unidentified men, women and youths who insulted, pushed, punched and spat at them. The four managed to escape the attackers and return to their car. When they arrived at the prison entrance, others appeared who attacked them, preventing them from reaching the prison. Both attacks were carried out in the presence of police officers who failed to take any action to protect them or to apprehend the attackers.

AI country reports/ visits
Visit
AI delegates visited Tunisia in July and met human rights defenders, government officials and representatives of EU governments.

TURKEY

REPUBLIC OF TURKEY
Head of state: Ahmet Necdet Sezer
Head of government: Recep Tayyip Erdoğan
Death penalty: abolitionist for all crimes
International Criminal Court: not ratified

After the introduction of new legislation in previous years, there was little evidence of progress in the implementation of reforms. There were continued prosecutions of people expressing their peacefully held opinions. Human rights further deteriorated in the eastern and south-eastern provinces in the context of an increase in fighting between the security forces and the armed Kurdistan Workers' Party (PKK); there was an increase in attacks on civilians in other areas by armed groups. There were reports of excessive use of force against demonstrators by law enforcement officers during violent protests in the city of Diyarbakır in the south-east of the country. In spite of a general decrease in allegations of torture or ill-treatment, there were reports that such abuses were widespread in police custody against those detained during the protests. There were continued concerns about unfair trials and conditions in "F-type" prisons. Little progress was made in creating shelters for women victims of violence.

Background

In December the European Union (EU) partially froze Turkey's membership negotiations because of its refusal to open its ports and airports for trade with the Republic of Cyprus on the grounds of the EU's continuing embargo of the internationally unrecognized Turkish Republic of Northern Cyprus.

In June, Parliament revised the Law to Fight Terrorism, greatly widening the scope and number of crimes punishable as terrorist offences, introducing articles liable to further restrict freedom of expression, and failing to restrict the use of lethal force by law enforcement officials. In July the President approved the Law but applied to the Constitutional Court for the annulment of two articles relating to sanctions against the press. In September the Ombudsman Law was passed by Parliament after amendments. During the year, Turkey ratified both the (first) Optional Protocol to the International Covenant on Civil and Political Rights (ICCPR) and the Second Optional Protocol to the ICCPR, aiming at the abolition of the death penalty.

Official human rights mechanisms, such as the provincial human rights boards under the control of the Human Rights Presidency attached to the Prime Minister's Office, did not function consistently and failed to address grave violations.

Freedom of expression

Laws containing fundamental restrictions on freedom of expression remained in force, resulting in the prosecution, and sometimes conviction, of groups such as journalists, writers, publishers, academics, human rights defenders and students for the peaceful expression of their beliefs.

Many prosecutions were brought under Article 301 of the Turkish Penal Code (TPC) which criminalizes denigration of "Turkishness", the Republic and the institutions of the state. Most of these cases, such as that of Nobel Prize-winning novelist Orhan Pamuk, ended in acquittal.

▭ In July the General Penal Board of the Court of Cassation upheld a six-month suspended sentence against Hrant Dink, a journalist, who was tried after writing about Armenian identity in *Agos* newspaper.

Turkish and international human rights defenders campaigned for the repeal of Article 301 of the TPC on the grounds that it lacked "legal certainty of the crime". They rejected the arguments of the Ministry of Justice that the development of case law would signal an end to arbitrary prosecutions.

Other articles of the new TPC of 2005 also imposed restrictions on freedom of expression.

▭ In October Abdurrahman Dilipak, a journalist with *Vakit* newspaper, received a sentence of just under one year, commuted to a fine of 10,500 liras (approximately US$7,250), for insulting the President. The prosecutor had called for his acquittal.

▭ Birgül Özbarış, a journalist for *Özgür Gündem* newspaper, faced seven prosecutions for "alienating the population from military service" because of her writings on military service and conscientious objection. She faced possible prison sentences totalling 36 years.

Article 288 of the TPC restricting public comment on cases under judicial consideration was used in an arbitrary and overly restrictive way to hinder independent investigation and public comment on human rights violations.

Officials of the pro-Kurdish Democratic Society Party (DTP) and those joining pro-Kurdish platforms faced frequent prosecutions amounting to a pattern of judicial harassment.

▭ The trial of 56 mayors from the DTP began in October. The mayors had signed a letter in December 2005 to the Danish Prime Minister, arguing that the Denmark-based Kurdish television channel, Roj TV, should not be closed down. They were being prosecuted for "knowingly and willingly supporting the PKK."

People collecting signatures for a petition recognizing Abdullah Öcalan, imprisoned leader of the PKK, as a "political representative", received varying sentences, with students receiving the harshest punishments.

Killings in disputed circumstances

There were continuing reports of fatal shootings of civilians by members of the security forces. The usual explanation for these killings was that the victims had failed to obey a warning to stop, but such killings often demonstrated disproportionate use of force and in some cases may have amounted to extrajudicial executions. There were concerns about Article 16 in the revised Law to Fight Terrorism which failed to be explicit that lethal force could only be used when strictly unavoidable to protect life. There were fears that Article 16, which permitted the "direct and unhesitating" use of firearms to "render the danger ineffective", could further hinder thorough and impartial investigations into shootings by members of the security forces.

Members of the security forces continued to use excessive force during the policing of demonstrations. Demonstrations in March in Diyarbakır, to mark the funeral ceremony of four PKK members, escalated into violent protests. Ten people, including four minors, were killed, eight of them from gunshot wounds. Many demonstrators and police officers were injured. Investigations into the killings were continuing at the end of the year. The demonstrations spread to neighbouring cities; two demonstrators were shot dead in the town of Kızıltepe, a stray bullet killed a boy aged three in the city of Batman, and in Istanbul three women died when a bus crashed after being set on fire by demonstrators.

In September a bombing in a park in Diyarbakır resulted in 10 deaths. The perpetrators were unknown.

Attacks by armed groups

Bomb attacks targeting civilians increased. An armed group, the Kurdistan Freedom Falcons, claimed responsibility for bomb attacks including in Istanbul, Manavgat, Marmaris and Antalya, in which nine people died and scores were injured. In March, in the city of Van in the east of the country, a bomb exploded next to a minibus, leaving two civilians and the bomber, a PKK member, dead.

The PKK announced a unilateral ceasefire with effect from 1 October, and there was a subsequent decrease in armed clashes.

In May, an armed attack on judges at the Council of State (the higher administrative court) resulted in the death of a judge, Mustafa Yücel Özbilgin, and the wounding of four other judges. The trial of the gunman and of eight others for the attack and for three bomb attacks on the premises of the newspaper, *Cumhuriyet*, began in August in Ankara.

In February, former PKK executive Kani Yılmaz, one of the founders of the Patriotic Democratic Party of Kurdistan (PWD), and PWD member Sabri Tori were assassinated in a car bomb attack in Suleymanieh, northern Iraq, continuing a pattern of assassinations allegedly carried out by the PKK against the PWD.

Torture

There were continued reports of torture and ill-treatment by law enforcement officials, although fewer than in previous years. Detainees alleged that they had been beaten, threatened with death, deprived of food, water and sleep during detention. Some of the torture and ill-treatment took place in unofficial places of detention.

▭ In October, Erdal Bozkurt reported that he was abducted in Alibeyköy in Istanbul by men identifying themselves as police officers, put into a car, blindfolded and handcuffed, beaten and threatened with death, and taken to a place where he was tortured and interrogated for a whole day about his and other people's involvement in a local group which had been protesting against drug dealers and social problems in their neighbourhood. He was released the following day.

There were widespread allegations by adults and minors of torture and ill-treatment during the mass detentions in the course of riots in Diyarbakır in March.

◻ Two 14-year-old boys reported that they were held for around nine hours at the Çarşı police station, stripped naked, made to pour cold water over each other, were threatened with rape, made to lie on a concrete floor, and were forced to kneel down with their hands tied behind their backs while being repeatedly beaten with fists and truncheons and kicked by police officers. Medical reports showed signs of their ill-treatment. They were later transferred to the Children's Department of the Police in another district.

Impunity
Investigations into violations by members of the security forces continued to be deeply flawed and there was a general unwillingness among elements of the judiciary to bring those responsible to justice.

◻ In February, a decision was made not to pursue an investigation into the alleged torture of five male teenagers in October 2005 in the town of Ordu.

◻ Two gendarmerie intelligence officers and an informer received prison sentences of over 39 years for the bombing of a bookshop in the town of Şemdinli in November 2005, in which one man died. The court's verdict stated that the men could not have acted without the involvement of their seniors. Pending appeal at the end of the year, the case exposed the serious obstacles to bringing to justice senior members of the security forces suspected of committing violations.

Interference in justice system
The Şemdinli bombing trial (see above) proceeded after an investigation into the bombing which appeared to have been mired by political interference by members of the government and senior military personnel. The Public Prosecutor's indictment was made public in March, and implicated the head of the army's land forces and other senior local military personnel in Hakkari province. The Public Prosecutor requested a separate investigation by the military prosecutor to establish whether the bombing was part of a wider conspiracy. The Ministry of Justice investigated the Public Prosecutor for possible misconduct and in April the Higher Council of Judges and Prosecutors dismissed him from office. An appeal by the Public Prosecutor was unsuccessful.

Fair trial concerns
Those charged under anti-terrorism legislation continued to face lengthy and unfair trials in the special Heavy Penal Courts which replaced the State Security Courts abolished in 2004. Prosecutors relied on evidence based on statements allegedly extracted under torture. Retrials, following judgements by the European Court of Human Rights that trials were unfair, were not impartial and did not re-examine evidence. Proceedings were excessively prolonged, and provisions limiting pre-trial detention had not yet become law and did not adequately address the need to complete a trial within a reasonable time.

Prison conditions
Prisoners continued to report ill-treatment, arbitrary and harsh disciplinary punishments and solitary confinement or small-group isolation in "F-type" prisons. In September the European Committee for the Prevention of Torture (CPT) issued a report relating to its December 2005 visit to places of detention in Turkey, calling for a significant increase in the amount of time allowed for prisoners to associate with each other and commenting on the "very harmful consequences" of an isolation-type regime which could lead to "inhuman and degrading treatment". The CPT also reiterated the call it made in 2004 for a full-scale review of prison health care services.

Conscientious objectors
Conscientious objection was not recognized and no civilian alternative was available.

◻ In a retrial in October, Sivas Military Court sentenced Mehmet Tarhan to two years and one month's imprisonment on two charges of insubordination following his refusal on two occasions to perform military service.

Violence against women
There was little progress in implementing the provision in the 2004 Law on Municipalities, which stipulated the need for shelters for women victims of domestic violence in towns with a population of more than 50,000. Women's organizations called for additional funds from the government to implement the law. A circular from the Prime Minister in July, outlining measures to combat violence against women and children, and to prevent so-called "honour killings", represented a step towards acknowledging an entrenched and endemic problem. In December, Parliament passed revisions to the Law on the Protection of the Family, widening its scope.

AI country reports/ visits
Reports
- Europe: Partners in crime — Europe's role in US renditions (AI Index: EUR 01/008/2006)
- Turkey: Article 301 — How the law on "denigrating Turkishness" is an insult to free expression (AI Index: EUR 44/003/2006)
- Turkey: No impunity for state officials who violate human rights — Briefing on the Şemdinli bombing investigation and trial (AI Index: EUR 44/006/2006)
- Turkey: Briefing on the wide ranging, arbitrary and restrictive draft revisions to the Law to Fight Terrorism (AI Index: EUR 44/009/2006)

- Turkey: Justice delayed and denied – The persistence of protracted and unfair trials for those charged under anti-terrorism legislation (AI Index: EUR 44/013/2006)

Visits

AI delegates visited Turkey in March, April, May and October.

TURKMENISTAN

TURKMENISTAN
Head of state and government: Kurbanguly Berdymukhammedov (replaced Saparmurad Niyazov in December)
Death penalty: abolitionist for all crimes
International Criminal Court: not ratified

Despite improvements in a small number of individual cases, human rights violations continued on a large scale. The targeting of human rights defenders intensified. The authorities failed to open a prompt, thorough or impartial investigation into the death in custody of a human rights defender who died in suspicious circumstances. Measures to silence dissent included harassment, restrictions of the freedom of movement, arbitrary detention, torture or other ill-treatment and the targeting of relatives. Dozens of those imprisoned in connection with an alleged assassination attempt on President Saparmurad Niyazov in 2002 continued to be held incommunicado.

Political background

President Saparmurad Niyazov died on 21 December from a cardiac arrest. The same day the State Security Council and Cabinet of Ministers appointed Deputy Prime Minister Kurbanguly Berdymukhammedov as acting President. President Niyazov's constitutionally designated successor, the Chairman of the Mejlis (parliament), was dismissed, and criminal charges were reportedly brought against him.

On 26 December the Halk Maslahaty (People's Council) approved the nomination of six people, including the acting President, as candidates in presidential elections to be held in February 2007. All were members of the Democratic Party of Turkmenistan, the only registered party in the country. The interim government ignored calls by exiled opposition groups to allow opposition leaders to put forward candidates.

International scrutiny

The UN Secretary-General, reporting to the UN General Assembly in October, concluded that "gross and systematic violations of human rights continued in [Turkmenistan], notwithstanding gestures by the government." He highlighted the plight of human rights defenders and minorities, restrictions on freedom of expression and religion, the use of torture, the absence of an independent judiciary, and the limited access to health care and education. He called on Turkmenistan to invite the special mechanisms of the UN Human Rights Council to visit the country. Despite repeated resolutions by the General Assembly and the UN Commission on Human Rights, Turkmenistan has previously failed to invite them.

In June the UN Committee on the Rights of the Child stressed the crucial role of civil society in contributing to the full implementation of Turkmenistan's obligations under the Convention on the Rights of the Child, and recommended removing restrictions on independent civil society organizations. It called on the authorities to investigate allegations of torture and ill-treatment, in particular within the juvenile justice system, to bring the perpetrators to justice, and to ensure that children enjoyed freedom of religion and access to information from a diversity of national and international sources.

Violence against women

In May the UN Committee on the Elimination of Discrimination against Women raised concerns at Turkmenistan's lack of awareness of the urgent need to stem violence against women, to pass specific legislation, including on domestic violence, and to introduce measures to address trafficking in women. Among other issues, it urged Turkmenistan to criminalize domestic violence; bring to justice the perpetrators; ensure that the victims have access to appropriate redress; and ensure that shelters are set up. The Committee also recommended that the government provide an enabling environment for women's and human rights organizations.

Death in custody

Activists from the human rights group, the Turkmenistan Helsinki Foundation, were taken into custody in June: Annakurban Amanklychev, Sapardurdy Khadzhiev, Elena Ovezova and Ogulsapar Muradova, a journalist with the US-funded Radio Liberty, and her three adult children. Four were released on 1 July. Annakurban Amanklychev, Sapardurdy Khadzhiev and Ogulsapar Muradova were convicted of "illegal acquisition, possession or sale of ammunition or firearms" and sentenced to prison terms of between six and seven years after an unfair trial in August. The charges appeared to be fabricated. The defendants were reportedly ill-treated in detention, and Annakurban Amanklychev and Ogulsapar Muradova given psychotropic drugs in an attempt to extract "confessions".

In September, Ogulsapar Muradova died in custody in suspicious circumstances. The authorities failed to open a prompt, thorough and impartial investigation into her death.

Silencing dissent

Civil society activists, political dissidents, members of religious minority groups and their relatives were harassed, arbitrarily detained and tortured.

The Ministry of National Security summoned for questioning virtually all those who met journalists of the BBC and the French media production company Galaxie Presse who visited Turkmenistan and subsequently criticized the government's policies. Those questioned were barred from leaving Turkmenistan, and some put under house arrest.

◻ Kakabay Tedzhenov, aged 70, was forcibly confined in medical institutions, mostly in a psychiatric hospital in Garashsyzlyk district in the eastern Lebap region, from January until October, when he was released following international pressure. On release, he reportedly had to undertake not to make political statements in the future. AI believed he was being punished for protesting at government policies and adopted him as a prisoner of conscience. In February the Turkmenistan delegation at the Organization for Security and Co-operation in Europe told all participating states that he had never been detained or confined in a medical institution.

◻ Environmental activist Andrei Zatoka was detained on 17 December by local police at the airport in his home town of Dashoguz. He had been preparing to fly to the capital, Ashgabat, and then on to Moscow the following day, to meet members of the International Social and Ecological Union and holiday with his family in Russia. He was reportedly charged with breaching public order. However, there were allegations that he had been targeted because of his peaceful work as an environmental activist.

The authorities continued to restrict freedom of movement to punish and put pressure on dissidents and their families. Thousands of people were reportedly on a "black list" barring them from leaving the country. They included those perceived as critical of the authorities and their relatives, relatives of people imprisoned in connection with the 2002 alleged assassination attempt on the President, and the relatives and friends of government officials imprisoned in recent years.

◻ On 2 May, Ovez Annaev, the brother-in-law of Khudayberdy Orazov, leader of the opposition movement Watan (Fatherland) in exile, was forced by National Security officers to leave a plane he had boarded. They reportedly threatened to imprison him if he complained to international organizations or embassies. He was on his way to Russia for specialist medical treatment for a gastric ulcer. He and his wife had previously been barred from travel abroad and removed from a plane before take-off, apparently because of their relationship with Khudayberdy Orazov, and accused by the authorities of playing a key role in the alleged assassination attempt.

At least one member of a religious minority group was reportedly deported to his country of origin as part of the clampdown on religious freedom. Since the mid-1990s hundreds of foreign members of minority religious groups have reportedly been deported to their countries of origin.

◻ When Aleksandr Frolov, a Baptist and Russian citizen who had lived in Turkmenistan for many years, returned from a trip to Russia via Kazakstan in March, religious literature he had on him was confiscated by Turkmenistani border guards. Shortly afterwards three officers of the Migration Service came to his house and confiscated his residence permit. They reportedly accused him of attempting to import Christian literature, failing to notify the Migration Service of his exit from Turkmenistan, and holding religious services in his home. No charges were known to have been brought against him. In June he was deported to Russia, separating him from his wife, a Turkmenistani citizen, their three-year-old son and a five-month-old daughter.

Incommunicado imprisonment

Dozens of prisoners sentenced following unfair trials in connection with the 2002 alleged assassination attempt continued to be held incommunicado, denied all access to families, lawyers and independent bodies including the International Committee of the Red Cross. There were allegations that many had been tortured and ill-treated following their arrests, and that some had died as a result of torture, ill-treatment and harsh prison conditions. The authorities failed to conduct thorough or impartial investigations into the allegations, or to respond to inquiries by AI and other human rights organizations.

In October President Niyazov announced that eight prisoners serving sentences in connection with the alleged assassination attempt would be released in a forthcoming amnesty. The eight had repented, "were not involved much and did not use arms", he said. None of those prisoners known to have been convicted of involvement in the alleged coup attempt was included in the published amnesty list.

AI country reports/ visits

Reports

- Europe and Central Asia: Summary of Amnesty International's concerns in the region, January-June 2006 (AI Index: EUR 01/017/2006)
- Commonwealth of Independent States: Positive trend on the abolition of the death penalty but more needs to be done (AI Index: EUR 04/003/2006)
- Turkmenistan: Open letter from a coalition of human rights organizations (AI Index: EUR 61/010/2006)

UGANDA

REPUBLIC OF UGANDA
Head of state and government: Yoweri Kaguta Museveni
Death penalty: retentionist
International Criminal Court: ratified

There was progress in peace talks in Southern Sudan between the government and the armed group, the Lord's Resistance Army (LRA), promising a possible end to 20 years of conflict in northern Uganda. Elections passed off relatively peacefully. Opposition presidential candidate Dr Kizza Besigye was acquitted of rape but continued to face treason charges. Attacks on freedom of expression and press freedom continued, as did reports of torture of detainees and harassment of people on account of their sexual orientation. Violence against women was widespread. Military courts continued to impose death sentences.

Background
A law enacted in May required non-governmental organizations to reregister annually. A Board comprised overwhelmingly of government representatives was set up to approve registrations.

Parliamentary and presidential elections took place in February, the first multi-party elections for 26 years. They were monitored by more than 500 election observers and, despite shortcomings including media bias and incomplete voter registration lists, were generally found to be transparent and relatively peaceful. President Museveni won almost 60 per cent of the votes and his main opponent, Dr Kizza Besigye of the Forum for Democratic Change (FDC), took 37 per cent. On 7 March Dr Besigye filed a suit in the Supreme Court, seeking to have the election results nullified. The Supreme Court rejected his appeal on 6 April.

Election violence
There were some reports of violence and intimidation, mostly of opposition supporters, particularly in the last three weeks of the campaign. Military forces were seen around some polling stations on election day.
🗁 On 15 February, three FDC supporters were shot and killed in Kampala when a soldier opened fire at a crowd waiting for Dr Besigye.

Trials of Dr Kizza Besigye
During 2006, Dr Besigye faced three separate court cases on charges of terrorism, rape and treason. He was released on bail on 2 January.

On 31 January the Constitutional Court ruled that Dr Besigye could not be tried for terrorism by a military court when the High Court was pursuing a case against him based on the same facts. On 7 March, President Museveni stated that Dr Besigye and his 22 co-accused would not be tried in a military court for terrorism and illegal possession of weapons.

The trial of Dr Besigye for rape began on 4 January. He was acquitted on 7 March following a recommendation by the jury. The state indicated an intention to appeal against the acquittal but no appeal had been filed by the end of the year.

On 15 March the trial of Dr Besigye and 22 other men for treason started in the High Court in Kampala. Several witnesses testified, including Onen Kamdulu, a former LRA leader suspected of gross human rights abuses who had been granted an amnesty. Defence counsel contested his appearance, but in October the Constitutional Court ruled that he should be allowed to testify and that the judge would rule on the admissibility of evidence. The trial was stayed in May 2006 following the filing of a constitutional petition by the defence lawyers in the Constitutional Court. The petition challenged the continued detention of the 22 people who had been accused with Dr Besigye on the basis that they had been granted bail by an earlier court order. The petition was argued in October 2006 and judgement was pending.

In September, the government sought to overturn the decision to grant bail to Dr Besigye, but the Constitutional Court upheld the High Court decision.

Conflict in northern Uganda
President Museveni offered to grant amnesty to the top five LRA leaders, including Joseph Kony and Raska Lukwiya, if a peace deal was reached. This was despite arrest warrants against them for crimes against humanity and war crimes issued by the International Criminal Court (ICC) in 2005.

A series of talks between the government and the LRA took place from July, sponsored by the government of Southern Sudan.

On 1 August, Joseph Kony called for a truce. Raska Lukwiya was killed in battle on 12 August.

The government and the LRA agreed a ceasefire on 26 August. Under its terms, LRA forces were to gather in two areas in Southern Sudan. By mid-September LRA fighters had started gathering at the assembly areas in Southern Sudan, but they subsequently left, fearing attack by the Uganda People's Defence Force (UPDF).

On 2 September President Museveni asked the ICC to maintain the charges against the LRA until a comprehensive peace agreement was reached, but said that once this was agreed the government would intervene to keep the commanders "safe" from the ICC. Late in September, peace talks stalled over the issue of the ICC warrants, and in October the UPDF said it had resumed its offensive against LRA rebels who had failed to assemble in the required areas.

Despite breaches of the ceasefire, in November both sides agreed to prolong it and talks continued. As the peace process continued, a number of confidence building measures took place from November with the government facilitating visits by family members of the LRA leadership and by community leaders from northern Uganda for consultations with the LRA leaders.

AI condemned the offer of amnesty made by President Museveni to the LRA leaders and stated that the offer of "protection" was in violation of Uganda's obligations under international law, since it itself referred the cases to the ICC on the basis that national authorities were unable to deliver justice for crimes committed in northern Uganda.

Internally displaced people
There were 1.7 million internally displaced people in the north, most in camps or settlements around villages. Conditions in camps were poor, with high mortality rates as a result of malnutrition, lack of sanitation and insecurity.

After the ceasefire, some people began returning home and the government set a deadline of 31 December to clear the camps. A number of sites were identified as suitable for resettlement and by October UN officials estimated that more than 300,000 people had left the camps.

Refugees in Uganda
In March the government passed a new refugee bill incorporating provisions of international refugee law.

In March the Ugandan and Southern Sudanese governments signed an agreement to repatriate Sudanese refugees. In July, the UN refugee agency UNHCR announced that 10,000 refugees had returned.

Some Congolese refugees returned to the Democratic Republic of the Congo (DRC) early in 2006, but further insecurity in the DRC prompted new arrivals of refugees.

Attacks on freedom of expression
Attacks on freedom of expression and press freedom continued, in particular during the election campaign. The police intervened to prevent programmes relating to the presidential candidates being aired, and several journalists were arrested during the run-up to the election. Radio stations were banned from broadcasting any debate or programme about Dr Besigye's trial.

On 23 February, police stormed Radio Pacis and stopped a talk show featuring the FDC deputy secretary general Kassiano Wadri.

On 7 March, the offices of the independent radio station Choice FM in Gulu were raided by police. The station's programme manager was arrested and held overnight before being released without charge. Later in March police shut down the radio station, accusing it of operating without a licence, although it had applied for a renewal.

Torture and ill-treatment
There were reports of torture of detainees by police forces and the state security services, who reportedly used "safe houses" where suspects were detained and tortured for days at a time.

Some of the 22 men accused of treason with Dr Kizza Besigye filed a suit on 1 November against the authorities for torture and ill-treatment while in detention.

On 4 May, Abdu Smugenyi, a businessman, was reportedly tortured to death by electrocution in a "safe house" in Kampala. He had been arrested in April near Kasese, western Uganda, and accused of involvement with an armed group operating in the DRC.

Lesbian, gay, bisexual and transgender people
Abuses against lesbian, gay, bisexual and transgender (LGBT) people continued. Homosexuality is a criminal offence in Uganda, and the media, police and other groups, including teachers, targeted and harassed LGBT people.

In August, *The Red Pepper* newspaper published a list of men it asserted were gay. Several of those named reported subsequent harassment and ostracism. In September the newspaper published a similar list of 13 women it said were lesbians.

Violence against women
The threat of violence against women remained very high, particularly in the ongoing conflict in the north where many young girls have often been abducted by LRA rebels to serve as "wives" and slaves for combatants. Women and girls in displaced people's camps were also at high risk of domestic violence and of attacks when performing daily tasks such as collecting wood.

The police stated that at least 989 young girls had been raped in displaced people's camps in the five northern districts between January and July 2006.

Death penalty
No executions following conviction by a civilian court have been carried out since 1999.

Military courts continued to pass death sentences and order executions, although the exact numbers were not clear.

In February the Chief of Defence Forces stated that 26 UPDF soldiers had been sentenced to death and executed between 2003 and 2005 for killing civilians while on duty in northern Uganda.

A UPDF soldier, Private Abubaker Mugwanate, was sentenced to death by hanging in September for murdering a student.

AI country reports/ visits
Statements
- Uganda: Amnesty International calls for an effective alternative to impunity (AI Index: AFR 59/004/2006)
- Uganda: Lesbian, gay, bisexual and transgender people targeted (AI Index: AFR 59/006/2006)
- Uganda: Fear for safety/harassment – 13 women (AI Index: AFR 59/007/2006)

UKRAINE

UKRAINE
Head of state: Viktor Yushchenko
Head of government: Viktor Yanukovych (replaced Yuriy Yekhanurov in August)
Death penalty: abolitionist for all crimes
International Criminal Court: signed

Refugees and asylum-seekers were deported to countries where they were at risk of torture or ill-treatment. Torture and ill-treatment in police detention continued to be routine. Overcrowded conditions in police detention led to high levels of tuberculosis. There was widespread impunity for perpetrators of domestic violence. Antisemitic and racist attacks were reported in various parts of the country.

Background
Parliamentary elections on 26 March were found to meet international standards for democratic elections by the election observation mission of the Organization for Security and Co-operation in Europe.

In October the UN Human Rights Committee expressed concern about torture and ill-treatment in police custody, the rights of refugees and asylum-seekers, domestic violence and antisemitic and racist attacks.

Refugees and asylum-seekers
Ukraine violated international standards for the protection of refugees by forcibly sending asylum-seekers and registered refugees back to their countries of origin without right of appeal.

The UNHCR, the UN refugee agency, and non-governmental groups criticized the authorities for forcibly returning 10 asylum-seekers from Uzbekistan during the night of 14-15 February. Uzbekistan had issued extradition warrants for 11 asylum-seekers in Ukraine for alleged involvement in events in Andizhan, Uzbekistan, in May 2005 when the security forces fired on mainly peaceful demonstrators, killing hundreds of people. Ten of the men were forcibly returned, but one was reportedly allowed to stay as he had relatives in Ukraine. The fate of the deported asylum-seekers in Uzbekistan remained unknown. They were at risk of serious human rights violations, including incommunicado detention, torture or other ill-treatment and a flagrantly unfair trial. On 28 February the Ukrainian security services defended their action on the grounds that the asylum-seekers "were associated with an organization that has been recognized as a terrorist one by the UN."

Torture and ill-treatment
Steps towards the eradication of torture and ill-treatment included a Ministry of Internal Affairs order in April that all detainees must be informed of their rights. However, the police did not subsequently receive instructions on how to carry out the order. In September, Ukraine ratified the Optional Protocol to the UN Convention against Torture, which requires independent national preventive mechanisms to monitor all places of detention.

Of six cases of alleged torture or ill-treatment raised by AI with the authorities in Ukraine in September 2005, prosecutions were brought against police officers in only two cases.

Harsh detention conditions
Detainees in pre-trial detention were subjected to high rates of overcrowding and poor conditions, leading to greater exposure to tuberculosis. Ukraine has an estimated tuberculosis case rate of 95 per year per 100,000 people, the eighth highest in Europe and Eurasia, according to the World Health Organization.

In January there were between 30 and 40 detainees with tuberculosis in the Sevastopol temporary holding facility in the Crimea, according to the Sevastopol Human Rights Group, a non-governmental organization (NGO). They were held in the facility for the full period of their pre-trial detention, in violation of the Criminal Procedural Code, because a pre-trial detention centre in Simferopol, closer to their homes, had a long-standing practice of not accepting detainees with tuberculosis. In January, 20 infected detainees were reportedly held in a cell designed for six people and were not given the special food or the vitamins needed to counteract the effects of their medication.

In November the UN Human Rights Committee called on Ukraine to "guarantee the right of detainees to be treated humanely and with respect for their dignity, particularly by relieving overcrowding."

Update: the murder of Georgiy Gongadze
In January the trial opened of three police officers charged with murdering the investigative journalist, Georgiy Gongadze, in 2000. In July a Rapporteur for the Parliamentary Assembly of the Council of Europe expressed disappointment at the lack of progress in investigating the instigators and organizers of the killing, as opposed to the perpetrators. In August the journalist's mother announced that she would no longer attend court hearings because of her lack of confidence in the trial's outcome. The trial was ongoing at the end of the year.

Discrimination
In August the UN Committee on the Elimination of Racism and Discrimination (CERD) reviewed Ukraine's latest periodic reports. In its submission, the Ukrainian government had stated that "racial discrimination in all its forms [had] been eliminated in Ukraine and the equality of every person before the law [had] been secured." However, NGOs continued to report incidents of racist attacks and discrimination. The Union of Councils for Jews in the Former Soviet Union reported that between January and November there were seven antisemitic and racist attacks on individuals and 18 other incidents including vandalism of synagogues and Jewish schools. According to the European Roma Rights

Centre, Roma were denied access to education, health care and housing because they did not have identification documents. The CERD recommended, among other things, that Ukraine should "take preventative measures against acts directed against persons or religious sites belonging to minorities and that it investigate such acts and bring perpetrators to justice." The CERD also called for all Roma to be issued with identification documents.

🗁 In March a group of youths attacked a Jewish Yeshiva student on the Kyiv metro, who defended himself with a legally registered air gun. He was a friend of Mordechai Molozhenov, a Yeshiva student stabbed and wounded in August 2005 in Kyiv. The attackers were charged with "hooliganism".

🗁 In October, Kunuon Mievi Godi, a Nigerian man who had been living in Ukraine for many years, was stabbed and killed by a group shouting racist slogans near Poznyaki metro station on the outskirts of Kyiv. The attackers did not steal the US$400 that the victim was carrying. The investigation was ongoing.

Violence against women

Provisions in the Law on the Prevention of Violence in the Family allowed victims of domestic violence to be given a warning for "victim behaviour", perpetuating the myth that women are to blame for the violence inflicted on them, providing impunity for perpetrators and deterring the reporting of crimes of violence. Women who attempted to take perpetrators to court were hampered by widespread corruption in the criminal justice system or by the derisory punishments imposed by the courts.

The Ministry for Family, Youth and Sport's network of centres provided legal and psychological counselling and shelter for people up to the age of 35 and for families. However, the shelters did not target women specifically and could not provide the level of support and protection required for victims of domestic violence.

In November the UN Human Rights Committee called on Ukraine to "intensify efforts to combat domestic violence, and ensure that social and medical centres for rehabilitation are available to all victims."

AI country reports/ visits
Reports
- Europe and Central Asia: Summary of Amnesty International's concerns in the region, January-June 2006 (AI Index: EUR 01/017/2006)
- Commonwealth of Independent States: Positive trend on the abolition of the death penalty but more needs to be done (AI Index: EUR 04/003/2006)
- Ukraine: Briefing to the UN Human Rights Committee – June 2006 (AI Index: EUR 50/003/2006)
Visit
AI delegates visited Ukraine in September.

UNITED ARAB EMIRATES

UNITED ARAB EMIRATES
Head of state: Shaikh Khalifa bin Zayed Al-Nahyan
Head of government: Shaikh Mohammed bin Rashid Al Maktoum (replaced Shaikh Maktoum bin Rashid Al Maktoum in January)
Death penalty: retentionist
International Criminal Court: signed

A Bangladeshi national was sentenced to death by stoning and a female domestic worker was sentenced to be flogged. Two prominent human rights activists were subject to harassment and intimidation.

Background
Shaikh Mohammed bin Rashid Al Maktoum became Vice-President and Prime Minister of the United Arab Emirates (UAE) and Ruler of Dubai following the death of his brother, Shaikh Maktoum bin Rashid Al Maktoum, in January.

In February, the UAE Society for Human Rights was established as the country's first non-governmental human rights organization. Full membership of the organization was limited to UAE nationals but non-nationals could become associate members.

In November the Prime Minister announced measures to regulate the labour market and improve conditions for foreign migrant workers, including a health insurance scheme, fixed working hours for domestic workers and the establishment of a special court to resolve labour disputes.

Also in November, the President issued a federal law against human trafficking, which prescribes penalties ranging from one year to life imprisonment.

In December, nearly 6,600 UAE nationals selected by the rulers of the seven Emirates that make up the UAE voted in the first elections to be held since the country became independent in 1971. They elected 20 members to the 40-member Federal National Council (FNC), an advisory body with no legislative powers and whose other members are directly appointed by the rulers of the seven Emirates. Sixty-three women candidates stood for election but only one was voted onto the FNC.

Death penalty and cruel judicial punishments
In June, in the Emirate of Fujairah, a *Shari'a* (Islamic) court imposed a sentence of death by stoning on Shahin 'Abdul Rahman, a Bangladeshi national, after convicting him of adultery with Asma Bikham Bijam, a migrant domestic worker, who was sentenced to receive a flogging of 100 lashes and to be imprisoned for one year. Ten days later the sentence of death by stoning against Shahin 'Abdul Rahman was commuted on appeal and he received a one-year prison sentence followed by deportation to his home country. However,

the sentence of flogging against Asma Bikham Bijam was upheld on appeal. It was not known whether it was carried out.

Risk of forcible return

In March Gazain Marri, a Pakistani national from the Baloch community, was arrested in Dubai and detained in Abu Dhabi. No charges were known to have been brought against him and there was concern that he might be forcibly returned to Pakistan where he would be at risk of serious human rights violations including torture. However, he was reported to have been released at the end of August.

There was similar concern after Riad 'Abdullah Laila, a Syrian national and member of the Muslim Brotherhood, was detained on arrival at Dubai airport in April, reportedly at the request of the Syrian authorities. He had been living as a refugee in Iraq since 1980. However, he too was reported to have been released uncharged and allowed to travel to a third country in May.

Human rights defenders

Two prominent human rights activists, who had been barred from giving interviews or writing articles for the local media for several years, were subjected to harassment.

⌐ Mohamed 'Abdullah al-Roken, a lawyer and former President of the UAE's Jurists' Association, was detained twice, in July and August, by State Security (Amn al-Dawla) officials. During his three-day detention in August, his interrogators reportedly threatened to close down his office and drugged his food. He was prevented from using the bathroom. Mohamed 'Abdullah al-Roken was released without charge but his passport was confiscated.

⌐ In June an arrest warrant was issued against human rights activist Mohamed al-Mansoori, a lawyer and President of the Jurists' Association, after he was accused of "insulting the Public Prosecutor". He had given several interviews to international news media in which he criticized the human rights situation in UAE. Mohamed al-Mansoori was abroad and was not arrested.

In August, attempts were made to bring criminal charges against Sharla Musabih, founder of the City of Hope Women's shelter in Dubai. She and others alleged the charges were politically motivated and intended to force the closure of the shelter, which provides support for women and children survivors of violence.

UNITED KINGDOM

UNITED KINGDOM OF GREAT BRITAIN AND NORTHERN IRELAND
Head of state: Queen Elizabeth II
Head of government: Tony Blair
Death penalty: abolitionist for all crimes
International Criminal Court: ratified

The government continued to erode fundamental human rights, the rule of law and the independence of the judiciary, including by persisting with attempts to undermine the ban on torture at home and abroad, and by seeking to enact legislation inconsistent with fundamental human rights. Measures taken by the authorities with the stated aim of countering terrorism led to serious human rights violations, and concern was widespread about the impact of these measures on Muslims and other minority communities. Public judicial inquiries into cases of alleged state collusion in past killings in Northern Ireland were ongoing, but the government continued to fail to establish an inquiry into the killing of Patrick Finucane.

'War on terror'

The Terrorism Act 2006, the fourth piece of legislation passed since 2000 with the stated aim of countering terrorism, became law in March. Some of its provisions were inconsistent with fundamental human rights. It created new offences, including "encouragement of terrorism", whose scope significantly exceeded international law provisions that the government claimed it would implement. The Act also extended the maximum period of police detention without charge from 14 to 28 days for people held under terrorism legislation.

Instead of bringing people to justice, the authorities continued to seek to deport individuals they asserted posed a threat to "national security", and to impose "control orders" under the Prevention of Terrorism Act 2005 on others allegedly involved in "terrorism-related activity". Consequent judicial proceedings were profoundly unfair, denying individuals the right to a fair hearing, including because of heavy reliance on secret hearings in which intelligence information had been withheld from the appellants and their lawyers of choice, as well as a particularly low standard of proof.

In August the Home Secretary lost his appeal against a ruling quashing "control orders" he had made against six foreign nationals. The court held that the obligations imposed on the men amounted to deprivation of liberty and that, in the circumstances, he had made the orders unlawfully. However, the same court allowed his appeal against a ruling that proceedings under the Prevention of Terrorism Act were incompatible with the right to a fair hearing.

During the year, charges were brought in connection with alleged breaches of "control orders". As a result, at least one man was held in custody. However, since his original "control order" had been ruled unlawful, his subsequent detention for alleged breaches of it was also unlawful. In December, 16 "control orders" were in force, seven of which were against UK nationals.

Appeals continued against the deportation on national security grounds of a number of men. A ruling was awaited on a lead case involving reliance by the UK authorities on a memorandum of understanding concluded in 2005 with Jordan. The government continued to assert that "diplomatic assurances" featured in this and other memorandums of understanding concluded with other countries could be relied on to relieve the UK of its human rights obligation not to send people to countries where they would face a real risk of torture or other ill-treatment. However, having failed to secure a memorandum with Algeria, and despite acknowledging such a risk upon return to that country, the government claimed that assurances obtained from Algeria on a case-by-case basis would eliminate the risk in any event.

◻ In August, an Algerian torture survivor and refugee, known for legal reasons only as "Y", lost his appeal against his deportation on national security grounds. Despite ample evidence to the contrary, the court ruled that "Y" would not face a real risk of torture if deported to Algeria. The authorities were allowed to present their case that "Y" would not face such a risk largely in secret hearings, from which "Y" and his lawyers of choice were excluded. Pending further appeal, at the end of 2006 he had not been deported.

In August the European Committee for the Prevention of Torture (CPT) published the reports on its visits to the UK in July and November 2005. It found that the Special Security Unit in Full Sutton Prison was inappropriate for holding people who had previously been interned, in some cases for more than three years; that the threat of deportation to countries where people had apparently suffered torture or other ill-treatment increased the possibility of self-inflicted deaths in custody; that the detainees' medical examination always took place within the hearing of prison officers; that some detainees had not had prompt access to a lawyer following arrest; and that during transport detainees were handcuffed despite being locked inside metal cages. The CPT found that people detained under terrorism legislation were not physically brought before a judge, even for the initial authorization to extend police custody beyond 48 hours. Instead, conferences by video link were held, with the detainee guarded by police officers on one end of the link and the judge on the other end. It recommended that legislation be amended to ensure that anyone arrested has access to a lawyer from the outset of their detention. The CPT also reiterated that the conditions at Paddington Green High Security Police Station were inadequate for prolonged detention.

Guantánamo detainees with UK links

At least eight former UK residents continued to be held at the US detention camp in Guantánamo Bay, Cuba.

◻ In October, the Court of Appeal of England and Wales refused to order the UK authorities to make representations seeking the return to the UK of Bisher Al Rawi, an Iraqi national and long-term UK resident; Jamil El Banna, a Jordanian national with refugee status in the UK; and Omar Deghayes, a Libyan national also with refugee status in the UK.

◻ In April the December 2005 ruling that David Hicks, an Australian national detained in Guantánamo Bay, was entitled to be registered as a UK citizen and therefore to receive assistance from the UK authorities was upheld, and the government was refused permission to further appeal. However, the government had successfully introduced measures to thwart the import of the ruling. As a result, in July David Hicks was granted UK citizenship but stripped of it hours later. His appeal against this decision was pending.

Renditions

Despite the emergence of further evidence implicating the UK in the unlawful transfer of Bisher Al Rawi and Jamil El Banna to US custody (see above) and in other known cases of renditions (illegal transfer of people between states outside of any judicial process), the government failed to instigate an independent and impartial inquiry.

Torture

◻ In June the Appellate Committee of the House of Lords (the Law Lords) granted immunity to Saudi Arabia and its officials at whose hands four UK citizens alleged they had suffered systematic torture. The UK government intervened in the case in support of the Saudi Arabian government's argument that it enjoyed state immunity. AI intervened in the case jointly with other non-governmental organizations, arguing that there should be no immunity for torture.

◻ In November leaked internal official reports revealed that more than 160 prison officers were implicated in allegations of torture of inmates at Wormwood Scrubs Prison that had come to light in the late 1990s. Reportedly, many of the incidents that the authorities had publicly refused to admit were acknowledged in the reports, and some managers had colluded in the abuse by ignoring it. The author of one of the reports allegedly stated that officers implicated in the abuses continued to pose an ongoing threat to inmates.

Police shootings

◻ In June police officers mounted a massive operation against a perceived terrorist threat that included forced entry into the home of Muhammad Abdulkahar and his family in Forest Gate, London, during which they shot and wounded him. It emerged that the operation was based on erroneous intelligence. In August an investigation concluded that the shot had been fired accidentally and that, in the circumstances, the officer involved had not committed any criminal or disciplinary offence.

◻ In July the prosecuting authorities announced that no individual police officer would be prosecuted for any criminal offence in connection with the fatal shooting of Jean Charles de Menezes in London in 2005. Instead, they decided to prosecute the Office of the Commissioner of Police of the Metropolis under health and safety legislation, a prosecution which, if successful, could result in a financial penalty only. In September the inquest into the death of Jean Charles de Menezes was adjourned indefinitely pending completion of ongoing criminal proceedings against the Office of the Commissioner of Police. In December a legal challenge brought by the family of Jean Charles de Menezes against the prosecuting authorities' decision not to bring criminal charges against any individuals in connection with his killing was dismissed.

◻ In July the prosecuting authorities announced that there was insufficient evidence to prosecute any police officer for any offence in connection with the fatal shooting of Azelle Rodney. In April 2005 the vehicle in which Azelle Rodney was travelling was intercepted by police who shot him in the ensuing operation.

◻ In December the sister of Christopher Alder, who in 1998 had choked to death on the floor of a police station while handcuffed, won the right to sue the prosecuting authorities for racial discrimination in connection with their handling of the case.

Prisons

In England and Wales alone, the prison population soared to nearly 80,000, among the highest per capita worldwide. Police cells were used as a result of the overcrowding crisis. Among other things, overcrowding continued to be linked to self-harm and self-inflicted deaths, greater risks to the safety of staff and inmates, and detention conditions amounting to cruel, inhuman and degrading treatment.

◻ In June the report of the public inquiry into the killing of Zahid Mubarek by his cellmate, a known racist, at Feltham Young Offenders Institution in March 2000 was published. Among other things, it found that 186 failings, either institutional or by 19 named individuals, had led to his death, which could have been prevented had appropriate action been taken.

Freedom of expression

◻ In December the Law Lords confirmed that detaining Jane Laporte to forcibly return her to London had been unlawful and violated her right to liberty. She was among three coach-loads of anti-war protesters who were prevented from reaching the air force base at Fairford – used by US B52 bombers to fly to Iraq – and forcibly returned to London in March 2003. The court also found that by preventing the coaches from reaching Fairford the police had violated Jane Laporte's right to freedom of peaceful assembly and expression.

Northern Ireland

Direct rule continued. In January the government withdrew the Northern Ireland (Offences) Bill after concern was expressed that, if enacted, it would have sanctioned impunity for past human rights abuses committed by state agents and paramilitaries, and would have deprived victims of effective redress. Despite concern about its lack of independence, the Police Service of Northern Ireland continued to investigate unresolved conflict-related deaths.

Collusion and political killings

The government continued to fail to establish an inquiry into allegations of state collusion in the 1989 killing of prominent human rights lawyer Patrick Finucane. The Secretary of State for Northern Ireland stated that a Finucane inquiry would only be constituted under the Inquiries Act 2005. The Irish government and the US House of Representatives stated that the Act would be incapable of delivering an independent and impartial inquiry into the killing.

In December David Wright won his legal challenge against the government's decision to convert the inquiry into allegations of state collusion in the killing of his son, Billy Wright, into an inquiry constituted under the Inquiries Act 2005. AI intervened jointly with other non-governmental organizations, asserting that the legislation was inadequate to fulfil the requirements of human rights law for such inquiries. On the same grounds, AI had opposed the move in March by the Secretary of State for Northern Ireland to convert the inquiry into allegations of state collusion in the 1997 killing of Robert Hamill into one constituted under the Inquiries Act 2005.

Allegations of collusion between UK security forces and loyalist paramilitaries in many human rights abuses, including bombings at Dublin airport and Dundalk in 1975 and at Castleblayney, County Monaghan, in 1976, were once again raised in an Irish Parliament report in November.

Refugees and asylum-seekers

The Immigration, Asylum and Nationality Act 2006 became law in March. It contained measures that could exclude from the protection of the UN Refugee Convention those seeking asylum on grounds of political persecution.

The vast majority of asylum applications were ultimately refused. Tens of thousands of rejected asylum-seekers who had not left the UK, often through no fault of their own, were condemned to live in abject poverty, living on the charity of others. A minority of rejected asylum-seekers received the statutory provision available to those left destitute who faced a temporary barrier to their removal. However, the majority of rejected asylum-seekers refused to apply, or were not eligible, for statutory provisions available to those left destitute. Rejected asylum-seekers were also not allowed to work, were not eligible for free health care in hospitals unless for emergency treatment, and were not allowed to continue with treatment they were already receiving during the asylum process.

In September, 32 Iraqi Kurds were forcibly returned to northern Iraq despite concern for their safety there.

In December, the government announced that the Independent Police Complaints Commission would be charged with investigating complaints arising from incidents involving immigration officials exercising police-like powers.

In July the European Court of Human Rights found that the UK had violated an asylum-seeker's right to be informed promptly of the reasons for his detention. He had been detained for some 76 hours before his representative had been informed of the reasons for his detention.

Violence against women
The government failed to address the lack of any strategic work on prevention of violence against women and did not provide adequate financial support to women subject to immigration control to enable them to leave abusive personal or employment situations. Women subject to immigration control – other than asylum applicants – were denied public funds, including for emergency housing.

Conviction rates for different forms of gender violence other than domestic violence remained very low. The conviction rate for the crime of rape was 5.3 per cent of all reported incidents in England and Wales.

AI country reports/ visits
Reports
- United Kingdom: Human rights – a broken promise (AI Index: EUR 45/004/2006)
- United Kingdom: Deepcut and beyond – high time for a public inquiry (AI Index: EUR 45/008/2006)
- United Kingdom: Justice denied for British survivors tortured in Saudi Arabia – A major leap backwards in the fight against impunity (AI Index: EUR 45/010/2006)
- United Kingdom: The Killing of Jean Charles de Menezes (AI Index: EUR 45/015/2006)
- United Kingdom: The Killing of Jean Charles de Menezes – let justice take its course (AI Index: EUR 45/021/2006)
- Europe: Partners in crime – Europe's role in US renditions (AI Index: EUR 01/008/2006)

Visits
AI delegates observed judicial hearings in the UK, including those held under terrorism legislation.

UNITED STATES OF AMERICA

UNITED STATES OF AMERICA
Head of state and government: George W Bush
Death penalty: retentionist
International Criminal Court: signed but declared intention not to ratify

Thousands of detainees continued to be held in US custody without charge or trial in Iraq, Afghanistan and the US naval base in Guantánamo Bay, Cuba. In June, the US Supreme Court struck down the military commissions established by President Bush and reversed the presidential decision not to apply Article 3 common to the four Geneva Conventions to detainees suspected of links with the Taleban or al-Qa'ida. Congress passed the Military Commissions Act stripping the US federal courts of the jurisdiction to hear habeas corpus appeals from such detainees, providing for trials by military commission, and amending the US War Crimes Act. In September, President Bush confirmed the existence of a programme of secret detentions run by the Central Intelligence Agency (CIA). There were reports of possible extrajudicial executions by US soldiers in Iraq, with a number of soldiers facing prosecution. There was a continued failure to hold senior government officials accountable for torture and other ill-treatment of "war on terror" detainees despite evidence that abuses had been systematic. There were reports of police brutality and ill-treatment in detention facilities in the USA. More than 70 people died after being struck by police tasers. Fifty-three people were executed in 14 states.

Military Commissions Act
In June, in *Hamdan v. Rumsfeld*, the US Supreme Court ruled that the military commissions established under a November 2001 Military Order to try foreign nationals held as "enemy combatants" in the "war on terror" were unlawful. Ten foreign nationals had been charged to stand trial before the commissions prior to the ruling. The ruling also reversed the presidential decision not to apply to detainees suspected of links with the Taleban or al-Qa'ida Article 3 common to the four Geneva Conventions of 1949 which requires fair trials and humane treatment for detainees in armed conflict. In September, President Bush confirmed that the CIA had been operating a secret detention programme in which some detainees in the "war on terror" had been held incommunicado and subjected to "alternative" interrogation techniques. He asserted that the Supreme Court ruling had put the secret programme in jeopardy.

In late September, Congress passed the Military Commissions Act (MCA). If found to be constitutional, the MCA would strip US courts of the jurisdiction to consider habeas corpus appeals challenging the lawfulness or conditions of detention of any non-US citizen held as an "enemy combatant" in US custody, regardless of location. On 13 December, a federal judge dismissed the habeas corpus petition of Guantánamo detainee Salim Ahmed Hamdan, who by then had been in US custody for more than five years without trial. The judge found that the MCA applied retroactively, blocking Salim Ahmed Hamdan's statutory access to habeas corpus, and that as a foreign national held outside US sovereign territory, he had no constitutional right to habeas corpus.

The MCA also provides for the President to establish new military commissions to try "alien unlawful enemy combatants" – broadly defined to include civilians captured far from any battlefield. The new commissions would have the power to hand down death sentences, under procedures which appeared highly unlikely to guarantee fair trials.

The MCA barred detainees from invoking the Geneva Conventions in any court action. It also narrowed the scope of the US War Crimes Act (and backdated this to 1997) by not expressly criminalizing acts violating common Article 3's prohibition of unfair trials or "outrages on personal dignity", particularly humiliating and degrading treatment. At a Senate hearing in July, six former and current military lawyers agreed that some of the interrogation techniques used by the USA in the "war on terror" had violated common Article 3.

Renditions and secret detention

In September President Bush announced that 14 "high-value" detainees held incommunicado for up to four and a half years as part of the secret CIA programme had been transferred to Guantánamo. AI considered that at least some of them had been victims of enforced disappearance. The fate and whereabouts of individuals other than the 14 who had been held in the CIA programme remained unknown at the end of the year.

In litigation in federal court, the government sought to ensure that whatever details the 14 recently transferred detainees knew about the secret CIA programme – such as the location of secret detention facilities or what interrogation techniques had been used – remained secret.

In June, the Council of Europe's Committee on Legal Affairs and Human Rights released a report of its inquiry into secret detention and renditions (the secret and unlawful transfer of detainees between countries) in Europe. The report concluded that the USA – an observer state of the Council of Europe – had been the "chief architect" of a "reprehensible" system of secret detentions and renditions. It confirmed AI's findings that several cases of rendition occurred with the involvement or co-operation of Council of Europe member states. The Committee urged the USA and European states to put an end to renditions and to conduct independent investigations into the practice.

Guantánamo

At the end of 2006, approximately 395 detainees of around 30 nationalities continued to be held without charge or trial at the US naval base in Guantánamo. Some had been held there for nearly five years.

In February, five UN experts, including the Special Rapporteur on torture, issued a report of their investigation into conditions at Guantánamo, calling for the facility to be closed. They found that some of the alleged treatment of detainees, including the use of solitary confinement, excessive force and the brutal manner of force-feeding during a hunger strike, amounted to torture.

In May the UN Committee against Torture also called for the closure of Guantánamo, noting that holding people indefinitely without charge constituted a violation of the UN Convention against Torture. In July, the UN Human Rights Committee urged the USA to ensure that all those held in Guantánamo were able "without delay" to challenge the lawfulness of their detention before a court.

In June, three detainees died in Guantánamo, apparently as a result of suicide. They included Abdullah Yahia al-Zahrani who was reportedly aged 17 when he was taken into custody. The deaths heightened concerns about the severe psychological impact of the indefinite detention regime.

Detentions in Afghanistan and Iraq

Hundreds of detainees were held without charge or trial at the US air base in Bagram, Afghanistan, with no provision for judicial review. Some had been detained for more than two years without access to lawyers, their families or the courts. In November, the US authorities said that a "significant percentage" of the Afghan detainees at Bagram might be transferred to the custody of the Afghan government within a year. It also said that some Afghans and other nationals would be kept at Bagram or transferred to Guantánamo.

Thousands of people were held by the US forces in Iraq, including several hundred "security internees" detained since before the handover of power to the interim Iraqi government in June 2004. There were no formal review procedures applying in such cases. Detainees arrested after that date had their detentions reviewed initially by a magistrate (often without the presence of the detainee) and thereafter by a non-judicial body at six-monthly intervals.

Unlawful killings by US forces outside the USA

There were a number of incidents of alleged extrajudicial executions or unlawful killings of civilians by US soldiers in Iraq.

▢ In November, a soldier pleaded guilty before a military court to charges of raping a 14-year-old Iraqi girl and murdering her and three members of her family in Mahmudiya in March. He was sentenced to life imprisonment. Three other soldiers faced charges of rape and murder in the same case, and arson for burning the girl's body to conceal the evidence. A fifth soldier, who had already been discharged from the army on mental health grounds when the charges arose, pleaded not guilty in a civilian federal court.

▢ Eight soldiers were charged with the kidnap and murder of 52-year-old Hashim Ibrahim Awad in the town of Hamdania in April. They were accused of dragging him from his home and shooting him while he was restrained. Four soldiers pleaded guilty to charges relating to the murder and were sentenced to between five and 10 years' imprisonment. However, in line with pre-trial agreements, their sentences were reduced to between 12 and 21 months' confinement. Other trials were pending at the end of the year.

In Pakistan, between 13 and 18 people, including five children, were killed when Hellfire missiles were fired into three houses in the village of Damadola Burkanday in northwestern Pakistan on 13 January. Reports suggested that US aircraft fired the missiles and that their intended target was Ayman al-Zawahiri, a high-ranking al-Qa'ida operative.

Detention of 'enemy combatants' in the USA

Ali Saleh Kahlah al-Marri, a Qatari national, continued to be held without charge or trial in military custody in South Carolina. He remained in isolation and had been denied family visits or phone calls for more than three years. In November, the US government filed a court motion seeking to have Ali al-Marri's appeals challenging the lawfulness of his detention dismissed on the grounds that under the MCA the federal courts no longer had jurisdiction in the case. The issue had not been decided by the end of the year.

In October, lawyers for José Padilla, a US citizen formerly detained as an "enemy combatant", sought to have criminal charges against him dismissed on the grounds that he had been tortured during more than three years of incommunicado detention in US military custody. A decision on the petition was pending at the end of the year.

Torture and other ill-treatment

A general lack of accountability for torture and other ill-treatment by US personnel in the "war on terror", including under interrogation techniques authorized by senior administration officials, continued. Although some generally low-ranking soldiers were court-martialled, by the end of the year no US personnel had been charged with torture under the USA's extraterritorial anti-torture statute or with war crimes under its War Crimes Act. Both the UN Committee against Torture and the UN Human Rights Committee expressed concern at the apparent leniency and impunity being enjoyed by US personnel.

By the end of the year, only one CIA employee had been brought to trial for abuses committed in the "war on terror". In August, David Passaro, a CIA contractor, was convicted of assault in connection with the beating of Afghan detainee Abdul Wali, who died in a US military base in Afghanistan in 2003. By the end of the year no other charges had been brought in relation to 19 cases of alleged abuse involving civilian or CIA personnel referred to the US Department of Justice.

A revised Army Field Manual was published in September, reiterating the ban on cruel, inhuman or degrading treatment of any detainee, a position the government had previously held not to apply to "unlawful enemy combatants". The Manual also expressly banned certain techniques during interrogation, including sexual humiliation, use of dogs, hooding, "water-boarding" (simulated drowning), mock executions and deprivation of food and water. The Army Field Manual did not apply to CIA interrogations conducted outside a military-run facility.

On 6 December, US citizen Roy Belfast Jr (also known as Charles Taylor Jr), son of former Liberian President Charles Taylor, became the first person to be charged with torture under the USA's extraterritorial anti-torture statute. He was charged in relation to the torture of an individual in Monrovia, Liberia, in July 2002.

Ill-treatment in jails and police custody

There were reports of ill-treatment of suspects in jails and police custody, involving abusive use of restraints and electro-shock weapons. More than 70 people died after being shocked with tasers (dart-firing electro-shock weapons), bringing to more than 230 the number of such deaths since 2001.

In June the Justice Department announced that a two-year study of taser deaths would be undertaken by the National Institute of Justice. Meanwhile many police departments continued to use tasers in situations that fell far below any threat of deadly force. The UN Committee against Torture called on the USA to deploy tasers only as a non-lethal alternative to using firearms.

In August, Raul Gallegos-Reyes died in Arapahoe County Jail, Colorado, after being repeatedly tasered and strapped into a restraint chair for screaming and banging on his cell door. The coroner concluded he had died from "positional asphyxia" due to restraint and ruled the death a homicide.

A lawsuit filed against Garfield County Jail, Colorado, in July, alleged that prisoners were frequently strapped into restraint chairs and left for hours in painful positions after being tasered or drenched with pepper spray. Guards were also alleged to have taunted and threatened to shock prisoners wearing remote-controlled electro-shock belts while being transported to court. The jail reportedly had no clear policies governing use of restraints.

There were reports of police ill-treatment of lesbian, gay, bisexual and transgender people, and of a failure to respond adequately to identity-based crimes against them.

Mariah López, a transgender woman, was allegedly subjected to verbal and physical abuse by New York Police Department officers and city jail employees after she was arrested. She reportedly sustained a broken cartilage in her nose, a broken tooth and numerous abrasions after being beaten by officers. She was also subjected to humiliating strip searches.

Christina Sforza, a transgender woman, was reportedly assaulted in a New York restaurant. Police responding to the scene arrested her and refused to accept her complaint against her assailant. Assault charges filed against her were eventually dropped.

'Supermax' prisons

Thousands of prisoners continued to be held in long-term isolation in "supermaximum" security facilities in conditions that sometimes amounted to cruel, inhuman or degrading treatment.

In November a federal appeals court condemned as unconstitutional alleged conditions in a "Behavioral Modification Program" in a Wisconsin "supermax" prison. A lawsuit brought on behalf of an inmate confined under the programme in 2002 claimed he was stripped of clothes and bedding, confined to a small bare cell and fed only ground-up food formed into a "loaf". The conditions were alleged to have had a severe adverse effect on his mental health. The case was referred to a lower court for a ruling on the facts, some of which were in dispute.

Women in prison

In May, Vermont became the last of the 50 states to pass a law protecting women in prison from sexual abuse by guards, by criminalizing all sexual contact between inmates and correctional staff. However, many women prisoners in the USA remained at risk of abuse through policies allowing male staff to conduct "pat-down" searches of women prisoners and observe women washing or dressing in their cells. Most US states allowed male guards unsupervised access to women's prisons, contrary to international standards.

Twenty-three states and the Federal Bureau of Prisons allowed women prisoners to be shackled during labour, a practice AI considers to be inhuman and degrading as well as potentially dangerous for the health of the mother or her baby.

Prisoners of conscience

Army National Guard Specialist Katherine Jashinski served one month in jail after being sentenced to 120 days' imprisonment in May for refusing to serve in Afghanistan on conscientious grounds.

Kevin Benderman, a US Army sergeant, was released from prison in August after serving 12 months of a 15-month sentence for refusing to deploy to Iraq on grounds of his conscientious objection to the war.

Several other soldiers refusing to deploy to Iraq because of their opposition to the war faced possible prosecution at the end of the year.

Death penalty

In 2006, 53 people were executed in 14 states, bringing to 1,057 the total number of prisoners put to death since executions resumed in 1977. The number of executions in 2006 was the lowest for a decade and the number of people sentenced to death continued to decline from its peak in the mid-1990s. There were ongoing legal challenges to the constitutionality of the lethal injection process, and in December executions were suspended in California and Florida pending resolution of problems with execution procedures. People with serious mental illness continued to be subjected to the death penalty.

⌕ Clarence Allen, a Native American, was executed in California on 17 January, a day after his 76th birthday. He had been on death row for 23 years, was confined to a wheelchair and nearly blind; he had advanced heart disease and diabetes, and had suffered a major heart attack in 2005.

⌕ Bobby Wilcher was executed in Mississippi on 18 October after more than two decades on a death row notorious for its bad conditions, including poor mental health care, profound isolation of inmates and low standards of hygiene. He suffered from bipolar disorder, a serious mental illness, and had a long history of psychological problems, including suicide attempts. On 24 May, he had filed a motion in court seeking to drop all his remaining appeals. In July he informed his lawyer that he had changed his mind, and subsequently signed two affidavits to that effect. However, the courts refused all attempts to have his appeals reinstated.

⌕ Angel Nieves Diaz was executed by lethal injection in Florida on 13 December, proclaiming his innocence after two decades on death row. The execution went ahead despite the fact that a key prosecution witness from the trial had recanted his testimony. The execution required 34 minutes and two doses of the drugs to kill Angel Diaz. Witnesses described Angel Diaz grimacing in pain and gasping for air during the execution.

Other concerns

Daniel Strauss and Shanti Sellz, charged with transporting illegal aliens, had the charges against them dismissed by a federal judge in September. The charges arose because they had transported three undocumented Mexican migrants for urgent medical care after finding them injured and suffering from heat exhaustion in the Arizona desert.

Several bills to tighten immigration enforcement were pending before Congress at the end of the year. They included measures which would expand summary deportation procedures known as "expedited removal". In October Congress passed a law authorizing funding for the construction of fortified fencing along around a third of the US border with Mexico.

AI raised concern with the US government about its refusal to allow the Cuban wives of René Gonzáles and Gerardo Hernández, Cuban nationals serving long prison sentences in the USA, visas to travel to the USA to visit them in prison.

UN Committee against Torture and UN Human Rights Committee

The Committee against Torture and the Human Rights Committee issued recommendations to the US authorities in May and July. They included calls for an end to secret detention and enforced disappearances and for the closure of Guantánamo. The Committee against Torture also called for cruel interrogation techniques to be rescinded, and for thorough and impartial investigations into torture and other ill-treatment, including the role of senior government officials.

On domestic policy, both Committees called for strict limitations on the use of electro-shock devices; a review of cruel conditions in "supermaximum" security prisons; and measures to prevent sexual abuse of prisoners and the shackling of women prisoners during childbirth. The Human Rights Committee also called for a moratorium on executions and a ban on "life without parole" sentences for children. It expressed concern that poor people, and in particular African Americans, were disadvantaged by the rescue and evacuation plans in the aftermath of Hurricane Katrina in August 2005, and continued to be disadvantaged under the reconstruction plans. It urged the government to ensure their rights were fully taken into account with regard to access to housing, education and health care.

AI country reports/ visits
Reports
- USA: Stonewalled – still demanding respect: Police abuses against lesbian, gay, bisexual and transgender people in the USA (AI Index: AMR 51/001/2006)
- USA: The execution of mentally ill offenders (AI Index: AMR 51/003/2006)
- USA: Guantánamo: Lives torn apart – The impact of indefinite detention on detainees and their families (AI Index: AMR 51/007/2006)07/2006)
- USA. Amnesty International's continuing concerns about taser use (AI Index: AMR 51/030/2006)
- USA: Below the radar – Secret flights to torture and "disappearance" (AI Index: AMR 51/051/2006)
- USA: Amnesty International's supplementary briefing to the UN Committee against Torture (AI Index: AMR 51/061/2006)
- USA: Memorandum to the US Government on the report of the UN Committee against Torture and the question of closing Guantánamo (AI Index: AMR 51/093/2006)
- USA: More about politics than child protection – The death penalty for sex crimes against children (AI Index: AMR 51/094/2006)
- USA: Updated briefing to the Human Rights Committee on the implementation of the International Covenant on Civil and Political Rights (AI Index: AMR 51/111/2006)
- USA: Justice at last or more of the same? Detentions and trials after Hamdan v. Rumsfeld (AI Index: AMR 51/146/2006)
- USA: Rendition – torture – trial? The case of Guantánamo detainee Mohamedou Ould Slahi (AI Index: AMR 51/149/2006)
- USA: Military Commissions Act of 2006 – Turning bad policy into bad law (AI Index: AMR 51/154/2006)
- USA: Five years on 'the dark side' – A look back at 'war on terror' detentions (AI Index: AMR 51/195/2006))

Visits
AI delegates visited the USA in February and interviewed former Guantánamo detainees in France and Germany in November.

URUGUAY

EASTERN REPUBLIC OF URUGUAY
Head of state and government: Tabaré Vázquez Rosas
Death penalty: abolitionist for all crimes
International Criminal Court: ratified

Progress was recorded in cases of past human rights violations. Prisons were reportedly overcrowded and conditions were inadequate. Sugar cane workers demonstrated against poverty.

Background
Social exclusion continued during the year. For example, in January sugar cane workers and members of social welfare organizations demonstrated in the capital, Montevideo, in favour of land rights and against poverty. This followed the occupation of disused land at Colonia España, Bella Unión area, Artigas Department, by more than 50 people urging the authorities to provide land and housing to six working families.

In November Uruguay ratified the Agreement on the Privileges and Immunities of the International Criminal Court. The Agreement provided the framework for the Court to function effectively.

Uruguay has not submitted its periodic report to the UN Committee on Economic, Social and Cultural Rights since 1996.

Justice for past human rights violations
Although the Expiry Law of 1986 preventing legal proceedings against members of the security forces from the military period (1973-1985) remained in force, some judicial decisions revealed progress in the fight for justice for victims of past human rights violations.

In September, a Penal Judge in Montevideo found six military officers and two former policemen guilty of organized crime and of kidnapping Uruguayan members of the opposition group Party for People's Victory (Partido por la Victoria del Pueblo) in Argentina in 1976 as part of Operation Condor. They had not been sentenced by the end of the year.

In November, the 11th Penal Judge ordered the detention and trial of former President Juan María Bordaberry (1971-1976) and the former Minister of Foreign Affairs Juan Carlos Blanco. They were charged with the murders of legislators Zelmar Michelini and Hector Gutierrez Ruiz, along with two members of the Tupamaro guerrilla group Movement of National Liberation (Movimiento de Liberación Nacional), Rosario Barredo and William Whitelaw, in Argentina in 1976. The decision was under appeal at the end of the year.

Prisons
There were reports of overcrowding, lack of medical attention, inadequate food and ill-treatment by prison guards.

In February, the Parliamentary Commissioner for Prisons reported the results of a visit to Libertad prison, San José Department. He found that detainees were subjected to degrading treatment while being searched by guards, and that the use of rubber bullets was excessive.

Following a visit in March, the Parliamentary Commissioner confirmed complaints of overcrowding in Las Rosas prison, Maldonado Department, which had led to a number of prisoners sleeping on the floor.

Intergovernmental organizations

In November, the Inter-American Commission on Human Rights expressed concern at the persistent and systematic violation of women's human rights in Uruguayan prisons. It criticized discrimination against women prisoners, inadequate health care and obstacles encountered by female detainees in complaining about abuses by prison guards and inmates.

UZBEKISTAN

REPUBLIC OF UZBEKISTAN
Head of state: Islam Karimov
Head of government: Shavkat Mirzioiev
Death penalty: retentionist
International Criminal Court: signed

The authorities continued to reject calls for an independent, international investigation into the killing of hundreds of unarmed people in May 2005 in Andizhan. Freedom of expression and access to information became increasingly restricted. Human rights activists and local independent journalists continued to face threats, harassment and imprisonment on apparently fabricated criminal charges. Many were reportedly tortured or ill-treated in detention. Scores of people were sentenced to long prison terms for alleged involvement in the Andizhan events, including several prominent human rights defenders, most after closed or secret trials. Suspected members of banned Islamic movements forcibly returned from other countries were held in incommunicado detention, and several were sentenced to long prison terms after unfair trials.

Background

In March the World Bank announced that it was suspending new lending to Uzbekistan. President Islam Karimov accused the Bank of taking part in a "shameless information war" against Uzbekistan.

In March the authorities ordered the UN refugee agency, UNHCR, to leave the country within four weeks.

In April UNHCR complied, expressing serious concern about some 2,000 refugees from Afghanistan whom it had been assisting.

In the build-up to the anniversary of the May 2005 Andizhan killings, when hundreds of people were killed when security forces fired on mainly peaceful demonstrators, the authorities sought to ensure that only the official version of events would be heard. The authorities continued to refuse to allow an independent international investigation into the Andizhan events. However, they apparently addressed some of the concerns of the European Union (EU) in bilateral discussions in the second half of the year. The EU reviewed the 2005 visa and arms bans imposed on Uzbekistan in November and extended them by six and 12 months respectively. The EU resumed bilateral meetings with Uzbekistan under the Partnership and Cooperation Agreement and held an expert meeting on the Andizhan killings in Uzbekistan in December. In October President Karimov conceded publicly that failures by local and regional authorities in Andizhan might have contributed to the Andizhan events. He dismissed the regional governor of Andizhan over his failure to stop the unrest in Andizhan.

Pressure on international media and non-governmental organizations (NGOs) increased throughout 2006. Several mostly US-based or US-funded organizations had their accreditation withdrawn and were forced to close their operations in Uzbekistan.

In November Uzbekistan protested at the US State Department's decision to add Uzbekistan to its list of "countries of particular concern" for violating religious freedom.

In its September session the UN Human Rights Council reviewed Uzbekistan under a confidential procedure and decided to keep Uzbekistan under review. The UN General Assembly, however, voted not to adopt a country resolution on Uzbekistan. In its response to the UN's concerns at grave human rights violations published in August, the Uzbekistani authorities denied any grave and systematic human rights violations. They rejected claims by the UN Special Rapporteur on torture that torture was still systematic and reports that the International Committee of the Red Cross (ICRC) had been denied access to places of detention. In November the ICRC stated that it had not had access for two years and that negotiations with the authorities to resume visits were difficult.

Human rights defenders

The situation for human rights defenders continued to deteriorate. Threats, house arrest and detention by police prevented six of 11 human rights defenders reaching a meeting at the German embassy in Tashkent in September. In November human rights defenders were detained and placed under house arrest when they demonstrated outside the Ministry of Foreign Affairs calling for dialogue with the authorities.

◻ Tolib Yakubov, head of the independent Human Rights Society of Uzbekistan (HRSU), and Abduzhalil Boimatov, his deputy, left the country in August after repeated threats. In August Bakhtior Khamroev, head of the HRSU Dzhizzakh section, was attacked by a group of about 20 women who burst into his apartment, called him a traitor and beat him. Two British diplomats were visiting Bakhtior Khamroev at the time. Nevertheless, police officers intervened only after he had been hit on the head. He was reportedly refused medical assistance at the local hospital. Bakhtior Khamroev's 21-year-old son was detained in August on reportedly fabricated charges of hooliganism. He was sentenced to three years' imprisonment after an unfair trial in September.

☐ Saidzhakhon Zainabitdinov, chairperson of the independent Andizhan-based human rights group Appeal, was sentenced to seven years' imprisonment by a court in Tashkent in January, after a closed trial. Reports in December indicated that he was being held incommunicado in Tashkent prison.

☐ In January Dilmurod Muhiddinov, a human rights activist from Andizhan, was sentenced to five years' imprisonment for being in possession of a statement on the Andizhan events published by the secular opposition party Birlik.

☐ Mutabar Tadzhibaeva, chairwoman of the human rights organization Fiery Hearts Club and a founder of the national movement Civil Society, was sentenced to eight years' imprisonment by a court in Tashkent in March. Her appeal was turned down in May. She was held in the Women's Prison in Tashkent. She was transferred to the psychiatric wing of the prison in July for 10 days, allegedly to punish her for speaking out from prison. One of her lawyers said in August that she could not represent Mutabar Tadzhibaeva any more after repeated threats against herself and her family. Family members and lawyers stated that their visits were obstructed, that Mutabar Tadzhibaeva was regularly placed in punishment cells for up to 10 days and that her health was deteriorating.

☐ Azam Farmonov and Alisher Karamatov, two HRSU members from Sirdaria region, were arbitrarily detained in April in the city of Gulistan. Both men had been defending the rights of local farmers who had accused district officials of extortion and corruption. Azam Farmonov and Alisher Karamatov were taken to the pre-trial detention centre in the town of Khavast. They were held incommunicado for at least a week and alleged that they were tortured during that time, including by suffocation and beatings on their legs and heels with truncheons. They were sentenced in June to nine years' imprisonment for extortion after a trial in which they had no legal representation.

Restrictions on freedom of expression

New regulations adopted at the end of February made it illegal for Uzbekistani citizens to work for or contribute to foreign-owned media unless they were accredited journalists. Foreign journalists would have their accreditation withdrawn if their reporting was found to be "interfering in domestic affairs". In March the Ministry of Foreign Affairs revoked the accreditation of a local correspondent of the German radio station Deutsche Welle for allegedly filing a false report about a fatal bus accident in Bukhara region.

☐ In September Ulugbek Khaidarov, an independent journalist, was arbitrarily detained at a bus stop in Dzhizzakh and charged with extortion. A woman had reportedly brushed past him and put US$400 into his pocket. He immediately dropped the money to the ground, but law enforcement officers appeared and detained him. In October he was sentenced to six years' imprisonment after an unfair trial. He was released on appeal in November. Two days before Ulugbek Khaidarov's detention, his colleague, journalist Dzhamshed Karimov, disappeared in Dzhizzakh after visiting his mother in hospital. His family believed that his enforced disappearance was linked to his journalistic activities. In October sources reported that he had been forcibly confined to a psychiatric hospital. Local authorities continued to deny any knowledge of his whereabouts. His family were intimidated by local officials and their phone was cut off after they alerted international organizations. Both Dzhamshed Karimov and Ulugbek Khaidarov had expressed fears for their safety and were preparing to leave the country.

☐ On 8 September Dadakhon Khasanov, a well-known singer and songwriter, was given a suspended three-year prison sentence for writing and performing a song about the Andizhan events. The trial, although announced as open to the public, was in fact closed. Earlier in the year, two men who had listened to recordings of Dadakhon Khasanov's songs received long prison sentences for being in possession of subversive materials.

Forcible returns of terrorism suspects

The authorities continued to seek the extradition of suspected members of banned Islamic parties or movements, such as Hizb-ut-Tahrir and Akramia, from neighbouring countries as well as Russia and Ukraine. Most of the men forcibly returned to Uzbekistan were held in incommunicado detention. The governments of the Russian Federation, Ukraine, Kazakhstan and Kyrgyzstan apparently co-operated with Uzbekistan in the name of regional security and the "war on terror", in disregard of their obligations under international human rights and refugee law not to return anyone to a country where they would be at risk of serious human rights violations.

☐ Rukhiddin Fakhruddinov, an imam (religious teacher), was sentenced to 17 years' imprisonment in September following a closed trial in Tashkent. He had been forcibly returned from Kazakstan in November 2005 and held incommunicado until March 2006.

In August the General Procuracy of the Russian Federation suspended the extradition order of 13 Uzbeks detained in Ivanovo, pending a review of the men's appeals by the European Court of Human Rights.

A group of 12 people who fled the country after the Andizhan events returned from the USA in mid-July. Forty-one Andizhan refugees evacuated by UNHCR first to Romania and then to the USA returned home in August. A third group of refugees resettled to Idaho, USA, were reportedly preparing to return but had not done so by the end of the year. Two refugees who had resettled in Idaho died in August and September in mysterious circumstances. Some of the refugees were reportedly pressured into returning to Uzbekistan, where their movements were closely monitored and they had to report regularly to the local law enforcement agencies. UNHCR and other agencies and diplomats had not been granted access to them by the end of the year. In November reports emerged that two returnees had been detained.

Arbitrary detentions and unfair trials

Arbitrary detentions and unfair trials of suspected members of banned Islamic organizations continued. In many cases, there were credible allegations of torture and ill-treatment.

There were dozens of trials of multiple defendants in Tashkent and Tashkent Region alone in 2006. At least 257 people were sentenced to long prison terms for their alleged involvement in the Andizhan events, the vast majority after closed or secret trials. Several thousand people convicted of involvement with banned Islamic organizations continued to serve long prison terms in conditions which amounted to cruel, inhuman and degrading treatment.

In March a court in Tashkent sentenced Sanzhar Umarov, the leader of the secular opposition political coalition Sunshine Uzbekistan, to ten and a half years' imprisonment for fraud, embezzlement, money laundering and tax evasion. He had been detained in October 2005 upon his return from a trip to the USA. Sanzhar Umarov alleged that the case against him had been fabricated by business rivals, and coalition supporters claimed that the charges were politically motivated. Human rights observers at the trial asserted that the prosecution failed to prove the charges. In April an appeal court in Tashkent reduced his sentence by three years. At the appeal hearing, his health appeared to have greatly deteriorated. In May he was transferred to a prison colony in Bukhara, where he was confined in a punishment cell for 16 days in June. His family and lawyers complained that they had not been able to visit him and that he continued to be confined to punishment cells. An appeal was pending before the Supreme Court.

In May the coordinator of Sunshine Uzbekistan, Nodira Khidoiatova, was released after an appeal hearing commuted her 10-year prison sentence to a seven-year suspended sentence. Friends and relatives had reportedly paid 120 million soms (approximately US$ 100,000) in compensation to the Uzbekistani state to secure her release. Nodira Khidoiatova had been sentenced on 1 March for tax fraud, embezzlement and participation in a criminal group.

Death penalty

Although the President issued a decree in August 2005 abolishing the death penalty from January 2008, there were no moves to introduce a moratorium on executions or death sentences. The authorities insisted that no death sentences had been passed in Uzbekistan over the previous couple of years. NGOs, however, reported that at least eight death sentences were passed.

In March Aleksei Buriachek, a prisoner on death row in Tashkent prison, died from tuberculosis (TB), raising fears for the health of fellow death row inmates and prison staff. Iskandar Khudaiberganov, for example, was diagnosed with TB in 2004 and reportedly was receiving inadequate treatment.

AI country reports/ visits
Reports
- Commonwealth of Independent States: Positive trend on the abolition of the death penalty but more needs to be done (AI Index: EUR 04/003/2006)
- Uzbekistan: Health Professional Action – Tuberculosis in Prison: Case of Iskandar Khudaiberganov (AI Index: EUR 62/009/2006)
- Uzbekistan: Impunity must not prevail (AI Index: EUR 62/010/2006)

VENEZUELA

BOLIVARIAN REPUBLIC OF VENEZUELA
Head of state and government: Hugo Chávez Frías
Death penalty: abolitionist for all crimes
International Criminal Court: ratified

Most human rights violations committed by members of the security forces remained unpunished. Human rights defenders and journalists were threatened, intimidated and attacked.

Background

Hugo Chávez was elected President in December for a third six-year term. In April Venezuela abandoned the Andean Community of Nations trading block, after Colombia and Peru signed free trade agreements with the USA, and joined the South American trade group Mercosur. The government continued to establish social programmes aimed at the most vulnerable, including programmes to improve access to education, health and housing. The independence and impartiality of the judiciary continued to be questioned. There were serious concerns that the proliferation of small arms was fuelling an increase in violence.

Impunity, intimidation and harassment

Human rights violations, including torture, extrajudicial executions and enforced disappearances perpetrated by members of the security forces remained unpunished.

In July the bodies of eight people, including two children, were found on a ranch in the villages of La Victoria and El Nula in Alto Apure region, on the border with Colombia. Their hands were tied and they had been shot and their bodies burned. Witness accounts and initial evidence obtained by the police indicated that several members of the military had been involved in the killings. Despite this, only one member of the military was charged and tried for this crime. Human rights organizations alleged that this was part of a wider pattern of human rights violations by the same military unit against rural communities in Apure state.

▭ Melquiades Villaroel was threatened in February after a judge sentenced five police officers to 25 years' imprisonment for the killing of her son Rafael Moreno Villaroel and two others, including a child, in El Tigre, Anzoátegui state, in March 2001.

▭ There were concerns for the safety of the Mendoza family in Araure, Portuguesa state, following a shooting at their house in March. The Mendoza family had taken part in the trial of 11 police officers accused of the killing of seven people, including three members of their family.

Human rights defenders
Human rights defenders continued to be threatened and intimidated. In May the Inter-American Commission on Human Rights reiterated its concern at threats and other open hostility towards human rights defenders by government officials who publicly referred to human rights defenders as "coup plotters" and agents of instability.

▭ In April, María del Rosario Guerrero and her husband, Adolfo Martínez Barrios, were victims of an attempted assassination in Guárico state. They had been the subject of a campaign of defamation and intimidation since 2001, apparently linked to María del Rosario Guerrero's allegations of human rights violations by the police in Guárico state. By the end of the year, María del Rosario Guerrero was receiving protection, following a ruling by the Inter-American Court of Human Rights.

▭ In September, the Public Ministry recommended the dismissal of the case and closure of the investigation into the threats and acts of intimidation against members of the human rights organization COFAVIC (Comité de Familiares de Víctimas de los sucesos de Febrero-Marzo de 1989). A court ruling on the recommendation was pending at the end of the year. Staff from COFAVIC feared for their safety as the dismissal of this case might mean the withdrawal of police protection.

There were concerns that a draft law on international co-operation which would allow government officials to decide which non-governmental organizations could access international funds, could be used to restrict the work of human rights defenders.

Violence against women
Violence against women remained a concern. In November the National Assembly passed the Organic law on the right of women to a life free of violence. The law criminalized physical, sexual and psychological violence in the home, the community and at work, as well as forced sterilization, trafficking, forced prostitution, and sexual harassment and slavery. The law established tribunals specializing in cases of gender-based violence.

Attacks against journalists
Threats and attacks against journalists continued.

▭ The Special Rapporteur for Freedom of Expression of the Organization of American States expressed concern about the killing in April of Jorge Aguirre, a photographer for the newspaper *El Mundo*. He was reportedly shot dead at a demonstration in Caracas protesting against high levels of crime and insecurity, following the kidnapping and killing of three students. A former police officer was charged with the shooting. At the end of the year he was awaiting trial.

▭ In August, Jesús Flores Rojas, Co-ordinator of the newspaper *Región* in El Tigre, Anzoátegui state, who had exposed corruption by local civil servants, was shot eight times in the head while he was parking his car in front of his house. The men allegedly responsible for the shooting were reportedly shot and killed by police. Three police officers were reportedly detained, accused of involvement in the killing of Jesús Flores Rojas. At the end of the year it was not known whether the Public Ministry had pressed charges.

AI country reports/ visits
Statement
- Venezuela: Open letter to candidates in the December 2006 presidential elections (AI Index: AMR 53/008/2006)

Visit
AI delegates visited Venezuela in July.

VIET NAM

SOCIALIST REPUBLIC OF VIET NAM
Head of state: Nguyen Minh Triet (replaced Tran Duc Luong in June)
Head of government: Nguyen Tan Dung (replaced Phan Van Khai in June)
Death penalty: retentionist
International Criminal Court: not ratified

Restrictions on freedom of expression and association continued. Members of unauthorized churches seen as opposing state policies faced harassment. Dissidents using the Internet were harassed, threatened and imprisoned. Small groups of ethnic minority Montagnards continued to flee human rights violations in the Central Highlands and seek asylum in neighbouring Cambodia; at least 250 remained imprisoned after unfair trials in Viet Nam. Despite proposals to limit the scope of the death penalty, at least 36 death sentences and 14 executions were reported.

Background
In February the ruling Communist Party of Viet Nam (CPV) for the first time invited public comments on the draft Political Report before its adoption at the party's National Congress. The report outlined guidelines and policies for national construction, party building and a law-governed socialist state until 2010. In April the Congress elected a new politburo and central committee.

A major reshuffle of the government leadership took place in June, with the appointment of a new President, Prime Minister and Chairperson of the National Assembly.

Public concern about corruption scandals increased, in particular one involving senior officials at the Ministry of Transport and police officials.

Four prisoner amnesties resulted in the release of 19,914 prisoners, including two prisoners of conscience.

The Supreme Patriarch of the banned Unified Buddhist Church of Viet Nam, Thich Huyen Quang, 87, exiled for 24 years in remote provinces, was allowed to travel to Ho Chi Minh City for medical treatment and to recover briefly at the Giac Hoa Pagoda there. His deputy, Thich Quang Do, 77, was awarded Norway's Rafto Prize in November for his "personal courage and perseverance through three decades of peaceful opposition".

International relations
Trade negotiations were a major focus during the year. Viet Nam hosted APEC (Asia Pacific Economic Cooperation) meetings, culminating in a November summit of economic leaders including US President Bush for the first time. During this time harassment and threats against leading dissidents increased and attempts were made to ensure that they could not meet or talk with foreigners. The US Congress voted to confer Permanent Normal Trade Relations (PNTR) in December. Negotiations for entry into the World Trade Organization were finalized in November.

Restrictions on freedom of expression and the Internet
Political dissidents, including those using the Internet to talk about human rights, democracy and political change, were harassed, threatened and imprisoned under national security legislation. The authorities increased efforts to tighten control of the Internet through new regulations, monitoring by Internet café owners and Internet Service Providers, and by filtering and blocking websites.

Bloc 8406
Despite these constraints, in April activists launched an online petition signed by 118 democracy activists calling for peaceful political change and respect for human rights. This Internet-based pro-democracy movement became known as Group 8406, or Bloc 8406. A further 2,000 people went on to sign the petition. Several of the original signatories subsequently faced harassment, interrogation, restrictions on movement and confiscation of computers for attempting to publish a bulletin named *Freedom and Democracy* (*To Do Dan Chu*).

🖾 Truong Quoc Huy, 25, was arrested with two of his brothers and a young woman in October 2005 after taking part in a chat room hosted by the PalTalk website entitled "The voice of people in Viet Nam and Abroad". He was detained incommunicado for nine months until his release in July. After his release he publicly supported Bloc 8406 and was rearrested in an Internet café in Ho Chi Minh City in August after logging on to the PalTalk website. He has reportedly been charged under Article 88 of the Criminal Code for "conducting propaganda against the Socialist Republic of Viet Nam."

🖾 Internet dissident Nguyen Vu Binh, arrested in September 2002 and sentenced to seven years' imprisonment, remained in prison at the end of the year. Dr Pham Hong Son and Nguyen Khac Toan were released from prison under amnesties into a three-year period of "probation", including interrogations, severe restrictions on freedom of movement, association and expression.

Central Highlands/Montagnards
Human rights violations against ethnic minority Montagnards in the Central Highlands continued. These included restrictions on movement and forcing Christians belonging to unauthorized house churches to renounce their religion. Reports of arrests and ill-treatment continued. More than 250 Montagnards sentenced to lengthy prison terms in connection with the 2001 and 2004 protests around land ownership and religious freedom remained imprisoned.

In April, two Montagnard students were reportedly arrested and detained for 18 days in a district prison in Dak Lak province, where they were interrogated and beaten by police. The two were accused of sending lists of political prisoners abroad via the Internet.

Small groups of Montagnards attempted to seek asylum in neighbouring Cambodia, where their situation was precarious. The Memorandum of Understanding (MOU) between Viet Nam, Cambodia and the UN refugee agency UNHCR, signed in January 2005 to resolve the situation of asylum-seekers, remained in place. It appeared to have been violated by the Vietnamese authorities, with reports that in some cases people who had returned from Cambodia to Viet Nam under the MOU were detained, interrogated and ill-treated.

◻ In June, six members of the E De and M'nong ethnic groups were sentenced to between three and seven years' imprisonment on charges of violating "national unity policies" and organizing illegal migration. They were accused of inciting people to public unrest and assisting others to flee to Cambodia.

Death penalty

In February the Ministry of Public Security proposed limiting the scope of the death penalty. A proposal submitted for consideration to the central judicial reform commission recommended that economic crimes such as fraud and embezzlement, smuggling, counterfeiting and bribery should no longer be capital offences. It was reported that this would reduce the number of capital offences from 29 to 20. Some discussion by legislators took place in the National Assembly. However, by the end of the year the proposal had not become law. At least five women and six men convicted of economic crimes were believed to remain on death row.

According to media monitoring at least 36 death sentences were imposed and 14 executions carried out, including five women, the majority for drug trafficking offences. The true number is believed to be much higher. Classification of statistics on the death penalty as a "state secret" prevented full and transparent reporting.

◻ Phung Long That, the former head of the anti-smuggling investigating division of Ho Chi Minh City customs department, was executed by firing squad in March. He had been sentenced to death in April 1999 after being convicted of accepting bribes and smuggling goods worth US$70 million.

AI country reports/ visits

Reports

- Socialist Republic of Viet Nam: Duong Quang Tri – Sentenced to death for fraud (AI Index: ASA 41/004/2006)
- Socialist Republic of Viet Nam: A tightening net – Web-based repression and censorship (AI Index: ASA 41/008/2006)

YEMEN

REPUBLIC OF YEMEN
Head of state: 'Ali 'Abdullah Saleh
Head of government: 'Abdul Qader Bajammal
Death penalty: retentionist
International Criminal Court: signed

Dozens of people arrested in previous years in the context of the "war on terror" remained in indefinite detention without trial. Two escaped prisoners were killed by the security forces in circumstances that suggested they may have been extrajudicially executed. Political prisoners were tried in special courts whose proceedings fell far short of international standards. Dozens of detainees were released in Sa'da Province, but hundreds were believed to be still detained at the end of the year. Death sentences continued to be imposed and at least 30 people were reported to have been executed.

Background

Presidential and local elections in September were accompanied by sporadic clashes between rival party supporters, some arrests and the blocking of at least two independent websites by the government. However, the elections were assessed as generally "open and genuine" by a European Union observer mission. President 'Ali 'Abdullah Saleh was re-elected with a large majority. Before the election, women's groups rallied in the capital Sana'a to call for more women candidates in the local elections, in which women comprised only 2 per cent of candidates.

Unrest in Sa'da Province

Dozens of members of the Zaidi community and followers of Hussain Badr al-Din al-Huthi, a Zaidi cleric killed in 2004, were released following negotiations between members of the Zaidi community and the government. Some had been detained after violent clashes between Zaidis and government security forces in previous years in Sa'da Province. Despite a ceasefire and presidential amnesty in September 2005, there was further violence early in 2006 in which dozens of people were reported to have been killed. However, few details emerged and a government clampdown prevented access to the region by the media and independent observers.

The trial of the so-called Sana'a cell – 37 members of the Zaidi community alleged to belong to the Faithful Youth organization and charged with causing explosions and plotting to kill military and political leaders – concluded in November. One defendant, Ibrahim Sharaf al-Din, was sentenced to death, 34 others received prison terms of up to eight years, and two were acquitted. Both the prosecution and defence reportedly lodged appeals.

'War on terror'

Dozens of people continued to be detained without charge or trial as suspects in the "war on terror". They were denied access to lawyers and had no recourse to the courts to challenge the legality of their detention.

The authorities divulged no information about the legal status or whereabouts of Hadi Saleh Bawazir, who was reportedly detained by Political Security officers in early 2005 when he sought to travel to Iraq.

▭ Five foreign nationals reportedly studying in Yemen were arrested on 15 October in connection with an alleged plot to smuggle arms into Somalia. They were held at the Political Security prison in Sana'a where they were denied access to their families but given some access to consular officials. On 16 December, 'Abdullah Mustafa bin 'Abdul Rahim Aiob and his brother, Mohammed Illias bin 'Abdul Rahim Aiob, and Marek Samouslki, all Australian nationals, as well as Rasheed Shams Laskar, a UK national, and Kinith Sorenson, a Danish national, were released without charge. The men, along with their families, were said to have been told to leave the country. The Aiob brothers had been released on 2 December but were rearrested on 13 December.

Salah Addin al-Salimi, a Yemeni national captured by US forces in Afghanistan in 2002, was one of three detainees who died in detention at Guantánamo Bay, Cuba, in June. The US authorities said the three had committed suicide (see United States of America entry).

Releases

▭ In March, the authorities released Muhammad Faraj Ahmed Bashmilah, Salah Nasser Salim 'Ali Qaru and Muhammad Abdullah Salah al-Assad, all of whom had been detained since they were returned to Yemen in May 2005 after they had been imprisoned for at least 18 months at undisclosed locations abroad by or at the behest of US authorities. In February, they were tried and convicted on forgery charges but released on account of the time they had already spent in prison.

▭ Two former Guantánamo inmates who had been detained since they were returned to Yemen were released. Walid Muhammad Shahir Muhammad al-Qadasi, returned in April 2004, was released without charge in March. Karama Khamis Khamisan, returned in August 2005, was tried and acquitted of drug trafficking charges in March and released in May.

▭ Zaidi clerics Yahia al-Dailami and Mohamed Miftah, both outspoken critics of the US-led invasion of Iraq, were released in May apparently after receiving presidential pardons. The former had been sentenced to death after an unfair trial in 2005, the sentence later being commuted by the President to a prison term. The latter had been serving an eight-year prison term. Both were prisoners of conscience. Muhammad 'Ali Luqman, a Zaidi judge serving a 10-year prison sentence, was also pardoned by the President and released in May.

Use of lethal force

Fawaz Yahya al-Rabi'ee and Mohamed Dailami, who escaped in February from the Political Security prison in Sana'a together with 21 other suspected members of al-Qa'ida, were killed on 1 October when Yemeni security forces reportedly fired from a helicopter gunship at two locations in which the men were hiding. It appeared that the security forces made little or no effort to apprehend the two men or to offer them an opportunity to surrender.

Special Criminal Court on Terrorism

The Special Criminal Court on Terrorism continued to be used to try terrorism-related cases despite concerns that it failed to meet international fair trial standards. Defendants were often held incommunicado in extended pre-trial detention before being charged and brought to trial. The court failed adequately to investigate defendants' torture allegations and convicted defendants on the basis of contested confessions. Defendants' rights to legal counsel were also severely constrained – they were denied access to lawyers while detained incommunicado for interrogation, and defence lawyers were reportedly denied access to case files. The authorities said that the court's proceedings were open, but defendants' relatives reported that they were prevented from attending hearings.

Prisoners of conscience

A leading human rights activist was detained as were relatives of people being sought by the authorities.

▭ 'Ali al-Dailami, executive director of the non-governmental Yemeni Organization for the Defence of Democratic Rights and Freedoms, was arrested at Sana'a airport on 9 October as he was about to travel abroad. He was detained at the Political Security prison, where he was held in solitary confinement, until 5 November. His detention was believed to be connected to his human rights work, including on behalf of his brother Yahia al-Dailami (see above).

▭ Mohammed al-Kazami, aged 15, was reportedly arrested in February and detained without charge or trial at the Political Security prison in Abyan, apparently with the aim of inducing one of his relatives to surrender to the authorities.

▭ Saddam Hussein Abu Saba'ah, Naif Abdulah Abu Saba'ah and Naji Abu Saba'ah were reportedly arrested in Sana'a on 15 July near to the US Embassy, where they apparently planned to seek asylum. In September, they were charged with "harming the reputation of Yemen" and "insulting the President".

▭ Ibrahim al-Saiani, aged 14, was released without charge in March. He had been held since May 2005 when security forces stormed his family home in Sana'a, apparently seeking one of his relatives. While in detention, his health gave serious cause for concern.

Freedom of expression curtailed

In February, three newspapers – the *Yemen Observer*, *al-Hurriya* and *al-Ray Al'am* – were suspended for allegedly publishing images offensive to Islam. The suspension order was overturned in May by the Prime Minister. However, the papers' editors-in-chief – respectively Muhammad al-Asadi, Akram Sabra and Kamal al-Olofi – were detained and reportedly charged with insulting the Prophet Muhammad in connection with their publication of Danish cartoons. They were tried before the Court of Publications and Press. All three denied the charges and said that they had reproduced only small, censored versions of the cartoons in the context of articles devoted to praising the Prophet. In December, Kamal al-Olofi was sentenced to one year's imprisonment suspended and Muhammad al-Asadi was fined. In December, Akram Sabra' was sentenced to a four-month suspended prison sentence and banned from writing for a month. Both the defence and prosecution appealed against the sentence.

Death penalty
The authorities did not make public the number of people who were executed, but there were unconfirmed reports of at least 30 executions and several hundred prisoners were believed to be held under sentence of death. Although Article 31 of the Penal Code, Law 12 of 1994, provides that no one under the age of 18 may be sentenced to death, in February the Supreme Court upheld the death sentence of Adil Muhammad Saif al-Ma'amari, who was convicted in 2002 of a murder committed when he was 16. He was reported to have confessed under torture.

▭ Ismail Lutef Huraish, who is deaf and had not had the assistance of a sign language interpreter since he was arrested in October 1998 in Taiz, and his cousin Ali Mussara'a Muhammad Huraish, both of whom were convicted of murder, remained under imminent threat of execution at the end of the year.

▭ Amina Ali Abdulatif was 16 when sentenced to death for the murder of her husband. Her execution, scheduled for May 2005, was stayed pending a review of her case by a committee appointed by the Attorney General. The committee's findings had not been disclosed by the end of the year. A co-defendant, Muhammad 'Ali Said Qaba'il, was also sentenced to death and remained on death row.

▭ Fatima Hussein al-Badi and her brother, Abdullah Hussein al-Badi, were sentenced to death in February 2001 for the murder of her husband. Their death sentences were confirmed by the Court of Appeal but the Supreme Court then commuted Fatima Hussein al-Badi's sentence to a four-year prison term before reinstating the death penalty. Her brother was executed in May 2005. She appealed to the President to commute her sentence on the basis that her trial was unfair.

In at least one case, a prisoner under sentence of death was released after family members of a murder victim accepted *diya* (financial compensation). Hammoud Murshid Hassan Ahmad, a former army officer who had been held since 1994, was freed in February.

Update: 2005 killings of refugees
No investigation was known to have been held into the actions of Yemeni security forces who violently dispersed a number of refugees and asylum-seekers taking part in a sit-in protest outside the Sana'a offices of UNHCR, the UN refugee agency, in December 2005. Seven people were killed and others sustained serious injuries.

AI country reports/visits
Report
· Terror and counter-terror: Defending our human rights (AI Index: ACT 40/009/2006)
Visits
AI delegates visited Yemen in March and June.

ZAMBIA

REPUBLIC OF ZAMBIA
Head of state and government: Levy Mwanawasa
Death penalty: retentionist
International Criminal Court: ratified

There was a marked increase in the number of civilian deaths as a result of police shootings. New legislation constrained the media's ability to report on elections in September. Violent attacks on women remained common. No death sentences were carried out.

Background
Incumbent President Levy Mwanawasa delayed the constitutional review process until 2007. This ensured that proposals for the reduction of presidential powers, greater freedom of expression, and electoral reform, did not come into play before general elections held in September 2006. The election campaign was largely peaceful.

President Mwanawasa and his ruling Movement for Multi-Party Democracy party won the presidential and the parliamentary election. Urban frustration at the poor performance of Michael Sata, widely expected to win the presidential race, resulted in violent clashes in Lusaka and on the Copperbelt. Over 100 people were formally arrested and charged with riotous behaviour.

The corruption case against former President Frederick Chiluba remained unresolved. After winning the election, President Mwanawasa signalled his intention to complete the case during his second term of office. In November, Samuel Musonda, a former director of the bank alleged to have been fraudulently used by Frederick Chiluba, was sentenced to two years' imprisonment with hard labour.

Freedom of expression and the media
In general 2006 saw less harassment of the media by the government than 2005, although the press remained subject to censorship, especially around election time. In July, ahead of the elections, a new electoral act was passed which prohibited the reporting

of "speculative analysis, unsourced opinion polls, and predictions of the result before the official announcement."

The government resisted pressure to pass the Freedom of Information Bill, which would compel public officials to release certain types of government information.

☐ In February, the government decided not to prosecute Fred M'membe, editor of the independent newspaper *The Post*. He had been charged with insulting the President in November 2005.

☐ In March, two journalists working for Radio Chikuni in the Southern Province were arrested and charged with publishing false news with intent to cause fear and alarm to the public. They were detained overnight and then provisionally released. The charge stemmed from a broadcast about a young boy found dead after going missing. The body was said to be mutilated, and local residents suspected that the boy was the victim of a ritual killing.

☐ In September, senior police officers visited the Lusaka-based Q-FM Radio and demanded that it cease its coverage of the elections which police claimed was "inciting the nation". The radio station had been carrying live broadcasts of press conferences, election results and post-election events.

☐ In November the government moved to restrict the activities of Michael Sata and his Patriotic Front party. On 22 November, President Mwanawasa instructed the police not to grant Michael Sata permission to hold post-election rallies, but the Solicitor-General, Sunday Nkonde, overruled the ban. In response, the President called on the Solicitor-General to resign. On 5 December, Michael Sata was arrested and charged with making a false declaration of his assets in August when being nominated for the presidential elections. The charge carried a minimum penalty of two years in jail.

Violence against women
A UN report released in November found that 49 per cent of Zambian women said they had been abused during their lives.

The death penalty
In November, the Supreme Court rejected a petition by two death row inmates which sought the abolition of capital punishment on the grounds that it contravened Christian values. There were 200 people on death row but there have been no executions since President Mwanawasa came to power.

Policing
There was a marked increase in the number of police shootings.

☐ In early September, two teenagers were shot dead by police in Lusaka's Ng'ombe compound. Following protests by local residents, the police officer involved in the shooting was arrested and was under investigation at the end of the year.

☐ In early October, one man was killed and another severely injured as police opened fire on a group of angry residents in Matero.

☐ In mid-November, three former street children were shot and wounded by police officers shooting into the air to disperse a crowd. The Acting Police Chief of Copperbelt Province condemned the shootings and announced an investigation.

In October the use of firearms on general duty patrols was prohibited, and plans were announced to retrain police officers in crowd management techniques.

ZIMBABWE

REPUBLIC OF ZIMBABWE
Head of state and government: Robert Mugabe
Death penalty: retentionist
International Criminal Court: signed

The human rights situation continued to deteriorate, in a context of escalating poverty. Freedom of expression, assembly and association continued to be curtailed. Hundreds of people were arrested for participating or attempting to engage in peaceful protest. Police were accused of torturing human rights defenders in custody. The situation of thousands of people whose homes were destroyed as part of Operation Murambatsvina (Restore Order) in 2005 continued to worsen, with no effective solution planned by the authorities. The government continued to obstruct humanitarian efforts by the UN and by local and international non-governmental organizations.

Background
In January the African Commission on Human and Peoples' Rights (African Commission) submitted to the Executive Council of the African Union a critical resolution on the human rights situation in Zimbabwe that it had passed in late 2005. In its response, the government of Zimbabwe asked the African Commission to revoke the resolution, arguing that procedures had not been followed. The government's arguments were entirely procedural, and did not address the serious human rights concerns raised. The government had repeatedly failed to implement the recommendations contained in the 2002 report of the African Commission's Fact Finding Mission and the 2005 report by the UN Secretary General's Special Envoy on Human Settlement Issues in Zimbabwe.

In August the Reserve Bank of Zimbabwe introduced new banknotes to replace the old ones, reducing their face value by a factor of 1,000. For example, a Z$20,000 note was replaced by a Z$20 note. People were given 21 days to exchange their old notes before they stopped being legal tender, but a limit of Z$100 million (US$400) was imposed on the amount of cash people could carry. Nationwide roadblocks were established to enforce the programme, known as Project Sunrise. Human rights abuses were reported at roadblocks manned by police officers, Reserve Bank officials and in some cases members of the pro-government youth militia. People were reportedly assaulted and subjected to degrading and inhuman treatment, including being forced to remove clothing during searches. Police at some roadblocks confiscated money, even when the victims had less than the stipulated maximum.

By the end of the year inflation was running at more than 1,000 per cent.

Right to adequate housing
Operation Garikai/Hlalani Kuhle (Better Life), a house-building programme launched in 2005 ostensibly to provide housing to victims of mass forced evictions, failed to provide a remedy for the majority of them.

By May, one year after the programme's launch, only 3,325 houses had been built, compared to 92,460 housing structures destroyed in Operation Murambatsvina. Construction in many areas appeared to have stopped. Many of the houses designated as "built" were unfinished, without access to water or sewage facilities, and uninhabited.

Moreover, the new houses were largely inaccessible to the hundreds of thousands of victims of the forced evictions. They were too expensive for the majority to afford, even if they were offered the chance to purchase them, which frequently they were not. The process for allocating the new — albeit largely incomplete — houses and bare residential plots lacked transparency. Houses and land plots were allocated to people who had not lost their homes during Operation Murambatsvina and at least 20 per cent of the houses built were earmarked for civil servants, police and soldiers.

Despite the government's repeated claims that Operation Garikai/Hlalani Kuhle was a programme under which houses would be built by government for victims of mass evictions, in reality people were allocated small bare plots of land, without access to adequate water or sanitation, on which they had to build their own homes with no assistance.

The government continued to forcibly evict groups of people, often from the place where they had moved after their homes were demolished during Operation Murambatsvina. These forced evictions were traumatic for victims and resulted in further loss of possessions. At least three small-scale evictions were reported in Harare alone.

⌂ In April and May the police threatened to forcibly acquire 200 plots of land at Hatcliffe Extension New Stands settlement just outside Harare to extend a nearby police boarding school. Fifteen families would be affected. After protests by AI and the Zimbabwe Lawyers for Human Rights, the authorities reversed the decision.

⌂ On 15 June municipal police forcibly evicted a group of approximately 150 internally displaced households who were living in makeshift shacks along the Mukuvisi river in Harare. The group had been living there since the brick cottages they had been renting were destroyed a year before. The police pulled down their structures with crowbars and set them alight. They told the people they had to move, but provided no alternative accommodation.

Obstruction of humanitarian aid
The government continued to hinder and frustrate humanitarian efforts to provide emergency shelter. After repeated rejections of UN temporary shelter solutions during 2005, in March the UN was finally given permission to erect some temporary shelters. By the end of 2006 approximately 2,300 shelters had been erected. This compared with a UN target for the provision of emergency shelter, based on need, of 40,000 households in August 2005, reduced to a target of 23,000 households in 2006.

The right to food
Despite a somewhat better harvest, millions of people continued to experience serious food insecurity. Inflation continued to place basic food items beyond the reach of many poor people. According to the UN World Food Programme (WFP), maize prices increased by 25 per cent between September and October. The WFP's limited emergency feeding programme for vulnerable groups experienced shortages of cereals and pulses, resulting in just 331,000 people being assisted against a planned 800,000 people for October.

Freedom of association and assembly curtailed
The Public Order and Security Act (POSA) and the Miscellaneous Offences Act continued to be used selectively to prevent the political opposition and civil society groups from meeting or engaging in peaceful protest. Hundreds of human rights activists were arrested or detained under these laws during the year.

Freedom of expression
Repressive laws, including the Access to Information and Protection of Privacy Act and the Broadcasting Services Act, were used to curtail freedom of expression. In July the government introduced the Interception of Communications Bill in Parliament which if passed into law would further restrict freedom of expression. It would allow the authorities to intercept both telecommunications and mail, and raised fears that the government would use it to spy on the activities of human rights organizations and the political opposition.

⌂ The trial of trustees and staff of Voice of the People, an independent radio station that broadcast from outside Zimbabwe but maintained offices in the country, started on 25 September. The state withdrew charges against the individuals and was to charge the Voice of the People Trust under the Broadcasting Services Act for broadcasting without a licence.

Human rights defenders

Human rights defenders came under sustained attack by the authorities and the police. Repressive legislation continued to be used to obstruct their work, and hundreds were subjected to arbitrary arrest, torture, ill-treatment and harassment.

⌐ In the early hours of 18 January, two police officers and a soldier arrived at the Mutare home of prominent human rights lawyer Arnold Tsunga, demanding to see him. When they were told that he was not there, they detained his domestic staff. The workers were later released without charge after Zimbabwe Lawyers for Human Rights, of which Arnold Tsunga is Executive Director, intervened. On 21 January, police visited his house in the capital, Harare, apparently to arrest him as a Voice of the People trustee. Arnold Tsunga was not there, and police arrested a driver and a caretaker, allegedly for obstructing investigations when they said they did not know where he was. On 26 January, Arnold Tsunga received a credible warning that the Zimbabwe Military Intelligence Corps had been ordered to kill him.

⌐ On 11 September, over 100 members of the activist group Women of Zimbabwe Arise (WOZA) were arrested ahead of a planned peaceful sit-in at Town House in Harare to protest against deteriorating services. Among those arrested and detained were five mothers with babies and a pregnant woman, who reportedly went into labour while in police custody. Many were detained in deplorable conditions for longer than the 48 hours allowed in law, and were held until 14 and 15 September. The women were charged with "participating in a public gathering with the intent to cause public disorder, breach of peace or bigotry." They were acquitted on 23 October.

⌐ On 13 September police arrested Lovemore Matombo, President of the Zimbabwe Congress of Trade Unions (ZCTU), Wellington Chibebe, the ZCTU Secretary General, Lucia Matibenga , ZCTU First Vice-President, and 12 other activists from the ZCTU and the Movement for Democratic Change, the main opposition party. They had been attempting to undertake a peaceful protest about deteriorating social and economic conditions in Zimbabwe. All 15 were reportedly tortured in custody at Matapi police station on 13 September. They were transferred to Harare Central Police Station on 14 September and released. Medical reports confirmed that they had injuries consistent with beatings with blunt objects, heavy enough to cause fractures to hands and arms, and severe multiple soft tissue injuries to the backs of the head, shoulders, arms, buttocks and thighs. The doctors also stated that eight of the activists had injuries consistent with the torture method called *falanga* (beatings on the soles of the feet), which can cause permanent problems with walking. The beatings were so severe that Lucia Matibenga had one of her ear drums perforated as a result.

Scores of ZCTU members were also arrested and detained in Harare, Beitbridge, Bulawayo, Mutare and other urban centres. On the eve of the protests, on 12 September, in an apparent pre-emptive action, police had also reportedly arrested a number of ZCTU leaders at their homes and offices in Rusape, Gweru, Chinhoyi and Kariba.

Domestic Violence Bill

The Domestic Violence Bill was passed by the House of Assembly (lower chamber of Zimbabwe's Parliament) in November and awaited transmission to the Senate. If the bill became law it would outlaw harmful cultural practices including pledging of women or girls for the purposes of appeasing spirits, female genital mutilation, forced wife inheritance, and forced virginity testing. A council mandated to deal with domestic violence issues would be established and it would be mandatory for all police stations to establish a section to deal with cases of domestic violence.

Human rights commission

In September the government embarked on a consultation process for the establishment of a human rights commission. The process was facilitated by the United Nations Development Programme. The government's proposal to establish a human rights commission was widely seen as yet another move by the government to divert attention from the serious human rights crisis unfolding in the country.

AI country reports/ visits

Reports
- Zimbabwe: No justice for the victims of forced evictions (AI Index: AFR 46/005/2006)
- Zimbabwe: Quantifying destruction – satellite images of forced evictions (AI Index: AFR 46/014/2006)
- Zimbabwe: Shattered lives – the case of Porta Farm (AI Index: AFR 46/004/2006)

Visit
AI delegates visited Zimbabwe in April/May.

Former child soldiers in the Democratic Republic of the Congo burn their uniforms to mark the end of their time in the military.   © AI

AMNESTY INTERNATIONAL
REPORT 2007
PART 3

Alaudin Sadykov, a schoolteacher whose ear was severed while he was tortured by federal forces in Grozny in 2000, honours murdered journalist Anna Politkovskaya, Chechnya, Russian Federation. © Kazbek Vakhayev/AP/Empics

SELECTED INTERNATIONAL AND REGIONAL HUMAN RIGHTS TREATIES

(AT 31 DECEMBER 2006)

SELECTED INTERNATIONAL HUMAN RIGHTS TREATIES
PAGES 294 – 305

SELECTED REGIONAL HUMAN RIGHTS TREATIES
PAGES 306 – 310

States which have ratified or acceded to a convention are party to the treaty and are bound to observe its provisions. States which have signed but not yet ratified have expressed their intention to become a party at some future date; meanwhile they are obliged to refrain from acts which would defeat the object and purpose of the treaty.

	International Covenant on Civil and Political Rights (ICCPR)	(first) Optional Protocol to the ICCPR	Second Optional Protocol to the ICCPR, aiming at the abolition of the death penalty	International Covenant on Economic, Social and Cultural Rights	Convention on the Elimination of All Forms of Discrimination against Women (CEDAW)	Optional Protocol to CEDAW	Convention on the Rights of the Child (CRC)	Optional Protocol to the CRC on the involvement of children in armed conflict	International Convention on the Elimination of All Forms of Racial Discrimination	Convention against Torture and Other Cruel, Inhuman or Degrading Treatment or Punishment
Afghanistan	●			●	●		●	●	●	●28
Albania	●			●	●	●	●		●	●
Algeria	●	●		●	●		●		●	●22
Andorra	◐	◐	◐		●	●	●	●	◐	◐22
Angola	●			●	●		●			
Antigua and Barbuda					●	◐	●		●	●
Argentina	●	●	○	●	●	○	●	●	●	●22
Armenia	●	●		●	●	◐	●	●	●	●
Australia	●	●	●	●	●		●	◐	●	●22
Austria	●	●	●	●	●	●	●	●	●	●22
Azerbaijan	●	●	●	●	●	●	●	●	●	●22
Bahamas					●		●		●	
Bahrain	◐				●		●	●	●	●
Bangladesh	●			●	●	●10	●	●	●	●
Barbados	●	●		●	●		●		●	
Belarus	●	●		●	●	●	●	◐	●	●
Belgium	●	●	●	●	●	●	●	●	●	●22
Belize	●			○	●	●10	●	●	●	●
Benin	●	●		●	●	○	●	●	●	●
Bhutan					●		●	○	○	
Bolivia	●	●		●	●	●	●	●	●	●22
Bosnia and Herzegovina	●	●	●	●	●	●	●	●	●	●22
Botswana	●				●		●		●	●
Brazil	●			●	●	●	●	●	●	●22
Brunei Darussalam					◐		●			
Bulgaria	●	●	●	●	●	◐	●	●	●	●22
Burkina Faso	●	●		●	●	●	●	○	●	●
Burundi	●			●	●	○	●	○	●	●22
Cambodia	●	○		●	●	○	●	●	●	●
Cameroon	●	●		●	●	◐	●	○	●	●22
Canada	●	●	●	●	●	●	●	●	●	●22
Cape Verde	●	●	●	●	●		●	●	●	●
Central African Republic	●	●		●	●		●		●	
Chad	●	●		●	●		●	●	●	●
Chile	●	●	○	●	●	○	●	●	●	●22
China	○			●	●		●	○	●	●28

Optional Protocol to the Convention against Torture	Convention relating to the Status of Refugees (1951)	Protocol relating to the Status of Refugees (1967)	Convention relating to the Status of Stateless Persons (1954)	Convention on the Reduction of Statelessness (1961)	International Convention on the Protection of the Rights of All Migrant Workers and Members of their Families	Rome Statute of the International Criminal Court	
	●	●				●	Afghanistan
●	●	●	●	●		●	Albania
	●	●	●		●	○	Algeria
						●	Andorra
	●	●				○	Angola
	●	●	●			●	Antigua and Barbuda
●	●	●	●		○	●	Argentina
◐	●	●	●	●		○	Armenia
	●	●	●			●	Australia
○	●	●		●		●	Austria
○	●	●	●	●	●		Azerbaijan
	●	●				○	Bahamas
						○	Bahrain
					○	○	Bangladesh
			●			●	Barbados
	●	●					Belarus
○	●	●	●			●	Belgium
	●	●	◐		●	●	Belize
◐	●	●			○	●	Benin
							Bhutan
◐	●	●	●	●	●	●	Bolivia
	●	●	●	●	●	●	Bosnia and Herzegovina
	●	●	●			●	Botswana
○	●	●	●			●	Brazil
							Brunei Darussalam
	●	●				●	Bulgaria
○	●	●			●	●	Burkina Faso
	●	●				●	Burundi
○	●	●			○	●	Cambodia
	●	●				○	Cameroon
	●	●		●		●	Canada
		●			●	○	Cape Verde
	●	●				●	Central African Republic
	●	●	●	●		◐	Chad
○	●	●			●	○	Chile
	●	●					China

● state is a party
◐ state became party in 2006
○ signed but not yet ratified
○ signed in 2006, but not yet ratified

10 Declaration under Article 10 not recognizing the competence of the CEDAW Committee to undertake confidential inquiries into allegations of grave or systematic violations

22 Declaration under Article 22 recognizing the competence of the Committee against Torture (CAT) to consider individual complaints

28 Reservation under Article 28 not recognizing the competence of the CAT to undertake confidential inquiries into allegations of systematic torture if warranted

12 Declaration under Article 12(3) accepting the jurisdiction of the International Criminal Court (ICC) for crimes in its territory

124 Declaration under Article 124 not accepting the jurisdiction of the ICC over war crimes for seven years after ratification

* Signed the Rome Statute but have since formally declared their intention not to ratify

	International Covenant on Civil and Political Rights (ICCPR)	(first) Optional Protocol to the ICCPR	Second Optional Protocol to the ICCPR, aiming at the abolition of the death penalty	International Covenant on Economic, Social and Cultural Rights	Convention on the Elimination of All Forms of Discrimination against Women (CEDAW)	Optional Protocol to CEDAW	Convention on the Rights of the Child (CRC)	Optional Protocol to the CRC on the involvement of children in armed conflict	International Convention on the Elimination of All Forms of Racial Discrimination	Convention against Torture and Other Cruel, Inhuman or Degrading Treatment or Punishment
Colombia	●	●	●	●	●	○	●	●	●	●
Comoros				●	●		●		●	○
Congo, Republic of	●	●		●	●		●		●	●
Cook Islands					●		●			
Costa Rica	●	●	●	●	●	●	●	●	●	●22
Côte d'Ivoire	●	●		●	●		●		●	
Croatia	●	●	●	●	●	●	●	●	●	●22
Cuba				●	●	○	●	○	●	●28
Cyprus	●	●	●	●	●	●	●		●	●22
Czech Republic	●	●	●	●	●	●	●	●	●	●22
Democratic Republic of the Congo	●	●		●	●		●		●	●
Denmark	●	●	●	●	●	●	●	●	●	●22
Djibouti	●	●	●	●	●		●	○	○	●
Dominica	●			●	●		●			
Dominican Republic	●	●		●	●	●	●	○	●	○
Ecuador	●	●	●	●	●	●	●	●	●	●22
Egypt	●			●	●		●		●	●
El Salvador	●	●		●	●	○	●	●	●	●
Equatorial Guinea	●	●		●	●		●		●	●28
Eritrea	●			●	●		●	●	●	
Estonia	●	●	●	●	●		●	○	●	●
Ethiopia	●			●	●		●		●	●
Fiji					●		●	○	●	
Finland	●	●	●	●	●	●	●	●	●	●22
France	●	●	●	●	●	●	●	●	●	●22
Gabon	●			●	●	●	●	○	●	●
Gambia	●	●		●	●		●	○	●	○
Georgia	●	●	●	●	●	●	●		●	●22
Germany	●	●	●	●	●	●	●	●	●	●22
Ghana	●	●		●	●	○	●	○	●	●22
Greece	●	●	●	●	●	●	●	●	●	●22
Grenada	●			●	●		●		○	
Guatemala	●	●		●	●	●	●	●	●	●22
Guinea	●	●		●	●		●		●	●
Guinea-Bissau	○	○	○	●	●	○	●	○	○	○
Guyana	●	●		●	●		●		●	●

Optional Protocol to the Convention against Torture	Convention relating to the Status of Refugees (1951)	Protocol relating to the Status of Refugees (1967)	Convention relating to the Status of Stateless Persons (1954)	Convention on the Reduction of Statelessness (1961)	International Convention on the Protection of the Rights of All Migrant Workers and Members of their Families	Rome Statute of the International Criminal Court	
	●	●	○		●	●124	Colombia
					○	●	Comoros
	●	●				●	Congo, Republic of
							Cook Islands
●	●	●	●	●		●	Costa Rica
	●	●				○12	Côte d'Ivoire
●	●	●	●			●	Croatia
							Cuba
○	●	●				●	Cyprus
●	●	●	●	●		○	Czech Republic
	●	●				●	Democratic Republic of the Congo
●	●	●	●	●		●	Denmark
	●	●				●	Djibouti
	●	●				●	Dominica
	●	●		○		●	Dominican Republic
	●	●	●		●	●	Ecuador
	●	●			●	○	Egypt
	●	●	○		●		El Salvador
	●	●					Equatorial Guinea
						○	Eritrea
●	●	●				●	Estonia
	●	●					Ethiopia
	●	●	●			●	Fiji
○	●	●	●			●	Finland
○	●	●	●	○		●124	France
○	●	●			○	●	Gabon
	●	●				●	Gambia
●	●	●				●	Georgia
○	●	●	●	●		●	Germany
○	●	●			●	●	Ghana
	●	●	●			●	Greece
							Grenada
○	●	●	●	●	●		Guatemala
○	●	●	●		●	●	Guinea
	●	●			○	○	Guinea-Bissau
					○	●	Guyana

● state is a party

● state became party in 2006

○ signed but not yet ratified

○ signed in 2006, but not yet ratified

10 Declaration under Article 10 not recognizing the competence of the CEDAW Committee to undertake confidential inquiries into allegations of grave or systematic violations

22 Declaration under Article 22 recognizing the competence of the Committee against Torture (CAT) to consider individual complaints

28 Reservation under Article 28 not recognizing the competence of the CAT to undertake confidential inquiries into allegations of systematic torture if warranted

12 Declaration under Article 12(3) accepting the jurisdiction of the International Criminal Court (ICC) for crimes in its territory

124 Declaration under Article 124 not accepting the jurisdiction of the ICC over war crimes for seven years after ratification

* Signed the Rome Statute but have since formally declared their intention not to ratify

	International Covenant on Civil and Political Rights (ICCPR)	(first) Optional Protocol to the ICCPR	Second Optional Protocol to the ICCPR, aiming at the abolition of the death penalty	International Covenant on Economic, Social and Cultural Rights	Convention on the Elimination of All Forms of Discrimination against Women (CEDAW)	Optional Protocol to CEDAW	Convention on the Rights of the Child (CRC)	Optional Protocol to the CRC on the involvement of children in armed conflict	International Convention on the Elimination of All Forms of Racial Discrimination	Convention against Torture and Other Cruel, Inhuman or Degrading Treatment or Punishment
Haiti	●				●		●	○	●	
Holy See							●	●	●	●
Honduras	●	●	○	●	●		●	●	●	●
Hungary	●	●	●	●	●	●	●	○	●	●22
Iceland	●	●	●	●	●	●	●		●	●22
India	●			●	●		●		●	○
Indonesia	●			●	●	○	●	○	●	●28
Iran	●			●			●		●	
Iraq	●			●	●		●		●	
Ireland	●	●	●	●	●	●	●	●	●	●22
Israel	●			●	●		●	●	●	●28
Italy	●	●	●	●	●	●	●	●	●	●22
Jamaica	●			●	●		●		●	
Japan	●			●	●		●		●	●
Jordan	●			●	●		●	○	●	●
Kazakstan	●			●	●	●	●	●	●	●
Kenya	●			●	●		●	●	●	●
Kiribati					●		●			
Korea (Democratic People's Republic of)	●			●	●		●			
Korea (Republic of)	●	●		●	●	●	●	●	●	●
Kuwait	●			●	●		●	●	●	●28
Kyrgyzstan	●	●		●	●	●	●	●	●	●
Laos	○			○	●		●	●	●	
Latvia	●	●		●	●		●	●	●	●
Lebanon	●			●	●		●	○	●	●
Lesotho	●	●		●	●	●	●	●	●	●
Liberia	●	○	●	●	●	○	●	○	●	●
Libya	●	●		●	●	●	●	●	●	●
Liechtenstein	●	●	●	●	●	●	●	●	●	●22
Lithuania	●	●	●	●	●	●	●	●	●	●
Luxembourg	●	●	●	●	●	●	●	●	●	●22
Macedonia	●	●	●	●	●	●	●	●	●	●
Madagascar	●	●		●	●	○	●	●	●	●
Malawi	●	●		●	●	○	●	○	●	●
Malaysia					●		●			
Maldives	●	●		●	●	●	●	●	●	●

Optional Protocol to the Convention against Torture	Convention relating to the Status of Refugees (1951)	Protocol relating to the Status of Refugees (1967)	Convention relating to the Status of Stateless Persons (1954)	Convention on the Reduction of Statelessness (1961)	International Convention on the Protection of the Rights of All Migrant Workers and Members of their Families	Rome Statute of the International Criminal Court	
	●	●				○	Haiti
	●	●	○				Holy See
●	●	●	○		●	●	Honduras
	●	●	●			●	Hungary
○	●	●				●	Iceland
							India
					○		Indonesia
	●	●				○	Iran
							Iraq
	●	●	●	●		●	Ireland
	●	●	●	○		○*	Israel
○	●	●	●			●	Italy
	●	●				○	Jamaica
	●	●					Japan
						●	Jordan
	●	●					Kazakstan
	●	●				●	Kenya
			●	●			Kiribati
							Korea (Democratic People's Republic of)
	●	●	●			●	Korea (Republic of)
						○	Kuwait
	●	●			●	○	Kyrgyzstan
							Laos
	●	●	●	●		●	Latvia
							Lebanon
	●	●	●	●	●	●	Lesotho
●	●	●	●	●	○	●	Liberia
			●	●	●		Libya
●	●	●	○			●	Liechtenstein
	●	●	●			●	Lithuania
○	●	●	●			●	Luxembourg
○	●	●	●			●	Macedonia
○	●		**			○	Madagascar
	●	●				●	Malawi
							Malaysia
●							Maldives

● state is a party

● state became party in 2006

○ signed but not yet ratified

○ signed in 2006, but not yet ratified

10 Declaration under Article 10 not recognizing the competence of the CEDAW Committee to undertake confidential inquiries into allegations of grave or systematic violations

22 Declaration under Article 22 recognizing the competence of the Committee against Torture (CAT) to consider individual complaints

28 Reservation under Article 28 not recognizing the competence of the CAT to undertake confidential inquiries into allegations of systematic torture if warranted

12 Declaration under Article 12(3) accepting the jurisdiction of the International Criminal Court (ICC) for crimes in its territory

124 Declaration under Article 124 not accepting the jurisdiction of the ICC over war crimes for seven years after ratification

* Signed the Rome Statute but have since formally declared their intention not to ratify

** Acceded in 1962 but in 1965 denounced the Convention; denunciation took effect on 2 April 1966

	International Covenant on Civil and Political Rights (ICCPR)	(first) Optional Protocol to the ICCPR	Second Optional Protocol to the ICCPR, aiming at the abolition of the death penalty	International Covenant on Economic, Social and Cultural Rights	Convention on the Elimination of All Forms of Discrimination against Women (CEDAW)	Optional Protocol to CEDAW	Convention on the Rights of the Child (CRC)	Optional Protocol to the CRC on the involvement of children in armed conflict	International Convention on the Elimination of All Forms of Racial Discrimination	Convention against Torture and Other Cruel, Inhuman or Degrading Treatment or Punishment
Mali	●	●		●	●	●	●	●	●	●
Malta	●	●	●	●	●		●	●	●	●22
Marshall Islands					●		●			
Mauritania	●			●	●		●		●	●28
Mauritius	●	●		●	●	○	●	○	●	●
Mexico	●	●		●	●	●	●	●	●	●22
Micronesia					●		●	○		
Moldova	●	○	●	●	●	●	●	●	●	●
Monaco	●		●	●	●		●	●	●	●22
Mongolia	●	●		●	●	●	●	●	●	●
Montenegro	●	●	●	●	●	●	●		●	●22
Morocco	●			●	●		●	●	●	●
Mozambique	●		●		●		●	●	●	●
Myanmar					●		●			
Namibia	●	●	●	●	●	●	●	●	●	●
Nauru	○	○					●	○	○	○
Nepal	●	●		●	●	○	●	○	●	●
Netherlands	●	●	●	●	●	●	●	○	●	●22
New Zealand	●	●	●	●	●	●	●	●	●	●22
Nicaragua	●	●	○	●	●		●	●	●	●
Niger	●	●		●	●	●	●		●	●
Nigeria	●			●	●	●	●	○	●	●
Niue							●			
Norway	●	●	●	●	●	●	●	●	●	●22
Oman					●		●	●	●	
Pakistan				○	●		●	○	●	
Palau							●			
Panama	●	●		●	●	●	●	●	●	●
Papua New Guinea					●		●		●	
Paraguay	●	●	●	●	●	●	●	●	●	●22
Peru	●	●		●	●	●	●	●	●	●22
Philippines	●	●	○	●	●	●	●	●	●	●
Poland	●	●	○	●	●	●	●	●	●	28●22
Portugal	●	●	●	●	●	●	●	●	●	●22
Qatar							●	●	●	●
Romania	●	●	●	●	●	●	●	●	●	●

Optional Protocol to the Convention against Torture	Convention relating to the Status of Refugees (1951)	Protocol relating to the Status of Refugees (1967)	Convention relating to the Status of Stateless Persons (1954)	Convention on the Reduction of Statelessness (1961)	International Convention on the Protection of the Rights of All Migrant Workers and Members of their Families	Rome Statute of the International Criminal Court	
●	●	●			●	●	Mali
●	●	●				●	Malta
						●	Marshall Islands
	●	●					Mauritania
●						●	Mauritius
●	●	●	●		●	●	Mexico
							Micronesia
●	●	●				○	Moldova
	●					○	Monaco
						●	Mongolia
●	●	●	●		○	●	Montenegro
	●	●			●	○	Morocco
	●	●				○	Mozambique
							Myanmar
	●	●				●	Namibia
						●	Nauru
							Nepal
○	●	●	●	●		●	Netherlands
○	●	●		●		●	New Zealand
	●	●			●		Nicaragua
	●	●		●		●	Niger
	●	●				●	Nigeria
							Niue
○	●	●	●	●		●	Norway
						○	Oman
							Pakistan
							Palau
	●	●				●	Panama
	●	●					Papua New Guinea
●	●	●			○	●	Paraguay
●	●	●			●	●	Peru
	●	●	○		●	○	Philippines
●	●	●				●	Poland
○	●	●				●	Portugal
							Qatar
○	●	●	●	●		●	Romania

● state is a party
● state became party in 2006
○ signed but not yet ratified
○ signed in 2006, but not yet ratified

10 Declaration under Article 10 not recognizing the competence of the CEDAW Committee to undertake confidential inquiries into allegations of grave or systematic violations

22 Declaration under Article 22 recognizing the competence of the Committee against Torture (CAT) to consider individual complaints

28 Reservation under Article 28 not recognizing the competence of the CAT to undertake confidential inquiries into allegations of systematic torture if warranted

12 Declaration under Article 12(3) accepting the jurisdiction of the International Criminal Court (ICC) for crimes in its territory

124 Declaration under Article 124 not accepting the jurisdiction of the ICC over war crimes for seven years after ratification

* Signed the Rome Statute but have since formally declared their intention not to ratify

	International Covenant on Civil and Political Rights (ICCPR)	(first) Optional Protocol to the ICCPR	Second Optional Protocol to the ICCPR, aiming at the abolition of the death penalty	International Covenant on Economic, Social and Cultural Rights	Convention on the Elimination of All Forms of Discrimination against Women (CEDAW)	Optional Protocol to CEDAW	Convention on the Rights of the Child (CRC)	Optional Protocol to the CRC on the involvement of children in armed conflict	International Convention on the Elimination of All Forms of Racial Discrimination	Convention against Torture and Other Cruel, Inhuman or Degrading Treatment or Punishment
Russian Federation	●	●		●	●	●	●	○	●	●22
Rwanda	●			●	●		●	●	●	
Saint Kitts and Nevis					●	◐	●		◐	
Saint Lucia					●		●		●	
Saint Vincent and the Grenadines	●	●		●	●		●		●	●
Samoa					●		●			
San Marino	●	●	●	●	●	●	●	○	●	◐
Sao Tome and Principe	○	○	○	○	●	○	●		○	○
Saudi Arabia					●		●		●	●28
Senegal	●	●		●	●	●	●	●	●	●22
Serbia	●	●	●	●	●	●	●	●	●	●22
Seychelles	●	●	●	●	●	○	●	○	●	●22
Sierra Leone	●	●		●	●	○	●	●	●	●
Singapore					●		●	○		
Slovakia	●	●	●	●	●	●	●	◐	●	●22
Slovenia	●	●	●	●	●	●	●	●	●	●22
Solomon Islands				●	●	●	●		●	
Somalia	●	●		●			○	○	●	●
South Africa	●	●	●	○	●	●	●	○	●	●22
Spain	●	●	●	●	●	●	●	●	●	●22
Sri Lanka	●	●		●	●	●	●	●	●	●
Sudan	●			●			●	●	●	○
Suriname	●	●		●	●		●	○	●	
Swaziland	●			●	●		●		●	●
Sweden	●	●	●	●	●	●	●	●	●	●22
Switzerland	●		●	●	●		●	●	●	●22
Syria	●			●	●		●	●	●	●28
Tajikistan	●	●		●	●	○	●	●	●	●
Tanzania	●			●	●	◐	●	●	●	
Thailand	●			●	●	●	●	◐	●	
Timor-Leste	●		●	●	●	●	●	●	●	●
Togo	●	●		●	●		●	●	●	●22
Tonga							●		●	
Trinidad and Tobago	●			●	●		●		●	
Tunisia	●			●	●		●	●	●	●22
Turkey	●	◐	◐	●	●	●	●	●	●	●22

Optional Protocol to the Convention against Torture	Convention relating to the Status of Refugees (1951)	Protocol relating to the Status of Refugees (1967)	Convention relating to the Status of Stateless Persons (1954)	Convention on the Reduction of Statelessness (1961)	International Convention on the Protection of the Rights of All Migrant Workers and Members of their Families	Rome Statute of the International Criminal Court	
	●	●				○	Russian Federation
	●	●	◐	◐			Rwanda
	●					◐	Saint Kitts and Nevis
						○	Saint Lucia
	●	●	●			●	Saint Vincent and the Grenadines
	●	●				●	Samoa
						●	San Marino
	●	●			○	○	Sao Tome and Principe
							Saudi Arabia
◐	●	●	●	●	●	●	Senegal
◐	●	●	●		○	●	Serbia
	●	●			●	○	Seychelles
○	●	●			○	●	Sierra Leone
							Singapore
	●	●	●	●		●	Slovakia
	●	●	●			●	Slovenia
	●	●				○	Solomon Islands
	●	●					Somalia
○	●	●				●	South Africa
◐	●	●	●			●	Spain
					●		Sri Lanka
	●	●				○	Sudan
	●	●					Suriname
	●	●	●	●			Swaziland
●	●	●	●	●		●	Sweden
○	●	●	●			●	Switzerland
					●	○	Syria
	●	●			●	●	Tajikistan
	●	●				●	Tanzania
						○	Thailand
○	●	●			●	●	Timor-Leste
○	●	●			○		Togo
							Tonga
	●	●	●			●	Trinidad and Tobago
	◐	●	●	●			Tunisia
○	●	●			●		Turkey

● state is a party

◐ state became party in 2006

○ signed but not yet ratified

◌ signed in 2006, but not yet ratified

[10] Declaration under Article 10 not recognizing the competence of the CEDAW Committee to undertake confidential inquiries into allegations of grave or systematic violations

[22] Declaration under Article 22 recognizing the competence of the Committee against Torture (CAT) to consider individual complaints

[28] Reservation under Article 28 not recognizing the competence of the CAT to undertake confidential inquiries into allegations of systematic torture if warranted

[12] Declaration under Article 12(3) accepting the jurisdiction of the International Criminal Court (ICC) for crimes in its territory

[124] Declaration under Article 124 not accepting the jurisdiction of the ICC over war crimes for seven years after ratification

[*] Signed the Rome Statute but have since formally declared their intention not to ratify

	International Covenant on Civil and Political Rights (ICCPR)	(first) Optional Protocol to the ICCPR	Second Optional Protocol to the ICCPR, aiming at the abolition of the death penalty	International Covenant on Economic, Social and Cultural Rights	Convention on the Elimination of All Forms of Discrimination against Women (CEDAW)	Optional Protocol to CEDAW	Convention on the Rights of the Child (CRC)	Optional Protocol to the CRC on the involvement of children in armed conflict	International Convention on the Elimination of All Forms of Racial Discrimination	Convention against Torture and Other Cruel, Inhuman or Degrading Treatment or Punishment
Turkmenistan	●	●	●	●	●		●	●	●	●
Tuvalu					●		●			
Uganda	●	●		●	●		●	●	●	●
Ukraine	●	●		●	●	●	●	●	●	●22
United Arab Emirates					●		●		●	
United Kingdom	●		●	●	●	●	●	●	●	●
United States of America	●			○	○		○	●	●	●
Uruguay	●	●	●	●	●	●	●	●	●	●22
Uzbekistan	●	●		●	●		●		●	●
Vanuatu					●		●	○		
Venezuela	●	●	●	●	●	●	●	●	●	●22
Viet Nam	●			●	●		●	●	●	
Yemen	●			●	●		●		●	●
Zambia	●	●		●	●		●		●	●
Zimbabwe	●			●	●		●		●	

Optional Protocol to the Convention against Torture	Convention relating to the Status of Refugees (1951)	Protocol relating to the Status of Refugees (1967)	Convention relating to the Status of Stateless Persons (1954)	Convention on the Reduction of Statelessness (1961)	International Convention on the Protection of the Rights of All Migrant Workers and Members of their Families	Rome Statute of the International Criminal Court	
	●	●					Turkmenistan
	●	●					Tuvalu
	●	●	●		●	●	Uganda
◐	●	●				○	Ukraine
						○	United Arab Emirates
●	●	●	●	●		●	United Kingdom
		●				○*	United States of America
●	●	●	●	●	●	●	Uruguay
						○	Uzbekistan
							Vanuatu
		●				●	Venezuela
							Viet Nam
	●	●				○	Yemen
	●	●	●			●	Zambia
	●	●	●			○	Zimbabwe

● state is a party
● state became party in 2006
○ signed but not yet ratified
○ signed in 2006, but not yet ratified

10 Declaration under Article 10 not recognizing the competence of the CEDAW Committee to undertake confidential inquiries into allegations of grave or systematic violations

22 Declaration under Article 22 recognizing the competence of the Committee against Torture (CAT) to consider individual complaints

28 Reservation under Article 28 not recognizing the competence of the CAT to undertake confidential inquiries into allegations of systematic torture if warranted

12 Declaration under Article 12(3) accepting the jurisdiction of the International Criminal Court (ICC) for crimes in its territory

124 Declaration under Article 124 not accepting the jurisdiction of the ICC over war crimes for seven years after ratification

* Signed the Rome Statute but have since formally declared their intention not to ratify

SELECTED REGIONAL HUMAN RIGHTS TREATIES
AFRICAN UNION

	African Charter on Human and Peoples' Rights (1981)	Protocol to the African Charter on the Establishment of an African Court on Human and Peoples' Rights (1998)	African Charter on the Rights and Welfare of the Child (1990)	Convention Governing the Specific Aspects of Refugee Problems in Africa (1969)	Protocol to the African Charter on Human and Peoples' Rights on the Rights of Women in Africa (2003)
Algeria	●	●	●	●	○
Angola	●		●	●	
Benin	●	○	●	●	●
Botswana	●	○	●	●	
Burkina Faso	●	●	●	●	● (became party 2006)
Burundi	●	●	●	●	○
Cameroon	●	○	●	●	○
Cape Verde	●		●	●	●
Central African Republic	●	○	○	●	
Chad	●	○	●	●	○
Comoros	●	●	●	●	●
Congo (Republic of)	●	○	● (became party 2006)	●	○
Côte d'Ivoire	●	●	○	●	○
Democratic Republic of the Congo	●	○		●	○
Djibouti	●	○	○	○	●
Egypt	●	○	●	●	
Equatorial Guinea	●	○	●	●	○
Eritrea	●		●		
Ethiopia	●	○	●	●	○
Gabon	●	●	○	●	○
Gambia	●	●	●	●	●
Ghana	●	●	●	●	○
Guinea	●	○	●	●	○
Guinea-Bissau	●	○	○	●	○
Kenya	●	●	●	●	○
Lesotho	●	●	●	●	●
Liberia	●	○	○	●	○
Libya	●	●	●	●	●
Madagascar	●	○	●	○	○
Malawi	●	○	●	●	●
Mali	●	●	●	●	●
Mauritania	●	●	●	●	●
Mauritius	●	●	●	○	○
Mozambique	●	●	●	●	●
Namibia	●	○	●		●
Niger	●	●	●	●	○

This chart lists countries that were members of the African Union at the end of 2006.

● state is a party
● state became party in 2006
○ signed but not yet ratified
○ signed in 2006, but not yet ratified

SELECTED REGIONAL HUMAN RIGHTS TREATIES
AFRICAN UNION

	African Charter on Human and Peoples' Rights (1981)	Protocol to the African Charter on the Establishment of an African Court on Human and Peoples' Rights (1998)	African Charter on the Rights and Welfare of the Child (1990)	Convention Governing the Specific Aspects of Refugee Problems in Africa (1969)	Protocol to the African Charter on Human and Peoples' Rights on the Rights of Women in Africa (2003)
Nigeria	●	●	●	●	●
Rwanda	●	●	●	●	●
Sahrawi Arab Democratic Republic	●		○		○
Sao Tome and Principe	●				
Senegal	●	●	●	●	●
Seychelles	●	○	●	●	◐
Sierra Leone	●	○	●	●	○
Somalia	●	○	○	○	○
South Africa	●	●	●	●	●
Sudan	●	○		●	
Swaziland	●	○	○	●	○
Tanzania	●	◐	●	●	○
Togo	●	●	●	●	●
Tunisia	●	○	○		
Uganda	●	●	●	●	○
Zambia	●	○	○	●	◐
Zimbabwe	●	○	●	●	○

This chart lists countries that were members of the African Union at the end of 2006.

- ● state is a party
- ◐ state became party in 2006
- ○ signed but not yet ratified
- ○ signed in 2006, but not yet ratified

SELECTED REGIONAL HUMAN RIGHTS TREATIES ORGANIZATION OF AMERICAN STATES

	American Convention on Human Rights (1969)	Protocol to the American Convention on Human Rights to Abolish the Death Penalty (1990)	Additional Protocol to the American Convention on Human Rights in the Area of Economic, Social and Cultural Rights	Inter-American Convention to Prevent and Punish Torture (1985)	Inter-American Convention on Forced Disappearance of Persons (1994)	Inter-American Convention on the Prevention, Punishment and Eradication of Violence Against Women (1994)	Inter-American Convention on the Elimination of All Forms of Discrimination against Persons with Disabilities (1999)
Antigua and Barbuda						●	
Argentina	●62	○	●	●	●	●	●
Bahamas						●	
Barbados	●62					●	
Belize						●	
Bolivia	●62		◐	◐	●	●	●
Brazil	●62	●	●	●	○	●	●
Canada							
Chile	●62	○	○	●	○	●	●
Colombia	●62		●	●	●	●	●
Costa Rica	●62	●	●	●	●	●	●
Cuba*							
Dominica	●					●	○
Dominican Republic	●62		○	●		●	○
Ecuador	●62	●	●	●	◐	●	●
El Salvador	●62		●	●		●	●
Grenada	●					●	
Guatemala	●62		●	●	●	●	●
Guyana						●	
Haiti	●62		○	○		●	○
Honduras	●62			○	●	●	
Jamaica	●					●	○
Mexico	●62		●	●	●	●	●
Nicaragua	●62	●	○	○	○	●	●
Panama	●62	●	●	●	●	●	●
Paraguay	●62	●	●	●	●	●	●
Peru	●62		●	●	●	●	●
Saint Kitts and Nevis						●	
Saint Lucia						●	
Saint Vincent and the Grenadines						●	
Suriname	●62		●	●		●	
Trinidad and Tobago						●	
United States of America	○						
Uruguay	●62	●	●	●	●	●	●
Venezuela	●62	●	○	●	●	●	◐

This chart lists countries that were members of the Organization of American States at the end of 2006.

● state is a party
◐ state became party in 2006
○ signed but not yet ratified
○ signed in 2006, but not yet ratified

62 Countries making a Declaration under Article 62 recognize as binding the jurisdiction of the Inter-American Court of Human Rights (on all matters relating to the interpretation or application of the American Convention)

* In 1962 the VIII Meeting of Consultation of Ministers of Foreign Affairs decided to exclude Cuba from participating in the Inter-American system.

SELECTED REGIONAL HUMAN RIGHTS TREATIES
COUNCIL OF EUROPE

	European Convention for the Protection of Human Rights and Fundamental Freedoms (ECHR) (1950)	Protocol No. 6 to the ECHR concerning the abolition of the death penalty in times of peace (1983)	Protocol No. 12 to the ECHR concerning the general prohibition of discrimination (2000)	Protocol No. 13 to the ECHR concerning the abolition of the death penalty in all circumstances	Framework Convention on the Protection of National Minorities
Albania	●	●	●	○	●
Andorra	●	●		●	
Armenia	●	●	●	○	●
Austria	●	●	○	●	●
Azerbaijan	●	●	○		●
Belgium	●	●	○	●	○
Bosnia and Herzegovina	●	●	●	●	●
Bulgaria	●	●		●	●
Croatia	●	●	●	●	●
Cyprus	●	●	●	●	●
Czech Republic	●	●	○	●	●
Denmark	●	●		●	●
Estonia	●	●	○	●	●
Finland	●	●	●	●	●
France	●	●		○	
Georgia	●	●	●	●	◐
Germany	●	●	○	●	●
Greece	●	●	○	●	○
Hungary	●	●	○	●	●
Iceland	●	●	○	●	○
Ireland	●	●	○	●	●
Italy	●	●	○	○	●
Latvia	●	●	○	○	●
Liechtenstein	●	●	○	●	●
Lithuania	●	●		●	●
Luxembourg	●	●	◐	◐	○
Macedonia	●	●	●	●	●
Malta	●	●		●	●
Moldova	●	●	○	◐	●
Monaco	●	●		●	
Netherlands	●	●	●	◐	●
Norway	●	●	○	●	●
Poland	●	●		○	●
Portugal	●	●	○	●	●
Romania	●	●	◐	●	●
Russian Federation	●	○	○		●

This chart lists countries that were members of the Council of Europe at the end of 2006.

● state is a party
◐ state became party in 2006
○ signed but not yet ratified
○ signed in 2006, but not yet ratified

SELECTED REGIONAL HUMAN RIGHTS TREATIES
COUNCIL OF EUROPE

	European Convention for the Protection of Human Rights and Fundamental Freedoms (ECHR) (1950)	Protocol No. 6 to the ECHR concerning the abolition of the death penalty in times of peace (1983)	Protocol No. 12 to the ECHR concerning the general prohibition of discrimination (2000)	Protocol No. 13 to the ECHR concerning the abolition of the death penalty in all circumstances	Framework Convention on the Protection of National Minorities
San Marino	●	●	●	●	●
Serbia	●	●	●	●	●
Slovakia	●	●	○	●	●
Slovenia	●	●	○	●	●
Spain	●	●	○	○	●
Sweden	●	●		●	●
Switzerland	●	●		●	●
Turkey	●	●	○	◐	
Ukraine	●	●	◐	●	●
United Kingdom	●	●		●	●

This chart lists countries that were members of the Council of Europe at the end of 2006.

● state is a party
◐ state became party in 2006
○ signed but not yet ratified
○ signed in 2006, but not yet ratified

An Iraqi soldier looks at photos of victims of an April suicide bombing at a mosque in northern Baghdad, Iraq. © Muhannad Fala'ah/Getty Images

Gay Pride marchers challenge discrimination against lesbian, gay, bisexual and transgender people, Warsaw, Poland. © Reuters/ Katarina Stoltz

A YEAR OF CAMPAIGNING

"They carried guns all the time. I was afraid of the guns. Actually, I was in constant fear." These are the words of Fereh Musu Conteh, who was abducted by an armed group during the conflict in Sierra Leone when she was just 13 years old.

"When there are guns, there are more victims," said Malya, a woman from Port-au-Prince, Haiti, describing the level of violence in her neighbourhood.

Gun violence afflicts countries around the world – armed conflict and violent crime claim the lives of men, women and children every day. AI is part of a worldwide coalition campaigning for a global Arms Trade Treaty in order to prevent the proliferation and misuse of arms and so reduce the number of victims. In 2006, activists achieved a major victory when the UN voted overwhelmingly to start work on a treaty – a goal many thought unrealistic when the campaign started.

The success of the Control Arms campaign shows what can be achieved with determination, clarity and imagination.

AI's uniqueness among human rights organizations is its strategic channelling of the passion and outrage of ordinary people around the world. AI's members and supporters exert influence on governments, armed political groups, companies and intergovernmental bodies. They change the lives of individuals – of victims and survivors of human rights abuses, of human rights activists and defenders, and even of the abusers.

The activism of AI's 2.2 million members and supporters, working alongside international and local partners, converts AI's research into a force for change. Activists confront governments, other institutions and individuals, not only through letters, emails and petitions but by mobilizing public pressure through street protests, vigils and direct lobbying. Thousands of AI members respond to Urgent Action appeals on behalf of individuals at immediate risk. Publicity through the news media and online takes AI's message swiftly and in a range of languages to millions more.

AI members invent creative and innovative forms of activism, both online and on the streets. In 2006, for example, AI Paraguay organized "toy gun swaps" in the run-up to Christmas, offering new toys to children in exchange for toy weapons, and street theatre to persuade parents not to buy them. AI Morocco carried out a survey on poverty and government responsibility, and AI Australia sought the public's view on the country's new anti-terror laws. AI Norway prepared to launch its online "pledge banking", where activists pledge to undertake a campaigning activity if enough others join in.

The key areas of focus for AI in 2006 were Control Arms; Stop Violence against Women, in particular domestic violence; torture and other abuses in the "war on terror"; the need for a peacekeeping force to protect civilians in Darfur, Sudan; and the conflict between Israeli forces and Hizbullah fighters based in Lebanon.

Among many other country and region-specific campaigns, AI focused on forced evictions in Africa. In countries such as Angola, Equatorial Guinea, Ghana, Kenya, Nigeria, Sudan and Zimbabwe, evictions are often carried out illegally, with excessive and sometimes lethal force, and without provision of adequate alternative accommodation. Forced evictions disproportionately affect people living in poverty and often lead to a wide range of other human rights being denied (*Africa: Forced evictions reach crisis levels*, AI Index: AFR 01/009/2006).

Successes continued in AI's global campaign for a world free of executions. In June, the Philippines became the 88th country to totally abolish the death penalty. This development was particularly welcome in the Asia-Pacific region where a disproportionately high proportion of the world's executions take place. In July, AI played a role in bringing together human rights groups, activists, lawyers and parliamentarians from 21 countries to form the Anti-Death Penalty Asia Network (ADPAN) as a united regional voice against the death penalty. In Europe and Central Asia, after vigorous AI campaigning in recent years, Moldova amended its Constitution to formalize its complete abolition of the death penalty and ratified international treaties that require abolition. Kyrgyzstan signed into law a new Constitution that no longer included, and therefore no longer authorized, death as a punishment.

In 2006 at least 1,544 people were executed in 25 countries worldwide. At least 3,861 people were sentenced to death in 55 countries. The true numbers are believed to be considerably higher. By far the majority of executions – 90 per cent – were carried out in just five countries: China, Iran, Iraq, Pakistan and the USA. Countries that executed people convicted of crimes committed while they were under 18 were Iran and Pakistan.

THE INDIVIDUAL AT THE CORE

At the heart of all AI's campaigns is the individual – as the victim and survivor of human rights abuses, as the partner in the defence of human rights, and as the activist speaking out and working with and for other individuals. Whether global or local, aimed at governments or multilateral institutions, focusing on one person in danger of torture or on a police service that needs training in responding effectively to domestic violence, all campaigns are generated and fired by the individual at their centre in need of protection or support.

The global connection between individuals is a motivating force behind all AI campaigns. It lies behind much of the activism of new human rights groups working at local, grassroots and community level. Such human rights defenders may be both victims and activists, struggling to achieve their own rights as well as those of their family or community. Working with such human rights defenders is as much about seeking structural changes to create the space in which people can organize and protest as it is about helping the individuals themselves.

Campaigning can achieve real improvements in the lives of individuals. Individual members of AI forge global links of solidarity with survivors, human rights defenders and their families. The human face in AI's work inspires and mobilizes members, and attracts wider support in society and from governments. AI presents the cases of individuals not as advocates working solely for one beneficiary, but to benefit all individuals experiencing similar abuses, to shift public opinion or to focus attention on mass violations, and to win changes in policy and practice. Offering that human context demonstrates starkly to governments and the public the consequences of failing to protect human rights.

> **IN 2006 AT LEAST 1,544 PEOPLE WERE EXECUTED IN 25 COUNTRIES WORLDWIDE. MOST WERE CARRIED OUT IN CHINA, IRAN, IRAQ, PAKISTAN AND THE USA.**

CONTROL ARMS

A UN vote in October marked a massive victory for AI and its partners in the Control Arms campaign, Oxfam and the International Action Network on Small Arms (IANSA). After three years of campaigning around the world and three weeks of concerted campaigning in New York before the vote, 139 governments were persuaded to vote in favour of a UN resolution to start work on an Arms Trade Treaty. In December, 153 governments voted for the resolution's formal adoption by the UN General Assembly, with only one state – the USA – voting against.

Under the resolution, the UN must collect states' views on the feasibility, scope and parameters of a treaty, then in 2008 set up a group of experts to establish the basis of a comprehensive, legally binding treaty. As a direct result of the campaigning before the vote, the UN resolution contains an explicit reference to governments' obligations under human rights and humanitarian law. While AI is eager for rapid advances, in UN terms progress has been extraordinarily swift. The resolution could be a key first step towards a worldwide ban on transfers of arms that devastate the lives of hundreds of thousands of people.

■ More than a million people around the world posted pictures of themselves on the Control Arms website for the Million Faces Petition. Supporters ranged from Archbishop Desmond Tutu to the entire French football team. The millionth face was that of Julius Arile, an athlete working for peace in Kenya, who presented the petition to UN Secretary-General Kofi Annan in New York in June. To lobby governments before the UN debate, the Control Arms campaign published *Arms without borders* (AI Index: POL 34/006/2006), a report on the globalized arms trade.

■ As part of the "100 days Countdown" before the crucial General Assembly vote, representatives from 70 AI Sections around the world travelled to New York to campaign and lobby a UN Review Conference on small arms and light weapons. Control Arms activists lobbied with a campaign report, *The AK-47: The world's favourite killing machine* (AI Index: ACT 30/011/2006), and a booklet entitled *Compilation of global principles for arms transfers* (AI Index: POL 34/004/2006) published by AI and its partner organizations. Although agreement at the Conference was stalled by a small group of governments led by the USA, the UN Secretary-General in his opening statement endorsed the call for an Arms Trade Treaty, as did many governments.

Other campaigning initiatives in 2006 targeted the export of arms to areas of the world in conflict where human rights abuses and war crimes are rife.

■ In January, AI published testimonies from individuals in Haiti (AI Index: AMR 36/001/2006) and during the conflict in Sierra Leone (AI Index: AFR 51/001/2006). Conflicts and mass killings in Sierra Leone and neighbouring states in West Africa were sustained by the supply of weapons funded by the illegal sale of diamonds. In Haiti armed violence has spread from armed political groups to criminal gangs that kill and rape hundreds of people every year with arms smuggled from neighbouring countries, including the USA.

■ Developing countries now absorb more than two thirds of world defence imports, increasingly using private contractors in diverse supply chains. Just before the UN Review Conference, AI and Transarms, the Research Centre for the Logistics of Arms Transfers, published a report in May, *Dead on time: Arms transportation, brokering and the threat to human rights* (AI Index: ACT 30/008/2006). The report documented unaccounted arms flights from Bosnia and Herzegovina to Iraq by the US Department of Defense, as well as shipments from Brazil to Saudi Arabia and from China to Liberia using foreign brokers and shippers while disregarding patterns of human rights abuse by the recipients.

■ While international debate has focused on the transfer of nuclear or long-range missile technology to countries such as Iran, North Korea and Pakistan, the routine export of conventional weapons and small arms that contribute to human rights violations and armed violence has received far less attention. In the July-August conflict involving Israel and Lebanon, Israeli forces used aircraft, bombs, missiles, cluster and other munitions supplied particularly by the US, while Hizbullah attacked northern Israel with Katyusha and other rockets said to have been produced with the assistance of Syria and Iran. An AI report on China's role in arming conflicts and sustaining human rights abuses in such countries as Myanmar, Nepal, South Africa and Sudan was published in June (*People's Republic of China: Sustaining conflict and human rights abuses*, AI Index: ASA 17/030/2006).

STOP VIOLENCE AGAINST WOMEN

Domestic violence was a focus for AI campaigning. AI's campaign was part of a wider worldwide movement to address violence against women as a human rights issue. The UN Secretary-General published an in-depth study of violence against women in all its forms in October. The report called on states to secure gender equality, bring laws and practices in line with international standards, collect data to strengthen policy and planning, and allocate adequate resources and funding. In November, AI members welcomed a Council of Europe campaign on domestic violence, and urged member states to deliver on the campaign's goals of abolishing discriminatory laws, strengthening services for survivors and challenging social prejudices.

AI holds the state responsible when it takes inadequate measures to protect women from domestic violence – by not introducing or implementing specific laws or procedures, not providing specialist training or health care, or not making available or supporting shelters or other services. If a state does not make sufficient effort to prevent, investigate and punish acts of violence against women, then it shares responsibility for the abuses.

■ AI called on governments to implement its new 14-Point Programme for the Prevention of Domestic Violence, which calls on governments to protect the physical and mental wellbeing of women who have been abused. It insists that government policies, practices and laws must not discriminate against women, and calls on governments to consult and work closely with women victims and survivors, and with organizations with experience of addressing domestic violence.

■ The need for a place of safety was the focus of AI's 16 Days of Activism to mark the International Day for the Elimination of Violence against Women on 25 November. Through 16 web-based appeal cases, AI urged governments to set up and fund shelters for women fleeing violence in the home. Some governments provide no shelters or support for women facing domestic abuse, such as in

Saudi Arabia. In other countries, for example Belgium or Mongolia, official support is sporadic or insufficient. AI highlighted the particular difficulties of migrant women in Denmark, at risk of losing residency rights if they leave an abusive marriage, and of Native American and Alaska Native women in the USA who cannot access shelters that provide culturally appropriate forms of help.

■ In August, the Director General of the State Police in Albania reported that he had directed the police to implement AI's recommendations published in March in *Albania: Violence against women in the family – "It's not her shame"* (AI Index: EUR 11/002/2006). AI had called for the police to treat seriously and investigate reports of family violence, to protect women complainants and witnesses, to facilitate the work of women's organizations, and to discipline police officers who "neglect or treat with indifference" complaints of violence against women.

■ In *Sierra Leone: Women face human rights abuses in the informal legal sector* (AI Index: AFR 51/002/2006), published in May, AI showed how powers exercised by traditional rulers through customary courts can deprive women of rights. Failures by police to respond to appeals for help and by local courts to exercise their jurisdiction frequently leave women at the mercy of discriminatory customary laws.

■ Failure to tackle high levels of sexual violence reflect social and cultural attitudes that trivialize the crimes and entrench discrimination against women, AI reported in June in *Sexual violence against women and girls in Jamaica: "Just a little sex"* (AI Index: AMR 38/002/2006). Jamaican law leaves women without the protection of the law in cases of marital rape, incest or sexual harassment, and in court, women's testimony is explicitly given less weight than that of men.

■ The threat of sexual violence in the home and community affects women's ability to travel to market or to work and to access health and education services, AI reported in September in *Papua New Guinea: Violence against women – not inevitable, never acceptable!* (AI Index: ASA 34/002/2006). In meetings with AI, police and other officials showed little understanding of the state's obligations to protect women.

■ In October, Hamda Fahad Jassem Al-Thani was allowed to join her husband, and thanked AI for its appeals. "I ask you to help end my suffering and to help me return to my husband, whom I chose entirely of my own accord, this being the most fundamental of my God-given rights, as enshrined in international human rights conventions," she had said to AI. A member of the ruling family in Qatar, she had been abducted from Egypt by the state security services and detained in secret following her marriage without her family's consent in 2002.

'I ASK YOU TO HELP END MY SUFFERING AND TO HELP ME RETURN TO MY HUSBAND... THIS BEING THE MOST FUNDAMENTAL OF MY GOD-GIVEN RIGHTS.'

'WAR ON TERROR'

In its international campaign against abuses in the "war on terror", AI exposed and denounced hundreds of cases of torture and other grave violations of human rights claimed by states to be a necessary response to security threats. AI also strongly condemned deliberate attacks on civilians and indiscriminate attacks by armed groups.

■ AI convened a two-day gathering of human rights organizations from the Middle East in Lebanon in January. The participants concluded that no detainees should be transferred from one country to another on the basis of mere diplomatic assurances that they would not be tortured or otherwise ill-treated after transfer, and that memorandums of understanding to that effect between the UK government and governments in the Middle East and North Africa undermined the absolute prohibition of torture and other ill-treatment.

■ AI and other human rights groups submitted a brief to the European Court of Human Rights in the case of *Ramzy v. the Netherlands*, seeking to uphold the absolute prohibition in law against transferring a person to a state where they risk torture.

■ The US programme of renditions — the secret transfer of individuals from one country to another, bypassing judicial and administrative due process — was analysed in April in *USA: Below the radar — Secret flights to torture and "disappearance"* (AI Index: AMR 51/051/2006). Since 2001, hundreds of terror suspects have been transferred to states where physical and psychological brutality and coercion feature prominently in interrogations. Many detainees have been subjected to enforced disappearance, a crime under international law.

■ Three Yemenis detained for more than 18 months by the USA or at its behest, then for over nine months without charge in Yemen — Muhammad Abdullah al Assad, Muhammad Faraj Bashmilah and Salah Nasser Salim 'Ali Qaru — provided unique insights into the workings of covert US-run detention centres known as "black sites". AI members campaigned for their trial or release, and AI delegates observed the trial that eventually took place in February 2006, leading to the final release of all three men in March.

■ The active involvement of European states in US rendition flights, or their denial of any knowledge about them, was spotlighted in AI's June report, *Partners in crime: Europe's role in US renditions* (AI Index: EUR 01/008/2006). AI lobbied Council of Europe (CoE) member states to investigate these abuses themselves and to cooperate fully with CoE investigations, and called for CoE guidelines on controls of domestic and foreign secret services and of transiting air traffic.

■ AI France created an online viral campaign to spread the message against renditions, also working closely with rap artist Leeroy Kesiah (www.terrorairlines.com). AIUSA hosted an online discussion in August after Peter Bauer and other former interrogators told the US Congress that torture and other ill-treatment were unnecessary to win the "war on terror". In December, AI Jordan campaigned with cartoonist Khaldoon Gharaibeh and former detainee Khaled Al-

Asmar for the closure of the US detention facility in Guantánamo Bay, Cuba.

■ In *Terror and counter-terror: Defending our human rights* (AI Index: ACT 40/009/2006), published in August, AI detailed how the widespread backlash against human rights in the "war on terror" has been vigorously challenged by AI and other activists around the world. The report drew attention to the conflicts and other contexts in which human rights abuses are ignored as states concentrate on national security issues.

■ "He is now again in the circle of his family. Their joy at embracing their lost son again is indescribable," said the lawyer for Murat Kurnaz, a Turkish national and resident of Germany released from Guantánamo in August 2006. Murat Kurnaz was detained without charge or trial for nearly five years before the German authorities acted on his behalf following intense and sustained pressure by his family, lawyers and AI members.

SUDAN: CIVILIANS UNPROTECTED

Despite a peace agreement in May, fighting escalated in Darfur as the government and the only other signatory, a rebel armed faction, launched a new offensive against the non-signatory armed groups. Cross-border attacks by government-backed Janjawid militias took the devastation of war and attendant human rights abuses into Chad, threatening growing destabilization in the region. Hundreds of civilians were believed killed and tens of thousands forced from their homes in direct and targeted attacks by government and allied forces. AI's campaigning focused on the need for international peacekeepers to protect the civilians of Darfur and eastern Chad despite the resistance of the Sudanese government.

■ Denied access to Darfur by the Sudanese authorities, AI delegates visited Chad in May, July and November. In camps in eastern Chad, they heard harrowing accounts from refugees from Darfur and from Chadians attacked as vast areas of eastern Chad were depopulated in cross-border raids (*Chad/Sudan: Sowing the seeds of Darfur – Ethnic targeting in Chad by Janjawid militias from Sudan*, AI Index: AFR

20/006/2006). In November AI delegates recorded the deaths of over 500 individuals in eastern Chad – the numbers killed as attacks continued were undoubtedly many times higher. They went to destroyed villages and spoke to the survivors of attacks and rapes. Numerous witnesses testified to the failure of the Chadian government to deploy its troops to protect civilians, even those stationed near the scene of attacks. AI renewed calls to the UN Security Council to deploy an international peacekeeping force in eastern Chad.

MURAT KURNAZ WAS RELEASED IN AUGUST 2006 FROM NEARLY FIVE YEARS' DETENTION AT GUANTÁNAMO AFTER PRESSURE FROM HIS FAMILY, LAWYERS AND AMNESTY INTERNATIONAL.

■ In March the African Union called for the peacekeeping duties of the African Union Mission in Sudan (AMIS) in Darfur to be transferred to a UN force. AMIS forces lacked equipment and funding, and the Sudanese government had restricted their activity. In July, AI produced a briefing on the resources, authority and mandate that a peacekeeping force needed, and in December developed an *Agenda for effective protection of civilians in Darfur* (AI Index: AFR 54/084/2006).

■ AI members protested at attacks on individuals and communities by the government and allied forces in North Darfur through Urgent Actions and appeal cases, including after 70 men, women and children were killed in attacks in July in Korma, and 67 people died in the Jebel Moon area in October. From September, hundreds more civilians were killed, tortured and raped, and thousands forcibly displaced in a renewed counter-insurgency offensive in northern and west Darfur.

■ On a Day for Darfur in September, AI campaigned in coalition with other human rights organizations for UN peacekeepers to be allowed to protect civilians in Darfur. In three weeks, 23,000 people had signed AI's online petition to the UN Security Council and the number continued to rise. Another day dedicated to campaigning on Darfur in

December focused the campaigning of AI and other groups on the plight of women (*Sudan/Chad: 'No one to help them' — Rape extends from Darfur into eastern Chad*, AI Index: AFR 54/087/2006).

■ The effective imprisonment by Janjawid of hundreds of thousands of displaced people in the camps was reported in October in *Sudan: Crying out for safety* (AI Index: AFR 54/055/2006). In November, as Sudanese forces carried out indiscriminate aerial bombardment using Russian- and Chinese-supplied planes and helicopters, AI called for the 2005 UN Security Council arms ban on all parties to the Darfur conflict to be implemented and fully enforced (*Sudan/China: Appeal by Amnesty International to the Chinese government on the occasion of the China-Africa Summit for Development and Cooperation*, AI Index: AFR 54/072/2006).

■ In November, AI called on the African Union to press the government of Sudan to consent to the deployment of a UN peacekeeping mission (*The African Commission: Amnesty International's oral statement on the human rights situation in Africa*, AI Index: AFR 01/012/2006). AI reported on the tens of thousands of people at risk as insecurity and restrictions imposed on humanitarian organizations by the Sudanese government forced cutbacks in the aid operation in Darfur in *Sudan: Darfur — Threats to humanitarian aid* (AI Index: AFR 54/031/2006).

■ In December, AI protested at the timidity of the resolution adopted by the UN Human Rights Council in a Special Session on Darfur. The Council agreed to send its own assessment mission to Darfur, but failed to respond to the urgency and magnitude of the human rights crisis on the basis of the existing, compelling evidence of close government links to Janjawid abuses.

■ AI was given the names of people killed in a Janjawid attack from Sudan on the town of Koloy in eastern Chad, November 2006. "In parting the Imam thanked me, thanked Amnesty International for coming," an AI delegate reported. "He stressed that he had gone to the capital two times to speak with authorities. He speaks frequently with local government and military officials, various international agencies have been by, but no one had ever asked for the names before. And he stressed: that matters so much."

THE IMAM THANKED AMNESTY INTERNATIONAL. NO ONE HAD EVER ASKED FOR THE NAMES OF CIVILIANS KILLED BEFORE.

ISRAEL AND LEBANON: CIVILIANS UNDER FIRE

In July a major military conflict erupted between Israeli forces and Hizbullah forces based in Lebanon after Hizbullah fighters crossed into Israel and attacked an army patrol. By the time a ceasefire was agreed 34 days later, Israeli attacks had killed more than 1,000 civilians in Lebanon, displaced around a million people, and destroyed thousands of homes and much of Lebanon's civilian infrastructure. Hizbullah launched missiles into civilian areas of Israel, causing the deaths of 43 civilians, displacing many thousands of people from their homes in northern Israel and damaging hundreds of buildings.

■ AI delegates visited both Israel and Lebanon during the fighting and in the immediate aftermath to research violations of international humanitarian law, including war crimes, by both sides. AI delegates interviewed hundreds of people whose lives had been devastated by unlawful attacks, visited numerous sites where rockets, artillery shells and bombs, including cluster munitions, had struck, and spoke to non-governmental organizations. AI met and obtained information from senior Israeli military and government officials, the Lebanese authorities and Hizbullah. It also repeatedly requested information about specific military operations from Israel and Hizbullah.

■ From the outset of the conflict AI called on both sides to respect their obligations under international humanitarian law (the laws of war), particularly those relating to the protection of civilians. However, civilians were bearing the brunt of the conflict and AI joined the call for a ceasefire made by UN Secretary-General Kofi Annan and other world leaders. In July, AI published *Israel/Lebanon: Israel and Hizbullah must spare civilians – Obligations under international humanitarian law of the parties to the conflict in Israel and Lebanon*, a reminder to the parties of their legal obligations (AI Index: MDE 15/070/2006).

■ Following the end of the hostilities, and after conducting further research and discussions with officials, AI issued two briefings covering aspects of the conflict. In August it published *Israel/Lebanon: Deliberate destruction or "collateral damage"? Israeli attacks against civilian infrastructure* (AI Index: MDE 18/007/2006). AI found that Israeli forces had committed indiscriminate and disproportionate attacks, pursuing a strategy that appeared intended to punish the people of Lebanon and their government for not turning against Hizbullah, as well as harming Hizbullah's military capability.

■ In September, AI published *Israel/Lebanon: Under fire – Hizbullah's attacks on northern Israel* (AI Index: MDE 02/025/2006). This concluded that Hizbullah had committed serious violations of international humanitarian law, including war crimes. Its rocket attacks amounted to deliberate attacks on civilians and civilian objects, and indiscriminate attacks. The attacks also violated other rules of international humanitarian law, including the prohibition of reprisal attacks on the civilian population.

■ In November, AI published *Israel/Lebanon: Out of all proportion – civilians bear the brunt of the war* (AI Index: MDE 02/033/2006). This covered further aspects of the conduct and consequences of Israeli military actions in Lebanon. It analysed patterns of Israeli attacks and a number of specific incidents in which civilians were killed in Lebanon. It highlighted the impact on civilian life of other Israeli attacks, including the legacy of the widespread cluster bomb bombardment of south Lebanon by Israeli forces in the last days of the war. It also summarized AI's conclusions with regard to the overall conduct of both Israeli forces and Hizbullah fighters.

■ "I have lost all my children, my mother, my sisters. My wife is in a very serious condition... How do you tell a mother that she has lost all her children?" Ahmad Badran spoke to AI delegates in al-Ghazieh village in south Lebanon after watching the bodies of eight members of his family being dug from under a pile of rubble. On 7 August an Israeli missile hit his home, killing his four children, his mother, his two sisters and his niece, and critically injuring his wife.

■ AI called for the UN to set up an international commission empowered to investigate the evidence of violations of international law by both Hizbullah and Israel, and to make provision for reparations for the victims. AI also called for an arms embargo on both sides, and an immediate moratorium on the use of cluster weapons. It urged all parties involved in the conflict to investigate alleged violations of international human rights law and ensure reparation for the victims.

■ After the conflict, AI members around the world focused their energy on calling for Israel immediately to hand over to the UN maps showing the areas in which it had used cluster munitions, in order to assist the clearance of unexploded cluster bomblets which continue to kill and maim Lebanese civilians. Up to a million unexploded bomblets littered south Lebanon when the ceasefire came into effect, presenting a long-term threat to the civilian population.

■ In December an AI delegation, including Secretary General Irene Khan, visited Lebanon and Israel and the Occupied Territories for high-level talks with officials. To coincide with the visit, AI published a campaign briefing, *Israel and the Occupied Territories: Road to nowhere* (AI Index: MDE 15/093/2006) that focused on the spiralling human rights crisis in the Occupied Territories over the previous six years.

> **'I HAVE LOST ALL MY CHILDREN, MY MOTHER, MY SISTERS. MY WIFE IS IN A VERY SERIOUS CONDITION... HOW DO YOU TELL A MOTHER THAT SHE HAS LOST ALL HER CHILDREN?'**

INTERNATIONAL JUSTICE

AI continued to take its work on behalf of individuals up to the international arena, campaigning for universal support for the International Criminal Court and for an end to impunity. It pushed hard for those responsible for the most serious crimes known to humanity to be brought to justice before international or national courts.

■ After years of campaigning by AI and others, Nigeria surrendered former Liberian President Charles Taylor in March to the Special Court for Sierra Leone on charges of war crimes and crimes against humanity, relating to his involvement in the country's civil war.

■ In March, Thomas Lubanga Dyilo, charged with enlisting and recruiting child soldiers in the Democratic Republic of the Congo, became the first person to be arrested and surrendered to the International Criminal Court.

■ Years of campaigning by AI and others saw progress in July when the Assembly of the African Union requested Senegal to promptly prosecute former Chadian President Hissène Habré, who is charged with crimes against humanity, war crimes and torture. AI urged Senegal to enact the necessary legislation, and Senegal's Council of Ministers in November adopted a law to permit Hissène Habré to be tried.

Holding to account those responsible for human rights abuses in the past not only gives justice to the victims and survivors. It is an essential part of AI's struggle to protect against abuses of other individuals' rights in the present, and to prevent them in the future.

AI members in Nepal campaign on behalf of the thousands of women and girls forced into sexual slavery by the Japanese military before and during the Second World War.

© AI

CONTACT AI

AI SECTIONS

Algeria Amnesty International,
47 rue Mohamed Zekkal, (en face Salle Harcha),
16004 Alger
email: amnestyalgeria@hotmail.com
www.amnestyalgeria.com

Argentina Amnistía Internacional,
Av. Rivadavia 2206 - P4A,
C1032ACO Ciudad de Buenos Aires
email: administracion@amnesty.org.ar
www.amnesty.org.ar

Australia Amnesty International, Locked Bag 23,
Broadway, New South Wales 2007
email: servicecentre@amnesty.org.au
www.amnesty.org.au

Austria Amnesty International, Moeringgasse 10,
A-1150 Vienna
email: info@amnesty.at
www.amnesty.at

Belgium Amnesty International (Flemish-speaking),
Kerkstraat 156, 2060 Antwerpen
email: amnesty@aivl.be
www.aivl.be
Belgium Amnesty International (francophone),
Rue Berckmans 9, 1060 Bruxelles
email: aibf@aibf.be
www.aibf.be

Benin Amnesty International, Sikecodji, Carré 880,
Immeuble Nobime, 2ème étage,
Non loin du Ciné OpkeOluwa, Cotonou
email: aibenin@leland.bj

Bermuda Amnesty International, PO Box HM 2136,
Hamilton HM JX
email: aibda@ibl.bm

Canada Amnesty International (English-speaking),
312 Laurier Avenue East, Ottawa, Ontario, K1N 1H9
email: info@amnesty.ca
www.amnesty.ca
Canada Amnistie Internationale (francophone),
6250 boulevard Monk, Montréal, Québec, H4E 3H7
email: info@amnistie.ca
www.amnistie.ca

Chile Amnistía Internacional, Oficina Nacional,
Huelén 164 - Piso 2, 750-0617 Providencia, Santiago
email: info@amnistia.cl
www.amnistia.cl

Côte d'Ivoire Amnesty International, 04 BP 895,
Abidjan 04
email: aicotedivoire@yahoo.fr

Denmark Amnesty International, Gammeltorv 8, 5,
DK - 1457 Copenhagen K.
email: amnesty@amnesty.dk
www.amnesty.dk

Faroe Islands Amnesty International, Hoydalsvegur 6,
FO-100 Tórshavn
email: amnesty@amnesty.fo
www.amnesty.fo

Finland Amnesty International, Ruoholahdenkatu 24,
D 00180 Helsinki
email: amnesty@amnesty.fi
www.amnesty.fi

France Amnesty International,
76 Boulevard de la Villette, 75940 Paris, Cédex 19
email: info@amnesty.fr
www.amnesty.fr

Germany Amnesty International, Heerstrasse 178,
53111 Bonn
email: info@amnesty.de
www.amnesty.de

Greece Amnesty International, Sina 30,
106 72 Athens
email: info@amnesty.org.gr
www.amnesty.org.gr

Guyana Amnesty International,
Palm Court Building, 35 Main Street,
Georgetown
email: rightsgy@yahoo.com

Hong Kong Amnesty International, Unit D, 3/F,
Best-O-Best Commercial Centre, 32-36 Ferry Street,
Kowloon
email: admin-hk@amnesty.org.hk
www.amnesty.org.hk

Iceland Amnesty International, Hafnarstræti 15,
101 Reykjavík
email: amnesty@amnesty.is
www.amnesty.is

Ireland Amnesty International,
Sean MacBride House, 48 Fleet Street,
Dublin 2
email: info@amnesty.ie
www.amnesty.ie

Israel Amnesty International, PO Box 14179,
Tel Aviv 61141
email: amnesty@netvision.net.il
www.amnesty.org.il

Italy Amnesty International,
Via Giovanni Battista De Rossi, 10,
00161 Roma
email: info@amnesty.it
www.amnesty.it

Japan Amnesty International, 4F Kyodo Bldg.,
2-2 Kandanishiki-cho, Chiyoda-ku,
Tokyo 101-0054
email: info@amnesty.or.jp
www.amnesty.or.jp

Korea (Republic of) Amnesty International,
Gwanghwamun PO Box 2045, Chongno-gu,
Seoul, 110-620
email: info@amnesty.or.kr
www.amnesty.or.kr

Luxembourg Amnesty International,
Boîte Postale 1914, 1019 Luxembourg
email: info@amnesty.lu
www.amnesty.lu

Mauritius Amnesty International, BP 69,
Rose-Hill
email: amnestymtius@intnet.mu

Mexico Amnistía Internacional,
Insurgentes sur 327 Oficina C,
Col. Hipódromo Condesa, CP 6100,
Mexico DF
email: informacion@amnistia.org.mx
www.amnistia.org.mx

Morocco Amnesty International,
281 avenue Mohamed V, Apt. 23, Escalier A,
Rabat
email: amorocco@sections.amnesty.org

Nepal Amnesty International, PO Box 135,
Amnesty Marga, Basantanagar, Balaju,
Kathmandu
email: info@amnestynepal.org
www.amnestynepal.org

Netherlands Amnesty International,
Keizersgracht 177, 1016 DR Amsterdam
email: amnesty@amnesty.nl
www.amnesty.nl

New Zealand Amnesty International,
PO Box 5300, Wellesley Street,
Auckland
email: info@amnesty.org.nz
www.amnesty.org.nz

Norway Amnesty International,
Tordenskiolds gate 6B, 0106 Oslo
email: info@amnesty.no
www.amnesty.no

Peru Amnistía Internacional,
Enrique Palacios 735-A, Miraflores, Lima
email: admin-pe@amnesty.org
www.amnistia.org.pe

Philippines Amnesty International, 17-B,
Kasing-kasing Street, Corner K-8th, Kamias,
Quezon City 1101
email: section@amnesty.org.ph
www.amnesty.org.ph

Poland Amnesty International, ul. Piêkna 66a,
lokal 2, I pietro, 00-672, Warszawa
email: amnesty@amnesty.org.pl
www.amnesty.org.pl

Portugal Amnistia Internacional,
Av. Infante Santo, 42, 2º, 1350 - 179 Lisboa
email: aiportugal@amnistia-internacional.pt
www.amnistia-internacional.pt

Puerto Rico Amnistía Internacional,
Calle Robles 54, Oficina 11, Río Piedras, 00925
email: amnistiapr@amnestypr.org
www.amnistiapr.org

Senegal Amnesty International,
35a Boulevard du Général de Gaulle,
Allée du Centenaire, BP 35269 Dakar Colobane
email: aisenegal@sentoo.sn
www.amnesty.sn

Sierra Leone Amnesty International, PMB 1021,
16 Pademba Road, Freetown
email: aislf@sierratel.sl

Slovenia Amnesty International, Beethovnova 7,
1000 Ljubljana
email: amnesty@amnesty.si
www.amnesty.si

Spain Amnistía Internacional, Fernando VI, 8,
1º izda, 28004 Madrid
email: info@es.amnesty.org
www.es.amnesty.org

Sweden Amnesty International, PO Box 4719,
S-11692 Stockholm
email: info@amnesty.se
www.amnesty.se

Switzerland Amnesty International, PO Box,
3001 Berne
email: info@amnesty.ch
www.amnesty.ch

Taiwan Amnesty International, 3F., No. 14, Lane 165,
Sec. 1, Sinsheng S. Rd, Da-an District,
Taipei City 10656
email: amnesty.taiwan@gmail.com
www.aitaiwan.org.tw

Togo Amnesty International, 2322 Avenue du RPT,
Quartier Casablanca, BP 20013, Lomé
email: aitogo@cafe.tg

Tunisia Amnesty International,
67 Rue Oum Kalthoum, 3ème étage, Escalier B,
1000 Tunis
email: admin-tn@amnesty.org

United Kingdom Amnesty International,
The Human Rights Action Centre, 17-25 New Inn Yard,
London EC2A 3EA
email: info@amnesty.org.uk
www.amnesty.org.uk

United States of America Amnesty International,
5 Penn Plaza, 16th floor, New York, NY 10001
email: admin-us@aiusa.org
www.amnestyusa.org

Uruguay Amnistía Internacional,
Wilson Ferreira Aldunate 1220, CP 11100,
Montevideo
email: oficina@amnistia.org.uy
www.amnistia.org.uy

Venezuela Amnistía Internacional,
Edificio Ateneo de Caracas, piso 6,
Plaza Morelos Los Caobos, Caracas 1010A
email: admin-ve@amnesty.org
www.amnistia.org.ve

AI STRUCTURES

Bolivia Amnistía Internacional, Casilla 10607,
La Paz
email: perescar@ceibo.entelnet.bo

Burkina Faso Amnesty International,
303 Rue 9.08, 08 BP 11344,
Ouagadougou 08
email: aiburkina@fasonet.bf

Czech Republic Amnesty International,
Palackého 9, 110 00 Praha 1
email: amnesty@amnesty.cz
www.amnesty.cz

Hungary Amnesty International, Rózsa u. 44, II/4,
1064 Budapest
email: info@amnesty.hu
www.amnesty.hu

Malaysia Amnesty International,
E6, 3rd floor, Bangunan Khas,
Jalan 8/1E, 46050 Petaling Jaya,
Selangor
email: amnesty@tm.net.my
www.aimalaysia.org

Mali Amnesty International,
Badala Sema 1,
Immeuble MUTEC (Ex Jiguissèmè),
Rue 84, porte 14,
BP E 3885, Badalabougou, Bamako
email: amnesty.mali@ikatelnet.net

Moldova Amnesty International,
PO Box 209,
MD-2012 Chişinău
email: info@amnesty.md
www.amnesty.md

Mongolia Amnesty International,
PO Box 180, Ulaanbaatar 210648
email: aimncc@magicnet.mn
www.amnesty.mn

Paraguay Amnistía Internacional,
Tte. Zotti No. 352 casi Emilio Hassler,
Barrio Villa Morra, Asunción
email: ai-info@py.amnesty.org
www.py.amnesty.org

Slovakia Amnesty International,
Benediktiho 5, 811 05 Bratislava
email: amnesty@amnesty.sk
www.amnesty.sk

Thailand Amnesty International,
641/8 Vara Place, Ladprao Road,
Soi 5, Ladyao, Bangkok 10900
email: info@amnesty.or.th
www.amnesty.or.th

Turkey Amnesty International,
Müeyyitzade Mh. Galipdede Cd. No. 149 Kat:1,
D:4, Beyoğlu, Istanbul
email: posta@amnesty.org.tr
www.amnesty.org.tr

Ukraine Amnesty International,
Ukrainskaia Assotsiatsia
"Mezhdunarodnaia Amnistia",
Chokolovsky bulvar, 1, kv. 12, Kiev
email: office@amnesty.org.ua

Zambia Amnesty International,
Room 715, 7th Floor, Lotti House,
Cairo Road North-End, PO Box 30603,
Lusaka
email: amnesty@zamtel.zm

AI GROUPS

There are also AI Groups in:
Angola, Bahamas, Bahrain, Barbados, Belarus, Botswana, Cameroon, Chad, Curaçao, Dominican Republic, Egypt, Gambia, Jamaica, Jordan, Kuwait, Kyrgyzstan, Lebanon, Liberia, Malta, Palestinian Authority, Pakistan, Russian Federation, Uganda, Yemen.

AI SPECIAL PROJECTS

There are AI Special Projects in the following countries:
Croatia, Ecuador, Ghana, India, Kenya, South Africa, Zimbabwe.

More information and contact details on both AI groups and AI Special Projects can be found online at www.amnesty.org.

AI OFFICES

International Secretariat (IS)
Amnesty International,
Peter Benenson House,
1 Easton Street, London WC1X 0DW,
United Kingdom
email: amnestyis@amnesty.org
www.amnesty.org

ARABAI (Arabic translation unit)
c/o International Secretariat,
Peter Benenson House,
1 Easton Street, London WC1X 0DW,
United Kingdom
email: arabai@amnesty.org
www.amnesty-arabic.org

Éditions Francophones d'Amnesty International (EFAI)
17 Rue du Pont-aux-Choux, 75003 Paris, France
email: ai-efai@amnesty.org
www.efai.org

Editorial de Amnistía Internacional (EDAI)
Calle Valderribas 13, 28007 Madrid,
Spain
email: mlleo@amnesty.org
www.edai.org

European Union (EU) Office
Amnesty International, Rue d'Arlon 37-41,
B 1000 Brussels, Belgium
email: amnesty-eu@aieu.be
www.amnesty-eu.org

IS Beirut – Middle East and North Africa Regional Office
Amnesty International, PO Box 13-5696,
Chouran Beirut 1102 - 2060, Lebanon
email: mena@amnesty.org

IS Dakar – Development Field Office
Amnesty International,
SICAP Sacré Coeur Pyrotechnie, Extension No. 25,
BP 47582, Dakar, Senegal
email: Kolaniya@amnesty.org

IS Geneva — UN Representative Office
Amnesty International, 22 Rue du Cendrier,
4ème étage, CH-1201 Geneva, Switzerland
email: gvunpost@amnesty.org

IS Hong Kong – Asia Pacific Regional Office
Amnesty International, 16/F Siu On Centre,
188 Lockhart Rd, Wanchai, Hong Kong
email: admin-ap@amnesty.org

IS Kampala – Africa Regional Office
Amnesty International,
Plot 20A Kawalya Kaggwa Close, PO Box 23966,
Kampala, Uganda
email: ai-aro@amnesty.org

IS Moscow — Russia Resource Centre
Amnesty International, PO Box 212, Moscow 119019,
Russian Federation
email: msk@amnesty.org

IS New York – UN Representative Office
Amnesty International, 777 UN Plaza, 6th Floor,
New York, NY 10017, USA

IS Paris – Research Office
Amnesty International, 76 Boulevard de la Villette,
75940 Paris, Cédex 19, France
email: pro@amnesty.org

IS San José – Americas Regional Office
Amnistía Internacional,
Del ICE de Pavas 100 metros al Oeste,
50 metros al Norte y 25 metros al Este,
Apartamentos Cherito No. 4, Barrio Rohrmoser,
San José, Costa Rica
email: ybautista@amnesty.org

A football match during the World Social Forum in Mali in support of the Control Arms campaign. The campaign won a major victory in December when the UN voted to start work on a global Arms Trade Treaty. © AI

WHETHER IN A
HIGH-PROFILE CONFLICT
OR A FORGOTTEN
CORNER OF THE GLOBE,
AMNESTY
INTERNATIONAL
CAMPAIGNS FOR JUSTICE
AND FREEDOM FOR ALL
AND SEEKS TO
GALVANIZE PUBLIC
SUPPORT TO BUILD A
BETTER WORLD...

...I WANT TO HELP

WHAT CAN YOU DO?

Activists around the world have shown that it is possible to resist the dangerous forces that are undermining human rights. Be part of this movement. Combat those who peddle fear and hate.

● Join Amnesty International and become part of a worldwide movement campaigning for an end to human rights violations. Help us make a difference.

● Make a donation to support Amnesty International's work.

Together we can make our voices heard.

I am interested in receiving further information on becoming a member of Amnesty International

name

address

country

email

I wish to make a donation to Amnesty International (donations will be taken in UK£, US$ or euros)

amount

please debit my ☐ Visa ☐ Mastercard

number

expiry date

signature

Please return this form to the Amnesty International office in your country.
(See pages 324-327 for further details of Amnesty International offices worldwide.)
If there is not an Amnesty International office in your country, please return this form to the International Secretariat in London:
Peter Benenson House, 1 Easton Street, London WC1X 0DW, United Kingdom

www.amnesty.org

AMNESTY INTERNATIONAL PUBLICATIONS

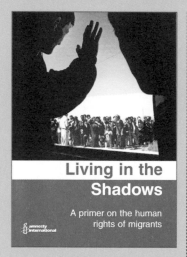

Living in the Shadows: A primer on the human rights of migrants
Designed to counter prejudice and misinformation, this 90-page handbook outlines the rights of migrants on all stages of their journey, and sets out a human rights campaigning agenda.

ISBN 978-0-86210-409-2
AI Index: POL 33/007/2006

Human rights for human dignity: A primer on economic, social and cultural rights
This 80-page introduction to economic, social and cultural rights explains the duties of governments, international organizations and businesses, and gives examples of campaigning successes in areas such as health, housing, education, land rights and labour rights.

ISBN 0-86210-383-5
AI Index: POL 34/009/2005

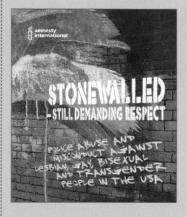

Stonewalled — Still demanding respect: Police abuse and misconduct against lesbian, gay, bisexual and transgender people in the USA
This full colour, 82-page campaigning report looks at how lesbian, gay, bisexual and transgender people remain at risk of gender-based violence in the USA, despite significant steps forward in recent years. It also makes detailed recommendations on what can be done to end the abuses.

ISBN 0-86210-393-2
AI Index: AMR 51/001/2006

Amnesty International produces a wide range of materials, including campaigning and country reports, focus sheets, legal briefings and policy papers.

The six below are a selected sample from our recent back catalogue. For more information on these and to view our full list, please visit www.amnesty.org

To order any of them, please contact the Amnesty International office in your country (addresses on pp324-327). Or if there is no office in your country, please contact the Marketing and Supply team at the International Secretariat:
Peter Benenson House, 1 Easton Street,
London WC1X 0DW, United Kingdom
Tel: 00 44 20 7413 5814 / 5507
Email: orderpubs@amnesty.org
Visit http://web.amnesty.org/shop

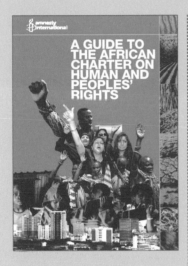

A Guide to the African Charter on Human and Peoples' Rights

An attractive, colourful and easy-to-use guide on the wide range of rights that the African Charter on Human and Peoples' Rights promotes and protects.
ISBN 978-0-86210-407-8
AI Index: IOR 63/005/2006

Israel and the Occupied Territories: Road to nowhere

An incisive 38-page analysis of the past six years of spiralling violence, humanitarian crisis and despair in the Palestinian Occupied Territories, illustrated throughout with photos.
ISBN 978-0-86210-423-8
AI Index: MDE 15/093/2006

Close Guantánamo: Symbol of injustice

An illustrated 16-page briefing that describes the unlawful transfer of hundreds of men from around the world to the USA's offshore detention centre at Guantánamo Bay, Cuba, and the subsequent abuse of their dignity, humanity and other fundamental rights.
ISBN 978-0-86210-420-7
AI Index: AMR 51/001/2007

COUNTRY INDEX

Page references in bold refer to the main chapter entry for that country.

A

Afghanistan 7, 8, 9, 10, 11, 22, 28, 29, **47-9**, 80, 119, 123, 174, 202, 273, 274, 275, 276, 278, 284
Albania **49-50**, 118, 122, 125, 174, 175, 187, 226-8, 316
Algeria 39, 41, 42, **50-3**, 68-9, 180, 188, 189, 190, 197, 271
Angola 16, **53-5**, 193, 232, 313
Argentina 25, **55**, 277
Armenia 5, **56**, 119, 262
Australia 2, 28, **57**, 138, 229, 256, 271, 284, 313
Austria 5, 6, **58**
Azerbaijan 31, 34, 36, 41, 42, **58-9**, 139

B

Bahamas **60**
Bahrain 40, 42, **60-1**
Bangladesh 11, 27, 29, 61, **61-2**, 202, 269
Belarus 7, 35, 36, **63-4**, 173, 185
Belgium **64-5**, 225, 316
Bermuda 229
Bhutan 196
Bolivia 11, 24, **66**
Bosnia and Herzegovina 33, **67-9**, 95, 187, 226, 259, 260, 315
Brazil 4, 5, 11, 22, **69-72**, 207, 315
Bulgaria 31, **72-4**, 125, 171, 173, 251, 259
Burkina Faso 94
Burundi 15, 16, 18, **74-6**, 101, 221, 237, 254

C

Cambodia 6, **77-8**, 282, 283
Cameroon **78-9**, 83-4
Canada 8, 9, **80**, 87, 156, 229
Canary Islands 3
Central African Republic 15, **80-2**
Chad 7, 15, 16, 19, 81, **82-4**, 198, 225, 242, 244, 246, 318, 318-9, 321
Chile 11, 24, 25, **84-5**
China 4, 7, 8, 27, 27-8, 29, **85-7**, 154, 156, 156-7, 159, 160, 161, 223, 231, 246, 314, 315, 319
Colombia 6, 22, 24, **88-91**, 105, 106, 280, 281
Congo, Republic of 15, 16, **91-2**
Côte d'Ivoire 15, 16, 20, **93-4**, 150, 169
Croatia 67, **95-6**, 226
Cuba 6, 21, **96-7**, 276, 318

D

Cyprus 31, **97-8**, 261
Czech Republic **99-100**, 232

D

Democratic Republic of the Congo 11, 12, 15, 16, 18, 19-20, 65, 91, 92, **100-3**, 110, 254, 267, 321
Denmark 5, 42, **103-4**, 168, 177, 262, 284, 285, 316
Dominican Republic 3, **104-5**, 130, 131, 198

E

Ecuador 22, 24, **105-6**
Egypt 7, 9, 33, 39, 40, 41, 42, 80, **106-9**, 125, 151, 214, 248, 317
El Salvador 22, 24, **109-10**
Equatorial Guinea 16, 18, **110-11**, 313
Eritrea 15, 16, 18, **112-13**, 115, 234, 243, 248
Estonia 34, **114**
Ethiopia 15, 16, 18, 19, 112, **114-17**, 118-19, 233, 234, 235

F

Fiji 27
Finland **117**
France 5, 8, 34, 81, **118-19**, 168, 221, 225, 227, 229, 238, 265, 277, 317

G

Gabon 110, 111
Gambia 8, 58, **120-1**, 225
Georgia 31, 35, 166, **121-2**, 219
Germany 9, 33, 59, **122-4**, 174, 251, 278, 279, 318
Ghana 20, **124**, 150, 258, 313
Greece 33-4, 49, **124-6**
Grenada **126**
Guatemala 7, 22, 24, 25, **126-7**
Guinea 65, **127-8**
Guinea-Bissau **128-9**, 225
Guyana **129**

H

Haiti 22, 60, 104, 105, **130-1**, 313, 315
Honduras 22, 24, **131-2**
Hungary **132-3**, 232, 261

I

India 3, 8, 11, 27, 28, 29, 124, **133-6**, 162, 192, 202, 214, 224, 241
Indonesia 29, 57, **136-8**, 224, 257
Iran 5, 7, 8, 12, 37, 39, 40-1, 41, 42, 47, **139-41**, 150, 168, 198, 248, 314, 315